The Complex World of Teaching

Perspectives from Theory and Practice

ETHAN MINTZ & JOHN T. YUN

Editors

Harvard Educational Review
Reprint Series No. 31

Library of Congress Catalog Card Number 98-75466

ISBN 0-916690-34-2

Harvard Educational Review
Gutman Library Suite 349
6 Appian Way
Cambridge, MA 02138
http://gseweb.harvard.edu/~hepg/her.html

Cover Design: Alyssa Morris
Cover Artwork: Barrington Edwards
Editorial Production: Dody Riggs
Typography: Sheila Walsh

To our Moms, Dads, Sisters, Brothers, and Grandparents . . .
our first and best teachers.

Contents

Introduction

Geologists study volcanoes for years and yet cannot predict exactly which will be the next to erupt and in what pattern the lava will flow. Meteorologists study weather patterns in order to come up with an accurate five-day forecast and, as we all know, often fail. Economists study global markets to predict and advise on the financial state of the world, and yet economic surges and collapses still take Wall Street by surprise. Physicists, try as they might, cannot even predict when the next drop of water will fall from a leaky faucet — and what appears more predictable than water dripping from a faucet? Similarly, teachers may present identical lessons to two classes, not knowing why one time the lesson works and the next time it falls flat. Ultimately, the work of teachers is no more predictable than erupting volcanoes, the weather, the economy, or a dripping faucet. Why is there such variability and uncertainty in these circumstances? Because these are all complex systems in which many factors come into play to create fundamentally unpredictable outcomes.

The beauty of complex systems lies in the fact that they amount to much more than the sum of their parts. You can break them apart, look at the pieces, analyze what has happened when similar conditions have previously existed, put all the parts back together, and have something entirely new. Why? Because, as Brent Davis and Dennis Sumara write in "Cognition, Complexity, and Teacher Education," complex systems are "more dynamic, more unpredictable, more alive" than other kinds of systems. There is an element of "magic" — the unexplainable and unpredictable — operating in complex systems.

Such is the complex world of teaching, in which teachers face numerous unpredictable challenges, where some lessons work and some are disasters. What creates this complex world? In any given classroom, there is at least one teacher and several students, each of whom brings a history, personality, learning style, ideology, culture, race, ethnicity, gender, and class background, along with the experiences they have had in the moments and hours before entering that classroom. Societal influences — economic, social, historical, and cultural — also shape the practice and nature of teaching. All of these forces come together in the teaching and learning environment, creating the complex classroom.

Sara Lawrence-Lightfoot, in the introduction to Part One of *Beyond Bias: Perspectives on Classrooms* (1979), writes:

> Teaching is an extremely demanding job that requires a complex mixture of intellectual capacities, pedagogical skills, personality characteristics, and organizational talents. The interactions between teachers and children seldom have a clear, singular purpose; they encompass a range of meanings and messages. . . .

Teachers seldom act alone. They must work within the context of the schools — highly ritualized and bureaucratic social environments that shape their behaviors, restrict their choices, and often provide sources of support, guidance, and reinforcement. And these schools, of course, exist within communities whose culture, history, physical dimensions, and political life have influence on what goes on inside classrooms.[1]

What are the implications of this reality for teachers? Teaching is a complex, dynamic, and continuously evolving profession, in which teachers must constantly learn, adapt, and stay attuned to the multiple relationships and interactions affecting their work in the classroom. Teaching, ultimately, is about uncertainty. As in all complex systems, this uncertainty is a source of excitement, and carries the potential for every teacher in every classroom to play a part in shaping the profession as well as profoundly influencing their own lives and the lives of their students.

In this volume, we bring together some of the most provocative theoretical perspectives, analyses, and reflections from practice published in the *Harvard Educational Review*. We believe this collection captures the environment in which teaching and learning happen and explores the complex relationships and interactions between teachers and students. Understanding the complexity of this system is crucial for teachers in their work.

As such, we have divided *The Complex World of Teaching* into three major parts. Part One, "Inner Worlds," is divided into two sections: "The Inner Worlds of Students" and "The Inner Worlds of Teachers." Through the voices of students, teachers, and researchers, we explore aspects of teachers' and students' lives that, while often hidden from one another, have a great impact on teaching and learning in the classroom. Part Two, "Outer Worlds: Beyond the Classroom," shifts the focus from the personal to the societal level, exposing how powerful forces from outside the classroom — economic, social, political, and cultural — influence the work of teachers and students. Part Three, "The Complex World of Teaching," focuses on the intersection of the inner and outer worlds, illuminating the multiple challenges that are part of the actual work of teaching.

When reading this volume, you may find chapters in one part that connect to and explore themes in other parts. Precisely because the work of teachers is so complex, it is neither possible nor accurate to neatly group these chapters in discrete parts. We have organized the book to highlight particular themes, in the hope that readers will make connections within and among the chapters and appreciate the complexity of the work of teachers.

One part of this complexity is embedded in the histories that students bring to the classroom, as well as in the experiences they have in the classroom — both have a great impact on how they learn and how they interact with other students and teachers at that particular time and place. Part One begins with "The Inner World of Students," presenting three chapters that explore various aspects of this important — and often hidden — world from differing points of view. Chapter one, "Voices of Youth," opens this volume with a short poem written by Kari Larsen, a young woman who lost her family when her village in Vietnam was destroyed in 1973. Her voice emerges from the shadows, no longer hidden by choice or indifference, exposing a side of her that we as teachers might never see, but must neverthe-

[1] Jean V. Carew and Sara Lawrence Lightfoot, *Beyond Bias: Perspectives on Classrooms* (Cambridge, MA: Harvard University Press, 1979), pp. 1-2.

less be sensitive to. How would it affect Kari if we presented a lesson on the plight of Vietnamese refugees without knowing or understanding her history? What important insights would we be losing, through ignorance, by not taking advantage of the knowledge and wisdom stockpiled in her experiences? Kari, like all students, deserves more. Students need us to understand that their lives and experiences are as important as curricular objectives, and that their experiences may interact with ours in unexpected ways that we must be prepared to deal with and understand.

Student histories aren't the only aspect of classroom life that teachers often miss. Chapters two and three examine two other classroom experiences that can greatly influence teaching and learning — peer sexual harassment and unnoticed student interactions. Nan Stein, in "Sexual Harassment in School: The Public Performance of Gendered Violence," explores peer sexual harassment through the voices of students who have experienced harassment, through court cases that have addressed the issue, and through the responses of school officials. She concludes that teachers and other school employees often overlook the antecedents of the harassment — such as bullying and teasing — and at times even overlook the acts themselves, making students' school lives more painful and greatly affecting the opportunity for many students to learn. In chapter three, "Reframing Classroom Research: A Lesson from the Private World of Children," Adrienne Alton-Lee, Graham Nuthall, and John Patrick explore the difference between what teachers believe their lessons are accomplishing and how students are actually affected by them. The disconnect between what teachers believe to be happening and what actually happens is illustrative of the message throughout this entire section — that we, as teachers, must be sensitive to the effects of what we are teaching, who we are teaching, and what is happening to our students. We also need to realize that even the most aware teacher, using the best pedagogy, misses educational opportunities, and that students may be suffering as a result; if this is true, imagine what happens in classrooms where teachers pay only lip-service to understanding the world in which students live. To teachers who avoid deeper understandings of these connections and relationships, simple classroom events must seem disconnected and random.

In the second section of Part One, "The Inner Worlds of Teachers," two teachers and one teacher educator point out the importance of bringing their whole selves to their work. The work of teachers does not begin upon entering the classroom, or even on the first day of official "teacher education." Rather, their personal lives and experiences, as well as their reflections on their work, all influence who they are and how they are as teachers.

Simon Hole, in "Teacher as Rain Dancer," reflects on his teaching and questions the idea that there is a method — like the steps of the rain dance — that will work consistently in the classroom. He reflects on the tension he feels when trying to meet both his students' needs and his own in the classroom — how, he wonders, can he turn this tension caused by conflicting needs into opportunity? These private dilemmas are rarely shared with students though they profoundly affect the work of teachers. In the second chapter of this section, "Zen and the Art of Reflective Practice in Teacher Education," Robert Tremmel makes a theoretical case in support of Hole's approach, asserting that teachers — in order to improve their teaching through a process of self-awareness and critical self-reflection — must "pay attention" to their inner worlds as they teach, and that teacher education programs need to focus much more on this aspect of teaching. In "Cacophony to Symphony: Memoirs in Teacher Research," Karen Hale Hankins rounds out this section by reflecting on her life through her journal, looking to her family experiences for guidance in her current work with students.

Although many teachers wish they could, no one can control all of the influences on our teaching. In Part Two, "Outer Worlds: Beyond the Classroom," we juxtapose theories about how particular aspects of the world outside the classroom can subtly (and not so subtly) affect teaching in the classroom with chapters that depict how sensitive and insightful teachers manage to deal with this reality in practice. In three theoretical chapters, R. W. Connell, Deborah Britzman, and Lilia Bartolomé examine the societal problems of poverty, social reproduction, and racial misunderstandings with respect to their effects on education. Connell, in "Poverty and Education," demonstrates how compensatory programs may reinforce the very patterns of inequality they were designed to counter by forcing children to compete within a structure that is fundamentally unequal. He further argues that at the core of this conflict lies a socially biased curriculum that controls teachers' work in favor of the status quo. In "Cultural Myths in the Making of a Teacher: Biography and Social Structure in Teacher Education," Britzman follows up on Connell's points, showing how the structure of teacher education programs actually works to reinforce that same status quo. Bartolomé, in "Beyond the Methods Fetish: Toward a Humanizing Pedagogy," brings her perspective to this issue by adding the dimensions of race and power. She contends that the current fascination with finding the "right methods" for teaching minority children masks the deeper power structures referred to by Connell and Britzman.

All three authors offer hope for overcoming these obstacles. These hopes are embodied in chapters penned by J. Alleyne Johnson, Carol Stumbo, and Robert Moses, Mieko Kamii, Susan McAllister Swap, and Jeff Howard, which focus primarily on how to apply these ideas in a living, breathing classroom. These chapters focus on three very different strategies. In "Life After Death: Critical Pedagogy in an Urban Classroom," Johnson brings the world of her students into her classroom, incorporating their world into her pedagogy so that both teacher and student can deal with, and focus on, the ways in which outside forces affect how and what they learn. Stumbo uses a different structure to bring the outside world to her students; as she describes in "Beyond the Classroom," she moves them out into that world. By going out and challenging the structures and forces that the outside world places on her classroom, Stumbo comes to a new understanding of how schools function, and how an understanding of the outside world can transform students' lives. Finally, in "The Algebra Project: Organizing in the Spirit of Ella," Moses, Kamii, Swap, and Howard present a third model for facing the limits placed on children by the outside world. This model, based on civil rights–era community organizing, uses parents, teachers, and community members to support and encourage the acquisition of mathematical skills in order to give children, who otherwise would not have had the skills to go to college, the option to someday realize that dream. Each of these teaching models both challenges and illustrates the theoretical structures described by Connell, Britzman, and Bartolomé; having them together in a single section highlights the connections in a way that is clear, concise, and helpful in understanding the complex classroom.

Part Three, "The Complex World of Teaching," explores the ways in which the inner worlds and the outer worlds come together in the classroom. The work of teaching takes place at the convergence of historical, societal, personal, and pedagogical influences; this part of the book captures the different ways these influences play out in the classroom. In the first chapter, "Cognition, Complexity, and Teacher Education," Brent Davis and Dennis Sumara lay a theoretical foundation for the section, asserting that teaching must be explored as the complex, whole system that it is, not as the compilation of separate pieces. Teacher education and practice should not be designed as "if you do X in the classroom, then Y will happen." Rather, teachers and teacher educators must consider the complex and unpredictable connections and relationships that comprise the teaching and learning environment to continue improving practice.

In "How Do Teachers Manage to Teach? Perspectives on Problems in Practice," Magdalene Lampert applies Davis and Sumara's philosophy by looking at what happens when she is faced with dilemmas in the classroom. Rather than simply choosing one solution or another, neither of which actually and completely solves the problem, Lampert chooses to "manage" the situation by working simultaneously with conflicting options. She argues that there is a great deal to learn from teachers who use conflict in the classroom rather than trying to resolve it. Melinda Fine, in "'You Can't Just Say That the Only Ones Who Can Speak Are Those Who Agree with Your Position': Political Discourse in the Classroom," and Kathe Jervis, in "'How Come There Are No Brothers on That List?': Hearing the Hard Questions All Children Ask," also argue for teachers to engage difficult issues in the classroom openly, constructively, and in complex ways, identifying the serious educational pitfalls of avoiding or missing the opportunities for learning through these issues.

Three chapters in Part Three vividly illustrate how aspects of the inner and outer worlds come together around three important areas of the work of teachers: power, teaching methodology, and special education. While each of these chapters focuses on one of these areas, they all contribute in multiple ways to an understanding of the complex classroom. The issue of power pervades Lisa Delpit's chapter, "The Silenced Dialogue: Power and Pedagogy in Educating Other People's Children"; she asserts that the "culture of power" that exists in schools and society is used in the classroom to either maintain the status quo or create change. According to Delpit, it is crucial to teach students — particularly poor students and students of color, and others who don't have access to the dominant culture — the rules of the "culture of power" in order to begin to create opportunities for equitable educational opportunities for all students. Karen Gallas, in "Arts as Epistemology: Enabling Children to Know What They Know," explores the complexity of her classroom through her teaching methodology. Gallas uses the arts in her classroom as a way of connecting to her students and tailoring the curriculum to their learning styles; she finds that being creative with her teaching methodology leads to students discovering a greater understanding of the curricular content. Joseph Cambone, in "Tipping the Balance," reveals many layers of complexity in the work of a special education teacher — the school context, the challenges her students face, societal expectations, and her own desperate desire to find success for herself and her students in this classroom. Cambone's portrait of this teacher and her classroom illustrates and illuminates, in a profound and insightful way, the complexity of the work of teachers.

Finally, Sonia Nieto, in the last chapter of the book, brings us full circle. Talking to students of a variety of racial, ethnic, cultural, and religious backgrounds,

Nieto, in "Lessons from Students on Creating a Chance to Dream," finds that they have a great deal to teach all of us about education. Nieto's chapter ends the book where it starts, the lens focused on the voices of students.

In the end, this volume does not offer solutions; in fact, it is quite clear that the search for a single solution to the challenges teachers face every day is futile. Teaching is not a simple endeavor; there is no recipe that will guarantee success in every classroom. Teaching is incredibly complex, as all teachers will attest. The excitement of teaching is rooted in its unpredictability, the "magic" that teachers and students experience when all of the complex dimensions align in the classroom.

The Complex World of Teaching, rather than joining the search for a "magic bullet," emphasizes the enormous potential inherent in unpredictability and provides a way of thinking about the work of teachers that focuses on understanding the multiple dimensions of teaching. Through exploring the inner worlds of teachers and students, the societal forces that influence teaching, and the convergence of all these aspects of teaching in the classroom, we hope that teachers and teacher educators will find the ideas and strategies that work for them in their own complex classrooms.

ETHAN MINTZ
JOHN T. YUN
Editors

We are grateful to Karen Maloney, Dody Riggs, Joan Gorman, Kelly Graves-Desai, Claire Scott, Kathy Gallagher, and the Editorial Board of the *Harvard Educational Review* for all of their work and support in the creation of this collection.

We also thank Nikki A. Merchant for her help in shaping the content and concept of this volume.

PART ONE

Inner Worlds

SECTION ONE

Inner Worlds of Students

Voices of Youth

This chapter includes eight short pieces written by a diverse group of high school students. Their pieces range from a cry for a mother lost, to a young man's loyalty to his neighborhood, to the loss of teenage innocence. These intensely personal stories, which can be found in every U.S. classroom, are seldom seen or heard by the teachers who are charged with guiding the education of these same students. Students' histories often remain masked — sometimes through the student's choice, sometimes by the overwhelming demands of teaching, and sometimes by the teacher's choice. We present these voices first in this volume to emphasize that every student has a history, and that this history affects every facet of who they are and how they learn. Hearing this point of view is integral to understanding how the complex strands of teaching come together in a classroom. Behind these few voices clamor many more asking for attention and understanding: if we do not hear them, we cannot hope to fully understand or teach the students in our care.

Untitled

KARI LARSEN

this is a poem to my birth mother
whom I never knew

whose sorrow filled Asian eyes,
lovely golden brown complexion,
and raven black hair
are all a figment of my imagination;
for I was too young then,
to now recall your face

I have felt your presence and love often
and you will never be forgotten,
I am a part of you
and I hope you haven't forgotten me

the Vietnam War, the war that separated us,
the war that killed millions
the war that left millions lonely and homeless

it's about you, mother,
about how I wondered
how you are
if you're content, sad, or lonely

I wish that I had a memory of you
a memory of you and I together
so I write this poem to you,
my birth mother whom I never knew

Harvard Educational Review Vol. 58 No. 3 August 1988, 331
Copyright © by Kari Larsen
Published and distributed by *Harvard Educational Review*

The Phone Call

JOY C.

When I look into our photo albums, I often wonder at the innocence and trust apparent in my old photographs. How is it that the baby I was has become the person I am now? It almost seems pointless to ask. Looking at the dozens of photographs, I take note of what I look like: I have my father's hands and his smile, I have the broad powerful frame of both my parents. We are so alike, yet so different. Our similarities are only on the surface, and I think my parents may wonder where this daughter of theirs has come from. I can almost note to the day when I began to diverge from the path they expected of me, or rather, when they noticed that I was headed somewhere they could not follow. I was expected, like my brothers before me, to go to college where I would meet someone (of the opposite gender) to marry. However, by the time I was fifteen, I had realized that I would not be following in my brothers' footsteps, and at this point my parents began to notice that I was not communicating my hopes for the future.

Both my brothers moved away when I was little, and my mom, dad, younger sister, and I live in separate worlds, spheres actually, that occasionally intersect but rarely meet for long. Part of this is due to my independence; I resent asking for anything and rarely do, even when I desperately need help or advice. They did not understand my world, my path, and I did not want them to. Therefore, when I was thirteen I began to withdraw from my parents, stopped talking to them much, except about silly superficial things, like, "How was your day?" "Fine." That was my reply to nearly every question, except for the big one; the question that seemed to tear my entire world apart.

It was my junior year, and I had just turned sixteen in August. School had been in session for a couple of months, and, in general, my life was miserable. Everyone seemed on my back. My relationship with my parents became worse as I began to withdraw more and more. I was trying to drown myself in work in order to keep out of my head. I didn't mind the stress. As long as I didn't have to deal with myself

I was okay. Then, as I was passing by the administration office between classes, the school secretary gave me a message. "Your Mom wants you to call, she says it's important." I didn't really think much about the message. I just figured that she wanted me to run to the store or go to the pharmacy, so when I got a chance I went over to the phone in the office. Standing there staring at the spare, white phone, I suddenly got a strange feeling that this was really not a phone call that I wanted to make. The phone seemed to stare up at me threateningly. I steeled my nerves; it was just a phone call — no reason to worry. Slowly I reached for the phone and dialed. The ring of the phone was unnaturally loud, breaking the silence.

"Hello."

A slightly out of breath voice picked up on the other line.

"Hi Mom, it's me. They said you wanted me to call."

"I went into your room today." At that moment I wanted to sink into the brown carpet beneath me. Every square inch of my being longed to run as far away from that phone as possible. My hand clenched the bone-white receiver in a painful grip and I clung to the edge of the desk like a sailor clinging to a life raft. With that brief statement, I knew that what I had been trying to hide for so long was out. She knew. There was nothing I could do about it. Through my own carelessness I would never be able to face my parents again.

I keep journals obsessively. They help me organize my feelings. They are an outlet for everything I cannot say to anyone. With those words I knew that mom had done the unthinkable: she had read my thoughts. I glanced at the clock; "Mom, I have math. I really have to go. Please."

"No, I need to know something; when I went into your room to open the curtain, I found something, and I need to know if it's true." Her words were choppy and pained. Slowly I spoke.

"What?" The room seemed to be getting smaller, and my breath quickened as I clenched my fist and felt my fingernails dig into my palm. Everything seemed to spin about me as she read my own words back to me verbatim. I could vividly remember writing that page in my journal and at that moment I regretted ever laying pen to paper, ever living, ever breathing, ever thinking.

"It says here 'I'm a lesbian' and I want to know if that's true."

I released the breath that had turned stale in my lungs. Shakily I spoke into the receiver.

"Mom, I have class, I have to go." What could I say? I clenched my fist harder, rocking back and forth in my shoes.

"No, I need to know. No matter what I still love you." I could almost hear the tears in her voice and I, too, was close to the edge.

"No . . . Mom, I have to go, I'm on the school phone." I felt my voice grow firm as I struggled to regain control.

"Then why did you write it?"

"Mom, I have to go." Then, for the first time in my life, I hung up on her. Conversation over. Picking up my books I rushed out of the room, her words echoing again and again throughout my head, driving out thought of all else. As I looked out at the brilliant blue sky I felt so small, and the world outside seemed so big. It was a beautiful view that left no escape. I knew that I could not hide forever, and the rest of my life stretched out before me — a new era.

The next few weeks were hard on all of us as my mom searched for a concrete reason for my lesbianism. I was grounded for several months and sent to a psychiatrist in hopes that I would change. Because I was not prepared to come out to my parents, I was unable to explain to my mother that my sexuality was not anybody's fault. Several of our discussions dissolved into screaming matches as she accused me of tearing our family apart. My dad, on the other hand, pretended nothing had happened and refused to even say the word "lesbian." My parents did not want me to tell my sister or brothers, and I agreed because I was not ready to deal with their reactions.

Since the initial day of my mom's discovery, we've talked a lot, and now, more than a year and a half later, my mom still has difficulty accepting my sexuality. But, coming to terms with being out to my parents has taught me to respect the strength it takes to be myself when so many stand against me. Gradually I have learned to love and respect myself for the strengths I have. I never want to have to hide again.

Maybe someday my mom will be able to see me as my friends do: opinionated, verbose, feminist, bookworm, writer, philosopher, actress, and idealist who also happens to have a crush on Melissa Etheridge. Maybe someday she will realize that my lesbianism is just one part of a very complex whole — something that has contributed to my identity and broadened my horizons. Whether or not "someday" ever comes, I know that I have the strength to continue to be who I am. So, on the first day of the fall semester, listen for my contagious laugh and look for the rainbows I wear with pride.

Harvard Educational Review Vol. 66 No. 6 Summer 1996, 175–177

When Things Get Hectic

JUAN AZIZE

Last summer I was headed to the bodega around my block to get a hero when I saw my boy Deps step to some kid I'd never seen before. Being the nosy friend that I am, I went over to see what the problem was. "Yo Deps, what's going on man?" I said.

"This b—ch ass n—ga got an eye problem." Deps answered.

"Whatever man," said the kid. I noticed he got scared when I came over, knowing there were two of us now and this wasn't his neighborhood.

But fighting over a bad look wasn't exactly the move. "Yo, forget about that sh-t man," I said. "He don't want no beef."

"So why he trying to scope if he don't want none?" said Deps.

"I wasn't scoping at you man," answered the kid.

"Yo man, squash this bullsh-t already so I could get my sandwich," I told Deps. "My stomach is growling."

"Aaiight man, just don't be trying to act like you represent around here," Deps told the kid. They both gave each other the hand along with dirty looks and slow moves.

After the fake pound, I went inside the store to get my salami and cheese and Deps tagged along. About 15 minutes later there we were chilling in front of my

Glossary

Beef — a problem or dispute.

Shank — a boxcutter or any sharp object other than a knife. Also the act of cutting someone.

Crib — house, apartment . . . the place where you live.

Bodega — corner grocery store.

Scope — look or stare at somebody.

Squash — the process of solving a problem without violence.

Represent — the act of standing up for something, a neighborhood, a certain place, for yourself, etc.

Pound — the hand change of two people when greeting.

Fair one — a fair fight, one on one.

Catch their back — back somebody up, being there for them.

Blasted — get shot up bad.

Trooping out to a jam — to go to a party.

Rolling deep — hanging out with a lot of people.

Finesse — the style or way people carry themselves.

Riff — to argue or dispute over something.

Get hectic — get wild, violent, or out-of-hand.

5-0s — the cops, police.

Hype — the excitement or the high feeling inside during a wild event.

Front — back down or hide from the truth, pretend to be something you're not.

Strapped — armed with a gun.

Glock — a powerful type of gun.

Nine — a 9-mm handgun.

Jansport — a brand name of backpacks.

house. It was really hot and we were trying to throw girls in front of the hydrant and munching down that delicious hero when, all of a sudden, a blue Corolla with tinted windows rolled up in front of us.

Drive-By Time

I knew right away this was the kid Deps was riffing to. I remember the hero losing its delicious taste. The girls were still teasing us, trying to get us to chase them, when Deps tapped my leg cause he knew what time it was. Before I could yell "duck," I saw the back window roll down enough for a gun to fit through. I grabbed Deps like a reflex and we both hit the floor at the same time two bullets hit the side of my house.

The car was long gone before me and Deps had a chance to feel burnt. All of a sudden the girls didn't want to play anymore and it wasn't that sunny. I never knew things could get to that point so fast. A dirty look setting bullets off didn't make any sense. What if they had caught us from behind? What if they had shot one of the girls? What if my mother had been standing there?

It really made me think deep. I wanted to kill those guys, I was so steamed. I was confused. I was flipping. I rode around with my friends looking for that blue Corolla for that whole week. Deps got a gun that same day hoping they were going to come back, which didn't happen.

Blasted over Something Stupid

This kind of thing goes on all the time: "Yo, you heard who got shot?" "I ran into some beef today." "Yo man, bring a shank just in case." I am sick and tired of hearing it. Violence surrounds us everywhere: school, work, even in front of your crib. That's the number one reason for deaths among teens in New York City. Kids nowadays are ready to kill each other over the dumbest things.

I know a lot of kids who are scared one day they are just going to get blasted for something stupid like that. There are so many other kids out there with guns, knives, and short tempers.

I live in Corona, Queens and when the weekends come I feel like I am in a battle zone. Before trooping it out to a jam I always have to make sure I am rolling with my little crew in case things get hectic. Most of the jams I've been to end up with a shootout or a rumble.

And this stuff doesn't just go down where I live. In school all the gossip in the hallway is about things happening in the streets. I know lots of people also carry weapons to school but the beef is outside most of the time.

There was this time, last year in my old school, when my boy Duzer was supposed to shoot a fair one with another kid in school, so my little crew got together to keep it a fair fight.

Shanked over a Girl

When eighth period came we all hit the handball courts. While Duzer hopped around to get ready, I saw kids pulling shanks and hammers out of their Jansports. I knew this wasn't going to be no fair fight, fake gangstas put that out of style trying to find the easy way out.

It started to get hectic: people were getting shanked up and hammered down. I was playing it safe and taking them sucker punches every chance I had. It was an even rumble, not counting the fact that they had more weapons. (I admit I was scared to death about them hammers.)

When the 5-0's rolled up we were gone with the wind. A couple of kids couldn't run so they stayed on the floor covering their sore spots. My boy Eliester had a thin slice on his neck and had to get 11 stitches. The rest of us had shanked jackets and arms, nothing serious (thank God).

We ran to the hospital about 10 blocks away. About a half hour later, after the hype went down, I stopped Duzer in the waiting room and asked him what the beef was all about. I almost started to laugh when I heard the answer: "He was trying to tell me who I wasn't allowed to talk to," answered Duzer. "Yo, I was up on that b—ch way before that n—ga even dreamed about it."

A girl! I didn't understand. One of our boys gets sliced in the neck with 11 stitches and three other kids were left on the floor bleeding like cold. This sh-t was pathetic, killing each other over a girl who's probably ready to move on to the next man. Eight tracks make better sense than that.

Your Boys Are Your Boys

I am not gonna front though. If my boys get into more senseless beef, I am still going to catch their backs and I won't stop to ask them what the problem is. Adrenalin flows faster than questions, and my boys have always been there for me when I needed them without asking questions and trying to talk it out.

I guess it must be written in that invisible book that knows everything, the one where ladies go first and actions speak louder than words. The funny thing is, I follow that book. If my boys have beef again I'll be there asking mute questions that come out too late. It's like a reflex. It shouldn't be, but it is. Your boys are your boys. I do stop to think about it, but only after it's too late, after the damage is already done.

Harvard Educational Review Vol. 65 No. 2 Summer 1995, 262–264

From Fighta to Writa:
How a Friend Changed My Life

KENYETTA IVY

I came into the system in '92. It was in the summer. I remember the night I went to Light St., my first group home.

I arrived at 1:30 in the morning. When I entered the house I was scared, 'cause I always heard that people died in group homes. When I got inside, the girls were all sitting in the lounge. There were 25 girls in the house.

I stayed there for only a month, because I started hanging with the wrong crowd. I was smoking weed, drinking, and fighting. I was considered the baddest girl in the house. They had to get me out of there, so they moved me to another group home.

This one was called Coney Island Diagnostic. It had four girls living there. But I was kicked out 'cause I broke a girl's jaw. Me and the girl were screaming in the hall after the staff went to bed. The next day the girl told the staff it was my fault. I got in trouble for that, so I hit her. When I left for school the staff said don't come back, so I didn't.

America's Most Wanted

I went to my grandmother's house and stayed there for two weeks. I was getting badder and badder. My friend's mother said I would be on "America's Most

Wanted" at age 16. I told her, "Ha, I fooled you, I'm in a group home." I thought everything was a joke.

When I left my grandmother's house, I went to my old group home, Sheltering Arms. My male friends would pay me to get them girls they could have sex with. They called me a female pimp. I was asking myself, "How can I do this to another girl?" But I didn't care.

In October, 1992, I went to court to get placed into another group home. It was a few days after my 17th birthday. They placed me in a 30-day transitional center in Brooklyn.

This was a group home I fell in love with. I loved it so much 'cause all we did was smoke weed and have fun. I had a crew in there called B.M.P. (Blunt Master Possie). We broke every rule in the book.

I eventually had to leave because my 30 days were up.

This time they moved me to a lockdown in Queens. It was a co-ed group home, boys and girls. I went there with the intention of leaving. I was going to leave "By Any Means Necessary," so that's just what I did.

Me and the few friends I made in the three weeks I was there beat up this girl. The girl thought she was all that. My friends grabbed the girl outside the house. We beat her so bad she pressed charges.

When we got to the police station, they said I was going to jail. I was scared but I really didn't care. I stayed at the station for a few hours, then was let go. I went back to the group home. The next day I got moved again.

Eight Group Homes

Moving from place to place was fun at first. By February of '93 I had been in eight group homes, picked up a tag name, and had over 20 fights. (My tag name was Bonnie, as in "Bonnie and Clyde," the bank robbers.)

My last group home was back in the Bronx again. When I got there, I was wondering how long I would stay — a month, a week, a day, or at the rate I was going, an hour.

Staff seemed nice at first. Most of the time I stayed to myself, because the girls didn't come home until night time.

The coolest girl in the house was Kathy. I thought she was cool from the first time I met her because she was so quiet. But when I would start fights with the girls in the house, if they said something wrong to me, Kathy would jump right in.

The staff in the house said that Kathy acted like my mother or something. She would always get me out of trouble. I still fought, but I was starting to slow down. See, every time I got into a fight, Kathy would take me for a walk.

Kathy was the only one who ever (I mean ever since I was born) encouraged me to make something out of myself. She told me fighting was not the move. I looked at her as a mother figure, because she treated me like she really cared and I knew she did.

I always thought that the people I hung out with cared, but I was wrong. Kathy said that if they cared for you, they wouldn't tell you to do bad things, such as smoking and stuff, but the right things. I knew she was right, because when I followed her advice I always had a positive outcome.

Could It Be She Was Changing Me?

Kathy and I were hanging out more and more. After a while, I started calling her my best friend. The staff became jealous, because at one point Kathy had been close to them. She used to tell them her problems, but now she was confiding in me.

Staff started calling me "sneaky" and told the other residents not to trust me. Kathy said, "Bonnie, you're not sneaky, they just don't understand you."

In the system, residents understand other residents 'cause they have almost the same problems. Staff thinks and looks at it another way. So they put us down mentally, emotionally, sometimes physically. Kathy said that I just needed someone to care for me.

She would always tell me it was positive over negative, and that if you respect a person, you will get the same respect back. I became a positive person. I was given a single room. When I first arrived I was on restriction every day, and now I was never on restriction.

It came to the point that when I saw a fight, I would try to break it up. I never knew a person could change someone that much, but Kathy changed me. She gave me a heart I could not get anywhere else. I think that if I hadn't met Kathy, I would still be listening to those people who call themselves my "friends."

Me and Kathy made big plans to go to college and then into the health field. I stayed in my room and wrote poems while she practiced dancing.

We were chosen to see Mayor Dinkins for a special discussion on youth. (Back in the days, the only person I thought I would be chosen to see was the judge.)

A Friendship Lost

Every night before I went to bed, I would thank God for a friend like her. Now I think that maybe that wasn't enough.

One day me and Kathy got into a fight because I called her a b-tch. I was only playing, but she took it the wrong way. We got into a verbal fight. I got mad and said a lot of things that hurt her.

She always told me you can't break up a true friendship, but I now realize that you can after I felt the pain of losing a friend.

I miss Kathy and still love her dearly. After a while I gave up on getting our friendship back, 'cause I kept trying and it wasn't working.

Now I'm still on the right track and still thinking of the advice she gave me. I thank God for the good times as well as the bad. Although we are no longer friends, I just don't know where I would be without her.

I know if God wants it, we will be friends again, and I hope that day is soon.

Harvard Educational Review Vol. 65 No. 2 Summer 1995, 276–278

Celebrate Humanity Day Speech

KATHRYN ZAMORA-BENSON

One Friday afternoon I was sitting with a group of my peers at a Sexual Preference Awareness Group (SPAG), when the possibility of presenting a piece on homophobia at my school was mentioned by one of our student sponsors. SPAG is a group of students who have the opportunity to exchange feelings, questions, and stories with others undergoing similar experiences. The group had been active for several years in my school and had a reputation among the handful of students who attended weekly lunches as being a valuable asset.

I had been waiting for an occasion like speaking at Diversity Day for quite a while. Three years earlier, my school had a series of fraudulent bomb threats and hate-mail given to several African American faculty members on campus. From that time on, I have noticed an increasing effort from my school, mainly the administration, to open the campus to culturally diverse students, faculty, and ideas. However, several groups, such as the homosexual/bisexual population on campus, have been ignored. Because the new trend was to be politically correct, SPAG decided it was an ideal time to be heard. Together, as a group, we would present the strong voice for sexual preference diversity that we felt our school lacked.

For the next several weeks I prepared to stand in front of a gymnasium full of my peers, mentors, friends, and enemies (if I can even call them that), and give a speech on essentially . . . me. The following manuscript is the speech I gave at Diversity Day last year at my school. It is an invitation to youth and adults alike to search within themselves to see if they might be, like me, scared of or trapped by who they are. My purpose was to say that I am in a state of constant questioning of who I am, and I wanted to let anyone in the audience who might be feeling my feelings know that it was OK.

My speech was a plea for change, a request for tolerance, and an offer of myself. I hope reading this evokes thought and questioning within you.

Celebrate Humanity Day Speech

To those of you who do not know me, my name is Kathryn Zamora-Benson and I am a junior at this school. I stand here not as a stranger, plucked from society and placed before you on a stage in yet another forum, but as your peer, your student, your friend, someone you see every day in the halls, in the quad, or in the classroom. Sadly, I do not stand here in trust and comfort, but in fear. Fear that you who befriend me today will turn your backs to me tomorrow. Fear that those same people who whispered "Go home, Dyke!" to Erin Best during a forum a few weeks ago will now say that to me. Fear that I will be left alone.

I want to talk to you all about homophobia, something important to me, something that hurts a lot of people here at the Academy. Our school is in the long process of eliminating discrimination from our community, and I do see an honest effort being made regarding the issue of color. However, the Academy stops there. Other minorities and oppressed groups are hushed, as if they do not exist. Contrary to its "Commitment To Diversity" statement, the Academy does not provide an environment where people of differing gender, religion, ethnicity, or sexual orientation can grow fully. No healthy person can thrive in the midst of a sea of sexism, homophobia, and other types of prejudice. Diversity at Albuquerque Academy is Black and White . . . literally.

Homophobia at Albuquerque Academy may be hidden under layers of polite surface smiles and monotonous mottoes and mission statements, but it lies there nevertheless. Homophobia, although subtle, is present. I have felt it breathing down my neck, my soft blond hairs rising defensively in the victim's agitations. I have heard it on the tongues of those who speak to me, I have seen it in the gaze of spectators waiting to see who wins the next round, I have felt it in the sympathetic concerns I am dished out daily. The monster, the beast, invades not me, in spite of the majority's opinion of who I am. The monster is not homosexuality. The monster is not bisexuality. The monster is not heterosexuality. The monster at Albuquerque Academy is fear and ignorance.

Oppression is the child of these. The beginning of a breed of imp-like creatures from the copulation of this monster came not as an order of the Universe, not as a part of the Common Good, but as an accident, maybe even as a lesson to be found and learned. I could feign compassion for the oppressors, I could be sympathetic to the victims, but I am not. I will not pretend to know how to judge the opinions, to say who will win and who will lose. I know that I hurt when the monster makes decaying stew of something that was benign and simple-hearted. I could cry out for help as do swarms of the world's victims or I could stand my ground and let it roll off of my back. I am shaking in the torrent of the waterfall, almost pulled under into the rotating whirlpool of the waters, but I stand still. I stand because I can, because my identity is not tainted, but pure. I stand because I must.

The best way I can represent and stand up for the overwhelming fear felt not only by homosexual and bisexual students, but also by heterosexual students aware of the ignorance and indifference to alternative sexualities, is to use my fear and my experience as examples.

I believe that while we are constantly shifting and floating in a three-dimensional universe, we engage and attach to others floating with us. Some unions are brief and connected with the most unreliable mortar. With others, the roots of the grass we lie on grow together, entwine, and become the same lawn, the same rising stalk of plant. So it was with my friend, and, in spite of the world around and within us, I believe it is still.

On an October Sunday morning, my female friend and I had no conversational boundaries between us on the fast track home on I-40. It is unbelievable how natural the sexual experience was. We both realized that we had shared something unique and beautiful, a one-time occurrence that brought us closer as friends. With any other person, this experience would have broken the delicate footing, the bond that is created when your slab of grass fits with that of another. Contradictory to all the impurities commonly associated with any homosexual or bisexual act, the experience was without any overtones of animalistic lust or sexuality. All that was present was the love and friendship I felt for her and the love and friendship she felt for me.

Now, I can imagine one question burning in your minds right now: "Is she gay? Is Kathryn Zamora-Benson gay?" I will tell you that for me, the question is, "Is she bi?" And while I make it a general rule to never respond to that question, I will do so now, in order to mirror the answer of high school students across this campus and across this country: "I don't know." As a sixteen-year-old girl, I am confused as to what I feel, and what I am allowed to feel. Because of the lack of space for questioning one's sexuality here at the Academy, the only honest answer I have is, "I don't know." I am not given the opportunity to discover and learn fully who I am, nor is any other student here at the Academy.

My situation at this school is precarious. I am good friends with people involved in the theater, which is commonly associated with drugs. This puts me at odds with the administration. I am adamantly against tobacco, alcohol, hallucinogens, Advil, and any other drug that manipulates our senses and erodes away our bodies, putting me at odds with many of the students. I need not another reason to become excluded, hated, or oppressed, yet I have one: homophobia. It runs rampant through the actions and words of people at my school. This hunt of hate must stop.

When I looked into my friend's eyes that frosted Sunday morning, I was looking into the naive goodness of love. How is it that love is categorized? I do not know. How is it that someone else would take a love and twist it into something cruel? I cannot answer. But, I know that love is love, with or without a sexual relationship. The loyalty and passion of soul I feel for all of my friends is a love that is greater than any I have ever had for a "boyfriend," for whom it is considered "normal" and "commendable" to have such feelings. I have never understood who made the distinction between loves, who conceived the unspoken agreement for what is "normal" and what is "weird." However, because the monster is here to stay, for all of our noble intentions, I recognize that I must work to open the eyes and hearts of the few whom I can reach.

This is my hope for the future at the Academy: I ask the administration to give a statement saying where they stand specifically on the issue of homophobia. I believe that by starting with the teachers and the policies of this school, eradication of prejudices, hurt, and fear will one day free the hearts and minds of the students. I try not to let the monster hurt me as it manipulates my brain and oozes over my community. I try not to be oppressed, as has every person at this school. I have tried, and will continue to try.

Harvard Educational Review Vol. 66 No. 2 Summer 1996, 178–180

Building 860

CHRISTIAN NEIRA

When trying to live in two different worlds, one is in peril of not belonging to either of them. One is left in a state of confusion. The morals, behavior, thinking, and perspective of the world of a New York City housing project are radically different from those of an elite preparatory school in the same city. Being put in the position of changing one's character every morning and afternoon to adapt to two different worlds endangers one's identity.

I remember one incident during high school that demonstrates the tightrope that I walked. I was coming out of my home when I saw one of my neighbors also leaving for school. While waiting for the elevator, we began to talk. I was dressed in compliance with the dress code of my school: tie and jacket. She told me she went to Joan of Arc, the public junior high school across the street from my school. I told her I was dressed like this because I went to the Trinity School. Her expression was one of deep shock and pity. She asked, "How do you survive?" I first thought she meant how did I survive living in the projects, but later that day in school I came to the realization that she meant to ask how I survived at the preparatory school.

Each of the two cultures considered me a foreigner, one who did not belong. Where my allegiance resided was their question. Neither world fully understood me because these two cultures almost never meet, and when they meet on the street, violence and suspicion are their common language.

The Week

Monday morning. It begins with a distant rumbling sound that intensifies as it approaches. The walls begin to vibrate. The sound reaches a crescendo of steel against steel as the New York City subway rolls by my window. I look at the graffiti-covered train as it passes, and I remember the kid at school whose parents are art collectors and collect graffiti paintings. The worst vibrations occur when two subways pass simultaneously. The only benefit of having an elevated train so close by is that it is a most effective alarm clock on a Monday morning.

There are three locks and a chain on my apartment door. As I open the door, the wind rushes in from the hallway, and with it comes the odor of rotten food. Outside, the hall is barely five feet wide, not enough space for two people to walk along side by side. The ceiling always leaks and pieces of paint and plaster sometimes fall on you as you walk along. The hall was recently painted, painted by someone with a spray paint can, that is. He left his street name painted on the floor.

As I walk toward the elevators I can only pray that they will be working this morning. One has been out since Saturday. I look through the hole in the elevator door to see if any cables are moving, the indicator that the elevator is working. After a few minutes of waiting for any signs, I resign myself to taking the stairs. Waiting any longer is futile.

The door to the stairs scrapes the floor as I try to push it open; it is held in place by only one hinge. Something is blocking the door from swinging open. As I squeeze through the opening, the odor of discarded food, plastic wrappers, and cans strikes me in the face. I quickly turn away in disgust and run down the stairs.

The best way to get down the stairs is to run, but it is not the safest way. Taking the stairs is like plunging into the darkness of a cave hoping to emerge at the other end. There are no lights; the bulbs have either burned out or the sockets simply do not work. As you run down you have to be careful not to lose your balance on the crack vials that litter the floor.

On the first floor I see a mother with a stroller waiting for the elevator. As I push the front door open and emerge onto the street, I yell to her that the elevators aren't working. My friend Mike is already waiting for me at the train station.

Monday lunch. The usual bunch of us sit together. The only thing we all have in common is that we eat lunch together. Some of us have shared experiences; others in the group have experiences and backgrounds that are foreign.

The discussions on Mondays start with Jonathan Swaine III telling the rest of us about his weekend. It is all very predictable, something about a country house somewhere. I never pay much attention to his stories because they do not seem real and tangible to me. They are very much a part of his life, but the stories of weekend country houses are not meaningful to me. I don't think he tells us his weekend stories to impress us; he must have gotten the impression long before that his stories had no effect on the rest of us in either a positive or negative ways. He sits with us because he wants to learn from our experiences, which are different from his own. We are a "good experience" that somehow reveals to him a different world. He takes advantage of the "diversity" of the school to have an "interesting experience."

Ragavendra is supposed to give Jonathan that unique experience. The name Ragavendra was Americanized into Rags by the teachers. Since reading the *Autobiography of Malcolm X*, Rags had become a fervent Indian nationalist. He tells us that he did not do anything exciting over the weekend. "The usual," he said. Translated this means that he spent the weekend working as a stock boy at the small bodega (grocery store) only three blocks from where I live.

Rags lives just north of me. I once visited his home. It is in a five-story tenement building next to a vacant lot. There were kids having a snowball fight in the lot; they would hide behind piles of discarded ties and abandoned cars. Another group of kids climbed a dumpster and jumped onto an old box spring that they used as a trampoline to fly into the sky.

To enter Rags's home you had to walk through the kitchen. There were four large pots of boiling water giving off heat, and the oven was turned to broil. The landlord refused to give any steam, saying that the boiler was broken. The tenants had retaliated with a rent strike, but were being served with eviction notices. A white sheet hung outside the window of the apartment, emblazoned with the words, "SUPPORT OUR RENT STRIKE."

The next person down the table is my friend Mike, who waits for me every morning at the train station. He spends his weekends and some week nights patrolling the buildings of the Frederick Douglass Housing Projects. A group of tenants wear jackets that read on the back, "Tenant Patrol." They set up a desk in the front lobby of a building which has no lock on the front door and try to ensure that only tenants enter the building. There are more than two dozen buildings in the Douglass Projects, and their efforts are, to a large degree, futile. No amount of time or effort could ensure any degree of safety to the people who enter these buildings.

No lunch group like ours would be complete without a person who desperately needs to be around people very different yet similar to himself. his real name is Eduardo Fernandez, but he wants people to call him Edward. I compromise and call him Ed. His mother is on the school's Board of Trustees and his father is a bank executive. They grew up in El Barrio (Spanish Harlem), but now live in a penthouse on Fifth Avenue. In many ways, Ed's parents' success is what Mike, Rags, and I hope to duplicate. Yet we fear Edward; he has what Rags once called the "Oreo disease." Trying to hide his real name is only a small part of the confusion he has about his cultural background. He would never call himself Latino, but he knows he cannot call himself a WASP. His parents shelter him so much from the environment that they grew up in that he is reduced to hearing about El Barrio over the lunch table. Ed gropes to understand his Latino background but at the same time denies it, trivializing it in order to move within the WASP culture of the school.

By the time the conversation reaches me, lunch is almost over, so I simply tell them I gardened. There is a neighborhood community garden on what was once the site of a dope house that the city tore down. So, in the minds of city officials the problem was resolved, but the rubble of the building was left in the lot. The community finally cleared the lot and established a garden on the site. It was planted with flowers and assorted plants. Still, the garden is not a pretty sight. Cardboard, pieces of plywood, and a chain-linked fence serves as a fence around the lot. The bricks that once littered the lot are used for pathways through the garden. Tires are used to hold up some plants.

One section is devoted to vegetables. Urban kids who have never seen the plants that vegetables come from always try to guess what each plant produces. Once, one boy pointed to a plant and said with a great deal of authority, "That's a pickle plant!" An older girl snapped back, "No, no, dummy, there's no such thing as a pickle plant. It's a tomato plant."

One section of the garden is devoted to food and medicinal herbs. Señora Rosa works in the herb section; she is the "country doctor" of the community. After people have tried countless doctors and their ailments persist, they consult Señora Rosa. The patient makes an offering (usually money) to Señora Rosa's statue of the Virgin Mary, and she prescribes the necessary herbs. The herb section also serves as the community bulletin board; people gather there to pick the herbs Señora Rosa recommends and to exchange neighborhood gossip.

Monday afternoon. There is a large crowd in front of my building as I approach. No one can get into the building because the front door is locked. Management decided to put a lock on the door because residents had complained that people could just walk in off the street. The problem was that management had forgotten to give anyone the key to the lock. In every group, someone has a bright idea. One kid reaches for the fire hose and uses the metal part to break the glass part of the door, reaches in, and opens the door.

Now a second wait begins, the wait for the elevator. One of them is rumored to be working so everyone waits in anticipation. Everyone tries to listen for the sound of chains rattling that indicates the elevator is moving. The waiting crowd grows, as more people enter, using the new doorknob. After what seems like an interminable wait, one elevator reaches the first floor. Before anyone can get off, the crowd presses forward. Three boys file out. One man in the waiting crowd accuses them of holding up the elevator. They snap back, telling the old man to mind his own business.

Close to fifteen people file into the completely dark elevator. The light bulb is missing. We all take a breath of air before the door swings shut. Our bodies are pressed so close together that no one can move. At every stop, everyone must file out to let someone off and then file back in. By counting the glimpses of light that reflect off other people's faces, I count the number of floors passed.

Tuesday night. Outside on the street are voices yelling at each other over the noise of their boom-box radio. Someone from the building yells at them to go away; it is two in the morning. The yelling and music continue, only louder. After a few minutes, I see a bottle sailing through the air. It came from above me and I live on the eleventh floor. The bottle crashes on one of the yelling men, and I say to myself, "Good hit!"

A couple of hours later while I am writing an English paper, I hear the fire alarm go off. I run toward the living room and see smoke coming through the racks in the front door. Outside, the hallway is filled with people and smoke. I run to call the fire department. After I give the operator my address, the first questions she asks is whether I'm calling form the projects. "Yes, yes," I scream into the receiver, "just hurry — there's a fire in the building!"

By the time the fire department arrives, we have extinguished the fire in the garbage chute. People passed buckets of water and poured them down the chute. The garbage had been backed up to the fifth floor and had caught on fire. The entire scene reminded me of a nineteenth-century bucket brigade.

Wednesday English class. I recount last night to my English teacher because I do not have my creative writing assignment. He simply stares at me, neither in surprise not disbelief. He is clueless; he does not know how to judge my story. No amount of training in preparatory schools has equipped him with the tools to evaluate this excuse. The rest of the class files into the room, and they begin to read out loud the stories they had written the night before. One story keeps ringing in my mind:

> This was one of the scariest experiences of my life. I was walking along 72nd and Park Avenue heading downtown. I stopped at the curb to wait for the light to change. On my left there appeared three guys about my age. I continued to walk along and crossed towards Fifth. I looked back and realized that those same three guys were following me. I started to walk a little faster, then run, but they were still following me. On 66th and Fifth one of the guys grabbed me from behind. I turned around and looked at this greasy, hairy, slimy Rican right in the eyes.

My chest tightens. The entire class is looking straight into Mike's eyes — the Puerto Rican in the class. There is a long, tense pause and only Mike can break the silence. He say, "Oh, was that you we got? Sorry."

There is a laughter of relief.

Thursday afternoon. By the end of the day the incident in English class has spread throughout the school. The story and reaction are slightly different in every version I hear. One version had Mike picking up his desk and throwing it across the room.

Rags and I walk home together. We retell the story over and over again, laughing at the incident in the beginning but becoming more and more angry with each retelling. "That's what they think of Blacks and Latinos. They have no other image," he says. "The only contact they have with any Black or Latino is as their doorman or their housecleaner. Then you have people like Edward that, instead of being a positive image of a Chicano, is wrapped up in trying to be a WASP. A double-stuffed Oreo is what he is! The rest of us are there to legitimize their White institution. You know the building they are building across the street from the school? Ten years ago the school sued the city not to build a low-income building on the lot. Now the school has gotten its way; they are building a luxury building on the lot. So, to 'improve relations with the neighborhood' they let the kids in the community center use the pool, and they let in a handful of Blacks and Latinos to add color to the place."

As we approach home, Rags and I start to laugh again at the story; there is not much of anything else we can do. We stop in front of the garden to see if anything has grown. From behind me I hear an echoing noise and then some screams. Before I can figure out that the noises I hear are gun shots, I am pushed to the ground. All I can do is hold my bookbag tightly over my head. My face is buried in Rags's back as we both crouch behind a car not knowing where the noises are coming from.

One man kneeling beside me yells in my ear that there is a pusher shooting madly into the air in front of 860.

"I will never get home," I think to myself, "860 is my building." After a few noiseless minutes, people start to run toward their buildings and up the stairs.

A couple of hours later when I am trying to get some schoolwork done, I look at my social studies paper topic: "In light of our discussion on the rights and protections afforded to citizens by the Constitution, discuss the question of the 'right' of the government to make certain drugs illegal and whether these drugs should be legalized." I tear up the paper in disgust.

Friday night. I get off the crosstown bus on 96th and start to walk down Fifth. As I approach the building on 88th, the door swings open and the doorman asks if I am here for Edward's party.

"Right, for Eduardo's party," I reply.

He directs me to the elevator on the left. The elevator is already waiting for me. On the way up I begin to talk to the elevator man; his name is Señor Manuel. I know him from other visits I have made and because he is the husband of Señora Rosa. We talk about how the garden is growing this year and how it needs a fence. The lights on the elevator panel finally reach PH. The elevator door opens onto another door. There is no hallway to walk, just another door. Inside, the entire school is having a party.

In need of some air, I walk onto the terrace. Mike is leaning against the wall looking out toward the lighted skyline and over Central Park. We do not say much for a while. Then he asks, "What you think of the story yesterday? I mean, you think I said the right thing?"

I look across the park uptown toward the group of buildings where we live. They are easily differentiated from the other buildings if you know what to look for.

"What else was I suppose to say? If I hit the guy like I wanted, out I go. One less Puerto Rican in the school is not going to bother them. These people have no sense that we exist in that school. No matter what they do or say we are simply nameless bodies that walk the halls. No name. No character. It is beyond the stage where they don't want us there; now they simply are oblivious to our presence. We only figure in their minds when we are called upon to agree that their notions of us are the right ones."

On the way home, we walk across Central Park in silence. The scenery changes very quickly when you walk uptown. We reach my building. I push the door open; the lock has been taken off, and pieces of glass are still on the floor. Ms. Johnson is waiting in front of the elevators. She is in a wheelchair.

"I've been waiting for the elevators for more than an hour and I can't get home," she says.

Mike gets into the elevator and presses all the buttons. It does not move. "Maybe if we call the cops they can do something," I say. "A woman that was here earlier called but they haven't come. Housing cops never come," she says. "Well, it's close to midnight and we can't leave her here," Mike says to me. Mike needs to prove something to himself tonight.

Before I know what I have gotten myself into we are carrying Ms. Johnson up the stairs, all twenty flights. It takes us over three hours to carry Ms. Johnson in her wheelchair. She never stops talking during those three hours. She tells us that she is going to City College and studying to become a social worker. Mike and I can barely talk as we concentrate on moving up the stairs.

A Closing Thought

Poised between two different worlds, I have learned that the emotional power of some experiences can never be conveyed to another. Outsiders can only begin to appreciate that which is foreign to them when they realize that they will never fully understand.

Harvard Educational Review Vol. 58 No. 3 August 1988, 337–342

A Dream Guy, a Nightmare Experience

ANONYMOUS

I'm lying on the floor, in a dark room, unable to move. Then I see him, standing over me, laughing. I try to move, but I'm paralyzed. He gets closer and closer and right when he's about to kiss me, I wake up, screaming. After that I'm too upset to go back to sleep, so I sit up and cry all night.

My nightmares aren't as vivid as before, but they're there. Just when I think it's finally over, the memories come back to haunt me. I keep thinking that maybe I could have done something to prevent it. Maybe if I hadn't been such a sucker for a happy ending. Maybe if I had thought ahead. Maybe . . . Maybe . . .

I Was 13

We didn't go to the same schools but he lived in the neighborhood, and was always hanging around. I used to see him in the morning, before school. He was about 16, kind of tall, with short, dark hair, and the most beautiful grey eyes I've ever seen. He'd say "hi" when he saw me and even though I didn't really know him, I started to like him. Occasionally, I'd stop and talk to him — nothing too personal. We talked about the movies we'd seen, music and stuff like that. I began to look forward to our little talks, and was disappointed when I didn't see him around the school. I was 13 at the time.

One day, after school, he was waiting for me. I was with my friend Charlene. We were talking outside the school and I pretended that I didn't see him. He kept trying to get my attention, but I pretended not to notice. I don't know why — maybe I didn't want Charlene to know I had a crush on him.

He Carried My Books

When I said goodbye to my friend, I walked slowly to the end of my block. "Hello," he called out to me. I turned, slowly, and smiled at him. "Hi, Eric," I said shyly. "Where are you going?" he asked. I told him I was going to the train station.

He asked if he could walk me there, and, being the lovesick puppy that I was, I said, "Sure."

He carried my books and we talked all the way to the train station. When we arrived, he asked if he could have my phone number. I was so excited that I gave it to him without any hesitation.

He called that night. We talked for at least two hours. He told me that he lived with his aunt and his brother. He said he'd been wanting to talk to me for a while, that he liked me and wanted to get together sometime. That phone call made me the happiest person in the world. After I got off the phone with him, I called some of my friends and told them. Being liked by a guy made me feel important.

A Small Kiss

The next time I saw him, he walked me to the train station again, and we talked some more. Then he kissed me goodbye. It was just a small kiss, but it made me feel wonderful. I was convinced he was a great guy.

He called me again that night. We talked for a while, and just as I hoped, he "popped the question."

"Yes! I'll go out with you!" I half screamed. For the rest of the night, I was practically floating in mid-air, I was so happy. "Somebody loves me," I thought.

We were "boyfriend and girlfriend" for a grand total of five days. He called me and we saw each other throughout the week. Then after school on Friday, he was waiting for me in our usual meeting place, on the corner by the schoolyard. He said he wanted to take me someplace special that afternoon. I was thrilled. I thought maybe we would go to the movies or something. "But first," he said, "we have to stop by my house for a minute."

It was a pretty big apartment, but it looked like it hadn't been cleaned in years. He brought me into the kitchen and got a class of water. Then we went into the living room and sat on a sofa with the stuffing coming out of it. He told me to leave my books on the floor. Then he turned on the television and shut off all the lights and said, "We'll go in a minute. I'm tired. I want to rest for a second. Sit down with me." So, I did.

This Doesn't Feel Right

We sat in the darkness and watched TV for a while. I asked him where his aunt and his brother were. He stared at me with those eyes and replied, "out" plain and simple. He was acting kind of weird, but I didn't want to say anything, because I thought he might get mad or something. He took my hand and started to kiss me. At first it was kind of nice. But then he started getting too aggressive, putting his hands in places they didn't belong.

I remember thinking to myself, "This doesn't feel right. What's he doing?" I started getting scared and told him to stop. But he didn't. I tried pushing him away, but I was too small. He was a lot bigger than me. He forced himself on top of me and pulled my pants down. No matter how much I struggled, he wouldn't let up. He held me down by the shoulders and raped me. I was crying and screaming, "No! Stop! Please stop!" But he wouldn't. Exhausted from crying and trying to get him off me, I stared into the blackness, tears sliding off of my cheeks.

It all happened very fast. As soon as I could, I fixed my pants, tried to wipe the tears away, and got the hell out of there. I walked the eight blocks to the train station and waited for the train in a daze. I kept telling myself that it didn't really happen, that it couldn't really happen — not to me.

The Trip Home

On the train this guy pressed up against me and tried to talk to me. I just turned around and walked through to the other car. Then I caught this girl looking at me, like she knew. I gave her a really ugly stare and she looked away, embarrassed.

When I finally made it home, the first thing I did was jump in the shower. I washed my entire body, but I just couldn't seem to feel clean. I dried myself off and put on some clean clothes. Then I looked at the clothes I was wearing at the time it happened. I noticed blood on my pants and shirt. I had a small cut on my chest and my legs were scraped up — I guess from struggling. I took the clothes, balled them up and put them in a plastic bag. I carried them to the incinerator and threw them out. Then I went into my room, lay down on my bed and cried. Thank God my mother wasn't home.

I didn't want to think about it, but I couldn't help it. I'll never forget the look he gave me afterwards. It was like he was proud of what he had done. Then something else popped into my mind: What if I get pregnant? I closed my eyes and tried to block the thought. (Thankfully, I wasn't, but I was really scared for a while.)

Playing Sick Seemed the Only Escape

I saw him once more afterwards when I went to the store with Charlene one day after school. I was getting some juice and, while I was walking up to the counter to pay for it, he and two of his friends came into the store. My heart raced and I dropped the bottle. It smashed on the floor, but I didn't hear it. Charlene grabbed me and pulled me out of there. She knew something was wrong, but she kept her mouth shut. I didn't leave my house for a few weeks after that. I was afraid I might see him again. I was staying home more and more. Playing sick seemed to be the only escape.

One day, my best friend was over at my house, and I decided to tell her. I just couldn't keep this horrible secret inside of me any longer. "Kate, I need to tell you something," I said. I took a deep breath and sat down. "Kate," I tried to go slowly, but the words raced out of my mouth. "I was going out with this guy and I thought he was really nice but he wasn't. Kate, you're my best friend and I want you to help me. I was raped."

Kate just stared at me, in shock. Then the expression on her face changed to one of disbelief. "Well," she said, "How do you know if he really raped you?" I couldn't believe it. My best friend, doubting me, almost accusing me of lying. Things between us were never the same from then on. I can't say that I hate her, because I don't. I just don't talk to her — about anything.

Telling Someone — Getting Help

Eventually, I told some friends and a few adults. I am happy to say that all of them really helped me. They always listened when I needed to talk, anytime. Even if it was 3:30 in the morning, and I had trouble sleeping, I could call them up and they'd help me get through it. Now I really regret not speaking to anyone sooner.

It happened almost three years ago, but I still think about it as though it were yesterday. I have to stop asking myself if it was my fault, if I "asked for it." It wasn't my fault, I didn't ask for it. I had no control over the situation. The only thing I did wrong was wait so long to get help.

Rape is a horrible thing, I know that now. You have to be aware. You have to be careful. It can happen to anyone. And yes, you can be raped by someone you know. One minute you're watching TV, riding along in a car, getting help with homework. The next minute you're fighting to get away, gasping for breath, staring off into the blackness. If it does happen to you, remember, it's not your fault. Tell someone fast. Get help. It'll really make a difference later on.

Harvard Educational Review Vol. 65 No. 2 Summer 1995, 258–261

"*Educate Us*"

LIVEDA C. CLEMENTS

From the back of my closet I retrieved my black dress and shoes. This attire was one I rarely liked to wear. While I was driving to the church, various scenes jogged through my mind, reminding me of my friend. Yet, at that very instant, images of what I might see today collided with each and every scene. My train of thought was immediately broken when I saw the mass of people crowding the church doorway. We had gathered to give our respects to another young, black male who had become an innocent victim of circumstance and in so doing had become an inspiration of many of my future goals.

When I was inside the church, a feeling of amazement overwhelmed me. Each pew, chair, and standing area was occupied by a soul filled with sorrow. I would have thought it was a Sunday service if I had not heard the shrilling cries of loss.

As I walked closer to the casket my legs became like rubber bands, tears descending from my eyes like water dripping from a leaking faucet. Then, there rested before me my friend. I had only known him for a brief period, yet long enough to realize that he and I shared many similar goals and expectations.

He had a great dream of becoming a criminal justice lawyer. He had chosen this career because the belligerent attitudes that have been generated by today's black youth worried him tremendously. He wanted to be a contributor to the rehabilitation of those who commit immoral acts. He wanted to assist in restoring the remains of the inner city. He had many goals which he intended to accomplish. Many of his immediate concerns centered around preparing for a successful future. He anticipated finishing high school with complementary grades and subsequently attending a university.

He expressed himself by transforming endless thought into elaborate pictures. Many of his pictures were abstract drawings, which told a story that only he could understand. Other pictures exemplified the suffering of black people. He was a perfect example of who I am today, not only because our dreams, goals and choices of expression joined hand in hand, but also because we faced an everyday obstacle — living in the inner city of Boston. Boston is an environment that shares only a small portion of its success with Black America, and it is a locality where drugs and lawless acts become synonymous with life for many.

Unfortunately all of his great dreams of success, of goals and opportunities, were shattered by one bullet. Now I am here to pursue both his dreams and my goals.

Education, acquiring general knowledge and developing the power of reasoning and judgment, is the solution to the problem of violence. If the student population were better educated their perception of life, motivation, and sense of destination would be generated toward success, as opposed to the existing conditions of: gaining respect by committing unlawful acts, selling drugs in order to make easy money, and maintaining a nonchalant attitude in an effort to survive. Further steps need to be taken in order to thoroughly supply schools with proper materials, effectively keep drugs and weapons out of the schools, productively decrease the student drop-out rate, and continuously offer students with the potential to progress and succeed better opportunities. Education is and will ultimately be the solution to the existing problem.

Harvard Educational Review Vol. 65 No. 2 Summer 1995, 269–270
Copyright © 1995 Liveda C. Clements
Published and distributed by *Harvard Educational Review*

Sexual Harassment in School:
The Public Performance of
Gendered Violence

NAN STEIN

Many things happen that go undetected by teachers' radar in every school around the country. Seeing the unseen and opening up to the world in which today's students live can be a valuable asset for those charged with guiding their education. In this chapter, Nan Stein exposes one of the more damaging things that can go unheard and unseen in our schools — peer sexual harassment. She argues that sexual harassment is a form of gendered violence that often happens in the public arena. She presents the voices of girls and boys as they describe their harassing experiences, and finds parallels with cases documented in court records and depositions. While highly publicized lawsuits and civil rights cases may have increased public awareness of this issue, inconsistent findings have sent educators mixed messages about ways to deal with peer sexual harassment. The antecedents of harassment, Stein suggests, are found in teasing and bullying, behaviors tacitly accepted by parents and teachers. Stein makes a case for deliberate adult intervention and the inclusion of a curriculum in schools that builds awareness of these issues.

"Ask Beth," the nationally syndicated teenage advice column, often includes letters from youngsters describing their experiences of sexual harassment at school. On February 3, 1994, the column in the *Boston Globe* contained this letter:

> Dear Beth: I am 11 years old and there's a boy in my class who just won't leave me alone. He chases after me and my best friend during recess. He hits and kicks me on the behind, stomach and legs. Once he slapped me so hard it brought tears to my eyes.
>
> I try to tell my teacher, but she just laughs and tells him, "If you like her so much, ask her for her phone number." Is this sexual harassment? If it is, what should I do?
>
> *Hates Being Harassed* (Winship, 1994, p. 50)

When I read this letter aloud to middle school and high school students, from Maryland to Alaska, and ask them, "If these people were older, what might we call

Harvard Educational Review Vol. 65 No. 2 Summer 1995, 145–162

these behaviors?" I receive answers like "dating violence," "assault," "domestic violence," and "stalking." Yet, this teacher, this *woman* teacher, infantilized these assaultive behaviors, maybe perceiving them as flattery or as efforts from a youthful suitor. Do kids know something that adults don't want to know?

In this article on sexual harassment in schools I will document the allegations and the lawsuits, the surveys, the voices of adolescents and the panicked reactions from school personnel, and the popularization of the issue in the mainstream press. Although sexual harassment among K-12 students is now recognized as a form of sex discrimination and the rush to litigation has begun in earnest, sexual harassment is still not considered to be "violence" — not by most teachers or school administrators, not by most law enforcement or public health officials, and not by most nationally appointed or elected political leaders.

Seeing Is Not Believing

Thousands of preteen and teenage girls, responding to two open-ended questions in a self-report survey published in the September 1992 issue of *Seventeen* magazine (Stein, Marshall, & Tropp, 1993), revealed stories about the tenacity and pervasiveness of sexual harassment in schools. Letters by the thousands, with messages scribbled on envelopes — "Open," "Urgent," "Please Read," — and handwritten on lined notebook paper or perfumed stationary, all begged for attention, for answers, and, above all, for some type of acknowledgment and justice (Stein, 1992a). The following testimonials are girls' voluntary elaborations, which we received in response to the questions, "What do you think schools should do to prevent sexual harassment?" and "If you've been sexually harassed at school, how did it make you feel?":

> Of the times I was sexually harassed at school, one of them made me feel really bad. I was in class and the teacher was looking right at me when this guy grabbed my butt. The teacher saw it happen. I slapped the guy and told him not to do that. My teacher didn't say anything and looked away and went on with the lesson like nothing out of the ordinary had happened. It really confused me because I knew guys weren't supposed to do that, but the teacher didn't do anything. I felt like the teacher (who was a man) betrayed me and thought I was making a big deal out of nothing. But most of all, I felt really bad about myself because it made me feel slutty and cheap. It made me feel mad too because we shouldn't have to put up with that stuff, but no one will do anything to stop it. Now sexual harassment doesn't bother me as much because it happens so much it almost seems normal. I know that sounds awful, but the longer it goes on without anyone doing anything, the more I think of it as just one of those things that I have to put up with.[1]
>
> *14 years old, White*

> In my case there were two or three boys touching me, and trust me they were big boys. And I'd tell them to stop but they wouldn't! This went on for about six months until finally I was in [one] of my classes in the back of the room minding my own business when all of them came back and backed me into a corner and started touching me all over. So I went running out of the room and the teacher yelled at me and I had to stay in my seat for the rest of the class. But after the class

I told the principal, and him and the boys had a little talk. And after the talk was up, the boys came out laughing cause they got no punishment.

12 years old, Mexican American

The guys would want you to let them touch you all over. But I was one of the girls that would not do that. Then one day they thought they would do it anyway. So I defended myself like you should. I kind of hurt him. The teacher caught me hitting him. And I got in trouble for hitting him. The teacher took him out of the room for his story and he lied and said he did nothing. My teacher wouldn't believe my story. I was the one getting in trouble. The school and the principal wouldn't listen to me.

13 years old, Mexican

Sometimes, I would look at the teacher and think "help," but I was afraid to say anything because maybe it wasn't as bad as I thought it was.

15 years old, White

These girls recognized that incidents of sexual harassment are often witnessed by adults, and they expect the adults to see and feel these violations as they do. Yet, many girls cannot get confirmation of their experiences from school personnel, because most of those adults do not name it as "sexual harassment" and do nothing to stop it (Stein, 1992b). These chilling stories and others like them reveal girls' repeated efforts to get adults to see and believe what is happening right before their eyes, and to do something about it. These young women begin to sound ominously like battered women who are not believed or helped by the authorities and who feel alone and abandoned. Listen again to the voices of students speaking about the public nature of sexual harassment:

At first I didn't really think of it because it was considered a "guy thing," but as the year went on, I started to regret going to school, especially my locker, because I knew if I went I was going to be cornered and be touched, or had some comment blurted out at me. I just felt really out of place and defenseless and there was nothing I could do.

14 years old, Black

It was like fighting an invisible, invincible enemy alone. I didn't have a clue as to what to do to stop it, so I experimented with different approaches. Ignoring it only made it worse. It made it easier for them to do it, so they did it more. Laughing at the perpetrators during the assaults didn't dent the problem at all, and soon my friends became tired of doing this. They thought it was a game. Finally I wrote them threatening letters. This got me in trouble, but perhaps it did work. I told the school administrators what had been happening to me. They didn't seem to think it a big deal, but they did talk to the three biggest perpetrators. The boys ignored the administrators and it continued. And they were even worse.

14–15 years old, White

I took a photography class, and the majority of the class was boys. A lot of the boys were my friends but three of them were after something different than friendship. On several occasions I was in the dark room developing pictures and they would come in and corner me. They would touch me, put their hands on my thighs and slide their hands up my shirt. They also often tried to put my hand down their pants. I often told my friends but no one believed me. One day I was in the room alone and one of the boys came in. When I went to leave he grabbed me and threw me down and grabbed my breast. I felt I was helpless but I punched him and he ran out. The teacher (who was a man) came in and yelled at me. When I tried to explain why I had hit him the teacher told me I deserved it because I wore short skirts. I was sent to the principal and I had to serve detention. I didn't want to tell the principal because I feared he would do the same and tell me it was my fault. I felt so alone. Everyday I had to go to class and face it. No girl should have to be uncomfortable because of what she wears or how she acts.

15 years old, White

I have told teachers about this a number of times; each time nothing was done about it. Teachers would act as if I had done something to cause it. Once I told a guidance counselor, but was made to feel like a whore when she asked me questions like "do you like it?" and "they must be doing it for a reason. What did you do to make them do it?"

13 years old, White

These stories illustrate injustices of considerable magnitude and suggest that schools may be training grounds for the insidious cycle of domestic violence. Girls are taught that they are on their own, that the adults and others around them will not believe or help them; in essence, they are trained to accept the battering and assault. Girls (and sometimes boys) who are the targets of sexual harassment find that when they report sexual harassment or assault, the events are trivialized while they, the targets, are simultaneously demeaned and/or interrogated. Boys, on the other hand, receive permission, even training to become batterers, because many of their assaults on girls are not interrupted or condemned by the adults in the school environment. Indeed, if school authorities, by not intervening, sanction the students who sexually harass, the schools may be encouraging a continued pattern of violence in relationships. This encouragement goes beyond those directly involved; it also conveys a message to those who observe these incidents that engaging in such behavior is acceptable. Other bystanders may receive the message that they may be the next to be harassed, and that no one will do anything to prevent it (Stein, 1992b).

Sexual harassment, when it occurs in schools, is unwanted and unwelcome behavior of a sexual nature that interferes with the right to receive an equal education. It is a form of sex discrimination that is prohibited by Title IX, the federal civil rights in education law that addresses issues of sex discrimination and, by judicial precedent, sexual harassment.

Both the courts and the Office for Civil Rights (OCR) of the U.S. Department of Education recognize two forms of unlawful sexual harassment: 1) "quid pro quo" cases, in which a person's entitlement to enjoyment of a particular benefit (such as an educational opportunity) is conditioned on sexual favors; and 2) "hostile environment" cases, in which unwelcome conduct has the purpose or effect of unreasonably interfering with a person's right or benefit (such as education) by creating an intimidating, hostile, offensive environment. In school settings, allegations, particularly between students, typically concern the hostile-environment claim.

According to OCR memorandums:

To find that a hostile environment exists, OCR must find that the alleged victim was subjected to verbal or physical conduct imposed because of the victim's gender, that the conduct was unwelcome, and that the conduct was sufficiently severe, persistent or pervasive as to alter the conditions of the victim's education and create an abusive environment. In cases of student-to-student harassment, an educational institution will be liable for hostile environment sexual harassment where an official of the institution knew, or reasonably should have known, of the harassment's occurrence and the institution failed to take appropriate steps to halt the conduct. (Nashoba, 1993)

In schools, harassment often happens while many people watch. This public enactment of sexual harassment may have more damaging ramifications than harassment that happens in private, because of the potential for public humiliation, the damage to one's reputation, the rumors targeted individuals must fear and combat, and the strategies that they implement in an effort to reduce or avoid the encounters. When sexual harassment occurs in public and is not condemned, it becomes, with time, part of the social norm.

Teasing and Bullying, or Back to the Future

The antecedents of peer sexual harassment in schools may be found in "bullying" — behaviors children learn, practice, and experience beginning at a very young age. Children know what a bully is, and many boys as well as girls have been victims of bullying. Much of the bullying that takes place at this age is between members of the same sex (Kutner, 1993, 1994; Olweus, 1993; Slaby & Stringham, 1994; Whitney & Smith, 1993). Teachers and parents know about bullying, and many accept it as an unfortunate stage that some children go through on their way to adolescence and adulthood.

Despite its prevalence in U.S. culture, bullying remains an under-studied phenomenon in this country.[2] Public interest in bullying has been raised, however, by recent press accounts documenting horrific incidents in Japan that have ended in either suicide or murder (Nickerson, 1993; Pollack, 1994; Sanger, 1993). I was drawn to the problem of bullying through my work on sexual harassment in junior high and high schools, beginning in 1979. It became clear to me that, left unchecked and unchallenged, bullying might in fact serve as fertile practice ground for sexual harassment (Keise, 1992; Stein, 1993). I began a search for appropriate strategies, interventions, and a conceptual framework that might help elementary educators bring this subject into their classrooms.

In late 1992, I received support from the Patrina Foundation, a private foundation located in New York, to conduct a small pilot project that involved seven classrooms in three elementary schools. Working with fourth- and fifth-grade teachers and their students in two schools for one year and in a third school for a period of more than two years, I developed and implemented eight to ten sequential classroom lessons, writing activities, reading assignments, and role plays that engaged children to think about the distinctions between "teasing" and "bullying." These activities helped the children focus on the boundaries between appropriate and inappropriate, hurtful behavior. In this unit, eventually named "Bully-proof," children gained a conceptual framework and a common vocabulary that allowed them to find their own links between teasing and bullying, and eventually sexual harassment.[3] The following reflections, written anonymously at the end of the unit by fifth-grade students between the ages of ten and eleven, in a multiracial classroom, displayed new conceptual connections and insights about themselves and their classmates:

> Well, since we started this, people in my class and I learned a lot. Now they stopped doing mean things to each other. Like now that people know how I felt when they called me "shrimp" and "shorty" and other mean things they stopped doing that. Now we don't hurt other people's feelings and respect one another even if the person is short, tall or opposite sex. (male)

> I see a big difference in myself since we started discussing bullying, teasing and sexual harassment. Example: when it was my turn to be captain of the kickball game I picked x as a player. As soon as I picked x, he started to pick all the players and suddenly x was the captain. Not only that but x also picked who was pitcher and the batting order (all stuff a captain does). So, I stood up to x reminded him that I was captain (I would have never done that before). It made me feel good inside. (female)

> I do see a difference in the way that all of the boys in the class are treating the girls now. 1) they have mostly stopped teasing us and chasing us down the hallways while we are coming back from recess. 2) The boys have also mostly stopped insulting all of the girls and trying to dis us. I think that the girls have also mostly stopped teasing and bullying all of the shrimpy or short boys. (female)

> I really think sexual harassment can hurt because sometimes people may tease you about your body parts and it really hurts your feelings because you can't change them in any way. It can also interfere with your school work because all your thoughts are on your anger and then you can't concentrate. If I am harassed in the future, I will stand up for my rights and if a teacher doesn't care, I will pressure him or her to punish my harasser. (male)

Bullying and its connections to sexual harassment in schools are of critical importance. This link is one that educators need to make explicit and public by deliberately discussing these subjects in age-appropriate ways with children (Stein, 1996). If educators and advocates pose and present the problem as "bullying" to young children, rather than labeling it immediately as "sexual harassment," we can engage children and universalize the phenomenon as one that boys as well as girls will understand and accept as problematic. Hopefully, such an approach will go a long way toward developing compassion and empathy in the students. Moreover, we can simultaneously avoid demonizing all little boys as potential harassers by initially presenting these hurtful and offensive behaviors as bullying.

The Surveys and the Lawsuits: From Many to One and Back Again

The media's attention to the problem of sexual harassment in schools has in large part been generated by lawsuits and surveys on sexual harassment in schools. Results from three recent national surveys on this topic illustrate its pernicious, persistent, and public nature, and demonstrate that it is a widespread, endemic phenomenon. The first survey, developed by the Wellesley College Center for Research on Women and cosponsored by the National Organization for Women's (NOW) Legal Defense and Education Fund, was published in the September 1992 issue of *Seventeen* magazine (the most widely read magazine for teenage girls in the country, with 1.9 million subscribers and a "pass-along" circulation of 8 to 10 million girls). The results were compiled from a nonscientific, random sample of 2,000 girls aged nine to nineteen, selected from a total of 4,300 surveys received by the deadline of September 30, 1992. They were released in March 1993 (Stein, Marshall, & Tropp, 1993).

In two-thirds of the reports of incidents of sexual harassment in the *Seventeen* study, the girls reported that other people were present. The most frequently cited location of witnessed incidents was the classroom: 94 percent of the girls who indicated that others were present when harassment occurred reported that it occurred in the classroom; 76 percent of those who reported that other people were present during the harassment cited the hallway, and 69 percent cited the parking lot or the playing fields (note that respondents often cited more than one location).

The second survey, conducted by the Harris Poll, was commissioned by the American Association of University Women (AAUW) Foundation and released in June 1993 (AAUW, 1993). The study used a random sample of 1,600 boys and girls in eighth through eleventh grade in seventy-nine public schools. The boys and girls sampled in the Harris poll painted a similar portrait of sexual harassment, one that included public incidents occurring throughout the school. Of the 81 percent of the students who reported some experience of sexual harassment in school, 66 percent said they had been harassed at least once in the hall; 55 percent reported the classroom as the site of their harassment; 43 percent said it happened outside the school, on school grounds (other than the parking lot); 39 percent reported harassment in the gym, playing field, or pool area; 34 percent were harassed in the cafeteria; and 23 percent named the parking lot as the site of the harassment. Interestingly, students indicated that locker rooms (19%) and rest rooms (10%), presumably gender-segregated sites, were also locations for sexual harassment.

At least four important findings emerged from these surveys: 1) sexual harassment is pervasive in secondary schools (experienced by 85% of the girls in the Harris Poll/AAUW study and 89% of the girls in the *Seventeen* survey); 2) students consider sexual harassment a serious problem (75% from the Harris Poll/AAUW survey, 70% in the *Seventeen* survey); 3) the behavior occurs in public places (two-thirds of the situations reported in both studies); and 4) students have difficulty getting help, even though a majority in both surveys reported trying to talk to someone about the harassing behavior (Lee, Croninger, Linn, & Chen, 1996).

"In Our Own Backyard: Sexual Harassment in Connecticut's Public High Schools," a study of sexual harassment during the 1993–1994 school year, was released on January 26, 1995 (Permanent Commission, 1995).[4] In this survey, 78 percent of a random sample of high school students (308 girls and 235 boys) in grades ten through twelve reported experiencing at least one incident of sexual harassment in high school. The researchers found that girls were nearly twice as likely to report experiencing the problem as boys: 92 percent of the female students and 57 percent of the male students reported that they had been the targets of unwelcomed sexual conduct since they started high school.

The statistics that emerged from these three surveys might have dropped quickly into oblivion were it not for the complaints and lawsuits that girls and young women have been filing, and winning, in state and federal courts in the past few years. It takes only one influential case to change the landscape and the discourse about sexual harassment. Such a change occurred in February 1992 with the landmark 9-0 U.S. Supreme Court decision in *Franklin v. Gwinnett County (GA) Public Schools*. In this case, the Court decided that schools could be held liable for compensatory damages if they failed to provide an educational environment that was free from sex discrimination. This decision has caused school personnel to pay increased attention to the problem of sexual harassment and sex discrimination in schools.

Prototypical Lawsuits and Complaints: Sexual Harassment as Public Behavior

In one case that is often cited in popular magazines and teen literature and on television talk and news shows, Katy Lyle, a fifteen-year-old high school student in Duluth, Minnesota, was targeted through nasty graffiti that covered the walls of one stall in the boys' bathroom at her high school (*Lyle v. Independent School District #709*, 1991). Statements like "Katy does it with farm animals," "Katy is a slut," "Katy gives good head," and "Katy sucked my dick after she sucked my dog's dick," remained up on the walls for a period of sixteen months, despite repeated requests from Katy and her parents to the principal to have them removed. His responses included, "No one reads it anyhow," and "It'll make you a stronger person." He also claimed that his hands were tied by the custodians' union contract, which only makes provision for painting the walls once every two years; since they had just completed a painting assignment, they could not paint over that graffiti. Boys would yell out across the hallways, "Hey, Katy, I took a leak in your stall today," and girls would wonder aloud what Katy had done to "deserve" this.[5] Katy was tormented daily on the school bus and as she entered the school. Finally, her older brother, home from college during a vacation, removed the graffiti in a matter of minutes. Although the physical evidence was removed, the taunting continued.

In a 1991 settlement with the Minnesota Department of Human Rights, Katy and her family were awarded $15,000, and the school district agreed to implement training programs for staff and students to develop and disseminate a sexual harassment policy. They also agreed to appoint an administrator to coordinate these efforts.

In another widely publicized case from Minnesota (*Mutziger v. Independent School District #272*, 1992), both the Minnesota Department of Human Rights and the Office for Civil Rights (OCR) of the U.S. Department of Education (Eden Prairie, 1993) found that six-year-old Cheltzie Hentz (and eventually several other girls) had been sexually harassed on the bus, on the school grounds, and in the classroom by boys who ranged in age from six to thirteen. The perpetrators were accused of making lewd remarks and sexual taunts, including references about girls' body parts and explicit suggestions about Cheltzie having oral sex with her father. This case became notable for the age of the target and the age of the perpetrators; Cheltzie was and remains the youngest child to file and win a sexual harassment complaint. In the stunning decision rendered by OCR, the "reasonable woman standard" was invoked to apply to six-year-olds:[6]

From the standpoint of a reasonable female student participating in district programs and activities, . . . the sexually offensive conduct was sufficiently frequent, severe, and/or protracted to impair significantly the educational services and benefits offered. . . . In this case, there is no question that even the youngest girls understood that the language and conduct being used were expressions of hostility toward them on the basis of their sex and, as a clear result, were offended and upset. (Eden Prairie, 1993, p. 12)

In Cheltzie's case, all of the events occurred in the presence of adults — either the bus driver or bus monitors, or the classroom teacher. As part of the investigation, other girls were interviewed about the same boys who were accused of harassing Cheltzie. According to the OCR finding:

During a social studies class, a seventh grade male student repeatedly made remarks of a sexual nature . . . touched the girls, and on one occasion, physically restrained one of them so that she could not escape his lewd remarks. According to the female students, the teacher witnessed the harassment, but was unresponsive to their requests for assistance. The teacher's response was to offer to change the boy's seat. According to the students, the boy's seat already had been changed numerous times as girls reported that he was bothering them. (p. 9)

Again, adults watched, students appealed for help, and adults offered only innocuous and insipid solutions.

The behavior of school personnel is mentioned in several lawsuits that have been filed in federal district courts. For example, in a 1992 lawsuit in Connecticut, Johana Mennone, a student at Amity Regional High School in Woodbridge, Connecticut, alleged that "in the presence of her teacher and a roomful of classmates, a male student grabbed her hair, legs, breasts, and buttocks nearly every day. He repeatedly made remarks about her breasts and told her that he was going to rape her" (Lawton, 1993). Again, a teacher watched while outright assaults took place in the classroom. Motions continue to be filed in this case. A case in Milford, Connecticut, with similar facts but with middle school students as the plaintiff and defendants, is underway in another complaint filed in both federal district court and state court.[7] In federal court, the complaint draws on provisions included in Title IX; in state court, the suit is framed around tort actions of negligence on the part of the teacher, principal, and superintendent.

At least seven other federal Title IX actions involving student-to-student sexual harassment are pending in federal district courts in California, Georgia, Kansas, New York, and Texas (Lewin, 1994). Three more complaints have been filed in federal district courts in Iowa (Fuson, 1994).

Three contradictory rulings have emerged from three different federal court jurisdictions. In a case in Georgia, *Aurelia Davis v. Monroe County Board of Education*, U.S. District Judge Wilbur D. Owens, Jr. of Macon ruled on August 29, 1994, that the school district was not liable for a fifth-grade student's alleged harassment of another student (*Aurelia Davis*, 1994). He dismissed the case on the grounds that the school did not have a special custodial relationship with its students and had no special duty to protect them from other students (Walsh, 1994). The complainant had alleged that school officials were slow to react to the harassing conduct by a boy who repeatedly tried to touch a girl's breasts, rubbed his body against hers, and used vulgar language. The complainant and her family decided to appeal the decision.

However, an opposite decision was rendered in federal court in New York State. On November 15, 1994, Thomas J. McAvoy, Chief Federal Court Judge for the Northern District of New York in Albany, issued a ruling that held teachers and administrators liable and responsible for preventing student-to-student sexual harassment in schools. In this case, *Bruneau v. South Kortright (NY) Central School District*, the court ruled that a sixth-grade girl who was taunted with sexual comments ("prostitute," "dog-faced bitch," and "lesbo") and physically abused by boys in her class could sue her teacher and an assistant superintendent under Section 1983 of the Civil Rights Act of 1871 (*Bruneau*, 1994).[8] She was also able to bring a suit against the school district under Title IX and recover compensatory damages, punitive damages, and attorney fees. The school district was found liable in the New York case because teachers and administrators were alerted to the assaults but took no action. In fact, when the girl's parents complained of the abusive behavior to their daughter's teacher, they were told "that their daughter was a beautiful child and they had nothing to worry about because boys would be all over her in a few years" (Jones, 1994). The parents requested assistance from the assistant superintendent of the school district following this meeting with the teacher, but again, no attempts to remedy the situation were made. When the parents asked that their daughter be allowed to transfer to another class, their request was denied. At that point, the girl transferred to another school and the parents took legal action. The judge's ruling in this case provides that a plaintiff can proceed against a school district if the district's inaction (or insufficient action) in response to complaints of student-to-student sexual harassment is the result of an actual intent to discriminate against the student on the basis of sex (*Bruneau*, 1994).

Yet, in October 1994 in Utah, the U.S. Federal District Court refused to allow a locker room incident, directed at one football player by his fellow teammates, as an actionable case of hostile environment sexual harassment. In Judge Dee V. Benson's decision, the lawsuit against the Sky View High School and the Cache County (UT) School District was dismissed on the grounds that the boy failed to prove that he had been a victim of any concerted discriminatory effort (*Seamons v. Snow*, 1994).

By any stretch of the imagination, the facts of this case give one pause. After a football game, the young man, Brian Seamons, was restrained by four of his teammates and painfully taped naked to a towel rack after he left the shower area. He was humiliated further when a girl was involuntarily dragged in to view him (Brown, 1995; "Court Dismisses," 1994). Brian claimed that this team ritual was well known to the coach and school officials.

The school authorities continued to either excuse the behavior as gender appropriate (i.e., "boys will be boys") or merely a case of team hazing; Brian was blamed for bringing the incident to the public's attention. The football coach reacted to Brian's complaints by first suspending and then dismissing him from the team. The next day, the superintendent canceled the remaining football games, prompting the coach, Douglas Snow, to demand that Brian apologize to the team for this course of action. Neither Snow nor any of the football players were disciplined for their behaviors in this incident. In fact, Snow stated publicly that "it was inappropriate to impose discipline on the other players for hazing." The judge in this case found no fault on the part of the coach or school administrators:

It may have been wrong, or right, or ethical, or unethical, or noble, or ignoble, but no plausible treatment theory could construe it as an act intended to treat Brian negatively because he is a boy. . . . Because plaintiffs have not alleged that defendants' conduct was sexual in any way . . . [the] allegations are not sufficient to base a claim of sexual harassment. (*Seamons v. Snow,* 1994, p. 1118)

It is clear that if this incident had been directed at a female, not only would it have been viewed as sexual harassment, but there would also have been criminal assault charges pending against the perpetrators. The question remains: Why should the sex of the target make any difference when the behavior is publicly performed, seemingly school-approved, gendered violence?

Despite troubling and contradictory rulings from federal courts, students continue to file Title IX complaints with OCR. Although OCR cannot award compensatory damages, it can compel the school district to pay for costs incurred from counseling, tutoring, transportation, and tuition for the complainant. They can also require the district to provide training for staff and students on the subjects of sex discrimination and sexual harassment. Among the hundreds of districts that OCR has investigated, letters of findings and/or settlement agreements have been issued to school districts in Millis, Massachusetts; Petaluma, California; Meridian, Texas; Reno, Nevada; Sweet Home, Oregon; Mason City, Iowa; Albion, Michigan; and, Victorville, California.[9]

Notable among OCR's letters of findings are two in which the sexual harassment incidents involved students of the same sex. Both complaints involved high school girls who sexually harassed other girls, one case from San Jose, California, and the other from Bolton, Massachusetts. The facts in both cases are strikingly similar: a single girl at each site was subjected to verbal and written sexual harassment over a period of many months. The harassment consisted of sexually explicit taunts, graffiti, and rumors of the girl's alleged sexual behavior with male students. Both young women's grades fell, while one cut classes and altered her walking route to avoid further harassment (San Jose) and the other required private counseling (Bolton). In both cases, school officials had been informed of the harassment but failed to treat it as such. According to the letter of finding from OCR in the Massachusetts case,

> the student evidenced an extensive record of her numerous and repeated efforts to end the conduct. The student immediately reported the graffiti to her counselor upon discovering it in the bathroom. On her own initiative, the student weekly, and sometimes daily, reported new graffiti to the principal or her counselor, and she kept detailed notes of verbal harassment incidents. The student herself removed some of the graffiti from the bathrooms and walls. (Nashoba, 1993, p. 9)

The San Jose school staff had a different response and rationale; they assumed that sexual harassment could only occur "when a student approaches another student of the opposite sex and makes lewd gestures or asks for sexual favors" (East Side Union High School District, 1993, p. 5). Moreover, they did not consider the conduct between members of the same sex to be possible sexual harassment, especially since the target and her harassers had once been friends. For all of these reasons, the school district did not investigate the complaint.

In both of these complaints, OCR concluded that there had been pervasive, persistent, and severe sexual harassment in violation of Title IX, and that the school districts had inadequate grievance procedures for prompt and equitable resolution of complaints of sexual harassment.

Despite clear rulings in these two same-sex cases, another regional office of OCR refused to investigate a Minnesota third-grade student's claim that he was sexually harassed by other boys at school for several months. Jonathan Harms of the Sauk Rapids–Rice School District, who taped his verbal harassment by concealing a small tape recorder, was sexually taunted over a period of months by about a dozen of his male classmates in the third grade. The harassment escalated to an assault when his pants and underwear were pulled down to below his knees. Yet, OCR responded in June 1993 to the parents' complaint, stating that it found "no indication that the student was singled out for harassment because of his sex" (Sauk Rapids–Rice, 1993).[10]

Protests about OCR's decision came from expected and unexpected quarters. Jonathan's parents responded by saying that "their son's case sends a 'disturbing' message: while girls are protected from the sexual taunts of their male peers, boys are not" (Brown, 1994a). Minnesota Attorney General Hubert H. Humphrey III sent a letter on January 6, 1994, to U.S. Secretary of Education Richard Riley, seeking an explanation for OCR's decision not to investigate: "I would appreciate clarification of whether boys are covered under Title IX. I ask that the OCR reconsider its decision not to investigate the . . . case" (Brown, 1994a). In an October 17, 1994, letter to Senator Durenberger of Minnesota, Norma Cantu, the Assistant Secretary for Civil Rights of the U.S. Department of Education's Office for Civil Rights, indicated that the investigation might be reopened (Pitsch, 1994). This decision was undoubtedly influenced by the Minnesota Department of Human Rights September 1994 decision that found "probable cause" in the Harms case; the Department has decided to investigate Jonathan's claim as sexual harassment under Minnesota state law.

The outcomes in two California cases (Modesto City Schools, 1993, and Newark Unified School District, 1993) investigated by the Office for Civil Rights provide sharp contrast to the outcome in the Jonathan Harms complaint in Minnesota. In both of the California cases, OCR found against the schools and in favor of the complainants.

In the California cases, elementary school children were also involved, this time with boys as the alleged harassers and girls as the targets. The Modesto case began in January 1993, when several girls were restrained in chokeholds, pinched, tripped, and touched repeatedly on their chests, genitalia, and buttocks by some male classmates. The school officials treated the incidents as routine misbehavior and followed their standard disciplinary procedures without determining if a sexually hostile environment existed. Nor were the parents informed of their rights under federal law Title IX. In May 1993, a group of boys, some of whom had been involved in the earlier incidents, threw two girls to the ground, forcibly kissed and fondled them, made lewd statements, and attempted to remove their clothing (Brown, 1994b). OCR's finding, issued on December 6, 1993, found that the school district had violated Title IX when it treated sexual harassment by elementary school students as a matter of misconduct and mischief rather than as a violation of federal anti-discrimination law.

The Newark case involved behavior classically viewed and typically dismissed as mutual, voluntary, and playful playground behavior. "Friday flip-up" days were an institution at this school: on Fridays, the boys in the first through third grades flipped up the dresses of their female classmates. OCR found that this practice subjected the girls to teasing and touching based on their gender, created different treatment for them, and limited their enjoyment of the educational program.

The California and Minnesota cases, which involve elementary school children, raise perplexing and disturbing questions: Are the ages of the targets and perpetrators the most salient factors that OCR considers when it decides to investigate a case? Or is it the sex of the target(s) and perpetrator(s)? Are incidents that involve children of the same sex ruled out if the students are in elementary school? What difference could the sex of the harassers or the target make when a student's clothes are pulled off? Are these acts not assaults, let alone sexual harassment? Or is it that gendered violence doesn't register with some federal and school officials as real violence?

Hopes, Actions, and Recommendations

As powerful and inspirational as legal decisions can be, we can't expect them to either enlighten educators or guarantee educational environments free from sex discrimination and sexual harassment. We need to promote nonlitigious remedies and to transport the lessons of the lawsuits into the classroom. Lawsuits can be preempted through preventive and sensible measures employed in the schools.

Hope and impetus for change come from schoolwide efforts to normalize the conversation about sexual harassment and other forms of gendered violence. This may best be achieved by inserting age-appropriate and sequential materials into class discussions and school curricula. The traditional practice of addressing sexual harassment only through disciplinary action has had little effect on the frequency of gendered violence. Recent attempts to enlist draconian prohibitions against handholding and other forms of affectionate behavior (Maroney, 1995) are also sure to fail.

Prior to initiating such classroom conversations, educators need to recognize sexual harassment in schools as a form of gendered violence that is often performed in public, sometimes in front of adults whose legal responsibility is to provide equal protection and equal educational opportunity. Sexual harassment can provide the impetus for opening the conversation about gendered violence.

Ultimately, a strategy to eliminate and prevent sexual harassment in schools needs to aim at a transformation of the broader school culture. Dealing effectively with sexual harassment is much easier if a school has committed itself to infuse a spirit of equity and a critique of injustice into its curriculum and pedagogy. On the other hand, harassment flourishes where children learn the art of doing nothing in the face of unjust treatment by others. When teachers subject children to an authoritarian pedagogy, they don't learn to think of themselves as moral subjects, capable of speaking out when they witness bullying or other forms of harassment. If youngsters have not been encouraged to critique the sexism of the curriculum, hidden and overt, then they are less likely to recognize it when they confront it in their midst. Too often, the entire school structure offers children no meaningful involvement in decision making about school policy, school climate, or other curriculum matters. Children rehearse being social spectators in their school lives (Stein, 1993).

We can make a difference in the classroom and beyond when we take up the subjects of teasing, bullying, and sexual harassment. When we frame the issue of sexual harassment as one of injustice and civil rights, and see the problem from the vantage points of the targets, the harassers, and the observers, we can teach empathy as we also teach children to emphasize and employ intervention strategies. In this way we teach children to see themselves as "justice makers," as opposed to social spectators (hooks, 1989).

I end this article in the same way I began it, with the words of children. This time, however, we hear from boys who confirm the experiences of the girls cited at the beginning of this article — that sexual harassment is present and very public in schools.[11] Even for the boys who are observers, sexual harassment is sometimes scary, troubling, and certainly disruptive to the educational environment.

> Today, as usual, I observed sexist behavior in my art class. Boys taunting girls and girls taunting boys has become a real problem. I wish they would all stop yelling at each other so that for once I could have art class in peace. This is my daily list of words I heard today in art that could be taken as sexual harassment: bitch, hooker, pimp, whore.

> Today for the first time I was witness to sexual harassment in my gym class. A couple of girls came into the exercise room today and suddenly, almost like a reflex, some of the boys began to whistle at them and taunt them. I was surprised since I had never seen this kind of behavior from my gym class before. Some of the boys that I considered my friends even began to do it. It felt awful to watch, but if I said anything it would not stop them and would only hurt me.

> Today in class people reported their findings as ethnographers; that is, they told the class about the examples of sexual harassment they had witnessed. There were some pretty bad examples. It's amazing that this stuff goes on at our school. I think that part of the problem is that some kids don't know what sexual harassment is, so they don't know when they are doing it. One of the things that scared me was that no one said they had any trouble finding examples. Everybody had found at least one or two examples, and most people found many more. I found out that it happens everywhere: in the halls, the cafeteria, or even at basketball try-outs. It happens everywhere that teachers are not in direct supervision of students.

> I think it's good that the eighth-graders are doing the curriculum at the same time, because then we can discuss it during lunch and stuff. I really do think that people are learning a lot from it. I mean, the person at our table at lunch who used to really be a sexual harasser has stopped and actually turned nice when all the girls at our table told him to stop or we would get [teacher] into it. I don't think he realized that what he was doing was really making us uncomfortable.

> The sexual harassment [curriculum] is really doing the school some good. One of the harassers who has been always harassing any girl at all has stopped. X has stopped goosing and touching girls. I never thought I'd see the day — he no longer pinches girls and rubs up against them in the hall. Now I feel a lot more comfortable in art class. I have art with him, and now I don't have to always, literally,

watch my back. And O has seen a lot of improvement. People are more conscious about what they say, and how they use words like gay, faggot, and lesbian. They realize that some people could really be offended by it.

These journal entries are hopeful in the way that they point out the impact that age-appropriate, deliberate, teacher-led conversations and curriculum can have on the lives of students. By creating a common classroom vocabulary and offering nonpunitive and nonlitigious ways to probe controversial and troubling subjects, educators and their students can confront and reduce sexual harassment and gendered violence in the schools. The first step is to recognize that sexual harassment is a common feature in children's school lives, and that the students — both boys and girls — recognize that most adults are sitting back, watching it happen. The next step is for the adults to name it as the kids see it, and to take it on — publicly, in the classroom, and throughout the whole school community.

Notes

1. Ethnic and racial descriptors that accompany the quotes are in the girls' own words.
2. Studies that have been done tend to focus on the sexually deviant child (Cunningham & MacFarlane, 1991) or on school violence (National Center for Education Statistics, 1988, and Search Institute, 1990, cited in Stepp, 1992). Most of the research on bullying has been conducted in Norway and Sweden (Olweus, 1993) and the United Kingdom (Keise, 1992; Whitney & Smith, 1993).
3. *Bullyproof* is copyrighted to Nan Stein (1996).
4. This report was published by the Permanent Commission on the Status of Women based upon research conducted by the University of Connecticut School of Social Work (research on incidents of sexual harassment) and the Connecticut Sexual Assault Crisis Services (research with Title IX coordinators).
5. Interviews with Carol and Katy Lyle conducted by Katie Couric on *Today* (NBC, October 7, 1992); and LeBlanc (1992).
6. "For both *quid pro quo* and *hostile environment* harassment, whether or not sexual harassment exists is to be judged from the perspective of the 'reasonable person.' That is, would a reasonable person view the behavior complained of as sexual harassment? There is some uncertainty among federal courts and agencies as to whether the 'reasonable person' standard takes into account the circumstances of the victim, and if so, to what extent. Federal agencies, such as the EEOC and OCR, as well as several lower courts that have addressed the issue, have adopted a 'reasonable woman' or 'reasonable person in the victim's situation' standard that would appear to favor the complainant more than the 'reasonable person' perspective. . . . Moreover, in several Title IX Letters of Finding, OCR states that the existence of a sexually hostile environment is determined from the viewpoint of a reasonable person in the victim's situation" (Sneed & Woodruff, 1994, p. 10).
7. The case is *Courtney Stern v. City of Milford (CT) Board of Education*; in Superior Court, Judicial District of Ansonia/Milford, filed January 29, 1993.
8. Civil Rights Act of 1871, 42 U.S.C. section 1983:

   Every person who, under color of any statute, ordinance, regulation, custom, usage, of any state or territory, subjects or causes to be subjected, any citizen of the United States or any person within the jurisdiction thereof to the deprivation of any rights, privileges, or immunities secured by the Constitution and laws, shall be liable to the party injured in an action at law, suit in equity, or other proper proceeding for redress.

   Section 1983, which is a federal statute, provides an avenue of redress for individuals who have been deprived of their federal constitutional or statutory rights at the behest of state authority. Section 1983 provides redress for violation of explicit constitutional rights (e.g., the right to due process) and also of federal statutory rights passed pursuant to constitutional authority.

9. Office for Civil Rights' Letters of Findings and/or Settlement Agreements obtained through Freedom of Information Act (FOIA): Millis, MA (#01-93-1123, issued May 19, 1994); Petaluma, CA (#09-89-1050, May 5, 1989); Meridian, TX (#06-92-1145, July 29, 1992); Washoe County School District, Reno, NV (09-91-1220, March 27, 1993); Sweet Home, OR (#10-92-1088, November 15, 1991); Mason City, IA (#07-93-1095, March 28, 1994); Albion, MI (#15-94-1029, April 7, 1994); and Victor Valley Union High School District, Victorville, CA (09-90-1143, August 8, 1990).

10. Letter from Kenneth A. Mines, Regional Director of the Office for Civil Rights, U.S. Department of Education, Chicago office, to Mr. and Mrs. Harms (June 28, 1993), p. 1, re: case #05-93-1142, Sauk Rapids–Rice (MN) School District #47.

11. Selections are from the ethnographies that these White, middle-class, eighth-grade students kept as part of a pilot curriculum development project. This pilot project, which involved approximately fifty Massachusetts classroom teachers in grades six through twelve in the fall of 1993, resulted in the publication, *Flirting or Hurting? A Teacher's Guide on Student-to-Student Sexual Harassment in Schools* (for grades six through twelve) by Nan Stein and Lisa Sjostrom (1994).

References

American Association of University Women (AAUW). (1993). *Hostile hallways: The AAUW survey on sexual harassment in America's schools*. Washington, DC: Author.

Aurelia Davis v. Monroe County (GA) Board of Education, 862 F.Supp. 863 (M.D. GA, 1994)

Brown, A. (1994a, February). OCR declines to investigate male student's harassment claim. *Educator's Guide to Controlling Sexual Harassment, 5,* 1–2.

Brown, A. (1994b, May). Same-sex harassment by students proves a tough issue for U.S. enforcement agency. *Educator's Guide to Controlling Sexual Harassment, 8,* 1–3.

Brown, A. (1995, January). Hazing or sexual harassment? Football player appeals ruling. *Educator's Guide to Controlling Sexual Harassment, 2,* 5.

Bruneau v. South Kortright (NY) Central School District, 94-CV-864 (N.Dist. NY, November 15, 1994).

Court dismisses male student's Title IX harassment claim. (1994, November 18). *School Law News, 22*(23), 7.

Cunningham, C., & MacFarlane, K. (1991). *When children molest children: Group treatment strategies for young sexual abusers*. Orwell, VT: Safer Society Press.

East Side Union High School District, CA, No. 09-93-1293-I. Office for Civil Rights, U.S. Department of Education, San Francisco, CA (November 19, 1993).

Eden Prairie School District #272, MN, No. 05-92-1174. Office for Civil Rights, U.S. Department of Education, Chicago, IL (April 27, 1993).

Franklin v. Gwinnett County Public Schools, 112 S. Ct. 1028 (1992).

Fuson, K. (1994, August 5). Teens suing 3 schools over harassment. *Des Moines Register,* pp. 1, 3A.

Harms v. Independent School District #47 (Sauk Rapids–Rice), file #ED1990019, Minnesota Department of Human Rights, Minneapolis, MN (May 14, 1993).

hooks, b. (1989). *Talking back: Thinking feminist, thinking Black*. Boston: South End Press.

Jones, M. M. (1994, December 19). Student sues school for sexual harassment by other students. *Lawyer's Weekly USA, 94*(26), 1, 12–13.

Keise, C. (1992). *Sugar and spice? Bullying in single-sex schools*. Staffordshire, Eng.: Trentham Books.

Kutner, L. (1994, Spring/Summer). Everybody's teasing me. *Parent's Digest,* pp. 34–37.

Kutner, L. (1993, October 28). Bullying: A test of the limits of one's power and control. *New York Times,* p. C12.

Lawton, M. (1993, February 10). Sexual harassment of students target of district policies. *Education Week,* pp. 1, 15–16.

LeBlanc, A. (1992, September). Harassment in the halls. *Seventeen,* pp. 162–165, 170.

Lee, V. E., Croninger, R. G., Linn, E., & Chen, X. (1996). The culture of sexual harassment in secondary schools. *American Educational Research Journal.*

Lewin, T. (1994, July 15). Students seeking damages for sex bias. *New York Times,* p. B12.

Lyle v. Independent School District #709, file #ED341-GSS5-6N Minnesota Department of Human Rights, Minneapolis, MN (September 18, 1991).

Maroney, T. (1995, January 21). Coming unhinged over hand-holding ban. *Boston Globe,* pp. 1,9.

Modesto City Schools, CA, No. 09-93-1319. Office for Civil Rights, U.S. Department of Education, San Francisco, CA (December 10, 1993).

Mutziger v. Independent School District #272 (Eden Prairie), file #ED19920006, Minnesota Department of Human Rights, Minneapolis, MN (September 3, 1992).

Nashoba Regional School District, MA, No. 01-92-1327. Office for Civil Rights, U.S. Department of Education, Boston, MA (October 22, 1993).

Newark Unified School District, CA, No. 09-93-1113. Office for Civil Rights, U.S. Department of Education, San Francisco, CA (July 7, 1993).

Nickerson, C. (1993, January 24). In Japan, "different" is dangerous. Fatal attack in school casts light on bullying. *Boston Sunday Globe,* pp. 1, 19.

Olweus D. (1993). *Bullying at school: What we know and what we can do.* Oxford: Blackwell.

Permanent Commission (CT) on the Status of Women. (1995). *In our own backyard: Sexual harassment in Connecticut's public high schools.* Hartford, CT: Author.

Pitsch, M. (1994, November 9). O.C.R. stepping up civil-rights enforcement. *Education Week,* pp. 15, 20.

Pollack, A. (1994, December 18). Suicides by bullied students stir Japanese furor. *New York Times,* p. 20.

Sanger, D. E. (1993, April 3). Student's killing displays dark side of Japan schools. *New York Times,* pp. 1, 3.

Sauk Rapids–Rice School District #47, MN, no. 05-93-1142. Office for Civil Rights, U.S. Department of Education, Chicago, IL (June 23, 1993).

Seamons v. Snow, 864 F. Supp. 1111 (D. Utah, 1994).

Slaby, R., & Stringham, P. (1994). Prevention of peer and community violence: The pediatrician's role. *Pediatrics, 94,* 608–616.

Sneed, M., & Woodruff, K. (1994). *Sexual harassment: The complete guide for administrators.* Arlington, VA: American Association of School Administrators.

Stein, N. (1992a, November 4). Sexual harassment — an update. *Education Week,* p. 37.

Stein, N. (1992b). *Secrets in public: Sexual harassment in public (and private) schools* (Working Paper No. 256). Wellesley, MA: Wellesley College Center for Research on Women.

Stein, N. (1993). No laughing matter: Sexual harassment in K-12 schools. In E. Buchwald, P. R. Fletcher, & M. Roth, *Transforming a rape culture* (pp. 311–331). Minneapolis: Milkweed Editions.

Stein, N. (1996). *Bullyproof.* Wellesley, MA: Wellesley College Center for Research on Women.

Stein, N., Marshall, N., & Tropp, L. (1993). *Secrets in public: Sexual harassment in our schools* (A report on the results of a *Seventeen* magazine survey). Wellesley, MA: Wellesley College Center for Research on Women.

Stein, N., & Sjostrom, L. (1994). *Flirting or hurting? A teacher's guide on student-to-student sexual harassment in schools.* Washington, DC: National Education Association.

Stepp, L. S. (1992, December 1). Getting tough with the big, bad bullies. *Washington Post*, p. C5

Study calls schools lax on sexual harassment. (1993, March 24). *Wall Street Journal*, p. 8.

Walsh, M. (1994, October 19). Harassment suit rejected. *Education Week*, p. 10.

Whitney, I., & Smith, P. K. (1993). A survey of the nature and extent of bullying in junior/middle and secondary schools. *Educational Research, 35*(1), 3–25.

Winship, B. (1994, February 3). Teacher is wrong to dismiss boy's actions as flirting. *Boston Globe*, p. 50.

The author would like to thank Susan Bailey, executive director of the Center for Research on Women at Wellesley College, for her editorial comments, many impromptu discussions, and a vibrant place in which to write. Helpful legal consultation and documents were provided by Kathryn Woodruff, Esq. of Hogan and Hartson, in Washington, DC; the New England regional office of the U.S. Department of Education, Office for Civil Rights; and the National Women's Law Center in Washington, DC. Deb Tolman delivered inspiration; Theresa and Imani Perry offered support, ideas, challenges, and many shared meals; and Donaldo Macedo's friendship and loyalty lived beyond his many voice-mail messages. Finally, thanks to e-mail and fax, editorial comments came from David Leshtz of the University of Iowa, a friend since high school, whose support and critical eye were invaluable, and who kept me laughing.

Reframing Classroom Research: A Lesson from the Private World of Children

ADRIENNE ALTON-LEE
GRAHAM NUTHALL
JOHN PATRICK

Much of what happens in classrooms between students goes unobserved by even the most vigilant teachers. In this chapter, Adrienne Alton-Lee, Graham Nuthall, and John Patrick attempt to expand our vision to include a glimpse of some of those unseen interactions. Using small microphones worn by students to record conversations in the classroom, the authors analyze the children's words and use them to reflect on the children's cognitive and emotional responses to the ongoing lesson. The data reveal how these students perceive and respond to cultural and gender biases in the curriculum and in the teacher's presentation. Their data also underscore how much can be missed by any teacher, regardless of the attention they give to pedagogy or classroom interactions. This study allows us to better understand children's actual experiences as they struggle with the overt and covert messages of the curriculum, and, perhaps, provides a reason to listen more carefully to what is taught, and to think about its potential effects on our students.

In this article we explore children's public and private experiences during a lesson in an intermediate (sixth-grade) classroom in Aotearoa New Zealand. In the *Handbook for Research on Teaching*, Courtney Cazden described "two interpenetrating worlds: the official world of the teacher's agenda, and the unofficial world of the peer culture" (1986, p. 451). Although children in the classroom experience both of these worlds simultaneously, the unofficial, private world has been largely hidden from teachers and researchers. By exploring both the official and public, and the unofficial and private utterances of individual children, we can open a window onto the child's experience of both worlds.

We are unlikely to come to such a window with open minds. In both educational practice and research, children's talk in the unofficial world has frequently been "considered a nuisance; literal noise in the instructional system" (Cazden, 1986, p. 448). Children's talk, even when it involves engagement with curriculum content, may be judged off-task because it contravenes the rules of order in a classroom.

Harvard Educational Review Vol. 63 No. 1 Spring 1993, 50–84

The "official world" of the teacher's agenda has become not only the focus of classroom research, but also the lens through which children's behavior is observed and judged.

The unofficial children's talk that occurred during the class lesson we focus on in this article would have been categorized as off-task in most classroom observation schedules. There is now evidence, however, that observer judgments about children's "on-task" behavior are not a valid index of children's engagement with content (Blumenfeld & Meece, 1988; Peterson, Swing, Stark, & Waas, 1984), and that children's spontaneous talk during time "off-task" can contribute to their intellectual development (Dyson, 1987).

A fundamental challenge for educational researchers has been the inaccessibility of the learning processes that take place in the mind of the child. The early behaviorists resolved the issue by denying the significance, or even the existence, of internal processing. In contrast, more recent research in cognitive science and artificial intelligence has attempted to develop functional models of these internal processes. In the field of classroom research, techniques such as stimulated recall (Peterson et al., 1984) and eliciting children's reports of their own internal processing strategies (Blumenfeld & Meece, 1988) have been used to provide insights about classroom learning. These techniques, however, depend on children's conscious and selective recall of their mental processing. In the study reported here, we have employed a new technique, in which children's utterances are recorded by individual broadcast microphones during the course of classroom activities. These utterances provide a unique and concurrent source of data about children's learning processes and allow us to identify individual children's responses to curriculum content, their use of prior knowledge and experience, their existing misconceptions, and their strategies for engaging with curriculum.

In our larger research program, the Understanding Learning and Teaching Project, we have traced children's learning during their interaction with specific test-item content in the course of instructional units (Alton-Lee & Nuthall, 1992a; Nuthall & Alton-Lee, 1991, 1992).[1] We have explained knowledge acquisition in classrooms as a developmental process in which children generate specific knowledge constructs as they participate in the enacted curriculum. We define the enacted curriculum as the actual ways in which students encounter curriculum content as they participate in individual, group, and whole-class activities and tasks.

Utterance data can be a rich source of information about the ways in which children experience and negotiate the instructional, social, and cultural contexts of the classroom. If the purpose of educational research is to improve classroom practice, then we need to understand how teachers influence these contexts. Children's utterances, when triangulated with other data, can illuminate the hidden cognitive and cultural processes that mediate their learning and well-being.

In this article, we use several data sources from a single class lesson to demonstrate the interplay between instructional, social, and cultural contexts that influence children's experience. In particular, we focus on cultural processes mediating gender and race. We report a detailed analysis of four case-study children's experience of one lesson, using multiple sources of data: transcripts of the public enacted curriculum and of children's private utterances (transcribed from audio recordings); continuous observational records of case-study children; tests of short- and long-term learning outcomes; and interviews with the teacher and with the children. We explain how the utterance data helped in the development of a model of classroom learning. Finally, we consider the implications of our analysis for developing an understanding that takes into account both the psychological and sociocultural dimensions of classroom learning processes.

Gathering Utterance Data in the Classroom

We began each of the studies in our project by finding a teacher who was aware of the nature of the research and was eager to participate. Each teacher decided which curriculum unit we would study. We negotiated prior permission with the local education board and the principal and obtained written permission from the children's parents. The purpose of the research was explained to the children, and they were given the opportunity to decide whether or not to participate.[2]

The Understanding Learning and Teaching Project now comprises a series of six studies of children's learning in schools selected for racial and social-class contrasts in student population. This article focuses on an introductory lesson taught in a sixth-grade classroom in a suburban intermediate school (sixth- and seventh-grade students only) serving a predominantly *Pakeha* (White) middle- to upper-middle-class population.[3] Four case-study children in the classroom were selected from those who had parental permission, wanted to participate, and were easily accessible to the video camera. Any child the teacher believed might be adversely affected by the intensive observation was not chosen as a case-study student.

Individual broadcast microphones were used to record the private and public utterances of the children. Public utterances were those audible to the teacher and the class, including comments and exclamations that were called out during the lesson and recorded on the public transcript of the lesson. Private utterances included private conversations between children and the whispers and comments that children made to themselves. Each private microphone and transmitter was encased in a small plastic box and hung by an elastic band around the child's neck and under his or her sweater. Each day the children put on their microphone transmitters at the beginning of the unit and switched on the transmitters. The children were shown how to turn off the transmitters if at any time they wished to keep their conversation entirely private. All the children in the class who wished to participate wore the microphone transmitters, but only the transmitters worn by the case-study children were live. The children rarely switched off the microphone transmitters during teacher-directed lessons. There is evidence that they often forgot they were wearing the microphones but monitored their behavior when they did remember. For example:

> Child (talking to peer): Don't give me that shit! — Nice little microphone.

The children appeared to disregard the recording process after the familiarization period, perhaps because they did not receive any reactions from the researchers to what was recorded.

The Lesson

To illustrate the value of utterance data in revealing the processes that mediate children's experience in both the official and unofficial worlds, we selected a thirty-six-minute introductory whole-class lesson from a social studies unit entitled "New

York City: A Study in Cultural Differences."[4] One of the teacher's goals in teaching the unit was for the children to develop more tolerance and appreciation for different races as they learned about the cultural mix in New York City. The teacher was a *Pakeha* (White) male.

Throughout the lesson the children were seated in a semicircle around the teacher, who used an overhead projector and a map as visual aids. During the first two minutes the teacher introduced the unit topic, and then the lesson itself began. The teacher began with a brainstorming activity, asking the children to respond to the question, "What does New York make you think of?" His purpose was to get "a word, a reaction, just to tune them in . . . getting them to bring to their awareness what they think about New York." The task difficulty increased slightly when he then asked, "What do you know about New York?" The teacher recorded the children's public responses on the overhead projector. The children were then asked to reflect on their responses and to consider a third question, "What would it be like to live in New York?"

After this brainstorming activity, which lasted nine minutes, the lesson continued with teacher-led discussions about New York's European settlement, its geography, the reasons for its growth, and the location of boroughs, landmarks, and prominent buildings. While discussing the European settlement, the teacher emphasized key dates as "coat hangers or signposts" to help the children with the concept of time. He made frequent comparisons between New York City and Aotearoa New Zealand in order to relate the new information to the children's prior knowledge. Throughout the lesson the teacher interspersed brief reviews in which he asked the children to recall factual details from the foregoing introductory lesson. At the end of the lesson he provided instructions for two follow-up map-labeling tasks to be done individually by the children.

Utterance Data as a Window on Children's Experience of the Lesson

We focused on four case-study children in order to trace the ways in which individual children participated in and were influenced by classroom processes.[5] The case-study children were selected to include children of different achievement levels and both boys and girls: Ann (average), Joe (low), Jon (high), and Mia (high).[6] All four children came from families in which both parents were in paid employment. Mia and John came from upper-middle-class families in which both parents were professionals (teacher and lawyer, teacher and scientist); Ann's and Joe's parents were in middle-class occupations (small business management, sales, and nursing). All were *Pakeha* (of European descent). The only Maori child in the class, Ricky, was not chosen for the case study because he was one of the children the teacher thought would be unsettled by the observational process.

We classified each utterance of each case-study child according to whether it was public or private and whether it was related to the curriculum content.[7] Public utterances were then classified in relation to the teacher's designation within the enacted curriculum: that is, whether the child was publicly answering the question when called upon ("public nomination"), calling out the answer without being called on ("call out"), responding in chorus with other children ("choral response"), or reading with the group ("unison reading"). Private utterances were initially classified by audience: whether the child was speaking or listening to a peer, talking to his or her self, or, in the case of one child, singing.

During the 36-minute lesson, the four case-study children produced 318 utterance strings, 86 percent of which occurred in the unofficial or private dimension of the children's experience of the lesson (see Table 1). For Ann, Joe, and Jon, public utterances comprised only 12 to 13 percent of their total utterances during this time. Mia engaged in much less private talk: 41 percent of her comparatively infrequent seventeen utterances were public.

Table 1 also shows the number of private utterances that were unrelated to curriculum content. These were: 16 percent for Ann, 11 percent for Jon, and 10 percent (one utterance) for Mia. Mia's private utterance that was unrelated to curriculum content concerned the task, as did half of Ann's and a third of Jon's. Private utterances that were unrelated to either the curriculum content or to the ongoing tasks were infrequent, except for those by Joe; even for Joe over two-thirds of his private utterances were related to curriculum content.

Beyond "Off-Task"

A comparison of the audio recordings and the observers' records revealed that fewer than a quarter of the private utterances recorded by the children's microphones were apparent to the observers. The simple finding that children's hidden classroom talk was far more prevalent than was apparent to the observers, who were each continuously watching one case-study child, reflects the children's expertise in hiding their private interactions. This is not surprising, given that private pupil talk is officially "off-task" during a teacher-directed lesson because it contravenes the rules of order. Doyle (1986) noted that in both secondary and elementary classrooms, quiet private talk between peers, although permitted in other task contexts, contravened the rules for teacher-directed lessons.

Indeed, the common assumption in the official classroom world is that during a lesson children should talk only when they participate publicly, and the teacher should nominate who talks publicly. Classroom research, however, shows a discrepancy between the official rules and actual behavior patterns. Doyle (1986) reviewed a series of studies that found that teachers are not always consistent in enforcing rules against "call-outs," and Cazden (1986) noted that in the course of curriculum enactment the rules of turn-taking are relaxed as the momentum of a lesson increases. Kounin (1970) explained that teachers risk sacrificing the instructional flow and momentum of a lesson if they engage in too many reprimands to achieve rule enforcement.

During the lesson we studied, the teacher did not consistently reprimand children for the private talk he appeared to notice. We should note that, because the teacher was attending primarily to the instructional flow, he noticed much less of the private talk than did the observers. However, the teacher enforced the rules of order when he found private talk disruptive.

The data in Table 1 indicate that much officially "off-task" talk was not only actually task-relevant, but also directly relevant to the children's engagement with the curriculum content.

Before we move on to consider the children's curriculum-relevant utterances during the teacher-directed lesson, we briefly consider a further problem with the use of "on-task" and "off-task" classifications of children's talk. This problem is the prevalence of "on-task" talk that shows preoccupation with task organization

TABLE 1

Frequency of Public Talk, Peer Interaction, and Talking or Singing to Self for the Case-Study Children (36 Minutes)

	Number of Utterances			
Utterance Type/Audience	*Ann*	*Joe*	*Jon*	*Mia*
Public Talk				
Public nomination	2	3	7	3
Call out	5	11 (1)	3 (1)	1 (1)
Chorus response	2	0	1	1
Unison reading	2	0	2	2
Table				
Talks to peer	23 (14)	36 (17)	26 (10)	1 (1)
Listens to peer	3	18 (11)	8	1
Talks to self	49	37	53 (1)	8
Sings	0	0	10	0
Total	86 (14)	105 (29)	110 (12)	17 (2)

Note: The number of utterances in each category that were unrelated to curriculum content are indicated in parentheses.

or presentation (for example, printing headings and coloring maps) but that displaces the academic work the teacher intended the task to involve.

For example, in the map-labeling tasks that followed the lesson we described earlier, the teacher had asked the children to locate New York City on a map of the world and to identify and label the Hudson River, the Atlantic Ocean, Mexico, and Canada. The second task involved labeling the boroughs and key landmarks on a map of New York City. Compare Jon's and Ann's utterances over a parallel time period while working at these tasks:[8]

Ann:

Ann (talking to peer): Mine [felt-tipped pen] hasn't been used that much . . . it goes a bit funny.

Ann (talking to peer): Can I use your navy? Can I use your navy please? Are you going around the edge in navy blue? What are you going to do there?

Peer (talking to Ann): Blue. But not with blue felt. Blue pencil.

Ann (talking to peer): In pencil. Yeah! Can I use your green or are you using it? Rose, have you got a blue-green?

[Two minutes later]

Ann (talking to peer): Are you definitely using pencil? I'll tell you which blue I did. I'm not going to take long. Remember we had to do the map in social studies. It's not going to take as long as that.

[Two minutes later]

Ann (talking to peer): That blue works marvelous. My blue works hopeless.

Jon:

Jon (singing to self): New York! Hot in the city! Hot in the city tonight!

Jon (talking to self): New York. Hudson River. Atlantic Ocean is here.

[Two minutes later]

Jon (talking to self): Mexico. Mekiko. Mehico.

Peer (talking to Jon): Statue of Liberty, eh?

Jon (singing to self): Mehico Ga-la-la!

Jon (talking to peer): Do you like Canada? Do you like Canada, the place?

Peer (talking to Jon): Do you know their cops are the worst in the world?

Jon (talking to peer): They're nasty.

Jon (talking to self): Mounties? . . .

Jon (talking to peer): Man, I've lost track of this map. That must be the Bronx up there. Bronx, Queens. Aw man, this map's hard to follow. It's badly drawn.

Peer (talking to Jon): No it's not. It's easy . . .

Jon (talking to peer): Well, that's your opinion, Mark. New Jersey! New Jersey man [attempts accent].

Peer (talking to Jon): That's the Bronx, isn't it?

Jon (talking to peer): Yeah. That's the Bronx . . . uh, Queens is across from the Bronx.

Peer (talking to Jon): That big bit down there. Queens, Manhattan, Brooklyn, it's down there.

Jon (talking to self): Brooklyn . . .

Jon (talking to peer): Staten Island. That's it. Here it is.

These examples reveal that during the map-labeling task, Ann was largely preoccupied with the coloring process, while Jon systematically attempted to locate and label each place specified by the teacher in his instructions. A pattern found across our classroom studies is that children often become preoccupied with task presentation rather than engaging with the curriculum content. From our detailed records of children's experience of curriculum in the classrooms we studied, it is clear that off-task behavior played a relatively minor role in inhibiting learning, as compared with on-task behavior that did not involve engagement with curriculum concepts.

We now turn to the case-study children's public and private utterances during the teacher-directed lesson, a high proportion of which were directly relevant to the curriculum content (Ann, 84%; Joe, 72%; Jon, 89%; and Mia, 88%). We cannot know whether these utterances were facilitating or even mediating learning processes; some utterances may simply reflect some of the thinking processes used by the children during the lesson. Alternatively, verbalization in itself may facilitate children's learning.

Interpreting the Utterance Data

We needed to develop a framework for interpreting the educational significance of the children's utterances. The prevalence of children's private talk that was not directed at *any* audience led us away from a traditional view that utterances are always a form of communication. Much of the children's talk did involve communication, but a significant proportion involved the children's personal and hidden verbal responses to the classroom processes.

We developed a framework within which utterances are interpreted as a source of information about the ways in which children are responding to the classroom context (see Figure 1). The framework is grounded in our data and evolving theoretical work in the Understanding Learning and Teaching Project (Alton-Lee, 1984; Alton-Lee & Nuthall, 1990, 1992a; Nuthall & Alton-Lee, 1990, 1991, 1993) and derived from a process of theoretical triangulation with the work of Doyle (1983) and Apple and Weiss (1983) and with recent information-processing theory (Howard, 1987). Central to our framework is a concern with the children's process of knowledge construction; this process we frame not only within the larger classroom context, but also within the wider sociocultural context of which the classroom is a part.

In this framework, the four major dimensions of official classroom culture are: the rules of order, the task routines, the curriculum, and the criteria by which children's performance is evaluated. As in any culture, many elements of these dimensions are implicit. The participants are enculturated over time (Berwick-Emms, 1989); it is the language, content, and perspectives of the curriculum that shape the classroom culture. For any particular classroom task, the task routines used by the teacher moderate the rules of order and shape the evaluative climate, creating particular contextual demands to be negotiated by the children (Doyle, 1983, 1986). The official agenda is that all children should acquire the same skills and knowledge through their participation in the classroom tasks. The teacher and children, however, have their own cultural perspectives, shaped by their gender, class, and race. These cultural perspectives influence their negotiation of the classroom culture and their public and private participation in curriculum enactment. The outcomes for children include not only how much they are able to learn from the official curriculum, but also what they learn about their own identity, value, and capability. The process of curriculum enactment itself is critical because children experience and learn culturally specific ways of participating that influence their learning and their well-being.

Our framework allows us to interpret the functions of children's utterances during a class lesson. Whether or not children talk privately is in itself significant, because private utterances contravene the rules of order in the lesson context. Accordingly, it is necessary to interpret the significance of silence. How a child negotiates the classroom culture during any lesson will influence the likelihood that she or he will participate, publicly or privately, in the lesson. Children's participation is also constrained by the evaluative dimension of classroom lessons. There is risk involved in responding publicly and failing. Individual children are more or

FIGURE 1   *A Framework for Interpreting the Contextual Influences on a Child's Experience of a Classroom Lesson*

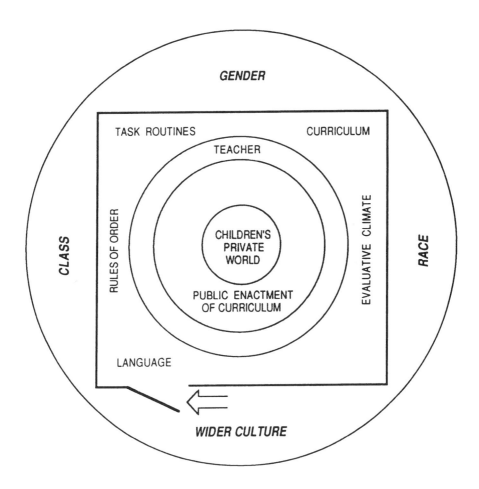

less likely to be able to lower the risk and accomplish tasks successfully because of differences in their prior knowledge, experience, and the particular skills and resources available to them both within and outside of the classroom. For children, participation in classroom lessons involves negotiating risk publicly and managing the social consequences of succeeding or failing.

In addition to whether or not a child talks publicly or privately, we must pay particular attention to the audience of an utterance. Even within the private utterance data for this lesson, there were three distinct audience categories. At the most private level, the case-study children engaged in whispers to themselves that were inaudible to peers; the second level involved private interactions with a single peer that were hidden from other peers and the teacher; and the third level involved verbalizations accessible to a few peers but not public. By identifying audience, we can learn much about the way a child negotiates the culture of the classroom and sociocultural processes.

Using this framework, we explain a child's experience during a lesson as a unique process involving three concurrent strands: 1) responding to curriculum content, 2) managing the classroom culture, and 3) participating in sociocultural processes.

Responding to Curriculum Content: Developing Knowledge Constructs

Our understanding of the way children acquire knowledge in the classroom is that they generate specific knowledge constructs as they engage in the process of making meaning out of curriculum content. The term "knowledge construct" is used to refer to a unit of knowledge that is constructed in memory as the child interprets classroom experience in relation to prior knowledge. It is less generic than a schema (see Howard, 1987) and more general than a mental model (Johnson-Laird, 1983).

We developed a model of the processes by which children generate specific knowledge constructs during instructional units by comparing the developmental progression of children's experience of curriculum content they learned with that for content that they failed to learn. Elsewhere we have described the model (Nuthall & Alton-Lee, 1991, 1992), the success of that model in predicting children's learning in three studies with children of different ages studying different curriculum areas (Nuthall & Alton-Lee, 1993), and the rationale for the methodology used (Alton-Lee & Nuthall, 1992b).

According to our model, in order to generate a specific knowledge construct, a student needs to be exposed to a sequence of appropriate, topic-relevant information within a limited period of time. Knowledge-construct generation involves the child in a series of cognitive processes: obtaining information, creating associative links, elaborating the content, evaluating the truth and consistency of information, and developing metacognitive awareness (Nuthall & Alton-Lee, 1993).

The utterances recorded during the teacher-directed lesson in this study illuminate the ways in which the case-study children created associative links to their existing knowledge, evaluated the truth of their emerging understandings, and elaborated the content. It should be noted that, because the lesson we focus on in this article was only an introductory one (almost seven hours of class time were spent on the New York City unit), the utterances often reflect the preliminary stages of the children's knowledge-construct generation.

Creating associative links between new information and prior knowledge The following utterances are examples of the ways in which the case-study children made connections with their prior knowledge and experience as they responded to the content of the enacted curriculum:

Teacher: . . . a whole 102 stories high. Imagine running up the stairs.

Mia (whispers to self): Cross country.

. . .

Teacher: . . . and the Dutch people under a Mr. Peter Stuyvesant, who of all things had a wooden leg.

Pupil (calls out): Smokes!

Teacher: If that helps.

Joe (talking to Ricky): Smokes! Ciggies!

. . .

Teacher: . . . Staten Island sometimes called Richmond.

Ricky (talking to Joe): I used to go to that school.

Joe (talking to Ricky): Richmond School.

. . .

[Teacher asks question about subway routes on map]

Ann (talking to self): Streams. Boats. In Lyttelton they have those boats.

. . .

Teacher: It's on . . . a little wee island. What is it, Jon?

Jon: Statue of Liberty.

Bart (talking to Jon): See that island there. That's where they dump their rubbish at the tip.

Jon (talking to Bart): I know 'cause they put rubbish barges down the Hudson River.

The teacher's invitation to imagine climbing the Empire State Building by the stairs reminded Mia of the school cross-country race scheduled for later in the day. Joe associated the name of Peter Stuyvesant with cigarettes (the brand his father smoked) after the teacher publicly validated another child's use of the association as a memory device. Joe realized that Ricky was making an association between Richmond Borough and Richmond School, which Ricky had attended previously. Ann's prior experience was insufficient to help her identify the subway route on the map, but she guessed, from her knowledge of a local seaport, that the symbols represented some kind of transport route. Jon's response to the teacher's question about an island near Manhattan was not only a public answer, but also a private display (to Bart) of extraordinarily specific prior knowledge about the use of barges for Manhattan rubbish disposal.

By identifying and making associations with personal experience and knowledge, children connect the new with the familiar in order to make sense or meaning out of the curriculum. Children's success at this process depends on the extent and availability of their general and topic-specific knowledge. The following excerpt illustrates the critical role that general knowledge can play in enabling a child to make sense of curriculum content:

Teacher: Brett?

Brett: The average stay for a visitor is two days.

Julia (talking to Ann): Are you only allowed to stay for two days?

Ann (talking to Julia): No that's an average. How long they do stay.

Although not every association made by the children occurred in response to a direct cue from the teacher, these associations were more likely to occur following the teacher's questions, cues, and hesitations. When reviewing the video record of the lesson, the teacher commented, "I'm pleased to see that I'm not only getting a pause, a 'wait-time,' but also that I was consciously doing it. . . . I'm asking them to think."

In addition to the logical associations the children made between their prior knowledge and the curriculum content, they also made idiosyncratic, playful, and joking associations; this was particularly true of the boys. These associations were sometimes linked to the meaning of curriculum material and sometimes to the sound of a name or an alternative meaning. For example:

Teacher: Manhattan.

Joe (talking to self): Madhattan!

. . .

Teacher: . . . sitting right on a fault line.

Joe (talking to self): Yeah! The line going across the motorway.

Jon's singing also illustrates this process:

Teacher (introducing the unit): We'll be handing out a map of New York . . .

Jon (singing to self): Cool, New York, hot in the city! Hot in the city! Hot in the city, tonight!

Teacher: Can you have a look [at map of New York City]?

(Jon singing to self): . . . from Central Park to Shanty Town. . . . New York . . . do do!

The process of making links to the curriculum content is not always consistent with the public curriculum. Inappropriate links lead to misconceptions. The utterance data showed not only children's extant misconceptions, but also the development of misconceptions during the lesson. For example, Ann inappropriately linked the notion of East Indies (where the English explorers were intending to go when they "found" New York) and the Indians who lived in New York. As a result, she mistakenly generated the name "Eastern Indians" to refer to the Manhattan Indians.

Evaluating and validating emerging understandings The children's utterances also demonstrated that they were integrating curriculum content. This involved identifying the implications of the new material and checking its coherence and validity in relation to their existing knowledge. In this monitoring process, they might identify their own misconceptions and explore evidence or reasons to support their emerging understandings. For example:

Teacher: 1664? . . . Charles?

Ann (talking to self) : American Revol-

Charles: Ah, um the English took over from the Dutch . . .

Ann (talking to self): Oh!

. . .

Teacher: Where did we start prior to 1600?

Jon (provides sound effects of gun fire): K.K.K.K.k.k.k.k.k . . .

Jon (talking to self): No machine guns . . . wouldn't have even been pump-action muskets.

. . .

Teacher: Yes, it [New York City] grew to a million people. It grew to more than . . .

Mia (talking to self): Eighty million.

Pupil: Eight million.

Teacher: What made you say eight million?

Ann (talking to peer): I guessed that because I just thought that New Zealand is three million and New York's bigger than that.

. . .

Teacher: 1609?

Mia (talking to self): The Dutch [precedes the correct answer in public lesson by half a minute].

There is evidence to suggest that this monitoring and integration process is an internalization of the model of teacher-student interactions that the children experience in the public discussion. This cycle of question-answer-reaction has been well-documented as the traditional pattern of teacher-student verbal interaction in the classroom (Aschner, 1959; Bellack, Hyman, Smith, & Kliebard, 1966). Empirical evidence indicates that students who participate publicly in the discussion cycle do not learn more than students who only listen to the cycle, and that listening to a discussion cycle is more effective than listening to a teacher lecture (see Hughes, 1973; Nuthall & Church, 1973). The utterances in this study suggest that the children are not only learning how to respond in an acceptable manner, but are also learning the teacher's role of reacting to responses. In their private utterances, both Mia and Ann responded to the teacher's cues and reacted like the teacher to their own covert utterances and to other children's overt responses. The evaluative climate of the lesson became their own internal evaluative process.

Developing and extending knowledge constructs   Once children have generated a specific knowledge construct, they develop and extend its content. Because the lesson we.selected was the introductory session to the unit, the children were interacting with primarily new information; thus this process was only infrequently evident in their utterances. There was one example in Ann's utterances:

Teacher: What did they use the river as?

Ann (talking to Julia): Exporting.

Teacher: Neil?

Neil: A road.

Teacher: Thank you. They used the river as a road.

The notion that the Hudson River had been used to transport people was discussed in the public lesson, but the idea was not developed to include the commercial function that Ann privately suggested to Julia.

Jon had the most relevant prior knowledge of all the case-study children (he already knew the content of over three-quarters of the items in the pre-test), so it is not surprising that his utterances frequently involved comments that developed, extended, and provided his personal perspective on the curriculum content:

> Teacher: The English took over from the Dutch, and they said, "We'll blow you up if you don't give us the island!"
>
> *Jon (talking to self): Threatened them!*
>
> . . .
>
> Pupil (in response to first question, "What does New York make you think of?"): Nukes.
>
> *Jon (talking to self): Nuclear. There's none in New York. They're all in Washington.*

As the unit progressed, these comments became more frequent. For example, in a later lesson about reasons for early immigration to New York, Jon found the teacher's explanation ironic:

> Teacher: So wars meant that some folk said, "Let's shift from Europe and go to where there are no wars," so they went to America.
>
> *Jon (talking to self): Now America's king of war.*

While there is danger in over-interpreting the utterance data, there are reasonable grounds for believing that, because they are spontaneous and private, they represent an externalization of normally covert processes; that is, that they represent spontaneous thinking aloud.

Jon's utterances during the introductory lesson reflected his higher prior knowledge: his utterances involved associative links, elaborations, evaluations of the truth and consistency of information, and metacognitive processes.[9] Ann's utterances were mainly concerned with monitoring her own misconceptions and emerging understandings. Joe frequently related the new curriculum content to his own knowledge, but did little monitoring or integrating of the new knowledge. Mia was very quiet, but her characteristic response was to monitor her own answers.

It may be that these differences between the children reflect differences in their ability to organize their experiences and generate relevant knowledge constructs. But what constitutes "ability" here? What the utterances do reveal is the critical role of **cultural capital**[a] in enabling the children to engage in the process of generating constructs.[10] This is apparent in both the topic-specific and general knowledge that the children brought to the lesson, or which they gained access to by interacting with peers and with the teacher during the lesson.

---

[a] **Cultural capital** refers to some types of cultural understanding — such as language, modes of social interaction, knowledge about the functioning of a system — that are valued commodities in a particular society or structure and can be used by an individual for advancement.

The utterances also reveal a difference between the children in the extent to which they incorporated into their processing a teacher-like role of monitoring the validity of their emerging understandings. Evidence of monitoring is least apparent in the utterances of Joe, the low achiever, suggesting that monitoring one's own understandings may be particularly critical to the knowledge-construct generation process.

It is important to remember, however, that with our focus on this one lesson we have opened only a partial window on the processes with which children generate knowledge constructs. Our studies indicate that such constructs are generated across a number of occasions throughout the course of a unit (Nuthall & Alton-Lee, 1992, 1993).

Managing the Classroom Culture

As is apparent in the section above, the children's ability to make meaning out of curriculum content was dependent on the extent to which they could draw upon relevant prior knowledge, skills (such as map interpretation), and experiences. When a child lacks these resources, she or he finds it difficult to manage the evaluative climate. In the following accounts, we consider what the utterances reveal about the ways in which the teacher and the case-study children managed the evaluative climate. Our findings should be interpreted with the proviso that our presence as observers almost certainly heightened the children's perception of the risk of replying.

Ann   Ann appeared to manage the evaluative climate with accurate judgment about the adequacy of her answers. Her public answers were consistently correct or appropriate and her eleven wrong answers were kept private. She was able to draw on considerable relevant prior knowledge during the lesson, including her recent television viewing of a news item about the Statue of Liberty. Almost 10 percent of Ann's utterances involved her friend Julia in a shared process of interacting with the curriculum content. When Ann was overwhelmed by new curriculum content and no longer able to engage in making associations to relevant prior knowledge and experience, she used an apparently deliberate strategy of repetition of key words:[11]

Teacher: The Dutch . . .

Ann (talking to self): The Dutch.

Teacher: . . . started a town on Manhattan; they called it New Amsterdam.

Ann (talking to self): New Amsterdam.

. . .

Teacher: There are three buildings I would like you to identify: United Nations, Empire State, and World Trade Center.

Ann (talking to self): World Trade, World Trade, Empire State, United Nations, Empire State.

Ann's style of participation in the lesson indicated almost total continuous involvement in the tasks or with the content. Of all the case-study children, she was most often observed to be focused on the teacher or on a relevant resource. Ann received no positive feedback from the teacher for her two publicly nominated responses, and she appeared frustrated in her desire to participate publicly more frequently. Of the four children, she was least likely to elicit teacher nomination with her hand raises: her fifteen hand raises during the lesson only elicited two teacher nominations. Ann responded by calling out her answers five times and by talking privately at a rate of two to three utterances per minute. A third of these utterances involved cooperative interactions with her friend, Julia. This private peer interaction appeared to play an important, mutually supportive role in both girls' management of the evaluative climate during the lesson. Julia sought Ann's help with strategies to remember the dates presented by the teacher. Ann shared her misconceptions with Julia. This talk was hidden, enabling Ann to give and receive peer support during the lesson, yet allowing her to avoid being seen by the teacher as contravening the rules of order.

Her management (masking) of her contravention of the rules of order was so effective that even when the teacher reviewed the video (long after the unit), Ann's private utterances were hidden, and he commented that "Ann doesn't offer as much as some of the others in terms of an active type of learning. . . . She learns just sitting and soaking it up."

Joe   Joe did not appear to manage the evaluative climate as carefully as Ann: his only two wrong answers were public responses. This can be explained partly by the absence of self-monitoring in Joe's interaction with curriculum content during the lesson; he did not appear to check the validity of his own answers.

Both Joe's utterances and the interview with Joe reveal that his free associations drew extensively on his prior knowledge and experiences, particularly on his television viewing: "Oh yeah! 'The Equalizer' program. The one just starting, there was this . . . picture of a subway and there was all this yukky stuff and rubbish." His background knowledge, however, was insufficient to enable him to answer public questions correctly:

Teacher: Can you think of any city, say in New Zealand or anywhere else, that has got this type of [name]?

Joe (talking to self): No, damn!

When another boy, Sean, gave information about the average stay for a visitor to New York being two days, Joe's retort was a scathing, "How do you know that?" But when the teacher then acknowledged Sean's prior reading as a valuable source of information, Joe grabbed a book from a nearby display. Throughout much of the rest of the lesson, Joe attempted to use the book to find answers to the teacher's questions:

Teacher: What else is there in New York?

Joe (calling out): Yeah, I know! I know! It's in this book!

. . .

Teacher: What did they use the river as [in the context of discussing the commercial growth of New York City]?

Joe (talking to self): It said canoeing here.

Joe's determination to get right answers preoccupied him to the point that he failed to follow the meaning of the public discussion; hence his response of "canoeing" in the instance above. The process finally became public after a sequence when Joe called out and pleaded with the teacher to choose him to participate:

Teacher: Why did New York grow, whereas the cities at the time that were a bit down there didn't grow nearly as much?

Joe (calling out): I know!

Teacher: You've got everything you need, Joe. Go!

Joe: Well it says in this book. It may not be right, but it says that European settlers had a habit of pulling it out — of pulling something out.

Teacher: Well! [pupils laugh] Let's just say you pulled it out of a book and I'm not certain what it is, but just leave it there, Joe.

The consequences of his public mistake did not seem to worry Joe excessively, and the teacher later commented, "I think it was a general humorous laugh and Joe was laughing as well. I don't think it was a ridicule laugh."

Though the social consequences of public failure were not serious for Joe, his inability to provide right answers seemed both to frustrate him and to motivate him to copy an effective strategy used by his peer — reading a book. Not only did Joe contravene the rules of order by getting the book, he also flicked through it in an attempt to get answers during the lesson. This strategy reduced the possibility of his making meaning of the ongoing curriculum content according to the teacher's agenda. During the lesson, Joe focused on the teacher or a relevant resource less than half as frequently as did both girls, though unlike them, he appeared to take great pleasure in the lesson, making jokes, word plays, and humorous free associations. He was the only case-study child to engage in more peer interactions than talking to himself.

Although a large proportion (41.5 percent) of Joe's social interactions involved a shared process of interacting with curriculum content, he also used the private world to abuse his peers. He engaged in serious breaches of the rules of order — kicking and name-calling. He was, however, very skilled at hiding his contraventions and was never individually reprimanded by the teacher. Actually, early in the lesson he was rewarded for breaking the public participation rule:

Teacher: That is, homework as opposed to what you do while you are?

Joe (calling out before the teacher opened up the turn to other children): At school!

Teacher: I want to hear a voice — "at school." Brilliant!

Joe's public response during the brainstorm, "Oh, what is, yeah . . . lots of violence," was rewarded with the affirmation, "He thinks, he does!" Joe made ten more public call-outs during the lesson.

Mia Mia appeared to be the case-study child most concerned about the evaluative climate and the rules of order. Her private utterances were rare and mostly inaudible to her peers. Mia's only comment to a peer, "He always says 'Brilliant!'," concerned the teacher's feedback to other children and revealed Mia's sensitivity to the evaluative climate. He never said "brilliant" to Mia. Mia watched or glanced at the teacher or appropriate visual resource at least three times per minute, but she also glanced around at a rate of twice a minute. She appeared to be very attuned to other children's private talk — particularly to Jon's evaluative comments, even when he was not directing them to peers.

Mia contravened the rules of order for public participation only once, when she called out to the teacher that she and the other girls around her could not see the visual resource. Her desire to see the screen overcame her characteristic reticence.

When Mia raised her hand, she was less likely to elicit a teacher nomination than were the boys. However, she gave two publicly nominated responses. The teacher's response to her contribution to the brainstorm indicated that he was using a more stringent criteria for Mia than for the other case-study children. Unlike the other case-study children, Mia (for both public responses) used an interrogative intonation, suggesting that she was attempting to diminish the risk. This was surprising, given the apparently low-risk status of a brainstorming session. However, her anxiety was justified. Instead of accepting the response, the teacher probed further, thereby changing the level of risk when Mia was already the focus of public attention:

Mia: The Empire State Building, Sir?

Teacher: Something about the Empire State Building. Can I just ask another question? What do you know about the Empire State Building?

Mia: Um, it's the tallest building in the world, isn't it?

Teacher: Ah, no; it's not.

Mia (talking to self): I thought it was.

The public correction of her incorrect response was remembered by Mia a year after the New York City unit:

Interviewer: Do you remember quite well when you said something in class?

Mia: Yeah, 'cause I was wrong (laugh) so I remember that. . . . I always thought what I said was the highest building, so I was surprised when he said to me I was wrong.

Jon   Of the four case-study children, Jon was the one who, when he raised his hand, was recognized most often by the teacher: approximately one out of four times that he raised his hand he was called on. He was nominated publicly seven times and called out on three occasions. Jon appeared to be less constrained by the evaluative climate and more at ease than the other case-study children:

Teacher: What's his name?

Pupil: Oh, I'm not sure.

Teacher: I should have written it down. I'm being a wee bit nasty asking you to remember these things.

Jon: Starts with a C. Was it Cooligan or something?

Neil: I know! Peter Stuyvesant.

Jon (talking to self): Oh yeah!

Jon (talking to Neil): How did you know it was a cigarette, Neil? Ooohhh!

In the example above, Jon was prepared to take the risk to give a public response that he knew he was unsure about. When Neil gave the correct response, Jon's self-monitoring was private. Within the unofficial peer culture, he mocked Neil for having knowledge of cigarettes, suggestively implying that his knowledge may have been acquired illicitly. Jon effectively took the evaluative focus off himself.

Of all the case-study children, Jon had the most specific topic-relevant knowledge, much of which came from television. His most frequent private utterance response to the lesson was to give an answer. Out of sixteen of Jon's private answers, only one was incorrect.

The contribution of television to Jon's learning was extraordinarily specific. The mystery of his knowledge of Manhattan's barge rubbish disposal was revealed in an interview when he explained how he knew about the Hudson river:

Interviewer: How did you learn that?

Jon (laughing): "Yogi Bear" and "Top Cat"!

Interviewer: Tell me more. Educate me about "Yogi Bear" and "Top Cat."

Jon: Oh no! I don't think it was "Yogi Bear." I think it was "Top Cat." And one day he wanted to take a cruise down the Hudson River and the only way he could do that was on a garbage boat, and he got put in a garbage can or something and by accident he got taken away by the garbage man, and at the end all his friends sort of say, "Oh well, you got what you wanted T.C.! A cruise down the Hudson!" or something like that!

Another source of topic-specific prior knowledge, a magazine, was revealed in the interview with Jon:

Jon: . . . in the magazine (*Mad Magazine*) where . . . on a deserted New York subway at 3:00 in the morning . . . there's three dark figures creeping up behind with knives . . .

Jon's confidence about his own prior knowledge was reflected in his next-most frequent utterance type, which involved an evaluative commentary on the adequacy and shortcomings of public answers offered by other pupils. For example:

Pupil: It's [New York] sitting on a fault line.

Jon (talking to self) : It's not. That's San Francisco.

Teacher: OK. What did they name New Amsterdam?

Jon (talking to peer): New York. Everyone tends to forget that.

He was confident enough of his own topic-relevant prior knowledge to qualify information given by the teacher:

Teacher: The very first people who may have lived in this area would have been?

Pupil: Indians.

Jon (talking to self): Red Indians actually.

Jon's response to Charles's challenge to the teacher about historical inaccuracy in the curriculum indicated that he himself was evaluating his peers and the teacher:

Charles: The Vikings were there [America] first because they saved all those copies of bits of paper and they said the Vikings were there in 1300.

Teacher: Yes. So, what?

Charles: So you said they were there first but they weren't.

Jon (talking to self): Guilty, man!

Jon not only evaluated peer responses and the teacher's information, he also argued about public information with a male peer:

Mia: It's [Empire State Building] the tallest building in the world.

Jon (talking to self): No, it's not. It's the second tallest.

Frank (talking to Jon): It's not the second highest.

Jon (talking to Frank): I know what the highest is.

Frank (talking to Jon): There are lots of buildings higher than the Empire State. It was a few years ago it was.

Jon (talking to Frank): It's the second highest.

[Argument continues]

Jon (talking to Frank): It's got eighty-six floors!

Jon, like Mia, was prepared to contravene the rules of order in order to interact with curriculum content. He directly contravened the teacher's direction not to use any other resource to solve a subway route problem by using a map key to locate the requisite answer.

Toward the end of the lesson, Jon complained to a peer that he wanted to be getting on with his own agenda — writing his own story about New York. However, overall he appeared to derive great enjoyment and entertainment from the lesson:

Jon (talking to self, attempting American accent): West of the Mississippi.

[Teacher discusses reasons for expansion of New York City]

Jon (talking to peer): It also became big because it's a seaport . . .

Jon (talking to peer): Because the Bronx Warriors were doing good!

Jon's private utterances gave us the impression that he was covertly directing his own movie version of the lesson, providing his version of a vocal sound track, relevant sound effects, and a commentary with corrections and modifications when he judged the enacted curriculum to be falling short of the needs of the topic.

The differences in the case-study children in their management of the classroom culture reflect not only differences in the resources they were able to bring to their participation, but also differences in the ways in which the teacher operated the official agenda for different children. Irrespective of achievement level, the case-study boys were more easily able to participate publicly, were more likely to be praised, and more likely to take the risk of offering answers of which they were uncertain. The girls were careful to keep answers they were unsure of covert. Mia's strategy of remaining comparatively silent contrasted with Ann's strategy of managing much of the lesson through hidden supportive interactions with her friend, Julia.

Participating in Sociocultural Processes: Learning within the "Lived Culture" of the Classroom

Children's responses to curriculum occur within a cultural context that is also shaped by the wider society. This cultural context is described by Apple and Weiss as the "lived culture" of the classroom: "Lived culture refers to culture as it is produced in ongoing interactions and as a terrain in which class, race, and gender meanings and antagonisms are played out" (1983, p. 27). The records of the enacted curriculum and the children's utterance data provided us with a unique perspective on the specific processes through which the lived culture was produced by the teacher and the children and influenced the children's interaction with curriculum content during this lesson.

Cultural bias in the curriculum   Because teachers' agendas have shaped our perspectives on classroom practice, the unofficial world of the students has been invisible; in addition, the cultural dimensions of classroom processes in the official world have been invisible. Spender (1982) argued that the school curriculum is strongly biased towards a White male perspective. The content of the enacted curriculum of the lesson we studied included not a single mention of a female, but fifty mentions of males (for example, Peter Stuyvesant, Henry Hudson, the Duke of York, Englishmen, Englishman, the "man in charge").[12] Pronounced gender bias is not uncharacteristic in the enacted curriculum of the social studies units we have studied in the Understanding Learning and Teaching Project. For the entire "New York City" unit, references to females comprised only 2.4 percent of the references to people. In the enacted curriculum for a study of the Middle Ages, references to females comprised only 3.9 percent of the references to people (81.7 percent were references to males) in more than fifty-two hours of class time (Alton-Lee, Densem, & Nuthall, 1991; Alton-Lee & Densem, 1992). The few women mentioned in the New York City unit were characteristically derogated or marginalized.[13] Clearly, if particular groups of people are omitted from curriculum content or characteristically marginalized or derogated, the curriculum conveys a message about relative cultural valuing of those groups.

The role of the teacher   How does bias become so pronounced in the enacted curriculum? The school resources available to teachers and historical reference books contribute to this bias, but the teacher is instrumental in shaping the lived culture of the enacted curriculum beyond the initial selection of lesson content and resources.

During the lesson studied, the teacher unconsciously structured the children's experience of curriculum by race and gender as he identified with a particular cultural group — White men of European descent. Although he began by calling each group of people or men who lived in New York City "they," as the momentum of the lesson increased, he began to use the term "we" occasionally. The following examples, spread over a six-minute period, show the teacher's use of "we" when referring to White people:

Teacher: The very first people who may have lived in this area may have been?

Child: Indians.

Teacher: They gave their names to one of the islands because they spoke of the Manhattan Indians . . .

. . .

[Forty-five seconds later]

Teacher: When White men first came they found Indians. . . . They were called Manhattan Indians. Because White people, Europeans, we were . . .

Teacher: Before we, or the Dutch people could get this island where we wanted to build our city . . .

. . .

[Five minutes later]

Teacher: Wouldn't that have been lovely if we had have owned it [New York City]?

The teacher's use of pronouns conveyed not only his own unconscious identification with the European men who colonized New York, but also an implied positioning of the children in the class as "White people, Europeans, we." He went on to mention the Treaty of Waitangi, which was the original (broken) agreement between the Maori and Europeans (*Pakeha*) in Aotearoa New Zealand, but he did so from the perspective of a White (*Pakeha*) male strongly identified with English settlers:

Teacher: In terms of Christchurch, what is the approximate date the first lot of boats, the first four ships — the big ones — where all of our ancestors came from? You know we all came . . .

This evidence illustrates the claim made by Apple and Weiss (1983) that "what counts as school knowledge . . . tends to embody the interests and culture of the group or groups who have power to distribute and legitimate their worldview through educational institutions" (p. 28). The teacher plays an unknowing but critical role in the **hegemonic**[b] cycle, and the White male bias becomes so customary it seems normal. In this lesson, the teacher's intention was to increase the children's appreciation of cultural diversity, but his unconscious assumption of "we" to refer to White males in the official enacted curriculum was in conflict with his overall aim. Although his conscious intent was to convey tolerance and cultural in-

---

[b] **Hegemonic** refers to a system that is designed to keep present power structures in place, and supports the oppression of one or more groups by others.

clusiveness, the teacher inadvertently excluded Maori from "our ancestors . . . we all came" (a reference to the English settlement of Christchurch) during the process of curriculum enactment.

Cultural bias can also influence the enacted curriculum through the teacher's split-second decisions about who can contribute to the enacted curriculum through public participation. If a teacher unwittingly favors the participation of a particular group of children, then that group's knowledge, experiences, and cultural perspectives shape the curriculum content. Marked gender bias was apparent in who was nominated to participate and in who participated in the lesson. The boys' perspectives on New York City were twice as prominent as the girls' in the enacted curriculum. Eighty-five (70 percent) of the public contributions were made by boys compared with thirty-six (30 percent) by girls. There were fourteen girls and fifteen boys in the class, making the average public participation rate for a girl 2.6 responses, and for a boy 5.7 responses. Our analyses of the experiences of the case-study children suggest that this imbalance occurred partly because the teacher was more likely to nominate boys. Also, the evaluative climate was more stringent for the girls with respect to the responses of both the teacher and their male peers. We consider that the bias in the curriculum content may itself contribute to the imbalance through affirming and supporting the participation of those children who are White and male.

Like curriculum-content bias, gender bias in public participation, although not usually so pronounced, has been shown to be characteristic of much educational practice (Kelly, 1988; Sadker, Sadker, & Klein, 1991). Research in Aotearoa New Zealand has uncovered pronounced gender bias even in the practice of feminist teachers (Newton, 1988) and shown patterns of cultural bias, with White (*Pakeha*) girls participating publicly more than Polynesian girls (Jones, 1985), and teachers giving more attention to both White (*Pakeha*) and Samoan children than to Maori children (Clay, 1985).

The curriculum enactment was not structured by gender just in the content and public participation. The children were physically segregated by gender, with the boys in a semicircle at the front and the girls in a semicircle behind. This segregation was normal in this classroom, and the teacher appeared to keep the boys close as a means of proximity control. After his introduction, the teacher began the lesson proper with the comment, "Let's boot off!" — a football analogy close to the heart of male culture, both *Pakeha* and Maori, in Aotearoa New Zealand. Although the analogy is used by the teacher inclusively — "Let [u]s" — the prior experience of the children will have been influenced by gendered practices in sporting participation. For the boys, the analogy cued prior experience as active participants. For the girls, who were most unlikely ever to have played on a football team, the analogy cued either their experience as spectators or their lack of experience.

The role of popular culture in classroom learning   The utterances highlighted the ways in which images from and associations to popular culture and the media were integral to the children's classroom learning processes and their generation of knowledge constructs. For this particular topic, the children drew extensively on prior knowledge they had gained from their television viewing. For example, in the post-unit interview, Jon described a documentary that he had watched before the unit:

Jon: It [a documentary] was about the poor side and the rich side of New York, and that there was a street down the middle that divided them, 49th Street or something. Oh yeah, it was called "The Streets of New York" and it was all about crime and everything in New York.

The children did not focus only on television programs about New York City. Television advertisements and general programs also provided a common source of general prior knowledge that they linked to new curriculum content.

This background knowledge was also predominantly male-focused (for example, with references to male cartoon characters, male television stars, male police, male baseball teams, male basketball players, male gangs, male brand names). There was also a difference in the television-viewing patterns of the female and male case-study children. For example, the boys reported watching more late-night American police shows than did the girls. Mia explained:

Mia: Well, from the television I thought all of New York was like "Diff'rent Strokes." I thought it was all very posh and things. I had no idea about all the sort of slum areas and things.

Interviewer: Have you ever seen anything on television about crime in New York?

Mia: Crime in New York?

Mia: Mmm . . . I don't think so . . . no . . . Dad doesn't like television much and especially he doesn't like American programs, so we don't watch them.

Children's responses to cultural bias in the curriculum How did the children respond to the teacher's unconsciously positioning them by using the pronoun "we" to mean White and male? During the following interview, the female researcher was startled when Mia showed her unconscious identification with White males in the curriculum by using the pronoun "us." This occurred when she was asked about the early settlement of New York City:

Mia: I think it's the Indians. I think they were the first people to have it.

Interviewer: Mm.

Mia: 'Cause they just, see you don't um Indians came before sort of today sort of wearing, wearing all them facepaints and things and you sort of think of them being first there because they're before us. You can tell sort of. You think of Indians and you think of long hair and headbands and weapons . . . and . . .

Interviewer: Yeah. And you say, you don't think of them — you think of them being there before us?

Mia: Mm.

Interviewer: And do you feel, when you say us, do you mean that the people who came to settle New York after the Indians were people like us?

Mia: Mm. Mm. [nods]

Interviewer: How were they like us?

Mia: Well, they didn't wear um, war paint and carry weapons around. They just sort of had, they wore clothes like us, sort of [laugh] civilized clothes.

Interviewer: When you say us do you think of women or men?

Mia: I think of men really 'cause like, sort of early Canterbury you have visions of people wearing sort of long suits and things. You know I don't really, yeah, that's right! I only think of the men. [giggle] I don't think of the women. [giggle]

Mia's identification with White colonists contrasted with the perspective taken by Ricky, the only Maori boy in the class. Ricky also remembered the men who colonized New York City, but spoke of them as culturally distant — "they" as opposed to "we" or "us":

Ricky: Oh well, first it was the Indians and then I think it was Englishmen, and ever since they have lived there, I think.

Interviewer: And you say Englishmen. Who are you thinking of? What sort of people?

Ricky: Well they were a bit greedy and more advanced than the Indians, so they just made towns and that started from there. They got rich and that.

The utterance data revealed that Ricky's exclusion from the White male "we" in the enacted curriculum also influenced Joe during the lesson:

Teacher: Because White people . . .

Joe (talking to Ricky): Honkies.

Ricky (talking to Joe): Shut up!

Teacher: Europeans, we were . . .

Joe (talking to Ricky): Nigger!

Teacher: Watch this way please, Ricky! — were often wanting to get things . . .

Joe (talking to Ricky): Black man! Samoan!

. . .

Teacher: East Indies.

Joe (talking to peer): Ricky, they're going to play cricket![14]

. . .

Joe (talking to Ricky): Shut up! Prove it! Get stuffed, Ricky!

. . .

[Joe kicks Ricky]

Joe (talking to Ricky): Ricky hurt his foot!

Teacher: . . . the English took over from the Dutch and . . .

Joe (talking to self): They built a ship.

. . .

Ricky (talking to Joe): Idiot! You get out!

Joe (talking to Ricky): You kicked me first you, nigger!

Ricky (talking to Joe): Did not you honky honk. I'm not a nigger you flippin' honky honk!

. . .

Joe (talking to Ricky): Shut up!

Teacher: Ricky, could you try and watch here please?

. . .

Joe (talking to Ricky): Ow! You kicked me!

Ricky (talking to Joe): I haven't! I haven't! Prove it! Prove it!

Joe (talking to Ricky): God, you're dumb! Now I'll prove that you're dumb!

Ricky (talking to Joe): Prove it! You don't know!

. . .

Joe (talking to Ricky): All right! I will! . . . What's fifty-nine divided by sixteen . . . ?

Joe immediately responded to the teacher's inadvertent exclusion of Ricky from "White people, Europeans, we" and compounded the teacher's positioning of Ricky as "other" by directing racist abuse — *"Nigger!"* — at him. His provocative challenge after he first kicked Ricky — *"Prove it!"* — suggests that he felt inviolable even from the rules of order in the classroom. Joe's confidence was well-placed. The teacher reprimanded Ricky repeatedly. The victimization experienced by Ricky culminated in a crisis when a group of White (*Pakeha*) boys, including Joe, went to the teacher after school to ask him to remove Ricky from the class because his "bad behavior" was "interfering" with their work. From the teacher's perspective, Ricky was always the child associated with trouble, since Joe was particularly skilled at hiding his racist provocation. Neither the teacher nor the observers ever heard instances of the racist abuse revealed later in the broadcast microphone transcripts, and in a later interview Ricky appeared to be surprised that the interviewer was aware of the racism.[15] When asked about the abuse he had experienced, Ricky attributed the cause of the racism to himself and revealed his solution to the problem:

Ricky: Well sometimes people be racist to me 'cause I annoy them. Sometimes they . . . That's how I know. . . . Sometimes I just get up and hit them and they stop.

Although physical abuse contravened the rules of order in the classroom, the message that superior violence prevails was conveyed by the colonial perspective on history in the curriculum content. For example, the history of New York City provided in the enacted curriculum was a military history in which the English were seen as triumphant and superior conquerors of the Dutch. Ricky referred not only to the New York City unit, but also to other social studies units as the source of his definition of "advanced" meaning possessing superior military strength:

Interviewer: You say they [the English] are more advanced?

Ricky: Oh well, the Indians just had bows and arrows I think, and they had guns.

We suggest that the cultural bias in the curriculum enactment created a climate wherein the White (*Pakeha*) boys used their culturally privileged position to speak out more, contravene the rules of order more frequently, and to derive more pleasure and entertainment from the lesson. When the teacher used the football term to initiate the lesson, Jon repeated the phrase and laughed. Mia watched Jon laughing.

The cultural climate triggered Joe's *private* racial abuse of Ricky, but allowed the boys to engage in *public* sexist behavior involving sexual innuendo and verbal harassment of the girls. One girl in the class, Sarah, had high status among the children because she was a class councilor.[16] This status appeared to enable her to respond publicly more frequently than any other girl in the class, thereby breaking the pattern of male dominance. During the brainstorming session, however, when she responded that New York made her think of breakdancing, Joe called out, labeling her "New Zealand Knickers!" (referring to underpants), making her the focus of a sexual innuendo and silencing her: she stopped participating after he made that remark. The introduction (by boys) of information involving sexual content or sexual innuendo was the major threat to orderliness during the lesson and gave rise to much joking among the boys while the girls watched. When one of the boys gave the response "flashers" (men who expose themselves) to one of the brainstorming questions, the ensuing disturbance brought the lesson to a halt. Although the teacher attempted to go on with the brainstorming session, his attempts failed, and he introduced a disciplinary measure — asking the boys to stand and sit down again. The football analogy appeared apt, as the teacher managed the behavior of the boys while the girls were spectators.

The low status of women in the curriculum was also reflected throughout the unit in the private utterances of both case-study boys. For example, during the introductory lesson, Joe responded "prostitutes" to the teacher's question about the first people to settle in New York, and "prostitutes" was the first public mention of women on the second day of the unit.

The language as well as the content and perspectives of the enacted curriculum play a powerful role in structuring cultural norms in the classroom. Who is included, how they are portrayed, and how the children are positioned in relation to them convey to the children messages about who is valued in society. The consequences for the well-being of children who are not White and male are profound. Mia accommodated to the norm by identifying as a White male at the cost of her own cultural identity as a White (*Pakeha*) female. Ricky admired the White male cultural norm, but became victim to it while blaming himself for the victimization. We do not have data to explain the ways Maori girls experience the enacted curriculum. However, in a lived culture featuring a curriculum in which White and male is valued and privileged, Maori girls are confronting bias against both their race and their gender.

The process worked both ways: the lived culture in the classroom contributed to the focus on male experience and interests in the enacted curriculum, and the curriculum significantly influenced power relations in the lived culture. Though the teacher intended to increase the children's tolerance of cultural differences, the hidden curriculum of differential cultural valuing was more powerful in the lesson we selected than his official agenda.

The Effect on the Teacher

In our experience, teachers who are prepared to open up their classrooms to the intensive audio and video recording and observational processes that these studies entail do so because of their deep commitment to children and to improving their educational practice. The experience, however, can be deeply disturbing when the evidence that is uncovered shows the impact of destructive cultural processes on individual children. The teacher involved in the New York City unit said that the data had a "devastating" effect on him, and that it was

> heart-rending because I would have liked to have thought that I was tuned in to what was happening in the class. . . . I just didn't know. . . . Prior to doing this research . . . I would've said "Yes, you know, I'm fully aware of all these things whether it's the race issue or the gender issue, whatever." . . . It comes as a real blow to find that in actual fact you're not necessarily doing things that are in line with what you believe. . . . You're faced with this discrepancy.

This teacher worked with us to disseminate the early findings and to make the research integral to his and our continuing work in teacher education; he has since taken up issues of gender and race in his own in-service teacher education courses. The following quote describes his perception of the influence of the research on his practice:

> The important things in the long run are the outcomes. . . . The outcomes for me of taking part in this research are not what we originally [foresaw]. I believe that they're extremely positive because they've increased my level of awareness. They've altered my action. . . . It's altered the things that I think are important when I'm devising a curriculum. . . . It's altered the way I treat other people too.

He has also discussed the implications of involvement in the research with the teachers who have chosen to participate in two subsequent studies. They, in turn, have used the opportunity to evaluate their own curriculum reforms that address issues raised by earlier research.

Toward a Constructivist Perspective on Curriculum Learning

There are profound questions to be addressed about the value of curriculum knowledge. Traditional classroom research has bypassed the question of the value, asking instead questions about quantity and efficiency. Sociologists have framed the curriculum content children learn as a commodity (Apple & Weiss, 1983) of which children get more or less — as if it is external, material, and given. But the constructivist view of learning we have taken here renders the concept of curriculum as commodity inappropriate. The findings from our analyses suggest that children do not *receive* various proportions of that commodity. Rather, they construct their own knowledge as they struggle to make sense of the enacted curriculum within the lived culture of the classroom. Unless they resist, they learn to construct a worldview that undermines their gender if they are female and their race if they are non-White. In the kind of contexts we have studied, the knowledge they construct is a Trojan horse for those children who are not White and male. Those children who fail do not receive the certification that allows them a better chance of paid employment in the mainstream of society. Those who achieve do so by coming to construct within their own minds a worldview that legitimates White male power and their own subordination.

While cultural bias in the classroom context is framed by the curriculum, it permeates the entire classroom culture. We cannot adequately explain how cultural bias influences children's experience and learning unless we include the critical role of social class in mediating classroom processes. The role of social-class membership has been extensively documented in input-output studies of educational achievement and in studies showing how parental education and out-of-school access to curriculum-relevant cultural resources and experiences advantage upper-middle-class children (Apple & Weiss, 1983; Bowles & Gintis, 1976; Densem, Wilton, & Keeling, 1988; Lauder & Hughes, 1990). Shirley Brice Heath's (1982) study of the match between children's experiences of language and books at home and at school revealed the importance not just of resources, but also of culturally specific (by race and social class) ways of linking written material to experience. Heath explains that "the *culture* children learn as they grow up is, in fact, ways of taking meaning from the environment around them" (p. 49).

Although the social-class differences between the case-study children in this study were small relative to the range of social-class differences in Aotearoa New Zealand, these class differences were reflected in the children's curriculum-appropriate prior knowledge, experience, and resource access (cultural capital), and in the ways in which they interacted with the curriculum content. When we take into account the complex ways in which class, race, and gender mediate classroom processes, we have the potential for a more coherent explanation for the contradictions and conflicts in children's experiences in classrooms.

Although Mia's race and class privileged her in the classroom, and she learned more as measured by the unit test than the other case-study students, her secondary status as a female within the classroom culture shaped her reticent way of participating and her identification with male experience. Joe was generally perceived as a low achiever by the teacher, and his long-term learning as measured by the unit test was lowest. In spite of his privileged position participating as a White male in the classroom culture, he did not have access to sufficient prior knowledge or ways of monitoring his own cognitive processes to succeed in the class discussions. He was able, however, to use his powerful position to abuse privately his Maori peer and to harass publicly his female peers with no official consequence. Ricky experienced private abuse and unjust public reprimands, but was engaged by Joe in a shared male culture, revealing the contradictions that arose from his being both male and Maori. Jon's participation in the lesson from a position of class, race, and gender privilege seems to have afforded him both freedom from the kind of anxiety evident in the girls' behavior and obvious pleasure as he sang and joked, impatiently correcting his peers. Ann's attempts to participate publicly were least successful and least rewarded, even though her private answers revealed that she successfully grappled with much of the new curriculum content despite having less prior knowledge than Jon. She participated instead by talking privately with her friend, Julia, taking refuge and offering support in a shared and hidden female world.

A child's class, race, and gender have a powerful and often contradictory effect on the way the child negotiates the sociocultural context of the classroom and shape the child's experience in the lived culture. These cultural dimensions also have a profound effect on the way the enacted curriculum is translated into the child's personal beliefs and knowledge. Our model of the way children acquire knowledge through a process of generating knowledge constructs is based on the premise that children are more or less constantly engaged in trying to make sense of the curriculum. But making sense of curriculum content in the classroom is itself a cultural process. It involves the child in making links to prior knowledge and personal experience, and in integrating and evaluating new experiences to conform to his or her developing understanding of what constitutes coherent and valued knowledge.

It is critical to understand not only the extent to which classroom learning is culturally constructed, but also the consequences for some children when they attempt to manage the problem this cultural construction may pose for them. For example: some children may reject the enacted curriculum as alien, as belonging to "them," and not "us," to be kept at a distance from personal understandings and beliefs. Some children may respond to the enacted curriculum as something to be memorized or circumvented to avoid public humiliation. Some children may actively engage in accommodating to the enacted curriculum by identifying with "them" and learning to be dismissive of their own experiences and perspectives. Some children may feel "at home" and able to pursue a model of "truth" that empowers them to evaluate and be critical of even the teacher's knowledge.

We have demonstrated that children's utterances in the private world raise fundamental questions about bias in research. To focus on the instructional dimension without attending to the lived culture of the classroom context makes invisible some of the most significant questions about both the learning and the well-being of children in classrooms. Our approach promises to allow the detailed records of children's experience to speak directly to teachers, to illuminate teaching practice, to lead to more adequate theoretical perspectives on classroom learning, and to inform theories about the role of schools in our society.

Notes

1. Our project, the Understanding Learning and Teaching Project, consists of a series of six studies of children's learning from integrated instructional units in fourth, sixth, and seventh grades (Alton-Lee, 1984; Alton-Lee & Nuthall, 1990, 1991, 1992a, 1992b; Nuthall & Alton-Lee, 1991, 1992, 1993). An instructional unit is a series of lessons and tasks through which students experience curriculum content relevant to a particular topic. The term "integrated" is used when different subject areas are integrated into the unit. For example, language, reading, and social studies were integrated into the New York City unit taught in the sixth-grade class we studied.
2. In this article and in all our research reports, the names of the children are changed.
3. *Pakeha* is the Maori term for White New Zealanders. We use the term as a mark of respect for the right of the indigenous people to name those who came after them. The term *Pakeha* is widely used in Aotearoa New Zealand. *Aotearoa* is the Maori word for New Zealand.
4. For the sake of simplicity, we use the term "lesson" to describe the 36-minute teacher-directed task sequence.
5. Although this article focuses predominantly on the four case-study children's participation in a single lesson, we traced their experience of the enacted curriculum throughout the entire unit in order to investigate their learning from their total in-class opportunity to learn specific item content (Alton-Lee & Nuthall, 1992b).
6. The achievement levels were determined using a variety of measures, including the teacher's prior assessment of each child's general achievement level and scores on the New Zealand Council for Educational Research standardized achievement tests (administered in schools at the beginning of each school year). The teacher's assessments of the case-study children's

achievement levels were consistent with the children's performance on the standardized tests and with the children's actual learning from the unit, as measured by the unit test. However, the case-study children's prior knowledge, as measured by the unit pre-test, indicated a possible gender difference rather than a general achievement difference. Out of 99 items, Jon scored 76 on the pre-test, Joe scored 57, Ann scored 54, and Mia scored 53.

7. Utterances were defined by speaker and topic. Where the topic of an utterance string remained constant within a quarter-minute interval, the utterance string of a single speaker was counted as one utterance. We located the continuous data in quarter-minute intervals because they were the smallest practical time intervals for the synchronized transcriptions and observational data in the Understanding Learning and Teaching Project. When the topic of an utterance changed within a quarter-minute interval, the number of topics determined the number of distinct utterances counted. When utterance strings (for example, peer conversations) persisted across quarter-minute intervals, they were counted as additional utterances with the same topic. We use the term "utterance" rather than "utterance string" for simplicity. When the same utterance served more than one function, the content-relevant meaning took precedence in the coding. For example, Joe's utterance, "Hi Mom," was a response to the video camera and a free association to the U.S. usage of "Mom"; this utterance was categorized as content-relevant, whereas an utterance such as "look at the camera" would have been classified as relevant only to our observational procedures (in substance, off-task).

8. Throughout the article, private utterances are shown in italics and public utterances are shown in regular type.

9. On the unit pre-test, consisting of 99 items, Jon already knew 19 items more than Joe, 23 items more than Ann, and 24 items more than Mia.

10. See Bourdieu (1977) for early arguments about cultural capital and habits. There is cultural bias in the cultural experiences that are publicly linked to new information in the enacted curriculum.

11. Our exploratory analyses of the relation between occurrence of utterance type and learning outcome revealed that Ann's repetition strategy was used more frequently during time she spent on content she did not learn (Nuthall & Alton-Lee, 1990).

12. There were 112 mentions of people in which gender was not specified.

13. The first mention of a woman in the unit, and the only mention of a woman given in response to the teacher's question about occupations of New Yorkers, was "a prostitute." Another female mention was of a girlfriend of a boy who was the subject of a picture-book story set in New York City. The children suggested that the problems of children living in poverty in New York could be caused by bad mothers. One child explained that young mothers needed to be confined to their apartments because of the violence in the city, and a joke was made about men's ability to be more successful than women, even when they attempt suicide. By contrast, White men such as Henry Hudson and Peter Stuyvesant, portrayed as intrepid and conquering, were central throughout the main lessons in the unit.

14. Male sports teams in Aotearoa New Zealand have traditionally played cricket against West Indian teams. The topic of cricket plays a significant role in social communication throughout the country.

15. Both the school principal and the teacher agreed to allow us to interview Ricky because of their concern about the abuse he had experienced. When Ricky initially expressed reservation about participating, he was assured by the principal that he could choose either not to participate, or to participate with the option to end the interview at any time. Ricky did choose to be interviewed, and when he was answering a question about how he learned the concept of racism, he referred to his own experience. At this point the White (*Pakeha*) interviewer acknowledged that she knew about the abuse because of the audio recordings. Ricky appeared to be deeply surprised that an adult believed him, but then began to talk openly about his feelings about the racist abuse. He prolonged the interview through a recess period (a request unprecedented in our studies) and asked that he be allowed to continue in the long-term interview.

16. Sarah received more votes than any other child in the class on a sociometric questionnaire we designed to identify the children's status among their peers.

References

Alton-Lee, A. G. (1984). *Understanding learning and teaching: An investigation of pupil experience of content in relation to immediate and long term learning.* Unpublished doctoral dissertation, University of Canterbury, Christchurch, New Zealand.

Alton-Lee, A. G., & Densem, P. A. (1992). Towards a gender-inclusive school curriculum: Changing educational practice. In S. Middleton & A. Jones (Eds.), *Women and education in Aotearoa* (Vol. 2, pp. 197–220). Wellington: Bridget Williams.

Alton-Lee, A. G., Densem, P. A., & Nuthall, G. A. (1991). Imperatives of classroom research: Understanding what children learn about gender and race. In J. Morss & T. Linzey (Eds.), *Growing up: Lifespan development and the politics of human learning* (pp. 93–117). Auckland: Longman Paul.

Alton-Lee, A. G., & Nuthall, G. A. (1990). Pupil experiences and pupil learning in the elementary classroom: An illustration of a generative methodology. *Teaching and Teacher Education: An International Journal of Research and Studies, 6*(1), 27–46.

Alton-Lee, A. G., & Nuthall, G. A. (1991). *Understanding Learning and Teaching Project: Phase Two* (Report to the Ministry of Education). Wellington: Ministry of Education.

Alton-Lee, A. G., & Nuthall, G. A. (1992a). Challenges in developing a methodology to explain "Opportunity to Learn." *Classroom Interaction Journal, 27*(2), 1–9.

Alton-Lee, A. G., & Nuthall, G. A. (1992b). A generative methodology for classroom research. *Educational Research Methodology, 24*(2), 29–55.

Apple, M., & Weiss L. (Eds.). (1983). Introduction. In M. Apple and L. Weiss, *Ideology and practice in schooling* (pp. 3–33). Philadelphia: Temple University Press.

Aschner, M. J. (1959). *The analysis of classroom discourse: A method and its uses.* Unpublished doctoral dissertation, University of Illinois, Urbana.

Bellack, A., Hyman, R., Smith, F., & Kliebard, H. (1966). *The language of the classroom.* New York: Columbia University Press.

Berwick-Emms, P. E. (1989). *Classroom interaction patterns and their underlying structure: A study of how achievement in the first year of school is influenced by home patterns of interaction.* Unpublished doctoral dissertation, University of Canterbury, Christchurch, New Zealand.

Blumenfeld, P. C., & Meece, J. L. (1988). Task factors, teacher behavior, and students' involvement and use of learning strategies in science. *Elementary School Journal, 88*(3), 1–9.

Bourdieu, P. (1977). Cultural reproduction and social reproduction. In J. Karabel & A. Halsey (Eds.), *Power and ideology in education* (pp. 487–511). New York: Oxford University Press.

Bowles, S., & Gintis, H. (1976). *Schooling in capitalist America.* London: Routledge & Kegan Paul.

Cazden, C. B. (1986). Classroom discourse. In M. Wittrock (Ed.), *Handbook of research on teaching* (3rd ed., pp. 432–463). New York: Macmillan.

Clay, M. (1985). Engaging with the school system: A study of interactions in new entrant classrooms. *New Zealand Journal of Educational Studies, 20*(1), 20–38.

Densem, P., Wilton, K., & Keeling, B. (1988). Community, residential and family indicators of psychosocial retardation. *Mental Handicap in New Zealand, 11*(4), 4–26.

Doyle, W. (1983). Academic work. *Review of Educational Research, 53,* 159–199.

Doyle, W. (1986). Classroom organization and management. In M. Wittrock (Ed.), *Handbook of research on teaching* (3rd ed., pp. 392–431). New York: Macmillan.

Dyson, A. H. (1987). The value of "time off task": Young children's spontaneous talk and deliberate text. *Harvard Educational Review, 57,* 396–420.

Heath, S. B. (1982). What no bedtime story means: Narrative skills at home and school. *Language in Society, 11,* 49–76.

Howard, R. W. (1987). *Concepts and schemata.* London: Cassell.

Hughes, D. C. (1973). An experimental investigation of the effects of pupil responding and teacher reacting on pupil achievement. *American Educational Research Journal, 10,* 21–37.

Johnson-Laird, P. N. (1983). *Towards a complex science of language, inference and consciousness.* Cambridge, Eng.: Cambridge University Press.

Jones, A. (1985). Which girls are "learning to lose"? Gender, class, race in the classroom. *New Zealand Women's Studies Journal, 1*(2), 15–27.

Kelly, A. (1988). Gender differences in teacher-pupil interactions: A meta-analytic review. *Research in Education, 39,* 1–23.

Kounin, J. S. (1970). *Discipline and group management in classrooms.* New York: Holt, Rinehart & Winston.

Lauder, H., & Hughes, D. (1990). Social inequalities and differences in school outcomes. *New Zealand Journal of Educational Studies, 25*(1), 37–60.

Newton, K. (1988). *Gender differences in classroom interaction.* Unpublished master's thesis, University of Auckland, New Zealand.

Nuthall, G. A., & Alton-Lee, A. G. (1990). Research on teaching and learning: Thirty years of change. *Elementary School Journal, 90,* 547–570.

Nuthall G. A., & Alton-Lee, A. G. (1991, April). *Making the connection between teaching and learning.* Paper presented at the Annual Meeting of the American Educational Research Association, Chicago.

Nuthall, G. A., & Alton-Lee, A. G. (1992). Understanding how students learn in classrooms. In M. Pressley, K. Harris, & J. Guthrie (Eds.), *Promoting academic competence and literacy in school.* San Diego: Academic Press.

Nuthall, G. A., & Alton-Lee, A. G. (1993). *Understanding learning and teaching: A theory of student knowledge construction in classrooms.* Unpublished manuscript.

Nuthall, G. A., & Church, R. J. (1973). Experimental studies of teaching behavior. In G. Chanan (Ed.), *Towards a science of teaching* (pp. 9–25). Slough, Eng.: National Foundation for Educational Research.

Peterson, P. L., Swing, S. R., Stark, K. D., & Waas, G. A. (1984). Students' cognitions and time on task during mathematics instruction. *American Educational Research Journal, 21,* 487–515.

Sadker, M., Sadker, D., & Klein, S. (1991). The issue of gender in elementary and secondary education. *Review of Research in Education, 17,* 269–334.

Spender, D. (1982). *Invisible women: The schooling scandal.* London: Readers & Writers.

We acknowledge the Social Science Research Fund Committee, the University of Canterbury, the Ministry of Education, and the New Zealand Employment Service for providing funding for this project. We are deeply grateful to Roger Corbett for creating the broadcast microphone transmitters and to Greta Bowron, Anthea Warren, and Kerry Hancock for their meticulous work in assisting with the transcription and coding of data.

PART ONE
Inner Worlds

SECTION TWO
Inner Worlds of Teachers

Teacher as Rain Dancer

SIMON HOLE

*In this chapter, Simon Hole examines one facet of his inner world as a teacher —
the tension he feels in the classroom as he tries to balance his needs as a teacher
with his students' needs. Hole's inquiry begins when he observes his teaching partner attempting to democratically elect reporters for a school newsletter; a dilemma
emerges when the teacher's desire to satisfy one student's interest in this position
collides with her goal for the class to elect the reporters by nomination and majority vote. After presenting this story, Hole shares a dilemma from his own practice,
in which he struggles with how to handle the inner tension he feels when faced with
this conflict of competing needs in the classroom. As he explores the complexities
of his inner struggle, a struggle that may never become publicly known to students
but will certainly have an impact on his work as a teacher, Hole raises important
questions about whose needs are being met in the classroom — teachers' or students'.*

> [Teaching seemed] too much magic, mystery. I always felt nervous, even afraid. If
> I got the steps right for the rain dance, rain came, but I never knew till I was wet
> whether I was close. I never seemed to have any sense of what a good rain dance
> looked like.
>
> — *Peter Elbow*[1]

I, too, have found the act of teaching to be filled with magic and mystery. I've
spent twenty-plus years as a fourth-grade teacher in a small suburban community on the southern coast of Rhode Island, and I've gotten wet often enough to
keep me in the game. Watching a class puzzle out some meaning from a Robert
Frost poem or seeing the proverbial light bulb go on for an individual student has
always been a joyful experience for me.

Yet even during those times I've been drenched, I've found myself wondering
what brought the rain. Why does one student make so much progress while another seems to flounder? How can one class come together as a tight-knit learning
community and the next never seem to be more than a group of individuals working within a shared space? There's always been a sense of uncertainty surrounding
what I do, a feeling of impending doom: one wrong step, a slight miscalculation,
and everything could come unraveled.

---

[1] Peter Elbow, *Embracing Contraries* (New York: Oxford University Press, 1986), p. xi.

Harvard Educational Review Vol. 68 No. 3 Fall 1998, 413–421

For much of my career I've focused on the nature of the rain dance. What is it that we teachers do? How do we structure our lessons, choose the content, maintain control in the classroom? What order do we give to the day? Which students do we put together in groups? How do we keep everything together?

In the early 1990s, my involvement with the Coalition of Essential Schools, a national school reform effort founded by Ted Sizer and housed at Brown University, caused me to become more reflective about the role of the teacher. A course in qualitative research methodology introduced me to the concepts of phenomenology as a search for the essence of lived experiences and raised the question, "What is it like to be a teacher?" Finally, a year-long sabbatical allowed me to spend time observing classrooms and engaging in conversations concerning what I was seeing.

Most of these observations and conversations took place at my own elementary school, although I also spent one day a week in a nearby high school. Much of my observation was done in the classroom of my teaching partner, with whom I've taught for over a decade. "Mrs. Morris's Dilemma" is an account of one observation I made of my teaching partner.[2] It is followed by an attempt to relate the conversations that arose when I shared this story with teachers and administrators. The final section is my attempt to sort out some of the complex issues that have emerged while I have been watching and listening to my colleagues.

Mrs. Morris's Dilemma

Mrs. Morris's efforts to engage students in democratic processes while choosing reporters for a school newsletter created a dilemma for her. The following vignette is based on my observation of the event and on my conversations with Mrs. Morris following the incident. I tell the story in Mrs. Morris's voice in an attempt to engage the reader and to better capture the essence of the event:

From the beginning, I wasn't particularly happy about the newsletter project. It felt as if the parameters established by the advisors, that each fourth-grade class would have two reporters, could easily turn this into a project for "gifted" students, and I strongly object to the philosophy that only "bright kids" get to do special projects. So, right away, I felt that the decision concerning who would represent our class would be a good place for us to practice the democratic process.

The students must have been especially sleepy Tuesday. When I called for them to sit in the circle, there was very little of the normal bustle and chatter. We were soon settled in on the floor, some cross-legged, some sprawled out. I began by explaining that we had another decision to make and that I would start by sharing everything I knew about a new schoolwide project. They would then have a chance to ask questions before deciding how they would choose two class reporters.

I think I did a fairly good job of presenting the project. I began to get more animated and the kids responded. They stopped picking at their shoestrings, leaned forward to catch the words of their classmates, and asked lots of questions: Who would be reading the newsletter? Where would the articles come from? How many pages would the newsletter have? Would it have jokes and artwork? I was especially excited when I saw Janeen "stand up" on her knees and wave her hand as if

---

[2] "Mrs. Morris" is a pseudonym.

it were a flag in a Fourth of July parade. I called on her immediately, wondering what burning question would cause her to be so physically engaged.

"Mrs. Morris, can I be a reporter?"

I live in the same neighborhood as Janeen and I'm aware of how difficult her home life is. Her parents have been divorced for years and she has almost no contact with her father. I see her here in the classroom, acting out occasionally, but mostly just not engaging in any of the activities. She often looks very sad and rarely volunteers to share her thoughts or feelings during class discussions. I've been trying to find something that would spark her interest, but we're six weeks into the school year, and so far nothing seems to hold her attention for more than a few moments.

So it was difficult for me. She's a bright girl. Her writing is among the best in the class, when I can get her to finish a piece. I'm desperate to find something that she can connect to, something that she can be excited about and that she wants to be engaged in. When I heard her ask to be chosen, I wanted to cry. It would have been perfect for her—a chance to be special and to shine not only in front of her classmates, but also the whole school.

At that point, I wanted so much to be able to start over, to tell the kids that I would be choosing the reporters. But I couldn't. We had worked too hard establishing the purpose and importance of the democratic process. I had already told them they would be involved in making this particular decision. I had to let them go through with the process they had decided on—discussing the criteria for a "good" reporter, making nominations, and voting.

And of course Janeen wasn't elected. She knew she wouldn't be. I could see her face fall as I explained again that the class would have to make the decision. I asked her about it afterwards, how she was feeling about the process we used and if her non-election hurt. She smiled, which I guess was a good sign, and said that it was okay, that the two who were going to be the class reporters would probably do a better job than she could have done, anyway. "Besides," she said, "it was a fair election."

As she walked off to lunch, shoulders rolled forward, feet shuffling over the dusty hallway tiles, I wondered how long it would be before something else might spark Janeen's interest. I think that she was right, it was a fair election, but was it fair that she didn't get a chance to participate in something that had sparked her interest?

"Mrs. Morris's Dilemma" represents a narrow slice from one classroom, two minutes of a half-hour lesson, and it occupies but a single line in my observation notes: "J on her knees, waving hand madly." It was later in the day while discussing the lesson with Mrs. Morris that I began to sense that this incident captured something about what it means to be a teacher. We talked about Janeen and how difficult the situation was for Mrs. Morris as her teacher. Mrs. Morris described the tension she felt during the lesson. "I could feel a lump form in my throat and my mouth got dry." I remarked that I remembered her sitting up straighter after Janeen had expressed her desire to be a reporter, and Mrs. Morris talked about how often that happens when she is faced with this kind of dilemma.

As I left the building that day, Janeen was still with me. Passing other teachers in the hallway, I wondered what they would say about this moment that seemed to me so significant. I decided to convene a series of focus groups—four to six educators engaged in a substantive conversation based on Janeen's story.

The Focus Group

The voices heard in the following section are those of participants from three separate focus groups merged to create a more coherent story. Each group was composed of four to six staff members from my school, including teachers, administrators (including the superintendent), and aides. They were all invited to participate and agreed to do so to help me with my research. I've included voices representing certain themes that struck me as I listened to the conversations and as I wrote this section.

The night before the group was to meet, each participant was given a copy of "Mrs. Morris's Dilemma" with the following questions attached:

This vignette exemplifies one of the dilemmas teachers constantly face, that of trying to meet both the needs of the individual and the needs of the group. Have you ever found yourself in a similar situation? Can you imagine yourself in Mrs. Morris's shoes? How does it feel to be in the middle of the tension this dilemma creates? How does it affect you as a person and as a professional?

We straggle in, an hour before the students, coffee cups filled, the caffeine yet to kick in. Sitting at hexagonal tables in chairs built for nine-year-olds, we talk quietly, waiting for the last group member to arrive so we can make a start at whatever this meeting will be. The others are here to help me with my research project; although I am responsible for convening the group, I know little more than they what direction the conversation will take.

Listening to the chatter, I check my tape recorder once again and glance at the clock. If Carlye doesn't show soon, we'll have to start without her. The others seem a bit nervous, facing the unknown. Then we hear footsteps in the hallway and Carlye seats herself through an apology for her lateness. We are ready. Seven faces turn expectantly to me, and I find I've completely forgotten how I wanted to start. I turn on the recorder, look at the group, and ask, "Did you all have a chance to read the vignette?" I'm met with silence, and then, amidst nods, Connie's soft voice: "Poor little girl."

Connie's is not the only voice to express sympathy for Janeen. "I just felt badly that that happened to her. She would have—it would have been a nice thing for her." "You are a caregiver for a big part of the student's day. It's heartbreaking when things like this happen." Tony is especially eloquent, speaking passionately and including Mrs. Morris in his sympathies: "I mean, we've all been there. We've been in this teacher's spot. It's devastating to both the student and the teacher."

Diane sums up many of these feelings while explaining how she is affected by the need to take care of her students. "I see myself as having to be the teacher and the counselor, the therapist, the mother. The children's needs are just so intense. So sometimes I find myself doing things and thinking, am I doing a little God-thing here? You know, the boy comes in and says, 'My father hit me,' and I want to fix it. I want to take away those hurts. I want to make that better. So it is like a savior-thing."

I have little to do but listen as the members of the group draw themselves into the conversation. They seem to enjoy themselves, breaking into easy laughter and good-natured ribbing. But there is also a serious and thoughtful quality to their responses. At times the speakers lean forward, addressing various members of the group, presenting their ideas. Other times they lean back and seem to be speaking to themselves, thinking out loud.

The path of the conversation widens as new thoughts are added to the mix. Several threads seem to weave in and out of the discussion, and we end up revisiting certain ideas or themes. Throughout the conversation the teachers express a desire to take care of Janeen: "I wanted to jump in and solve the problem." They suggest a number of strategies that Mrs. Morris could have used: "Might the reporter job be rotated on a monthly basis, or could Janeen be an alternate?" "Perhaps Mrs. Morris could have started a classroom paper, and let Janeen have a position on that." Some seem to feel that the teacher should have changed directions, taken back control of the decisionmaking process, and given Janeen the reporter job. Ronnie wonders what might have happened if the teacher had stopped the process and explained to the class why she thought Janeen should be the reporter.

Several participants feel that Mrs. Morris should have anticipated a problem with the parameters set forth by the advisors. One acknowledges that "you get a lot of things that you can't deal with up front. You go into your classroom and just do what you think is right." Another disagrees: "I would do it up front. I think you have to be honest and negotiate. Tell them that you have a problem with the parameters and negotiate. If they insist, you can tell them that they don't need reporters from your classroom."

For some, storytelling becomes a way to express their thoughts. Connie recounts an experience she and her teaching partner had with first-graders, of searching with them for a fair way to make choices. She speaks slowly, almost hesitantly, as if she is exploring the story for the first time:

> Each spring we establish our own classroom country. Each of the students draws a flag, and we put them all on the board to select the one that will represent our society. There are no names on the flags, but as we examine them, I hear one of the "popular" boys whisper to another, "Mine is number twelve, vote for mine." Pretty soon it is going around the room, "Vote for number twelve." Sure enough, flag twelve wins the election, even though it was really a mediocre flag.
>
> So we try to talk with the kids about how we make a decision like this. Should we vote? But that always becomes a popularity contest. Should the best behaved student get it, or should the smartest, etc.? Whatever way you look at it, it's based on opinion, pretty much. So a lot of times they end up picking out of a hat or a random thing like that. It never works perfectly.

Carlye offers, "It does when you fix it." When the laughter subsides, she explains, "I have been known to do that. I find that the children accept the random, or the idea that it was random, a lot better than they would accept the results of an election, which can pretty much be a downer. So I have been known to [deep sigh] fix the election, or make it look like it was random when we picked out of the hat."

Geri's voice continues in the same vein. "It's definitely a struggle everyone has been in. I remember some situations like this, and I was thinking how often teachers can really affect the vote so that it comes out the way you want it to." Others agree. Someone notes that it depends on the age of the children: "The younger kids, they would be more apt to do what the teacher wants to do. They really want your approval."

Amidst the nods, Ida begins speaking. Her voice is strong, and it is apparent that she is sharing deeply held beliefs. "That's why my classroom is a monarchy. That's exactly why I don't have a democratic classroom. I probably once did something like what Mrs. Morris did. I would have been devastated the first time, and I would have never put myself in that position again. In similar situations, I tell my students about the 'job' and what it will entail. I ask who would be interested and then I choose. I try to pick the ones who would benefit most, who need the extra boost or the enrichment."

Later, as I reexamine the transcripts of the focus groups and read my attempts to render them as one conversation, the complex and varied issues begin to coalesce and certain themes arise. The voices swirl around me, blending together, and I seem to hear them as one speaker, bringing a new focus to my research: "I'm a teacher. It's my job to take care of these kids, to see to it that they have every opportunity to learn and grow. That's my responsibility. But more than that, I care about them. When I see a kid like Janeen walk away, feeling like that, I ask myself, 'Have I failed? What more could I have done?' So I play the God game, or I make sure her name comes out of the hat. I know I can't fix everything, that the child's life beyond school is out of my control. But here, in my classroom, I am in control, and I'll do whatever it takes."

Reflections

After observing Mrs. Morris and listening to the voices of my colleagues, I'm beginning to understand how futile it is to mimic the chants and movements of the rain dancer. Even if I could get the steps right, could I bring forth the rain? If I could create lesson plans as taught in teacher education courses, would every lesson be perfect? No, for being a rain dancer is so much more than just knowing the dance. Being a teacher is so much more than an extensive repertoire of strategies and techniques. Teaching is a way of life, a way of orienting the self to the world. So my focus changes from the act of teaching to the nature of "teacher." What does it mean to be a teacher?

One thing my research seems to be telling me is that to be a teacher is to find a way to live within an environment filled with dilemmas. These dilemmas create an inner tension that is compounded by our expectation that we should be able to "get the steps right" every time. In the case of Mrs. Morris, the needs of the individual student were at odds with the needs of the class as a whole. The dilemma created by not being able to meet the needs of both created the tension within Mrs. Morris.

These months of research have brought as much confusion as clarification, as many questions as answers. The multitude of issues, the felt need to do the right thing, to not hinder the growth of the students, and the sometimes overwhelming number of variables create a web of complexity difficult to sort through. Out of my attempt to simplify, to create an order out of the seeming chaos emerge only more questions. Do teachers, in general, allow the needs of the individual to take precedence over the needs of the group? If so, is it because individual needs are somehow more important, or because the needs of the individual are more easily identified, easier to attempt to meet? Creating monarchies, making sure the "right" person is chosen, changing the parameters of the reporter's job . . . are these strategies we adopt to lessen the tension and discomfort? And underlying all of this is a question of whose needs are being met—our own or those of our students. For whom does the tension and discomfort decrease?

It's been over a year now since Mrs. Morris watched Janeen shuffle off down the dusty hallway, since I listened to the voices of my colleagues in the focus groups. Yet the search for meaning is still fresh, all the more so as my sabbatical ends and I return to the daily madness that is teaching. I wonder what it means to live within the tension that is so much a part of education. How does my awareness of these tensions affect my practice?

Within my colleagues' discussion of "Mrs. Morris's Dilemma," I'm beginning to view their need to take care of their students, their need to control, as a reaction to the tension, a struggle to lessen the discomfort that invariably accompanies it. Upon reflection, I come to see my own past practice as such a struggle. My need to know the nature of the rain dance, to be able to "get the steps right" every time, may have been a manifestation of my need to diminish the pain that I feel when the rain doesn't come.

Can we exorcise the tension? Should we? What if tension itself is essential to the process of learning for both our students and ourselves? Could I learn to see the tension and discomfort not as a negative thing to be avoided but as a marker, a kind of signpost that says, "pay attention here, something important is happening"? If I cannot do away with the tension, might it at least allow me to better understand the dilemmas facing me in my teaching?

The following incident occurred just three weeks after my return to the classroom. The tension produced was strong enough to require a journal entry that night:

Wednesday, September 24, 9:30 A.M. I stand to one side of the classroom, getting the morning housekeeping out of the way, taking attendance and lunch count, collecting notes for the office. One student glances out the window and sees a dozen Canada geese grazing on the playground. Hopping from his seat, he calls out as he heads to the window for a better view. Within moments, six students cluster around the window. Others start from their seats to join them. I call for attention, ask them to return to their seats. When none of the students respond, I walk to the window and lower the blinds.

Even as I lowered the blinds, I was kicking myself. Here was a natural opportunity to explore the students' interests. Had I stood at the window with them for five minutes, asking questions to see what they knew about geese, or even just listening to what they might have to say, I'd be telling a story of "seizing the moment," of taking advantage of a learning opportunity. I knew, even as I lowered the blinds, that the tension was getting the better of me and that my response was keeping the rain from falling.

So why did I lower the blinds? The answer, I think, lies in finding the source of the tension and begins with a closer examination of a dilemma caused by a conflict between my own needs and those of the children. As I reflect back on that September morning, the thing that stands out concerns the day's schedule. On Wednesdays the class is out of the room for most of the morning. On this particular Wednesday, I had to be out of the classroom all afternoon attending a meeting, and so I knew that first half hour was all the time I would have with the kids. And as this was the first time I was to be out of the classroom this year, I needed to be sure the kids were prepared for the substitute.

Could I have met my need to prepare the class for a substitute while still meeting the students' spontaneous need to explore another aspect of their world? In a climate of "kids first," it is difficult to think that as a teacher I might sometimes let my needs take precedence over theirs. The dilemma surrounding the question of whose needs are being met creates an incredible amount of tension for the teacher.

While I am often out of the classroom for various meetings, committees, and workshops, I never feel completely comfortable leaving my students with a substitute teacher. I tend to watch the clock and wonder how my kids are doing, if they are giving the sub a difficult time. My need to be in control of the class even when I am not there is strong.

Even as the geese incident was occurring, I knew something about what was going on. The lessons learned from my research were in my head and setting off all kinds of alarms; I just didn't recognize them yet. That night, as I wrote about the geese and reflected on the discomfort I had felt, I thought again of Mrs. Morris and the voices of my colleagues. Lowering the blinds met *my* need to have the class prepared for the substitute, but had nothing to do with meeting the needs of my students.

Being aware of the tensions didn't help me much this time. After all, I did lower the blinds. But in a sense, I lifted my personal blinds, if just a bit. It only took me twelve hours or so to analyze the dilemma and the needs that were driving my actions. Perhaps next time, or the time after that, I'll be able to notice the tension, identify the source as the incident occurs, and leave the blinds up for a bit, letting the rain in.

Zen and the Art of Reflective Practice in Teacher Education

ROBERT TREMMEL

"What really drives us forward is still the persistent hope that somewhere 'out there' is THE answer, THE formula, THE technology, THE research technique that will solve all our problems and meet all our needs. Until we are seriously and equally willing to look within, I am afraid we will see little beyond what we have already seen." Robert Tremmel writes this passage in this chapter, in which he brings a theoretical perspective to the types of dilemmas Simon Hole struggles with in his practice. Tremmel asserts that teachers must "pay attention" to what is going on within themselves as they teach, and that teacher education programs need to focus much more on the inner worlds of teachers in order for teachers to be able to improve their teaching through a process of self-awareness and critical self-reflection. Tremmel explores Donald Schön's concept of "reflection-in-action," and then looks to Zen philosophy for guidance on the concept of "mindfulness," building his argument that teachers must constantly reflect as they teach in order to be able to respond to what is happening in their classrooms at any given moment.

> You should therefore cease from practice based on intellectual understanding, pursuing words, and following after speech, and learn that backward step that turns your light inwardly to illuminate yourself.
> — *Eihei Dogen (1200–1253)*

In the midst of a growing interest in "reflection" and "reflective practice" in teacher education over the last few years, there is one serious limitation in how both of these notions tend to be defined. Renee T. Clift and Robert Houston (1990) sum up the limitation in this way:

> Current definitions of reflection are strongly influenced by the Western cultural heritage, which emphasizes analysis and problem-solving as opposed to negotiation, contemplation, or enlightenment. (p. 211)

Clift and Houston suggest that more attention be paid to both non-Western and Western approaches to reflection as a way of enriching what they call the "paucity of thought that has gone into the conceptualizing of many teacher education pro-

Harvard Educational Review Vol. 63 No. 4 Winter 1993, 434–458

grams" (p. 212), including, apparently, some programs that claim to be based on notions of reflective practice.

In this article, I discuss some of the limitations of the one-dimensional, analytic view of reflection most commonly held in the educational community by focusing on Donald Schön's alternative, broader approach to reflection, and on the difficulties that can occur when narrow conceptions of reflection are instituted into teacher education programs. I consider how a perspective that includes attention to the Zen Buddhist tradition of "mindfulness" might help broaden teacher educators' understanding of reflection and deepen efforts to define reflective practice for teachers and student teachers. While I do not advocate the abandonment of our Western traditions, I do seek some common ground between these two traditions in human thought. Finally, I draw on my own practice as a teacher educator to discuss how I teach students the art of "paying attention" as a way of nurturing reflective practice.

Donald Schön and Technical Rationality

Although many educational writers (Cruikshank, 1987; Tom, 1984, 1985; Van Manen, 1977; Zeichner & Liston, 1987) have helped shape views of what reflection in teacher education is and might be, the liveliest center of action has been two books by Donald A. Schön, *The Reflective Practitioner* (1983) and *Educating the Reflective Practitioner* (1987). In the first book, Schön sketches a "crisis of confidence in professional knowledge" (p. 3) that he attributes to "technical rationality," which is the "dominant **epistemology**[a] of practice" in professional education (p. 21). Schön defines technical rationality as an unreflective overreliance on technology and the scientific method. He traces its origins to the rise of science in Western civilization and to the prominence of problem-solving methods and linear, analytic forms of thought.

Schön argues that single-minded attachment to this **positivistic**[b] view is the cause of the curious and destructive tendency in Western education to separate the authorities and sources of knowledge from knowledgeable practice. This tendency leads to the mistaken notion that knowledge gained by scientific research and represented in abstract technical formulations is the only legitimate knowledge available to inform and shape practice. According to Schön, this technical form of knowledge does not provide a sufficient basis for practitioners' actions, especially when they are acting in the "swampy lowland where situations are confusing 'messes' incapable of technical solution" (1983, p. 42).

Learning to operate in the "swampy lowland," according to Schön, calls for a kind of knowledge that reaches beyond the knowledge available from the methods of technical rationality. To explain this kind of knowledge, Schön introduces the concept of "knowing-in-action" (1983, p. 49). Knowing-in-action reaches beyond what we can say we know to what we know but cannot say. This idea resonates in interesting ways with Plato's teaching that "learning" is really "recollection of what the soul has encountered in other worlds" (Plato, 1961, p. 81). It is also akin

[a] **Epistemology** is the study of the nature of knowledge, its limits and validity.
[b] **Positivistic** is the notion that a verifiable "truth" exists and can be tested using data gathered from the real world.

to Michael Polanyi's (1958) notion of "personal knowledge," which departs from what Polanyi refers to as "the well-known fact that the aim of a skillful performance is achieved by the observance of a set of rules which are not known as such to the person following them" (p. 49). Similarly, Schön maintains that the process that underlies knowing-in-action is "reflecting-in-action" or "reflecting-in-practice." Schön compares reflecting-in-action to "thinking on your feet" (1983, p. 54). He ties it to such abilities as "feeling," "seeing," or "noticing" what it is you are doing; then learning from what you feel, see, or notice; and, finally, intelligently, even intuitively, adjusting your practice.

Even though Schön's ideas have attracted a great deal of attention and support over the years, he is sometimes criticized for not articulating the specific structures of reflection-in-action (see, for example, Court, 1988; Hills & Gibson, 1988; Pugach & Johnson, 1990; Selman, 1988). I suspect that one unacknowledged but important reason for the critics' objections is the "unpreparedness" of many of us in education to enter into Schön's way of looking at action in the teaching process. This unpreparedness stems from not being formally taught to think in this way, from misunderstanding Schön's concepts, or even from a resistance to the challenge that Schön's way of looking at teaching demands. His ideas have challenged educational theorists who have been accustomed to thinking in terms of analytical and theoretical systems and who look toward technically rational research as the primary, if not the sole, source of professional knowledge. It does no disservice to Schön to simply admit that he does, in fact, fail the tests of the technical rational paradigm.

In Schön's view, even the most fundamental elements of traditional educational research must be looked at differently. Take "student" and "teacher," for example. In Schön's extended presentation of teaching in the architectural design studio, teacher and student do not operate as two separate entities or categories who respond to separate sets of imperatives. Rather, Schön pictures them working together in a dancelike pattern, simultaneously involved in design and in playing various roles in virtual and real worlds, while at the same time remaining detached enough to observe and feel the action that is occurring, and to respond. In such teaching situations, Schön emphasizes, "the whole is at stake in every partial move" (1987, p. 64):

> When the practitioner reflects-in-action in a case he perceives as unique, paying attention to phenomena and surfacing his intuitive understanding of them, his experimenting is at once exploratory, move testing, and hypothesis testing. The three functions are fulfilled by the very same actions. (1987, p. 72)

One of the possible reasons Schön might frustrate some educational theorists is that he uses metaphors, rather than relying on conceptual language to describe the processes of reflection-in-action. One of these metaphors referred to above is "experiment." Unlike the more familiar knowledge born of technical rationality, which is based on external criteria and on the results of research conducted off the scene, the knowledge gained by means of reflection proceeds directly from the experience of the practitioner acting as a researcher on the scene (1983, p. 68). Whereas technical rationality applies the results of research to a general category of situations, reflection-in-action makes a laboratory of practice and brings research immediately to the pressure of the moment, the current situation. The present moment — which is the essence of "in-action" — is important above all else.

Another metaphor is "artistry." Schön understands that using a term like artistry creates problems because it is hard to specify exactly what it means (1987, p. 13). Indeed, what we *can* specify by virtue of the explicit structures of technical rationality is not important to Schön in the context to which he refers. When we are immersed in practice, technical rationality can only tell us what we already know. The beginning point, Schön says, should be to respond artistically to what we are doing and to bring our insights from that to bear on what it is we do not know. This is not to say that technical rationality is of no value, but rather that "in the terrain of professional practice, applied science and research-based technique occupy a critically important though limited territory, bounded on several sides by artistry" (1987, p. 13).

Ultimately, the mind that Schön is trying to represent is not the theoretical mind that has been schooled to contain its operations within the familiar patterns of rational thought. It is instead the mind of the athlete, the jazz musician, or the poet (1983, pp. 53, 54), which is flexible and pliable. It is a mind that can attend to what is happening in the moment and respond directly, not by means of "research based theory," but rather with its "repertoire of themes and examples," "transforming moves," or "exploratory probes" (1987, pp. 78, 79). It is, moreover, the mind that has the capacity to reach into the center of confusing situations, to see itself, and to shift the base of its operations or pull up stakes altogether and follow the flow of the action. What follows are some examples of what can happen when we try to embrace the attractive notion of reflection without first preparing our minds.

Putting Reflection in Practice

Schön's work has been enthusiastically cited since the mid-eighties, and aspects of it have been put into practice in classrooms and teacher education programs. One reason for this enthusiasm is the appeal of an idea that appears to cut through the increasing bulk and weight of often ineffective standards, procedures, and formulas that have proliferated in the name of technical rationality. Despite decades of unremitting scientific research, educational institutions in this country still appear to be struggling and are continually being attacked. It is natural under such circumstances to want to look in new directions for solutions. However, the "quest for certainty" is every bit as intense and every bit as dangerous today as when John Dewey warned against it (Dewey, 1929). In Schön's terms, it is exactly this desire for *solutions* that hinders efforts to establish reflective practice in education.

As Peter Grimmett (1988) has pointed out, Schön is headed in exactly the opposite direction from those who are seeking generalized solutions. At the heart of his notion of reflective practice is neither prescribed solutions nor certainty, but action and paradox. Schön's notion of action focuses attention on the artistry of the practitioner in the present moment, simultaneously doing and learning and coming to know. The paradox is that of the practitioner acting as if she knew, but being willing not to know until she acts. Schön draws the basis for this paradox from Plato's *Meno*. In Plato's dialogue, the young man Meno tries to explain to Socrates what virtue is and, failing that, to learn what it is from Socrates. After Socrates repeatedly frustrates him by refusing to give him the kind of answer he seeks, Meno responds angrily that Socrates is like the stingray in the ocean that numbs anyone who comes in contact with it (in Plato, 1961, p. 363). Obviously an early proponent of outcomes-based education, Meno describes the bind he is in this way:

> But how will you look for something when you don't in the least know what it is? How on earth are you going to set up something you don't know as the object of your search? To put it another way, even if you come right up against it, how will you know that what you have found is the thing you didn't know? (p. 363)

Schön's response to Meno's paradox is that reflective learners, in order to move forward, must move into the center of the learning situation, into the center of their own doubts (Schön, 1987, p. 83). Grimmett (1988) offers the following commentary on the nature of this paradox as it is represented in Schön's understanding of reflection and learning:

> Action is the necessary precursor to reflection. It is in reflection-in- and on-action that the willing suspension of disbelief is temporarily abated until further learning dictates the call for renewed action. The Meno paradox creates in most students a sense of being at risk. Their autonomy to act as they see fit, the hallmark of professionals, is temporarily disallowed so that they can learn how to function as professional practitioners. In order to gain that sense of competence, control, and confidence that characterizes professionals, students of professional practice must first give it up. As they act and reflect in situations of perplexing uncertainty, mystery, and frustration, that which is given up for the sake of experimenting begins to emerge in their development. Out of the darkness of student unknowing comes the light of professional practical knowledge. (p. 11)

What Grimmett is describing with his use of the metaphor of enlightenment is very much out of step with the usual linear, forward-moving approach. According to Grimmett, Schön wants beginning practitioners to take a step backward in order to be able to take a step forward as independent, reflective professionals. However, this idea is much easier to appreciate in the abstract than it is to put into practice. Some teachers and students are unprepared to take this risk, to let go of the security of technical rationality and make the leap of faith backward to reflective practice. Instead, we cling like Meno to the creature comforts of a prescribed process to a solution — even, sometimes, while protesting otherwise. Purposeful attempts to teach reflective practice often become confused as they implicitly encourage linear processes.

Encouragement of linear processes is often reflected in how the components of the teacher education programs are articulated. For example, Doreen D. Ross's (1989, 1990) description of a program to prepare "reflective teachers" begins by articulating the five "elements" of the reflective process.[1] And the heart of Marleen C. Pugach and Lawrence J. Johnson's (1990) program to develop reflective practice is the attention paid to the process of encouraging teachers' reflection through peer collaboration, a process that involves four steps aimed toward reaching a "solution."[2] Both of these descriptions represent linear series that are set in motion by a "problem" or "dilemma" and are impelled forward by separate movements devoted to the sort of "exploratory, move testing, hypothesis testing" activities that Schön, in contrast, posits as a holistic process, not reducible to separate elements.

In my opinion, the source for both of these views of process can be traced to Dewey's "analysis of a complete act of thought" articulated in the 1910 edition of *How We Think*. In that book, Dewey identifies "five distinct steps in reflection."[3]

Neither Ross nor Pugach and Johnson explicitly associate their system with Dewey's, nor do they directly cite Dewey in the context of presenting their "elements" or "steps," although Ross does cite both the 1910 and 1933 editions of *How We Think* in her article. There are, no doubt, many good reasons for such a rhetorical strategy, but most important is that it helps disassociate both of these programs from an otherwise useful model that has over the years become misinterpreted as a narrow problem-solving formula.

I do not want to be understood as objecting to Ross's or Pugach and Johnson's programs, or to the overall efforts of these writers. On the contrary, I am grateful for the insights they provide that help me in my work with student teachers. I recognize that what I interpret as their unwillingness to let go of a safe and familiar formula is my own unwillingness as well. It is a sign of the limitations that restrict us all that at the heart of both these programs devoted to advancing the cause of reflection there lies a pattern of scientific analysis that has come to represent what Schön believes is nothing other than the unreflective mind of technical rationality itself. Dewey was aware of this limitation and saw the potential dangers of such a deceptively simple formula. In his 1933 "restatement" of *How We Think,* his five "steps" become five "aspects" (p. 107), and he declares while discussing them that "there is nothing sacred about the number five" (p. 116).

As I have noted already, Schön understands that one of the primary qualities distinguishing reflective practice is its emphasis on the need for students, as well as teachers, to give themselves up to the learning situation and to the action of the moment, and to be joint experimenters and artists in the laboratory of practice. Schön communicates in numerous ways the need for teachers and students to take this stance. For example, he talks about reflective practice as being intuitive and as emerging out of the self rather than being rule bound (1983). He cites Polanyi's notion of tacit knowledge (Schön, 1983) and the Platonic idea that practitioners must first of all discover what it is "they already understand and know how to do" (Schön, 1991, p. 5). He also extensively quotes Carl Rogers (Schön, 1987), whose intention was to empower and free the learner to learn, rather than to rely entirely on external goals and objectives that may or may not have anything to do with the learning situation at hand.

A third example of a program that intends to be reflective comes from Kenneth Zeichner and Daniel Liston's (1987) oft-cited description of the student-teaching program at the University of Wisconsin. Like Ross and Pugach and Johnson, Zeichner and Liston put forth a powerful argument in favor of reflective practice; but I believe that they, too, get caught in the snares of technical rationality even while trying to avoid them. This time, however, the difficulty does not lie in a problem-solving model; instead, it lies in the best intentions of the program designers.

Zeichner and Liston, even while reaching in the direction of reflective practice, build into their program a strong emphasis on technical and analytical abilities, as well as an agenda of moral attitudes they want to foster among students. Early in their article, they outline four "qualities" they seek to "develop" in their students.[4] These "qualities" were instituted into the program in 1979, and eight years later were raised to the level of "criteria" (1987, p. 23). Although these criteria are indeed worthwhile for a program in teacher education, they contradict Schön's notions of reflective practice and the teaching of reflective practice. By preestablishing criteria that designate outcomes for professional values and behaviors, Liston and Zeichner create a program that shares with technically rational models the quality of imposing requirements from outside the dynamics of specific learning situations. In contrast, reflective practice must begin in-action and be built up interactively in the details of situations as they unfold. In this light, it is no wonder that Zeichner, Liston, and their colleagues were left looking for the reasons (1987, pp. 40–45) that troublingly large numbers of students resisted their program for reflective teaching, did not change their minds about teaching, and "left at the end of their student teaching experience with essentially the same perspective [with which they began], albeit a more refined one" (p. 36). Encouraging students to reflect does not mean just leading them to change their minds in the sense of changing perspective; it means, rather, trying to help them change the way their minds work so that they are prepared for reflection.

It is illuminating to see that, in subsequent work with their program in reflective teacher education, Liston and Zeichner (1990) have changed the tone of their discourse considerably and have moved closer to Schön's idea of reflection. In an effort to help their students move toward a deeper and more profound understanding of the social and moral contexts and implications of practice, Liston and Zeichner have come to advocate the use of "action research" projects during student teaching. One of the main purposes of this research is to provide students a tool with which they might be able to locate and to articulate their *own* values and practices within "the central traditions of educational thought and practice" (p. 240). Although, as the educational theorist Susan Adler (1991) points out, Liston and Zeichner are working within a conceptual framework distinct from Schön's (and, she believes, superior to it), the effect of the research project on their program is to bring it much closer to the action-centered, intuitive, self-sponsored spirit of Schön's idea of reflection. One sign of this shift is Liston and Zeichner's agreement with the point that "action probably initiates reflection" and that self-reflective practice arises "naturally in the work of teachers" (1990, p. 246).

Thus, in the process of their own teaching and research over a period of several years, Liston and Zeichner come to exemplify in the most positive way how reflection can support change and move practitioners closer and closer to the center of their own practice.

The Way of Zen

The habits of mind that support technical rationality date back to ancient times and to the genesis of language, and are of inestimable value to human beings (see Tremmel, 1992). A problem arises, however, when we realize, as Clift and Houston (1990) suggest in the passage I quoted early in this article, that everything that we know of reflection and technical rationality — our very awareness of them — is embedded in the same epistemological traditions that gave rise to them and that continue to shape our understanding. We are caught in a circle of our own mind's making. Thus I agree with Clift and Houston that one important step toward a more complete understanding of the promise reflective teaching might hold is to try to gain a perspective from outside the diameter of that circle — a perspective born entirely of a different epistemological tradition.

In the rest of this article, I focus on the perspective of a particular school of Buddhism called Zen. Among the many reasons for working with Zen is that it has already proven to be widely and transculturally accessible.[5] An initial barrier for many in coming to an understanding of Zen is the paradox that, even though Zen is accessible, it resists definition in terms of language and conceptual thought. Alan Watts (1957) put it this way:

> Zen Buddhism is a way and a view of life which does not belong to any of the formal categories of modern Western thought. It is not religion or philosophy; it is not a psychology or a type of science. It is an example of what is known in India and China as a "way of liberation," and is similar in this respect to Taoism, Vedanta, and Yoga. . . . A way of liberation can have no positive definition. (p. 3)

D.T. Suzuki (1959/1989) summed up the paradoxical quality of Zen this way:

> Zen is not necessarily against words, but is well aware of the fact that they are always liable to detach themselves from realities and turn into conceptions. And this conceptualization is what Zen is against. . . . Zen insists on handling the thing itself and not an empty abstraction. (p. 5)

Thus, in a general way, Zen shares with Schön's idea of reflection the quality of being ungraspable in the form of the conceptual frameworks and structures traditional in technical rationality and academic discourse. Another quality shared by Zen and Schön's idea of reflection is that both are best understood in-action and in the midst of everyday practice. Another passage from D.T. Suzuki illustrates this point:

> The object of Zen training consists in making us realize that Zen is our daily experience and that it is not something put in from the outside. . . . Dōgo . . . (748–807) . . . illustrates the point most eloquently in his treatment of a novice monk. . . .
>
> Dōgo had a disciple called Soshin. When Soshin was taken in as a novice it was perhaps natural of him to expect lessons in Zen from his teacher the way a schoolboy is taught at school. But Dōgo gave him no special lessons on the subject, and disappointed Soshin. One day he said to the master, "It is some time since I came here, but not a word has been given me regarding the essence of the Zen teaching." Dōgo replied, "Since your arrival I have ever been giving you lessons on the matter of Zen discipline."
>
> "What kind of lesson could it have been?"
>
> "When you bring me a cup of tea in the morning, I take it; when you serve me a meal, I accept it; when you bow to me, I return it with a nod. How else do you expect to be taught in the mental discipline of Zen?"
>
> Soshin hung his head for a while, pondering the puzzling words of the master. The master said, "If you want to see, see right at once. When you begin to think you miss the point." (1959/1989, p. 13)

On first glance, this concrete, day-to-day quality of Zen would seem to disqualify it from any academic discussion of reflection. However, the fact that Zen comes at the problem of knowing and reflecting from an entirely different perspective than those that currently inform discussions of reflection in education is what makes its potential contribution to our understanding unique. As Schön points out, we are not lacking for traditional academic, technically rational views. What we do lack is the power to move outside the limits of such views, and Zen, which is not totally dissimilar to Schön's approach to reflection-in-action, helps us ascend to that wider range of practice.

The specific Zen practice that best illuminates Schön's idea of reflection is that of mindfulness. A basic metaphor for mindfulness is "to return." When the Zen practitioner sits in meditation or engages in the everyday activities of living, thoughts will naturally arise and the mind will have a tendency to wander. When this happens, the practitioner needs to "return" to mindful awareness of the present moment. This might be done by a variety of means, such as returning to mindfulness of breathing, mindfulness of the posture as a whole, or mindfulness of the present activity at hand, such as washing dishes, making tea, or even working with students. Whatever the specific action, though, mindfulness in simplest terms means to pay attention to "right here, right now" and to invest the present moment with full awareness and concentration. The practice of mindfulness in Zen is based on study and discipline that date back to early Buddhist teachings in the *Sutra on the Four Establishments of Mindfulness,* first collated in the fifth century B.C.E. (Before the Common Era). The general methods of practice are laid out in the *Sutra,* along with the specific skills, the physiological, psychological, and philosophical grounds and conditions for mindfulness (Nhat Hanh, 1990).

Mindfulness is a central component in Zen meditation, or *zazen, which is the basic practice in Zen. Twentieth-century Zen teachers such as Shunryu Suzuki (1970), Dainin Katagiri (1988), and Robert Aitken (1982) begin their books about Zen practice by describing the physical and mental postures for zazen.* In this they follow the approach of Eihei Dogen, the thirteenth-century teacher who was instrumental in bringing Zen to Japan from China (where it was called Ch'an). Dogen's collected writings — his whole teaching, in fact — rest on a short essay entitled "Zazen-Gi," or "Rules for Zazen." This is because *zazen* (literally "sitting meditation") is the basis for Zen Buddhist practice as it came to Dogen from his teachers in China and as he passed it on to his students in Japan. Kazuaki Tanahashi, who translated Dogen's writings, points to mindfulness as being central to Dogen's teaching of Zen meditation:

> Zen meditation — sometimes described as mindfulness or concentration in serenity — is done sitting upright in a cross-legged position. Dogen teaches that this practice . . . is not merely a method by which one reaches awakening, but is itself awakening. (Dogen, 1985, p. 12)

Although mindfulness should not be equated with reflection in the broad sense, there is an important common ground between mindfulness and reflection-in-action. Mindfulness is reflection-in-action moved from the sphere of professional practice in which Schön located it and extended to encompass the whole practice of living. Thich Nhat Hanh, a Vietnamese Zen Buddhist monk, writes:

> The Sutra of mindfulness says, "When walking the practitioner must be conscious that he is walking. When sitting, the practitioner must be conscious that he is sitting. . . . No matter what position one's body is in, the practitioner must be conscious of that position. Practicing thus the practitioner lives in direct and constant mindfulness of the body. . . ." The mindfulness of the positions of one's body is not enough, however. We must be conscious of each breath, each movement, every thought and feeling, everything which has any relation to ourselves. (1975, pp. 7–8)

The purpose of mindfulness, insofar as it can be said to have a purpose, is not to analyze experience or thought processes or to evaluate, but to help the practitioner "study the mind" (see Dogen & Uchiyama, 1983, p. xi), to come to know and understand the mind in a direct and immediate way that is not possible simply with analysis or evaluation. Shunryu Suzuki describes mindfulness this way:

> The important thing in our understanding is to have a smooth, free thinking way of observation. We have to think and to observe things without stagnation. We should accept things as they are without difficulty. Our mind should be soft and open enough to understand things as they are. . . . Thinking which is divided in many ways is not true thinking. Concentration should be present in our thinking. This is mindfulness. (1970, p. 115)

Despite the fact that Zen sometimes has the reputation of being esoteric, this view of mindfulness represents a very direct and concrete approach to experience. Mindfulness moves away from mindless absorption in the endless parade of thoughts through the mind. When one is mindful, one lives in the present and pays attention — pure and simple. Dainin Katagiri writes:

> When you walk on the street, be mindful of walking. Mindfulness is to go toward the center of whatever you are doing. Usually the mind is going in many directions; instead of going out in all directions, let's go in. This means, look at the walking you are doing now. (1988, p. 30)

Mindfulness is most closely associated with its 2,500-year heritage in Zen practice and other Eastern disciplines, but it is not an alien notion in contemporary Western thought. Let me cite two examples. First, in a book entitled *Mindfulness*, based on psychological research, Ellen Langer (1989) draws a distinction between what she calls "mindfulness" and "mindlessness." She defines "mindlessness" as thought and action "entrapped" by reified categories and habitual and "automatic behavior." According to Langer, one particular form of mindlessness that plagues education is an "outcome orientation" that forces attention away from *present* "processes" and toward fixed requirements for the future: once an outcome is determined, it becomes possible to stop thinking much at all about what one is doing and why one is doing it — except as it bears on the end preordained by the outcome — and to act, as it were, mindlessly.

In contrast, Langer's idea of "mindfulness" pictures an open mind that focuses on the processes of thought and action in the present, on "awareness of the processes of making real choices along the way" (p. 75). Although Langer is correct to point out that her idea of mindfulness differs in significant ways from what she refers to as mindfulness in Eastern disciplines, she does acknowledge sharing with those disciplines an understanding of mind that is in-action and in-process, and that is not bound by the "old categories" and "rigid distinctions" (p. 79) that are by-products not only of mindlessness, but, as Schön would surely agree, of overreliance on technical rationality as well.

The second example comes from what is perhaps an unexpected source for a discussion of educational theory, and that is the two-volume, posthumously published work of the historian and political philosopher Hannah Arendt, entitled *The Life of the Mind* (1971/1977–1978). In volume one, whose title *Thinking* names exactly the basic challenge in Zen practice, Arendt speaks of what she refers to as the "immovable present," the "gap between past and future," or the *nunc stans*. For Arendt, the present — what I have been calling the "here and now" of Zen —

"opens only in reflection whose subject matter is what is absent — either what has already disappeared or what has not yet appeared" (p. 206). *Nunc stans* (literally "standing now") represents for Arendt a sort of metaphysical "time out" for the thinking ego in the continuing tension between past and future. She writes:

> What are this dream and this region but the old dream Western metaphysics has dreamt from Parmenides to Hegel, of a timeless region, an eternal presence in complete quiet, lying beyond human clocks and calendars altogether, the region precisely of thought. (p. 207)

Arendt's further characterization of this moment in the center of constant change as "the immobile quiet in which the mind is active without doing anything" (p. 206) invites quite an interesting comparison with Dogen's (1985) description in "Zazen-Gi" of the attitude of the mind in *zazen* — that is, sitting meditation:

> Sit silently in [concentration] and think not-thinking. How do you think not-thinking? Nonthinking. This is the art of zazen. (p. 30)

Arendt's idea does not escape Schön's attention. Just as Arendt refers to a Zen-like "time out," so does Schön (1988) refer to a particular "mode of research activity, undertaken in tranquillity, off-line, which Hannah Arendt has called a 'stop-and-think' " (Schön, 1988, p. 29). And even though Langer, Arendt, and Schön do not refer to Zen in their writing, there are many further echoes between these particular ideas and passages in their works and Zen texts. Take, for example, the following three passages from Dainin Katagiri's book, *Returning to Silence* (1988), which center on themes of process, of quiet, and of standing (in addition to the fundamental Zen practice of sitting) in the present and paying attention:

> [*Zazen*] is "sit down and just be present" right now, right here. Become one with the present. This is a continual process. Process is really dynamic energy; it is not a concept of energy or concept of process. Process is process. If there is even a slight gap between process and us, it is not process. We must be process. (p. 126)

> But if we focus on countless lives in an immensely long span of time all we have to do is focus on right now, right here, without looking around. This is to practice in the eternal world. (p. 161)

> We have to stand up continuously, in whatever realm of existence, suffering, pain we find ourselves, and then, very naturally, we can see something omnipresent. (p. 147)

Reflecting on Mindfulness

The link between mindfulness in Zen and reflection-in-action helps us move beyond the "paucity of thought" to which Clift and Houston (1990) refer and beyond the limitations of concepts such as "reflection-as-problem-solving." This link introduces the issue of mind into the discussion of practice and leads us to focus on the mental processes that support practice. Being able to make this link has been particularly helpful to me in my work with education students and student teachers. James Calderhead (1989) puts it in familiar terms by using a metaphor common in both Eastern and Western literature. He distinguishes the mental act of reflection from the "random stream of consciousness of everyday experience" (p. 44). Attending to this stream of consciousness is a main focus of Zen, and is the raw material of mindful practice. This stream running out of control is a great hindrance to reflective practice; Calderhead notes that many elements of it, such as uncertainty or "ego involvement" (p. 46) (to say nothing of anxiety and outright fear), stand in the way of education students' and student teachers' efforts to engage in clear-minded action and reflection. For these reasons, he suggests that the ability to teach reflectively does "not appear to be developed easily," and can be approached only with the right disposition and sufficient experience:

> Some student teachers, for instance, seem to have great difficulty acquiring the detachment from their own practice that enables them to reflect upon it critically and objectively. . . . Reflection, in the general sense of an appraisal of one's own work, may require not only the possession of certain knowledge, critical skills, and a way of conceptualizing one's own learning as a reflective process, but also a basic practical competence together with some degree of self-confidence. (p. 47)

I am not entirely sure what Calderhead means here by "basic practical competence," but in my own work with student teachers I would use this term to refer to mastering not only the basic skills of functioning in the classroom, but the basic skills of using the mind as well. That begins with paying attention. I am beginning to see that paying attention, not only to what is going on around us but also within us, is not only a necessary step toward mindfulness and Zen, but is also the better part of reflective practice. For both Zen students and education students, no skillful action of any kind can occur without paying attention,.

Unfortunately, paying attention is an idea that teacher educators — responding to the demands of the academic marketplace — tend to move right past in order to develop more elaborate systems and theories. Ross, Pugach and Johnson, and Zeichner and Liston certainly do, although Liston and Zeichner eventually reconsider their position.

Louise Wetherbee Phelps (1991) gives an example of how the art of paying attention gets lost as she applies Schön's metaphor of the "ladder of reflection" to the field of composition.[6] Phelps, a college composition program director, applies Schön's notion in the process of mapping out an elaborate view of theory, practice, and knowledge-making in composition:

> Schön places these stances toward action along a continuum called the "ladder of reflection." At the bottom is activity itself, insofar as it is intelligent but not steadily self-critical: at the top is thinking (about knowledge) at its most abstract removed from material activity (epistemology, metacognition). The ladder thus symbolizes a continuity from practice itself to formal inquiry and from lore to theory and metatheory. (p. 873)

Phelps's schema for knowledge-making in composition, which she sketches out in this passage, is highly useful and has been influential in helping compositionists' understand their field. However, Schön's own rendering of the ladder of reflection defines levels of reflective activity rather than defining levels of abstraction and theorizing.

Schön does not mention concepts such as "most abstract remove from material activity," "formal inquiry," "theory," or "metatheory." Instead, he is interested is reflection and the process of moving deeper into the physical and mental operations of reflecting. To put it another way, what Schön is interested in is awareness — awareness of the world, awareness of the self acting in the world, and awareness of being aware. Schön is interested in paying attention.

There are others besides Calderhead and Schön who do not overlook the importance of paying attention. One of these, who like Phelps comes from the field of composition, is Howard Tinberg (1991). Tinberg puts it simply. He says that none of the problems of teaching or learning to teach will ever be resolved until teachers do a better job of paying attention. Tinberg goes right to the heart of the mental art of awareness. "To observe our classroom," Tinberg says, "is to reclaim it," and "observing our observations we teachers will find ourselves both inside and outside the setting we are studying. . . . We . . . must study ourselves as we study others" (pp. 41–42).

One of the terms Tinberg uses in explaining his position on paying attention is "seeing." Philip W. Jackson (1986), from the field of education, echoes Tinberg's language and his focus on paying attention when he refers to "seeing more" as a central practice that distinguishes skilled teachers:

> Expert teachers "see more" than do non-experts. They are alive to the latent pedagogical possibilities in the events they witness. Within a classroom setting, they anticipate what is going to happen. They can spot an inattentive student a mile off. They can detect signs of incipient difficulty. Their senses are fully tuned to what is going on around them. They are not easily rattled. As younger students sometimes swear is true, they behave as though they had eyes in the back of their heads. (p. 87)

For me, arriving at the fundamental point of paying attention both simplifies and complicates my work with student teachers. It simplifies my work, first of all, because it lets me know that I am not dealing with any great mystery that requires a high-tech, high-dollar solution: my first task is simply to bring up mindfulness in the context of reflective action — that is, to help my students pay attention. At the same time, it complicates my work because, despite how simple the task might seem, when it comes to actually working with teachers and student teachers, the challenge and difficulty of experiencing and helping others to experience reflective practice becomes clear.

Teaching Students the Art of Paying Attention: Insights from My Own Practice as a Teacher Educator

The first thing I try to keep in mind in teaching students the art of paying attention is Calderhead's point that education students and student teachers (to say nothing of other human beings in every place and every time) may be only dimly aware of the actions of their minds. They *use* their minds, often very well, but they may have no more than intermittent awareness of the moment-to-moment activities of mind. One of the reasons Calderhead refers to the stream of consciousness as random is because many human beings dip into it randomly and bring it into focus only when some special need arises or something unusual occurs. In fact, given the need that many people have to ignore their minds and let their attention be pulled to and from by distractions, getting students merely to consider how mind and attention work can be a big step — even a little teaching about mind can be a lot.

The second thing I keep in mind in teaching students to pay attention is that the way *not* to proceed is by teaching students and student teachers the practice of Zen. To begin with, I am not a certified Zen teacher, and only certified teachers with the proper credentials can teach Zen. Even more important, though, is that the specific practices of a discipline like Zen are difficult and slow to develop, and they are not for everyone. This is especially true for students who would interpret Zen Buddhism as a religious practice in conflict with their own beliefs.

In my own teaching, I have found three ways of introducing students to paying greater attention and reflective practice. These ways are illuminated by my familiarity with Zen's notions of mindfulness, but also by other sources. The first of these approaches is based on Peter Elbow's (1970) *Writing Without Teachers,* which I often use in a rhetoric and composition methods course. The central writing practice Elbow elaborates in this book is called "freewriting," which is an **heuristic**[c] technique that calls for the writer to write down everything that comes to mind without interposing editorial comments. What can happen in freewriting is that the writer's stream of consciousness is suddenly brought to attention and put on paper. What is most interesting about teaching freewriting is that even though it is a demonstrably useful technique that can be of great value in the process of composing, some students strongly resist it because it unsettles them to reveal the workings of their minds — even if they are revealing those workings only to themselves. The surprise, the shock, even the revulsion some students experience when they confront what is going on in their minds reflects the difficulty many of us have directing our attention inward toward ourselves. But it is important to be able to do this; for in order to begin to be mindful and truly reflective, one must have the skill and the courage to begin to know the self. (For views and techniques related to Elbow's, see Moffett, 1982, and Rico, 1983.)

A second way to introduce students to paying attention is to refer to it directly when responding to students' teaching and classwork. As a teacher educator, my attention was for a long time directed entirely toward helping students and student teachers understand such important topics as educational theories, course and curriculum planning, and classroom management techniques. Even though I still spend a great deal of time on such matters, I find myself focusing more and more on paying attention. Explaining this shift is not easy, since it occurs in the form of countless comments, responses, and small bits of writing, notes, and so forth. However, one concrete instance comes to mind. A student of mine recently presented a 30-minute lesson in a literature methods class. His lesson plan was an elaborate — and indeed impressive — combination of interactive set-up, informal writing, lecture, oral performance, and discussion. As one might expect, despite its excellent qualities, thirty minutes was much too short a time in which to present such a lesson. As this student saw his time slipping away and large sections of his lesson still looming ahead of him, his reaction was to try rapidly to complete his plan; this attempt made him visibly upset. When he finished the class, we had a workshop session during which the student expressed a great deal of anger at not having enough time to teach his lesson. His frustration was aimed in many directions — toward himself for over planning, toward me for allowing only 30-minute

---

[c] **Heuristic** refers to experiences, methods, or objects that aid in learning.

time periods for teaching, and even toward his classmates for what he perceived as their failure to contribute to the efficient dispatch of his lesson.

I tried to provide this student with two kinds of teachings. The first was obvious. I talked with him — and his classmates also talked with him — about the need to fit one's classroom plans to the time one has available, and then to remain loose and flexible if things don't work as planned. The second teaching I tried to give him was that he should work on paying attention. By this, I meant not only that he needed to become more mindful of his "students," in this case his classmates and me, but also that he needed to become more mindful of the thoughts and feelings that arose for him during and after teaching his lesson. After all, the real problem he had wasn't with his planning. In a classroom anything can happen, and all teachers have experienced implementing a plan that is thrown off track by unexpected responses from students. The real problem was the panic and anger that overtook this student and that overcame him while he was teaching and afterwards. The real problem was being unable to see what was happening with his students or with himself *when* it was happening, and thus not being able to respond at the moment in order to make necessary adjustments.

Several years ago I never would have thought that addressing distracting thoughts and feelings, such as wandering attention and anger, would become part of my teaching. However, today I can think of no more important and difficult lesson to learn. Sometimes slowly, and sometimes through the haze of my own distractions, I am beginning to recognize not only the importance of teachers' skills and knowledge, but also the importance of how their minds work. What follows is the written response I made to this student after his teaching experience:

> As you know [from class discussion], there was much in your lesson that I liked. The oral reading you did was very effective. . . . Most students — at all levels — will respond positively to such a reading. On paper your lesson is very complete and very well put together. You obviously know a lot about and have a good command of [your topic and its literature.]
>
> I was not kidding around in class when I talked to you about *patience* and learning to recognize those kinds of thoughts and feelings that you said led you to rush and to focus on *doing the lesson* rather than *working with* your students. When those thoughts and feelings arise, find a way to focus your attention back on what is happening in the classroom with your students — at the moment. (I know this is not easy. All the more reason to begin working on it right now.)

Even though it was not my intention when I wrote this, and even though I have absolutely no competence or ambition as a Zen teacher, in retrospect I do see that there is some common ground between my comments to this statement and a basic teaching of Zen. This connection is encouraging the practitioner not simply to become more adept at the basic skills of teaching, but also to pay attention, to avoid getting caught up in thoughts as they arise, and to return to the present moment, to the classroom and the students right "here and now." Paraphrasing the passage from Dainin Katagiri I cited earlier, what I tried, in my own way, to tell this student was: When you teach, be mindful of teaching. Mindfulness is to go toward the center of whatever you are doing. When you begin teaching the mind will go in many directions; instead of going out in all directions, let's go in. This means, look at the teaching you are doing now.

I have no concrete idea how useful these teachings were to my student. His frustration and anger were slow to pass. However, he did his next teaching exercise much more comfortably, and his attention to the actions of teaching, his planning, and his posture were much more settled.

A third way I introduce my students to paying attention is to ask them to write what I call "slices of classroom life" — informal, two-part writings (see Tremmel, 1992). Part one consists of a detailed narration of some specific and limited "event" in school. I ask students to think of themselves as anthropologists who observe closely and write in detail about their findings in the process of investigation. Part two is given over to reflection, to writing about the thoughts and feelings that arise during and after the event. I have three purposes for assigning these slices of life. The first one is to give students an opportunity, as researcher and rhetorical theorist James Britton (1970) would say, "to represent the world to themselves" in a loosely structured way that permits them to shape their understanding during the action of composing (or, as Britton might put it, to "shape at the point of utterance"). The second purpose is to introduce students to the idea of paying close attention to the details of specific events as they unfold, which they must do if they are going to be able to write about them afterwards. It is remarkable how difficult some students find it to look for details, preferring instead to look broadly and to think in terms of summaries (ironically, a practice traditionally encouraged in U.S. schools as a sign of higher-order thinking). Sometimes it takes several tries before a student teacher is able to focus closely enough to produce a slice of life that satisfies the requirements. The third purpose of the slices of life is to create an occasion for my students and me to explore together the various — sometimes unexpected — ways in which paying attention reveals the practice of teaching. Below are three very different examples.

Slice of Life No. 1:

They chit-chat and giggle with one another. I can only say "Listen Up" so many times. I realize that my silence drives them crazy. Allowing each other to quiet the group works much better. They are a very energetic group and when on task work very well. They are creative, fun, interesting, and intelligent. But also noisy. Usually it's "good" noise, but at times I would prefer my 1st hour students who are afraid of their own voices.

I really like my energetic 5th hour. Some days are better than others. But individually they are good kids so I just have to "warn" him/her about the talking during class and it helps. Just a quick moment after class making them aware of my feelings really can do the trick. I'll really miss these kids when I leave and I honestly believe some will miss me too.

This is a slice of life that was written near the beginning of the student teaching term. The student teacher who wrote it had not yet come to terms with the requirements for a slice of life. She is caught up with the broad observations, uncertainties, and with convincing me that she had these "good kids" and her teaching situation under control. When I received this slice it told me that this student teacher's attention was skipping over the general scene of the classroom and that she was concerned about the impression her fifth-hour class created. In response to this piece of writing, I encouraged her to focus more closely on particular students, events, and details of action and reaction, without being critical of her work during what was for her a confusing and anxious time.

Slice of Life No. 2:

I was confronted with an anxiety I hoped I could avoid. A boy in my . . . English class gave me no choice but to prove my authority. I sent him to the office for misbehavior.

It all took place during a lesson over rhyme and meter. By its very nature, this subject matter is hard to comprehend. But to deepen the heartache, a few boys in the class kept making "smart" comments, which in turn got the class riled up. My approach was initially to ignore it.

But then it escalated. Warnings shot out of my mouth left and right. Still no luck. I had a choice: let the students who misbehaved take control or I take control. I opted for the latter.

I sent one of the "leaders" to the office. I simply told him to get out of the classroom. The students know they are supposed to go see the principal when these things happen.

Afterwards, I felt guilty. I kept thinking if there wasn't something I could have done to prevent that step. But after thinking about it I realize I made the right decision for two major reasons: 1) the student was invading other students' rights to an education, and 2) I had to show I would keep my promise to carry out my warnings.

While I still regard sending kids to the office a final resort, I am a little less reluctant to do it because I realize it can both help students who do behave and help me to regain control in the classroom.

This is a slice of life written by a student teacher in a desperate situation. Not only had she been having discipline problems in her classes, but the school she was working in was having discipline problems too: there was tension between faculty and administration, political tension among faculty members, and a general lack of collegiality and mutual support. Even though the student teacher had been encouraged several times to remove this particular student from her class, she did not do so because she feared the response of administrators and disliked having to resort to such a measure, which she interpreted as a sign of failure. Finally, she did send the student to the office.

Even though this slice of life ignores the format I assigned, it does show how this student's attention, in the midst of a crisis in her environment, turns inward to establish a basis for action. "This past week I was confronted with an anxiety," she begins. She does not begin by saying that she was confronted with an unruly student. This seems significant to me, because many teachers' first inclination in such a situation would be to put the blame "out there" on the student. Not so in this case. Consciously or unconsciously, this student knows right from the start that finding and applying appropriate means of discipline is only part of her challenge; she knows that an equally important part is for her to recognize and pay close attention to her own anxious state of mind, which arises as a reaction to her students' behavior.

This slice of life contains additional signs that this student teacher is gaining insight into the fact that the action in the classroom is not the only problem, but that her own reactions also contribute to the situation. She is becoming aware of the value of self-discipline as part of the overall classroom discipline. "But to deepen the heartache" is an unusual comment for one of my student teachers to make. She knows she is in deep trouble and in the midst of a painful situation that is escalating out of control. She understands that she is losing control of herself by getting as "riled up" as her students, and that that loss is a significant part of the situation. "Warnings shot out of my mouth left and right" is a powerful figure of speech that suggests a loss of control. When this student teacher says, "I had a choice: let the students take control or I take control, I opted for the latter," she is not simply saying that she took control of the class, but that her decision to send the student to the office was also intended to help her regain control of herself. In this way, this slice of life suggests her awareness of the need to pay close attention to the self.

Of course, what is missing in this slice of life are signs that this student teacher is attending closely to the particular actions of her students. Attending to herself leads her to get caught up in herself. I would hope for this student teacher and all teachers, including myself, to be able also to pay attention to our students. I believe, however, that the ability to pay attention to oneself in order to maintain a calm mind is a necessary initial step. This slice of life suggests to me that, with more time and reflection, this student teacher may be capable of paying attention to both.

Slice of Life No. 3:

Part I.

The balding man strides across the bright tile floor. Wearing a pin striped grey suit, he carries a piece of white and green paper in his hand as he approaches the table I sit at with my cooperating teacher. He greets us and sits down in the small wooden chair. "My name is _____'s father." "Well," he [the father] says, "looks like he's getting a B?" "Yes," my teacher says, "a good strong one." "Yes, [the father replied] but he's an A student." She takes out a bunch of papers, digs through them and finally pulls one out. "Here is a sample of his writing. He's done real well so far." He glances at the first page, looks up and answers "Yes, but he's capable of doing 'A' work." He laughs. She tells him what's planned for the rest of the year. He still laughs and says "Yes. Okay. I'm sure he'll bring the grade up since I know he's capable of it." This was his last reply as he moves on to the next table.

Part II.

Parent/Teacher conferences. It's the first night, and I'm anxious to meet the parents of students I've been teaching. As [the] father introduces himself, [the teacher] tells him that his son is doing well. The father keeps repeating to us that his son is capable of "A" work and is an "A" student. Much more so than I described above. Probably four to five times. But, he's not saying it in a way like he demands it of his son, but more like — Why didn't we give him the "A" he deserves! His son is a decent student, but not real cooperative in class, or real motivated. He seems to do the work and get what he should from it, but not willingly. If he put more effort into it, I would probably agree — he is an "A" student. The way his father acted, though, you'd think he was the greatest, smartest kid who was a perfect angel. *Wrong.* He is easily distracted and often disrupts others. In fact I made a new seating chart and put him in front so I could make sure he was more on task. It has helped some. [The teacher] did point out the reasons she did not give an "A" but his father still seemed positively convinced of what he was saying. I wondered why. Was it because in the past he has been? Or because he seems to believe his son is able to really earn that grade? I don't think he would put an *over abundance* of pressure on him (my own opinion after listening to him) to earn a better grade, but I could see how he *might*.

This is a more typical slice of life. No early term jitters and no crisis. The author of this slice has worked and progressed at paying attention. This piece is characteristic of her practice. In this and other slices she attends to physical traits, actions, mannerisms, and dialogue. Her attention to these matters in this slice leads her to focus on the student and to reflect on his actions in class. In slice after slice she followed the same pattern: her attention to the details of the situations and the people she is writing about lead her to reflect compassionately on her students' needs.

The Journey Itself

Once I knew a Chinese doctor. He had credentials in both Western and Eastern medicine and taught at a major midwestern medical school while maintaining a private, off-campus practice in acupuncture and traditional medicine. He compared the two cultures he practiced in this way: "In the East," he said, "there is good understanding of internal ecology; in the West there is good understanding of external ecology. What is now necessary is to bring the two together." In education we have done well with external ecology, constructing a prodigious edifice built up by means of technically rational research and theory. However, we are still pretty much at a loss when it comes to the internal field of the mind and the art of paying attention in practice.

I remember reading somewhere that to study Zen is to study the self. In education, self as an area of study and study of the self as a way of knowing have often been misplaced in the rush forward to new theories and techniques. Yet, they have not been lost, as evidenced in the increased interest in research techniques like ethnography and teacher research, which encourage paying attention to and recognizing the influence of self. Another piece of evidence is the work of educators who seem willing to take a step back from theoretical entanglements and ask fundamental questions about what and how teachers are thinking and why they are doing what they are doing. Calderhead and Tinberg certainly do this, as do Liston and Zeichner. Pugach and Johnson, in an article that contains many aspects of technical rationality, are nevertheless able to write: "Listening to one's own processes of thinking and having those processes modeled provides a structured means for encouraging reflective practice among teachers" (1990, p. 203). "Listening to one's own processes of thinking" is a beautiful if deceptively simple idea that seems to show some understanding of what it is Zen teachers try to teach.

Signs of this growing awareness of the need for reflection occur unexpectedly. Recently, the chair of the National Council of Teachers of English Committee on Teacher Preparation sent me a packet of articles to prepare for an upcoming convention. One article, written by Amy Bernstein Colton of the National Board for Teaching Standards and Georgia M. Sparks-Langer of Eastern Michigan University, was entitled, "A Conceptual Framework to Guide the Development of Teacher Reflection and Decision Making." Even though the idea of a conceptual framework does not rest too comfortably with either Schön's view of reflection or Zen, Colton and Sparks-Langer do recognize "consciousness" as a main "attribute of reflective decision making" (1993, p. 50). Interestingly, they also include a speculative example of the need for mindfulness in the midst of practice that parallels the second of the "slices of life" that I presented:

Feelings often have a huge influence on one's ability to reflect — to interpret and respond to a situation. . . . For example, a teacher who is disrupted for the ump-teenth time may become angry and ask the student to leave the classroom with little reflection as to why the student is acting in that manner. Sometimes such frustration and anger make it impossible to delve into the professional knowl-edge base or construct new meanings — in effect, reflective thought is tempo-rarily "frozen" by these intense feelings. Until one recognizes those feelings and deals with them, it is impossible to think of alternative interpretations of the event. (p. 48)

When I see educators rediscovering the ancient and fundamental need for pay-ing attention, I feel hopeful that the educational community might welcome non-traditional, non-Western practices, as Clift and Houston suggest, and thus enrich current teaching practices. Such enrichment has the potential to lead to a balanced and powerful blend of thought and action. However, in much of the literature on reflection that I read, I still see too few signs that our profession is willing to revise the way it regards the grand promises of technical rationality and the agendas that arise from pursuing theory. Indeed, sometimes as I read, the nagging suspicion grows that what really drives us forward is still the persistent hope that somewhere "out there" is THE answer, THE formula, THE technology, THE research tech-nique that will solve all our problems and meet all our needs. Until we are seriously and equally willing to look within, I am afraid we will see little beyond what we have already seen. Looking within is part of preparing ourselves for — and actually engaging in — reflective and mindful practice.

Perhaps the main difficulty that many programs and exercises in reflective prac-tice have is the expectation that students be able to develop subtle and complex abilities in a one- or two-year period, based on a handful of courses and practicums. This is unrealistic, especially for students raised in a society that has perfected the arts of distraction as thoroughly as ours has. The ability to reflect mindfully in- and on-action is not an ability that most students can master in their undergraduate experiences or in a semester of teaching. It is, rather, the practice of a lifetime that can only *begin* with what we call "pre-service" education (a term that oddly implies a clear-cut difference between preparing to do and doing). To become reflective and mindful practitioners, we need to learn to become aware of the workings of our own minds and, simultaneously, to let go of involvement in our thoughts and feelings while plunging ourselves, mind and body, into the center of teaching and learning. This is no easy task.

Basho, the seventeenth-century Zen poet, captured this practice of learning to leave the self behind while staying in the center when, in the beginning of a travel journal, he wrote: "Each day is a journey, and the journey itself, home" (Corman & Susumu, 1986, n. p.). The practice of teaching is demanding, and the making of a teacher is not something that can happen in a short time, bounded by the sorts of stages we use to mark out academic life. Like all rigorous practice, the way of teaching demands a long journey that does not have any easily identifiable destina-tion. It does not end with "pre-service," or graduation, or after one year, or after all the criteria are met. It is beyond all criteria. It is a journey that I believe must in-clude a backward step into the self, and it is a journey that is its own destination.

Notes

1. Ross (1990) articulates the five elements of the reflective process as follows:
    1. recognizing educational dilemmas;
    2. responding to a dilemma by recognizing both similarities to other situations and the unique qualities of the particular situation;
    3. framing and reframing the dilemma;
    4. experimenting with the dilemma to discover the implications of various solutions;
    5. examining the intended and unintended consequences of an implemented solution and evaluating it by determining whether the consequences are desirable. (p. 98)
2. Pugach and Johnson (1990) describe the four steps as follows:
    1. clarifying problems of practice by self-questioning in a guided learning situation, a strategy in which particular questions are posed and responded to as a means of reframing the nature of those problems;
    2. summarizing the redefined problems;
    3. generating possible solutions and predicting what might happen should they be utilized;
    4. considering various ways of evaluating the effectiveness of the solution chosen. (p. 189)
3. Dewey (1910) articulates the five steps as follows:
    1. a felt difficulty;
    2. its location and definition;
    3. suggestion of possible solutions;
    4. development by reasoning of the bearings of the suggestion;
    5. further observation and experiment leading to its acceptance or rejection. (p. 72)
4. Zeichner and Liston (1987) outline the four qualities as follows:
    1. technical competence in instruction;
    2. ability to analyze practice;
    3. awareness of teaching as an activity that has ethical and moral consequences;
    4. sensitivity to the needs of students with diverse characteristics and ability to play an active role in developing a respect for individual differences within their classrooms and schools. (p. 25)
5. Founded in the last millennium on the teaching of Shakyamuni Buddha and developed in the process of moving to Japan and other Eastern nations through China from India, Zen is now spreading through the United States and Western Europe, where dozens of Zen centers have been established and are attracting growing memberships. These centers, for the most part, were established after World War II by Japanese, Korean, and Vietnamese teachers and have now passed to a second generation of Western and Eastern teachers educated in both the West and the East (see, for example, Aitken, 1982; Beck, 1989; Kapleau, 1980; Katagiri, 1988; Loori, 1988; Mountain, 1983; Nhat Hanh, 1975, 1988; Sahn, 1982; S. Suzuki, 1970; Thien-An, 1975).

    In addition to the establishment of formal practice centers, Zen has also penetrated the culture of both the East and the West. In Japan, for example, many aspects of culture can be traced directly to the influence of Zen (see D.T. Suzuki, 1959/1989). In the United States, Zen figures in twentieth-century literary consciousness. For example, Robert Pirsig's *Zen and the Art of Motorcycle Maintenance,* first issued in 1974, has gone through over two dozen printings and has been read by large numbers of readers throughout the English-speaking world. Pulitzer Prize winning poet Gary Snyder (1980), who spent several years practicing Zen at Daitoku-ji Monastery in Japan in the 1960s, has incorporated many aspects of Zen into his poetry. In addition, the currently popular Eastern martial arts are based in part on disciplines that are closely linked to Zen and Zen teaching.
6. Schön (1987) articulates the four levels of reflective activity in the "ladder of reflection" as follows (the reverse order of the numbers reflects the bottom to top nature implicit in the metaphor):
    4. Reflection on reflection on description of designing
    3. Reflection on description of designing
    2. Description of designing
    1. Designing (where "designing is, . . . in its own way, a process of reflection in action") (p. 115)

References

Adler, S. (1991). The reflective practitioner and the curriculum of teacher education. *Journal of Education for Teaching, 17,* 139–150.

Aitken, R. (1982) *Taking the path of Zen.* San Francisco: North Point Press.

Arendt, H. (1971/1977–1978). Thinking. In *The life of the mind.* New York: Harcourt Brace Jovanovich.

Beck, C. J. (1989). *Everyday Zen.* New York: Harper & Row.

Britton, J. N. (1970). *Language and learning.* Hammondsworth, Eng.: Penguin.

Calderhead, J. (1989). Reflective teaching and teacher education. *Teaching and Teacher Education, 5*(1), 43–51.

Clift, R. T., & Houston, W. R. (1990). The potential for research contributions to reflective practice. In R. T. Clift, W. R. Houston, & M. C. Pugach (Eds.), *Encouraging reflective practice in education* (pp. 208–222). New York: Teachers College Press.

Colton, A. B., & Sparks-Langer, G. M. (1993). A conceptual framework to guide the development of teacher reflection and decision making. *Journal of Teacher Education, 44*(1), 45–54.

Corman, C., & Susumu, K. (Eds.). (1986). *Back roads to far towns: Basho's Oku-no-hosomichi.* Fredonia, NY: White Pine Press.

Court, D. (1988). Reflection-in-action: Some definitional problems. In P. P. Grimmett & G. L. Erickson (Eds.), *Reflection in teacher education* (pp. 143–146). New York: Teachers College Press.

Cruikshank, D. R. (1987). *Reflective teaching.* Reston, VA: Association of Teacher Educators.

Dewey, J. (1910). *How we think.* New York: D. C. Heath.

Dewey, J. (1933). *How we think: A restatement of the relation of reflective thinking to the educative process.* Boston: D. C. Heath.

Dewey, J. (1929). *The quest for certainty.* New York: G. P. Putnam's Sons.

Dogen, E. (1985). Rules for zazen (D. Welch & K. Tanahashi, Trans.). In K. Tanahashi (Ed.), *Moon in a dewdrop: Writings of Zen Master Dogen* (pp. 30–31). San Francisco: North Point Press. (Original work published 11th month, 1st year of Kangen, 1243)

Dogen, E., & Uchiyama, K. (1983). *Refining your life from the Zen kitchen to enlightenment* (T. Wright, Trans.). New York: Weatherhill. (Original work published 1237)

Elbow, P. (1970). *Writing without teachers.* London: Oxford University Press.

Grimmett, P. P. (1988). The nature of reflection and Schön's conception in perspective. In P. P. Grimmett & G. L. Erickson (Eds.), *Reflection in teacher education* (pp. 5–15). New York: Teachers College Press.

Hills, J., & Gibson, C. (1988). Reflections on Schön's reflective practitioner. In P. P. Grimmett & G. L. Erickson (Eds.), *Reflection in teacher education* (pp. 147–176). New York: Teachers College Press.

Jackson, P. W. (1986). *The practice of teaching.* New York: Teachers College Press.

Kapleau, P. (1980). *The three pillars of Zen.* Garden City, NY: Anchor Books.

Katagiri, D. (1988). *Returning to silence: Zen practice in daily life.* Boston: Shambala.

Langer, E. (1989). *Mindfulness.* Reading, MA: Addison-Wesley.

Liston, D. P., & Zeichner, K. M. (1990). Reflective teaching and action research in preservice teacher education. *Journal of Education for Teaching, 16,* 235–254.

Loori, J. D. (1988). *Mountain record of Zen talks.* Boston: Shambala.

Moffett, J. (1982). Writing, inner speech, and meditation. *College English, 44,* 231–246.

Mountain, M. (1983). *The Zen environment.* New York: Bantam.

Nhat Hanh, T. (1975). *The miracle of mindfulness.* Boston: Beacon Press.

Nhat Hanh, T. (1988). *The sun my heart.* Berkeley, CA: Parallax Press.

Nhat Hanh, T. (1990). *Transformation and healing: Sutra on the four establishments of mindfulness.* Berkeley, CA: Parallax Press.

Phelps, L. W. (1991). Practice wisdom in the geography of knowledge and composition. *College English, 53,* 863–885.

Pirsig, R. M. (1974). *Zen and the art of motorcycle maintenance.* New York: Bantam.

Plato. (1961). *The Meno* (W. K. C. Guthrie, Trans.). In E. Hamilton & H. Cairns (Eds.), *The collected dialogues of Plato* (pp. 353–384). Princeton, NJ: Princeton University Press.

Polanyi, M. (1958). *Personal knowledge: Towards a post-critical philosophy.* Chicago: University of Chicago Press.

Pugach, M. C., & Johnson, L. J. (1990). Developing reflective practice through structured dialogue. In R. T. Clift, W. R. Houston, & M. C. Pugach (Eds.), *Encouraging reflective practice in teacher education* (pp. 186–207). New York: Teachers College Press.

Rico, G. L. (1983). *Writing the natural way.* Los Angeles: J. P. Tarcher.

Ross, D. D. (1989). First steps in developing a reflective approach. *Journal of Teacher Education, 40*(2), 22–30.

Ross, D. D. (1990). Programmatic structures for the preparation of reflective teachers. In R. T. Clift, W. R. Houston, & M. C. Pugach (Eds.), *Encouraging reflective practice in education* (pp. 97–118). New York: Teachers College Press.

Sahn, S. (1982). *Only don't know: The teaching letters of Zen Master Seung Sahn.* San Francisco: Four Seasons Foundation.

Schön, D. A. (1983). *The reflective practitioner: How professionals think in action.* New York: Basic Books.

Schön, D. A. (1987). *Educating the reflective practitioner: Toward a new design for teaching and learning in the professions.* San Francisco: Jossey-Bass.

Schön, D. A. (1988), Coaching reflective teaching. In P. P. Grimmett & G. L. Erickson (Eds.), *Reflection in teacher education.* New York: Teachers College Press.

Schön, D. A. (Ed.). (1991). *The reflective turn: Case studies in and on educational practice.* New York: Teachers College Press.

Selman, M. (1988). Schön's gate is square: But is it art? In P. P. Grimmett & G. L Erickson (Eds.), *Reflection in teacher education* (pp. 177–192). New York: Teachers College Press.

Snyder, G. (1980). *The real work: Interviews and talks.* New York: New Directions.

Suzuki, D. T. (1959/1989). *Zen and Japanese culture.* Princeton, NJ: Princeton University Press.

Suzuki, S. (1970). *Zen mind, beginner's mind.* New York: John Weatherhill.

Thien-An, T. (1975). *Zen philosophy, Zen practice.* Berkeley, CA: Dharma.

Tinberg, H. B. (1991). An enlargement of observation: More on theory building and composition. *College Composition and Communication, 42,* 36–44.

Tom, A. R. (1984). *Teaching as a moral craft.* New York: Longman.

Tom, A. R. (1985). Inquiring into inquiry-oriented teacher education. *Journal of Teacher Education, 36*(5), 35–44.

Tremmel, R. (1992). A habit of mind. *English Education, 24*(1), 20–33.

Van Manen, M. (1977). Linking ways of knowing with ways of being practical. *Curriculum Inquiry, 6,* 205–228.

Watts, A. W. (1957). *The way of Zen.* New York: Vintage Books.

Zeichner, K. M., & Liston, D. P. (1987). Teaching student teachers to reflect. *Harvard Educational Review, 57,* 23–48.

The author wishes to thank Robert Stein of Washburn University for his support in the early stages of this research.

Cacophony to Symphony:
Memoirs in Teacher Research

KAREN HALE HANKINS

In this chapter, Karen Hale Hankins explores her past, looking inward to her own history for guidance in learning how to reach and teach her current students. Hankins delves into her inner world through the journal she keeps, reflecting on her past experiences as they are sparked by events, feelings, and challenges in her present classroom. Using her journal to "listen to the wholeness of my life rather than just the present moment," Hankins finds ways to connect to the students in her class, particularly those who came into her kindergarten class already labeled negatively by the school system. Investigating and analyzing the inner worlds of her past and present — particularly her family relationships — Hankins pushes herself to persist with the students she teaches, maintaining high expectations, never giving up, and continually searching for what her students need in order to "find their place in the 'symphony' of the classroom."

The room was filled with the chatter of writing workshop. Nat[1] puzzled over two crayons in his hand, one of them blue: "Mrs. Hankins, ain't you had you a blue bicycle when you was a little-girl-teacher?" Nat had a way of naming me for what I was: always a teacher — or was it always a little girl? I answered Nat's present question, remembering my past blue bicycle and a childhood story about it that I had shared with the children recently.

Perhaps it was one of those "tell-me-about-when-you-were-little" moments that brought writing memoirs to the forefront of my teaching journal. Perhaps it was the need to make some sense of the cacophonous days with my three special students, Nat, Loretta, and Rodney, who had all been damaged in utero by crack cocaine or alcohol. The original impetus for these writings is lost to me now, but, as Lucy Calkins says, writing memoirs "has everything to do with rendering the ordinariness of our lives so that it becomes significant" (1991, p. 169). The past seemed to wrap itself around my present-day questions, and as the number of memoirs grew, my journal became a place for uncovering the significant.

I kept a journal of that full school year, documenting these three children's entry into school. In this article, I first share a sampling of my memoirs, which were an

---

[1] All names except Kathy's are pseudonyms.

Harvard Educational Review Vol. 68 No. 1 Spring 1998, 80–95

important part of that journal. I attempt to document the impact that recording the past had on my teaching that year. As Calkins writes, "The challenge of memoir is to discover memories no one talks about" (1991, p. 177), and to understand how they shape who we are.

I also document a bit of my struggle as a novice teacher-researcher to claim a voice in the definition of research. Events remembered from the past are, as a rule, not written into research reports, but I believe that they are a part of all of our questions.

Cacophony: Separate Voices

My assumption is that the story of any one of us is in some measure the story of us all. (Beuchner, 1991, p. xii).

Persons who become master teachers are likely to do so because of a tacit understanding of how to shape and reshape the materials of their craft. (Greene, 1985, p. 17)

Writing is really very simple; all you do is sit down at the typewriter and open a vein. (Red Smith, quoted in Beuchner, 1992, p. 77)

The three quotations read against each other may "sound" like the warm-up of a symphony orchestra: each instrument separately tunes up and runs its own independent agenda for a minute or two before coming to a common purpose. Then they make music!

Let me conduct you to the common purpose I hear in these statements. For me they represent the multiple foci of this writing. First, I came to understand that the children whose lives seemed so distant from mine were "in some measure the story of [myself]." Second, understanding that relationship helped me "to shape and reshape the materials of [my] craft" in order to teach them. Finally, it was in "opening the vein," in the composing and practicing process involving soul, pen, and paper, that I heard the "symphony."

My Journal: Memoirs Within

My father kept a journal for over twenty years. It was always open, and we were invited to read it. Most often it contained a daily log — of the weather, scribbles from a grandchild, his weight and how much he exercised, the basic mood of the family, and unusual occurrences. Many times he wrote reflections and memoirs as well. I wondered at the open and public nature of them. He even had his secretary type them up.

I have kept daily logs and a journal for years, but mine were messy in comparison, not for public view, and full of the things that bothered me. Most often the bothersome things revolved around incidents with children I taught. By the time teaching journals became popular, I was already using one. The various complaints and musings I recorded in them documented my growth as a teacher, my level of tolerance, and the tide of trends and issues in education. My early journals were primarily chronological documents in which I used words, poetry, and songs to chronicle my career — teaching.

After more than fifteen years of teaching in schools of varying sizes — in urban, rural, and suburban settings, and in three southern states and one foreign country — I went back to school to pursue a Ph.D. I took my first course while I was still in the classroom, and I decided to write the story of three special children I was teaching that year as part of my course work. Since I'd always kept a journal, I was delighted that my professor encouraged me to use it even more that I was. It was the natural place for me to record observations and to make notes of things I'd like to do next. That year, for the first time, my journal was filled with memoirs, written accounts that helped me explore the significance of my past.

My professor got me involved with a teacher-research group funded by the National Reading Research Center. One day at a meeting we shared some writings about coming into teaching. After I read my piece, which began with a story about my sister, someone asked me if I had more of this type of writing anywhere. My teaching journal was full of such stories, but I'd never revealed that before. My colleagues' interest caused me to review the stories in my journal, which helped me realize that the three children I was teaching that year put me in touch with my own past. It was a useful journey — one that helped me interpret and orchestrate my present.

I wrote up a study of Nat, Loretta, and Rodney's journey through kindergarten and presented parts of the study at a conference. After the presentation, I wrote the following reflection in my journal:

> So, I keep this journal. It was easier when no one else knew or cared that I wrote. It's a teaching journal. It's a personal journal. It's a research journal. It's both a personal and teaching journal because John Dewey first and Lucy Calkins later taught me to reflect on my day and my life in the same breath. It's both a Teaching and Research journal because I no longer believe that teaching can be separated from research. (Perhaps it CAN be but it shouldn't be.) The question is . . . I guess . . . Can it be both Personal and Research journal? That's what people really want me to defend. But how can I tell people what my heart and head do together in my classroom? For instance, today at a conference I talked to someone about my study. She "listened" politely and patiently. When I finished she had only one question, "But . . . did it help them learn to read better? "Yes," I said as I looked her square in the face. I think she meant — "there are no numbers." (Journal Entry, April 1995)

I remember the night I wrote that entry. I closed my journal and felt tears well up and spill slowly down my face. I wept because there was joy in my class's progress as readers and writers. But more than that, I cried because of that woman's question. I keep running into the feeling that because I'm a teacher, I'm doing research wrong. And in honesty, I want to be heard by that woman and others like her. I have a problem being controlled by formulated text and vocabulary. I wondered if there was a place for my research, my story, told my way.

Writing in my journal is like learning to play the cello, a process akin to practice time, full of starts, stops, and repeats. I practice knowing, indeed hoping, that no one hears. However, the only real drive to practice grows from the belief that someday someone will want to hear.

I kept the journal of my observations of Nat, Rodney, and Loretta privately, knowing no one would read it but hoping someday someone would want to know the essence of the notes recorded there. I wrote at nap time, while waiting for faculty meetings to begin, during the last ten minutes before turning out the light each night, and on the backs of church bulletins or napkins in restaurants. I had never heard of field notes at the time. I read recently a definition of ethnographic field notes as "the systematic ways of writing what one observes and learns while participating in the daily rounds of the lives of others" (Emerson, Fretz, & Shaw, 1995, p. 18). As the year progressed, I fell into a system of sorts as I recorded the "lives of others." My journal served, then, as the field notes of a teacher. Mine were records of what Emerson et al. (1995) call "headnotes" (mental notes), "hard notes" (direct observations), and "heartnotes" (my feelings and reflections). The more I observed and made notes, the more adept I became at documenting. Just as learning scales and études builds the foundation for making music, learning to record quickly and accurately built a foundation for my research. As I later fleshed out my quickly written notes, filling in half-written words and sentences, I often felt a keen connection to other stories from my past. At those times, I wrote long into the night or too long after school. That's when the stories from my own life surfaced. Writing my memoirs became a time when I allowed myself to listen to the wholeness of my life rather than just the present moment. "This is the very stuff of memoir . . . and it is the stuff that propels us forward with a sense of direction and momentum" (Calkins, 1991, p. 167).

Delving into these stories from my past felt a bit like stopping practice to play a piece of music I knew well enough to play with flair. When I played those pieces, I shifted my attention from the notes on the page and connected with my cello almost physically. The bow slid across the strings with no effort, my fingers following commands from deep inside. Invariably I chastised myself for digressing. It felt "too good to be practice," I confessed to my teacher one day. "Oh no," she responded, "it is *essential* that you digress every day. It reminds you that there is sense to the scales, that they connect later to something larger *and* that there are compositions yet to be born!" At the end of the year, as I reread my journal, I realized that the digressions — my memoirs — paralleled the stories of Nat, Rodney, and Loretta. Their stories demanded to be interpreted in light of my own. I began to see the connectedness of our stories, of our lives.

As I understand the idea of the "researcher as an instrument" (Emerson et al., 1995), it behooves me to know that instrument and to know it well, especially when the instrument is me. Writing memoirs while I documented the present helped me to know myself better and to understand Nat, Loretta, and Rodney better as a result. When I began to "chunk" (LeCompte & Preissle, 1993) the text of these memoirs into common themes, two themes emerged: prejudice and family denial. I began to see how interactions between the children and me triggered my own childhood memories.

Shared Denial: "Just don't talk about it"

I teach in a public school of six hundred K-5 students. It is a lovely school, built within the last eight years in the suburbs of a southeastern university town. I average twenty-three children per year in a regular heterogeneously grouped kindergarten. The year of this writing, I had a part-time teaching assistant. Our school population is about 50 percent African American, 45 percent European American, and 5 percent a variety of other ethnic origins. The children represent a cross-section of our city. The middle-class children come from neighborhoods that are close to the school, while the children from less affluent neighborhoods are bused in. All of our children, including kindergartners, begin the school day at 7:50 A.M. and leave at 2:30 P.M.

When I was given my class list, I was surprised to see that it was attached to three very thick folders. Kindergarten teachers don't usually receive permanent folders for students; we create them. These children had double folders, which meant that at age four they were already receiving special education services. I knew I needed more than I had at my immediate disposal, materially and emotionally, to promote success for these already labeled children. During the first few weeks of school, family members of each of the children informed me that the children had a common problem. Each was a product of Fetal Alcohol Syndrome (FAS) and/or crack cocaine exposure in utero. I wrote in my journal about this discovery:

> It has come to this has it? Real live "crack babies" in my classroom! I had been waiting for this to happen in some place like New York City or maybe even Atlanta. I thought I would read about it. But I suppose the world stays quiet about the things that embarrass us and that we have no immediate answers for. It doesn't mean it's not happening, it doesn't mean that the subject is not being sensationalized on some TV magazine show, it just means we refuse to admit that the problem is commonplace and with us all the time. It means that we walk beside the problem every day, bumping shoulders with it and never turning to look it directly in the face. Something like elevator etiquette; face forward and don't talk.

* * * * *

We seventh grade girls were all in the school bathroom trying to comb our hair in the bit of mirror each could claim. Connie Woods, the leader of our group said, "Hannah makes me sick bragging about her baby brother all the time. You'd think that is the only thing she could talk about. Why can't she be like Karen?" (I don't know why she found favor with me today, probably because I was in hearing distance unlike poor Hannah.)

"Karen," she said turning to allow me another inch of mirror, "you don't ever talk about your baby sister. How old is she now?" I blushed beet red and answered, "Six months," hoping she would continue attacking some absent class member and stop asking me questions. There was nothing to say.

For Mother's entire pregnancy I had talked of nothing else. The first month or two of my sister's life was the same way. But then I just stopped.

I was nearly 13 when she was born. That fragile year when dolls are permanently stored in the attic. The year I found my skate key had rusted and childhood began to be past tense most of the time. I was NOT ready to leave it. A new baby sister felt like the granted wish of a fairy godmother. A live baby doll to play with and a reason to keep the toys and best loved books on the shelves and out of the attic.

But I wasn't prepared to know HER. I was in love with the idea of it all. She was beautiful. So perfectly formed on the outside. But the fairy godmother turned out to be the tricking kind . . . something was very wrong. This baby sister had seizures that were frightening. She rarely, if ever, made eye contact with me and she never seemed any happier to be with us than with anyone else. But she could sit alone, pull up, and she crawled . . . right past us and the toys we waved in her path to get her attention.

"Well, why don't you talk about her?" My eyes were brimming with tears, I shrugged my shoulders. I hated Connie Woods and I hated Hannah Gallis and her baby brother too. As the tears blurred my square inch of mirror, the bell rang. I couldn't wait for the next bell to ring signaling dismissal, a way out . . . a solitary walk home. I love my baby sister. I do . . . really. Just don't talk about it. Just don't talk about it. It . . . my sister, the end of childhood for me and the beginning of a lifetime of childhood for her. (Journal Entry, October 1993)

I saw the folders before I saw the children. But I had met all three children when they were younger because I had taught their older siblings. But these younger siblings were different. They carried a label, and they were all in the same room — with *me*.

As I looked through Nat's folder, I remembered the first time I met him. He was about three years old the year I taught his sister. I went to visit the family in their home, where I met his mother. She was more like a sister, so young, full of chatter, and truly funny. Nat and the sister I was teaching were both cared for by the grandmother, but she was letting the mother have the conference. We were almost unable to talk together because Nat was all over the place. I asked how old he was, but his mother couldn't remember. She hollered back to her mother, the custodial grandmother, who was staying in the background, "Mama, how old Nat is?" The grandmother was so embarrassed. She must have realized the cover was blown. It was obvious that the grandmother wanted the children's mother to conduct the parent conference; that it wouldn't look right if the mother was a nonparticipating parent. I wondered how many times the grandmother had tried to deny the obvious. *Just don't talk about it. Just don't talk about it.*

I went through the other folders and had the same experiences of flashing back to visits with the families of Rodney and Loretta, of seeing them as very small children. Their brothers and sisters were not without noticeable problems, and I began to reflect on things I had observed in their behavior. I wondered about the time Loretta's brother had a huge scrape on his face and their mother called, so worried that we would think she had hit him. "He is just clumsy," she said, "and that's why I wouldn't get him a bicycle, so he go off on somebody else's bike, and see, he bust up his face!" I remembered Loretta's brother's stoic personality, coupled with his unpredictable outbursts, his perseverance on tasks, and the inconsistency of performance almost minute by minute. Why wasn't I suspicious of something — or was I? *Just don't talk about it. Just don't talk about it.*

I looked at Rodney's huge folder of papers and felt grateful that he had received early intervention. His brother, Michael, was much like Rodney. His face bore the marks of FAS. When his grandmother had come for conferences, I asked about the mother, whom I'd met only once (she had not been sober). "She's fine," the grandmother replied. Michael told me that he was living with "Mother" now, but the grandmother insisted that he did not. Michael claimed to witness domestic violence and repeated numerous anecdotes about his little brother Rodney, who at three years old "couldn't talk but shore can cuss!" The grandmother shook her head and remarked quietly that Michael could "sure tell a tale." Cover. *Just don't talk about it.*

Reflecting further, and trying to understand, I began to see a bit of my own story in the memories of those encounters. I recognized my family in them — not the drugs or the violence, but the pride and the need to keep it ours alone. *Just don't talk about it. Just don't talk about it.*

The day I saw myself in the folders of those children, their labels became less indicting, less formidable. At the same time that their labels grew less important, their personhood grew more important. The drive to get them comfortably contributing to the reading and writing work of our classroom community became paramount.

The day I saw my own middle-class White parents in the faces of these less affluent Black parents, I knew we had made some similar journeys. I recognized the unaddressed fear, I felt the cloak of words around explanations that would seem too raw if told point blank. I felt the accusation in their explanations and answers. "You wouldn't understand" was never spoken aloud, but it bathed every phrase they uttered to me about their children. I did understand, but only in part. I had been the big sister, not the parent. I had been the big sister, not the child who constantly walked into failure and non-acceptance. And I was not Black, never had been, never would be . . . Hold it! Don't talk about that! *Just don't talk about it.*

I know on reflection, and I think I knew then, that I was dealing with more than the obvious problem of the children's specific learning challenges. I was facing the distance between our two cultures in a new way. Somewhere along the way, I came to the realization that I could never fully understand their culture and their families until I understood my own. I could not embrace who they were until I was willing to embrace myself. That meant only one thing: I was going to have to *talk about it.* The journal was the place I talked about it, at first safely and later more painfully.

"Reshaping to Teach" from Memoirs

I am not sure I had "a tacit understanding of how to shape and reshape" my craft to meet the needs of Nat, Rodney, and Loretta, but I did know that I would have to make changes for them. I was looking specifically at how they would approach reading and writing, given the very low expectations expressed in their Individual Education Plans. When I saw them as part of myself, in some measure as part of my own story, my expectations for them rose, as did my ability to reshape my craft for them. I saw them differently, as more than children with thick folders or problem behavior. As I remembered and wrote about my family's dreams for my sister Kathy to become a reader, and her attempts to match her stride to our goals, I developed a new fascination and reverence for the varied ways that children learn to read and write (Dyson, 1986). Writing my memoirs helped me to identify reading and writing problems *in* my students, rather than identifying my students *as* reading and writing problems.

Each of these three children faced a different set of challenges in learning to read. A common problem, however, was their inability to pay attention to the books or games presented to them. The coming together of their physical ability to focus for more than a few moments and their emotional stamina to engage the material without losing control and to understand what I was teaching happened inconsistently and unpredictably. I had to learn to trust the children's natural desire to read. Taking lessons from my memories of Kathy — learning to read, to spell, to count — gave me the patience to wait for the teachable moment and then empowered me to capitalize on it, and kept me from giving up.

Rodney was not able to listen to or look at a book at the beginning of the school year. He especially hated to hear one read aloud. Sitting and listening seemed to cause him such pain that I wondered if the class would ever be able to read without being distracted by his wandering, by his rolling and moaning on the floor.

Remembering how Kathy hated the sound of a book being read gave me patience. I watched Rodney begin to stop and watch us from a distance when we "sang" a book, and one day he asked me to play the "meow-meow song." From those cues, and from remembering my mother setting spelling words to music, I began to sing books to Rodney. He became able to sit and listen, and even to say, "do it again." He was hooked! I reshaped whole-class activities to begin with a song. One of my teaching buddies lent me a set of books of illustrated songs, and the class learned all of them. Eventually I forgot what brought Rodney to join us; we grew accustomed to his presence in the group.

Loretta often wanted to hold and stack books in an apparent effort to possess them. She turned the pages and told her version of the story very quietly, in a whisper. She sat in the reading corner with a baby doll in her lap, looking intently at the pages of books. If someone else came to the reading corner, she carried the stack of books and the baby doll to another spot in the room. It hadn't always been like that. The first week of school she stood in the middle of the room, refusing to make contact with me or with other children during self-directed and small-group activities. However, she was mesmerized by stories the class read aloud together. Later in the week she went to the play area alone and rocked the baby doll until some other children came over. Then she took her spot in the middle of the room again, staring at nothing and daring me to make her move.

I have always thought that rules governing learning/activity centers were important in kindergarten, especially the ones about materials staying where they belong. I expected the books to stay in the book corner, the dolls in the house, and the blocks with the blocks. It makes sense that way, and it teaches order. One day, when Loretta challenged the rule about books remaining in the reading center, I recorded in my journal a memory of how Kathy had challenged a long-standing family rule and reshaped our weekends.

I wrote several journal entries that dealt with my strict Southern Baptist upbringing. We kept the Sabbath holy in many ways, including my parents' refusal to engage in paid-for entertainment on Sunday. That meant no swimming, no movies, no golf, etc. Now, Kathy was a precocious swimmer, mastering the water early. There she excelled, and it was wonderful to see her jumping off the diving board when she was two or three years old. Kathy could make no sense of the Sunday rule: she knew it was hot and she knew it was afternoon, which meant it was time to swim. She was miserable, which meant we were going to be miserable, too. Eventually my mother convinced my father that God surely would take more offense at Kathy's misery than at having the family enjoy each other on the Sabbath. The "no-swimming-on-Sunday" rule was dropped, and the whole family benefited from Kathy's challenge of the established order.

So when Loretta challenged the rule about where the dolls and books belonged in the classroom, I realized I could enforce the rules, or I could celebrate the way she read to her baby doll and change the rule about books staying in the book corner. I changed the rule, and the whole class benefited. Children began to create new places to read and write. The books began to wander to mats at nap time and to places to be "copied" in the children's own notebooks. I followed their lead, and brought big baskets to hold the books, which were now all over the room. The book corner was now only one place where children could read.

Nat was unable at first to pay attention in a large group, but he connected in a small group or with an individual reading to him. He was most drawn to books with "props." On the special days that I brought materials for children to use in telling stories, Nat went straight to the props he wanted to use and then loudly told his stories. One day my mother dropped by after school and saw the animal masks we used as props in telling *The Little Red Hen*. She said that she wished Kathy had been exposed to some of the things she saw happening in my classroom. Over twenty years later, she still had the leftover dream that Kathy could have been taught in a setting where she really belonged. That night in my journal, I didn't write how Kathy had helped me to reach Nat; instead I wrote how Nat had helped me to reach an understanding about Kathy.

The oldest questions about Kathy were feeding the immediacy of my questions about Nat, Rodney, and Loretta. Although I had recorded many connections between lessons learned in my classroom and those with Kathy, it was actually the fact that so much *didn't* work that kept me open to shaping and reshaping the materials of my craft.

I have felt responsible for Kathy all her life, and have had the nauseating experience of people telling us how we ought to handle her. People offered such "helpful" advice as "You *should* just slap her." "I'd knock her through the wall." "She would do that just once to me." Did people really believe that we gave Kathy no structure, no guidance, no counsel? Finding solutions to her behavior consumed us, and my parents spent years pushing aside the thought that Kathy's brain damage was their fault. Writing about that exposed-nerve feeling helped me focus on what I could do for Rodney, Nat, and Loretta, rather than merely blaming their birth circumstances for their problems. Recording stories of people who gave up on Kathy because she was difficult caused me to reexamine what I really expected from my special students.

Facing My Prejudices through My Memoirs

When a child comes to me prelabeled, stamped "lower socioeconomic, African American," how does that affect my expectations for that child? I began asking myself such tough questions as I began to feel burdened by my Whiteness. I was sometimes uncomfortable talking to my African American teaching assistant because I was so carefully trying not to offend him. I wanted to ask him questions, but I was always too careful practicing being "color blind." I wished I were able to talk freely with the African American parents like he did. Writing memories of my earliest encounters with people who were not "like me" caused me to look hard at my unexamined assumptions about Blackness.

Reading Lisa Delpit's (1995) *Other People's Children* made me aware that African American teachers have felt left out of the discourse on literacy education. I had to admit that I was part of what Delpit referred to as a "new prejudice." The legal system may have dispensed with "separate but equal," but we began using words that separate instead, that lower expectations of African American students — "low group," "culturally deprived," "language deficient," and "at risk." These words are different than those used in more segregated times, but they nevertheless leave African American children in a less equal place. Though I tried to deny it, through my writing I had to acknowledge my own place in the problem of racism.

The questions in my journal record some of my painful self-interrogation: How can you teach someone you don't expect to learn? How do you hand a child a piece of paper and tell him to write when you see a less-than-able child before you? How do you talk and partner with parents when you feel so sorry for their plight that you just gloss over their child's struggles? How do you teach a child that you have fallen in love with differently from one that you haven't? How do you hold your own sister's hand through a lesson differently from the way you hold another child's?

In February that year, during our school's celebration of Black History Month, I again experienced the discomfort of reliving civil rights memories differently from my African American colleagues. The following journal entry is an uncomfortable criticism of my own level of denial.

> I guess I always felt, being a child of the 60s, that if I sang the Coca-Cola commercial about teaching "the world to sing in perfect harmony" long enough, I would be an unbiased teacher.
>
> *"I'd like to teach the world . . ."*
> Hadn't I survived being called "nigger-lover" in high school?
> *"To sing in perfect harmony . . ."*
> Didn't I truly believe that all are created equal?
> *"I'd like to buy the world a home . . ."*
> Didn't I say over and over, "all people are the same only their color is different"?
> *"And furnish it with love . . ."*
> I mean, once I was going to be a missionary — to AFRICA! Now aren't they Black?
> *"Buy apple trees and honey bees and snow white turtle doves . . ."*
> Who would dare suggest that I should examine my feelings about race?
> *"It's the real thing . . . what the world wants today . . ."*
> (Journal Entry, February 1995)

* * * * *

We were standing in front of a large mirror playing dress-up at Kay's house.

As we changed from one gaudy outfit after another to try to transform our five year old bodies into something that resembled a starlet we saw our overly made up faces in stark contrast to our bare stark white chests marred only by suntan lines and two brown nipples. In my very southern accent I asked her, "Do colored children have brown ninnies or white ones?"

"Don't have neither one," she responded "'cause they don't make colored children."

"They most certainly do," I said. "Where do you think the grown up ones
come from?"

"Did you ever see a colored child?"

"No-o-o . . . don't guess so . . ."

Kay lived at the jail. Her Daddy was the sheriff. Her great tall house was half
jail and half residence of the sheriff. The court house was next door and the
church right across the alley. . . . The cooks were black women who were called
trustees. A sort of quasi prisoner, gentle as lambs and dressed in green uniforms.
The "nurse" (baby sitter) was also one of these black trustees as was the gardener
and the yard man and a number of others as I remember. Kay and I were allowed
to go into the jail [where] we delivered the plates [of food] and chatted with the
prisoners who were all black and all very nice to us. The doors were not locked
and the men were sitting on their beds playing cards or talking. This particular
day I noticed a man sleeping in a cell toward the back. The Sheriff told us to leave
him alone, "He's not ready to wake up yet. He'll eat later."

"But he's white," I whispered.

"You'll never guess what is down in that jail, Daddy," I said that night. "A
white man. In Jail!! Why are those people in jail Daddy?"

* * * * *

Where were the colored children? Why didn't we see one another and why were
the only colored people I ever saw prisoners? And if prisoners were bad people
what were they doing walking around out of the jail? Was the cook or the woman
who watched us out in the yard once bad but now good? Or did they wind up in
jail by mistake? Would they rather take care of little colored children than us?

Sometime later we began to get Little Rascals on TV. I had confirmation.
There were "colored children." Maybe not here but they were in television land.

* * * * *

"I wish I had me a little colored boy or girl to play with," I ventured to my own
baby sitter one rainy sit-inside day. "The very idea!! Don't be nasty." The look of
shock and disapproval said it all or at least more than I would undo in the next
40 years.

* * * * *

What does it mean to be prejudiced? How does it shape us as teachers of children
from another culture? Could I be operating through messages I logged in early in
my life? Does prejudice inform the way I address these children? Each of them
has a parent currently serving a jail sentence. Each of them live in what John
Ogbu (1977) calls a "caste-like" minority vested with little hope of walking out
of it. Each of us by social design and personal choices are celled off from truly
knowing each other's culture. Prisons can be self made I've come to understand.
(Journal Entry, February 1995)

It is possible that I viewed the ability to read and write in a kind of prisoner-
jailer metaphor, as if freedom and power came from the level of literacy a child had
reached. As a teacher, I hold the knowledge and serve it out my way, at a specified
time, denying the knowledge and history each child brings with them. I perpetuate
a White, middle-class school agenda that continues to sort children by race while

calling it "performance." It is my job to make available the power of the written word to all children. In order to do that I have to scrutinize the ideology of my White-female-southern-middle-class upbringing, to understand ways I may stand in the way of the equal dissemination of that power. If African American children consistently perform less well than their White counterparts in my classroom, could I be the problem?

From the time I learned that "colored children" existed and were brown underneath their shirts, I adamantly denied prejudice in myself. I had addressed the issue of skin pigmentation and I was done with it. But I became painfully aware that the burr of racism attaches to me still in my perceptions of children like Nat, Rodney, and Loretta. Maya Angelou described my feeling: "I envision racism to be like a blanket which sneaks up and covers me at night as I lie sleeping, and each morning when I awake and find it there yet again I must consciously make the effort to pull it off of me" (quoted in McKee, 1988, p. 14).

Through the process of writing in my journal, I made progress in crawling out from under the cover of racism. Accepting my previously unexamined attitudes was an important step in teaching Rodney, Loretta, and Nat. Was I just playing with them? Was I just in love with some romanticized idea left over from my 1960s idealism? Was I ready to accept them for all they were now, and not merely label them as crack babies? Finding answers to some of those questions was a necessary step in my recognizing their parents as coteachers, as partners in the education of their children.

> I had to walk out of my missionary mentality to become a questioning educator. I have addressed children as parts of my job, as pets, as vessels to be filled, as products, and as the little bearers of news from the classroom that would build my reputation in the eyes of their parents. When their parents were prestigious, it mattered more. It hurts me to write those words.   (Journal Entry, Spring 1995)

When I began seriously listening to my life, my teaching life, I also began to listen to my students' lives at a different level. When I looked behind the picture the public saw of my family, I became more tolerant of those who were different from me. When I began to stop and examine the flashes of memory that jolted me, I became a more patient teacher. I more often saw the students and their parents as people; people walking in and out of pain, in and out of joy, in and out of socially constructed prisons.

Examining Choices and Expectations

I saw myself, the teacher, walking in and out of the same pain and joy, and in and out of the same socially constructed alienation. The memoirs I was recording in my journal helped me to sort out, to clarify some of the confused messages I carried with me from my White childhood in the segregated South.

"Mill children," the townspeople had said of my parents, "don't need a good school; after all, they were bred to work the mill. Bunch of lint heads can't learn much beyond the basics." I wanted to be sure I did not make the same assessment of my students, did not have low expectations based on their home circumstances, or on their color. After all, my father failed the fifth grade and barely squeaked by in others. His teachers didn't expect much of him, and he didn't give them much, which makes his Ph.D. all the sweeter now. But, I wonder, how many children believe the negative messages we send?

> *I was standing in front of the mirror in my parents' bedroom while Mother fixed my hair. It was Sunday, and of course we would be going to Mama and Granddaddy's house after church. I thought about Granddaddy.*
> *"How does Granddaddy tie his shoe without his hand?"*
> *"Oh, he can do anything. I've never known him with his hand; he lost it when he was a young boy, working in the mill."*
> *"Lost it?"*
> *"It got cut real bad in a big machine when he was working."*
> *"Then what happened?"*
> *"He had to have it amputated and so the mill offered him a college education or $2000. He took the money because they needed it so bad. See, he couldn't work until his hand healed, so they needed the money."*
> *"Did he do right? Did he take the right thing?"*
> *"Well . . . I don't think he did, but I wasn't there. I don't know everything."*
> *And the far away look was there. The unspoken story about Granddaddy. The words that would stop when I entered the room. Sh-h-h. Just don't talk about it.*

* * * * *

Everybody in our very large family knew that Granddaddy had a drinking problem except me and my siblings. I didn't know until I was an adult. But I knew something was wrong. I could feel it. Low expectations of one who had big dreams. Money constraints that were so big and so socially unalterable that the choice was really not a choice. The money couldn't bring his arm back and it couldn't bring his twin brothers back either. They were much younger, in fact just infants, when he was a young adult. He came home from work one day and found that his mother had allowed them to be adopted. . . . He died in his 70's and the twins had not been mentioned in over fifty years. He wouldn't allow it. Just don't talk about it.

Well, times were different, I've been told. For whom? What do "the times" have to do with poverty? What do "the times" have to do with uninformed choices?

Alcohol was a way out for my granddaddy. Alcohol and crack were a way out for the parents of these children. Stupid choices? Looking for quick money and quick fixes? Surely they realize the fallacy of that thinking. Don't they realize what they've done to their children? All of those questions deserve thought but the people don't deserve condemnation. The bottom line is that I have children to teach who will never be able to walk away physically from the past. I have a grandfather who was never free from the haunting physical reminder of the kind of poverty that allowed children to become maimed and separated from families. (Journal Entry, Spring 1995)

When I looked at the physical deformities in Rodney's hands and feet, I thought of Granddaddy. With fused wrists and shortened fingers, Rodney learned to cut with scissors and paint and write and became the best builder in our community of learners. You see, if Granddaddy could do it with one hand, I was sure Rodney could do it with two, however limited they were.

Symphony: Voices in Context

When my problems with Nat, Loretta, and Rodney were most confusing, an image from my own family often appeared next to my observations of their disturbing behavior. It was easy to see only individuals and forget how they fit into the total "orchestra" of our class. It takes a collection of individual instruments all playing at once, carefully synchronized and interpreted, to make a symphony. Writing my memories of Kathy, Granddaddy, my parents' village, the whole of my living, gave context and meaning to my understanding of the children, my class of "instruments," and helped me hear Nat, Loretta, and Rodney find their place in the "symphony" of my classroom.

References

Beuchner, F. (1991). *Telling secrets.* San Francisco: HarperCollins.

Beuchner, F. (1992). *Clown in the belfry.* San Francisco: HarperCollins.

Calkins, L. (1991). *Living between the lines.* Portsmouth, NH: Heinemann.

Delpit, L. (1995). *Other people's children: Cultural conflict in the classroom.* New York: New Press.

Dyson, A. (1986). Individual differences in beginning composing. *Written Communication, 4,* 411–442.

Emerson, R., Fretz, R., & Shaw, L. (1995). *Writing ethnographic field notes.* Chicago: University of Chicago Press.

Greene, M. (1985). A philosophic look at merit and mastery in teaching. *Elementary School Journal, 86,* 17–26.

LeCompte, M., & Preissle, J. (1993). *Ethnography and qualitative design in educational research* (2nd ed.). San Diego: Academic Press.

McKee, K. (1988). Framing our past and crafting our present. In G. Wolfe (Ed.), *The program for the colored museum* (pp. 18–20). Atlanta: Tom Kepler.

Ogbu, J. (1977). *Minority education and caste.* New York: Academic Press.

I would like to thank Dr. JoBeth Allen for her insistence that I tell my stories and for her willingness to plow through a multitude of manuscripts. Thanks to Betty Shockley Bisplinghoff for calling me a writer.

PART TWO

Outer Worlds:
Beyond the Classroom

Life after Death:
Critical Pedagogy in an
Urban Classroom

J. ALLEYNE JOHNSON

Just as the inner worlds of students and teachers meet in the classroom, the world beyond the classroom often enters into and shapes what happens inside the classroom. In this chapter, J. Alleyne Johnson describes the evolution of her class into one in which the day-to-day realities of students' lives outside the classroom — particularly their encounters with death — are acknowledged and formally addressed as being central to the work of both student and teacher. She explains how her understanding of her teaching has been informed and transformed by a theory known as critical pedagogy. Johnson describes her journey with her students as they move from viewing her, the teacher, as "knowledge giver" to someone who uses the students' own knowledge and experiences as a basis for learning. In her attempt to translate critical pedagogy into practice, she also highlights the impact of violence and death in U.S. society on students' lives, using their life experiences to emphasize this important point. Johnson's experiences also help set the scene for the following chapters by Connell, Britzman, and Bartolomé, who provide theoretical perspectives on many of the issues that Johnson faces in her classroom.

Recently I saw a dead boy. I don't know for sure if he was dead. He looked dead. He laid on the ground in fetal position. Blood oozed from beneath him slowly changing the color of his shirt. I was craning my neck through the car window to see why there were so many policemen on Redding Blvd. when I saw him. Four police cars, lights flashing hysterically, surrounded the stilled body. People were everywhere. I scanned the crowd for any familiar adolescent faces. I wanted to get out of the car and gather with the crowd. I wanted to see if the boy was dead. What happened? Did anyone see? I knew I'd hear about it tomorrow. My students all lived around here. In the hood. It could be family, a homey I saw lying on the ground. I hoped not. It would be hard enough as it was to insist that we get back to the math problems, world history, and lessons in sentence structure for English. (Journal entry, April 18, 1993)

Harvard Educational Review Vol. 65 No. 2 Summer 1995, 213–230

When I wrote the above, I was a teacher of a combined seventh- and eighth-grade "special" class at Brent Junior High School in northern California's East Bay area. I taught social studies, math, English, and physical education during the first four periods of each day. My students' experience with violence and death was one of the first insights they shared with me about their realities of living in, around, or near a poor neighborhood, one not unlike many others in urban areas across the United States.

All of my students know someone who was murdered. One recent death was that of a young man who had attended our school two years earlier. The day after his death, everyone was whispering about it. Although only one person in my class was actually related to this young man, the death was felt personally by many of them. Not only was he a former student, this young man was a "homey," that is, someone from the flatland neighborhood where all of my students — and most of the others who attended Brent — lived. Another student in my class had witnessed the actual shooting. After listening a while to their quiet murmuring, I respectfully asked, "Did someone die?" The young people confirmed the death without giving me the details I had gathered from just listening. I then asked, "When was the funeral?" They responded that it would be that afternoon. They asked me, "Why you ask, are you going?" I replied, "Yes." I introduced my lesson after a brief pause. I waited to hear a reaction to my attending the funeral. None came. I was thinking about the colors I had worn to school that day: a black-and-yellow African print blouse with a bright yellow silk skirt. These were not colors that I would normally wear to a funeral. As I looked down and frowned at my attire, the student who was a relative of the deceased quietly said, "It don't matter what you have on. Anybody who want to come, can come." She had answered my unstated question. I nodded, grateful for the reassurance as I began the world history lesson.

Later that day, in English class, we continued the lesson we had started the day before. I was teaching the students about different kinds of narrative paragraphs and assigned students to construct a first-person narrative. Students had to interview each other and write these paragraphs using the information they collected. From past experience, I knew students liked talking into a microphone, so I used a tape recorder and an outside mike to make the interview process more exciting for them and to enhance the interactive process of the assignment.

I had an interview topic prepared, but I told them they could choose their own. As I moved about the room, I noticed, not surprisingly, that in their interview groups a number of students wanted to discuss the recent death. Salima, the eyewitness to the shooting, ended up being interviewed by Tavia, a classmate whose brother had died in a similar incident a year earlier:

Tavia: On the day that Hasan died, what happened?

Salima: It was a large crowd of people. One of the males had a gun. Everybody start running when he pulled it out, except for Hasan 'cause he didn't have no reason to run. Me and my cousin ran across the street and we watch the shooting of Hasan. He got shot in the stomach and he got up start walking. Then the man shot him in the chest. He got back up start walking. He shot him on the side of the head. He got up start walking. And the man finally shot him in the back of the head and Hasan just laid his coat down like a pillow and he laid his head down on it. He started saying 'bye to everybody cause he knew he was gon' die.

But [then] I didn't hear nothing about it. The story was not printed in the newspaper. Hasan's funeral is October 7, 1992. It was a sad tragedy for a lot of people. I felt bad about it because he was a cool person. He was cool with me.

Tavia: After it happen, did it take long for the ambulance to come?

Salima: Well, the police showed first. Then the ambulance come. I'll tell you like this: I felt like whupping them police A—, you know what. They just stood there, you know, they just stood there for a little while watching him. If it was me, if it was me being a police officer I'd be trying to put him in my police car and try to get him to the hospital so he wouldn't die. He was just a cool person. I don't know why this man shot him and this man got life in jail. If that was me, the judge or the jury, I would kill that M—. You know what? I would kill him 'cause he don't have no reason to take nobody life. 'Cause if he got that gall to take somebody life, I'd take his.

Tavia: But don't you think that if he get killed, if we just kill him, if we kill the people that killing other people, that's all they gon' do. is rest in peace, because they asking God for his forgiveness, we don't know if God gon' forgive them, but all he gon' do is rest in peace like everybody else resting in peace. 'Cause when the world end that's all God gon' look at, is our good side and our bad side. The guy who shot Hasan or whoever shot my brother, their good side probably be filled with good things and their bad side probably be filled with less and you know, they might just be resting in peace. It's good that he is suffering in jail and he gon' think about all what he did. I don't know.

We love him [Hasan] very much and you know we sorry for him to be dead. That's why we making this article like today, 'cause the damn newspaper people ain't doing nothing about it, so you know, we feel real sad about it, you know. We just love him. He gonna rest in peace.

Salima and Tavia finished their interview, but I did not immediately ask for the tape recorder's return. Later, Tavia spoke alone on the interview tape, recording some of her own thoughts about death and dying:

I just feel real sad that he's gone cause everybody's leaving like this. Because my brother died. Like A.B. that went to Harris Junior High. Like my cousin Shawn, Hario. Everybody's just dying like this. I just wish that I could be there for my cousin and everybody else that's gone. But he's going to be resting in peace now and we gon' let him go on and rest in peace. Because we do love him.

A year after the brutal death of her brother, Tavia still misses him and is struggling with the loss of an important influence in her life. Of her own volition, Tavia decided to give personal testimony about the frequency of death in her family and in her neighborhood. I did not know she had done this until I listened to the tape later that day.

Nationwide, nearly seven thousand people between the ages of ten and twenty-four died of gunshot wounds in 1991 ("Bleeding Colors," 1993). People, mostly men, specifically Black men, are being murdered.[1] This rising homicide rate is frequently mentioned in the news, and is usually followed by a more general report on violence, poverty, crime, unsafe neighborhoods. Occasionally, one hears about racism and the political, economic, social, and moral implications of these deaths. Rarely is it reported that someone's father or mother, son or daughter, brother or sister, aunt or uncle has been killed, or that the death has had a traumatic effect on the immediate and extended families. A family's trauma is especially silenced when the dead person was a "wrongdoer," someone who broke the law. Whether someone was a "gangsta" killed by cohorts or police usually receives more attention than whether someone was a "homey" — a friend, a loved one.

This 1993 release by the rap group GETO BOYZ acknowledges the death of all the homies:

> *Another homey got smoked but it's no surprise/ Everybody's trippin' 'cause the boy was too young to die/ A sad sight to see my homey take his last breath/ Everybody's trippin' 'cause they can't accept my homey's death/ Another killing was reported on the evening news/ Somebody's brother got killed behind a pair of shoes/ In the midst of all this shit I think about myself/ Wondering when somebody's gon' try to take me off the shelf.* (© 1993 N-the-Water, Inc., ASCAP; Straight Cash BMI)

The song reiterates the death and familial loss embedded in rising homicide rates in urban areas. It notes the mindless killing that takes place, and the trauma that family members suffer in the wake of personal tragedies. It also notes the questions faced by those in the midst of the violence about their own mortality. Death is at home, in the news, in the culture at large. And death is unquestionably in our schools.

Education: A Matter of Life and Death

> Education as the practice of freedom — as opposed to education as the practice of domination — denies that man is abstract, isolated, independent, and unattached to the world; it also denies that the world exists as a reality apart from men. (Freire, 1989, p. 69)

The purpose of this article is to assert the need to make connections between the day-to-day realities of students' lives and the day-to-day process of teaching and learning that takes place in urban public schools across the United States. In the small city where I lived, we had twenty-one homicides by the middle of 1993. I realized that this homicide rate had an impact on my students' lives and also spoke to societal issues of power and oppression. As such, the need for a critical pedagogy is vital. Henry Giroux (1992) describes critical pedagogy as an educational process that integrates issues of power, history, self-identity, and the possibility of **collective agency**[a] and struggle. In this article, I tell the story of one classroom community in which teacher-student interactions formally addressed and acknowledged death as an important issue in the lives of the students. This acknowledgment enabled the teacher (me) and students together to find power for ourselves in disempowering circumstances through the employment of critical pedagogy. I describe my journey as I came to realize that connecting school knowledge with the students' real-life issues is essential in my classroom.

This article evolves from my concurrent experiences as an urban middle school teacher in northern California and a graduate student at the University of Califor-

---

[a] **Collective agency** is a term from critical pedagogy that describes the work of people acting in concert to understand and change structures that define and support power, history, and oppression.

nia at Berkeley. The privilege of having time to write about my teaching is the result of my experience as a graduate student. In my writing, I struggle to combine several "languages": the language of my students, the language of secondary education teachers and schools, and the language of teachers and writers within the academy. The process of combining and balancing these languages as producers of different but equally important sets of knowledge is integral to my work, and represents the formation of my own critical pedagogy. Giroux (1992) points out that

> critical pedagogy needs a language that allows for competing solidarities and political vocabularies that do not reduce the issues of power, justice, struggle, and inequality to a single script, a master narrative that suppresses the contingent, the historical and the everyday as serious objects of study. (p. 75)

My struggle to combine these languages is also my struggle not to subsume the important issues related to my work. Issues such as the politics of authority and power (between, for example, university researchers and classroom teachers, teachers and students, etc.), class, and the "re-presentation" of race occupy my mind as I write this article.[2] Thus, I have carefully developed a language or re-presentation — written and spoken — that mirrors those languages utilized by my students and the teachers about whom I write. As Ngugi Wa Thiongo (1986) asserts, "From a word, a group of words, a sentence and even a name, one can glean the social norms, attitudes and values of a people" (p. 8).[3] The insistence, pervasive in university settings, on finding one voice, one definitive writing style is problematic in the face of my varied experience. I claim the languages of all those with whom I teach and work and study as a part of my own ethos and in my formation of a critical pedagogy.

Each of these languages speaks volumes on the state of U.S. schools, but unfortunately, conversations combining all three languages are rare. Across the nation, students who are failing or have "failed" at school can tell anyone who will listen why schools "didn't teach them anything." The "failing" students I have met, and their parents, are apt to point out the school's failure to educate all of its children. Practitioners struggle with the frantic rhythm of classrooms, which leaves little time to acknowledge or to record fleeting reflections on the act of teaching. In addition, in universities across the country, graduate teacher-researchers like myself struggle to translate solutions often hidden in convoluted academic writings into daily practice. I hope that this article will illustrate the power found in merging the conversations of the students, of teachers and schools, and of the academy.

Death in U.S. Society

Until recently, most discussions of death in the literature were of an existential nature; death was discussed only in relation to aging, terminal illnesses, or war, as opposed to death as a more general part of life, an everyday occurrence that threatens one's human existence. These limited discussions of death come, in part, from a fear of the inevitability of death (Corr & McNeil, 1986; Kubler-Ross, 1969; Schowalter, 1987). Partly as a way of coping, people subsume the impact of death in rhetoric about ageism, illness, violence, and moral issues. The view of death as oppositional to life, instead of as part of an inevitable, natural progression, makes it a difficult issue to discuss.

Discussions of adolescent death are even more complex and problematic. One significant factor is that the most common causes of adolescent death — suicide, accidents, and homicide — all occur unexpectedly (Schowalter, 1987). In addition to the shock of a loss, surviving adolescents often contend with the inability of the adults around them to discuss death. Audrey Gordon (1986) expands on this idea. She writes that

> at the point where the teen has a personal experience with the death of a signifi-
> cant person, all the [mainstream American] cultural messages about death as dis-
> tant, violent or beautiful are challenged. Nothing in previous experience has pre-
> pared the youth for the feelings of rage, loneliness, guilt and disbelief that
> accompany a personal loss. (p. 22)

For young African American adolescents, the difficulties of dealing with death are even further complicated by the brutal nature of homicide, which is the main cause of Black adolescent death. Furthermore, the literature and media have gener-ated certain perceptions of African American homicide. For instance, newspaper headlines scream: "MAN GUNNED DOWN IN . . . " — a headline that could de-scribe an event in a poor neighborhood in any major U.S. city. Television shows like *Cops, Crime Stories,* and *Hunter* sensationalize such acts of violence. The mu-sic industry commodifies the "romance" of violence frequently, but not only, in rap music.[4]

The response to the increase in deaths by homicide has been a public outcry for increased police surveillance, weaponry, and manpower, as well as prison construc-tion. Embedded in this response is what many scholars identify as a racist notion; that is, that the violence occurring in Black, low-income neighborhoods is entirely the fault of the people in those neighborhoods (Baldwin, 1985; Blackwell, 1985; Brown, 1988; Jordan, 1977; Wilson, 1990; Wright, 1987). Amos Wilson (1990) provides a rich discussion of the racist underpinnings in perceptions of crime and violence in Black communities. He locates this bias in many aspects of crime and violence reporting, from FBI reports to general attitudes and responses toward "crime in the streets," as "an African-American monopoly" (p. 19). Wilson views criminal justice statistics as having much less to do with accurate reports of crime in the United States than with what he sees as a generally held belief about the vio-lence-prone nature of Blacks. He quotes Evan Stark:

> [The] alternative view [to blacks being more violent-prone] is supported by na-
> tional surveys of crime victims, a far more accurate source of information about
> crimes committed than arrest reports. According to the FBI, for example, the pro-
> portion of blacks arrested for aggravated assault in 1987 was more than three
> times greater than the proportion for whites. But the National Crime Survey,
> based on victim interviews, found that the actual proportion of blacks and whites
> committing aggravated assault in 1987 was virtually identical: 32 per 1,000 for
> blacks; 31 per 1,000 for whites. (Stark, 1990, quoted in Wilson, 1990, p. 25)

The tragedy of homicides among Blacks is negated in this suggested framework of crime and violence. Violence becomes the word that both subsumes one event (the tragedy of the victim's death) and qualifies another action (a brutal homicide). In addition, this framework defines the actors as potential menaces to society, thereby undermining any sympathy when lives are taken by an act of violence. As a result, the public feels a macabre sense of relief when it is reported that the "menaces" kill each other.

Death framed as violence begs the question, "Where is the tragedy?" This framework leaves no room to mourn a family member lost to a brutal death. On an even more insidious level, the "violent" framing of African American homicide incriminates both the assassin and the deceased. Looking at death only through a lens of violence generates silence around the issue of this death as loss. Thus, the tragedy and overall impact of death felt by surviving African American adolescents is hidden by mainstream society's inability and unwillingness to deal with the issue of death or with the brutal way most Black adolescents encounter death.

In this harsh light and harsher silence stands the African American adolescent whose friend or loved one was gunned down. There are too few spaces where Salima and Tavia, the students quoted earlier, could deal with their emotions about witnessing a killing of a "cool person" or losing a sibling. Few are the spaces where Tavia could admit that she "just feel real sad that he's [her brother] gone 'cause everybody's leaving like this." Few are the spaces where the two young people can discuss different views of the tragedy. Salima's anger at her friend's death is directed at the policemen — their seeming lack of interest and their failure to act swiftly to save a life. She also expresses anger at the assassin and argues for his death. Tavia sympathizes with her friend, but responds to Salima's wish for vengeance by reminding her that "if we kill the people that killing other people, that's all they gon' do is rest in peace."

Tavia's and Salima's experiences with death reflect those of many African American students from low-income families living in poor neighborhoods across the country. The students at Brent are among these; therefore, I will examine how death entered my classroom. I am not referring to the rise in school crime and violence, but rather the long-term effects of experiencing frequent deaths on teaching and learning in urban classrooms.[5] I will show how I transformed the notions of teacher authority and **legitimated knowledge**[b] within my classroom. Through my approach to teaching and learning, I acknowledged one of the most traumatic life experiences survived by my students — the trauma of death.

Cluster Academy: Another Kind of Death

Brent Junior High School has a population of approximately nine hundred students. In the 1992–1993 school year, 62 percent of the students at Brent were African American. Some of these students are bused from poor neighborhoods of the city to the middle- and upper-class neighborhood where Brent Junior High is located. As these minority students, mostly African Americans, leave the flatlands and come up the hill to the school, they yell greetings, friend to friend, that formerly blended with the morning rhythms of their neighborhoods, but sound harsh in the quiet neighborhood surrounding the school. Nothing affirms their presence in the hill neighborhood, not even their roles as students at the school. As a Black woman ascending the hill, I too feel some sense of displacement, but, unlike them, I ascend the hill to a position of relative power. I am a teacher there.

[b] **Legitimated knowledge** is knowledge that is deemed important by schools, society, or individuals with authority.

In the 1992–1993 school year, the school district received Chapter I funding. With these federal dollars, they created Cluster Academies, which are classes that provide prevention/intervention services for students who have been promoted based on their age or retained in grades seven, eight, or nine. Each junior high school in the district had at least one Cluster Academy class. These classes are allowed to have a maximum of twenty-five students. Brent had only one Cluster class, which I taught. Twenty-one of my students were Black, two were Asian, and one was Mexican.

The general perception at Brent Junior High is that Cluster Academy is "a classroom for bad students" who are labeled "at risk," "learning disabled," "violent," "disruptive," and other debilitating terms, even by their own schoolmates. The general feeling around the school was that students who were placed in Cluster Academy could not function in regular classes, mainly because of "behavioral" problems, secondarily because of academics. My students were, in fact, the ones with the most reported disciplinary and behavioral problems in the school. Prior to being placed in Cluster, the best of these students averaged a C on their report cards, and many had received straight F's. By all of the school's indicators, any attempt to educate these students was hopeless. The Cluster teacher was not expected to make much headway with these students, and the students themselves were very aware of this. I once asked my students to write their perceptions of the school's view of Cluster Academy, and combined their individual responses into the following essay:

How People View Cluster

People look at Cluster as though we do not do anything, we are doomed, all we ever do is play, and we are bad all the time. That's how people look at Cluster. People say that Cluster kids are stupid. It's a class for dummies. Some people think that we are just dumb and just bad. I bet if we let someone from regular classes in for a day they would be shocked. Even a teacher. We do more work than in regular classes. People always pass judgment on each other and for what? Just to put someone down. To me it does not make any sense. Some people talk about the Cluster Kids every day, probably not just students. Maybe teachers. Maybe even the principal talk about us too.

People make it seem like we're those terrible kids. Every time we get sent out of class, they suspend us or give us SAC [suspension alternative class]. Some kids in regular classes are cutting classes and all they get is a note to get back to class. They don't even give the Cluster class a chance in the office. One time [counselor X] suspended me without hearing my side of the story. I think its because I'm in Cluster class. This counselor didn't used to act like that when I was in regular classes.

I think they look over us like we are bums in the street. I'll let them know how I feel about being looked over. I'm not saying that everybody looks over us. I'm saying that its people like [Mr. X (a teacher)] and a whole bunch of kids. I don't like when they say that Cluster is dumb. I get mad and curse and say "You dumb!" but I don't really mean it. I just get mad.[6]

Initially, the call for classes like Cluster Academy came from a desire of policy-makers, school officials, and concerned parents to aid educationally disadvantaged students (Fine, 1991; Levin, 1971; Minow, 1990; Ravitch, 1983). However, clearly the euphemistic title of the class did not impress the students and did not hide the reality of their being framed as a certain type of student by being placed in Cluster Academy class. By perceiving the negative label and the subsequent negative treatment, Cluster students experienced another reality, one that contradicted the original intent of the formation of the class.

It was my challenge, then, to change the Cluster students' negative self-perceptions of the Cluster Academy class and to liberate them from their images as Cluster students. I began to reflect on how other parts of their lives might impact the roles they see for themselves as students. Although there were many times when my students would criticize the way the school community viewed them, their critique was difficult for them to maintain in light of so few school experiences that affirmed their abilities and competencies as students.

It was true that a number of students experienced difficulty in reading and math; difficulties that I now believe were exacerbated by the way teachers "taught" the subjects. For example, I started the year with skills and drills in math because I, to some degree, also bought into the view that students' difficulties were due to their lack of math ability, as opposed to a range of causes, not the least of which might be my presentation of the material and the teaching method. I noticed, however, math in operation on the P.E. field, when students were playing baseball, setting up teams, and keeping score; I saw it in money and candy exchanges and bartering. I decided, therefore, to risk seeing how much of their difficulty with math was contextual and situational, or presentational and procedural, according to classroom norms. I let them take one of the Friday math tests in groups of four students. Some of the test questions were created by the students themselves, submitted in advance. I also included an applied math problem I'd found about setting up a basketball tournament schedule. The students responded well to making up the test questions and to having a problem on a familiar topic that they were interested in.

After this experience, I reflected on how well the students responded to acting as agents in their own learning process. This reflection was the avenue through which the issue of death entered our classroom and the advent of my attempts to transform the structure of education in our classroom. In the process of being "students," these young people might also find power in being themselves: who they were outside the classroom and away from the school.

Death

I first realized how much death was on the minds of these young people when I let them draw during a "rained-out" physical education period. I encouraged them to draw whatever they wanted. I noticed that the letters "R.I.P" were in almost every drawing. In some, "R.I.P" and the name of the person or persons who died comprised the drawing. In others, the words were located in corners or at the bottom of the drawing.

When I had looked at my students' artwork earlier in the year, the drawings didn't appear to me to have anything to do with death or resting in peace. One picture that especially impressed me was a detailed drawing of the artist's neighborhood. In the picture were two tall buildings, each with eighteen squares representing windows. A brick wall adjoined the second building. "R.I.P XIV" was drawn on the wall along with other graffiti. A "gangsta," wearing a XIV's hat ("XIV" is the name of a neighborhood gang), high-top sneakers, and a t-shirt with a marijuana plant on it, sat on the wall. An old car, its tires flat and the back window broken, was parked in front of the wall. Another homey, giving the peace sign, stood in front of the car. I was so impressed by the drawing's detail and depth that "R.I.P" initially seemed like only another detail. Yet as time passed, I noted that "R.I.P" was frequently scratched into the desks, and appeared in the young people's art and on their hats and t-shirts. I then began to acknowledge the presence of death in the classroom.

Later in the semester, my interactions with the students around the death of the former Brent student made it clear that I had to address the issue of death with my students. Something that mattered this much to them and was so prevalent in their thoughts could not be ignored. My challenge was to find a way to deal with death in the classroom.

Paulo Freire's (1989) work offered me ideas to begin the process of negotiating the issue of death in the classroom. Freire's "banking concept" of education critiques teacher-student relationships. The banking concept is the idea that "knowledge is a gift bestowed by those who consider themselves knowledgeable upon those whom they consider to know nothing" (p. 57). He describes the character of the teacher-student relationship as it traditionally operates in public schooling: "This relationship involves a narrative subject (the teacher) and patient, listening objects (the students)" (p. 57). As a person new to the role of teacher, I quickly realized that the burden of conveying specific information to the students is placed on teachers by the structure of the schooling process. In California, for example, there are restrictive curriculum guidelines for every grade level in public schools. Covering all of the topics dictated by the guidelines is virtually impossible, considering the many interruptions that occur daily during school, where students exit and enter the classroom continuously. Neither administrators nor teachers logically expect to complete all of the requirements, yet students are held accountable based on state guidelines as they move from one grade level to the next. The goal of having the students present every day to receive this "gift" of knowledge seems an even more insurmountable task if one acknowledges the many outside disruptions, including those caused by the prevalence of death, in students' lives.

Moreover, Freire questions the relevance of the gift of knowledge to the lives of students. He notes that in using the "banking concept" of education "the contents, whether values or empirical dimensions of reality, tend to become lifeless and petrified. Education is suffering from narrative sickness" (p. 57). The symptom of this sickness in my classroom was the students' response to lifeless, disengaging material, their blank faces staring back as I lectured. No learning was taking place. It became obvious that the superficial nature of teacher as the "giver of knowledge," and students as the "patient," listening receptors needed to be transformed.

At one point, in a desperate attempt to ignite some excitement in my students, I stopped "teaching" and started to talk about possible field trips that might bring to life the importance of the material I presented. The shutters of disinterest on students' faces lifted momentarily. I went on about where we would go, what we would do, and how we would do it. As I paused to catch my breath and rein in my own excitement, one student packed a powerful punch, asking loudly, "Did you ask us?" I was stunned into silence and had no reply. I realized that, as hard as I had tried not to, I had fallen back into the trap of teacher as authoritative knowledge-giver. I had not engaged the students, or asked what they might like to do with my idea. I merely brainstormed in front of them about what *I* thought *they* would find interesting without asking for their input. Not only did I realize my failure to engage students with my curriculum, I also realized that I was ignoring other issues that were occupying their thoughts — such as death and dying — as shown clearly in their art and in the earlier taped interview.

I began to see that education, real education, as Freire states, must begin with a solution to the teacher-student contradiction — where the teacher is the only conveyer of knowledge and the knowledge brought into the classroom by students is unrecognized and negated — by reconciling the poles so that both are simultaneously teachers and students. Once again, my awareness of the importance of death to my students returned to me, but I had no idea where to start: How could I broach the subject? What part of the discussion might be culturally taboo? In what lesson would the discussion fit? How would I grade it? How would I make up the time I would lose in covering "school knowledge" (the curriculum) if I used class time to discuss death? The conflict between teaching a prescribed curriculum and wanting to respond to students' realities became unbearable — and so I sought their help.

Renegotiating Death in the Classroom

We were halfway through the school year, and things were becoming really stale in the classroom. In despair, I wrote and read a letter to my students. The following is an abridged version of the letter:

> Something's happened to me. What happened is that I lost it. I get discouraged trying to teach you. I get caught up in the everyday — giving out referrals, teaching at you, forgetting that I had a bigger picture when I came into the room. There's a certain number of black kids (and the number is growing) that come into schools and just don't make it the way the schools say that you should. They make it in other ways but the school and the teachers do not care. So these kids get placed in classes like Cluster and Opportunity. That's why I chose to teach Cluster. I felt that I could turn things around, that I could prove the school wrong about these kids.
>
> But then I get down here and I get discouraged but this is where I went wrong. I think I know what's best. I bring in all the ideas and just expect you to do them. I stopped asking you what you want to do, what you want to be taught. What do you think will help you the most in the long run? . . . Anyway I propose or put to you that we think of a project or something to end the semester with. My idea is to first get each of you to write about what troubles you the most about your life that you would like to change and then we decide as a class what out of those things we can try to start changing before the semester ends. But we must make a plan *together*. It will take time but I believe that we can do it. Some of the things I thought about are: going to high school next year, dying, getting shot, clothes, sex, parents, brothers and sisters, the police, the hood, gangstas. But I don't know that any of these things are the most important. Whatever we decide, we must also think up a plan.
>
> That was my idea but I truly want to hear yours so that we are doing this together. I recently read this essay that a black student at Clark High wrote. She

wrote that one of her teachers "wallowed over the class like a bowl of jelly." I don't want to do that. I want to interact with you. I won't take people playing the fool, but I want to be sure I let everyone have a say in their education.

Thank you for listening.

The young people did not comment on the letter, except to ask me to read it a second time for the latecomers, and again the next day for the people who had been absent. At first, I thought they only wanted to hear it again because the word "shit" was in it (original version), but then I saw other reasons: I asked for their input, and I acknowledged that I, too, got tired of school every day the way it was.

The process to become a community where knowledge is expected from and acknowledged by all members, although trying at times, is one from which my students and I hoped to extract some value. I was attempting to undo or at least challenge a multiplicity of **hegemonic**[c] processes in the classroom simultaneously. In the weeks after I read my letter to the students, I allotted two English class periods per week to discuss the end-of-semester project. There was a lot of classroom conversation that did not necessarily include me, and I eventually had to "join" with the various groups to have a voice in the discussions.

The class eventually voted to create a newspaper. Students decided that anyone could write as many articles in as many sections as they wanted. I arranged time in one of the school's computer rooms so that students could type in their contributions. The students read and critiqued each others' writing for spelling and grammar. I did not impose any spelling or grammatical rules, but checked with individuals to verify that their use of other than standard English was a personal, informed choice. The first paper took about four weeks to complete, taking up all of their class periods in the last week for final editing changes and production.

The students became very involved in the process; everything started to matter, from how many pages the newspaper would be, to what color paper to use, to how it would be distributed. During the process of constructing the newspaper, I noticed that the students became less afraid of being vulnerable with me and with each other and of challenges they were initially hesitant to face. The writings for the "Special Memories" section brought out a lot of personal and sad exchanges in the classroom. I learned a lot about coping with the stresses of day-to-day living from these young people. They also showed me humor in the worst situations. A camaraderie grew between me and my students that extended into other class periods when we were not working on the paper.

This interaction resulted in the creation of the *Cluster Chronic*. The students decided to share their newspaper with the rest of the school community. In the first year, we distributed two editions and completed a third that was distributed only to members of the class. Creating this newspaper was powerful on many levels. First, I saw a change in how my students felt about Cluster Academy. For example, they decided to include the collaborative essay, "How People View Cluster," adding the following ending paragraph:

It's alright being in Cluster. Some teachers, they woo [say] "Cluster is so nice. They do all their work." This makes me feel very happy. People look at Cluster

---

[c] **Hegemonic** refers to a system that is designed to keep present power structures in place, and supports the oppression of one or more groups by others.

like its a messed up class but its not. It's a good class for me. Who puts on all the shows and do newspapers? Cluster kids are getting talked about because we made a newspaper and no one else did. We did a concert. I don't feel we get enough props [validation] for the things we do at Brent School and that's all I have to say.

Second was the response of the rest of the school community to the newspaper. Cluster students distributed the newspaper during their lunch break to students in the rest of the school. Teachers received any copies that remained. The following excerpts from my field notes illustrate the magic of the moment of distributing the first edition:

> We distributed the newspaper 4th & 5th period lunch to the students of the school. I announced it over the intercom that we were going to be doing this. It was great! The students were reading it. Some had it on their laps, reading it while they ate their lunch. Some were in the lunch line reading it while they waited to go in. GP [a security guard] sat down and read the whole thing. I did not see any papers thrown anywhere although D [the custodian] said that he picked up a few. Ms. M. [a teacher] came into the class for a copy. She said "the kids are all reading it." Ms. S. asked for a copy. Ms. H. [the vice principal] asked for 2 copies to take to the district office.
>
> My kids were walking tall when they distributed the newspaper. At first I kept a few copies for the teachers but the kids kept asking for them to give to other students. I ended up with only two copies for the teachers' room. M. immediately took one up as I put them down.
>
> One English teacher stopped me and told me how she enjoyed the paper. She said that she was an English teacher and she agonized about letting the kids write slang words. She said, "the kids would put slang words into the computer and the spell check would go crazy! Because she was an "English Teacher" the slang words worried her so much. Yet she recognized and appreciated the emotion, the realness in the kids' writing. (Journal entry, April 1993)

The act of creating a newspaper that was widely read by their peers in the school was empowering for the young people.

Finally, the most powerful experience for all of us in writing the newspaper was while revisiting the topic of death. To give respectful mention and remembrance to their loved ones who had died, the young people created a "Special Memories" section in the first edition of the newspaper. There were six articles in this section. In addition, the "Street Life" section, which included opinions on events that occur in students' neighborhoods, had two articles about death. In all, eight contributions in the *Cluster Chronic* discussed death in the young people's lives. Below are three of the eight.

SPECIAL MEMORIES

In Loving Memories

I love my cousin Trevel Jamison
He was one of the best
R.I.P. David Rogan and Hasan Bess

To all the birds we have to feed
Rest in peace Andre Reed
And all the ways we have to go
R.I.P. Gizmo
                    written by Sabrina Brown

James Roberts — Dec. 10, 1974 to Aug. 29, 1991

In loving memories of James Roberts. He attended Clarke and Brent Middle Schools and Sojourner High School. He loved to go fishing and riding around in his car. He was 18 years old when he died. He left us his beloved kids James Jr. and Jamilah. He loved football. He departed this life August 29, 1991. I really do miss him. We had our ups and downs but he still told me what was right from wrong.

I was hurt when my brother left me because he was my mother's only son. Now I don't have a big brother but its going to be all good, because he's going to see me again in the next life. We really do miss him.
                    written by Tavia Keller

STREET LIFE

My Opinion

There are more than two-hundred people getting killed because of gun wars. People are getting shot by mistake. More people should start a crime watch in their neighborhood. Some people are being killed over a word. Sometimes there are fights but mostly threats. A man was beaten to death with a baseball bat because of the part of town he lived in. I think this stuff is wrong because brothers are killing each other and by the year 2000 there will not be enough black men to communicate with.
                    written by Willis Irwin

On the day of the first edition, I made the following field note: "We talked about dying and family. Rodney, me, Damon, and some others said we did not know what we would do if our Moms died" (Journal entry, April 1993). I asked no questions about death, but instead shared my feelings about the subject. This enhanced my relationship with my students, as we acknowledged our whole selves, not only the roles of "student" and "teacher." It was also a relationship where knowledge was not mine alone; everyone gave and everyone received.

As I struggled to deal with death in the classroom, I gained clarity from another teacher's experience, which was less successful than mine. The following tells of this teacher's attempt to negotiate the issue of death without changing the operating norms and behaviors in her classroom, and emphasizes the difficulty of this endeavor as well as its necessity.

Critical Pedagogy: No Teaching as Usual

The day after the funeral of the student mentioned at the beginning of this article, I made copies of the funeral program for the students who had known the deceased but had not attended the service. Another of my students' teachers took one of the funeral programs and copied only the picture of the deceased. The following day, she handed out copies of this picture to her class, asking students to write a letter of condolence to the mother of the deceased.

The young people's reaction was swift. The girl who was related to the deceased screamed obscenities at the teacher, burst into tears, and ran out of the class. Other girls also cursed the teacher as tears fell from their eyes. Paralyzed with confusion, this well-meaning teacher dropped the subject and barely managed to get through the rest of the period. She was still shaken by the experience as she related it to me the next day.

Later, feeling more comfortable with the students after working with them on the first issue of the *Cluster Chronic,* I ventured to ask them what had occurred that day with the other teacher. Their indignation was still apparent in their responses:

She had the nerve to copy his picture on a ditto!

Coral ask her "why you put his picture on a ditto and ask us to write his momma a letter when his momma is having a hard time as it is, you stupid-ass b-t-h?!"

A school ditto! A school activity!

Don't nobody wanna keep feeling those memories!

It's like she making his death a joke.

It seemed that this teacher had assumed she had to "teach" the students how to cope with death. She had assumed the role of "knowledge-giver," and these students were not about to be "told" how to handle death. They coped with death on an almost daily basis. They and their communities were already coping the best way they knew how. These students were not about to compromise a lived experience to the banking concept of knowledge transference. The students' response was passionate, with the intent to hurt and insult the teacher the way they'd perceived themselves to be hurt and insulted. This well-intentioned teacher omitted an important part of the negotiation. She didn't ask them.

Conclusion

Death is one example of students' life experiences that enters the classroom whether a teacher chooses to acknowledge it or not. It is also one of many student experiences that debunk the notion of classroom teaching and education as neutral spaces or endeavors. It is important to find a way, with the help of the young people, to connect teaching in the school with life outside of school and, as Freire suggests, to find space for the emergence of teacher-students and student-teachers.

Although the classroom I share with the young people has come a long way, there are still days when education suffers from "narrative sickness," but now there are twenty-six of us acting as doctors on call, so diagnosis is possible. Cuban and Tyack (1989), who wrote a historical perspective on schools and the students who don't fit them, make two suggestions for policy reform relevant to this discussion. They state that "as hard as it may be to change the school to match the students of an 'imperiled generation,' it is a more promising strategy than trying to fit the student to the school" (p. 29). They propose further "to undertake comprehensive changes that take no features of schools for granted" (p. 29).

Our classroom is now an exciting place where learning and teaching takes place, bringing life to a usually lifeless curriculum. We've become a community of student-teachers and a teacher-student. We are a community of learners. Students have opinions about what they would like to get from their education. I have found that it is important to start from where they are. I ask them.

In this article, I attempted to demonstrate how our class moved from traditional one-way teaching to an interactive teaching and learning environment. I no longer want to acknowledge students only to the extent of how well they fulfill my expectations or their response to a prescribed, petrified curriculum. I believe that it is not effective or responsible to teach on a day-to-day basis as though nothing that happens outside of the school building impacts on the act of teaching. My students were empowered through the acknowledgment of knowledge acquired as a consequence of their lived experiences. They also taught teachers the benefits of respecting students' knowledge and incorporating it into their classroom pedagogy. Whether we as teachers choose to address it or not, students' lives come with them to school, death and other aspects of students' realities come into our classrooms. Instead of wishing for other students, let us gear our work toward the students we have.

Appendix

Following are the three other articles from the *Cluster Chronic* that deal with death.

In Loving Memories of Omont L. Wilson

Omont was a proud young man. He stayed in J.F.K manor. Omont had two brothers by the names of Marvin Wilson and Kiniko Wilson. Omont departed this life a few days after Christmas. He left behind loving memories of what he and his family used to do together. He left behind good and helpful friends that hang inside of "Easter Hill" on South 26th Street. Omont liked to ride bikes with me, Ree-Love, Ghetto "o", and other friends. Omont is badly missed by family and friends. May He Rest In Peace.

written by RJ Johnson

In Loving Memories Willie L. Bowie

On March 20, 1991 Willie L. Bowie departed this life leaving behind two little boys of his own by the names of Kamari and Larry Bowie. His family was badly hurt when they found out this tragedy. R.I.P. B-40.

written by RJ Johnson

In Loving Memories — Dameion D. West

In loving memories of Dameion. I love him from the bottom of my heart. He means something to me more than some of the other people I know. I know and you know that Dameion was a young, Black, intelligent teenager. Before he got laid in his grave he came over to my house and kissed my momma and everything, and then the next day his first cousin came over to my house and told my momma that Dameion just got killed. He said that he was out there fighting with his friend and his friend got beat up. After the fight was over the boy told Dameion that he was going to get killed. At the time Dameion wasn't tripping, because as I said before, Dameion was a young, loving Black boy. That boy just looked back and shot him. I'm glad that Dameion didn't have any kids because now they would be without a father and that's not what we want. Everyone needs a father, especially these little kids nowadays that don't have a mother, so you know they need a father.

written by Coral Wilson

Notes

1. See Wideman and Wideman (1984); McCall (1991); Blackwell (1985).
2. The writing of "re-presentation" in this way is a political act — creating an awareness of the politics of identity formation, particularly with regard to race, in the U.S. social context.
3. Ngugi's (1986) comment refers specifically to African culture, but language as the most powerful bearer of a culture has been posited by social scientists for centuries. See DuBois (1961); hooks (1989); Smitherman (1986); Sanchez (1970); and Bernstein (1971).
4. Rappers like Ice Cube, Too Short, Ice-T, and NWA (Niggas with a Attitude) made their mark on the music industry with a particular discourse of violence in their music. The irony of death in the African American community is sometimes played out in different songs from the same album. For instance, the GETO BOYZ's poignant rendering of death as a loss of a life in "Six Feet Deep" is followed by a rap tale justifying the murder of a Black woman.
5. For a critique of the impact of school crime and violence in urban schools, see Comer (1980).
6. The students who wrote this essay are Sabrina Brown, Kevin Henderson, James Porter, Danny Simpson, Coral Wilson, Rodney Walker, Stacey Willis, RJ Johnson ("Rodney" in the text), and Damon Marshall.

References

Baldwin, J. (1985). *The evidence of things not seen.* New York: Henry Holt.

Bernstein, B. (1971). *Class, codes and control.* New York: Schocken Press.

Bleeding Colors. (1993, September 26). *West County Times* [Special Report], pp. 1–18.

Blackwell, J. E. (1985). *The Black community: Diversity and unity.* New York: Harper & Row.

Brown, R. L. (1988). *The state of Black America.* New York: National Urban League.

Comer, J. (1980). *School power: Implications of an intervention project.* New York: Free Press.

Corr, C. A., & McNeil, J. N. (Eds.). (1986). *Adolescence and death.* New York: Springer.

Cuban, L., & Tyack, D. (1989). *Mismatch: Historical perspectives on schools and students that don't fit them.* Unpublished manuscript.

DuBois, W. E. B. (1961). *Souls of Black folk.* Greenwich, CT: Fawcett.

Fine, M. (1991). *Framing dropouts: Notes on the politics of an urban public high school.* Albany: State University of New York Press.

Freire P. (1989). *Pedagogy of the oppressed.* New York: Continuum.

Giroux, H. A. (1992). *Border crossings: Cultural workers and the politics of education.* New York: Routledge.

Gordon, A. K. (1986). The tattered cloak of immortality. In C. A. Corr & J. N. McNeil (Eds.), *Adolescence and death* (pp. 16–31). New York: Springer.

hooks, b. (1989). *Talking back: Thinking feminist, thinking Black.* Boston: South End Press.

Jordan, W. D. (1977). *White over Black: American attitudes toward the Negro, 1550–1812.* Chapel Hill: University of North Carolina Press.

Kubler-Ross, E. (1969). *On death and dying.* New York: Macmillan.

Levin, H. (1971). A decade of policy developments in improving education and training for low-income populations. In R. Herman (Ed.), *A decade of federal anti-poverty programs* (pp. 123–188). New York: Academic Press.

McCall, N. (1991, January 13). Dispatches from a dying generation. *Washington Post,* p. C1.

Minow, M. (1990). *Making all the difference: Inclusion, exclusion and American law.* New York: Cornell University Press.

Ngugi, W. T. (1986). *Decolonising the mind: The politics of language in African literature.* London: James Currey.

Ravitch, D. (1983). *The troubled crusade: American education 1945–1980.* New York: Basic Books.

Schowalter, J. E. (1987). Adolescents' concepts of death and how these can kill them. In J. E. Schowalter, P. Bushman, P. R. Patterson, A. H. Kutscher, M. Tallmer, & R. G. Stevenson (Eds.), *Children and death: Perspectives from birth through adolescence.* New York: Praeger.

Smitherman, G. (1986). *Talkin and testifyin: The language of Black America.* Detroit: Wayne State University Press.

Wideman, J. E., & Wideman, R. D. (1984). *Brothers and keepers.* New York: Henry Holt.

Wilson, A. N. (1990) *Black-on-Black violence: The psychodynamics of Black self-annihilation in service of White domination.* New York: Afrikan World Infosystems.

Wright, J. B. (1987). *Black robes, White justice.* Secaucus, NJ: L. Stuart.

Poverty and Education

R. W. CONNELL

One of the issues in the outer world that affects what goes on in the classroom is the issue of poverty. In this chapter, R. W. Connell examines the schooling of children who live in poverty. He demonstrates how compensatory programs may reinforce the very patterns of inequality that they were designed to counter, in that they function within existing institutions that force children to compete on a playing field with unequal resources. At the core of this conflict is a socially biased curriculum that controls teachers' work in favor of the status quo. Connell argues that changing the industrial conditions of teachers' work is central to addressing these issues of poverty and education because teachers are the workers most strategically placed to affect the relationship between poor children and schools. He further suggests that the accumulated practical experience of teachers and parents with children in poverty is essential to successful reform, and asserts that targeted programs are unlikely to have a major impact on poverty unless teachers and parents are part of a broader agenda for social reform. These larger insights into how poverty affects schooling are necessary to understand even part of the classroom struggles described by Johnson, Stumbo, and Moses in their chapters — struggles that are faced by thousands of other teachers every day in their own classrooms.

How schools address poverty is an important test of an education system. Children from poor families are, generally speaking, the least successful by conventional measures and the hardest to teach by traditional methods. They are the least powerful of the schools' clients, the least able to enforce their claims or insist that their needs be met, yet the most dependent on schools for their educational resources.

Since modern school systems persistently do fail children in poverty, a sense of outrage runs through much educational writing about disadvantage. Several authors have recently added a note of urgency to this discussion. Natriello, McDill, and Pallas (1990) give their survey of U.S. practice the subtitle, "Racing against Catastrophe." Kozol's (1991) book, *Savage Inequalities*, presents an even bleaker portrait of willful neglect and deepening tragedy. Korbin (1992) speaks of the "devastation" of children in the United States. This note has also been heard outside education in discussions of the urban "underclass" and is given strength by the 1992 violence in Los Angeles and the rise of neo-fascism in Europe.

Harvard Educational Review Vol. 64 No. 2 Summer 1994, 125–149

In its first year, the Clinton administration signaled no sharp break from the educational policies of the 1980s. But Clinton's election has created a political space in the United States for reconsidering compensatory programs, which were already gaining renewed support after a period of skepticism and narrowed horizons.[1] The secretary of education speaks, for instance, of a "revolutionary" plan for "reinventing" Chapter I, the major U.S. compensatory program (Riley, 1994). Rhetoric aside, there is certainly a need to rethink the underlying logic of compensatory programs, which have not changed in their basic design and political justification, either in the United States or in other countries, since the 1960s. Meanwhile, child poverty has grown dramatically, and the difficulties faced by some parts of the school system have reached crisis proportions.

Such rethinking can draw on two assets that were not available in the 1960s. The first is the accumulated practical experience of teachers and parents with compensatory programs. A great fund of such experience is found outside the United States, which Weinberg (1981) has documented in a vast "world bibliography." A more international perspective can help one to see both the deeper roots of the problems and a broader range of responses; however, participants in the debate in the United States rarely consider it.

The second asset is a much more sophisticated sociology of education. In discussion of how inequalities are produced, the focus has gradually shifted from the characteristics of the disadvantaged to the institutional character of school systems and the cultural processes that occur in them. Compensatory programs cannot be reinvented in isolation; the rethinking leads us inevitably to larger questions about education.

Education used to be represented in political rhetoric as a panacea for poverty. This is now rare, but education for the poor is still an arena for confident pronouncements by many economists and businesspeople, welfare specialists, and political and cultural entrepreneurs of various persuasions — some of whom are startlingly naive about the educational effects of what they propose. I hope to show that teachers' experience and educational reasoning are central to a strategy for reconstruction.

The purposes of this article are to question the social and educational assumptions behind the general design of compensatory programs; to propose an alternative way of thinking about the education of children in poverty, drawn from current practice and social research; and to explore some broad questions about the strategy of reform this rethinking implies. My focus is on the educational systems of industrialized, predominantly English-speaking, liberal-capitalist states (Australia, Britain, Canada, and the United States), though in broad outline the argument should also apply to other countries with comparable economic and political systems.

Poverties and Programs

"Poverty" is not a single thing, nor a simple concept. On a world scale, distinctly different situations are embraced in the term. MacPherson (1987) speaks of five hundred million children living in poverty in developing countries, most in rural settings. The quality of the schooling that reaches them is debated; Avalos (1992), for example, argues that the formal pedagogy conventional in their schools is profoundly inappropriate. Poverty in agricultural villages is different from poverty in the explosively growing cities, from Mexico City to Port Moresby, that now dominate the politics of the developing world. It was in the context of migration into such urban settings that Lewis (1968) formulated the idea of a "culture of poverty," which has had a profound effect on compensatory education in wealthy countries.

In industrial capitalist countries with high average incomes, poverty is the effect of unequal distribution, rather than the effect of absolute level of resources. Even in these countries, welfare researchers have pointed to the diversity of situations. As early as 1962, in *The Other America,* Harrington distinguished the aged, minorities, agricultural workers, and industrial rejects as belonging to different "subcultures of poverty." Such complexity is reemphasized in more recent and more systematic welfare research (for example, Devine & Wright, 1993).

There is complexity in two senses. The first lies in the very definition of poverty. Low incomes are part of everyone's concept of poverty, but incomes vary in character as well as amount: some are regular and others are intermittent; some are paid all in money and some are partly "in kind"; some are shared in a household (or a wider group) and some are individual. Further, people's economic situations depend on what they own, as well as on their current incomes. The distribution of wealth is known to be markedly more unequal than the distribution of income, so a simple income measure of poverty is likely to underestimate the severity or extent of deprivation. Further, there are other types of resources beyond income and wealth that cannot be cashed out on an individual basis, but where inequality is materially significant: for example, access to public institutions such as libraries, colleges, and hospitals; to public utilities; and to safety and community health.

Official statisticians generally throw up their hands at this complexity, and settle for a single index that allows a "poverty line" to be drawn. The most widely used is an austere income-based poverty line adopted in the United States in 1964 (based on earlier government calculations about emergency food needs for families), and subsequently applied in other countries. The great virtue of a poverty-line approach is that it allows a straightforward calculation of the number of people living in poverty. For example, in 1991 the United States counted fourteen million children in poverty (U.S. Bureau of the Census, 1992); extrapolating to the industrial capitalist countries as a group (United Nations Development Programme, 1992), we might estimate they have about thirty-five million children in poverty, which might be regarded as the potential target group for compensatory education.[2] The great disadvantages of the poverty-line approach are that it ignores important dimensions of deprivation and inequality and that it readily leads to political misperceptions of poverty, as I explain below.

The second aspect of complexity is that economic deprivation, however defined, is shared by people who are very different in other respects. Ethnic background is far from homogeneous. The poverty of indigenous peoples, still grappling with the consequences of invasion and colonization, is different from the poverty of recent immigrant groups. Political debate on poverty in the United States mainly addresses African-American urban "ghettos," but the majority of the people marked off by the poverty line in the United States are White. In a disadvantaged inner-city Australian school, there may be ten or twelve languages spoken on the playground. Further, poor people are not all of one gender. To note this is not merely to say we must count women as well as men. As with race relations, gender relations affect the creation of poverty and affect people's responses to poverty. Thus, women's overall economic disadvantage vis-à-vis men shapes the demography of poverty: female-headed households have higher poverty rates than male-headed households. The ways children and teenagers deal with gender affect their schooling. This is a familiar general point (Thorne, 1993). It should not be forgotten that it applies to children and teenagers in poverty; for both girls and boys, gender relations shape their difficult relationships with their schools (Anderson, 1991; Walker, 1988).

Schooling designed specifically for the poor dates back to the charity schools of the eighteenth century, and to the ragged schools of the nineteenth century that were established to tame the children of "the perishing and dangerous classes" (Clark, 1977). Modern compensatory programs date from the 1960s and have a specific history. Earlier in this century, most educational systems were sharply and deliberately stratified: they were segregated by race, by gender, and by class; tracked into academic and technical schools; divided among public and private, Protestant and Catholic. A series of social movements expended enormous energy to desegregate schools, establish comprehensive secondary systems, and open universities to excluded groups. As a result of this pressure, the expanding educational systems of the mid-century generally became more accessible. The idea of education as a right, which was crystallized in the 1959 United Nations Declaration of the Rights of the Child, was interpreted internationally as implying equal access to education (with notable exceptions like South Africa).

Yet equal access was only half a victory. Children from working-class, poor, and minority ethnic families continued to do worse than children from rich and middle-class families on tests and examinations, were more likely to be held back in grade, to drop out of school earlier, and were much less likely to enter college or university (for example, Curtis, Livingstone, & Smaller, 1992; Davis, 1948). Documenting this *informal* segregation within formally unsegregated institutions was the main preoccupation of educational sociology in the 1950s and 1960s. A mass of evidence built up, ranging from national surveys like the 1966 Coleman Report in the United States (see his retrospective account in Coleman, 1990) to case studies like Ford's (1969) *Social Class and the Comprehensive School* in Britain. The evidence of socially unequal outcomes continues to mount; it is one of the most firmly established facts about Western-style educational systems in all parts of the world.

Compensatory education programs were designed in response to this specific historical situation: that is, the failure of postwar educational expansion, despite its principle of equal access, to deliver substantive equality. The educational movement occurred within a broader context of social welfare reform. In the United States, the civil rights movement, the rediscovery of poverty by the intellectuals, and the political strategies of the Kennedy and Johnson administrations led to the War on Poverty. Its main designers were welfare economists, and its main success was the reduction of poverty among the elderly — not among children (Katz, 1989).

Education was brought into the welfare picture through the correlation between lower levels of education on the one side, and higher rates of unemployment and lower wages on the other. The idea of a self-sustaining "cycle of poverty" emerged, where low aspirations and poor support for children led to low educational achievement, which in turn led to labor market failure and poverty in the next generation. Compensatory education was seen as a means to break into this cycle and derail the inheritance of poverty.[3] Thus the failure of equal access was read outward from the institutions to the families they served. Families and children became the bearers of a deficit for which the institutions should compensate. This maneuver protected conventional beliefs about schooling; indeed, a wave of optimism about the power of schooling and early childhood intervention accompanied the birth of compensatory education.

With this rationale, publicly funded programs were set up in the 1960s and 1970s in a number of wealthy countries, starting with the United States and including Britain, the Netherlands, and Australia.[4] While the details of these programs vary from country to country, they do have major design elements in common. They are "targeted" to a minority of children.[5] They select children or their schools by formulae involving a poverty-line calculation. They are intended to compensate for disadvantage by enriching the children's educational environment, which they do by grafting something onto the existing school and pre-school system. And, finally, they are generally administered separately from conventional school funding.

The False Map of the Problem

The circumstances of the birth of compensatory programs and the political means by which some have survived — not all did — produced a false map of the problem. By this I mean a set of assumptions that govern policy and public discussion but are factually wrong, doubtful, or profoundly misleading. Three are central: that the problem concerns only a disadvantaged minority; that the poor are distinct from the majority in culture or attitudes; and that correcting disadvantage in education is a technical problem requiring, above all, the application of research-based expertise.

The Disadvantaged Minority

The image of a disadvantaged minority is built into compensatory education via the poverty line by which target groups are identified. Whatever the formulae used to measure disadvantage (they vary from country to country, from state to state, and from time to time, with a running controversy over the method), the procedure always involves drawing a cut-off line at some point on a dimension of advantage and disadvantage. Where the cut-off comes is fundamentally arbitrary. This is a familiar problem with defining poverty lines. In compensatory programs, determining the cut-off point leads to unending dispute over which children or schools should be on the list for funds. The procedure could label 50 percent of the population "disadvantaged" as logically as it could 10 percent or 20 percent. In practice, however, the cut-off point is always placed so as to indicate a modest-sized minority. This demarcation is credible because of the already existing political imagery of poverty, in which the poor are pictured as a minority outside mainstream society.[6] The policy implication is that the other 80 or 90 percent, the mainstream, are all on the same footing.

However, this is not what the evidence shows. Regardless of which measures of class inequality and educational outcomes are used, gradients of advantage and disadvantage typically appear across the school population as a whole (for one example among hundreds, see Williams, 1987). We can identify an exceptionally advantaged minority as well as an exceptionally disadvantaged one, but focusing on either extreme is insufficient. The fundamental point is that class inequality is a problem that concerns the school system *as a whole*. Poor children are not facing a separate problem. They face the worst effects of a larger pattern.

The Distinctiveness of the Poor

That the poor are not like the rest of us is a traditional belief of the affluent. This belief affected the design of compensatory education mainly through the "culture of poverty" thesis, in which the reproduction of poverty from one generation to another was attributed to the cultural adaptations poor people made to their circumstances (Lewis, 1968; for a later review, see Hoyles, 1977).

Though framed within the discourse of anthropology, this idea was immediately given a psychological twist. Cultural difference in the group meant psychological deficit in the individual; that is, a lack of the traits needed to succeed in school. With this twist, a very wide range of research could be read as demonstrating cultural deprivation, from studies of linguistic codes to occupational expectations to achievement motivation to IQ, and so on. In the 1960s and 1970s, the cultural deficit concept became folklore among teachers as well as policymakers (Interim Committee for the Australian Schools Commission, 1973; Ryan, 1971).

It was this tendency to reduce arguments about different situations to the idea of a cultural deficit that Bernstein (1974) protested against in a famous critique of compensatory education. Culture-of-poverty ideas were strongly criticized by anthropologists, linguists, and teachers, not to mention poor people themselves; yet these ideas have had tremendous resilience, persisting through two decades of changing rhetoric, as Griffin (1993) has recently shown in a detailed survey of youth research. The ideas survive partly because they have become the organic ideology of compensatory and special education programs. The very existence of such programs now evokes the rationale of deficit, as Casanova (1990) illustrates in heartbreaking case studies of two Latino children in a U.S. school system: battered by the system's languages policy, inserted into "special education" programs — with mandated, rigid, teacher-centered methods — these children's education was massively disrupted and their social selves assaulted with labels like "learning-disabled." More broadly, deficit ideas also survive because they fit comfortably into wider ideologies of race and class difference.

But the facts of the matter do not require us to adopt cultural deficit concepts. The bulk of evidence points to cultural *similarity* between the poorest groups and the less poor. This might be expected from facts about the demography of poverty not widely known to educators. Studies such as the U.S. Panel Study of Income Dynamics (PSID), which has followed the same families since 1968, show large numbers of families moving into and out of poverty (as measured by the poverty-line approach). Over a twenty-year period, nearly 40 percent of the families in the PSID spent some period in poverty, when the rate of poverty in any one year was only 11 percent to 15 percent (Devine & Wright, 1993). We should, then, expect those in poverty at any one time to have a lot in common with the broader working class, including their relations with schools. For example, attitude surveys produce little evidence that the poor lack other people's interest in education or in children (for a recent example in England, see Heath, 1992).

In the United States, the argument over cultural deficit has been refocused by the concept of the "underclass," which is defined as inhabitants of urban centers marked by massive unemployment, environmental decay, high numbers of births to single mothers, community violence, and the presence of the drug trade. It is clear that the most severe concentrations of poverty have the most severe impact on education (for statistical evidence, see Orland, 1990). Ethnographies in inner-city settings (Anderson, 1991) and in communities of the rural poor (Heath, 1983) show ways of life that do not mesh with the practices of mainstream schooling. Ogbu's (1988) argument that this bad mesh has roots in the history of imperialism, with "involuntary minorities" such as conquered indigenous peoples and enslaved labor forces resisting the institutions of White supremacy, is attractive.

But ethnography may not be the best guide to this issue. As a research method, it assumes the coherence of the group being studied, and ethnographic writing understandably tends to emphasize what is unique or distinctive about its subjects' way of life. We must counterbalance this by considering the interplay and interconnection of poor people with other groups. The cultural inventiveness of poor people (including the American "underclass") and their interplay with wider popular culture is hardly to be denied — witness music from jazz to rap, New Wave rock, punk fashion, contemporary street styles, and so on. And, further, close-focus research on schooling using interviews and participant observation documents a vigorous desire for education among poor people and ethnic minorities (for example, Wexler, 1992, from the United States; Angus, 1993, from Australia). Yet there is massive educational failure. Something is malfunctioning, but it is hardly the culture of the poor.

The Nature of Reform

The belief that educational reform is, above all, a technical question, a matter of assembling the research and deducing the best interventions, is embedded in the education world through the very hierarchy of teaching institutions. At the apex of this hierarchy are the universities, which both produce education research and train administrators for the schools in education studies programs. The dominant ideology in education studies is positivist. The 1966 Coleman Report (Coleman, 1990) was a monument to technocratic[a] policy research, and the "effective schools" and national testing movements continue to promote the belief that quantitative research will generate good policy more or less automatically. Teachers are defined within this framework as receiving guidance from educational science, rather than as producing fundamental knowledge themselves. The structure of educational funding in federal systems, where local institutions provide bread-and-butter school finance while higher level institutions fund policy innovation, further encourages a view of school reform as based on outside expertise.

While these are general conditions in educational policymaking, their effect on policy about poverty is especially strong. The poor are precisely the group with the

[a] **Technocratic** is a term that refers to governance by (or reliance on) methods and technology, rather than by values and ideology.

least resources and the least capacity to contest the views of policymaking elites. Social movements of the poor can win concessions, but only by widespread mobilization and social disruption, as shown in the classic study by Piven and Cloward (1979). Mobilization and disruption do not generally develop around the education of the poor.

As a consequence, policy discussions about education and poverty have frequently been conducted in the absence of the two groups most likely to understand the issues: poor people themselves and the teachers in their schools. A striking example is the 1986 conference held by the U.S. Department of Education to reconsider Chapter I programs, which was entirely composed of academics, administrators, and policy analysts (Doyle & Cooper, 1988). Teachers are expected to implement policies, but not to make them, while poor people are defined as the objects of policy interventions rather than as the authors of social change.

The broad effect of this "map" of the issues has been to locate the problem in the heads of the poor and in the errors of the particular schools serving them. Meanwhile, the virtues of other schools are taken for granted. The consequences of this policy, as Natriello et al. (1990) have perceptively pointed out, has been an oscillation among strategies of intervention that are mostly technocratic, all narrowly focused, all within a context of massive underfunding, and none making a great difference to the situation.

Re-Mapping the Issues

What can we offer instead — "we" meaning researchers, teacher educators, students, and administrators, the typical audience for academic journals in education? We cannot continue to offer what we usually do: proposals for fresh, expert interventions and for more research to support them. The exemplary research by Snow, Barnes, Chandler, Goodman, and Hemphill (1991) shows the limits that have been reached by this approach. This careful and compassionate study, which sought practical lessons for literacy teaching by comparing good and bad readers among poor children in a U.S. city, found on returning four years later that hopeful differences were overwhelmed by what one can only read as the structural consequences of poverty. The enrichments these researchers proposed certainly improved the children's quality of life, but they were not capable of altering the forces shaping the children's educational fates.

There are no great surprises in the research on poverty and education, no secret keys that will unlock the solution. If there is a mystery, it is the kind that Sartre (1958) called a "mystery in broad daylight," an un-knowing created by the way we frame and use our knowledge. Descriptive research on poor children by psychologists, sociologists, and educators will certainly continue — spiced by occasional claims from biologists to have found the gene for school failure. But that kind of research is no longer decisive. What we need, above all, is a rethinking of the pattern of policy, a reexamination of the way the issues have been configured.

This rethinking should start with the theme that comes through insistently when poor people talk about education: power. This issue leads to the institutional form of mass education, the politics of the curriculum, and the character of teachers' work. I develop each of these themes in the discussion that follows.

Power

Educators are uncomfortable with the language of power; to talk of "disadvantage" is easier. But schools are literally power-full institutions. Public schools exercise power, both in the general compulsion to attend and in the particular decisions they make. School grades, for instance, are not just aids to teaching. They are also tiny judicial decisions with legal status, which cumulate into large authoritative decisions about people's lives — progression in school, selection into higher education, employment prospects.

Poor people, like the rest of the working class, by and large understand this feature of schools. It is central to their more dire experiences of education. An example is Wexler's (1992) description of students' experiences at Washington High, where tardiness is policed by an intrusive patrolling of corridors, leading to the bureaucratic processing of students for expulsion.

Once again we must recognize that what students in poverty experience is not unique. Mass schooling systems were created in the nineteenth century as state intervention into working-class life, to regulate and partly take over the rearing of children. Legal compulsion was needed because this intervention was widely resisted.

From this history, public schools and their working-class clientele inherit a deeply ambivalent relationship. On the one hand, the school embodies state power; hence the most common complaint from parents and students is about teachers who "don't care" but cannot be made to change. On the other hand, the school system has become the main bearer of working-class hopes for a better future, especially where the hopes of unionism or socialism have died. Hence the dilemma, poignantly described by Lareau (1987), of working-class parents who want educational advancement for their children but cannot deploy the techniques or resources called for by the school. The extent to which school routines presuppose a gender pattern based on a certain level of affluence, the unpaid labor of a mother/housewife is particularly noteworthy.

Dealing with powerful institutions requires power. Some of the resources that families need to handle contemporary schools are the bread and butter of positivist research on children: adequate food, physical security, attention from helpful adults, books in the home, scholastic know-how in the family, and so on. Generally absent from positivist research (because they are hard to quantify as attributes of a person) are the collective resources that produce the kind of school system that favors a particular home environment for success. These resources are put into play when property owners cap taxes supporting public schools; or when university faculty dominate curriculum boards and corporations create textbooks; or when the professional parents at an upper income school meet with routine responsiveness from principal and teachers.

In the false map already discussed, poverty is constantly taken as the sign of something else, such as cultural difference, or psychological or genetic deficit. Educators need to be more blunt and see poverty as poverty. Poor people are short of resources, individually and jointly, including many of the resources that are deployed in education. The scale of material shortages is easily shown. For instance, an Australian study of household expenditure in families with dependent children found high-income couples spending an average of $8.82 per week on books and periodicals, while sole-parent pensioners (roughly equivalent to AFDC recipients in the United States) spent $2.06 (Whiteford, Bradbury, & Saunders, 1989).

Such differences in income and expenditure, not to mention the greater inequalities of wealth, mean both shortages of resources in the home and vulnerability to institutional power — such as derogatory labeling in the welfare system and streaming or tracking in the education system. There is no mystery about this to poor people. As an activist in a Canadian immigrant women's group put it:

> Streaming of low income, immigrant children is obvious. More well-to-do parents make sure their children are directed in the proper direction, they have much more pro-active involvement in the school system. Poor working-class families don't have the time or the wherewithal to fight. (quoted in Curtis et al., 1992, p. 23)

Poverty and alienation are likely to mean material disruptions of life, one of the points emphatically made in the "underclass" discussion. Disruptions can also be seen outside the United States: witness Robins and Cohen's *Knuckle Sandwich* (1978), about youth and violence in England, and Embling's look at *Fragmented Lives* (1986) in Australia. We do not need to assume cultural difference to understand the damaging effects of poverty on young people's lives. We certainly need to think carefully about power in order to understand the violence that has long been an undercurrent in schools for the urban poor, and which has taken a dramatic turn with the advent of guns in U.S. high schools.

Serious violence is more common from boys than from girls, not because of their hormones, but because Western masculinities are socially constructed around claims to power. Where this claim is made with few resources except physical force, and where boys have been habitually disciplined by force, "trouble" in the form of violence is eminently likely. A familiar course of events frequently develops in which boys' masculinity comes to be defined or tested in their conflict with the state power embodied in the school, a conflict that can turn violent. Losing this conflict, which is inevitable, is likely to end the boys' formal education.[7] The power relations of gender thus play out paradoxically in a context of poverty. To grapple with such a process means directly addressing the politics of masculinity — an issue, as Yates (1993) notes at the end of her review of the education of girls, still absent from educational agendas.

The School as an Institution

The young people who fight the school and find themselves bounced out on the street are meeting more than the anger of particular teachers and principals. They are facing the logic of an institution embodying the power of the state and the cultural authority of the dominant class. Fine's (1991) study of a New York inner-city school shows the dull bureaucratic rationality of encouraging students to drop out. In a school facing great difficulties in teaching and establishing its legitimacy, and with no prospect of getting the resources it needs or a change in its working methods, "discharge" of a student becomes the routine solution to a wide range of problems.

The role of institutional power in shaping pupil-teacher interactions has been clear in close-focus studies of schools for some time. It was vividly portrayed, for instance, in Corrigan's (1979) study of the struggle for control in two schools in a declining industrial area of England. What "school ethnographies" cannot show, however, is the institutional shape of the education system as a whole. Selectiveness at upper levels (selection cuts in at different ages in different countries) means a narrowing offer of learning that forces unequal outcomes, whether or not the system attempts to equalize opportunity. For instance, if a university system trains only one in ten of a particular age group, which is the current average for industrial countries (United Nations Development Programme, 1992), then nine must go without degrees. If unequal outcomes are forced, a struggle for advantage results, and the political and economic resources that can be mobilized in that struggle become important. The poor are precisely those with the least resources.

Policies to increase competitive pressures within the school system — including mandatory objective testing, parental choice plans, and "gifted and talented" programs — have a transparent class meaning, reinforcing the advantages of the privileged and confirming the exclusion of the poor. The fact that such policies deliver class advantages is not new knowledge; similar observations on the class meaning of testing programs have been made for half a century (for example, Davis, 1948). It seems to be a fact that has to be constantly rediscovered.

The legitimacy of educational competitions depends on some belief in level playing fields. Economic facts have been marginal in discussions of educational disadvantage, though educators periodically justify compensatory programs as contributing to a well-trained work force. In the United States, however, Kozol (1991) has recently made an issue of differences in school funding. Taylor and Piché (1991), in a study of per-pupil expenditure by U.S. school boards, found a range from $11,752 in the richest district to $1,324 in the poorest, with many states having a 2.5-to-1 or 3-to-1 ratio between high-expenditure and low-expenditure groups of districts. Further, current per capita spending is likely to understate differences, because background capital expenditure has also been unequal. And beyond public finance, as already noted, there are stark inequalities in what can be privately spent on educational resources.

Other wealthy countries have more centralized, and thus more uniform, funding of schools than the United States, but a more exclusive system of student selection for higher education. This, being more costly, weights overall per capita expenditure back in favor of advantaged groups who enter higher education in greater proportions. On the face of it, differences in the total social investment in the education of rich children and poor children appear to be much larger than any redistributive effect of compensatory education funds.

Curriculum

The importance of curriculum for issues of educational inequality has long been argued by Apple (1982, 1993), and the point is highly relevant to strategy about poverty. Compensatory programs were intended to lever disadvantaged children back into mainstream schooling. The success of these programs is conventionally measured by pupil progress in the established curriculum, especially as evidenced by the closing of gaps to system norms. This logic has been taken to a startling extreme in a program in Cleveland, Ohio, which consists of awarding pupils $40 for getting an A, $20 for a B, and $10 for a C (Natriello et al., 1990).

When progress in the mainstream curriculum is taken as the goal of intervention, that curriculum is exempted from criticism. However, the experience of teachers in disadvantaged schools has persistently led them to question the curriculum. Conventional subject matter and texts and traditional teaching methods and assessment techniques turn out to be sources of systematic difficulty. They persistently produce boredom. Enforcing them heightens the problem of discipline, and so far as they are successfully enforced, they divide pupils between an academically successful minority and an academically discredited majority (Connell, Johnston, & White, 1992; Wexler, 1992).

To teach well in disadvantaged schools requires a shift in pedagogy and in the way content is determined. A shift toward more negotiated curriculum and more participatory classroom practice can be seen in compensatory education in Australia, where it is a broad tendency in disadvantaged schools, not just a matter of isolated initiatives (Connell, White, et al., 1991). The effectiveness of similar practice in U.S. elementary classrooms is demonstrated by Knapp, Shields, and Turnbull (1992). However, such practices do not seem to be the main tendency in the United States. A survey of U.S. middle schools by MacIver and Epstein (1990) suggests a more conventional pedagogy, with less commitment to active learning methods and exploratory courses in disadvantaged schools than in advantaged schools. The push for "standards" and "basic skills" has fostered a rigid, teacher-centered pedagogy in compensatory and special education programs (for a striking illustration, see Griswold, Cotton, & Hansen, 1986).

To see "mainstream" curriculum as a key source of educational inequality raises the question of where it comes from. We are beginning to get an answer from the new social history of the curriculum produced by Goodson (1985, 1988) and others. The very concept of "mainstream" must be called into question, as it suggests reasoned consensus. What we are dealing with, rather, is a dominant, or **hegemonic,**[b] curriculum, derived historically from the educational practices of European upper class men. This curriculum became dominant in mass education systems during the last 150 years, as the political representatives of the powerful succeeded in marginalizing other experiences and other ways of organizing knowledge. It has been reorganized from time to time by struggles among interest groups; thus classics was replaced by physical science as the highest prestige knowledge, without disturbing the "subject" organization of knowledge. The competitive academic curriculum sits alongside other kinds of curricula in the schools — such as practical knowledge in music or in manual arts — but remains hegemonic in the sense that it defines "real" knowledge, is linked to teacher professionalism, and determines promotion in the education system (Connell, Ashenden, Kessler, & Dowsett, 1982).

The apparently remote discipline of curriculum history has made a key contribution to rethinking the issues of poverty and education. It has de-mythologized the hegemonic curriculum and shown it to be *only* one among a number of ways knowledge could have been organized for the schools (Whitty, 1985; Whitty & Young, 1976). Without this historical perspective, proposals for alternative curricula are easily discredited as abandoning real knowledge and educational quality. Different versions of this claim were made in turn by the "Black Papers" neoconservatives in England in the 1960s and 1970s, cultural literacy entrepreneurs in the United States in the 1980s, and professors attacking assessment reform in Aus-

---

[b] **Hegemonic** refers to a system that is designed to keep present power structures in place, and supports the oppression of one or more groups by others.

tralia in the 1990s. We can now see that the work of teachers in disadvantaged schools implies not a shift to different content (though there will be some of that), but, more decisively, a different organization of the field of knowledge as a whole.

Teachers' Work

Teachers are strikingly absent from much of the policy debate about schooling and poverty (so much so that a recent book reviewing the subject does not even list teachers in its index). This absence is an important consequence of the deficit interpretation of disadvantage and the technocratic style of policymaking.

But teachers are the frontline workers in schools. If exclusion is accomplished by schools, it is certainly in large measure through what teachers do. We may not wish to blame teachers, but we also cannot ignore them. Education as a cultural enterprise is constituted in and through their labor. Their work is the arena where the great contradictions around education and social justice condense.

Teachers' work has been studied in an international literature (surveyed by Ginsburg, 1995; Seddon, 1994), which, like curriculum history, has been little noticed in discussions of poverty. Nevertheless, its significance is clear. Lawn (1993), for example, shows the complexity of teachers' relationships to state power and the importance of teacher professionalism as a system of indirect control. Professionalism is an important factor attaching teachers to the hegemonic curriculum. The question of the "de-skilling" of teachers through tighter management control and packaged curricula is highly relevant to the prospects for good teaching in disadvantaged schools, which requires maximum flexibility and imagination.

Some activities included under the name "compensatory education" expand teachers' options and call for higher levels of skill. Others, as a condition of funding, constrict methods and de-skill teachers, generally pushing them toward more authoritarian styles. Where compensatory programs are accompanied by an active testing program, for example, a familiar pressure is created to teach to the test and thus narrow the curriculum. "Pull-out" classes are likely to disrupt the supportive classroom dynamics that good teachers try to establish. The whole model of expert intervention tends to disempower teachers. Given all these effects, it is likely that some compensatory interventions have worsened the educational situation in disadvantaged schools, not improved it. It is almost impossible for embattled schools to resist offers of resources, but the consequences are not always beneficial. (See the uneasy discussions in Doyle & Cooper, 1988; Knapp, Shields, & Turnbull, 1992; Savage, 1987; Scheerens, 1987.)

By looking at the industrial conditions of teachers' work, we might also begin to understand the paradox of the evaluations of compensatory education (for example, Glazer, 1986). In a nutshell, most intervention projects produce little change when measured in conventional ways, while those that do produce change follow no clear pattern. The technocratic approach to policymaking should be deeply embarrassed by this situation, though the usual reaction is to call for more research.

I suspect these findings reflect a "Hawthorne effect" in poverty programs, along the following lines.[8] Teaching practice is governed mainly by the institutional constraints of the school as a workplace. Compensatory interventions are generally far too small to change these constraints, a point that has been made throughout their history (see, for example, Halsey, 1972; Natriello et al., 1990). Accordingly, most educational practice in disadvantaged schools is routinely like practice in other schools (for evidence, see Connell, 1991), and produces the usual socially selective effects. Those programs that do produce changes happen to have found one of the variety of ways — which may be situational and temporary — of bolstering teachers' agency, increasing their capacity to maneuver around constraints and grapple with the contradictions of the relationship between poor children and schools.

Toward a Strategy of Change

Given a remapping of the issues along these lines, our concept of what constitutes a solution must also change. Solutions cannot consist of expert interventions from a central place. The educational authority that defines "expertise" must itself be contested. People in disadvantaged schools and poor communities do not lack knowledge. They do, however, often lack ways of putting their knowledge to use.

Does this mean that academics should simply get out of the way? There is a lot to be said for breaking the routines by which science legitimates intrusions in the lives of the poor. Nevertheless, researchers often do have information, resources, and skills that poor people and their teachers can use.

Rather than vacate the field, then, we should rethink the relationship between professional intellectuals and disadvantaged communities — as is done, for instance, in participatory action research in the welfare field (Wadsworth, 1983). It is possible to support strategic thinking in the schools rather than substitute for it, though the balance is not an easy one. That is to say, it is possible for researchers to refine, criticize, inform, and disseminate attempts to achieve educational purposes defined from below. In this spirit, I will briefly explore four issues that necessarily arise for democratic education strategies concerned with poverty: the goals of action, the direction of change in curriculum, the work force, and the political conditions of change.

Formulating Goals

Most statements of purpose for educational reform treat justice in distributional terms. That is, they treat education in much the way arguments about economic justice treat money: as a social good of standard character that needs to be shared more fairly. Even if the criteria for fair shares vary from one policy sphere to another, as in Walzer's (1983) sophisticated model of justice, the distributional approach governs the discussion of education.

If we have learned one thing from research on the interaction of curriculum and social context, it is that educational processes are not standard in this sense. Distributing equal amounts of the hegemonic curriculum to girls and boys, to poor children and rich children, to Black children and White children, to immigrants and native-born, to indigenous people and their colonizers, does not do the same thing for them — or to them. In education, the "how much" and the "who" cannot be separated from the "what."

The concept of distributive justice certainly applies to material resources for education, such as school funds and equipment. But we need something more to deal with the content and process of education: a concept of curricular justice (Connell, 1993). This idea is closely connected to the lesson curriculum history teaches: that there are always multiple ways to organize the knowledge content of schooling.

Each particular way of constructing the curriculum (i.e., organizing the field of knowledge and defining how it is to be taught and learned) carries social effects. Curriculum empowers and disempowers, authorizes and de-authorizes, recognizes and mis-recognizes different social groups and their knowledge and identities. For instance, curriculum developed from academic institutions controlled by men has, in a variety of ways, authorized the practices and experiences of men and marginalized those of women.[9] Curriculum defined by representatives of a dominant ethnic group is liable to exclude or de-authorize the knowledge and experience of dominated groups, or to incorporate them on terms that suit the dominant group.[10] Curricular justice concerns the organization of knowledge, and, through it, the justice of the social relations being produced through education.

There is nothing exotic about this idea. It is implied in a great deal of practical teaching that goes on in disadvantaged schools, teaching that contests the disempowering effects of the hegemonic curriculum and authorizes locally produced knowledge. This is the kind of "good teaching" Haberman (1991) has recently contrasted with the "pedagogy of poverty." As he observes, the challenge is how to institutionalize "good teaching" in disadvantaged schools. Initiatives of this kind remain marginal and are easily dismantled, unless they can be linked to larger purposes.

I think a concept of curricular justice makes the link to larger purposes possible and should be at the heart of strategic thinking on education and disadvantage. It requires us to think through curriculum-making from the point of view of the least advantaged, not from the standpoint of what is currently authorized. It requires us to think about how to generalize the point of view of the least advantaged as a program for the organization and production of knowledge in general.

Taking an *educational* view of poverty and education thus pushes us beyond the goal of "compensation" and toward the goal of reorganizing the cultural content of education as a whole. This goal is intimidating, given the difficulties encountered with much more limited goals. Yet clear thinking is helped if we put local initiatives in the perspective of the larger agenda they imply.

The Direction of Curriculum Change

Compensatory programs have mainly supplemented the hegemonic curriculum, adding extra activities or small-group instruction in core areas of conventional teaching — principally, mathematics and language skills. Add-on programs do not change the main patterns of teaching and learning in the school. A strategy that takes curriculum change seriously would base itself on another approach found in compensatory programs, the whole-school change approach, which uses compensatory funds to redesign the major activities of the school.

How we understand curricular change depends on what we take the basic social effects of education to be. Wexler (1992) sees the main effects as the **discursive formation of identities**.[c] This would focus strategies for justice on respect for diversity and on producing identities that are rich and solid — not far, indeed, from the concerns of multicultural education. I would argue, however, for a broader conception

---

[c] **Discursive formation of identities** is an explanation of identity formation that describes it as an imprecise process that shapes identity through numerous and discrete forces such as race, culture, ethnicity, class, time, region, etc.

of educational effects as the development of capacities for social practice (Connell, 1995). The social practices addressed by schooling include the winning of livelihood, a theme whose importance for youth still in school is documented by Wilson and Wyn (1987); the **construction**[d] of gender and negotiation of sexuality (Frank, 1993); and the mobilization of social power, which is a familiar theme in adult literacy work (see Lankshear, 1987).

Perhaps learning how to mobilize and use power is the clearest example of how a course of learning can open up ways of transforming the situation of the poor. The same point was made by the Australian Schools Commission, in stating objectives for its national compensatory education program; the objectives included "to ensure that students have systematic access to programs which will equip them with economic and political understanding so that they can act individually or together to improve their circumstances" (Australian Schools Commission, 1985, p. 98).

The idea of helping the poor "act . . . together" to change things is directly opposed to the divisive effects of a competitive assessment system. The link between exclusionary curricula and competitive assessment is very close. It is no accident that the Blackburn Report on post-compulsory education in the Australian state of Victoria, which pursued the principle of a socially inclusive curriculum, also laid the groundwork for an important democratic reform of secondary assessment (Ministerial Review, 1985). This report drew on the experience of disadvantaged schools to formulate a policy for the state's school system as a whole.

Curriculum and assessment reforms are not cheap, especially in the time and human energy they require. The level of material resources for schools serving the poor still matters, even if one agrees that the quality of education does not depend on the freshness of paint on the school buildings. Measures of current per capita funding are, as I have already suggested, inadequate measures of total social investment in the education of different groups of children. Given the educationally relevant inequalities of resources around schools, the consequences of unequal family and community wealth and income, distributive justice would require much higher levels of funding to the schools of the poor, and higher funding to working-class schools in general.

A curriculum focus, similarly, does not erase issues about the school as an institution. The curriculum as it is taught and learned, not just as it is in the manual, is the labor process of pupils and teachers, and, like other forms of labor, is powerfully affected by the surrounding social relations. Expanding the agency of teachers means moving toward industrial democracy at the level of the school. This is not easily achieved, as teachers' unions know; for a situation like that found in Britain after a decade of New Right government, it may sound utopian. But if we are serious about educational enrichment, then we need to produce the industrial conditions for richer forms of teaching.

The students, too, are working in more than a metaphorical sense. Democratization means expanding the agency of those normally overwhelmed by the agency of others or immobilized by current structures. Good teaching does this in an immediate, local way — as is vividly shown in the adult education for empowerment de-

---

[d] **Construction** is a process through which deep and unconscious influences combine to create a phenomenon such as personality, text, conversation, a film, etc.

scribed by Shor (1992), where the teacher functions as problem-poser and a critical dialogue replaces teacher-talk. An agenda for change must concern itself with how this local effect can be generalized.

The Work Force

Given the institutional and cultural forces that make for inequality in education, the case can be made that more can be done outside schools than inside them. This seems to be implied by postmodernist readings of educational politics by authors such as Giroux (1992). Acknowledging the cultural changes to which this reading responds, I would nevertheless argue that the profoundly ambivalent relationship between working-class people and educational institutions is central to contemporary cultural politics in industrial countries. This relationship has grown in importance with the growing weight of education as a part of the economy and the culture. Teachers in schools are the workers most strategically placed to affect the relationship. I have argued already for bringing teachers' work to the center of discussions of disadvantage. If the education of children in poverty is to be changed, teachers will be the work force of reform. This conclusion has two important corollaries.

First, teachers should be centrally involved in the design of reform strategies. Giroux (1988) earlier called our attention to the sense in which teachers are intellectuals. A capacity for strategic thinking certainly exists among the teachers of the poor. The Disadvantaged Schools Program in Australia, partly because of its decentralized design, encouraged the growth of an activist network that included teachers' unions and a group of experienced teachers in poor districts. This informal network, more than any formal agency, has transmitted experience and provided the forum for intense policy debates (White & Johnston, 1993). Such groups exist in other countries, too. A notable example is the network around the magazine *Our Schools/Our Selves,* which has brought teachers across Canada into a series of debates about educational reform. An intelligent approach to policymaking would regard such teacher networks as a key asset.

Second, a reform agenda must concern the shaping of this work force: the recruitment, training, in-service education, and career structures of teachers in disadvantaged schools. The 1966 Coleman Report, to its credit, raised this issue and collected data on teacher training, but the issue almost vanished from later discussions of disadvantage. In a recession, where education budgets are under pressure, funds for teacher preparation, and especially for in-service training, are likely to be cut. To an extent, compensatory programs themselves function as teacher educators. A potentially cost-effective reform would be to expand these programs' capacities to train teachers, to circulate information, to pool knowledge, and to pass on expertise.

The work force is not static. Families move into and out of poverty, and teachers move into and out of disadvantaged schools. For both reasons, issues about poverty *should* concern teachers in all parts of a school system. I would argue that these issues should be major themes in initial teacher training, and that competence in work with disadvantaged groups should be central to the idea of professionalism in teaching.

Political Conditions: The Poor and the Less Poor

Targeted compensatory education programs are based on definitions of disadvantage, which are always to some degree arbitrary and may also be stigmatizing — especially where, as in the United States, issues about poverty are interwoven with a volatile politics of race.

Special programs for the disadvantaged are most easily accepted where inequalities can be seen as accidental, or as consequences of neglect. They are not so easily accepted where the inequalities are intended. A recent court case showed the school system in Rockford, Illinois, to have been operating a covert system of racial segregation — via tracking, scheduling, and special programs — that subverted official desegregation policies to a startling degree ("'Integrated' Schools," 1993). This is a conspicuous example, but institutional racism is, of course, not unusual (for a recent British example, see Tomlinson, 1992.) We also cannot ignore the intention behind other forms of inequality and exclusion, whether along lines of class or gender or nationality.

Disadvantage is always produced through mechanisms that also produce advantage. The institutions that do this are generally defended by their beneficiaries. The beneficiaries of the current educational order are, broadly speaking, the groups with greater economic and institutional power, greater access to the means of persuasion, and the best representation in government and in professions. No one should imagine that educational change in the interests of the poor can be conflict-free.

That change happens at all is due to two facts. First, advantaged groups are far from monolithic. They are internally divided in a number of ways: for example, professionals versus capitalists, regional elites versus multinational elites, elite women versus elite men, new wealth versus old. These divisions affect educational stances, such as support for public expenditure on schooling. Members of advantaged groups differ in their judgments of short-term versus long-term interests, and in their willingness to take stances based on a notion of the common good. Their views of long-term interests are affected by pressure from below. United States elites, as Domhoff (1990) argues, conceded reforms in the 1960s and early 1970s — including compensatory education — under pressure of social disruption from the civil rights and other social movements. The reassertion of conservatism in U.S. public policy followed the decline of this pressure.

Second, the interests of the poor are not isolated. I emphasized earlier the statistical evidence that the most severe disadvantage is part of a much broader pattern of class exclusion. The poorest groups share an interest in educational reform with a broader constituency in the working class, even in very wealthy countries. However, it is not automatic that shared interest will be turned into any kind of practical alliance. Racism, regionalism, the weakening of the union movement, and the impact of New Right educational politics all stand in the way.

Targeted programs, however well-designed and lively, are unlikely to have a major impact unless they are part of a broader agenda for social justice. The problem of breadth is familiar in debates over social policy (see, for example, Skocpol, 1991). Narrowly targeted benefits appear more cost-effective than universal benefits, especially in a context of budget-cutting. But narrow targeting is likely to stigmatize the targeted group; the current political hostility to welfare dependents in the United States is a prime example. Because their beneficiaries are stigmatized minorities, the programs are politically weak, and the level of benefits is held down to a minimum. Continuing poverty is a common result. Broad entitlements to benefits (as illustrated by old-age pensions and health insurance in countries with universal systems) create larger constituencies and mobilize more political strength. Paradoxically, then, *less* targeted benefits (including universal benefits) are often more effective in producing redistribution: they "level up."

In education the case is somewhat different because the universal benefit already exists — compulsory schooling. The problem, as I have argued throughout this article, is that this universal benefit contains powerful mechanisms of privilege and exclusion; it does not *function* in a universal way. A social justice program in education must attempt to reconstruct the service that is formally available to everyone. Once we recognize this, the same strategic principle applies as in welfare politics: the broader the agenda, the more chance of a social justice outcome. The task is easier than welfare reform in that the idea of common schooling is well established, and more difficult in that the unequal functioning of education systems is defended by a formidable combination of class interest, professional routine, and institutional hierarchy.

To accomplish the institutional change needed by children in poverty requires greater social forces than poverty programs themselves generate. At the end of the day, then, the educational problems of compensatory education are political problems. Their long-term solution involves social alliances whose outlines are still, at best, emerging. Yet work on education can be one of the ways these very alliances are created.

Notes

1. The term "compensatory" has been rightly criticized for its association with deficit notions about the poor. However, it is the only common term for the special-purpose programs that are the focus of the policy discussion. It continues in official use, so I, too, use it.
2. I have counted the U.N. Development Programme's group of "industrial countries," excluding the communist or former communist countries. A more sophisticated calculation could adjust for known differences in the rates of child poverty — the United States appears relatively high — but a poverty line in any case has an element of arbitrariness; the order of magnitude would remain the same.
3. Useful histories of the compensatory idea have been written by Jeffrey (1978) and Silver and Silver (1991).
4. For their stories see Connell, White, and Johnston (1991); Halsey (1972); Peterson, Rabe, and Wong (1988); and Scheerens (1987).
5. In Australia, which is particularly explicit on this point, national compensatory education funds reach about 15 percent of school-age children. In the United States, where the situation is more complex, the figure appears to be about 11 percent, according to a careful estimate of the early 1980s (Kennedy, Jung, & Orland, 1986).
6. The emergence of the modern concept of poverty is traced by Dean (1991), and its impact on welfare policy by Katz (1989).
7. See, for example, the life histories of unemployed young men discussed in Connell (1989).
8. The "Hawthorne effect" is named for the factory where a famous experiment found industrial workers increasing output no matter how their work was arranged by the experimenters. The researchers finally realized that it was the experiment itself, not the manipulations within it, that was creating a supportive group and boosting the workers' morale.
9. For an excellent account of this process and the complexities of contesting it, see chapter five in Yates (1993).
10. For a striking historical example of debate within the dominant group about this issue, see Ball (1984).

References

Anderson, E. (1991). Neighborhood effects on teenage pregnancy. In C. Jencks & P. E. Peterson (Eds.), *The urban underclass* (pp. 375–398). Washington, DC: Brookings Institution.

Angus, L. (Ed.) (1993). *Education, inequality and social identity.* London: Falmer Press.

Apple, M. W. (1982). *Education and power.* Boston: Routledge & Kegan Paul.

Apple, M. W. (1993). *Official knowledge: Democratic education in a conservative age.* New York: Routledge.

Australian Schools Commission. (1985). *Quality and equality.* Canberra: Commonwealth Schools Commission.

Avalos, B. (1992). Education for the poor: Quality or relevance? *British Journal of Sociology of Education, 13,* 419–436.

Ball, S. J. (1984). Imperialism, social control and the colonial curriculum in Africa. In I. F. Goodson & S. J. Ball (Eds.), *Defining the curriculum: Histories and ethnographies* (pp. 117–147). London: Falmer Press.

Bernstein, B. B. (1974). A critique of the concept of "compensatory education." In D. Wedderburn (Ed.), *Poverty, inequality and class structure* (pp. 109–122). Cambridge, Eng.: Cambridge University Press.

Casanova, U. (1990). Rashomon in the classroom: Multiple perspectives of teachers, parents and students. In A. Barona & E. E. Garcia (Eds.), *Children at risk: Poverty, minority status, and other issues in educational equity* (pp. 135–149). Washington, DC: National Association of School Psychologists.

Clark, E. A. G. (1977). The superiority of the "Scotch system": Scottish ragged schools and their influence. *Scottish Educational Studies, 9,* 29–39.

Coleman, J. S. (1990). *Equality and achievement in education.* Boulder, CO: Westview.

Connell, R. W. (1989). Cool guys, swots and wimps: The interplay of masculinity and education. *Oxford Review of Education, 15,* 291–303.

Connell, R. W. (1991). The workforce of reform: Teachers in the disadvantaged schools program. *Australian Journal of Education, 35,* 229–245.

Connell, R. W. (1993). *Schools and social justice.* Philadelphia: Temple University Press.

Connell, R. W. (1995). Transformative labor: Theorizing the politics of teachers' work. In M. B. Ginsburg (Ed.), *The politics of educators' work and lives.* New York: Garland.

Connell, R. W., Ashenden, D. J., Kessler, S., & Dowsett, G. W. (1982). *Making the difference: Schools, families and social division.* Sydney: Allen & Unwin.

Connell, R. W., Johnston, K. M., & White, V. M. (1992). *Measuring up: Assessment, evaluation and educational disadvantage.* Canberra: Australian Curriculum Studies Association.

Connell, R. W., White, V. M., & Johnston, K. M. (1991). *"Running twice as hard": The disadvantaged schools program in Australia.* Geelong, Australia: Deakin University.

Corrigan, P. (1979). *Schooling the Smash Street kids.* London: Macmillan.

Curtis, B., Livingstone, D. W., & Smaller, H. (1992). *Stacking the deck: The streaming of working-class kids in Ontario schools.* Toronto: Our Schools/Our Selves Education Foundation.

Davis, A. (1948). *Social-class influences upon learning.* Cambridge, MA: Harvard University Press.

Dean, M. (1991). *The constitution of poverty: Toward a genealogy of liberal governance.* London: Routledge.

Devine, J. A., & Wright, J. D. (1993). *The greatest of evils: Urban poverty and the American underclass.* New York: Aldine de Gruyter.

Domhoff, G. W. (1990). *The power elite and the state: How policy is made in America.* New York: Aldine de Gruyter.

Doyle, D. P., & Cooper, B. S. (Eds.). (1988). *Federal aid to the disadvantaged: What future for Chapter I?* London: Falmer Press.

Embling, J. (1986). *Fragmented lives: A darker side of Australian life.* Ringwood, Australia: Penguin.

Fine, M. (1991). *Framing dropouts: Notes on the politics of an urban public high school.* Albany: State University of New York Press.

Ford, J. (1969). *Social class and the comprehensive school.* London: Routledge & Kegan Paul.

Frank, B. (1993). Straight/strait jackets for masculinity: Educating for "real" men. *Atlantis, 18*(1/2), 47–59.

Ginsburg, M. B. (Ed.). (1995). *The politics of educators' work and lives.* New York: Garland.

Giroux, H. A. (1988). *Teachers as intellectuals: Toward a critical pedagogy of learning.* Granby, MA: Bergin & Garvey.

Giroux, H. A. (1992). *Border crossings: Cultural workers and the politics of education.* New York: Routledge.

Glazer, N. (1986). Education and training programs and poverty. In S. H. Danziger & D. H. Weinberg (Eds.), *Fighting poverty: What works and what doesn't* (pp. 152–173). Cambridge, MA: Harvard University Press.

Goodson, I. F. (Ed.). (1985). *Social histories of the secondary curriculum: Subjects for study.* London: Falmer Press.

Goodson, I. F. (1988). *The making of curriculum: Collected essays.* London: Falmer Press.

Griffin, C. (1993). *Representations of youth: The study of youth and adolescence in Britain and America.* Cambridge, Eng.: Polity Press.

Griswold, P. A., Cotton, K. J., & Hansen, J. B. (1986). *Effective compensatory education sourcebook.* Washington, DC: U.S. Department of Education.

Haberman, M. (1991). The pedagogy of poverty versus good teaching. *Phi Delta Kappan, 73,* 290–294.

Halsey, A. H. (Ed.). (1972). *Educational priority: Vol. I. E. P. A. Problems and policies.* London: Her Majesty's Stationery Office.

Harrington, M. (1962). *The other America.* New York: Macmillan.

Heath, A. (1992). The attitudes of the underclass. In D. J. Smith (Ed.), *Understanding the underclass* (pp. 32–47). London: Policy Studies Institute.

Heath, S. B. (1983). *Ways with words: Language, life and work in communities and classrooms.* Cambridge, Eng.: Cambridge University Press.

Hoyles, M. (1977). Cultural deprivation and compensatory education. In M. Hoyles (Ed.), *The politics of literacy* (pp. 172–181). London: Writers and Readers Publishing Cooperative.

"Integrated" schools kept races separate. (1983, November 9). *San Francisco Chronicle.*

Interim Committee for the Australian Schools Commission. (1973). *Schools in Australia.* Canberra: Australian Government Publishing Service.

Jeffrey, J. R. (1978). *Education for children of the poor: A study of the origins and implementation of the Elementary and Secondary Education Act of 1965.* Columbus: Ohio State University Press.

Katz, M. B. (1989). *The undeserving poor: From the War on Poverty to the war on welfare.* New York: Pantheon.

Kennedy, M. M., Jung, R. K., & Orland, M. E. (1986). *Poverty, achievement and the distribution of compensatory education services: An interim report from the national assessment of Chapter I.* Washington, DC: U.S. Department of Education, Office of Educational Research and Improvement.

Knapp, M. S., Shields, P. M., & Turnbull, B. J. (1992). *Academic challenge for the children of poverty: Summary report.* Washington, DC: U.S. Department of Education, Office of Policy and Planning.

Korbin, J. E. (1992). Introduction: Child poverty in the United States. *American Behavioral Scientist, 35*, 213–219.

Kozol, J. (1991). *Savage inequalities: Children in America's schools.* New York: Crown.

Lankshear, C. (1987). *Literacy, schooling and revolution.* New York: Falmer Press.

Lareau, A. (1987). Social class differences in family-school relationships: The importance of cultural capital. *Sociology of Education, 60*(2), 73–85.

Lawn, M. (1993, April). *The political nature of teaching: Arguments around schoolwork.* Paper presented at American Educational Research Association Conference, Atlanta, 1993.

Lewis, O. (1968). *La vida: A Puerto Rican family in the culture of poverty — San Juan and New York.* London: Panther.

MacIver, D. J., & Epstein, J. L. (1990). *How equal are opportunities for learning in disadvantaged and advantaged middle grade schools?* Baltimore: Johns Hopkins University, Center for Research on Effective Schooling for Disadvantaged Students.

MacPherson, S. (1987). *Five hundred million children: Poverty and child welfare in the Third World.* Brighton, Eng.: Wheatsheaf.

Ministerial Review of Postcompulsory Schooling (Blackburn Committee). (1985). *Report.* Melbourne: Education Department, Victoria.

Natriello, G., McDill, E. L., & Pallas, A. M. (1990). *Schooling disadvantaged children: Racing against catastrophe.* New York: Teachers College Press.

Ogbu, J. U. (1988). Cultural diversity and human development. In D. T. Slaughter (Ed.), *Black children and poverty: A developmental perspective* (pp. 11–28). San Francisco: Jossey-Bass.

Orland, M. E. (1990). Demographics of disadvantage: Intensity of childhood poverty and its relationship to educational experience. In J. I. Goodlad & P. Keating (Eds.), *Access to knowledge: An agenda of our nation's schools* (pp. 43–58). New York: College Entrance Examination Board.

Peterson, P. E., Rabe, B. G., & Wong, K. K. (1988). The evolution of the compensatory education program. In D. P. Doyle & B. S. Cooper (Eds.), *Federal aid to the disadvantaged: What future for Chapter I?* (pp. 33–60). London: Falmer Press.

Piven, F. F., & Cloward, R. A. (1979). *Poor people's movements: Why they succeed, how they fail.* New York: Vintage.

Riley, R. W. (1994, January 27). Reinventing Chapter I deserves full support. *San Francisco Chronicle,* op ed page.

Robins, D., & Cohen, P. (1978). *Knuckle sandwich: Growing up in the working-class city.* Harmondsworth, Eng.: Penguin.

Ryan, W. (1971). *Blaming the victim.* New York: Vintage Books.

Sartre, J. P. (1958). *Being and nothingness.* London: Methuen.

Savage, D. G. (1987). Why Chapter I hasn't made much difference. *Phi Delta Kappan, 68,* 581–584.

Scheerens, J. (1987). *Enhancing educational opportunities for disadvantaged learners: A review of Dutch research on compensatory education and educational development policy.* Amsterdam: North-Holland.

Seddon, T. (1994). Teachers' work and political action. In T. N. Postlethwaite & T. Husén (Eds.), *International encyclopedia of education* (2nd ed.). Oxford, Eng.: Pergamon.

Shor, I. (1992). *Empowering education: Critical teaching for social change.* Chicago: University of Chicago Press.

Silver, H., & Silver, P. (1991). *An educational war on poverty: American and British policymaking, 1960–1980.* Cambridge, Eng.: Cambridge University Press.

Skocpol, T. (1991). Targeting within universalism: Politically viable policies to combat poverty in the United States. In C. Jencks & P. E. Peterson (Eds.), *The urban underclass* (pp. 411–436). Washington, DC: Brookings Institution.

Snow, C. E., Barnes, W. S., Chandler, J., Goodman, I. F., & Hemphill, L. (1991). *Unfulfilled expectations: Home and school influences on literacy.* Cambridge, MA: Harvard University Press.

Taylor, W. L., & Piché, D. M. (1991). *A report on shortchanging children: The impact of fiscal inequity on the education of students at risk.* Washington, DC: U.S. House of Representatives, Committee on Education and Labor.

Thorne, B. (1993). *Gender play: Girls and boys in school.* New Brunswick, NJ: Rutgers University Press.

Tomlinson, S. (1992). Disadvantaging the disadvantaged: Bangladeshis and education in Tower Hamlets. *British Journal of Sociology of Education, 13,* 437–446.

United Nations Development Programme. (1992). *Human Development Report 1992.* New York: Oxford University Press.

U.S. Bureau of the Census. (1992). *Poverty in the United States: 1991.* Washington, DC: Government Printing Office.

Wadsworth, Y. (1983). *Do it yourself social research.* Melbourne: Allen & Unwin.

Walker, J. C. (1988). *Louts and legends: Male youth culture in an inner-city school.* Sydney: Allen & Unwin.

Walzer, M. (1983). *Spheres of justice: A defense of pluralism and equality.* New York: Basic Books.

Weinberg, M. (1981). *The education of poor and minority children: A world bibliography.* New York: Greenwood.

Wexler, P. (1992). *Becoming somebody: Toward a social psychology of school.* London: Falmer Press.

White, V., & Johnston, K. (1993). Inside the disadvantaged schools program: The politics of practical policy-making. In L. Angus (Ed.), *Education, inequality and social identity* (pp. 104–127). London: Falmer Press.

Whiteford, P., Bradbury, B., & Saunders, P. (1989). Inequality and deprivation among families with children: An exploratory study. In D. Edgar, D. Keane, & P. McDonald (Eds.), *Child poverty* (pp. 20–49). Sydney: Allen & Unwin.

Whitty, G. (1985). *Sociology and school knowledge: Curriculum theory, research and politics.* London: Methuen.

Whitty, G., & Young, M. (Eds.). (1976). *Explorations in the politics of school knowledge.* Driffield, Eng.: Nafferton Books.

Williams, T. (1987). *Participation in education.* Hawthorn: Australian Council for Educational Research.

Wilson, B., & Wyn, J. (1987). *Shaping futures: Youth action for livelihood.* Sydney: Allen & Unwin.

Yates, L. (1993). *The education of girls: Policy, research and the question of gender.* Hawthorn: Australian Council for Educational Research.

My thinking on these issues has been profoundly influenced by my colleagues on the national study of the Disadvantaged Schools Program in Australia, Ken Johnston and Viv White, and by the other contributors to that project. This article is based on the 1992 Paul Masoner International Education Lecture; I am grateful to the University of Pittsburgh for the invitation to deliver this lecture and thus bring these ideas together for a North American audience.

Beyond the Classroom

CAROL STUMBO

In this chapter, Carol Stumbo illustrates another strategy for dealing with how the outer world affects classroom practice. In Johnson's chapter we saw a model that brings the history and context of the outside world into the classroom. Here, Stumbo turns the classroom inside out and takes her students out into that world. Drawing on her experience growing up as the daughter of an Appalachian coal miner in the region where she now teaches, Stumbo designed an oral history project meant to make the acquisition of writing skills more interesting to her students. Using interviews with people in the region that they published in a school magazine, she and her class described the changes that had taken place all around them. Stumbo examines the unexpected and far-reaching impact the project had on her view of her education, teaching, students, and community. We see her realization that her education had pulled her away from the roots of community and made her an "outsider in my own home." We also witness the profound changes that learning and writing about their own community made in her students. This chapter captures the seriousness and honesty with which Stumbo confronts these changes and reflects her deep commitment to, and belief in, her profession and her students.

Lisa, an eighteen-year-old senior, is sitting in the front seat of my car trying to clean the film off the passenger window so she can take photographs of the Virginia landscape. She is intent about it. Despite my attempts to tell her that she might not be able to take good photographs from a moving car, I know that she is not convinced. She assures me that she has done it before, and she works on each section with a tenacity that used to make me so impatient with her. Today I smile and watch the back of her blonde hair as she leans in and studies the pane of glass closely before she renews her assault. I know from past experience that she will stop only when she has finished the job, so I leave her to her battle. In the back seat, squeezed between some of our luggage, two other students of mine, Dorothy and Pam, are giggling about something that one of them has whispered to the other. For the moment, Lisa and I aren't part of their world. All of this has such a familiar feel to it.

For the last three years I have made many trips with my students, but most of them have been in and around Wheelwright, the small town in eastern Kentucky where I teach. Almost every afternoon, we have loaded tape recorders and camera equipment into my car and spent a couple of hours interviewing coal miners, ministers, and housewives. On this day, however, we are on our way to an Appalachian youth conference in Virginia where the girls will talk about *Mantrip*, the magazine that we do at our high school. We had left the school before daylight with the prediction of snow fresh in our minds, halfway believing that we might have to turn around and come back before we could cross the mountain at Norton. Large snowflakes began to fall as we pulled away from the deserted school building. I consoled myself with the thought that it was March and snows do not last in March — not in the hills.

We have at least a four- or five-hour drive in front of us, if we can make it. Now, at the Virginia border. the snow has turned into a spring rain that clouds the windows inside the car, but we are all relieved. There are long periods of time in which the girls just study the landscape. They have not been in this section of Virginia before, and they are interested.

I am reminded, as I drive, of trips I took at their age. I remember riding in the backseat of my father's car on the occasional trips we made out of the hills of eastern Kentucky into the Bluegrass Region of central Kentucky. We didn't make that many trips because we couldn't afford them. My father was a miner, and when he wasn't working he was usually on strike. But when we did go, I was always impressed by the large homes that sat back from the highway, secure somehow behind the fences that are used on horse farms. As we rode past them, I used to play a game inside my mind. I always thought I could imagine the families that lived in those houses. I believed I could strip back the exterior walls and see into their lives. I never had the chance to test out my belief, but I didn't have to. Although later, when I would read about artists such as Henry James, who had friends send him picture postcards of what they had seen in their travels in the belief that he could deduce the unknown from the known, I somehow knew that there are worlds that we do not know or understand. I learned that life was more complex than what I had believed as a child. It was Henry James who recognized the futility of attempting to live over other people's lives without living over their perceptions and the changes, growth, and intensity with which they experienced those lives. We all live in different worlds, and only in rare moments do we obtain a glimpse of another person's world.

The mood inside my car is in sharp contrast to the dialogue that had taken place earlier among the four of us. Shifts in mood and feeling seem to take place so abruptly with teenagers. Earlier that morning, the tone of our conversation had been more somber. As we prepared to leave, Dorothy had told us about her brother's decision to move out of the house that he and his family have lived in since the death of their father several years ago. Dorothy's brother and his wife have cared for her and her brothers since then. It is her home, too. Although she is eighteen and ready to graduate, she is upset about the decision. She feels that once again something is being taken away from her. Only in passing does she mention her mother, who was killed when Dorothy was young. Others have told me the details about the shooting. "Was Dorothy there when it happened?" I asked for some reason. I didn't expect that it could have happened that way, but I was told that she was there. For some unexplained reason, the mother had been killed by a man, and Dorothy's father was left with the care of four children. Then he died of complications from black lung. It is something Dorothy and I have never talked about. When Dorothy writes about her childhood in English class, it is about the apple trees and the wildness of the land around her and how it was the best of times for her. I do not know how she copes with that memory or how you stay young when you have to face a situation like that.

There is very little gentleness or quiet in the lives of most of my students. The place where I have chosen to teach leaves very little room for those two qualities, and a great deal of what is happening to my students is tied into the history of the town. Wheelwright is located in southeastern Kentucky, near the borders of West Virginia and Virginia. Before the early 1900s, people of the area made their living from farming and some logging. Otter Creek, as it was known then, was made up of the descendants of four or five families. People had to travel for a full day on wagons through creek beds and across hills to bring food and supplies into the settlement. But that isolation began to change in 1917 when the Elkhorn Coal Corporation began buying up large tracts of mining properties in the hills of eastern Kentucky. The coal seams were among the best ever to be discovered by geologists. A local man by the name of John C. C. Mayo recognized the wealth that was lying underneath the hills in the form of coal and created the broad-form deed, which gave businessmen control of all minerals on a piece of land, often for no more than the payment of fifty cents an acre. Before a transportation system was built to carry coal to the marketplace, it was dug out of the mountains and stockpiled outside the mines.

A town was built near the mining sites. In the old photographs of Wheelwright, you see what looks like a western town; most of the buildings were wooden structures. Even the sidewalks were wooden. The older people of the town remember when a bounty was paid by the company for every rat killed by the miners. Rats lived under the houses and the sidewalks. People in the camp, especially children, suffered from disease. Workers from the Deep South and Europe began to arrive in the hills. Men from Appalachia who were not accustomed to living in towns or working underground often found themselves embroiled in violence. Old-timers tell stories of the shootings or killings that took place almost every day. Soon a culture that had known only the sounds of the fiddle and the banjo began to feel the effects of the outside world.

In the early 1930s, Inland Steel Corporation of Chicago, Illinois, purchased the mining properties and the town of Wheelwright from Elkhorn and began extensive renovations of the town. The company based its operations on the theory that good living and working conditions made sound economic sense in the long run. Like other companies in the region, Inland Steel provided medical care, entertainment, and stores for the residents. It also hired law officials, set curfews for the town's young people, and asked troublemakers to move on. In time, Inland Steel began to call Wheelwright a "model coal town"; and for the next thirty-five years, the town prospered under the company's direction.

In 1965, citing economic reasons, Inland Steel sold its Wheelwright holdings. For a while it seemed that Wheelwright, like other coal towns, might die altogether. For the first time, the town was free of any company ownership, but the people didn't know what to do with their freedom. Some miners left to work for the company in Illinois, but most stayed in the town, hoping they could find work with the new company that had purchased the mining properties. But in time, that company also sold its interests, this time to independent coal operators. The coal industry began to decline, and many people were unemployed. Today the town is attempting to survive. Company houses were sold to people in the town, and many of them who are still living in Wheelwright are retired or disabled workers. Still others live on some form of state financial assistance. Too many of the young people I teach seem to be living with one parent or in the home of grandparents. A large number of these students are convinced that they will have to leave the area if they want to find a job or a future for themselves.

I think it is for these reasons that the teachers I am best able to identify with at conferences are those who teach in inner-city schools in urban areas. So many of the problems that they confront, such as student indifference to learning, vandalism, and fighting in school, are my concerns also. Students and teachers in some cases work in an atmosphere that borders on despair. Several years ago, I attended a summer institute where I got to know an experienced teacher from an urban school. As he described his problems of trying to teach students who had severe reading problems and really saw no reason to attend school, I realized that we shared more than just the problems inside our classrooms. Nothing in school seemed to matter to the students whom we taught, but their indifference had a great deal to do with the conditions that they faced when they left the school. Many came from poor families and went home each day to difficult lives. Did they really see any connection between what was going on in school and in their lives? In school, the students of this inner-city teacher were, like mine, hard kids, perhaps because they had to be. At times they were disrespectful, and as a teacher I always felt that I was working in a situation that could at any moment break into violence. I had seen students who had seemed to be all right suddenly erupt and begin to fight when one word too many had been spoken or some small incident had occurred.

As I sat and listened to the teacher from the urban school, I could feel his struggle. I knew what he was talking about, and I also knew that we could only deal with that kind of hopelessness for so long before something inside us as teachers began to give way. His kids were going back to the streets each day; mine, to homes in town and isolated hollows. But both groups faced poverty, some drug and alcohol usage, and too often lived in situations where violence became a solution to problems. Could we really expect them to find much in school that mattered? I was beginning to understand, but it had not always been that way.

I had come to high school teaching after working for eight years at a junior college. I am ashamed to say that I came with a great deal of confidence, the kind of empty confidence that was based on no real understanding of the problems that I would confront as a public school teacher. On my first day at Wheelwright, I asked all of my students to do a piece of writing. I remember walking into the teachers' lounge at the end of the day and looking for the first time at what I had asked them so casually to write. Most of it I couldn't read, yet they had filled page after page. Here and there, I was able to understand the thought and feeling of some of their writing, and it was beautiful, but most of them were locked away in a prison of sorts, unable to express their feelings in words. They simply didn't know how.

I soon knew that I was facing the hardest challenge of my life. My students let me know that I was going to have to prove myself. I came believing that I could reason with people. I had never hit anyone in my life, but the teachers around me kept telling me that if I wanted to remain in control, I was going to have to spank my students. Each day was a battle. Would I be able to hang onto my classes? There were horror stories of teachers being literally driven away from the school. My principal, realizing that I was floundering, supplied the discipline that kept me from losing total control of my classroom. One afternoon, he took me to visit some of the homes and families of the students I taught. It was then that my real education as a teacher began. Although I had grown up not more than ten miles from Wheelwright, I saw a world that day that I had not known really existed.

In one of the homes, six or seven adults were living in a crowded five-room house. At other stops, the principal told me about the brother or father of a student who was either in jail or had abandoned the family. When we pulled back into the school parking lot, he told me that I shouldn't really expect too much of most of the students, and that for some of them just coming to school was an accomplishment. I didn't doubt his word. During my first months there, I had seen some of what my principal was talking about. I knew one boy who had been locked in a closet for several hours at a time when he disobeyed his stepfather, and I knew there were other equally horrible situations. It was very seldom that I did not leave the school feeling totally defeated or in tears. But as inadequate as I was as a teacher, the one thing that never occurred to me was to follow the advice that the principal gave me on that day. I never intended to lower my expectations for my students. I knew there was nothing wrong with their ability to think, and I suppose I thought of myself. I wondered what would have happened to me if someone had decided that because I was the child of a coal miner I was not capable of doing very much. It was just not thinkable.

In time, I gained control of my classes, and I taught Chaucer and Shakespeare and writing skills to my students. With some I was successful; they went on to college and did well, but I knew that they would have done so with or without me. I still left school each day feeling that with the majority of them I was losing the battle. The few students with whom I was able to establish personal relationships endured my classes for that reason, but we all knew that what was happening in the classroom wasn't of any real importance to them.

And that was the way things continued until 1985, when I made what I thought was a simple decision to change what I was doing after I attended a Foxfire workshop at Berea College conducted by Eliot Wigginton. To be honest, I conceived of the project as simply a way to make the acquisition of writing skills more palatable to my students; I had no deep understanding of the changes that would take place once I began the process.

In my senior English class, I discussed the possibility of doing a magazine based on interviews with older people in the area. We would look at the changes that had taken place in the region with the arrival of the coal industry. At first, none of what was happening seemed too remarkable. We set up interviews and spent a great deal of time after school working on the project. Because I didn't know much about the subject we had chosen to study, I found myself asking my students more and more for help. Suddenly, the boys who sat in the back of the room creating problems for me were making real contributions to the class, and our time together began to change in deeper ways.

One morning after I left my class, I ran into one of the boys in my second-period English class and he told me that Tony, one of the students in the senior English class, was in trouble and was about to be suspended. Tony had been taking photographs for the magazine, and I found myself forgetting why I had left the classroom and going instead to the principal's office. We needed to take a crucial set of pictures for the magazine that week, but I don't think that is the reason I went. I didn't want the progress that Tony had made over the last few weeks to be lost because of one mistake. In front of Tony, I told the principal what a help he had been in class and what a good student he was. His friends were waiting just outside the office and in the hallway, as I discovered later. When we left the office, Tony was still in school and there was a quietness among the group that I had not seen before. On our way out, we talked about what we had to do to get the photography finished. If there had been any doubt that we were in this together, my visit to the principal's office settled the matter. I had never been to the principal's office before to plead that a second chance be given to a student and my students knew that, but there was also a sense that we had started something that we needed to finish. Tony graduated from high school that year, and there were teachers who told me that it never would have happened if it had not been for that class.

The first edition of our magazine appeared in the spring of that year and we celebrated its arrival as something of a miracle. One of the state newspapers did a story about the class and the magazine. For a while, the students struggled with their celebrity, not quite believing that they deserved recognition and praise, and then they accepted it as someone might who has gone without food or water for a long time. I first began to recognize that we had done something important when another student, who had helped me carry the magazines into the school from my car on the day they arrived, picked one of them up and said with surprise that he thought it looked really good. But even at that point I was not really aware of everything that was going on with my students.

The real success of the project was driven home to me, not by the community's acceptance and support, but by a visit the following fall from one of the seniors who had been in the class. He had come back to see me, and by the rock wall that runs alongside the school grounds separating the campus from the public highway, we stood and talked for a long time. He told me that he had not been able to find a job and that he was still living at home. Things were not going well for him. We talked about all this in the indirect manner that I know my students are comfortable with. In the hills of eastern Kentucky, people often do not express their feelings directly, except, perhaps, in moments of anger. I know, for example, that my father is pleased with something I have done not because he has ever told me so, for he has never once done that. I know that he is proud of me when he begins to tease me. It's almost as if we do not know how to deal with emotions that bring us close to each other, so we find other, safer ways of expressing our feelings to each other.

As our conversation continued by the rock wall, I realized that Charles, for some reason, was going to change that convention. At the point when we had almost finished talking, he turned and looked directly at me and said, "You know, I didn't get much out of this school, but our magazine class, that was all right." We both knew that what was being said was more than a casual offhand remark. It is a moment I have remembered and wondered at for two years. Putting together the magazine had been hard work, had involved struggle and the willingness to put in long hours, but it had been the only experience that meant anything to him in his four years at the school; and now as he began his real struggle with the world around him, it was a memory that he kept with pride. Perhaps it helped in some way. I remember standing by that rock wall after he left, thinking of how little we had given him: a few weeks out of years, and feeling — with the same fervor that I had felt eight years before when I first walked into the school — that these students were being cheated and that they deserved more than they were getting.

For the past two years, I have taught a class devoted exclusively to producing a magazine at our school, and, more important, one that allows me to work with students in the manner that I did that first year. I have sometimes told myself that I am only experimenting with this method during this one class period, but I know that is really not true. Even in those classes I believe I am teaching with traditional methods, I know that I have changed in some important ways. After the first year with the magazine class, I intuitively felt the rightness of what was happening in my classroom, but I had very little intellectual understanding of why any of it was working, or of whether it could be duplicated with another group of students. Why was this working when everything else that I had tried over the years had failed so badly?

I don't have all the answers yet, and that is one of the things that I value most about this process. I am a learner again, studying my classroom, always changing and adapting, searching for better ways to teach. But I am beginning to believe that 95 percent of the difference lies in the changes that have taken place within me. Growing up in the mountains of eastern Kentucky, I had in so many subtle ways been taught that the life I was leading at home was not as good as that of others. Neither of my parents had finished grade school, and at some point in my education, without realizing it, I began to dismiss their knowledge and experience as unimportant. In school we studied algebra and American literature and history, and none of it was connected with the world I came home to. My mother wanted to tell stories about the earlier days, full of information about signs and beliefs in witches and supernatural happenings. That was nothing like what I was learning in school. For as long as I can remember, I have loved words. I hid away for hours just reading, but in school my words were wrong. I learned not to use the words I heard at home. College outside the mountains only sharpened the differences, and without realizing what was happening, I was creating two worlds inside my mind — the one that dealt with the outside world and the one I shared with my family. I was always aware of the fact that one of those worlds could betray me in the other. When I returned home to teach, I taught in the manner I had been taught myself, with the deep-seated conviction that education could "save" the children from an environment that I basically viewed as inferior. I was at war with the culture that I came from in more ways than one. By now, I could technically construct sentences and paragraphs that were sound, but I no longer wanted to write; I had nothing that I wanted to say. In so many ways, I was an outsider in my own home. As an educated person, I thought I should be making a difference in the community I lived in, but I couldn't see that I was. I did not understand how decisions were made or how changes were brought about. One of the people who understood those things was my father, but I had shut him out of my life a long time ago as a source of information. I had cut myself off from the people who could have given me the information that I needed: my parents and the people around me.

At some point during the last three years, I realized that the world around me was the best classroom I could offer my students, and with that single realization, my battle with my own environment ended. In the communities outside our school, my students and I could study the effects of technology upon people. As mining moved into the Appalachian region, what happened to people's lifestyles and their values? What are the logical effects of overdependence on a single industry? Why did some towns survive the bust-and-boom cycle of coal mining while others died?

How had the people of Appalachia become the victims of economic development? What happens when a small group of people have a great deal of power? What were the people like who settled in the hills of eastern Kentucky? Who were the artists and writers? The possibilities for research and understanding are endless. We could bring all that information into the classroom and examine, analyze, and learn from it. I have not reached the point where I am willing to assert that we are blessed by the fact that the Appalachian region has so many issues and problems to deal with, but I do believe that we have many subjects worthy of study. I also believe that if we are sensitive enough and do our research well enough, then perhaps we can come close to understanding the perceptions and changes and growth in the lives of the people of the mountains. Like Henry James, by submerging ourselves in their lives we might be able to gain a sense of who we are as a people and create students who leave our high schools feeling whole about themselves and capable of having some impact upon their own communities. Education does not have to create a sense of separateness.

I had not in any way allowed for the experiences of my students in my classes. The structure did not permit that. I was the dispenser of knowledge, and for the most part they sat passively responding to literature that was far removed from their own experiences. All the time, many of my students were confronting problems that I would have had trouble dealing with as an adult, but when they entered the classroom I made the decisions for them. They had to fit their lives within the forty-five minutes and the manner in which I had organized that time. The knowledge and skills they had acquired had to be put aside while we went about the business of school. Now I have learned to listen to students and, whenever possible, bring all the strengths that they possess inside the classroom. Over the past two years, I have watched them attack problems, verbalize solutions to those problems and put them into action and, in the process, exceed even my expectations. As I have given up some of the control within the classroom, I have learned that my students, given the opportunity, can do more than even I had believed possible. They are continually surprising me. As I have watched them grow as they have worked on this project, this little voice inside me has continued to say, "You mean you can do that?" Does that mean that I don't believe in them? No. What my surprise does mean is that even in my best moments I had not really known how much they could do in a classroom if I would let them. In a very real sense they are teaching me about the possibilities of learning.

The traditional class structure does not demand that students be involved in the learning process; it does not require that students be problem-solvers or creative. This past winter, one of my students and I spent over a week working on a word processor. At the insistence of students from last year's class, we had located enough money to purchase a computer and word processor toward the end of the school year. And there it sat. We were feeding introductions to the interviews into it and using it to edit those, but because our interviews were so long, we didn't know how to use it to do our editing. Sometimes we needed to shift paragraphs from page sixty to page one of the edited version, and we could not, of course, display enough of the interview on the screen to do that or obtain a sense of the entire feel of the piece. I did not know how to do it. One of the students in the class loved working with the computer. He had the technical expertise, and I had some knowledge of how to organize written material. Together, the two of us created an outline and coding system that would allow us to go through the long interviews, identify and label sentences and paragraphs that belonged together, and move them.

As we worked together, I realized how much both of us were learning. We had to test for transitions and coherence. If we put sentence x here, would it logically lead into y? Would the reader be able to follow the meaning? Had we distorted in any way what our contact was attempting to say? As we worked together, we had to adjust to each other's methods of working and getting things done. I tended to want to move faster, make quicker decisions, and move on, while my student wanted to take time to review what he had done and consider it before he moved on. In the beginning, we disagreed a great deal and argued as much as we worked. We also laughed a great deal. In the end, he had learned some important aspects of outlining and organization, skills he did not have, and I knew more about our computer and understood what must happen each time two of my students work together. Adjustments and compromises must be made.

I have learned to respect the different ways that people learn and work. When Lisa works on the layout for our magazine, everything must have a certain order in her mind before she can work. Tools and equipment must be placed in certain spots. She sees things that I am not able to see. If a line is slightly off, she recognizes it immediately and corrects it. She is just as organized when she edits an interview. Every line is coded and labeled and then marked with different colors of ink before she begins to consider the order in which she wants the information. I must take time to explain details to her so she can get a sense of an entire assignment in her mind; she has to visualize it as a whole.

Other students in my class use entirely different approaches. One girl never labels anything as she works with an interview. She reads and rereads it until she has a sense of how she wants to organize it and then moves it in bits and pieces. I remember Lisa's reaction when she first saw this method. Believing her own method was so much better, she couldn't understand why the student was working in this manner. By the end of the year, Lisa had stopped trying to convince her that she should change her method. Lisa saw that it worked, and that, in the end, was what really mattered.

Because I work with the students, I know the difficulty of the assignments that they undertake. Last year, because of space limitations in the magazine, we had to take one of the longer interviews we had done and do an article based on the information, making use of key quotations. Most of the information seemed important, and we worked for several weeks on condensing it. Finally, during one session, one of the students working on the article turned to me and said, "This is like writing a poem." I had not thought of it that way, but she was right. We had to present the interview in seven pages rather than seventy, and in doing that we had to use skills that none of my college writing courses had demanded of me. I now fully recognize that my students are making use of some very complex writing and organizational skills.

It is very difficult for me to identify all the changes I see taking place in the students I work with. I have watched wonderful relationships develop between the students and the people in the community and witnessed my students deal with people who have become so emotional during an interview that they have cried. As I have watched them, I have realized that they are becoming sensitive to the reality and the needs of others, and in doing so they forget, for a while, about some of the problems in their own lives. And, through it all, I know that they are involved in the very best kind of learning. This is why I wanted to be a teacher. I want to know about the worlds that my students bring into the classroom with them. I have discoveries to make about them and the people that live in them. If teaching is the creative process that I believe it is, I have to listen; I have to understand that some of my students bring scars and terrible experiences into the classroom with them. But I believe with every fiber of my being that we cannot sell students short because of those experiences and scars. They have had the strength to deal with them, and I have to find ways to use that strength in my classroom. I cannot expect less from them or myself.

Inside the car, the girls are talking again. They are worried about the people they will be speaking to tomorrow. Dorothy and Pam have moved forward in their seats and have joined Lisa and me again.

"Will you tell them that we do good work?" Dorothy asks. I glance at her and smile.

"Yes, I will." For a moment, there is silence in the car, but Dorothy is smiling.

Cultural Myths in the Making of a Teacher: Biography and Social Structure in Teacher Education

DEBORAH P. BRITZMAN

Deborah Britzman's chapter expands the context of education beyond the economic realities that Connell addresses to the social realities embedded in the education of teachers. Britzman believes that recent theoretical discussions of the role of education in the reproduction of the social system need to start from descriptions of how teachers are educated. She addresses this need by drawing on her experiences as a teacher educator to offer an analysis of the reproductive mechanism at work in teacher education. She describes the way in which teachers' personal histories interact with common myths in our culture to maintain and reinforce current teaching practices. By becoming conscious of these mechanisms, Britzman argues, student teachers can gain a critical perspective, which they need to gain control of the social mechanisms that would otherwise control them. Within this chapter we see the teacher become the student, and — like Stumbo's experience — understand how teachers' own educational experiences reverberate through each classroom they occupy, ultimately shaping the learning experiences of all the children they teach.

Student teaching is routinely considered the ritual bridge between the student's world and the teacher's world. Fresh from university course work, the student teacher enters the classroom and attempts simultaneously to experience, incorporate, and interpret the teacher's perspective. Presumably, student teaching should be a time when the student teacher's practice begins to become informed by educational theory and where the metamorphosis from the role of student to that of teacher begins. Indeed, the dominant model of teacher education is organized on this implicit theory of immediate integration: the university provides the theories, methods, and skills; schools provide the classroom, curriculum, and students; and the student teacher provides the individual effort; all of which combine to produce the finished product of professional teacher. This training model, however, ignores the role of the social and political context of teacher education while emphasizing

Harvard Educational Review Vol. 56 No. 4 November 1986, 442–456

the individual's effort. Here, the social problem of becoming a teacher is reduced to an individual struggle. Furthermore, this problem is exacerbated by the dominant cultural view of the teacher as rugged individualist (Waller, 1961). Understanding the complex process of learning to become a teacher, however, requires a qualitatively different perspective on the context within which learning to teach occurs. Student teachers need to understand how the interaction between time, place, people, ideas, and personal growth contributes to the process of professional development. Critical consideration must be given to what happens when the student teacher's biography, or cumulative social experience, becomes part of the implicit context of teacher education.

The sense of time and place in which teacher education is currently rooted reflects its nineteenth-century origins. Then, as now, teacher education was largely designed as vocational training, based on an apprenticeship model of education (Gordon, 1985). Inherent in this apprenticeship model is a behavioristic view of learning: learning is achieved through imitation of working teachers and repeated practice. This model, however, ignores the cultural baggage carried by new student teachers: the mass experience of compulsory education has made teaching one of the most socially familiar professions in the United States. We have all played a role opposite teachers for a large part of our lives. It is taken for granted that we all know what a teacher is and does. Prospective teachers, then, bring to their teacher education more than their desire to teach. They bring their implicit institutional biographies — the cumulative experience of school lives — which, in turn, inform their knowledge of the student's world, of school structure, and of curriculum. All this contributes to well-worn and commonsensical images of the teacher's work and serves as the frame of reference for prospective teachers' self-images. But the dominant model of teacher education as vocational training does not address the hidden significance of biography in the making of a teacher, particularly as it is lived during student teaching.

The apprenticeship of student teaching is routinely considered in contradictory terms. It is both a time of "getting one's feet wet" and a "sink-or-swim" experience. This contradiction between gradual and abrupt experience reveals the tensions of learning to teach amid the immediate demands of classroom life. But learning to teach requires more than attending to the immediate present. The hidden work of the student teacher really involves negotiating past and present demands. While the student teacher's past informs her/his present teaching, the present generates its own constraints. The student teacher must try to understand his or her own institutional biography as it is evoked by the return to classroom life, while at the same time educating others and learning the teacher's world. Throughout student teaching, the tensions between biography, practice, and structure create a cacophony of conflicting demands. How does the student teacher make sense of them?

This article explores what prospective secondary teachers ostensibly learn about the work of teachers as they combine their own experience in compulsory education and teacher education with their student teaching practice. The words of two student teachers will be used to illustrate how they made sense of the dilemmas they confronted. I argue that the underlying values that coalesce in one's institutional biography, if unexamined, propel the cultural reproduction of authoritarian teaching practices and naturalize the contexts that generate such a cycle. My analysis rests upon the assumption that teacher education, like any education, is an ideological education. It promotes particular images of power, knowledge, and values by rewarding particular forms of individual and institutional behavior. The ways that prospective teachers understand and experience power throughout teacher education shape their acceptance or rejection of the status quo. Similarly, teacher education's conception of knowledge can promote a view of the teacher as either technician or intellectual, and the extent to which values are rendered explicit can either inhibit or encourage a more critical pedagogy. By situating the problem of becoming a teacher within a political and ideological framework, we can better understand how past teaching models are reproduced during student teaching and the consequences of cultural reproduction in the lives of those learning to teach.

The Structure of Experience and the Experience of Structure

To understand that school provides the context within which compulsory education occurs calls for an awareness of the power of its structure. Three important facts commonly shape our views and experiences of secondary school teaching and learning. First, social control is a significant dynamic in classroom life. Second, curriculum is compartmentally organized. Finally, schools are hierarchically ordered. While these statements appear simply to characterize the organization or the structure of experience, their consequences are ultimately political in that this structure supports particular social, economic, and ideological interests of the dominant society (Apple, 1982).

Within the United States, public education is compulsory. While the desirability of compulsory education is not disputed here, the influence of the compulsory context on the ways that students are organized accounts for many antagonisms between students and teachers. Within this context, power struggles are inevitable, and teachers are required to spend an inordinate amount of time orchestrating the practice of social control. It is the teacher's work to control large groups of students in order to get through classroom routine. This part of the teacher's work is so common as to be characterized by teachers as "mob-control." Yet what dominates the perceptions of both teachers and students is the individual teacher's ability to control the class rather than the institutional mandate to control. Indeed, for students, this structural feature of the teacher's work often appears as an extension of the teacher's personality (Everhart, 1983; Payne, 1984; Waller, 1932).

The compartmentalization of curriculum defines classroom structure, our images of knowledge, and the work, status, and roles of teachers and students. Curricular organization is fragmented into instructional activities reduced to discrete blocks of time, thereby isolating subject areas and **decontextualizing**[a] skills. This process of fragmentation severs knowledge from its sociopolitical context and consequences and obscures relationships that connect the student to her/his social world. For example, in studying the United States Constitution, students may memorize its structural features without acquiring an awareness of their own civil rights. Knowledge takes on the appearance of a product, something unrelated to the learner's experience and empowerment; as Freire's (1981) work demonstrates, it is as if the teacher "banks" education into the passive vessel of the student. As a

---

[a] **Decontextualizing** is the taking of incidents, statements, or actions out of the context in which they occurred, and in doing so altering the original intent of the incident, statement, or action.

product that is socially distributed by the teacher, it is privately acquired by the student.

While the hierarchical order of school creates and sustains specific institutionalized roles of unequal power and status, in the eyes of students the teacher's place in this hierarchy is often obscured by her/his seemingly autonomous classroom presence. Since students are segregated from the behind-the-scenes world of teachers and administrators and have no power to effect organizational change, they often reduce school hierarchy to that of classroom life. To students, school hierarchy looks more like a teacher's personal decision than a structural feature of the school (Everhart, 1983; Payne, 1984).

For students and teachers who remain in the same classroom day after day, the classroom does indeed take on the appearance of a separate and private world. Its relationship to school structure is taken for granted and thus becomes invisible, as do the underlying values of social control, hierarchical authority, and knowledge as external to the knower. Structure becomes personified by the teacher, since the teacher is the most accessible authority figure and distributor of school knowledge. The teacher's classroom appearance, however, as autonomous, charismatic, and in control (Descombe, 1982), tends further to cloak school structure by glorifying individual effort. But while the classroom represents the teacher's mandated authority, it also represents the teacher's isolation. Despite the reality that teachers share collective problems, in this individual world, asking for help is viewed as a sign of weakness. Within the culture of teachers, the combination of isolation and an emphasis on the value of autonomy functions to promote an "ethos of privacy" (Descombe, 1982, p. 257). As shared concerns become individualized as private concerns, privacy becomes valued as a source of teacher autonomy.

Within this context of school structure, students construct images of the teacher's world. In an ethnographic study of junior high school students, Everhart (1983) describes how students understand the work of teachers:

> From the student point of view, there was little else involved in what teacher did in the classroom other than represented in this simple 'factory model' of learning; that is, the teacher's pouring in the facts and the students pouring them back in the form of papers and tests . . . . The student picture of teachers provided little room for emotion, with the exception of that associated with student violation of school standards. The teacher's world, in the student's eyes, was straightforward and linear, hardly complex at all. (p. 74)

This simplification of the teacher's work is a direct consequence of the hierarchical context from which this work is viewed. Since students rarely have any structural mechanism for sharing decision-making power in determining school hierarchy, curriculum, or pedagogical style, they experience these factors as an accomplished fact. On the classroom level, it is a rare teacher who lends students insight into her/his own teaching struggles. Consequently, what students tend to observe is a pattern that results from the hidden influences of teacher preparation, school policy, curricular mandates, and state law. Beyond students' recognition that teachers have more police-like power in the classroom, students perceive the teacher's work as similar to their own work, and, as such, reduce it to mere classroom performance.

Years of classroom experience allow students to have very specific expectations of how teachers should act in the classroom. Students, for example, expect the teacher to maintain classroom control, enforce rules, and present the curriculum. Students expect teachers to be certain in both their behavior and in their knowledge, and students articulate these expectations if the teacher in any way deviates from this traditional image. In this sense, students do coach their teachers in ways that reinforce school structure and, as such, constitute an immediate source of teacher socialization (Britzman, 1985). So, while teachers are socializing the students, students are also socializing teachers.

Practical Experience and Remote Theory

Prospective teachers enter teacher education with practical theories about the work and stance of teachers. Grounded in their student perspectives, constructed from their prolonged experience of compulsory classroom life, their view of the teacher's work is incomplete insofar as it is simplified to mere classroom performance. Yet this partial view is a significant factor in shaping prospective teachers' desires for a practical training experience (Beyer, 1985; Buchmann & Schwille, 1983; Descombe, 1982). The problem, however, is not so much their desire for practical methods as it is their understanding, usually legitimated by vocational models of teacher education, of methods as ends rather than as means. The "methods as ends" model of teaching reduces the complexity of pedagogical activity to a technical solution (Beyer, 1985).

Emphasis on a utilitarian approach reinforces present school structure and legitimates the existing school reality as the only possible reality. Consequently, the dominant organization of teacher education, which presupposes an acceptance of the way things are, tends also to reinforce the ideas and images of education that prospective teachers bring to their training. It is a cycle that powerfully affects prospective teachers' understanding of the relationship between pedagogical practice and theory. Prospective teachers, then, want and expect to receive practical things, automatic and generic methods for immediate classroom application. They bring to their teacher education a search for recipes, and, often, a dominant concern with methods of classroom discipline, because they are quite familiar with the teacher's role as social controller. Education course work that does not immediately address "know-how" or how to "make do" with the way things are, appears impractical and idealistic. Real school life, then, is taken for granted as the measure of a teacher education program, and, as such, the student teaching semester is implicitly valued as the training ground that will fill the void left by theoretical course work.

These implicit needs and expectations of prospective teachers help determine which education courses are seen to be meaningful during student teaching. Courses in pedagogical theory, child psychology, educational history, and sociology generally do not inform the student teacher's practice, particularly if these courses are organized in lecture format (Iannaccone, 1963; Maddox, 1968; Seiferth & Purcell, 1980). Maddox's finding, based on sixty-two graduate student teacher interviews, reveal, for example, that student teachers depend more on learning by intuitive trial-and-error during student teaching than on knowledge presented in teacher education.

Indeed, theory informs only a small portion of the pedagogical practice that takes place during the student-teaching experience. This theoretical void is commonly explained by pointing to the nature of student teaching. Many researchers contend that student teachers are more concerned with survival than with theory (Fuller & Brown, 1975; Popkewitz, 1978). Because survival becomes a "sink-or-swim" situation, student teachers are more likely to consider what works in the classroom while ignoring the reasons for and consequences of activities that appear to work (Hooper & Johnson, 1973). What works in the classroom is usually congruent with bureaucratic expectations and norms. So when 162 student teachers in Sorenson's (1967) study were asked to list for their best friends the things one must do in order to get an A in student teaching, the following advice was frequently offered: Do as you are told without question, be well organized, and keep your class under control. As for theory, these student teachers warned their friends not to attempt to apply it (Sorenson, 1967).

The remoteness of educational theory, however, is not limited to the condition of student teaching. Within school settings, university theory counts for little. That is, teachers are usually evaluated on their ability to orchestrate classroom control rather than to articulate pedagogical theory (Descombe, 1982). In my own study on secondary student teacher socialization, all participants viewed their education courses as a waste of time (Britzman, 1985). In the words of two student teachers:

> I had instructional planning, which I despised. Instructional planning, I felt, could have merged with a methods course, or leave it to on-the-job training. . . . But I would rather just have gotten the information and go do it. Teacher training doesn't compare to actually being in school and learning. And I don't know how much help all those education classes gave me. (p. 120)

> They're all theory courses, outside of the one where you develop something. None of the courses are like, this is how you fill out a grade book, or this is how you teach. I think it's something I'm going to learn how to do myself. I don't think you learn to be a teacher by going to the university. You have to rely on your experience, develop your own style. (p. 255)

The apprenticeship model of teacher education implicitly encourages student teachers to look to on-the-job training, regardless of whether or not schools are designed to facilitate teacher education. In each of the above cases, education courses were not considered as real experience. Instead, in the minds of these student teachers, their education courses failed to demonstrate the value of theory, or even to shed light on their pragmatic needs.

The learning expectations brought to teacher education by these student teachers resembled the images of learning cultivated in their compulsory school lives. There, learning took the form of a concrete product, something acquired, possessed, and immediately applied. Consequently, the university-promoted theories, often dispensed in a language separate from the student teaching reality, appeared more like speculative idealism than concrete realism. Repeatedly, student teachers do leave their university course work with a concept of theory as abstract and untenable. Moreover, the student teacher's over-reliance on and glorification of practical firsthand experience tends to devalue theory even before it is encountered. Instead, student teachers internalize the pervasive cultural belief that experience makes the teacher. So, while firsthand classroom experience is a prerequisite to understanding the complex work of teachers, experience, like teaching methods, is a means for understanding rather than an end in itself (Feinman-Nemser & Buchmann, 1985). Unless teaching experience is critically analyzed in relation to educational theory, experience that is taken for granted tends to reinforce commonsensical perspectives prospective teachers bring to their teacher education.

Telling Experience and the Stuff of Myths

The student teacher enters the apprenticeship classroom armed with a lifetime of student experience. This institutional biography tells the student teacher how to navigate through the school structure and provides a foundation for the stock responses necessary to maintain it. Additionally, implicit in these stock responses are particular images of the teacher, mythic images that tend to sustain and cloak the very structure that produces them.

Early on, the student teacher learns that teaching is a lonely endeavor. The student teacher's isolation simultaneously suggests an overwhelming burden of responsibility as well as the promise of individual power. But while the structure of the teaching experience is characterized by isolation, it is also sustained and obscured by the value placed on individual effort. As structure fades into the background of daily activity and is "forgotten," the teacher's individualized effort appears as the sole determinant of educational matters. Consequently, while the teacher is a significant actor in the educational drama, the valorization of individual effort sustains a view of the teacher as the only actor. With this view, individual effort takes on mythic proportions.

Throughout the course of my study of secondary student teacher socialization, student teachers and the professionals who surrounded them held shared views about the work and power of teachers (Britzman, 1985). Evoked to somehow illustrate and explain their teaching intentions, these views, or what I have come to call "cultural myths," tended to rationalize and legitimize the existing school structure as well as to provide a semblance of order, control, and certainty in the face of the uncertainty of the teacher's world. Given the emphasis on social control in the school context, order and certainty are significant psychological and institutional needs. In the case of the student teacher, cultural myths contribute to the student teacher's taken-for-granted views of power, authority, and knowledge, while serving to mystify school structure. Cultural myths, then, provide a set of ideal images, definitions, justifications and measures for thought and activity and sustain a naturalized view of the reality it seeks to encode. As Barthes (1985) observed, a myth, as a language for codifying what a culture values, serves contradictory functions: "it points out and it notifies, it makes us understand something and it imposes it on us" (p. 177).

Three recurring cultural myths emerged throughout the course of my study: 1) everything depends on the teacher; 2) the teacher is the expert; and 3) teachers are self-made. While each cultural myth concerns a social aspect of the teacher's work — control, curriculum, and the presentation of self — they are all stated in highly individualistic terms. These myths valorize the individual and make inconsequential the institutional constraints that frame the teacher's work. The teacher is depicted as a self-contained world. Such myths transform the teacher's actual isolation into a valued autonomy that, in turn, promotes the larger social value of rugged individualism.

Everything Depends on the Teacher

Both teachers and students implicitly understand two rules governing the hidden tensions of classroom life: unless the teacher establishes control there will be no learning, and, if the teacher does not control the students, the students will control the teacher. This power struggle, predicated upon the institutional expectation that teachers individually control their classes, equates learning with control. Additionally, outside aid in controlling the class is perceived as a sign of professional incompetency (Descombe, 1982). Teachers tend to judge themselves, and others tend to judge them, on the basis of their success with this individual struggle. Everything — student learning, the presentation of curriculum, and social control — is held to be within the teacher's domain, while the teacher's isolated classroom existence is accepted as the norm.

Isolation thus creates a strong pressure to replace students' real learning with social control. This pressure is especially problematic for the student teacher, who is also engaged in his or her own process of learning. While spontaneity and the unexpected should be significant features of a student teacher's own learning experiences, the classroom requirement to present a stable appearance tends to make student teachers view the unexpected as a "bind" rather than as an opportunity for learning. The fact is, most student teachers hardly understand their own learning processes and therefore find it difficult to understand them in others. In the words of two prospective teachers:

> Today was the day when I really didn't know what to expect. It seems as a teacher, you're going to have to react then and there. (p. 345)

> Quick thinking . . . getting myself out of the bind I'm in seems like a requirement in teaching. To be able to know, what next, what next. If something isn't working, or to make those transitions really fast to avoid unpleasant silences. (p. 207)

The student teachers who made these statements believe they must master the art of premonition and instantaneous response — both of which depend on the teacher's ability to anticipate and contain the unexpected — to insure control as a prerequisite for student learning. Yet within the push to control learning, the student teacher also devalues her/his power to explore and be open to unknown teaching territory. Consequently, in classroom situations the student in each student teacher often becomes repressed and denied.

The pressure to control learning, however, affects more than the student teacher's immediate activity. As we saw above, it also sustains implicit views of learning and the learner. When the double pressures of isolation and institutional mandates to control force teachers to equate learning with social control, the teacher's role becomes one of merely instilling knowledge rather than engaging learners. Moreover, this pressure denies the webs of mutual dependency and the power relationships that characterize and give shape to classroom life. As such, student and teacher negotiations, an essential interaction throughout student teaching, are ignored when the student teacher feels compelled to predict, contain, and thus control student learning. A teacher-centered approach to learning is implicitly sustained, since this myth assumes that students are incapable of leadership, insight, or learning without a teacher's intervention. When everything depends on the teacher, the teacher's role is confined to controlling the situation. Consequently, the cultural myth that everything depends on the teacher compels the teacher to exert institutional authority. In the case of both the teacher and the student teacher, social control is the measure of establishing competency.

The Teacher as Expert

The fear most commonly articulated by prospective teachers is that they will never know enough to teach. Behind this fear is the larger cultural expectation that teachers must be certain in their knowledge. Teachers are supposed to know the answers. The stance of the expert is particularly problematic for the student teacher simultaneously being educated as a student while educating others. In the words of two student teachers:

> The pressure is there to know, whether it's from yourself, or the students or other teachers. I mean there's a category on the teacher-certification evaluation form: Is this person knowledgeable in her field? But when you're in the classroom, initially you're trying to prove yourself, and you want to know. And then someone asks a question. There is that tug, "Gee, why don't I know? I should know that." (p. 219)

> I didn't have much of a background in history and felt just a few pages ahead of the students. It was kind of strange to be put into a position where I'm supposed to know something to teach people and I don't know it myself and I have to hurry up and learn it so I could teach them. (p. 313)

While these student teachers felt the pressure to know and the corresponding guilt in not knowing, classroom performance prevented the deeper epistemological issues — about the nature of knowing and the values that knowledge promotes — from being explored. Instead, knowledge was reduced to a set of discrete and isolated units to be acquired, while not knowing — and indeed, any condition of uncertainty — became a threat to the teacher's authority.

Having been students themselves, teachers have internalized a view of knowing shaped by classroom life and governed by the compartmentalization of curriculum. The combined effects of compulsory schooling and university education have naturalized the image of the teacher as expert. Knowing answers appears to demonstrate the teacher's ability to "think on her/his feet," a seemingly significant ingredient in the making of a teacher. From the student teacher's point of view, the veteran teacher appears to know the material backward and forward. Knowledge, from this perspective, resides between the covers of textbooks and presumably becomes familiar with years of use. Many student teachers, then, tend to approach the problem of knowing, not as an intellectual challenge, but as a function of accumulating classroom experience. Acquiring classroom experience and therefore becoming an "expert" becomes the key to controlling knowledge and imposing it on students as a means of classroom control.

The view of the teacher as expert also tends to reinforce the image of teacher as autonomous individual. From this perspective, teachers seem to have learned everything and, consequently, have nothing to learn; knowledge appears as finite and unchanging. As a possession, knowledge also implies territorial rights, which become naturalized by the compartmentalization of curriculum. Knowledge as private property denies the emotional and social changes that accompany the process of reflective understanding. The cultural myth of teachers as experts, then, contributes to the **reification**[b] of both knowledge and the knower. In the case of the student teacher, any condition of uncertainty is viewed as a threat to becoming an expert.

Teachers Are Self-Made

The third cultural myth, that teachers are self-made, serves seemingly contradictory functions, since it supports the conflicting views that teachers form themselves and are "born" into the profession. This myth provides a commonsense explanation to the problem of how teachers are made. It is a highly individualistic explanation that reinforces the image of the "natural teacher." This natural teacher somehow possesses talent, intuition, and common sense, all internal and implicit features that combine to heighten the power of the subjective self. The value placed on these internal qualities diminishes recognition of the importance of social forces and institutional contexts in the teacher's process of growth.

More than any other cultural myth, the dominant belief that teachers "make" themselves functions to devalue teacher education, educational theory, and the social process of making value systems explicit. Here, since the teacher appears as a completed product, there is no need to change or even explain one's activity. This myth structures a suspicion of theory, which takes the form of anti-intellectualism. So while this myth may be a response to teachers' real alienation from their first-hand experience with the decontextualized theory so often dispensed in teacher education programs, a larger consequence concerns the rejection of any concept of theory. Instead of critiquing, generating, or grounding theory, there is a pervasive expectation that the individual generates everything that makes a teacher. For example, one student teacher remarked: "I think teaching is something that I'm going to learn how to do myself. Nobody is going to be able to teach me. You have to rely on your own experience. I think you have to do it and develop your own style." Sentiments like this, which reflect only a part of the reality, are distorted by cultural myth to occupy the whole picture of teacher education.

In the supposedly self-made world of the teacher, pedagogy becomes a product of one's personality. As such, pedagogy is replaced by teaching style. This teaching style, viewed as an extension of one's personality, functions to distinguish one teacher from the next and is valued as an important source of establishing one's individuality and autonomy (Descombe, 1982). Indeed, many in the field of teacher education promote the view that teaching style cannot be taught, but is considered a self-constructed product mediated only by personal choice. In the case of the student teacher learning to teach, the problem is not so much that teaching style can reflect something about the individual as it is the mystification of the process whereby teaching style develops.

The professional legitimation of teaching style over pedagogy denies both the social basis of teaching and the institutional pressure for teachers to exert social control. In reality, the activity of teaching is significantly influenced by the mutual social relationship between teachers and students. Within this compulsory relationship, both conflict and social dependency are inevitable features, creating an arena of struggle within which teaching style becomes subject to social negotiation.

[b] **Reification** refers to the process of making an idea or concept into a concrete, unchangeable thing.

Teaching style, then, turns out to be not so much an individually determined product as a complex movement between the teacher, the students, the curriculum, and the school culture. Thus, the myth that teachers are self-made serves to cloak the social relationships and the context of school structure by exaggerating personal autonomy. Like the other myths, this one provides the final brushstrokes on the portrait of the teacher as rugged individual: if one cannot make the grade, one is not meant to be a teacher.

Uncovering Biography

Mills (1959) argued that the individual has the capacity to understand critically his or her life experiences and present dilemmas by situating her/himself within history. This connection allows the individual critical insight into both the nature of her or his relationships to individuals, institutions, cultural values, and political events, and the ways in which these social relationships contribute to the individual's identity, values, and ideological perspectives. In this way, individuals do have the capacity to participate in shaping and responding to the social forces that directly affect their lives. In the case of student teachers, uncovering biography can empower student teachers through a greater participation in their own process of becoming a teacher and move them beyond the sway of cultural authority.

Exploring the internal world of prospective teachers requires a journey into biography and an understanding of the contexts through which the future teacher progresses. One such context is the historical experience of lives lived in compulsory education, since it is there that prospective teachers first experience the classroom life to which they return as student teachers. As previously described, life in the classroom is characterized by routine as well as disruption. Student teachers expect both and have had years of observing teachers' responses to these situations. But, while the situations are familiar, experiencing these tensions from the teacher's role is not. Indeed, the emotional world of the teacher is a new encounter. This is the difficult process of making sense of, and acting within, self-doubt, uncertainty, and the unexpected, while assuming a role that requires confidence, certainty, and stability. It is a painful experience, often carried out in a state of disequilibrium.

While disequilibrium is a necessary condition for transformation, the student teacher tends to deal with disequilibrium as a threatening experience. That is, given the immediacy of classroom life, student teachers often reduce conflicts in a way that minimizes the complexity of their work. The way we interpret a situation influences our response to that situation. The cultural myths previously described should be considered as a way to come to terms with such dissonance: they are not so much mechanical recipes as they are culturally provided ways of seeing the teacher's world, and guidelines for interpreting the teacher's stance. There may not be a direct correspondence between each myth and a specific pedagogy, but the underlying values each myth supports encourage compliance to bureaucratic expectations while obscuring the messier process of living these expectations.

Certainly cultural myths promote a view of the teacher as rugged individual, a stance that bestows valor on the lonely process of becoming a teacher but at the same time obscures the social forces that individualize this struggle. While individual effort is, of course, a necessary prerequisite to learning to teach, so too are social negotiation, interaction, and social dependence. However, the image of the teacher as rugged individual stigmatizes negotiation and views social dependency as a weakness while it promotes autonomy as a strength. The image of the rugged individual represents a familiar and admired legend in the dominant culture, a lesson, so to say, in the possibility of overcoming difficult circumstances through sheer ingenuity and individual effort. Usually, this lesson is used to illustrate economic success in the sense of the individual's ability to rise from "rags to riches." For the rugged individual, any context — be it history, race, class, sex, or society — is viewed as a mere handicap to be individually overcome. In this view, the rugged individual becomes competitive and possessive, uninterested in social change and obsessed with getting ahead. The ideology supporting this notion of the rugged individual is used to justify success or failure, social class, and social inequality. This brand of individualism infuses the individual with both undue power and undue culpability. Ryan (1971), in his analysis of how social problems become individualized while social context and history are trivialized, aptly termed the ideology fueling this individualistic stance as "blaming the victim." Propelled by the belief that the individual is responsible for what is in fact a product of complex social circumstances, the ideology of blaming the victim ignores the influence of social relationships and historical progression. In the case of learning to teach, the cultural myth of the self-made, isolated, expert teacher supports the ideology of blaming the victim and ultimately promotes a simplistic understanding of the operation of power in educational life.

What does it mean to individualize the process of becoming a teacher? Teaching is fundamentally a social relationship characterized by mutual dependency, social interaction, and social engagement. Individualizing the social basis of teaching dissolves the social context, establishing instead the supposed autonomy and very real isolation of the teacher in the current school structure. Once the student teacher is severed from the social context of teaching, the tendency is to reproduce rather than to challenge her or his institutional biography. The values embedded in the institutional biography become sedimented and serve as the foundation for the cultural myths that legitimize a hierarchical image of authority, a reified view of knowledge, and a rugged individualist stance. Each of these particular views of power helps maintain the institutional push for social control. The value of individualism, inherent in each of these myths, requires an over-reliance on the self, which actually mandates an over-dependence on one's institutional biography. Consequently, a significant social outcome of the individualization of learning to teach is the reproduction of school structure through worldview and teaching style.

Furthermore, this dynamic of cultural reproduction is made insidious by its involuntary nature. Student teachers don't set out to collude with authoritarian pedagogical principles. Just the opposite: they usually begin with intentions of enhancing the human potential of their students and find this intention thwarted by the socially patterned school routines. Student teachers often describe their involuntary collusion with authoritarian pedagogy as "learning what not to do." Their intentions about teaching are contradicted by their daily teaching activity. For example, student teachers may very well intend to create a participatory classroom, but they are at a real loss as to how to proceed. They possess no comparative perspective and lack either prior experience in, or institutional support for, challenging the status quo and understanding how institutional constraints become lived practice.

Student teachers thus see no way out of the reproductive cycle. The irony of this dynamic is that cultural myths are evoked to serve not only as an "ideological escape," in that they function to preserve a facade of power in a seemingly powerless situation, but also as an "ideological trap," in that they preserve the teacher's isolation and naturalize the institutional pressure for social control.

In exploring the relationship between institutional biography and school structure, I have identified three hidden contradictions that operate within teacher education: 1) the presentation of teaching as an individual act when it is necessarily a social relationship; 2) the reification of knowledge, which obscures the existential, social, and political problems of knowing; and 3) the internalization of school structure in what appears to be a personally determined practice of pedagogy. Each of these problems encompasses the movement between school structure, the social self, and curriculum. Yet, while these problems are experienced as individual predicaments, they are socially generated. The presuppositions of individualism, buttressed by the tacit acceptance of social control in a compulsory setting, result in the individualization of contradictions that are collective in origin.

Throughout this article, I have argued that making critical sense of educational experience in the process of learning to teach requires more than simply the prospective teacher's return to the classroom and assumption of the teacher's role. While experience is always instructive, the issue is whether the instruction empowers human agency or replicates the status quo. Prospective teachers need to participate in developing critical ways of knowing that can interrogate school culture, the quality of students' and teachers' lives, school knowledge, and the particular role biography plays in understanding these dynamics. Without a critical perspective, the relationships between school culture and power become "housed" in prospective teachers' biographies and significantly impede their creative capacity for understanding and altering their circumstances. Moreover, without a critical understanding of how forms of knowledge, commonsensical categories, and cultural myths provide the ideological foundations for hierarchical authority and social control, prospective teachers will continue to be naively trapped in a cycle of cultural maintenance without the means to challenge such a painful circumstance.

In this vein, Aronowitz and Giroux's (1985) concept of the teacher as transformative intellectual can enable prospective teachers to reconsider the cultural images student teachers bring to their teacher education. The teacher as transformative intellectual can provide a significant counterframework for envisioning what is possible rather than merely accepting what is probable. Moreover, when prospective teachers become concerned with possibilities, they are able to theorize critically about how their teaching experience shapes their construction of explanations used to inform pedagogical decision making and problem posing. Understanding the work of the teacher as transformative intellectual can empower prospective teachers to "examine their own histories, those connections to the past which in part define who they are and how they mediate and function in the world" (Aronowitz & Giroux, 1985, p. 160). But for this reconception of the teacher to have any import in teacher education, we can no longer view or organize it as a technical education producing technicians (Giroux, 1985). In order for prospective teachers to experience becoming a teacher as an activity of human agency, the structure of teacher education must begin in a social environment that enables prospective teachers to engage in their professional development as students and teachers.

References

Apple, M. (1982). *Education and power.* New York: Routledge & Kegan Paul.

Aronowitz, S., & Giroux, H. A. (1985). *Education under siege: The conservative, liberal & radical debate over schooling.* South Hadley, MA: Bergin & Garvey.

Barthes. R. (1985). *Mythologies.* New York: Hill & Wang.

Beyer, L. (1985). Aesthetic experience for teacher preparation and social change. *Educational Theory, 35,* 385–297.

Britzman, D. (1985). *Reality and ritual: An ethnographic study of student teachers.* Unpublished doctoral dissertation, University of Massachusetts, Amherst.

Buchmann, M., & Schwille, J. (1983). Education: The overcoming of experience. *American Journal of Education, 92,* 30–51.

Descombe, M. (1982). The hidden pedagogy and its implications for teacher training. *British Journal of Sociology of Education, 3,* 249–265.

Everhart, R. (1983). Reading, writing and resistance. New York: Routledge & Kegan Paul.

Feinman-Nemser, S., & Buchmann, M. (1985). Pitfalls of experience in teacher preparation. *Teachers College Record, 57,* 53–66.

Freire, P. (1981). *Pedagogy of the oppressed.* New York: Continuum.

Fuller, F., & Brown, O. (1975). Becoming a teacher. In K. Ryan (Ed.), *Teacher education: The seventy-fourth yearbook for the study of education. Part 2* (pp. 25–52). Chicago: University of Chicago Press.

Giroux, H. A. (1985). Critical pedagogy and the resisting intellectual, Part 2. *Phenomenology & Pedagogy, 3*(2), 84–97.

Gordon, B. (1985). Teaching teachers: "Nation at risk" and the issue of knowledge in teacher education. *Urban Review, 17,* 33–46.

Hooper, D., & Johnson, T. (1973). Teaching practice: Training or social control? *Education for Teaching, 92,* 25–30.

Iannaccone, L. (1963). Student teaching: transitional stage in the making of a teacher. *Theory into Practice, 2,* 73–80.

Maddox, H. (1968). A descriptive study of teaching practice. *Educational Review, 20,* 177–190.

Mills, C. W. (1981). *The sociological imagination.* New York: Oxford University Press.

Payne, C. (1984). *Getting what we ask for.* Westport, CT: Greenwood Press.

Popkewitz, T. (1978). Educational reform and the problem of institutional life. *Educational Researcher, 8,* 3–8.

Ryan, W. (1971). *Blaming the victim.* New York: Vintage.

Seiferth, B., & Purcell, T. (1980). Student teachers' perceptions of their preparation for student teaching. *Association for the Study of Perception, 15,* 17–23.

Sorenson, G. (1967). What is learned in practice teaching. *Journal of Teacher Education, 18,* 173–178.

Waller, W. (1932). *The sociology of teaching.* New York: Wiley.

This article originated with a paper given at the First Working Conference on Critical Pedagogy in Amherst, Massachusetts, February 1986. Special thanks must go to Marilyn Stocker and Laura Lamash for their critical suggestions and encouragement.

Beyond the Methods Fetish:
Toward a Humanizing Pedagogy

LILIA I. BARTOLOMÉ

Lilia Bartolomé's chapter is intimately related to points made by Britzman and Connell. While Britzman and Connell point out how societal values impact the education of teachers and the poor, Bartolomé examines the current obsession for finding the right "methods" to improve the academic achievement of students who have historically been oppressed. Bartolomé argues that this focus on methods hides the less visible but more important reasons for these students' performance: the asymmetrical power relations in society that are reproduced in the schools, and the deficit view of minority students that many school personnel uncritically, and often unknowingly, hold. As an alternative to the prevailing methods fetish, Bartolomé endorses a humanizing pedagogy that respects and uses the environment, history, and perspectives of students as an integral part of educational practice. Discussing two approaches that show promise when implemented within a humanizing pedagogical framework — culturally responsive education and strategic teaching — Bartolomé emphasizes the need for teachers to develop political awareness of their relationship with students as knowers and active participants in their own learning.

Much of the current debate regarding the improvement of minority student academic achievement occurs at a level that treats education as a primarily technical issue (Giroux, 1992).[1] For example, the historical and present-day academic underachievement of certain culturally and linguistically subordinated student populations in the United States (e.g., Mexican Americans, Native Americans, Puerto Ricans) is often explained as resulting from the lack of cognitively, culturally, and/or linguistically appropriate teaching methods and educational programs.[2] As such, the solution to the problem of academic underachievement tends to be constructed in primarily methodological and mechanistic terms dislodged from the sociocultural reality that shapes it. That is, the solution to the current underachievement of students from subordinated cultures is often reduced to finding the "right" teaching methods, strategies, or prepackaged curricula that will work with students who do not respond to so-called "regular" or "normal" instruction.

Recent research studies have begun to identify educational programs found to be successful in working with culturally and linguistically subordinated minority student populations (Carter & Chatfield, 1986; Lucas, Henze, & Donato, 1990; Tikunoff, 1985; Webb, 1987). In addition, there has been specific interest in identifying teaching strategies that more effectively teach culturally and linguistically "different" students and other "disadvantaged" and "at-risk" students (Knapp & Shields, 1990; McLeod, 1994; Means & Knapp, 1991; Tinajero & Ada, 1993). Although it is important to identify useful and promising instructional programs and strategies, it is erroneous to assume that blind replication of instructional programs or teacher mastery of particular teaching methods, in and of themselves, will guarantee successful student learning, especially when we are discussing populations that historically have been mistreated and miseducated by the schools.

This focus on methods as solutions in the current literature coincides with many of my graduate students' beliefs regarding linguistic-minority education improvement. As a Chicana professor who has taught anti-racist multicultural education courses at various institutions, I am consistently confronted at the beginning of each semester by students who are anxious to learn the latest teaching methods — methods that they hope will somehow magically work on minority students.[3] Although my students are well-intentioned individuals who sincerely wish to create positive learning environments for culturally and linguistically subordinated students, they arrive with the expectation that I will provide them with easy answers in the form of specific instructional methods. That is, since they (implicitly) perceive the academic underachievement of subordinated students as a technical issue, the solutions they require are also expected to be technical in nature (e.g., specific teaching methods, instructional curricula and materials). They usually assume that: 1) they, as teachers, are fine and do not need to identify, interrogate, and change their biased beliefs and fragmented views about subordinated students; 2) schools, as institutions, are basically fair and democratic sites where all students are provided with similar, if not equal, treatment and learning conditions; and 3) children who experience academic difficulties (especially those from culturally and linguistically low-status groups) require some form of "special" instruction since they obviously have not been able to succeed under "regular" or "normal" instructional conditions. Consequently, if nothing is basically wrong with teachers and schools, they often conclude, then linguistic-minority academic underachievement is best dealt with by providing teachers with specific teaching methods that promise to be effective with culturally and linguistically subordinated students. To further complicate matters, many of my students seek *generic* teaching methods that will work with a variety of minority student populations, and they grow anxious and impatient when reminded that instruction for any group of students needs to be tailored or individualized to some extent. Some of my students appear to be seeking what María de la Luz Reyes (1992) defines as a "one size fits all" instructional recipe. Reyes explains that the term refers to the assumption that instructional methods that are deemed effective for mainstream populations will benefit *all* students, no matter what their backgrounds may be.[4] She explains that the assumption is

> similar to the "one size fits all" marketing concept that would have buyers believe that there is an average or ideal size among men and women. . . . Those who market "one size fits all" products suggest that if the article of clothing is not a good fit, the fault is not with the design of the garment, but those who are too fat, too skinny, too tall, too short, or too high-waisted. (p. 435)

I have found that many of my students similarly believe that teaching approaches that work with one minority population should also fit another (see Vogt, Jordan, & Tharp, 1987, for an example of this tendency). Reyes argues that educators often make this "one size fits all" assumption when discussing instructional approaches, such as process writing. For example, as Lisa Delpit (1988) has convincingly argued, the process writing approach that has been blindly embraced by mostly White liberal teachers often produces a negative result with African-American students. Delpit cites one Black student:

> I didn't feel she was teaching us anything. She wanted us to correct each other's papers and we were there to learn from her. She didn't teach anything, absolutely nothing.
>
> Maybe they're trying to learn what Black folks knew all the time. We understand how to improvise, how to express ourselves creatively. When I'm in a classroom, I'm not looking for that, I'm looking for structure, the more formal language.
>
> Now my buddy was in a Black teacher's class. And that lady was very good. She went through and explained and defined each part of the structure. This [White] teacher didn't get along with that Black teacher. She said she didn't agree with her methods. But *I* don't think that White teacher *had* any methods. (1988, p. 287)

The above quote is a glaring testimony that a "one size fits all" approach often does not work with the same level of effectiveness with all students across the board. Such assumptions reinforce a disarticulation between the embraced method and the sociocultural realities within which each method is implemented. I find that this "one size fits all" assumption is also held by many of my students about a number of teaching methods currently in vogue, such as cooperative learning and whole language instruction. The students imbue the "new" methods with almost magical properties that render them, in and of themselves, capable of improving students' academic standing.

One of my greatest challenges throughout the years has been to help students to understand that a myopic focus on methodology often serves to obfuscate the real question — which is why in our society, subordinated students do not generally succeed academically in schools. In fact, schools often reproduce the existing asymmetrical power relations among cultural groups (Anyon, 1988; Gibson & Ogbu, 1991; Giroux, 1992; Freire, 1985). I believe that by taking a sociohistorical view of present-day conditions and concerns that inform the lived experiences of socially perceived minority students, prospective teachers are better able to comprehend the quasi-colonial[a] nature of minority education. By engaging in this critical sociohistorical analysis of subordinated students' academic performance, most of my graduate students (teachers and prospective teachers) are better situated to re-interpret and reframe current educational concerns so as to develop pedagogical structures that speak to the day-to-day reality, struggles, concerns, and dreams of these students. By understanding the historical specificities of marginalized students, these teachers and prospective teachers come to realize that an uncritical focus on methods makes invisible the historical role that schools and their personnel

---

[a] **Colonial** is a term that refers to a historical or political power relationship in which one group or set of ideas has been held separate or subservient to others by force or by structural impediments.

have played (and continue to play), not only in discriminating against many cultur-ally different groups, but also in denying their humanity. By robbing students of their culture, language, history, and values, schools often reduce these students to the status of subhumans who need to be rescued from their "savage" selves. The end result of this cultural and linguistic eradication represents, in my view, a form of dehumanization. Therefore, any discussion having to do with the improvement of subordinated students' academic standing is incomplete if it does not address those discriminatory school practices that lead to dehumanization.

In this article, I argue that a necessary first step in reevaluating the failure or suc-cess of particular instructional methods used with subordinated students calls for a shift in perspective — a shift from a narrow and mechanistic view of instruction to one that is broader in scope and takes into consideration the sociohistorical and political dimensions of education. I discuss why effective methods are needed for these students and why certain strategies are deemed effective or ineffective in a given sociocultural context. My discussion will include a section that addresses the significance of teachers' understanding of the political nature of education, the re-productive nature of schools, and the schools' continued (yet unspoken) deficit views of subordinated students. By conducting a critical analysis of the sociocultural realities in which subordinated students find themselves at school, we highlight the importance of the implicit and explicit antagonistic relations between students and teachers (and other school representatives).

As a Chicana and a former classroom elementary and middle school teacher, I encountered negative race relations that ranged from teachers' outright rejection of subordinated students to their condescending pity, fear, indifference, and apathy when confronted by the challenges of minority-student education. I find it surpris-ing that little minority-education literature deals explicitly with the very real issue of antagonistic race relations between subordinated students and White school personnel (see Ogbu, 1987, and Giroux, 1992, for an in-depth discussion of this phenomenon).

For this reason, I also include in this article a section that discusses two instruc-tional methods and approaches identified as effective in current education litera-ture: culturally responsive education and strategic teaching. I examine the methods for pedagogical underpinnings that — under the critical use of politically clear teachers — have the potential to challenge students academically and intellectually while treating them with dignity and respect. More importantly, I examine the ped-agogical foundations that serve to humanize the educational process and enable both students and teachers to work toward breaking away from their unspoken antagonism and negative beliefs about each other and get on with the business of sharing and creating knowledge. I argue that the informed way in which a teacher implements a method can serve to offset potentially unequal relations and discrimi-natory structures and practices in the classroom and, in doing so, improve the quality of the instructional process for both student and teacher. In other words, politically informed teacher use of methods can create conditions that enable sub-ordinated students to move from their usual passive position to one of active and critical engagement. I am convinced that creating pedagogical spaces that enable students to move *from object to subject position* produces more far-reaching, posi-tive effects than the implementation of a particular teaching methodology, regard-less of how technically advanced and promising it may be.

The final section of this article will explore and suggest the implementation of what Donaldo Macedo (1994) designates as an

> anti-methods pedagogy that refuses to be enslaved by the rigidity of models and methodological paradigms. An anti-methods pedagogy should be informed by a critical understanding of the sociocultural context that guides our practices so as to free us from the beaten path of methodological certainties and specialisms. (p. 8)

Simply put, it is important that educators not blindly reject teaching methods across the board, but that they reject uncritical **appropriation**[b] of methods, materials, curricula, etc. Educators need to reject the present methods fetish so as to create learning environments informed by both action and reflection. In freeing themselves from the blind adoption of so-called effective (and sometimes "teacher-proof") strategies, teachers can begin the reflective process, which allows them to recreate and reinvent teaching methods and materials by always taking into consideration the sociocultural realities that can either limit or expand the possibilities to humanize education. It is important that teachers keep in mind that methods are social constructions that grow out of and reflect ideologies that often prevent teachers from understanding the pedagogical implications of asymmetrical power relations among different cultural groups.

The Significance of Teacher Political Clarity[5]

In his letter to North American educators, Paulo Freire (1987) argues that technical expertise and mastery of content area and methodology are insufficient to ensure effective instruction of students from subordinated cultures. Freire contends that, in addition to possessing content-area knowledge, teachers must possess political clarity so as to be able to effectively create, adopt, and modify teaching strategies that simultaneously respect and challenge learners from diverse cultural groups in a variety of learning environments.

Teachers working on improving their political clarity recognize that teaching is not a politically neutral undertaking. They understand that educational institutions are socializing institutions that mirror the greater society's culture, values, and norms. Schools reflect both the positive and negative aspects of a society. Thus, the unequal power relations among various social and cultural groups at the societal level are usually reproduced at the school and classroom level, unless concerted efforts are made to prevent their reproduction. Teachers working toward political clarity understand that they can either maintain the status quo, or they can work to transform the sociocultural reality at the classroom and school level so that the culture at this micro-level does not reflect macro-level inequalities, such as asymmetrical power relations that relegate certain cultural groups to a subordinate status.

Teachers can support positive social change in the classroom in a variety of ways. One possible intervention can consist of the creation of heterogeneous learn-

---

[b] **Appropriation** is the taking of an idea, ideology, or item from one system or culture by a person of another system or culture without regard for its original context or use.

ing groups for the purpose of modifying low-status roles of individuals or groups of children.[6] Elizabeth Cohen (1986) demonstrates that when teachers create learning conditions where students, especially those perceived as low status (e.g., limited English speakers in a classroom where English is the dominant language, students with academic difficulties, or those perceived by their peers for a variety of reasons as less able), can demonstrate their possession of knowledge and expertise, they are then able to see themselves, and be seen by others, as capable and competent. As a result, contexts are created in which peers can learn from each other as well.

A teacher's political clarity will not necessarily compensate for structural inequalities that students face outside the classroom; however, teachers can, to the best of their ability, help their students deal with injustices encountered inside and outside the classroom. A number of possibilities exist for preparing students to deal with the greater society's unfairness and inequality; they range from engaging in explicit discussions with students about their experiences to more indirect ways (that nevertheless require a teacher who is politically clear), such as creating democratic learning environments where students become accustomed to being treated as competent and able individuals. I believe that the students, once accustomed to the rights and responsibilities of full citizenship in the classroom, will come to expect respectful treatment and authentic estimation in other contexts. Again, it is important to point out that it is not the particular lesson or set of activities that prepares the student; rather, it is the teacher's politically clear educational philosophy that underlies the varied methods and lessons/activities she or he employs that make the difference.

Under ideal conditions, competent educators simultaneously translate theory into practice *and* consider the population being served and the sociocultural reality in which learning is expected to take place. Let me reiterate that command of a content area or specialization is necessary, but it is not sufficient for effectively working with students. Just as critical is that teachers comprehend that their role as educators is a political act that is never neutral (Freire, 1985, 1987, 1993; Freire & Macedo, 1987). In ignoring or negating the political nature of their work with these students, teachers not only reproduce the status quo and their students' low status, but they also inevitably legitimize schools' discriminatory practices. For example, teachers who uncritically follow school practices that unintentionally or intentionally serve to promote tracking and segregation within school and classroom contexts continue to reproduce the status quo. Conversely, teachers can become conscious of, and subsequently challenge, the role of educational institutions and their own roles as educators in maintaining a system that often serves to silence students from subordinated groups.

Teachers must also remember that schools, similar to other institutions in society, are influenced by perceptions of socioeconomic status (SES), race/ethnicity, language, and gender (Anyon, 1988; Bloom, 1991; Cummins, 1989; Ogbu, 1987). They must begin to question how these perceptions influence classroom dynamics. An important step in increasing teacher political clarity is recognizing that, despite current liberal rhetoric regarding the equal value of all cultures, low SES and ethnic-minority students have historically (and currently) been perceived as deficient. I believe that the present methods-restricted discussion must be broadened to reveal the deeply entrenched deficit orientation toward "difference" (i.e., non-Western European race/ethnicity, non-English language use, working-class status, femaleness) that prevails in the schools within a deeply "cultural" ideology of White supremacy. As educators, we must constantly be vigilant and ask how the deficit orientation has affected our perceptions concerning students from subordinated populations and created rigid and mechanistic teacher-student relations (Cummins, 1989; Flores, Cousin, & Diaz, 1991; Giroux & McLaren, 1986). Such a model often serves to create classroom conditions in which there is very little opportunity for teachers and students to interact in meaningful ways, establish positive and trusting working relations, and share knowledge.

Our Legacy: A Deficit View of Subordinated Students

As discussed earlier, teaching strategies are neither designed nor implemented in a vacuum. Design, selection, and use of particular teaching approaches and strategies arise from perceptions about learning and learners. I contend that the most pedagogically advanced strategies are sure to be ineffective in the hands of educators who implicitly or explicitly subscribe to a belief system that renders ethnic, racial, and linguistic minority students at best culturally disadvantaged and in need of fixing (if we could only identify the right recipe!), or, at worst, culturally or genetically deficient and beyond fixing.[7] Despite the fact that various models have been proposed to explain the academic failure of certain subordinated groups — academic failure described as *historical, pervasive,* and *disproportionate* — the fact remains that these views of difference are deficit-based and deeply imprinted in our individual and collective psyches (Flores, 1982, 1993; Menchaca & Valencia, 1990; Valencia, 1986, 1991).

The deficit model has the longest history of any model discussed in the education literature. Richard Valencia (1986) traces its evolution over three centuries:

> Also known in the literature as the "social pathology" model or the "cultural deprivation" model, the deficit approach explains disproportionate academic problems among low status students as largely being due to pathologies or deficits in their sociocultural background (e.g., cognitive and linguistic deficiencies, low self-esteem, poor motivation). . . . To improve the educability of such students, programs such as compensatory education and parent-child intervention have been proposed. (p. 3)

Barbara Flores (1982, 1993) documents the effect this deficit model has had on the schools' past and current perceptions of Latino students. Her historical overview chronicles descriptions used to refer to Latino students over the last century. The terms range from "mentally retarded," "linguistically handicapped," "culturally and linguistically deprived," and "semilingual," to the current euphemism for Latino and other subordinated students: the "at-risk" student.

Similarly, recent research continues to lay bare our deficit orientation and its links to discriminatory school practices aimed at students from groups perceived as low status (Anyon, 1988; Bloom, 1991; Diaz, Moll, & Mehan, 1986; Oakes, 1986). Findings range from teacher preference for Anglo students, to bilingual teachers' preference for lighter skinned Latino students (Bloom, 1991), to teachers' negative perceptions of working-class parents as compared to middle-class parents (Lareau, 1990), and, finally, to unequal teaching and testing practices in schools serving working-class and ethnic minority students (Anyon, 1988; Diaz et al.,

1986; Oakes, 1986; U.S. Commission on Civil Rights, 1973). Especially indicative of our inability to consciously acknowledge the deficit orientation is the fact that the teachers in these studies — teachers from all ethnic groups — were themselves unaware of the active role they played in the differential and unequal treatment of their students.

The deficit view of subordinated students has been critiqued by numerous researchers as ethnocentric and invalid (Boykin, 1983; Diaz et al., 1986; Flores, 1982; Flores et al., 1991; Sue & Padilla, 1986; Trueba, 1989; Walker, 1987). More recent research offers alternative models that shift the source of school failure away from the characteristics of the individual child, their families, and their cultures and toward the schooling process (Au & Mason, 1983; Heath, 1983; Mehan, 1992; Philips, 1972). Unfortunately, I believe that many of these alternative models often unwittingly give rise to a kinder and more liberal, yet more concealed version of the deficit model that views subordinated students as being in need of "specialized" modes of instruction — a type of instructional "coddling" that mainstream students do not require in order to achieve in school. Despite the use of less overtly ethnocentric models to explain the academic standing of subordinated students, I believe that the deficit orientation toward difference, especially as it relates to low socioeconomic and ethnic-minority groups, is very deeply ingrained in the ethos of our most prominent institutions, especially schools, and in the various educational programs in place at these sites.

It is against this sociocultural backdrop that teachers can begin to seriously question the unspoken but prevalent deficit orientation used to hide SES, racial/ethnic, linguistic, and gender inequities present in U.S. classrooms. And it is against this sociocultural backdrop that I critically examine two teaching approaches identified by the educational literature as effective with subordinated student populations.

Potentially Humanizing Pedagogy: Two Promising Teaching Approaches

Well-known approaches and strategies such as cooperative learning, language experience, process writing, reciprocal teaching, and whole language activities can be used to create humanizing learning environments where students cease to be treated as objects and yet receive academically rigorous instruction (Cohen, 1986; Edelsky, Altwerger, & Flores, 1991; Palinscar & Brown, 1984; Pérez & Torres-Guzmán, 1992; Zamel, 1982). However, when these approaches are implemented uncritically, they often produce negative results, as indicated by Lisa Delpit (1986, 1988). Critical teacher applications of these approaches and strategies can contribute to discarding deficit views of students from subordinated groups, so that they are treated with respect and viewed as active and capable subjects in their own learning.

Academically rigorous, student-centered teaching strategies can take many forms. One may well ask, is it not merely common sense to promote approaches and strategies that respect, recognize, utilize, and build on students' existing knowledge bases? The answer would be, of course, yes, it is. However, it is important to recognize, as part of our effort to increase our political clarity, that these practices have *not* typified classroom instruction for students from marginalized populations. The practice of learning from and valuing student language and life experiences *often* occurs in classrooms where students speak a language and possess cultural capital that more closely matches that of the mainstream (Anyon, 1988; Lareau, 1990; Winfield, 1986).[8]

Jean Anyon's (1988) classic research suggests that teachers of affluent students are more likely than teachers of working-class students to utilize and incorporate student life experiences and knowledge into the curriculum. For example, in Anyon's study, teachers of affluent students often designed creative and innovative lessons that tapped students' existing knowledge bases; one math lesson, designed to teach students to find averages, asked them to fill out a possession survey inquiring about the number of cars, television sets, refrigerators, and games owned at home so as to teach students to average. Unfortunately, this practice of tapping students' already existing knowledge and language bases is not commonly utilized with student populations traditionally perceived as deficient. Anyon reports that teachers of working-class students viewed them as lacking the necessary cultural capital, and therefore imposed content and behavioral standards with little consideration and respect for student input. Although Anyon did not generalize beyond her sample, other studies suggest the validity of her findings for ethnic-minority student populations (Diaz et al., 1986; Moll, 1986; Oakes, 1986).

The creation of learning environments for low SES and ethnic-minority students similar to those for more affluent and White populations requires that teachers discard deficit notions and genuinely value and utilize students' existing knowledge bases in their teaching. In order to do so, teachers must confront and challenge their own social biases so as to honestly begin to perceive their students as capable learners. Furthermore, they must remain open to the fact that they will also learn from their students. Learning is not a one-way undertaking.

It is important for educators to recognize that no language or set of life experiences is inherently superior, yet our social values reflect our preferences for certain language and life experiences over others. Student-centered teaching strategies such as cooperative learning, language experience, process writing, reciprocal teaching, and whole language activities (if practiced consciously and critically) can help to offset or neutralize our deficit-based failure and recognize subordinated student strengths. Our tendency to discount these strengths occurs whenever we forget that learning only occurs when prior knowledge is accessed and linked to new information.

Beau Jones, Annemarie Palinscar, Donna Ogle, and Eileen Carr (1987) explain that learning *is* the act of linking new information to prior knowledge. According to their framework, prior knowledge is stored in memory in the form of knowledge frameworks. New information is understood and stored by calling up the appropriate knowledge framework and then integrating the new information. Acknowledging and using existing student language and knowledge makes good pedagogical sense, and it also constitutes a humanizing experience for students traditionally *de*humanized and disempowered in the schools. I believe that strategies identified as effective in the literature have the potential to offset reductive education in which "the educator as *the one who knows* transfers existing knowledge to the learner as *the one who does not know*" (Freire, 1985, p. 114, emphasis added). It is important to repeat that mere implementation of a particular strategy or approach identified as effective does not guarantee success, as the current debate in process writing attests (Delpit, 1986, 1988; Reyes, 1991, 1992).

Creating learning environments that incorporate student language and life experiences in no way negates teachers' responsibility for providing students with particular academic content knowledge and skills. It is important not to link teacher respect and use of student knowledge and language bases with a laissez-faire attitude toward teaching. It is equally necessary not to confuse academic rigor with rigidity that stifles and silences students. The teacher is the authority, with all the resulting responsibilities that entails; however, it is not necessary for the teacher to become authoritarian in order to challenge students intellectually. Education can be a process in which teacher and students mutually participate in the intellectually exciting undertaking we call learning. Students *can* become active subjects in their own learning, instead of passive objects waiting to be filled with facts and figures by the teacher.

I would like to emphasize that teachers who work with subordinated populations have the responsibility to assist them in appropriating knowledge bases and discourse styles deemed desirable by the greater society. However, this process of appropriation must be additive; that is, the new concepts and new discourse skills must be added to, not subtracted from, the students' existing background knowledge. In order to assume this additive stance, teachers must discard deficit views so that they can use and build on life experiences and language styles too often viewed and labeled as "low class" and undesirable. Again, there are numerous teaching strategies and methods that can be employed in this additive manner. For the purposes of illustration, I will briefly discuss two approaches currently identified as promising for students from subordinated populations. The selected approaches are referred to in the literature as culturally responsive instructional approaches and strategic teaching.

Culturally Responsive Instruction:
The Potential to Equalize Power Relations

Culturally responsive instruction grows out of cultural difference theory, which attributes the academic difficulties of students from subordinated groups to cultural incongruence or discontinuities between the learning, language use, and behavioral practices found in the home and those expected by the schools. Ana María Villegas (1988, 1991) defines culturally responsive instruction as attempts to create instructional situations in which teachers use teaching approaches and strategies that recognize and build on culturally different ways of learning, behaving, and using language in the classroom.

A number of classic ethnographic studies document culturally incongruent communication practices in classrooms where students and teachers may speak the same language but use it in different ways. This type of incongruence is cited as a major source of academic difficulties for subordinated students and their teachers (see Au, 1980; Au & Mason, 1983; Cazden, 1988; Erickson & Mohatt, 1982; Heath, 1983; Philips, 1972). For the purposes of this analysis, one form of culturally responsive instruction, the Kamehameha Education Project reading program, will be discussed.

The Kamehameha Education Project is a reading program developed as a response to the traditionally low academic achievement of native Hawaiian students in Western schools. The reading program was a result of several years of research that examined the language practices of native Hawaiian children in home and school settings. Observations of native Hawaiian children showed them to be bright and capable learners; however, their behavior in the classroom signaled communication difficulties between them and their non-Hawaiian teachers. For example, Kathryn Hu-Pei Au (1979, 1980) reports that native Hawaiian children's language behavior in the classroom was often misinterpreted by teachers as being unruly and without educational value. She found that the children's preferred language style in the classroom was linked to a practice used by adults in their homes and community called "talk story." She discusses the talk-story phenomenon and describes it as a major speech event in the Hawaiian community, where individuals speak almost simultaneously and where little attention is given to turn-taking. Au explains that this practice may inhibit students from speaking out as individuals because of their familiarity with and preference for simultaneous group discussion.

Because the non-Hawaiian teachers were unfamiliar with talk story and failed to recognize its value, much class time was spent either silencing the children or prodding unwilling individuals to speak. Needless to say, very little class time was dedicated to other instruction. More important, the children were constrained and not allowed to demonstrate their abilities as speakers and possessors of knowledge. Because the students did not exhibit their skills in mainstream accepted ways (e.g., competing as individuals for the floor), they were prevented from exhibiting knowledge via their culturally preferred style. However, once the children's interaction style was incorporated into classroom lessons, time on task increased and, subsequently, students' performance on standardized reading tests improved. This study's findings conclude that educators can successfully employ the students' culturally valued language practices while introducing the student to more conventional and academically acceptable ways of using language.

It is interesting to note that many of the research studies that examine culturally congruent and incongruent teaching approaches also inadvertently illustrate the equalization of previous asymmetrical power relations between teachers and students. These studies describe classrooms where teachers initially imposed participation structures upon students from subordinated linguistic-minority groups and later learned to negotiate with them rules regarding acceptable classroom behavior and language use (Au & Mason, 1983; Erickson & Mohatt, 1982; Heath, 1983; Philips, 1972). Thus these studies, in essence, capture the successful negotiation of power relations, which resulted in higher student academic achievement and increased teacher effectiveness. Yet there is little explicit discussion in these studies of the greater sociocultural reality that renders it perfectly normal for teachers to automatically disregard and disrespect subordinated students' preferences and to allow antagonistic relations to foment until presented with empirical evidence that legitimizes the students' practices. Instead, the focus of most of these studies rests entirely on the cultural congruence of the instruction and not on the humanizing effects of a more democratic pedagogy. Villegas (1988) accurately critiques the cultural congruence literature when she states:

> It is simplistic to claim that differences in languages used at home and in school are the root of the widespread academic problems of minority children. Admittedly, differences do exist, and they can create communication difficulties in the classroom for both teachers and students. Even so, those differences in language must be viewed in the context of a broader struggle for power within a stratified society. (p. 260)

Despite the focus on the cultural versus the political dimensions of pedagogy, some effort is made to link culturally congruent teaching practices with equalization of classroom power relations. For example, Kathryn Au and Jana Mason (1983) explain that "one means of achieving cultural congruence in lessons may be to *seek a balance between the interactional rights of teachers and students,* so that the children can participate in ways comfortable to them" (p. 145, emphasis added). Their study compared two teachers and showed that the teacher who was willing to negotiate with students either the topic of discussion or the appropriate participation structure was better able to implement her lesson. Conversely, the teacher who attempted to impose both topic of discussion *and* appropriate interactional rules was frequently diverted because of conflicts with students over one or the other.

Unfortunately, as mentioned earlier, interpretations and practical applications of this body of research have focused on the *cultural* congruence of the approaches. I emphasize the term *cultural* because in these studies the term "culture" is used in a restricted sense devoid of its dynamic, ideological, and political dimensions. Instead, culture is treated as synonymous with ethnic culture, rather than as "the representation of lived experiences, material artifacts and practices *forged within the unequal and dialectical relations* that different groups establish in a given society at a particular point in historical time" (Giroux, 1985, p. xxi, emphasis added). I use this definition of culture because, without identifying the political dimensions of culture and subsequent unequal status attributed to members of different ethnic groups, the reader may conclude that teaching methods simply need to be ethnically congruent to be effective — without recognizing that not all ethnic and linguistic cultural groups are viewed and treated as equally legitimate in classrooms. Interestingly enough, there is little discussion of the various socially perceived minority groups' subordinate status vis-à-vis White teachers and peers in these studies. All differences are treated as ethnic cultural differences and not as responses of subordinated students to teachers from dominant groups, and vice versa.

Given the sociocultural realities in the above studies, the specific teaching strategies may not be what made the difference. Indeed, efforts to uncritically export the Kamehameha Education Project reading program to other student populations resulted in failure (Vogt et al., 1987). It could well be that the teachers' effort to negotiate and share power by treating students as equal participants in their own learning is what made the difference in Hawaii. Just as important is the teachers' willingness to critically interrogate their deficit views of subordinated students. By employing a variety of strategies and techniques, the Kamehameha students were allowed to interact with teachers in egalitarian and meaningful ways. More importantly, the teachers also learned to recognize, value, use, and build upon students' previously acquired knowledge and skills. In essence, these strategies succeeded in creating a comfort zone so students could exhibit their knowledge and skills and, ultimately, empower themselves to succeed in an academic setting. Teachers also benefited from using a variety of student-centered teaching strategies that humanized their perceptions of treatment of students previously perceived as deficient. Ray McDermott's (1977) classic research reminds us that numerous teaching approaches and strategies can be effective, so long as trusting relations between teacher and students are established and power relations are mutually set and agreed upon.

Strategic Teaching:
The Significance of Teacher-Student Interaction and Negotiation

Strategic teaching refers to an instructional model that explicitly teaches students learning strategies that enable them consciously to monitor their own learning. This is accomplished through the development of reflective cognitive monitoring and metacognitive skills (Jones, Palinscar, Ogle, & Carr, 1987). The goal is to prepare independent and metacognitively aware students. This teaching strategy makes explicit for students the structures of various text types used in academic settings and assists students in identifying various strategies for effectively comprehending the various genres. Although text structures and strategies for dissecting the particular structures are presented by the teacher, a key component of these lessons is the elicitation of students' knowledge about text types and their own strategies for making meaning before presenting them with more conventional academic strategies.

Examples of learning strategies include teaching various text structures (i.e., stories and reports) through frames and graphic organizers. *Frames* are sets of questions that help students understand a given topic. Readers monitor their understanding of a text by asking questions, making predictions, and testing their predictions as they read. Before reading, frames serve as an advance organizer to activate prior knowledge and facilitate understanding. Frames can also be utilized during the reading process by the reader to monitor self-learning. Finally, frames can be used after a reading lesson to summarize and integrate newly acquired information.

Graphic organizers are visual maps that represent text structures and organizational patterns used in texts and in student writing. Ideally, graphic organizers reflect both the content and text structure. Graphic organizers include semantic maps, chains, and concept hierarchies, and assist the student in visualizing the rhetorical structure of the text. Beau Jones and colleagues (1987) explain that frames and graphic organizers can be "powerful tools to help the student locate, select, sequence, integrate and restructure information — both from the perspective of understanding and from the perspective of producing information in written responses" (p. 38).

Although much of the research on strategic teaching focuses on English monolingual mainstream students, recent efforts to study linguistic-minority students' use of these strategies show similar success. This literature shows that strategic teaching improved the students' reading comprehension, as well as their conscious use of effective learning strategies in their native language (Avelar La Salle, 1991; Chamot, 1983; Hernandez, 1991; O'Malley & Chamot, 1990; Reyes, 1987). Furthermore, these studies show that students, despite limited English proficiency, were able to transfer or apply their knowledge of specific learning strategies and text structure to English reading texts. For example, Jose Hernandez (1991) reports that sixth-grade limited-English-proficient students learned, in the native language (Spanish), to generate hypotheses, summarize, and make predictions about readings. He reports:

> Students were able to demonstrate use of comprehension strategies even when they could not decode the English text aloud. When asked in Spanish about Eng-

lish texts the students were able to generate questions, summarize stories, and predict future events in Spanish. (p. 101)

Robin Avelar La Salle's (1991) study of third- and fourth-grade bilingual students shows that strategic teaching in the native language of three expository text structures commonly found in elementary social studies and science texts (topical net, matrix, and hierarchy) improved comprehension of these types of texts in both Spanish and English.

Such explicit and strategic teaching is most important in the upper elementary grades, where students are expected to focus on the development of more advanced English literacy skills. Beginning at about third grade, students face literacy demands distinct from those encountered in earlier grades. Jeanne Chall (1983) describes the change in literacy demands in terms of stages of readings. She explains that at a stage three of reading, students cease to "learn to read" and begin "reading to learn." Students in third and fourth grade are introduced to content area subjects such as social studies, science, and health. In addition, students are introduced to expository texts (reports). This change in texts, text structures, and in the functions of reading (reading for information) calls for teaching strategies that will prepare students to comprehend various expository texts (e.g., cause/effect, compare/contrast) used across the curriculum.

Strategic teaching holds great promise for preparing linguistic-minority students to face the new literacy challenges in the upper grades. As discussed before, the primary goal of strategic instruction is to foster learner independence. This goal in and of itself is laudable. However, the characteristics of strategic instruction that I find most promising grow out of the premise that teachers and students must interact and negotiate meaning as equals in order to reach a goal.

Teachers, by permitting learners to speak from their own vantage points, create learning contexts in which students are able to empower themselves throughout the strategic-learning process. Before teachers attempt to instruct students in new content or learning strategies, efforts are made by the teacher to access students' prior knowledge so as to link it with new information. In allowing students to present and discuss their prior knowledge and experiences, the teacher legitimizes and treats as valuable student language and cultural experiences usually ignored in classrooms. If students are encouraged to speak on what they know best, then they are, in a sense, treated as experts — experts who are expected to refine their knowledge bases with the additional new content and strategy information presented by the teacher.

Teachers play a significant role in creating learning contexts in which students are able to empower themselves. Teachers act as cultural mentors of sorts when they introduce students not only to the culture of the classroom, but to particular subjects and discourse styles as well. In the process, teachers assist the students in appropriating the skills (in an additive fashion) for themselves so as to enable them to behave as "insiders" in the particular subject or discipline. Jim Gee (1989) reminds us that the social nature of teaching and learning must involve an apprenticeship in the subject's or discipline's discourse in order for students to do well in school. This apprenticeship includes acquisition of particular content matter, ways of organizing content, and ways of using language (oral and written). Gee adds that these discourses are not mastered solely through teacher-centered and directed instruction, but also by "apprenticeship into social practices through scaffolded and supported interaction with people who have already mastered the discourse" (p. 7). The apprenticeship notion can be immensely useful with subordinated students if it facilitates the acceptance and valorization of students' prior knowledge through a mentoring process.

Models of instruction, such as strategic teaching, can promote such an apprenticeship. In the process of apprenticing linguistic-minority students, teachers must interact in meaningful ways with them. This human interaction not only assists students in acquiring new knowledge and skills, but it also often fosters familiarity between individuals from different SES and racial/ethnic groups and creates mutual respect instead of the antagonism that so frequently occurs between teachers and their students from subordinated groups. In this learning environment, teachers and students learn from each other. The strategies serve, then, not to "fix" the student, but to equalize power relations and to humanize the teacher-student relationship. Ideally, teachers are forced to challenge implicitly or explicitly held deficit attitudes and beliefs about their students and the cultural groups to which they belong.

Beyond Teaching Strategies: Toward a Humanizing Pedagogy

When I recall a special education teacher's experience related in a bilingualism and literacy course that I taught, I am reminded of the humanizing effects of teaching strategies that, similar to culturally responsive instruction and strategic teaching, allow teachers to listen, learn from, and mentor their students. This teacher, for most of her career, had been required to assess her students through a variety of closed-ended instruments, and then to remediate their diagnosed "weaknesses" with discrete skills instruction. The assessment instruments provided little information to explain why the student answered a question either correctly or incorrectly, and they often confirmed perceived student academic, linguistic, and cognitive weaknesses. This fragmented discrete skills approach to instruction restricts the teacher's access to existing student knowledge and experiences not specifically elicited by the academic tasks. Needless to say, this teacher knew very little about her students other than her deficit descriptions of them.

As part of the requirements for my course, she was asked to focus on one Spanish-speaking, limited-English-proficient special education student over the semester. She observed the student in a number of formal and informal contexts, and she engaged him in a number of open-ended tasks. These tasks included allowing him to write entire texts, such as stories and poems (despite diagnosed limited English proficiency), and to engage in "think-alouds" during reading.[9] Through these open-ended activities, the teacher learned about her student's English writing ability (both strengths and weaknesses), his life experiences and worldviews, and his meaning-making strategies for reading. Consequently, the teacher constructed an instructional plan much better suited to her student's academic needs and interests. And, even more important, she underwent a humanizing process that allowed her to recognize the varied and valuable life experiences and knowledge her student brought into the classroom.

This teacher was admirably candid when she shared her initial negative and stereotypic views of the student and her radical transformation. Despite this teacher's mastery of content area, her lack of political clarity blinded her to the oppressive and dehumanizing nature of instruction offered to linguistic-minority students. Initially, she had formed an erroneous notion of her student's personality, worldview, academic ability, motivation, and academic potential on the basis of his Puerto Rican ethnicity, low SES background, limited English proficiency, and moderately learning-disabled label. Because of the restricted and closed nature of earlier assessment and instruction, the teacher had never received information about her student that challenged her negative perceptions. Listening to her student and reading his poetry and stories, she discovered his loving and sunny personality, learned his personal history, and identified his academic strengths and weaknesses. In the process, she discovered and challenged her own deficit orientation. The following excerpt from this student's writing exemplifies the power of the student voice for humanizing teachers:

My Father

I love my father very much. I will never forget what my father has done for me and my brothers and sisters. When we first came from Puerto Rico we didn't have food to eat and we were very poor. My father had to work three jobs to put food and milk on the table. Those were hard times and my father worked so hard that we hardly saw him. But even when I didn't see him, I always knew he loved me very much. I will always be grateful to my father. We are not so poor now and so he works only one job. But I will never forget what my father did for me. I will also work to help my father have a better life when I grow up. I love my father very much.

The process of learning about her student's rich and multifaceted background enabled this teacher to move beyond the rigid methodology that had required her to distance herself from the student and to confirm the deficit model to which she unconsciously adhered. In this case, the meaningful teacher-student interaction served to equalize the teacher-student power relations and to humanize instruction by expanding the horizons through which the student demonstrated human qualities, dreams, desires, and capacities that closed-ended tests and instruction never captured.

I believe that the specific teaching methods implemented by the teacher, in and of themselves, were not the significant factors. The actual strengths of methods depend, first and foremost, on the degree to which they embrace a humanizing pedagogy that values the students' background knowledge, culture, and life experiences, and creates learning contexts where power is shared by students and teachers. Teaching methods are a means to an end — humanizing education to promote academic success for students historically under-served by the schools. A teaching strategy is a vehicle to a greater goal. A number of vehicles exist that may or may not lead to a humanizing pedagogy, depending on the sociocultural reality in which teachers and students operate.

The critical issue is the degree to which we hold the moral conviction that we must humanize the educational experience of students from subordinated populations by eliminating the hostility that often confronts these students. This process would require that we cease to be overly dependent on methods as technical instruments and adopt a pedagogy that seeks to forge a cultural democracy where all students are treated with respect and dignity. A true cultural democracy forces teachers to recognize that students' lack of familiarity with the dominant values of the curriculum "does not mean . . . that the lack of these experiences develop in these children a different 'nature' that determines their absolute incompetence" (Freire, 1993, p. 17).

Unless educational methods are situated in the students' cultural experiences, students will continue to show difficulty in mastering content area that is not only alien to their reality, but is often antagonistic toward their culture and lived experiences. Further, not only will these methods continue to fail students, particularly those from subordinated groups, but they will never lead to the creation of schools as true cultural democratic sites. For this reason, it is imperative that teachers problematize the prevalent notion of "magical" methods and incorporate what Macedo (1993) calls an anti-methods pedagogy, a process through which teachers 1) critically deconstruct the ideology that informs the methods fetish prevalent in education, 2) understand the intimate relationships between methods and the theoretical underpinnings that inform these methods, and 3) evaluate the pedagogical consequences of blindly and uncritically replicating methods without regard to students' subordinate status in terms of cultural, class, gender, and linguistic difference. In short, we need

> an anti-methods pedagogy that would reject the mechanization of intellectualism . . . [and] challenge teachers to work toward reappropriation of endangered dignity and toward reclaiming our humanity. The anti-methods pedagogy adheres to the eloquence of Antonio Machado's poem, "Caminante, no hay camino, se hace camino al andar." (Traveler, there are no roads. The road is created as we walk it [together])." (Macedo, 1993, p. 8)

Notes

1. The term "technical" refers to the positivist tradition in education that presents teaching as a precise and scientific undertaking and teachers as technicians responsible for carrying out (preselected) instructional programs and strategies.
2. "Subordinated" refers to cultural groups that are politically, socially, and economically subordinate in the greater society. While individual members of these groups may not consider themselves subordinate in any manner to the White "mainstream," they nevertheless are members of a greater collective that historically has been perceived and treated as subordinate and inferior by the dominant society. Thus it is not entirely accurate to describe these students as "minority" students, since the term connotes numerical minority rather than the general low status (economic, political, and social) these groups have held and that I think is important to recognize when discussing their historical academic underachievement.
3. "Chicana" refers to a woman of Mexican ancestry who was born and/or reared in the United States.
4. "Mainstream" refers to the U.S. macroculture that has its roots in Western European traditions. More specifically, the major influence on the United States, particularly on its institutions, has been the culture and traditions of White, Anglo-Saxon Protestants (WASP) (Golnick & Chinn, 1986). Although the mainstream group is no longer composed solely of WASPs, members of the middle class have adopted traditionally WASP bodies of knowledge, language use, values, norms, and beliefs.
5. "Political clarity" refers to the process by which individuals achieve a deepening awareness of the sociopolitical and economic realities that shape their lives and their capacity to recreate them. In addition, it refers to the process by which individuals come to better understand possible linkages between macro-level political, economic, and social variables and subordinated groups' academic performance in the micro-level classroom. Thus, it invariably requires linkages between sociocultural structures and schooling.

6. Elizabeth Cohen (1986) explains that in the society at large there are status distinctions made on the basis of social class, ethnic group, and gender. These status distinctions are often reproduced at the classroom level, unless teachers make conscious efforts to prevent this reproduction.

7. For detailed discussions regarding various deficit views of subordinated students over time, see Flores, Cousin, and Diaz (1991); also see Sue and Padilla (1986).

8. "Cultural capital" refers to Pierre Bourdieu's concept that certain forms of cultural knowledge are the equivalent of symbolic wealth in that these forms of "high" culture are socially designated as worthy of being sought and possessed. These cultural (and linguistic) knowledge bases and skills are socially inherited and are believed to facilitate academic achievement. See Lamont and Lareau (1988) for a more in-depth discussion regarding the multiple meanings of cultural capital in the literature.

9. "Think-alouds" refers to an informal assessment procedure where readers verbalize all their thoughts during reading and writing tasks. See Langer (1986) for a more in-depth discussion of think-aloud procedures.

References

Anyon, J. (1988). Social class and the hidden curriculum of work. In J. R. Gress (Ed.), *Curriculum: An introduction to the field* (pp. 366–389). Berkeley, CA: McCutchan.

Au, K. H. (1979). Using the experience text relationship method with minority children. *The Reading Teacher, 32,* 677–679.

Au, K. H. (1980). Participant structures in a reading lesson with Hawaiian children: Analysis of a culturally appropriate instructional event. *Anthropology and Educational Quarterly, 11,* 91–115.

Au, K. H., & Mason, J. M. (1983). Cultural congruence in classroom participation structures: Achieving a balance of rights. *Discourse Processes, 6,* 145–168.

Avelar La Salle, R. (1991). *The effect of metacognitive instruction on the transfer of expository comprehension skills: The interlingual and cross-lingual cases.* Unpublished doctoral dissertation, Stanford University.

Bloom, G. M. (1991). *The effects of speech style and skin color on bilingual teaching candidates' and bilingual teachers' attitudes toward Mexican American pupils.* Unpublished doctoral dissertation, Stanford University.

Boykin, A. W. (1983). The academic performance of Afro-American children. In J. T. Spence (Ed.), *Achievement and achievement motives: Psychological and sociological approaches* (pp. 322–369). San Francisco: W. H. Freeman.

Carter, T. P., & Chatfield, M. L. (1986). Effective bilingual schools: Implications for policy and practice. *American Journal of Education, 95,* 200–232.

Cazden, C. (1988). *Classroom discourse: The language of teaching and learning.* Portsmouth, NH: Heinemann.

Chall, J. (1983). *Stages of reading development.* New York: McGraw-Hill.

Chamot, A. U. (1983). How to plan to transfer curriculum from bilingual to mainstream instruction. *Focus, 12.* (A newsletter available from the George Washington University National Clearinghouse for Bilingual Education, 1118 22nd St. NW, Washington, DC 20037)

Cohen, E. G. (1986). *Designing groupwork: Strategies for the heterogeneous classroom.* New York: Teachers College Press.

Cummins, J. (1989). *Empowering minority students.* Sacramento: California Association of Bilingual Education.

Delpit, L. (1986). Skills and other dilemmas of a progressive Black educator. *Harvard Educational Review, 56,* 379–385.

Delpit, L. (1988). The silenced dialogue: Power and pedagogy in educating other people's children. *Harvard Educational Review, 58,* 280–298.

Diaz, S., Moll, L. C., & Mehan, H. (1986). Sociocultural resources in instruction: A context-specific approach. In *Beyond language: Social and cultural factors in schooling language minority students* (pp. 187–230). Los Angeles: California State University, Evaluation, Dissemination and Assessment Center.

Edelsky, C., Altwerger, B., & Flores, B. (1991). *Whole language: What's the difference?* Portsmouth, NH: Heinemann.

Erickson, F., & Mohatt, G. (1982). Cultural organization of participation structures in two classrooms of Indian students. In G. Spindler (Ed.), *Doing the ethnography of schooling: Educational anthropology in action* (pp. 133–174). New York: Holt, Rinehart and Winston.

Flores, B. M. (1982). *Language interference or influence: Toward a theory for Hispanic bilingualism.* Unpublished doctoral dissertation, University of Arizona at Tucson.

Flores, B. M. (1993, April). *Interrogating the genesis of the deficit view of Latino children in the educational literature during the 20th century.* Paper presented at the American Educational Research Association Conference, Atlanta.

Flores, B., Cousin, P. T., & Diaz, E. (1991). Critiquing and transforming the deficit myths about learning, language and culture. *Language Arts, 68,* 369–379.

Freire, P. (1985). *The politics of education: Culture, power and liberation.* South Hadley, MA: Bergin & Garvey.

Freire, P. (1987). Letter to North-American teachers. In I. Shor (Ed.), *Freire for the classroom* (pp. 211–214). Portsmouth, NJ: Boynton/Cook.

Freire, P. (1993). *A pedagogy of the city.* New York: Continuum Press.

Freire, P., & Macedo, D. (1987). *Literacy: Reading the word and the world.* South Hadley, MA: Bergin & Garvey.

Gee, J. P. (1989). Literacy, discourse, and linguistics: Introduction. *Journal of Education, 171,* 5–17.

Gibson, M. A., & Ogbu, J. U. (1991). *Minority status and schooling: A comparative study of immigrant and involuntary minorities.* New York: Garland.

Giroux, H. (1985). Introduction. In P. Freire, *The politics of education: Culture, power and liberation* (pp. xi–xxv). South Hadley, MA.: Bergin & Garvey.

Giroux, H. (1992). *Border crossing: Cultural workers and the politics of education.* New York: Routledge.

Giroux, H., & McLaren, P. (1986). Teacher education and the politics of engagement: The case for democratic schooling. *Harvard Educational Review, 56,* 213–238.

Golnick, D. M., & Chinn, P. C. (1986). *Multicultural education in a pluralistic society.* Columbus, OH: Merrill.

Heath, S. B. (1983). *Ways with words.* New York: Cambridge University Press.

Hernandez, J. S. (1991). Assisted performance in reading comprehension strategies with non-English proficient students. *Journal of Educational Issues of Language Minority Students, 8,* 91–112.

Jones, B. F., Palinscar, A. S., Ogle, D. S., & Carr, E. G. (1987). *Strategic teaching and learning: Cognitive instruction in the content areas.* Alexandria, VA: Association for Supervision and Curriculum Development.

Knapp, M. S., & Shields, P. M. (1990). *Better schooling for the children of poverty: Alternatives to conventional wisdom: Vol. 2. Commissioned papers and literature review.* Washington, DC: U.S. Department of Education.

Lamont, M., & Lareau, A. (1988). Cultural capital-allusions, gaps and glissandos in recent theoretical developments. *Sociological Theory, 6,* 153–168.

Langer, J. A. (1986). *Children reading and writing: Structures and strategies.* Norwood, NJ: Ablex.

Lareau, A. (1990). *Home advantage: Social class and parental intervention in elementary education.* New York: Falmer Press.

Lucas, T., Henze, R., & Donato, R. (1990). Promoting the success of Latino language-minority students: An exploratory study of six high schools. *Harvard Educational Review, 60,* 315–340.

Macedo, D. (1994). Preface. In P. McLaren & C. Lankshear (Eds.), *Conscientization and resistance* (pp. 1–8). New York: Routledge.

McDermott, R. P. (1977). Social relations as contexts for learning in school. *Harvard Educational Review, 47,* 198–213.

McLeod, B. (Ed.). (1994). *Language and learning: Educating linguistically diverse students.* Albany: State University of New York Press.

Means, B., & Knapp, M. S. (1991). *Teaching advanced skills to educationally disadvantaged students.* Washington, DC: U.S. Department of Education.

Mehan, H. (1992). Understanding inequality in schools: The contribution of interpretive studies. *Sociology of Education, 65*(1), 1–20.

Menchaca, M., & Valencia, R. (1990). Anglo-Saxon ideologies in the 1920s–1930s: Their impact on the segregation of Mexican students in California. *Anthropology and Education Quarterly, 21,* 222–245.

Moll, L. C. (1986). Writing as communication: Creating learning environments for students. *Theory Into Practice, 25,* 102–110.

Oakes, J. (1986). Tracking, inequality, and the rhetoric of school reform: Why schools don't change. *Journal of Education, 168,* 61–80.

Ogbu, J. (1987). Variability in minority responses to schooling: Nonimmigrants vs. immigrants. In G. Spindler & L. Spindler (Eds.), *Interpretive ethnography of education* (pp. 255–280). Hillsdale, NJ: Lawrence Erlbaum Associates.

O'Malley, J., & Chamot, A. U. (1990). *Learning strategies in second language acquisition.* New York: Cambridge University Press.

Palinscar, A. S., & Brown, A. L. (1984). Reciprocal teaching of comprehension-fostering and comprehension-monitoring activities. *Cognition and Instruction, 1*(23), 117–175.

Pérez, B., & Torres-Guzmán, M. E. (1992). *Learning in two worlds: An integrated Spanish/English biliteracy approach.* New York: Longman.

Philips, S. U. (1972). Participant structures and communication competence: Warm Springs children in community and classroom. In C. B. Cazden, V. P. John, & D. Hymes (Eds.), *Functions of language in the classroom* (pp. 370–394). New York: Teachers College Press.

Reyes, M. de la Luz. (1987). Comprehension of content area passages: A study of Spanish/English readers in the third and fourth grade. In S. R. Goldman & H. T. Trueba (Eds.), *Becoming literate in English as a second language* (pp. 107–126). Norwood, NJ: Ablex.

Reyes, M. de la Luz. (1991). A process approach to literacy during dialogue journals and literature logs with second language learners. *Research in the Teaching of English, 25,* 291–313.

Reyes, M. de la Luz. (1992). Challenging venerable assumptions: Literacy instruction for linguistically different students. *Harvard Educational Review, 62,* 427–446.

Sue, S., & Padilla, A. (1986). Ethnic minority issues in the U.S.: Challenges for the educational system. In *Beyond language: Social and cultural factors in schooling language minority students* (pp. 35–72). Los Angeles: California State University, Evaluation, Dissemination and Assessment Center.

Tikunoff, W. (1985). *Applying significant bilingual instructional features in the classroom.* Rosslyn, VA: National Clearinghouse for Bilingual Education.

Tinajero, J. V., & Ada, A. F. (1993). *The power of two languages: Literacy and biliteracy for Spanish-speaking students.* New York: Macmillan/McGraw-Hill.

Trueba, H. T. (1989). Sociocultural integration of minorities and minority school achievement. In *Raising silent voices: Educating the linguistic minorities for the 21st century* (pp. 1–27). New York: Newbury House.

U. S. Commission on Civil Rights. (1973). *Teachers and students: Report V. Mexican-American study: Differences in teacher interaction with Mexican-American and Anglo students.* Washington, DC: Government Printing Office.

Valencia, R. (1986, November 25). *Minority academic underachievement: Conceptual and theoretical considerations for understanding the achievement problems of Chicano students.* Paper presented to the Chicano Faculty Seminar, Stanford University.

Valencia, R. (1991). *Chicano school failure and success: Research and policy agendas for the 1990s.* New York: Falmer Press.

Villegas, A. M. (1988). School failure and cultural mismatch: Another view. *Urban Review, 20,* 253–265.

Villegas, A. M. (1991). *Culturally responsive pedagogy for the 1990s and beyond.* Paper prepared for the Educational Testing Service, Princeton, NJ.

Vogt, L. A., Jordan, C., & Tharp, R. G. (1987). Explaining school failure, producing school success: Two cases. *Anthropology & Education Quarterly, 18,* 276–286.

Walker, C. L. (1987). Hispanic achievement: Old views and new perspectives. In H. T. Trueba (Ed.), *Success or failure: Learning and the language minority student* (pp. 15–32). New York: Newbury House.

Webb, L. C. (1987). *Raising achievement among minority students.* Arlington, VA: American Association of School Administrators.

Winfield, L. F. (1986). Teachers beliefs toward academically at risk students in inner urban schools. *Urban Review, 18,* 253–267.

Zamel, V. (1982). Writing: The process of discovering meaning. *TESOL Quarterly, 16,* 195–209.

The Algebra Project:
Organizing in the Spirit of Ella

ROBERT PARRIS MOSES
MIEKO KAMII
SUSAN McALLISTER SWAP
JEFF HOWARD

In this chapter, Robert Parris Moses, Mieko Kamii, Susan McAllister Swap, and Jeff Howard provide a third model of community integration to complement those of Johnson and Stumbo. The authors describe the interaction among parents, students, and teachers engaged in The Algebra Project, an ongoing seven-year effort to establish a mathematics curriculum that expects, encourages, and supports every student to study algebra at the middle school level. The project emphasizes the unique impact of civil rights organizing in the grassroots efforts of a community activist parent, Robert Moses. Moses, who is also a mathematician, argues that all children should have access to the college preparatory mathematics curriculum taught in high school, and that children without access to such programs are barred from acquiring the knowledge and skills necessary for participation in an economy driven by rapid technological change. The Algebra Project recognizes the importance of issues raised by Connell and Bartolomé and uses the commitment of the community to provide an impetus for sustaining a project that will give students a better chance to access the best that society has to offer.

The United States is beginning to address, in a fundamental way, the teaching of mathematics in its middle schools. The National Science Foundation (1989), for instance, has issued a request for proposals to develop materials for middle school mathematics instruction that sets out the technical elements of the problem in great detail. At the heart of math-science education issues, however, is a basic political question: If the current technological revolution demands new standards of mathematics and science literacy, will all citizens be given equal access to the new skills, or will some be left behind, denied participation in the unfolding economic and political era? Those who are concerned about the life chances for historically oppressed people in the United States must not allow math-science education to be addressed as if it were purely a matter of technical instruction.

The Algebra Project, a math-science program in Cambridge, Massachusetts, has organized local communities to help make algebra available to all seventh- and

Harvard Educational Review Vol. 59 No. 4 November 1989, 423–443

eighth-grade students, regardless of their prior level of skill development or academic achievement. The project's philosophy is that access to algebra will enable students to participate in advanced high school math and science courses, which in turn are a gateway for college entrance. The project offers a new curriculum and a five-step curricular process for sixth-graders that provides the following: a smooth transition from the concepts of arithmetic to those of algebra, increasing the likelihood of mastery of seventh- and eighth-grade algebra; a home, community, and school culture involving teachers, parents, community volunteers, and school administrators in activities that support students' academic achievement; and a model of intellectual development that is based on motivation rather than ability.

The belief that ability is the essential ingredient driving intellectual development and is necessary for mastering advanced school mathematics is the basis for the differentiation in mathematics curricula at the eighth-grade level as well as the widespread practice of offering eighth-grade algebra only to students who are "mathematically inclined" or "gifted." The developers of the Algebra Project have called upon the traditions of the civil rights movement to assist communities in organizing a challenge to the ability model and its institutional expressions.

Traditions of the Civil Rights Movement in Mississippi

Through the Public Broadcasting System's (PBS) *Eyes on the Prize* series, the American public has been given an opportunity to revisit the civil rights movement's community mobilization tradition. Masses of people were mobilized to participate in large-scale events such as the Birmingham campaign, the March on Washington, and the Selma-to-Montgomery March, which were aimed at achieving equal access for Southern Blacks to public facilities and institutions. The tradition is epitomized by Dr. Martin Luther King, Jr., who lifted the movement by inspiring immense crowds in vast public spaces.

Within the civil rights movement was an older, yet less well known, community organizing tradition. This tradition laid the foundation for Mississippi Freedom Summer (1964), which revolutionized race relations in Mississippi, and for the Voting Rights Act of 1965, which altered politics throughout the South during the last quarter of this century. Its leader was Ella Baker, a community organizer and *fundi* whose wisdom and counsel guided the Black veterans of the first wave of student sit-ins through the founding and establishment of the Student Nonviolent Coordinating Committee (SNCC).[1] She inspired in SNCC field secretaries a spiritual belief in human dignity, a faith in the capacity of Blacks to produce leaders from the ranks of their people, and a perseverance when confronting overwhelming obstacles. Baker symbolizes the tradition in the civil rights movement of quiet places and the organizers who liked to work in them.[2] Just as her spirit, consciousness, and teaching infused the Mississippi Movement, they permeated the Algebra Project from its inception.

Three aspects of the Mississippi organizing tradition underlie the Algebra Project: the centrality of families to the work of organizing; the empowerment of grassroots people and their recruitment for leadership; and the principle of "casting down your bucket where you are," or organizing in the context in which one lives and works, and working the issues found in that context.[3]

Families and Organizing

Of central importance to the Mississippi Movement was the capacity of Black families to adopt, nurture, love, and protect civil rights organizers as if they were family members. This practice, known in the literature as "informal absorption," allowed SNCC and CORE (Congress of Racial Equality) field secretaries and organizers to move from place to place in Mississippi with scarcely a dollar in their pockets, knowing full well that a family welcome awaited them at the end of their journeys. The absorption of civil rights organizers into Black families was spiritual gold for the Mississippi Movement, and it empowered movement organizers with the one credential that they could never earn: being one of the community's children. This credential contradicted the label of "outside agitator" used in Mississippi by the White power structure to negate the impact of the movement. By the same token, movement organizers empowered their adoptive families by reinforcing and enlarging the connections between them and the larger movement family, with its extensive networks across the land.

Grassroots People and Grassroots Leadership

The Mississippi Movement's message of empowerment for grassroots people was delivered to the entire country on national television at the 1964 Democratic National Convention by the Black sharecroppers, domestic workers, and farmers who formed the rank and file of the Mississippi Freedom Democratic Party (MFDP). Thereafter, the message of empowerment was carried by Black and White community organizers into many areas of community activity, including education, health, welfare, religion, and politics. However, neither the MFDP nor other grassroots organizations took root and flourished into a strong national movement for empowering Black people. The echoes heard — from the Democratic party to the federal government and from the religious sector to public school systems — were the same: institutionalizing empowerment in the hands of Black "folk" is too risky a notion to attract lasting political support.

The issue of community empowerment in the public schools, first raised by Black community organizers in Harlem in 1965, also found expression in White, liberal America. For example, in 1969 the Open Program of the Martin Luther King, Jr., School was established as a magnet program in the Cambridge public schools, in part because of the clamoring of Cambridge parents for more open education programs for their children, and in part because of the response to desegregation of the Cambridge schools.[4]

"Cast down your bucket where you are"

To master the art of organizing that strives to empower grassroots people, one needs to learn to "cast down your bucket where you are." In 1976, Bob and Janet Moses, both former organizers for SNCC in Mississippi, cast down their bucket in Cambridge and looked to the Open Program of the King School as a place to educate their children.[5] What would later become the Algebra Project began in 1982 when their eldest daughter, Maisha, entered the Open Program's eighth grade.

The Algebra Project

Before 1982, Moses, whose background included teaching secondary school mathematics in New York City and in Tanzania, had been teaching math to his children at home. Maisha, now a junior at Harvard University, recalls these lessons, conducted weekly during the school year and daily during the summer and vacations:

> Doing math at home was always a lot harder than math at school. It was somewhat like a chore. In our family, extra reading with my mom when we were much younger and math with my dad was part of our responsibility in the family, like taking out the garbage or doing the laundry.

Moses faced a familiar challenge: the resistance of adolescent children to performing what they regarded as a "household chore." Maisha explains:

> As we were getting older, it was a lot harder to get us to do math at home. We battled a lot more and complained. "Why do we have to do this? No one else has to do this." Dad would say, "It's important. I want you to do it. You need to do it." But we wouldn't be satisfied. I didn't really want to do it. Dad would have to sit there and force answers out of me. Finally he decided that the only way to get me to do algebra was to go into school.

In the fall of 1982, Mary Lou Mehrling, Maisha's eighth-grade teacher, invited Moses into her seventh/eighth-grade classroom to work with Maisha and three other eighth graders on algebra. That spring, Maisha and two others took the Cambridge citywide algebra test that was offered to students who wished to bypass Algebra I and go directly into honors algebra or honors geometry in the ninth grade. All three passed, becoming the first students in the history of the King School to be eligible to pursue the honors math and science curriculum at Cambridge's only high school, Cambridge Rindge and Latin.[6]

With one eye on his eldest son, who was about to enter the Open Program's seventh grade, Moses decided to continue working the next year (1983–1984) with Mehrling and another seventh/eighth-grade teacher. The number of eighth-graders studying algebra with Moses increased to nine. Partway through the year, the teachers selected seven seventh-graders they thought were likely to begin algebra the following year, creating the first group of "high-ability" seventh-graders for Moses to direct. That spring, all nine of Moses's eighth-graders took the citywide algebra test, and six passed.

In the following year the program expanded again, but it was no longer quite the same. As early as 1983–1984, it was evident that in spite of the commitment to meeting the educational needs of all its pupils, mathematics instruction in the Open Program was unwittingly skewed along racial lines.[7] Children in the two seventh/eighth-grade classrooms were clustered into separate ability groups: above-grade-level tracks primarily composed of middle-class Whites; below-grade-level tracks made up almost exclusively of Blacks and other children of color; and grade-level tracks that were racially mixed. The Open Program's system of ability groups effectively shunted most students of color onto the no-algebra track, imbuing too many youngsters with the self-fulfilling notion that little was expected of them.

Additionally, Moses and Mehrling became aware that some high-achieving Black males felt uncomfortable joining the algebra group, for it meant being separated from their friends who were on other math tracks. On the whole, young people feel the need to be as similar to their peers as possible. Separating academically talented adolescents from their peers for the sake of participation in the academic "fast track" potentially aggravates the anxiety that accompanies adolescents' identity development.[8] Moreover, enduring attitudes toward math are shaped by math instruction at the seventh- and eighth-grade levels. Traditionally, very few new math principles are introduced in these two grades, when attention focuses instead on review (Usiskin, 1987). Moses and Mehrling hypothesized that using the seventh and eighth grades to lay a groundwork of competence in algebra might enhance students' general self-confidence and provide them with the mathematical background necessary for advanced high school courses.

The Mississippi Movement's organizing tradition utilized everyday issues of ordinary people and framed them for the maximum benefit of the community. In Mississippi the issue was the right to vote; technically: "What are the legal, judicial, political, and constitutional obstacles to the right to vote? How can we initiate court cases, introduce legislation, and mobilize political support to remove these obstacles?" SNCC and CORE workers pursued this goal by establishing beachheads, through Black families, in the most resistant counties throughout the state. But the Mississippi organizers did something of even greater importance, and that was to conceive of the issue of voting in its broadest political sense. Midway through voter registration efforts, they began to ask themselves and the Black community: "What is the vote for? Why do we want it in the first place? What must we do right now to ensure that when we have the vote, it will work for us to benefit our communities?" After the organizers and key community groups had worked and reworked these and other questions, they shifted the organizing strategy from increasing voter registration to laying the basis for a community-based political party, which eventually became the Mississippi Freedom Democratic Party. Creating a new political party became the Mississippi Movement's focus, because of its greater potential for involving community people in a substantive long-term effort. Participants would come to own the political questions and their responses to them.[9]

In the Open Program the everyday issue was teaching algebra in the seventh and eighth grades. Moses, the parent-as-organizer in the program, instinctively used the lesson he had learned in Mississippi, transforming the everyday issue into a broader political question for the Open Program community to consider: What is algebra for? Why do we want children to study it? What do we need to include in the mathematics education of every middle school student, to provide each and every one of them with access to the college preparatory mathematics curriculum in high school? Why is it important to gain such access?

By linking the content of math education to the future prospects of inner-city children, Moses transformed what had previously been a purely curricular issue into a broader political question. Drawing on his experience as an organizer, educator, and parent, Moses transformed the dialogue among parents, teachers, and school administrators in the Open Program into one that centered on questions that would get at the heart of educational practice: How can a culture be created in the Open Program in which every child is expected to be as good as possible in his or her mathematical development? What should the content of middle school mathematics be? What curricular processes make that content available to all students?

A cornerstone of the evolving Algebra Project thus became the expectation that every child in the Open Program could achieve math literacy, an ethos powerful enough to suffuse both the peer and adult culture. The components of this effort included changing the content and methods of teaching math, involving parents in activities that would enable them to better support their children's learning, teaching students to set goals and motivating them to achieve, and reaching out to Black college graduates in the Boston area who would serve as tutors and role models of academic success.

Teachers as Learners

From the beginning, Mehrling and Moses modeled the notion that there is no shame in confessing ignorance — if it is the first step in learning. Mehrling, an ex-music teacher, took courses in mathematics, beginning with algebra, and eventually achieved state certification in math. But she did something more profound: she turned her inexperience with math content into a component of learning by adopting a position of mutual inquiry with her students and by presenting herself to them as a learner. As she states, she "developed methods of responding to students' questions that helped both the students and me to think through the problems." When she had questions, she would ask Moses for help, on the spot:

> Presenting myself as a learner, in front of my students, helped me to understand what they were experiencing, and helped them to feel comfortable asking for help. Students no longer felt threatened if they did not understand a problem or a concept, for they saw that we all were learners and we all learn in different ways.

Because Mehrling presented herself openly and honestly as a student of the subject she was teaching, she was able to help build her students' confidence. She overtly transmitted the message, "if I [your teacher] can risk embarrassment to learn this subject, surely you can, too." But she also conveyed to them a powerful latent message:

> I am confident that people who don't know this subject can learn it; to learn it they have, at all times, to be ready not to pretend to understand what they do not truly understand; to learn it they must be comfortable asking for help and willing to risk embarrassment.

Mehrling's message recapitulated a memorable message that Fannie Lou Hamer and others conveyed at the height of the MFDP challenge to the Democratic National Convention of 1964 — confidence that people who did not know the business of politics could learn it by asking direct questions and risking embarrassment. Each confronted their inexperience with honesty and integrity, turning potential liabilities into strengths.

Involving Parents

From its inception, the Open Program had evolved a set of policies and practices that encouraged parents' active involvement in staff hiring, curriculum development, observation and evaluation of teachers, and governance and administration of the school. Parental involvement in the Algebra Project grew naturally in this context.

Parents who served on the program's seventh/eighth-grade committee in 1984–1985 concluded that decisions about studying algebra in the seventh and eighth grades could not be left up to individual sixth-graders. These children were too young to fully understand the long-range implications of their decisions for college entrance. Nor should such decisions rest solely with the teachers, curriculum coordinators, or school or district-wide administrators, each of whom had their own ideas about who should study algebra and in which grade. Rather, parents needed to be involved in making educational choices for their children at both individual and policymaking levels. They also had to be better informed about details of the middle school math curriculum so that they would be able to make informed decisions and protect the best interests of their children.

During the spring of 1985, a parent from the Open Program's seventh/eighth-grade committee collaborated with Moses to distribute a letter to the parents of all the sixth-graders, asking whether they thought that every seventh-grader should study algebra, and whether they thought their own child should study algebra in the seventh grade. In reply, a few parents said they thought that some seventh-graders probably weren't ready, but no parent thought his or her own child should be denied access to algebra in the seventh grade. Exposing the contradictions between parental assessments of their children's capabilities and curricular assumptions at the community level provided a means for building consensus around educational outcomes for all children.

This was the catalyst for inviting all Open Program children entering the seventh grade in the fall of 1985 to study algebra three times a week. With the exception of a few eighth-graders who in their teacher's judgment were not ready, the invitation to study algebra was extended to the entire eighth grade as well. The consensus statement from parents launched a change in school policy and culture. Currently, every Open Program student is expected to study algebra in the seventh and eighth grades.

As the project evolved, parental participation increased as parents volunteered in classrooms and participated in workshops on student self-esteem and achievement. Parents from throughout the King School were invited to attend "Honors Bound" parent groups, which prepared students of color to accept the challenge of taking honors courses in high school and created a home-school culture that would nurture and support serious intellectual effort. A Saturday morning algebra course for parents was offered, teaching algebra in the same way that it was being taught to their children.

Parents who took algebra during the Saturday classes committed themselves to making the project "theirs" in a fundamental sense. A grateful parent captured the multiple dimensions of this experience in a 1987 letter to the Cambridge School Committee:

> . . . this program exemplifies to me all that I hope most for in the education of my daughter and other young people in our community: a positive orientation to learning; a rich understanding of advanced mathematics; recognition of the relationship between what is learned in the classroom and what goes on in life; and a sense of personal empowerment.

> As a sixth grader in her first year in the program, my daughter began to overcome her fear of math and distorted perceptions of what she is capable of doing

and why it is important. I believe this was due to several factors, including the climate of learning in the classroom (in part, a sense that students, teachers and aides alike were learning *together*); the demystification of the subject by relating it to life experiences; and by the fact that her mother, along with other parents and community members, was simultaneously overcoming latent math panic by taking the course on Saturdays.

This experience not only helped me understand the program (and learn math); it also greatly enhanced my comprehension of the life of the school and neighborhood community and of problems that as a citizen I can help to resolve. . . .

Parents were barraged with letters and opportunities to talk, to ask questions, and to join in planning, all as an acknowledgment of the centrality of parents in the construction of a home-school culture of high achievement.

Creating a New Teaching and Learning Environment for Math

As an adjunct to opening up algebra to all seventh and eighth graders in 1985, ability grouping was replaced with individual and small-group instruction. Students were taught skills for learning hard material "on their own." In conferences with teachers, students were asked to set their own short-term objectives (for example, deciding how many lesson sets they wished to complete each week), and longer-range goals (for example, deciding to prepare for the citywide test). Parents were informed about the goals and were asked to sign their child's goal statement each semester. The pace and scope of students' mathematical studies therefore came under student control. Mehrling tells a story that reflects the individual and group motivation that such goal-setting can foster:

Andrea spoke up at one of our first meetings and said, "I'm going to do four lessons a week because I want to finish such-and-such by the end of seventh grade, so I can finish the book by the end of eighth grade, so I can be in honors geometry in the ninth grade." This was a twelve-year-old. The others looked at her — this hadn't come from a teacher — and said, "Are you crazy?" She said, "That's what I'm going to do." Bob [Moses] was there, and he started to frame for them why what Andrea had just done was a very mature and farsighted act, and how maybe they weren't ready to do that yet. But it gave Andrea a lot of support and affirmation for having said that in the group. And it changed what the others were going to say next. Everything from then on was in terms of Andrea: "Well, I'm not going to do quite what Andrea is, but . . . ."

Students also learned to work harder than they had before. They were encouraged to develop habits of concentration, patience, and perseverance in approaching their daily math work. Students decided which of several resources to consult — the textbook, the instructor, or a peer — when they had a question or ran into difficulties in solving a problem. Teachers met with small groups for brief lessons on specific concepts and regularly held small-group review sessions. Reflecting on this decision, Mehrling recently explained:

Adolescent learners can sometimes interrelate with materials, and it's not nearly as threatening as interacting with an adult. If they can go to an adult to ask a question about the materials when they're ready to go to an adult, it's wholly different from being in a group, being pinpointed and put on the spot, and feeling vulnerable about the pieces they don't have in place yet. Once they start to inter-act with materials, they get not only very possessive of them, but very reluctant to go back to any kind of teacher-directed lessons. They're empowered, in a curious way, around materials — something I would never have even thought about. The Open Program generally is a very teacher-intensive kind of program. We moti-vate, we bring in materials from everywhere, and our teaching is interpersonal. We discovered at the seventh- and eighth-grade level that that was one of the problems with students who felt vulnerable: It put them on the spot.

As part of the new curricular, pedagogical, and social environment for studying math, the seventh- and eighth-grade teachers assumed the role of "coach" as op-posed to "lecturer" in their relationship with students.

The project produced its first full graduating class in the spring of 1986. When they entered high school the following autumn, 39 percent of the graduates were placed in Honors Geometry or Honors Algebra. Not a single student in that cohort ended up at Cambridge Rindge and Latin School in lower-level math courses, such as Algebra I.

Curricular Expansion

By 1986, attention turned to the preparation of students for seventh-grade algebra. With all students in the seventh and eighth grades taking algebra, lower grade teachers began to question the adequacy of their own math curricula as prepara-tion for algebra. To address this question systematically, the entire staff of the Open Program participated in a year-long institute centered on the question of math literacy.

After the institute, teachers at all levels (K–8) implemented new curricula in mathematics appropriate for the age and grade levels they taught. Some teachers found it unsettling to devise their own curricular practices around the needs of children and their own teaching styles. The results of the Algebra Project suggest that flexibility leads to better pedagogy. For example, when fifth/sixth-grade teach-ers tried a materials-centered approach with sixth-graders that had worked very well at the seventh/eighth-grade level, they found that younger children, accus-tomed to more teacher-centered instruction, needed more teacher-child and small-group interaction in the sixth-grade transition curriculum. The teachers modified their classroom technique, but retained the principle of encouraging greater self-reliance in finding answers to problems. Improved adaptation of curriculum was itself beneficial. But equally important, this process gave teachers the same sense of empowerment experienced by students. Teachers who participated in the innova-tion and trained themselves in how to present the curriculum were more likely to understand, appreciate, and foster the skill of self-education that was central to the Algebra Project. One teacher explained:

Bob was affirming what we were doing while he was helping us change. He didn't come in and say, "We're throwing this out, it's junk." He came in and said, "You guys are great. Wanna try something different?" When we asked, "How will it work?" he turned it around and asked, "Well, how do you think it should work? What do you want to have happen?" He didn't really give us a way, which admit-tedly was frustrating, but it also gave us ownership around it. Bob didn't have all of the answers. At first I was really annoyed that he was making me go through this process. I kept saying, "Bob has an agenda. Why doesn't he tell us? We're wasting so much time!" But he knew that it had to come from us. He knew he couldn't impose, because he didn't know what would work. He wasn't a classroom teacher. He just had the vision. If he could help us catch the vision, we would make it work.

A second outcome was that Moses agreed to develop a curriculum for the sixth grade that would provide a conceptual transition from arithmetic to algebra. The main features of what has come to be called the Algebra Project, and the philosophy that guided its construction, are discussed below.

What to Teach and How to Teach It

The opening of algebra to everyone in 1985–1986 gave Moses the opportunity to work closely with several students who had great difficulty with the initial chapters of the algebra textbook. In particular, one Black male student took many months to complete the first few lessons. Moses wondered precisely where the student's conceptual knot lay. Was it possible to lead the student from arithmetic to algebra by mapping a conceptual trail, beginning with concepts that were obvious and proceeding by equally obvious steps?

After working with a number of students who were having difficulty, Moses came to the conclusion that the heart of the problem lay in their concept of number. In arithmetic, the distinctive feature of a number is magnitude or quantity. In algebra, a number has two distinctive features: one is quantitative; the other is qualitative and must be explicitly taught. Students of arithmetic have in their minds one question that they associate with counting numbers: "How many?" Students of algebra need to have two: "How many?" and another questions, such as "Which way?" as points of reference for the intuitive concept of opposites. Children understand the question, "Which way?" from their early years, but it is not a question that they associate with numbers. The number concept used in arithmetic must be generalized in algebra, and failure to make this generalization blocks students' understanding. Once students have generalized their concept of number, they must also generalize their knowledge of basic operations such as subtraction.

Moses gradually arrived at a five-step teaching and learning process that takes students from physical events to a symbolic representation of those events, thereby accelerating sixth graders' grasp of key concepts needed in the study of algebra.[10] The five steps are:

1. Physical event
2. Picture of model of this event
3. Intuitive (idiomatic) language description of this event
4. A description of this event in "regimented" English
5. Symbolic representation of the event

The purpose of the five steps is to avert student frustration in "the game of signs," or the misapprehension that mathematics is the manipulation of a collection of mysterious symbols and signs. Chad, a young Black seventh-grader, recently looked up from reading a page in the first chapter of a traditional algebra text and said to his mother, "It's all just words." For too many youngsters, mathematics is a game of signs they cannot play. They must be helped to understand what those signs *really* mean and to construct for themselves a basis of evidence for mathematics. When middle-school students use the five-step process to construct symbolic representations of physical events (representations that they themselves make up), they forge, through direct experience, their own platform of mathematical truths. Their personally constructed symbolic representations enter into a system of mathematical truths that has content and meaning.

At the Open Program, students initiate this process with a trip on the Red Line of Boston's subway system (the physical event). This experience provides the context in which a number of obvious questions may be asked: At what station do we start? Where are we going? How many stops will it take to get there? In what direction do we go? These questions have obvious answers, forming the basis for the mathematics of trips. When they return, students are asked to write about their trip, draw a mural or construct a three-dimensional model, make graphs for trips that they create, and collect statistical data about them. The purpose is to fuse in their minds the two questions "How many?" and "which way?" and to anchor these questions to physical events.

Students then use this process to explore the concept of equivalence in the broad cultural context of everyday events, such as cooking, coaching, teaching, painting, and repairing. They explore any concept in which object A is substituted for object B to achieve a certain goal. They conclude the discussion of equivalence in subway travel with open-ended constructions of equivalent trips, leading to an introduction of displacements as "trips that have the same number of stops and go in the same direction."

Once displacements are introduced, they investigate the concept of "comparing" as a prelude to generalizing their concept of subtraction. Most algebra texts introduce subtraction as a transformed addition problem. Students are asked to think of subtraction $(3 - (-2) = +5)$ as "adding the opposite" or "finding the missing addend" $(3 - ? = 5)$, which provides one group of signs as a reference for another. But students look for concrete experiences, pictures, or at least a concept, to link directly to algebraic subtraction. The problem is compounded because students have over-learned "take-away" as the concept underlying subtraction. In algebra, "take-away" no longer has a straightforward application to subtraction. Within a couple of months of beginning algebra, students confront subtraction statements that have no discernable content, have only indirect meaning in relation to an associated addition problem, and are not at all obvious.

To give additional content, meaning, and clarity to subtraction in beginning algebra, students begin with the physical event of comparing the heights of two students, Coastocoast, who is six feet tall, and Watchme, who is four feet tall. The class works with a picture of this event, generating questions that can be used to compare heights:

1. Which one is taller?
2. What is the difference in their heights?
3. How much shorter is Watchme than Coastocoast?
4. Who is shorter?
5. How much taller is Coastocoast than Watchme?

In arithmetic there are two subtraction concepts, the concept of "take-away" and the concept of "the difference between." The latter provides the appropriate entry into subtraction in algebra, as illustrated in the above set of questions. Students will readily identify an answer to the second question by subtracting to find the difference in the heights. This prepares them to accept subtraction as the best approach to answering comparative questions — questions that belong to algebra and not arithmetic.

The answers to these questions are carefully processed in three stages: intuitive language, regimented English, and symbolic representations. "How much taller is Coastocoast than Watchme?" is explored in the following way:

- *Intuitive language:* "Coastocoast is two feet taller than Watchme."
- *Regimented English:* "The height of Coastocoast compared to the height of Watchme is two feet taller."
- *Symbolic representations:*

    (5a)   H(C) compared to H(W) is 2' ↑
    (5b)   H(C) – H(W) = 2' ↑
    (5c)   6' ↑ – 4' ↑ = 2 ↑
            (that is, 6' is 2' taller than 4')

"How much shorter is Watchme than Coastocoast?" proceeds along a similar track.

- *Intuitive language:* "Watchme is two feet shorter than Coastocoast."
- *Regimented English:* "The height of Watchme compared to the height of Coastocoast is two feet shorter."
- *Symbolic representations:*

    (3a)   H(W) compared to H(C) is 2' ↓
    (3b)   H(W) – H(C) = 2' ↓
    (3c)   4' ↑ – 6' ↑ = 2' ↓
            (that is, a height of 4' is 2' shorter than a height of 6')

This way of comparing physical quantities is easily reinforced with work stations at which students compare weights, lengths, temperatures, and speeds. They may return to their experience on the subway to compare positions of stations on the Red Line, using the following model:

Alewife	Davis	Porter	Harvard	Central	Kendall	Charles	Park
●	●	●	●	●	●	●	●
A	D	P	H	C	K	CH	P

When asked, "What is the position of Harvard compared to Kendall?" students work through the following steps:

- *Intuitive language:* "Harvard is two stops outbound from Kendall."
- *Regimented English:* "The position of Harvard compared to the position of Kendall is two stops outbound."

- *Symbolic representations:*

  (a) P(H) compared to P(K) is 2
  (b) P(H) − P(K) = 2

In a similar way the question, "What is the position of Kendall relative to Harvard?" yields

P(K) − P(H) = 2

As soon as integers are introduced as a system of coordinates, students are ready to generate their own subtraction problems. The notion of an arbitrary point of reference having been introduced earlier, systems of coordinates are assigned to the stations, with the zero point alternately assigned to various stations. Each assignment generates a different subtraction problem for the question, "What is the position of Harvard relative to Kendall?"

Alewife	Davis	Porter	Harvard	Central	Kendall	Charles	Park
●	●	●	●	●	●	●	●
A	D	P	H	C	K	CH	P
−6	−5	−4	−3	−2	−1	0	+1

  (a) P(H) compared to P(K) is 2
  (b) P(H) − P(K) = 2
  (c)   −3 − (−1) = −2

By similar reasoning, the question, "what is the position of Kendall relative to Harvard?" yields

P(K) − P(H) = 2
−1 − (−3) = +2

The opposite comparisons [P(H) compared to P(K), and P(K) compared to P(H)] lead to opposite expressions [(−3) − (−1), and (−1) − (−3)] as well as opposite integers [(−2) and (+2)], in a way that gives direct, intuitive meaning to subtraction of integers and provides students and teachers alike with control over the generation of simple subtraction problems and equations. The curriculum and curricular process used in the sixth grade have made algebra accessible for all middle school students. The project has demonstrated that all seventh- and eighth-grade students in the King School's Open Program can study algebra, and that the entire school community expects them to do so.

Community Participation in Creating a Culture of Achievement

For youngsters who have felt excluded from the culture of academic achievement in school, the expectation that they, too, can learn is crucial. During the 1987–88 school year, the project's response to children who did not think they were likely to succeed in math was to institute a series of measures designed to create a culture of mathematical and scientific literacy, not only in the Open Program, but in other programs within the King School as well. The Seymour Institute for Advanced Christian Studies, a service organization conceived by Black Harvard graduates to support community-based development in urban areas, provided Black role models to go into classes to tutor students and to run before-school algebra study halls four mornings a week. The study halls were open to seventh and eighth graders from all of the King School's four programs. The tutors, who came from Harvard, MIT, Wentworth Institute, and Boston University, established relationships with individual children and became role models of academically successful young adults for seventh and eighth graders to emulate. A Harvard Law School student and tutor wrote:

> I have been impressed by the fact that these seventh and eighth graders are able to read and understand their math textbooks, already have some understanding of algebraic concepts, and are willing to come out at 7:30 A.M. in order to work on their mathematical skills. . . . The students in the Algebra Project are able to help themselves, and each other, by using their books. Helping each other has another important role in the Project. I believe that it is their friendships that keep them coming to early morning study halls; relationships that support educational achievement are being established outside the classroom.

As the Algebra Project developed, the message that each child could learn was more systematically articulated by the Efficacy Institute.[11] Emphasizing confidence and effective effort as key ingredients in the process of intellectual development, the Efficacy model provides educators, parents, and students with an explicit alternative to the ability model of learning. Efficacy assumes that children, who are well enough endowed to master the fundamentals of language at an early age, are fully capable of learning mathematics. In order to learn, children are required to marshal effective effort. They must learn to work with commitment, focused attention, and reliable strategies. When learning is perceived as a function of effective effort, one seeks factors inhibiting children when they are having difficulties learning or understanding a concept, rather than looking for "disabilities" that prevent learning.

Many children of color learn from an early age that there are doubts concerning their capacity to develop intellectually. Messages communicated from school (low-ability placements in the primary grades), from peers (pervasive anti-intellectualism within the peer group), and the media (expectations of inferiority) all serve to impress upon them that they may not be up to the task of advanced studies. The lack of confidence engendered by the internalization of these messages shapes the meaning of any failure ("I guess this proves I'm not smart") and undermines the capacity to work ("Why bang my head against the wall if I'm unable to learn the stuff anyway?").

To redress these circumstances, Efficacy works to plant an alternative idea in the child's mind: "If I work hard enough, I can get smart."

Confidence	$\rightarrow$	Effective Effort	$\rightarrow$	Development
(Think you can)		*(Work hard)*		*(Get smart)*

Emphasis is placed on the process of development and some measure of control is returned to the child.

Teachers are the carriers of Efficacy ideas, and it is to them that responsibility falls for building confidence and shaping strong effort in children. Teachers attend an intensive, five-day seminar to learn the Efficacy model of development and study its implications for their own teaching. They are then provided with a formal curriculum to use with their students over the course of an academic year. The curriculum gives teachers and students a shared language and a conceptual framework for reworking questions, such as why a particular child has been unable to "do math" in the past. The teacher is able to impress upon the child that learning is a function of effort, not of innate ability. The curriculum helps the students to raise their consciousness so they can affirm for themselves their own need for self-development. Such affirmation on their part is a critical prerequisite to confronting obstacles to their own development and acquiring attitudes and habits that will ensure success in many endeavors, including the algebra program.

In 1988, a sixth-grade teacher in the Open Program began teaching the Efficacy curriculum to all the sixth graders twice a week. She explains:

> We all consider ourselves to be good teachers, and yet we know that we are failing some students. Bob talked to us about a way that could help us to help those children achieve. We realized what that will mean not only to those students but to all of the children in our classrooms, and from there, what that will mean to the community at large.

The Project Continues

The Algebra Project continues at the Open Program. The Efficacy and algebra curricula are taught to sixth-graders, and algebra is studied by all seventh- and eighth-graders. The project is now challenging other schools to make the political decision to alter their own math curricula. For example, discussions are proceeding with administrators and teachers in Boston, where three schools have volunteered to experiment with both the Efficacy and Algebra Project curricula and receive training in their implementation. Moses has also begun to train selected middle school teachers in Atlanta. Currently, the project is exploring relationships with school systems in other cities.

Conclusion

Community Organizing and Educational Innovation

The community organizing approach to educational innovation differs from traditional educational interventions in several important ways. The principle of "casting down your bucket where you are" stands in marked contrast to research programs originating in universities, where scholars design interventions they hypothesize will result in outcomes that they articulate in advance and that are replicable. Researchers in universities and consulting firms must have well-designed, highly articulated interventions in order to convince funding agencies that their projects have promise. Depending upon the focus of the investigation, the researcher generally targets selected neighborhoods, schools, or organizations for participation based on their demographic or similarly quantifiable characteristics. Additionally, researchers have intellectual roots in their own disciplines and view problems through lenses that are consonant with their disciplines, rather than through the eyes of a community.

In contrast to the university-based researcher, the organizer working in the tradition of Ella gradually becomes recognized by community members as having a commitment to their overall well-being. The organizer immerses himself or herself in the life of the community, learning its strengths, resources, concerns, and ways of conducting business. The organizer does not have a comprehensive, detailed plan for remedying a perceived problem but takes an "evolutionary" view of his or her own role in the construction of the solution. He or she understands that the community's everyday concerns can be transformed into broader political questions of general import. The form they will take is not always known in advance.

Once political questions are identified, the organizer's agenda must remain simultaneously focused and fluid — sharply focused on the long-range goal, but fluid with respect to how the goal will be attained. The organizer seeks out views of community participants who have strong interests in the issue and informally educates community members who are uninvolved but whose interests are at stake. It is the organizer's task to help community members air their opinions, question one another, and then build consensus, a process that usually takes a good deal of time to complete.

Improving the mathematics curriculum and curricular process in a middle school has gradually become the focus of the Algebra Project. At the outset, Moses did not know that the project would become a vehicle for raising questions about ability grouping, effective teaching for children of color, or the community's roles in educational decisionmaking. He did not imagine that it would trigger an interest in teaching algebra to inner-city middle school students beyond his daughter's classroom.

As we have seen, the program's innovations relied on the involvement of the entire community: teachers, parents, school administrators, students, tutors, and consultants from the Greater Boston community. In her review of programs that have been helpful in breaking the cycle of disadvantage, Lisbeth Schorr (1988) highlights the importance of comprehensive, flexible, and intensive approaches to reform:[12]

> Many interventions have turned out to be ineffective not because seriously disadvantaged families are beyond help, but because we have tried to attack complex, deeply rooted tangles of troubles with isolated fragments of help, with help rendered grudgingly in one-shot forays, with help designed less to meet the needs of beneficiaries than to conform to professional or bureaucratic convenience, with help that may be useful to middle-class families but is often irrelevant to families struggling to survive. (pp. 263–264)

The work of discovering new solutions, building a broad base of support, and overcoming barriers takes time. Moses's effort to work with teachers, parents, and administrators to transform the middle school mathematics curriculum and curricular process in the Open Program began seven years ago. We note that it took fifteen years for James Comer's efforts at comprehensive reform in two New Haven schools to yield striking improvements in test scores (Comer, 1980, 1988).[13] Durable reforms are possible, but there are no shortcuts in bottom-up implementation.

In the Open Program, faculty volunteered to participate, committing themselves to working together to discover better ways to teach math and struggling to reach consensus. Parents were deeply involved as learners, supporters, contributors, and decisionmakers. Students voluntarily set goals for themselves and came to 7:30 A.M. study halls four mornings a week. School administrators supported teachers as they tried out new strategies, worked to secure funding, and acted as spokespersons for the project. The strengths of various contributors were recognized, and they were empowered to adapt, create, and evaluate their progress in attaining a shared vision.

Others have learned that it is through struggling with a problem and shaping the solutions that commitment to change really occurs. Schorr (1988) reports:

> Dr. Comer wanted to make sure I understood that the essence of his intervention is a process, not a package of materials, instructional methods, or techniques. "It is the creation of a sense of community and direction for parents, school staff, and students alike." (p. 234)

Comer is pointing to the fact that significant innovations must transform the culture, and transformation requires a broad base of voluntary support. It is crucial that participants have time to understand an idea, explore their commitment, and adapt the innovation to their needs.

Henry Levin (1988) also emphasizes the importance of process.[14] He states:

> Underlying the organizational approach are two major assumptions: First, the strategy must "empower" all of the major participants rather than decrying their weaknesses. (p. 5)

Many will find it useful to follow the precept "cast down your bucket where you are," as Jaime Escalante did in Los Angeles when he began offering calculus to disadvantaged youth. The starting point for reform is less important than whether the issue is powerful and inspiring enough to generate enthusiasm, reveal broader political questions, compel devoted leadership, and serve as a vehicle for community commitment.

Funding to Support Innovation

The Algebra Project would not have developed as it did had it not been for the MacArthur "no strings attached" Fellowship that allowed Moses to work in the Open Program for five years without having to account for the way he spent his time. Subsequent funding has been difficult. For eighteen months, Wheelock College in Boston supported Moses as he looked for resources to provide release time for teachers, cover materials and reproduction costs, and secure consultation from the broader academic community. Moses is still spending an enormous amount of time trying to secure long-term funding to support the continuation and dissemination of the Algebra Project.

Finding support can be a depleting struggle for many innovative efforts. National funding sources are hesitant to fund projects with grassroots leadership, a community focus, a long timeframe, and a philosophy that casts educational issues in political as well as technical terms. Declining state and local budgets also threaten commitment to comprehensive, long-term reforms. But only when major political questions are addressed (for instance, that *all* children can benefit from and should have access to algebra in their middle school years) can we discover the most appropriate ways to organize knowledge, develop curriculum, and encourage home, school, and community participation.

Transforming School Culture

Teachers and parents in the Open Program came to believe that ability grouping in mathematics seriously impaired the capacity of middle school females and students of color to learn as well as they might. Questioning the policy was the first step toward comprehensive change. Others concur that differentiating students harms those who are disadvantaged or placed in lower tracks.[15] After articulating a vision of high expectations in algebra for all students, participants worked to transform the culture of the school, so that policies, teaching strategies, and the Efficacy curriculum could together help students.

The project speaks to the importance of family as a link to school success. Henderson (1987) concludes her review of research concerning parental involvement in student achievement by categorically stating that "the evidence is beyond dispute: parent involvement improves student achievement" (p. 1). This finding holds for middle- as well as low-income families, at different grade levels, and within a broad spectrum of interventions. As the U.S. population becomes more diverse, it is absolutely fundamental that schools join with families to define and support school success. Continuity between home and school must be forged for all children, and we must draw on the strengths and resources that families can provide.

Curriculum and Curricular Process

Among the strengths of the faculty and volunteers in the Open Program was their curiosity about why some children were not succeeding in mathematics and their willingness to explore the possibility that their own teaching strategies might be a factor. Moses and the teachers became classroom researchers — analyzing student errors, locating conceptual knots, and experimenting with materials and teaching processes that might improve students' mathematical development. A sixth-grade transition curriculum that allows students to relate everyday experiences to mathematical concepts represented symbolically should be disseminated widely.

In 1964, national attention was focused on the disenfranchised citizens of the South. In 1989, another kind of disenfranchisement exists, as many poor, indigenous, and immigrant children of color are denied access to programs and teaching that support their success in school. The success of the Algebra Project stands as a challenge to public school teachers, administrators, scholars, and, most important, those individuals who have traditionally advocated for the democratization of the society and schools: Will you wage a campaign for mathematical literacy, which acknowledges that every middle school student can and should learn algebra while simultaneously empowering the child's community and family? Will you organize in the spirit of Ella?

Notes

1. *Fundi* is a Swahili term for a person who has an expertise valued by society, and who passes on his or her art to the young by example and instruction. Ella Baker was a *fundi* to the SNCC workers learning the art of community organizing.
2. One such quiet place was Amite County, in a remote corner of southwest Mississippi, where E. W. Steptoe's family welcomed Bob Moses, SNCC's first field secretary, into the community in the summer of 1961. Mr. Steptoe was president of Amite County's NAACP chapter in the late 1950s when the county sheriff raided a chapter meeting and confiscated the group's books, thus exposing the members to economic reprisals and physical danger. By the time the first wave of SNCC organizers spread out across the rural South, activities at places like the Steptoe farmhouse had ground to a halt.
3. "Cast down your bucket where you are" was used by Booker T. Washington in an address at the Atlanta Exposition, September 18, 1895.
4. The King School is a large, modern facility built on the site of a school that had served Cambridge's Black community for many years. By the late 1970s, the King School housed four programs for grades K–8: a regular program composed of personnel from the former school; a magnet Open Program; and smaller bilingual and special needs programs.
5. Because some but not all authors of this article are also the subjects of discussion, we have chosen to use third-person references throughout to avoid confusion.
6. The fourth student opted to go to a private high school, and did not take the test.
7. See Delpit (1986) for a discussion of the differences between the instructional needs of mainstream and minority children.
8. See Fordham (1988) for a discussion of the tensions high-achieving Black students feel when they strive for academic success.
9. It was only in Mississippi, where the entire state was structured along a community organizing tradition, that the issue of the right to vote was perceived as a broad political question.
10. This model is a synthesis of ideas derived from three sources. The first was the Open Program itself. Moses observed teaching practices in the Open Program and attended workshops with teachers in which Virginia Chalmers and others explained the teaching and learning ideas that they had developed for primary grades. The second was Quine's (1981) notion of "mathematization in situ." "A progressive sharpening and regimenting of ordinary idioms: this is what led to arithmetic, symbolic logic, and set theory, and this is mathematization" (p. 150). Quine insisted that "set theory, arithmetic, and symbolic logic are all of them products of the straightforward mathematization of ordinary interpreted discourse . . . " (p. 151). The third source was Dubinsky (1987), who shared his insight that in the future, mathematics education would center on a "fixed curricular process" rather than a "fixed curriculum."
11. The Efficacy model of intellectual development is based on motivation. The role of motivation in self-development was studied by Jeffrey Howard, Director of the Efficacy Institute, who, in collaboration with educators, developed the model summarized here.
12. As a participant of the Harvard University Working Group on Early Life and Adolescence, Lisbeth Schorr believed that with the knowledge currently available, society could prevent the damaging outcomes for adolescents associated with disadvantage, such as teenage pregnancy, juvenile crime, school failure, and unemployment. She visited an array of health and education programs that were successful in interrupting the cycle of disadvantage and discovered that what the programs had in common was a comprehensive, flexible, and intensive approach to reform.
13. In 1968, James Comer, a psychiatrist at the Yale Child Study Center, began a program of reform in the two New Haven schools that had the lowest achievement scores and the worst attendance and behavior records in the system. Today, although the community is still impoverished, these demonstration schools now boast top achievement scores in the New Haven system (ranking third and fourth), no serious behavior problems, and superior attendance records. The critical components of the reform, now disseminated to fourteen other sites, include a school planning and management team (composed of the principal, parents,

and teachers), a mental health team that provides coordinated services to children in conflict, and extensive parent involvement.

14. Henry Levin is the director of the very successful Accelerated Schools Project in the San Francisco Bay Area, whose mission is "bringing children into the educational mainstream so that they can fully benefit from future schooling and their adult opportunities" (1988, p. 3).

15. Levin (1988) argued that the major reason for the failure of many disadvantaged children is low teacher expectation, which in turn leads to pull-out programs based on tedious drill-and-practice curricula. Peterson (1989) conducted a study in Utah, concluding that ability grouping is harmful to remedial students, and that participation in accelerated programs is a more effective route to higher achievement.

References

Comer, J. (1988). *Maggie's American dream.* New York: New American Library.

Comer, J. (1980). *School power.* New York: Free Press.

Delpit, L. (1986). Skills and other dilemmas of a progressive Black educator. *Harvard Educational Review, 56,* 379–385.

Dubinsky, E. (1987). *How Piaget's and related work should influence K–12 curriculum design.* Unpublished manuscript.

Fordham, S. (1988). Racelessness as a factor in Black students' school success: Pragmatic strategy or Pyrrhic victory? *Harvard Educational Review, 58,* 54–84.

Henderson, A. (1987). *The evidence continues to grow: Parent involvement improves student achievement.* Columbia, MD: National Committee for Citizens in Education.

Levin, H. (1988). Don't remediate: Accelerate. In *Proceedings of the Stanford University Centennial Conference, Accelerating the Education of At-Risk Students.* Stanford, CA: Stanford University, Center for Educational Research.

National Science Foundation. (1989). *Materials for middle school mathematics instruction.* Catalog of Federal Domestic Assistance no. 47.067, Materials Development, Research, and Informal Science Education.

Peterson, J. (1989). Remediation is no remedy. *Educational Leadership, 46*(6), 24–25.

Quine, W. V. (1981). *Theories and things.* Cambridge, MA: Harvard University Press.

Saxon, J. H., Jr. (1982). *Algebra I: An incremental development.* Norman, OK: Saxon Publishers.

Schorr, L. (1988). *Within our reach: Breaking the cycle of disadvantage.* New York: Anchor Press/Doubleday.

Usiskin, Z. (1987). Why elementary algebra can, should, and must be an eighth-grade course for average students. *Mathematics Teacher, 80,* 428–437.

The authors wish to thank the following people for their contributions to this article: Theresa Perry, Daniel Cheever, Barney Brawer, Ceasar McDowell, and, finally, the teachers and administrators of the Open Program of the Martin Luther King, Jr., School.

PART THREE

The Complex World
of Teaching

Cognition, Complexity, and Teacher Education

BRENT DAVIS

DENNIS J. SUMARA

*Brent Davis and Dennis Sumara build a theoretical case in this chapter for their be-
lief that teaching is "complex" rather than "complicated." Complicated systems
can be understood by breaking them down and analyzing their individual parts;
complex systems, by contrast, cannot be discerned by deconstructing them, as
these systems are often greater than the sum of their parts—they are "more dynamic, more unpredictable, more alive." Teaching, therefore, cannot be looked at
piecemeal; the web of relationships, experiences, outside influences, and unknown
factors that play into the teaching and learning situation must be explored as the
complex, whole system it is. As Davis and Sumara assert, "there is no direct,
causal, linear, fixable relationship among the various components of any community of practice" in education. Instead, all of the people and all of the elements that
create the teaching and learning environment are connected in complex, multiple,
and unpredictable ways. As a consequence, teachers and teacher educators must
reconceive the practice of teaching by blurring the lines between knower and
known, teacher and student, school and community.*

The question of how one learns to teach continues to be hotly debated. Despite the range of opinions being voiced on the matter, however, one mindset
seems to predominate that casts teaching in terms of management and me-
chanics. Corporate and computer metaphors appear to have finally become
literalized, and the *business* of teaching is now overwhelmingly cast in terms of
such techniques as sorting, organizing, categorizing, overseeing, and controlling.
Reflecting this trend, learning to teach has become a matter of mastering a set of
narrow competencies: lesson planning, questioning modes, test construction, assessment strategies.

Relying strictly on some of the popular "how-to" manuals that have been prepared for teacher education programs, one might come to the mistaken conclusion
that what it means to teach and how one learns to teach are largely settled matters.
The corporate slogans, the carefully articulated taxonomies, and the neatly dis-
sected structures present an image of a sound, unambiguous body of knowledge.
Yet, as one moves into the uncertain atmosphere of a pre-service teacher education

Harvard Educational Review Vol. 67 No. 1 Spring 1997, 105–125

class, considers the apprehension associated with practicum experiences, or examines the uncertainties announced by even the most seasoned of teachers, it is clear that there exists a stubborn dissatisfaction with our understandings of how one learns how to teach.

The purpose of this article is to take up this question. To this end, we begin by focusing on the first part of the question: how one *learns*. We develop our discussion around an exploration of popular and emerging conceptions of cognition, drawing our illustrations from an ongoing interrogation of our own experiences in teaching, learning, and research.

Our attention to learning is consistent with the theoretical work of Britzman (1991), as developed in her book *Practice Makes Practice*. She argues that, in learning to teach, practice does not make perfect. Rather, particular practices serve to perpetuate themselves. Consequently, much of the work in current teacher education — particularly in programs where the practicum is regarded as the principal location for learning about teaching — merely reproduces a set of teaching practices that are founded on somewhat limited conceptions of learning and cognition.[1] Hence, despite the widespread consensus that schooling must be reconceptualized, teacher education programs that emphasize *practice* are participating in the reproduction — rather than the transformation — of school settings in which both students and teachers find learning to be disconnected from their past, present, and projected worlds of experience. The issue of "learning" in "learning to teach" has thus been eclipsed by concerns about fitting into, coping with, and copying existing practices.

In this article we develop the theory of "enactivism," an interpretive framework that derives principally from Bateson's (1979, 1987) work in ecology, biology, and anthropology, and Varela, Thompson, and Rosch's (1991) work in phenomenology, neurology, and evolutionary theory.[2] This framework speaks to pressing issues in teacher education and to some of our own recent experiences of relearning how to teach. We interrogate some popular interpretations of cognition, then we draw upon current discussions in biology, ecology, and complexity theory that help frame current educational practices. Recent developments in these fields, we believe, have profound implications for those of us involved in the education of preservice teachers.

Popular Interpretations of Cognition and Learning

When one considers that educationists are confronted with such contrasting theories as behaviorism and radical constructivism, for example, it is perhaps not surprising that they have been unable to settle on curricula and models of instruction that have met with the approval of more than a small portion of the population. The implications and emphases of the many understandings of cognition are simply too varied. We often find ourselves with programs of study and teaching strategies that attempt to address the interests and the insights of as many theorists as possible, yet satisfy none. We thus find ourselves in a situation where, within virtually every speech or document intended to guide classroom practice, we can expect to hear calls for a renewed emphasis on the "basics" *and* for "student-centered instruction" *and* for the formal, standardized evaluation of individuals, *and* for collective learning activities — all with no apparent awareness of the contradictory nature of many of these notions. In our home province of British Columbia, for example, a recent curriculum initiative was undertaken by the Ministry of Education that explicitly insists on teaching approaches that can allow for group process, flexible programs, and varied assessment strategies, but which culminates in a battery of standardized, externally graded examinations at the end of the final year of schooling.

Small wonder, then, that new programs of study or "revolutions" in research have little impact on classroom practice. Confronted with a multitude of fragmented and incompatible recommendations for practice, some teachers continue to be informed by commonsense understandings of cognition and learning. What are some of these understandings, and what are the conditions that support their continued prominence in educational discourses and practices?

Within the conventional culture of schooling, learning tends to be seen as a matter of developing internal representations of a reality that is perceived to be external to and independent of the cognizing agent. Dubbed "representationism" by cognitive theorists (e.g., Varela et al., 1991; von Glasersfeld, 1990), this commonsense orientation to cognition defines understanding in terms of the level of correspondence between subjective (inner) representations and an objective (external) world.

Historically, representationist models of cognition have tended to draw on prevailing technologies for their defining imagery, with hydraulics, telegraphs, and telephone switchboards figuring prominently in more recent models of cognition. With the current prevalence of electronic technologies, a "mind as computer" metaphor has been taken up — and has, in fact, become so pervasive that it has become part of our common sense. We speak of "inputting" and "storing" information, of "processing" and "retrieving" data, of "compiling" and "structuring" knowledge. Further, it is not at all unusual to hear educators (among others) refer to the brain as if it were a computer — albeit a highly sophisticated one. As Lakoff and Johnson (1980) and Rorty (1989) have argued, the metaphors we use eventually become literalized and woven seamlessly into our everyday beliefs and practices — so completely that their figurative aspects dissolve into transparency. It is this process of becoming invisible, of "literalization," that helps to support the entrenchment of once-metaphorical imagery into routinized daily practices.

It is only when our experience deviates from our expectation that our literalized metaphors are once again presented for interrogation. In terms of the "mind as computer" notion, for example, such breeches are currently arising from a range of perspectives. Studies in psychology (Bruner, 1990; Merleau-Ponty, 1962) and neurology (Damasio, 1994; Sacks, 1995), for example, have alerted us to the limitations of a mechanically based model of a complex human mind.

This orientation to knowledge and to truth is the one that undergirds most of our actions within schools. Countless curriculum documents carefully delineate what is to be internalized. Shelves of textbooks lead students through an unambiguous journey of constructing appropriate subjective representations. A barrage of diagnostic and achievement tests promises objective assessments of the accuracy of the resulting inner conceptions. For teacher education programs, this emphasis has resulted in an effort to introduce prospective teachers to every aspect of the many-faceted role of the teacher — all in the absence of any deep understanding of the students who are expected to be taught and to learn, and of the as-yet unrealized world in which those students will be expected to function. In each case, the "real" world (of mathematics, of grammar, of teaching, etc.) is defined in opposition to — and given primacy over — the learner's world (which, inevitably, is regarded as incomplete and deficient).

This idea of knowledge consists of dichotomous constructions such as the "knowing-agent versus known-world." Self is made distinct from other, fact from fiction, right from wrong, and teacher from student — all with the same 1-0 binary logic upon which computers are constructed. Moreover, in making such tidy distinctions, and by equating the brain with a computer, knowledge is reduced to data or information that not only exists independently of knowing agents but, significantly, also comes to be regarded as personally and socially inert. Therefore, even though writers as diverse as Bakhtin (1981), Heidegger (1966), Merleau-Ponty (1962), Trinh (1992), and Vygotsky (1962, 1978) have insisted upon the inextricability of the cultural and the personal, the known and the knower, and the "experienced" and the "narrated," popular interpretations of cognition and learning continue to ignore such relations.

In many disciplines, however, a general resistance to framing phenomena in such cut-and-dry terms is emerging. Coupled with a growing awareness that we, quite simply, are *not* converging onto some coherent, universal theory of existence, this orientation has been widely rejected by educational and cultural theorists such as Grumet (1988), Kincheloe and Steinberg (1993), and Pinar (1994).

In the face of such critique, alternative models of cognition have risen to prominence over the last few decades. In particular, *constructivism* has become the focus of considerable discussion. While interpretations of this framework are varied, constructivist accounts tend to be framed in terms of nonlinear and dynamic evolutionary processes. Adequacy of function rather than optimality of representation becomes the criterion for appropriateness of understanding. Constructivist models thus reject the mechanistic metaphors of representationism and take up more organically based interpretations. This shift from the language of physics to the language of biology is an important one, as the images of forces, trajectories, and direct causes are replaced with thinking about thinking in terms of constant change and complex interdependencies. Cognition is thus understood as a process of organizing and reorganizing one's own subjective world of experience, involving the simultaneous revision, reorganization, and reinterpretation of past, present, and projected actions and conceptions.

However, while having served a critical role in interrupting commonsense assumptions about cognition and the modernist mindset, constructivist accounts tend to share a tenet with representationism. In both orientations, the cognizing agent is cast as fully autonomous. And so, like representationism, constructivism is a theory of knowledge and experience that seeks to bridge perceived gaps between knower and world and among knowers. The belief in the isolated subject further supports the notion that the "individual" is *contained* in a context rather than regarding the individual as an integral part of a relational fabric. This belief, we argue, is *monological;* that is, the idea of an isolated subject presumes a solitary truth-determining authority. The *relations* among knower and known are not considered the most important feature in the development of a theory of cognition.

Monologic thinking is divisive thinking, developed around the articulation of distinct and fixed boundaries. Cognizing agents are thus cast as separate — not only from the world, but from one another. While interaction among agents is deemed possible, it is reduced to coordinated mechanical action whereby subjects are unable to transcend their subjectivities. This, of course, has been the central target of those who have been critical of "modern" philosophies and the character of Western societies (for example, Borgmann, 1992; Lyotard, 1984; Taylor, 1991).

The difficulty here amounts to a deeply embedded cultural inability to rid ourselves of the notion that knowledge, in itself, has some sort of corporeal existence. Knowledge tends to be discussed as if it were an object — some *third thing* — to be grasped, held, stored, manipulated, and wielded, rather than being associated with our acting and existing in a biologically and phenomenologically constituted world. Depending on the theoretical stance, such *objective* knowledge is assigned a particular location.

What happens if we reject the pervasive knowledge-as-object (as "third thing") metaphor and adopt, instead, an understanding of knowledge-as-action — or, better yet, knowledge-as-(inter)action? Or, to frame it differently, what if we were to reject the *self*-evident axiom that cognition is located *within* cognitive agents who are cast as isolated from one another and distinct from the world, and insist instead that all cognition exists in the *interstices* of a complex ecology of organismic relationality?

An Enactivist Theory of Cognition

We might begin to answer these questions by comparing the notion of *monologue* to its complement, the *conversation*. In his exploration of the nature of communication, Gadamer (1990) suggests that conversations are distinct from other modes of interaction (such as debates, interviews, and discussions) because the topic of the conversation cannot be predetermined. Rather, it arises in the process of conversing.

We suggest that understanding emerges among people in a similar way. The conversation winds and wanders, arriving at places that, quite simply, could never have been anticipated. Given its unspecifiable path, Gadamer suggests that it is more appropriate to think of the participants as *being led* by the conversation than as leading it. The conversation is something more than the coordinated actions of autonomous agents — in a sense, it has us; we do not have it. Put differently, the conversation is not subject to predetermined goals, but unfolds within the reciprocal, codetermined actions of the persons involved. It is a collective activity that cannot be explained through either mechanistic models of human relationality or subjectivist accounts of cognition. The conversation might be thought of as a process of "opening" ourselves to others, at the same time opening the possibility of affecting our understandings of the world — and hence, our senses of our identities that are cast against the background of that world.

Merleau-Ponty (1962) has also studied such patterns of interacting, describing the relationships among persons engaged in conversation as "action-à-deux" or "coupling." Contrary to the privileged Western notion that selves are individual and autonomous, the idea of "coupling" suggests that a new transcendent unity arises when two or more persons come together in conversation or in any joint action. In the process, a possibility is opened for what Gadamer calls a "fusing of horizons," a movement toward consensus among persons whose thinking/acting can no longer be considered in strictly subjective terms. More recently this concept has been described by biologists Maturana and Varela (1987) as "structural coupling," and by Varela, Thompson, and Rosch (1991) as "co-emergence" or "mutual speci-fication." Although each of these phrases suggests a commingling of conscious-nesses, of cognitive abilities, and of lived actions, none suggests that personal integrities or subjectivities are abandoned. While there may be an experience of "self-forgetting" in the midst of shared action, it is in the fusing of consciousnesses, in the "coupling" of identities, in the "mutual specification" of forms and actions, that there arises a possibility for actions/understandings to emerge that likely could not have been achieved by either participant independently.

These ideas are not new. Some time ago, ecological theorists presented these concepts and extended them to the level of planetary dynamics (e.g., Bateson, 1979; Berry, 1977; Lovelock, 1979). Their assertions regarding the relationships of organisms with one another and with their environments have important implica-tions for studies of education because they render problematic the notion of learn-ers as situated *within* particular contexts. Rather, the cognizing agent is recast as *part of* the context. As the learner learns, the context changes, simply because one of its components changes. Conversely, as the context changes, so does the very identity of the learner. Cast against a different set of circumstances, caught up in different sets of relationships, how we define ourselves and how we act is inevita-bly affected. And so, learning (and, similarly, teaching) cannot be understood in monologic terms: there is no direct causal, linear, fixable relationship among the various components of any community of practice. Rather, all the contributing fac-tors in any teaching/learning situation are intricately, ecologically, and complexly related. Both the cognizing agent and everything with which it is associated are in constant flux, each adapting to the other in the same way that the environment evolves simultaneously with the species that inhabit it. In simplest terms, ecological thinking understands that the boundaries we perceive between different objects and different events are mere **heuristic**[a] conveniences. Everything is inextricably in-tertwined with everything else. This is not an understanding that Western societies have taken up readily, given our cultural emphases on personal freedoms and indi-vidual autonomy.

Sumara (1996) has described these ecological theories as the unity of the *us/not-us* relationship in an attempt to announce the inextricability of what we call "sub-ject" and what we call "context." The signifier, "us/not-us," acknowledges that we can *identify* individual cognizing agents while simultaneously announcing that we can only perceive and interpret their action by attending to the conditions of their existence. Figure and ground — *us* and *not-us* — are simultaneously defined. As such, us/not-us points to the significance of the contemporary project of **hermeneu-tic**[b] inquiry in understanding everyday lived experience, for as Gadamer (1990) has suggested, it is not so important that we come to understand who we are and what we do — what matters is that we come to interpret the *conditions* that circum-scribe identities and actions. This means, hermeneutically speaking, that the focus of inquiry is not so much on the components of experience (persons, objects, places), but, rather, on the relations that bind these elements together in action. Aligned with ecological thinking, the hermeneutics of us/not-us asks that interpre-tation occur in the interstices of things rather than within the things themselves.

[a] **Heuristic** refers to experiences, methods, or objects that aid in learning.
[b] **Hermeneutic** refers to the investigation of a text or phenomenon for the purpose of interpretation.

We have attempted to collect some of these ideas into what we, following Bateson (1987) and Varela, Thompson, and Rosch (1991), have called an *enactivist* theory of cognition (Davis, 1996; Davis, Sumara, & Kieren, 1996; Sumara, 1996). The starting point of such a theory is the assertion that each of us is, in the words of Merleau-Ponty (1962), a "complex fabric of relations," fundamentally and inextricably intertwined with all else — both physically/biologically and experientially/phenomenologically. This notion helps us to rethink what it means to teach — and to interpret the difficulties of enacting alternative conceptions of teaching. The oft-noted problems of taking on teaching actions that are known to be inappropriate and of coping with tacit pressures to behave in particular ways can, for us, be better understood through an ecological rather than a monological basis of action.

Enacting Different Teaching Practices

We recently conducted a year-long study that was informed by and that sought to explore the ramifications of enactivism. Our project began as a collaborative inquiry into the nature of learning that involved most of the teaching staff of a small, inner-city elementary school. We and these teachers began by gathering for semimonthly meetings, during which we inquired into our own learning processes. These "learning seminars" were developed around a range of reading, writing, and mathematical tasks intended to help uncover some of the usually hidden assumptions that frame classroom learning activities.

Through a series of unanticipated events — and true to the ecological sensibilities that informed the project — the research group soon expanded to include parents from the community. At their insistence, the research was extended to include teaching experiments in a few of the school's classrooms. Along with the regular classroom teachers, Davis cotaught an introduction to fractions unit in a grade-3/4 classroom, and Sumara cotaught a language arts unit developed around the reading of a popular novel in a grade-5/6 classroom. In this section, we recount the details of some of our learning and teaching experiences. In the process, we challenge some of the underlying assumptions of popular ideas of cognition and learning.

In particular, through this teaching example, we aim to present alternatives to the beliefs that learning can be predetermined and that it can be caused (in direct, linear terms) by teaching. Additionally, we hope to render problematic the belief that collective activity is a matter of the coordinated actions of autonomous agents, offering instead an interpretation of human activity as relational, codetermined, and existing in a complex web of events. Through this example, we also speak to the difficulties associated with efforts to affect long-held and uninterrogated practices. Overcoming the habits that are supported by taken-for-granted beliefs and that are woven into the collective character of a broader culture is a matter that enactivism, with its simultaneous attentiveness to the individual's activity and the group's dynamic, has helped us to address.

This issue was prominent for us during our recent teaching experiments. One of the most frustrating aspects of these experiences was the tendency each of us had to fall back on teaching behaviors that we felt were incompatible with (and even contradictory to) the enactivist theory of learning and understanding that had prompted us to undertake the project in the first place. In any given lesson, for example, we inevitably posed several questions to students for which we already had answers in mind. These are the sorts of questions that Gadamer (1990) has deprecatingly referred to as "pedagogic," a reference intended to underscore the fact that such questioning is rarely witnessed outside the modern classroom.

What is perhaps most interesting (and, for us, most disturbing) is that we were usually completely unaware that we had asked such irrelevant questions. Although we tended to notice this sort of behavior in each other and in the teachers with whom we were working, we seldom "caught ourselves in the act." The problem was not limited to just matters of questioning. Upon reflection, there were also elements of lesson structures, assignments, explanations, and assessments that were inconsistent with our espoused beliefs and announced intentions. In brief, not only did we tend to fall into conventional patterns of acting, we also were unable to notice and/or to attend to such patterns, let alone avoid them. Further, even when we were able to catch ourselves, the process of formulating and enacting alternatives proved to be quite challenging.

Teaching, like any other collectively situated experience, occurs in wholly embodied contexts that in some way must cohere. We began to notice that the teachers with whom we were working were "picking up" small, idiosyncratic qualities of our teaching, and we were doing the same of theirs. We found ourselves mimicking each others' particular ways of standing, moving around the room, reading, addressing students, and modulating voices. MacKinnon (1996) has suggested that it is the "teaching at the elbows" that fosters this sort of choreography of movement. It is perhaps not so surprising that we found ourselves uttering questions that were not really questions. As in most schools, such practices were common in the classrooms where we were teaching; we, as it were, were caught up in the existing current.

The commonsense response to concerns of this sort is to suggest that such behaviors are merely matters of unconscious action, supported by the momentum of habit. While we do not reject this explanation, we hardly regard it as an adequate account of our more general inability to be attentive to our unformulated actions — let alone to actively and continually interrogate the mindsets, prejudices, and tacit assumptions that underlie such actions. As we reviewed the video recordings and transcripts of these lessons, it became evident that our actions were not autonomously constituted. Rather, we were playing out parts in a larger whole, in many ways filling the roles we were expected to fill and behaving in the ways we were expected to behave. We were being conducted more than we were conducting. Thus, at the same time that we were striving to redefine appropriate action (for ourselves as teachers, for the teachers with whom we were working, and for the students we were teaching), we were drawn into *collective* patterns of expectation and behavior. In other words, contrary to the pervasive myth that the teacher is supposed to be in control of everything (Britzman, 1991), it is clear from the records of the research that our teaching was as much shaped and controlled by its context as by our own conscious intent. It was *not* primarily the individual teacher but the *collective* that set the standard for good teaching in the setting.

It is important to note that we are including not only our coteachers in this sense of "collective," but also the other teachers in the school and the students with whom we worked. In this "community of practice" (Lave & Wenger, 1991), there existed a general — and predominantly tacit — "understanding" of how things were done. As in many conventional school settings, these understandings were cast in a language of production, and they were evidenced in the pervasive concerns for efficient use of time, clear specification of objectives, and quality of outcomes, along with an overarching concern for accountability. Because we had spent considerable time in this community of practice (and in others that were strikingly similar) prior to beginning our teaching of these units, we had already been "caught up" in the prevailing conceptions of teaching and learning — even though our express purpose was to interrupt what was being taken for granted on these matters. At the same time, we were also having a shaping influence on this community, having participated with teachers in a number of activities that, as was later to become evident, were beginning to occasion[3] shifts in the communal fabric. Thus, although we were concerned that we were imitating and resurrecting teaching practices that we had hoped to counter, we were also noticing teachers making changes in their teaching. Our shared work in this community of practice, we believe, in part prompted these changes.

There is another dimension to this collective determination of appropriate action that is directly related both to the specific topics addressed in the classes taught and to the nature of the resulting understandings among the students and teachers in these classes. In each case, our actions were in part shaped by our belief that "learning" cannot be predicted or controlled. We thus approached our teaching with the assumption that, while we could present occasions that were rich with learning possibilities and in which we might participate with our students in the unfolding of understandings, we could not *prescribe* what would be learned. Learning, for us, is thus "occasioned" rather than "caused" — that is, we regard student learning as dependent on, but not determined by, the teaching (for a fuller explanation see Davis et al., 1996). As others have suggested (e.g., Lave & Wenger, 1991; Vygotsky, 1962, 1978), all of our "understandings" are situated in and co-emerge with complex webs of experience. As such, we can never discern the direct "causes" of any particular action. This is not to say, however, that our deliberate efforts to teach are all in vain. On the contrary, the teacher's activity continues to matter, as highlighted by the notion of occasioning. By occasioning action, the teacher participates in, but does not determine, student learning.

In the process of offering such occasions, it was not unusual for the activity in the classroom to take completely unanticipated but (in terms of the subject matter) appropriate turns. Insights would "spread" through the room. Conversations would begin with a few and grow to include most or all. Understandings would emerge that appeared to be shared and constructed by many. In the math class, for example, in response to the prompt, "What are some ways of making three fourths?" — a prompt that the teacher (Davis) expected to be answered in terms of the rather limited range of possibilities afforded by the "fraction kits" around which the unit was structured — students began to generate a potentially infinite list of combinations such as "one-and-a-half halves," "eleven-sixteenths and a fourth of a fourth." In the language arts class, in response to a prompt by Sumara to revisit their initial written responses to the novel in the midst of a second reading, students suggested that a baby who had been euthanized in the story had actually been only drugged and shipped to another community to be raised. This occasioned a large and continuing discussion about other possibilities that had not previously occurred to either the teachers or the other students. And even though these conjectures could not be supported through reference to the novel, they were soon a matter of common sense. Knowledge, then, was not some sort of object that was created *during* or *in* the interaction; rather, the ongoing, ever-evolving interaction was itself the form and substance of the collective knowledge.

Further, just as individual knowing could no longer be understood as being located within autonomous subjects, collective knowledge — or, as Rorty (1989) would call it, "patterns of acting" — could not be contained by the perceived boundaries of the classroom walls. It was not long before we became aware that the complex weave of classroom activity had spilled into other communities through what appeared to be a mix of deliberate communication, casual conversation, and unconscious imitation. Other teachers, for example, began to develop similar units of study for their own classrooms; students reported on their dinner table discussions of novels and fractions with parents and siblings; parents purchased copies of novels being used in school and discussed their interpretations in a range of community venues; reading groups and math clubs, not unlike the ones we helped to establish in the school, began to come together in nearby schools and communities.

The knowledge about fractions and the knowledge about the intersection of literature with other lived experiences that emerged during these learning events cannot be located within "individuals." Attempting to do so is futile, for it was not so much the opportunities for *individual* action that sponsored the unique paths of inquiry and understanding, but, rather, the opportunity for ongoing *interaction* that allowed such ideas to emerge and to continue to develop within these communities of practice. Conversely, attempting to locate the knowledge that arose in these school settings within the "real world" (i.e., in what is generally thought of as external to the school classroom) or to describe the students' actions as converging onto some objective understanding of a pre-given reality are inadequate, because in neither case were students converging onto some predetermined, preestablished "truths." Instead of trying to situate knowledge inside of or external to individuals, we contend that the mathematical and literary understandings that arose are better thought of as the products of *joint action*. The knowledge of fractions and the knowledge of the function of literary fictions was neither "outside of" nor "within" individual cognizing agents (i.e., students, teachers), but emerged with and existed in their ongoing interactions.

This interpretation prompts us to suggest that, in order to better understand cognition, the commonsense divisions that tend to be drawn among individuals and between "persons" and "contexts" must be abandoned. Just as the rejection of the parallel postulate by mathematicians gave rise to some powerful new geometries (see Boyer & Merzbach, 1991); just as poststructural reader-response theorists extinguished the boundaries between readers, texts, and contexts (Barthes, 1974; Derrida, 1992; Sumara, 1996); just as cultural critics have shown the overlapping and inextricable complexity of race, class, gender, ethnicity, and sexuality (Butler 1993; Haraway, 1991; Sedgwick, 1990); just as the recent rejection of the possibility of "crisp" distinctions among things has spawned the fruitful field of fuzzy logic (McNeill & Freiberger, 1994) and complexity theories (Casti, 1994; Waldrop, 1992); just as queer theory has further "queried" usually unquestioned cultural categories (Britzman, 1995; de Lauretis, 1991) — revisiting this axiom of cognitive theories, we suggest, opens the door to important new insights into thought and learning.

246

Enactivism also draws our attention to the knowledge that tends to remain unformulated — knowledge that we are constantly enacting as we move through the world, but which tends to be relegated to the backdrop, the ground of our conscious experience rather than the figure (Grumet, 1991). For the most part, we are unaware of the extent of such unformulated understandings. Engaging in a "thought experiment" of considering the difficulty of programming an android to behave "naturally" points to the expansive nature of what generally remains tacit. Such knowledge is embodied — that is, it arises from the fact that we have/are bodies that are parts of the organismic unity of an ongoing world. While our enacted or embodied knowledge is available to conscious formulation, it tends to go on unnoticed unless something occurs to draw our attention to it. Thus, according to enactivist theory, actions are not simply manifestations of (internal) understandings. They are themselves understandings.

The enactivist claim is that cognition does not occur in minds or brains, but in the possibility for shared action. Enactivism refuses to privilege the individual as the truth-determining authority. Truth and collective knowledge, for the enactivist, exist and consist in the possibility for joint action — and it is, necessarily, something larger than the solitary cognizing agent. That is, contrary to the Western tradition of consciousness, whereby the subject is seen as apart and distinct from the world (Smith, 1991), in enactivism the individual is understood to be part of — a subsystem to — a series of increasingly complex systems (such as a classroom, a school, a neighborhood, a culture, humanity, the biosphere). We might say that the notion of "embodied knowledge" extends to bodies that are much larger than our own.

Teaching and Learning: From "Complicated" to "Complex"

The word "complicated" is often used to describe what it means to fulfill the teacher's role. The various and overlapping tasks of responding individually and collectively to students, of "managing" material and human relationships, of organizing for instruction, and of assessing the merit of completed tasks, are all understood as activities that are enormously "complicated." However, informed by the field of "complexity theory" (Casti, 1994; Waldrop, 1992), we have come to understand that "complicated" does not offer an adequate description of the acts of teaching and learning. Rather, these are "complex" phenomena.

Complexity theorists draw a distinction between the descriptors *complicated* and *complex*. This new interdisciplinary field begins by rejecting the modernist tendency to use machine-based metaphors in characterizing and analyzing most phenomena. Machines, however complicated, are always reducible to the sum of their respective parts, whereas complex systems — such as human beings or human communities — in contrast, are more dynamic, more unpredictable, more alive. Spanning such areas of inquiry as physics, biology, neurology, economics, meteorology, and psychology, complexity theorists have begun to develop a rigorous alternative to the divisive, reductionist, and linear thinking that has dominated academic inquiry throughout the modern era. Like ecologists, these "complexivists" (Casti, 1994) focus on the interrelationships of things. More specifically, they study the manner in which subsystems come together to form larger, more complex systems. They contend that phenomena we normally think of as independent systems (our "selves," for example) are simultaneously comprised of subsystems that are intertwined and have their own integrities (e.g., organs and cells) while they are themselves subsystems of larger systems, with their own particular integrities (e.g., a family, a community, a society). Each of us is, all-at-once, a collective of wholes, a whole, and a part of a whole.

As Waldrop (1992) points out, complex systems have three distinguishing characteristics. First, they have the capacity to undergo spontaneous self-organization, in the process somehow managing to transcend themselves. Collective properties such as thought and purpose emerge, and these sorts of properties might never have been manifested by any of the subsystems. Simply put, the collective is much greater than the sum of its parts and much more "complex" than any of its components. Second, complex systems are adaptive. Species, marketplaces, and individual organisms evolve within changing environments. In fact, such entities and their environments can be seen as subsystems of larger complex systems. It is *not* the individual organism that shapes the environment, and it is *not* the environment that necessarily conditions the organism; rather, the two are engaged dialectically in a mutually specifying choreography where, all at once, each specifies the other. Third, complex systems are qualitatively different from systems such as clocks and computers, which are merely *complicated*. Complicated systems can be understood by analyzing their component parts and the ways they are assembled. An adequate understanding of their components, then, makes it possible to predict, with confidence, the manner in which the larger system will behave. In the case of complicated systems, the whole *is* the sum of the parts.

However, even the most profound knowledge of the subsystems that come together to form a complex system will not help us to predict or to control the behaviors of such systems. The most thorough understandings of hearts, livers, brain stems, and skin does not help us much in accounting for the emergence of such complex phenomena as consciousness and identity. Although these "components" all contribute to such phenomena, their interrelation is too complex to understand through a process of fragmented study. It is the *relations* among them, not the things themselves, that are productive and, as such, of interest.

An illustrative example of complex processes has been provided through recent studies of the human immune system. Occurring principally in conjunction with studies of HIV infection, these investigations have shown that, like any complex system, the immune system is continually "learning" — that is, evolving in response to and in conjunction with any "perturbation" or change in its environment (Varela & Coutinho, 1991). Consequently, attempts to "fix" an understanding of the functioning of the HIV virus have been in vain; like all phenomena it is always in a state of flux, always shifting, and always altering the boundaries of its identity. Studies of the human immune system's engagement with the HIV virus, along with other investigations of complex systems, have shown us that postmodern tropes (blurred edges, interweavings, unfixability) are more than mere metaphors. AIDS and the HIV virus cannot be understood without also considering their complex relations to a particular immune system: an immune system cannot be understood without also considering its complex and ever-shifting participation in the human physiological system. The parts and the whole must be understood in relation to one another. This notion calls to mind a tenet of both ecological and hermeneutic thought: the whole unfolds from and is enfolded in each of the parts.

Similarly, the most extensive knowledge of human psychology helps us little in forecasting the whims and movements of our society. While an understanding of the natures of and the relationships among the components of a complex system is helpful, it is simply inadequate. Conversely, a comprehensive knowledge of collective phenomena is inadequate for understanding the specificity of an individual's psyche. Such emergent phenomena must be studied *in all their complexity*, which implies an attentiveness not just to their subsystems, nor merely to the systems themselves, but to the larger systems in which the subjects of investigation are embedded. As examples, we point to the grade-3/4 students' unexpected ways of generating three-fourths and the grade-5/6 students' shared "rewriting" of a novel. These actions/understandings were not merely elements of individuals' knowledge structures. Rather, each student's conceptions were entwined with every other student's. Knowledge and understanding in this frame, then, cannot be thought of in strictly subjective terms; collective knowledge and individual understanding are dynamically co-emergent phenomena.

Enactivism takes these ideas one step further, focusing simultaneously on the *emergence* of the complex behaviors of a system (such as a student or a teacher) and on the *co-emergence* of such systems — that is, on the emergence of larger systems (such as the classroom, the community, the society). Using enactivism as an interpretive and analytic framework, it is possible to be attentive to how human subjects learn, how individual and collective identities emerge, and how participation in any shared action contributes to the very conditions that shape these identities. With reference to our classroom examples, for instance, rather than attempting to locate understanding and identity within individual agents, we might say that the knowledge is inactive and implicit in the activity — or, perhaps more descriptively, in the interactivity — of learners. As the events of the lesson are retraced, it becomes apparent that it was not so much the possibility for individual action as it was the opportunity for interaction that contributed to the character of the setting (and of the persons who were part of the setting). Teaching and learning are thus understood to occur in the relations between the individual and the collective, between accepted truth and emerging sense, and between actualities and possibilities. For the enactivist, therefore, what is imagined, what is fantasized, what is guessed at, what is intuited, are not marginalized to the fringes of valued thought and resulting actions, but are understood as vitally contributing to the conscious experience of everyday life. Further, enactivist thought is in many ways compatible with psychoanalytic theories that suggest that a usually unperceived *unconscious* participates in our psychosocial identities.[4] In so doing, enactivism is aligned with the radical hermeneutic (Caputo, 1987; Silverman, 1994) and the Eastern philosophic (Longxi, 1992; Suzuki, 1950; Trungpa, 1991; Varela et al., 1991) notion of the "presence of an absence"; that is, the belief that what is invisible and deferred is as influential as what is not.

The work of those who have adopted critical stances in educational theory have tended to emphasize the movement of the collective and the manner in which the individual is shaped by prevailing cultural conditions (Apple, 1993; Giroux, 1988; hooks, 1994). Unfortunately, such discourses, as valuable and powerful as they are, have been presented in opposition to educational perspectives that concentrate on individual learners. Thus, there exists a mutually critical relationship between studies of cognition and cultural commentaries — a debate rather than a dialogue. It is our contention that enactivism, which embraces the notion that there is a particular similarity (along with continuous mutual affect) between the cognitive processes of the individual and the evolutionary dynamic of the collective, helps us to bring such disparate discourses into conversation.

The cultural practice of "education" occurs within and among complex systems that span several phenomenal levels: there are individuals, there are collectives of individuals (including classrooms, schools, etc.), there are communities in which schools exist, and there are larger cultural contexts. These are but a handful of the complex systems that might be identified; such lists can be considerably extended in either direction. A complexified awareness of such levels, of how one exists simultaneously in and across these levels, and of how part and whole co-emerge and co-specify one another is needed by those who claim to be participating in the collectively and individually reproductive and transformative process known as formal education. Educational theories and practices that are inattentive to the particularities of context and, more specifically, that are inattentive to the evolving *relations* among such particularities, are no longer adequate. They might have been, at some point in the past when, for example, societies were more homogenous and less subject to rapid transformation. However, linear models of description and causality no longer help us much in our efforts to interpret our complex situations. Given the increased density of our populations, the more pronounced sociocultural diversity, the accelerated paces of change and movement, and the ability to more readily access and influence information through emerging technologies, those systems that we refer to as "community" and "culture" have become more complex. They are transforming themselves far more quickly than they once were. Correspondingly, "knowledge" and "teaching," as phenomena that are implicated in the communal, have themselves become more complex.

To state the point differently, like cognition, teaching has been cast as a *complicated* rather than as a *complex* phenomenon — one that can be understood by analyzing its component parts and one that, for all intents and purposes, does not vary across time, setting, and persons. Teaching tends not to be regarded in its original and irreducible complexity. It is our contention that until it is we will continue the ineffective and potentially damaging practice of regarding learners as isolated, detemporalized, and **decontextualized**[c] subjects. Knowledge will continue to remain separated from knowers, and educators will continue to be oblivious to their contributions to the formation and transformation of our culture. In a phrase, school will continue to be a place of mindless action, seeking to fit the inevitable complexity of existence into a framework of logical order.

This is not to suggest that all teacher education has been misdirected. That is certainly not the case. Our point, rather, is that the focus of educators has tended to be on only a small part of the picture — on coping in the classroom — hence, the preoccupations in control-oriented teacher education with *planning* for instruction and with the *management* of students. And, even with such a narrow scope, the issues tend to be fragmented and decontextualized. Such matters as the status of knowledge and the cultural context of education — two dynamic and fundamentally inextricable phenomena (which, we reemphasize, are matters of learning) — have tended to be treated as unproblematic givens within our schools. They arrive, completed, on

---

[c] **Decontextualizing** is the taking of incidents, statements, or actions out of the context in which they occurred, and in doing so altering the original intent of the incident, statement, or action.

the teacher's desk in the form of curriculum manuals and standardized textbooks, and their believed-to-be static natures are continuously announced in an unceasing barrage of examinations. "Covering the curriculum" can become all that is important. Everything else is eclipsed because there are few opportunities to move beyond the immediate concerns of the program manual, the impending practicum, and the perceived instrumental function of public schooling in our society.

An exclusive concern with the components of teaching, whether regarded in complicated or complex terms, has always been and continues to be inadequate for preparing teachers for the complex situations within which they will be working. We believe that we must strive to broaden our perceptions to include other levels of complex organization: to study teaching and learning within the contexts of which they are part. If we are to take seriously the enactivist notions of ecological situatedness, co-emergence, and varying degrees of complexity, it follows that we must be attentive to the ways in which teaching and learning are woven into, how they are shaped by, and how they contribute to their involvement in the unity of any us/not-us relation. We are thus suggesting that, consistent with our own attempts to change our pedagogical practices, teaching and learning must be understood as simultaneously shaping and being shaped by the circumstances in which they occur. Neither a simple process of enacting cultural standards nor a matter of subjective activity, teaching is a responsive choreography. Teaching is an active participant in the evolution of cultural forms and collective knowledge, just as it is a dynamic product and process of such forms. Teaching acquires its form within a complex relational web that seeks to affect the understandings and abilities of the individual members of that community. Of all these facets, we have tended to focus only on the last, and have thus failed to acknowledge that just as the cognizing agent cannot be understood as a solitary component (but must be regarded as a subsystem of a larger system), teaching and learning cannot be studied as though they occur in isolated and closed systems.

At first reading, such statements as these would seem to render teacher education an unmanageable task and, in a sense, that is true. Perhaps Freud (1930/1961) was correct when he suggested that teaching was one of the "impossible" professions. We cannot teach everything that must be known, for what is known and the circumstances of such knowledge are always shifting, evolving, unfolding. Teaching is not something that can be managed — especially when one considers, for example, that the nature of teaching changes simply by teaching. Thus, we argue that such notions as controlling learners and achieving pre-set outcomes must be set aside in favor of more holistic, all-at-once co-emergent curricula that are as much defined by circumstance, serendipity, and happenstance as they are by predetermined learning objectives.

With regard to the project of teaching teachers, an enactivist theory of cognition prompts us to assume a hermeneutic attitude, replacing mechanical and business metaphors with an interpretive mindset. In some ways, we are supporting the shared concern of cognitive theorist and cultural critic that teachers, in general, need to know more about the circumstances of schooling. But what we are adding is that these commentaries should not be cast as separate discourses — that is, the respective concerns of the educational psychology experts and the foundation experts. Such divisions locate pre-service teachers in the troublesome situation of being expected to learn about the varied discourses within a setting that is little different from the conventional high school classroom. Caught up in the same sorts of structures and practices, there are often few opportunities to interrogate popular conceptions of learning on other than a rhetorical level.

Rather than locating "learning to teach" activity in either the university lecture hall or in the public school classroom, enactivist theory prompts the suggestion that such learning must occur at points between these — in the various layers of community that include university and school. Rejecting the cultural arrogance underlying the belief that the formal educational setting is the principal location for the study of cultural knowledge, we are suggesting that other sites be seen as places of teaching and learning: shopping malls, restaurants, food banks, retirement homes, churches, festivals, hockey games, etc. In our desire to separate the schooled experience from life outside the classroom, such locations have not been regarded as an integral part of who we are. Instead, inside the classroom they are named "the real world," and nodding reference is made to this distanced realm through contrived word problems and fragmented discussions of social issues. Thus, at the same time that school and not-school are dichotomized, educators often delegitimize their own project by naming it as not part of the "real world."

In short, we are suggesting that the boundaries that currently define schools and universities be blurred so that the relations between that which we call "teaching" and that which we call "learning" might be better understood as mutually specifying, co-emergent, pervasive, and evolving practices that are at the core of our culture's efforts at self-organization and self-renewal. The task of the school is not to point to the "real world" as though these entities were somehow separable — and so teacher education needs to move away from a model that focuses on the mastery of classroom procedures and toward a more deliberate study of "culture making" (Bruner, 1986). This becomes possible, we believe, by focusing on the question of how one learns, as that emphasis inevitably pulls one away from the classroom desk, from solitary activity, and from the confines of the school. These and other categories dissolve within the inclusive and active space of learning.

Notes

1. The terms "cognition" and "learning" are used synonymously in this article — a linguistic move that is intended to trouble the notion that personal knowledge can be static. Thought is dynamic and always in flux — that is, it is always caught up in new learning. (Indeed, the word "cognition" derives from a Latin root that means "to learn.")

2. A more complete genealogy of enactivism, which includes its relationships to a diversity of academic disciplines (including physics, mathematics, cybernetics, and philosophy), is provided by Capra (1996).

3. According to the *Oxford English Dictionary,* the original Latin meaning of occasion (*occasion-em*) has to do with an opportunity arising from a "falling of things toward each other." To occasion is thus to open oneself to the possibility of the unpredictable, to lay down a new path of understanding — in brief, to forego the desires to predetermine teaching behaviors and learning outcomes. The use of the verb form of "occasion" was first brought to our attention by mathematics educator Thomas E. Kieren.

4. It is important to note that, consistent with our reading of psychoanalytic thought, the "unconscious" is not afforded an objective status here. We use it in reference to that category of (inter)action that generally escapes notice: the embodied, the enacted, the unformulated.

References

Apple, M. (1993). *Official knowledge: Democratic education in a conservative age.* New York: Routledge.

Bakhtin, M. M. (1981). *The dialogic imagination.* Austin: University of Texas Press.

Barthes, R. (1974). *S/Z.* New York: Hill and Wang.

Bateson, G. (1979). *Mind and nature: A necessary unity.* New York: E. P. Dutton.

Bateson, G. (1987). Men are grass. In W. I. Thompson (Ed.), *Gaia, a way of knowing* (pp. 37–47). Hudson, NY: Lindisfarne.

Berry, W. (1977). *The unsettling of America: Culture and agriculture.* San Francisco: Sierra Club Books.

Borgmann, A. (1992). *Crossing the postmodern divide.* Chicago: University of Chicago Press.

Boyer, C. B., & Merzbach, U. C. (1991). *A history of mathematics* (2nd ed.). New York: John Wiley.

Britzman, D. (1991). *Practice makes practice: A critical study of learning to teach.* Albany: State University of New York Press.

Britzman, D. (1995). "The question of belief": Writing poststructural ethnography. *Qualitative Studies in Education, 8,* 229–238.

Bruner, J. (1986). *Actual minds, possible worlds.* Cambridge, MA: Harvard University Press.

Bruner, J. (1990). *Acts of meaning.* Cambridge, MA: Harvard University Press.

Butler, J. (1993). *Bodies that matter: On the discursive limits of "sex."* New York: Routledge.

Capra, F. (1996). *The web of life: A new scientific understanding of living systems.* New York: Doubleday.

Caputo, J. (1987). *Radical hermeneutics.* Bloomington: Indiana University Press.

Casti, J. L. (1994). *Complexification: Explaining a paradoxical world through the science of surprise.* New York: HarperCollins.

Damasio, A. R. (1994). *Descartes' error: Emotion, reason, and the human brain.* New York: G. P. Putnam's Sons.

Davis, B. (1996). *Teaching mathematics: Toward a sound alternative.* New York: Garland.

Davis, B., Sumara, D. J., & Kieren, T. E. (1996). Cognition, co-emergence, curriculum. *Journal of Curriculum Studies, 28,* 151–169.

Derrida, J. (1992). *Acts of literature.* New York: Routledge.

de Lauretis, T. (1991). Queer theory: Lesbian and gay sexualities. *Differences: A Journal of Feminist Cultural Studies, 3,* iii–xviii.

Freud, S. (1961). *Civilization and its discontents.* New York: W. W. Norton. (Original work published 1930)

Gadamer, H.-G. (1990). *Truth and method.* New York: Continuum.

Giroux, H. (1988). *Schooling and the struggle for public life.* Minneapolis: University of Minnesota Press.

Grumet, M. (1988). *Bitter milk: Women and teaching.* Amherst: University of Massachusetts Press.

Grumet, M. (1991). Curriculum and the art of everyday life. In G. Willis & W. Schubert (Eds.), *Reflections from the heart of educational inquiry: Understanding curriculum and teaching through the arts* (pp. 74–89). Albany: State University of New York Press.

Haraway, D. J. (1991). *Simians, cyborgs, and women: The reinvention of nature.* New York: Routledge.

Heidegger, M. (1966). *Being and time.* New York: Harper & Row.

hooks, b. (1994). *Teaching to transgress.* New York: Routledge.

Kincheloe, J., & Steinberg, S. (1993). A tentative description of post-formal thinking: The critical confrontation with cognitive theory. *Harvard Educational Review, 63,* 296–320.

Lakoff, G., & Johnson, M. (1980). *Metaphors we live by.* Chicago: University of Chicago Press.

Lave, J., & Wenger, E. (1991). *Situated learning: Legitimate peripheral participation.* New York: Cambridge University Press.

Longxi, Z. (1992). *The Tao and the logos: Literary hermeneutics, East and West.* Durham, NC: Duke University Press.

Lovelock, J. (1979). *Gaia, a new look at life on earth.* New York: Oxford University Press.

Lyotard, J.-F. (1984). *The postmodern condition: A report on knowledge.* Minneapolis: University of Minnesota Press.

MacKinnon, A. (1996). Learning to teach at the elbows: The Tao of teaching. *Teaching and Teacher Education, 12,* 653–664.

Maturana, H., & Varela, F. (1987). *The tree of knowledge: The biological roots of human understanding.* Boston: Shambhala.

McNeill, D., & Freiberger, P. (1994). *Fuzzy logic: The revolutionary computer technology that is changing our world.* New York: Simon & Schuster.

Merleau-Ponty, M. (1962). *Phenomenology of perception.* London: Routledge.

Pinar, W. F. (1994). *Autobiography, politics, and sexuality: Essays in curriculum theory, 1972–1992.* New York: Peter Lang.

Rorty, R. (1989). *Contingency, irony, and solidarity.* New York: Cambridge University Press.

Sacks, O. (1995). *An anthropologist from Mars.* New York: Alfred A. Knopf.

Sedgwick, E. K. (1990). *Epistemology of the closet.* Berkeley: University of California Press.

Silverman, H. (1994). *Textualities: Between hermeneutics and deconstruction.* New York: Routledge.

Smith, D. (1991). Hermeneutic inquiry: The hermeneutic imagination and the pedagogic text. In E. Short (Ed.), *Forms of curriculum inquiry* (pp. 187–209). Albany: State University of New York Press.

Sumara, D. J. (1996). *Private readings in public: Schooling the literary imagination.* New York: Peter Lang.

Suzuki, D. (1950). *Living by Zen.* London: Rider Books.

Taylor, C. (1991). *The malaise of modernity.* Concord, ON: Anansi.

Trinh, T. M. (1992). *Framer framed.* New York: Routledge.

Trungpa, C. (1991). *Crazy wisdom.* Boston: Shambhala.

Varela, F., & Coutinho, A. (1991). Second generation immune networks. *Immunology Today, 12,* 159–166.

Varela, F., Thompson, E., & Rosch, E. (1991). *The embodied mind: Cognitive science and human experience.* Cambridge, MA: MIT Press.

von Glasersfeld, E. (1990). An exposition of constructivism: Why some like it radical. In R. B. Davis, C. A. Maher, & N. Noddings (Eds.), *Constructivist views on the teaching and learning of mathematics* (pp. 19–30). Reston, VA: National Council of Teachers of Mathematics.

Vygotsky, L. S. (1962). *Thought and language.* Cambridge, MA: MIT Press.

Vygotsky, L. S. (1978). *Mind in society: The development of higher psychological processes.* Cambridge, MA: Harvard University Press.

Waldrop, M. M. (1992). *Complexity: The emerging science at the edge of order and chaos.* New York: Simon & Schuster.

How Do Teachers Manage to Teach? Perspectives on Problems in Practice

MAGDALENE LAMPERT

Classroom conflicts create complex moments for teachers. In these situations, teachers, according to Magdalene Lampert, are often simply expected to choose among a number of contradictory alternatives, none of which is completely satisfactory. Lampert, however, when faced with a dilemma related to the social organization of her own classroom, shuns the traditional problem-solving role of the teacher and takes on the more complex work of managing the dilemma. In her desire to avoid making a choice that only partially addresses the problem at hand and simultaneously creates other problems, Lampert engages in an argument with herself, searching for the ways to "act with integrity while maintaining contradictory concerns." Looking at both the dilemma in her classroom and a dilemma involving the nature of knowledge in a colleague's classroom, Lampert argues against the beliefs that all problems in the classroom are solvable and that solutions to problems come from outside the classroom. Lampert asserts that the teacher, acting as dilemma manager, is the most important resource for dealing with conflict in the classroom, and that we can learn a great deal about teaching from teachers who engage and utilize conflict rather than trying to solve it.

In the classroom where I teach fourth-, fifth-, and sixth-grade mathematics, there are two chalkboards on opposite walls. The students sit at two tables and a few desks, facing in all directions. I rarely sit down while I am teaching, except momentarily to offer individual help. Thus the room does not have a stationary "front" toward which the students can reliably look for directions or lessons from their teacher. Nevertheless, an orientation toward one side of the room did develop recently in the fifth-grade class and became the source of some pedagogical problems.

The children in my classroom seem to be allergic to their peers of the opposite sex. Girls rarely choose to be anywhere near a boy, and the boys actively reject the girls whenever possible. This has meant that the boys sit together at the table near one of the blackboards and the girls at the table near the other.

Harvard Educational Review Vol. 55 No. 2 May 1985, 178–194

The fifth-grade boys are particularly enthusiastic and boisterous. They engage in discussions of math problems with the same intensity they bring to football. They are talented and work productively under close supervision, but if left to their own devices, their behavior deteriorates and they bully one another, tell loud and silly jokes, and fool around with the math materials. Without making an obvious response to their misbehavior, I developed a habit of routinely curtailing these distractions from the lesson by teaching at the blackboard on the boys' end of the classroom. This enabled me to address the problem of maintaining classroom order by my physical presence; a cool stare or a touch on the shoulder reminded the boys to give their attention to directions for an activity or to the content of a lesson, and there was no need to interrupt my teaching.

But my presence near the boys had inadvertently put the girls in "the back of the room." One of the more outspoken girls impatiently pointed out that she had been trying to get my attention and thought I was ignoring her. She made me aware that my problem-solving strategy, devised to keep the boys' attention, had caused another, quite different problem. The boys could see and hear more easily than the girls, and I noticed their questions more readily. Now what was to be done?

I felt that I faced a forced choice between equally undesirable alternatives. If I continued to use the blackboard near the boys, I might be less aware of and less encouraging toward the more well-behaved girls. Yet, if I switched my position to the blackboard on the girls' side of the room, I would be less able to help the boys focus on their work. Whether I chose to promote classroom order or equal opportunity, it seemed that either the boys or the girls would miss something I wanted them to learn.

This first-person account of a particular pedagogical problem is an unusual way to begin an analysis of the work of teaching. Commonly, such inquiries begin with general observations based on a consideration of several instances of teaching practice or with assertions about what teaching can or should be. I have taken a different tack, however, not because I believe these approaches cannot offer useful insights into what it is that teachers do, but because I believe they are incomplete. Efforts to build generalized theories of instruction, curriculum, or classroom management based on careful empirical research have much to contribute to the improvement of teaching, but they do not sufficiently describe the work of teaching.[1] Such theories and research are limited in their capacity to help teachers know what to do about particular problems such as the one I have just described. My intention, however, is not to build another kind of theory that can more adequately guide practice but to describe those elements of practice that are inconsonant with theoretical principles. To do this, I shall use both my experience as a classroom practitioner and the tools of scholarly inquiry.

The special and salient value of descriptions of teaching from the practitioner's perspective has been recognized by scholars and supported by researchers.[2] Moving back and forth between the work of practice and the work of scholarship in order to inquire into the nature of practice fosters in the inquirer a useful sort of deliberation; it enriches and refines both the questions one can ask about teachers' work and the attempts one can make to answer them.[3] In this essay, I shall present two cases, which first describe teaching problems from the teacher's point of view and then examine, from the scholar's point of view, the work involved in facing them.

The teacher's emphasis on concrete particulars in the description of a classroom problem distinguishes the perspective of practice from the perspective of the theory-builder. This distinction has received considerable attention in the literature on teaching.[4] Another fundamental though less familiar difference involves the personal quality of teaching problems as seen through the eyes of a practitioner.[5] Who the teacher is has a great deal to do with both the way she defines problems and what can and will be done about them.[6] The academician solves problems that are recognized in some universal way as being important, whereas a teacher's problems arise because the state of affairs in the classroom is not what she wants it to be. Thus, practical problems, in contrast to theoretical ones, involve someone's wish for a change and the will to make it.[7] Even though the teacher may be influenced by many powerful sources outside herself, the responsibility to act lies within. Like the researcher and the theoretician, she identifies problems and imagines solutions to them, but her job involves the additional personal burden of doing something about these problems in the classroom and living with the consequences of her actions over time. Thus, by way of acknowledging this deeply personal dimension of teaching practice, I have chosen not only to present the particular details of two teachers' problems but to draw one of these problems from my own experience.

In addition to recognizing the particular and personal qualities of the way teachers understand problems in their work, I would like to consider another distinction between practice and theory building in education. Some of the problems the practitioner is required to do something about might be defined as unsolvable. The work required to manage such problems will be the particular focus of my inquiry. It is widely recognized that the juxtaposition of responsibilities that make up the teacher's job leads to conceptual paradoxes.[8] I will argue further that, from the teacher's point of view, trying to solve many common pedagogical problems leads to practical dilemmas.[9] As the teacher considers alternative solutions to any particular problem, she cannot hope to arrive at the "right" alternative in the sense that a theory built on valid and reliable empirical data can be said to be right.[10] This is because she brings many contradictory aims to each instance of her work, and the resolution of their dissonance cannot be neat or simple. Even though she cannot find their right solutions, however, the teacher must do something about the problems she faces.

Returning to my own classroom at this point will serve to explicate more clearly these qualities of a teacher's work. One might think it possible to monitor the boys' behavior in my fifth-grade math class in a way that does not reduce my attention to the girls, or to involve the girls more in the math lesson without reducing my capacity to monitor the boys' behavior. But teaching dilemmas like this are often not so easily resolved in practice. For example, if I were to assign seats mixing the boys and the girls, it might be possible to give equal attention to everyone no matter which blackboard I use, but the silliness that results from proximity to the opposite sex in the fifth grade might then take so much away from the lesson that there would be less of my attention to go around. If I were to leave the boys and the girls where they choose to sit, and walk around the room to spread my attention, then the walking around might cause even greater disruption, because it would take me away from the boys who need my presence. It might be possible to use desks instead of tables and seat everyone facing in the same direction as a way of monitoring behavior, but that might make the students' valuable problem-solving discussions with one another impossible. All these possible "solutions" lead to problems. I felt I could not choose a solution without compromising other goals I wanted to accomplish. Yet, I knew that not implementing a solution would have negative consequences too. I was convinced that some action had to be taken.

When I consider the conflicts that arise in the classroom from my perspective as a teacher, I do not see a choice between abstract social goals, such as Excellence versus Equality or Freedom versus Standardization. What I see are tensions between individual students, or personal confrontations between myself and a particular group of boys or girls. When I think about rewarding Dennis's excellent, though boisterous, contributions to problem-solving discussions, while at the same time encouraging reticent Sandra to take an equal part in class activities, I cannot see my goals as a neat dichotomy and my job as making clear choices. My aims for any one particular student are tangled with my aims for each of the others in the class, and, more importantly, I am responsible for choosing a course of action in circumstances where choice leads to further conflict. The contradictions between the goals I am expected to accomplish thus become continuing inner struggles about how to do my job.

A Pedagogical Dilemma as an Argument with Oneself

The solutions I imagined to restrain the boys' boisterous behavior and to encourage the girls' involvement in class activities were contradictory. I could do neither without causing undesirable consequences, yet both were important to me. One way to think about the dilemma that I faced is to see it as a problem forcing a choice between equally undesirable alternatives. In this view, my job would be to grit my teeth and choose, even though choosing would bring problematic consequences.[11] Another way to think of a dilemma, however, is as an argument between opposing tendencies within oneself in which neither side can come out the winner. From this perspective, my job would involve maintaining the tension between my own equally important but conflicting aims without choosing between them. It may be true that some teachers do resolve their dilemmas by choosing — between excellence and equality, between pushing students to achieve and providing a comfortable learning environment, between covering the curriculum and attending to individual understanding; but I wish to argue that choosing is not the only way to manage in the face of self-contradictory alternatives. Facing a dilemma need not result in a forced choice. A more technical definition of a dilemma is "an argument that presents an antagonist with two (or more) alternatives, but is equally conclusive against him whichever alternative he chooses."[12] This definition focuses on the deliberation about one's alternatives rather than on a choice between them. The conflicted teacher is her own antagonist; she cannot win by choosing.

As I presented my case for leaving the boys' area of the room to be nearer to the girls, my argument for taking such an action was conclusive against me, because my students and I would be distracted from our lessons by my need to control overtly the boys' behavior. If I argued, on the other hand, for continuing to teach from the boys' side of the room, I would also lose the argument, because I would not be giving the girls at least equal amounts of my attention. Instead of engaging in a decision-making process that would eliminate conflicting alternatives and lead to a choice of which problem to solve, I pursued a series of such losing arguments with myself as I considered the consequences of various alternatives. One element of the teachers' work is having an argument with oneself — a speculative argument that cannot be won. The thinking involved in this sort of work is quite different from the kind of thinking that might go into concluding that one can make the correct choice between dichotomous alternatives. My arguments with myself served to articulate the undesirable consequences of each of my alternatives in terms of potential classroom confrontations. In order to hold the conflicting parts of my job and myself together, I needed to find a way to manage my dilemma without exacerbating the conflicts that underlay it.

Pedagogical Dilemmas and Personal Coping Strategies

My argument with myself resulted from a desire to do contradictory things in the classroom. My ambivalence about what to do was not only a conflict of will, however; it was a conflict of identity as well. I did not want to be a person who ignored the girls in my class because the boys were more aggressive in seeking my attention. I think of myself as someone who encourages girls to become more interested and involved in mathematical thinking. At the same time, I did not want to have a chaotic classroom as a result of turning away from the boys' behavior. But neither did I want to appear to have such a preoccupation with order that I discouraged enthusiasm; standing near the boys enabled me to keep them focused without attending to their misbehavior directly. Working out an identity for this situation was more than a personal concern — it was an essential tool for getting my work done. The kind of person that I am with my students plays an important part in what I am able to accomplish with them. Figuring out who to be in the classroom is part of my job; by holding conflicting parts of myself together, I find a way to manage the conflicts in my work.

The self that I brought to the task of managing this classroom dilemma is a complicated one. My personal history and concerns contributed to the judgment that it would not be wise simply to make a choice in this case. I felt sympathy for the girls who were seated in what had inadvertently become the "back of the room" because of the many pained moments I had spent with my raised hand unrecognized at the back of my own predominantly male trigonometry class in high school. But I was not of one mind about that experience. Competing for attention with the more aggressive boys in my math class had not been wholly negative; a significant amount of the satisfaction I derive from my work in mathematics is based on the knowledge that there are few women who are successful in this area. Although I believe girls are entitled to special encouragement in learning mathematics, this belief is entangled with my feeling of accomplishment from having developed an interest in the subject myself despite discouragement. Now, as part of my job, I had to accomplish a balance between these conflicting influences in what I chose to do about this classroom dilemma. There were similarly divergent personal concerns behind how I understood the actions I might take in relation to the boys in the class. In my teaching relationship with them I had to balance my own conflicting yet simultaneous desire for freedom and order.

My capacity to bring disparate aspects of myself together in the person that I am in the classroom is one of the tools I used to construct an approach to managing my dilemma. Because a teacher is present to students as a whole person, the conflicting parts of herself are not separable, one from another, the way they might be if we think of them as names for categories of persons or cultural ideals, like child oriented versus subject oriented, or democratic versus authoritarian.[13] A teacher has the potential to act with integrity while maintaining contradictory concerns. I did not want to be a person who treated girls unequally, as my high school trigonometry teacher had done. Nor did I want to be someone who gave special attention to girls just because they were girls. I did not want to be a person who had such a preoccupation with order that I discouraged enthusiasm. Nor did I want to try to do my work in a disorderly classroom. The person that I wanted to be — this ambiguous self-definition — became a tool to enable me to accomplish my pedagogical goals.

Constructing Solutions in the Face of Unsolvable Problems

When I met my class the morning after recognizing my dilemma, I had not resolved any of the arguments with myself about what to do, but I did have some sense of who I wanted to be. And that made a difference.

It happened that two of the more offending boys were absent that day, so I was able to leave everyone seated where they were, walk to the other side of the room, and do most of my teaching standing at the blackboard near the girls' table without any major disruptions occurring. I used this hiatus to construct a strategy for managing the conflict that did not involve stark choices.

While I taught the class, my thinking about the boys and the girls merged with my thinking about some other currently pressing matters in the classroom. I was about to begin a new instructional unit that involved using manipulative materials and had been wondering about how to organize the students' activities with those materials. I had also been talking with my student teacher, Sandy, about ways in which she might take on responsibility in the class. We had planned the next unit together, and she was prepared to do some of the teaching. So I divided the class into four small groups (two of girls and two of boys) and put Sandy in charge of instructing and managing one group of boys and one group of girls, while I took responsibility for the other two groups. This strategy depended heavily on specific elements in the context of my classroom. It enabled me to cope with the surface of my problem while keeping its more general conflicts submerged. It was not a general solution or a permanent one; it was an act of improvisation, a product of adjusting my ambivalent desires to the particular circumstances in which I was working.

I moved one group of boys to the area near the girls' blackboard and one group of girls to the other side of the room. This helped to avoid the distractions that would result from grouping the boys and girls together, but without geographically dividing the class along gender lines. Furthermore, because there were now two groups of boys and two of girls, both the class and I could identify other criteria for group membership besides gender. Instructing in small groups also means [meant] that neither the teachers nor the students would be performing in front of both boys and girls at the same time, so my attention would be less likely to be judged as preferential toward either the boys or the girls. Paradoxically, because I would be teaching boys only in the company of other boys, and girls only in the company of other girls, I would be able to respond to the children more as individuals than as members of one sex or the other, as I had done when I taught them all together while they were seated at opposite ends of the room.

What can we learn from this case about how a teacher works? I did not choose this strategy because it would solve problems. I managed my dilemma by putting the problems that led to it further into the background and by bringing other parts of my job further to the foreground. Although this meant that the problems remained, my strategy gave me a way to live with them, a temporary respite that would prevent the underlying conflicts from erupting into more serious, distracting discord.

A Second Case: Conflicts over the Nature of Knowledge as Another Source of Classroom Dilemmas

The adversity in my situation arose because of contradictory social goals in my teaching. One might imagine that if I had been able to put problems of social organization aside and had defined my job only in terms of whether my students learned the subject matter, then the dilemmas I described would have disappeared. In fact, some scholars have argued that by using an impersonal "technology of instruction" (more often called a curriculum) teachers can produce subject-matter knowledge in students without concern for social problems in or out of the classroom.[14] Others, who understand knowledge as a construction of the individual learner, leave social problems aside and focus on the teacher's work in fostering an individual child's understanding.[15] It may be true that if teaching and learning occur in a one-to-one encounter outside the classroom, the sort of dilemma I have described may not arise, but it is not possible in schools to separate social problems from subject-matter knowledge. In the teacher's job, at least as it is now understood, a clear distinction between tasks related to social organization and tasks related to instruction is unachievable. The following case study is intended to illustrate this point. Neither it nor the preceding case, however, is intended in any way to illustrate good or bad, skillful or skill-less teaching. Both cases presume a value in studying common teaching practice, however it may be evaluated, whatever its effects.

Rita Cerone is a fourth-grade teacher in a small, urban public school.[16] In the situation I am about to describe, she was faced with a set of problems that arose out of her use of a workbook to instruct students in science. Her concern for solving these problems led her into a pedagogical dilemma, and what she did to manage her dilemma raises issues about teachers' work that are similar to those already described.

Science lessons in Rita's classroom often consisted of students reading their workbooks, looking at the drawings and diagrams in them, and then answering questions and checking their answers with the teacher. The topic of one such exercise was "The Cycle of Water." The workbook presented the students with a picture of a cloud, and next to it a question: "Where does the water come from?" Rita said it seemed obvious to her from the illustration that the answer was "clouds," and so she had "marked it right" when students gave that answer. (She checked other answers which were not so obvious to her in the teacher's guide before she judged them right or wrong.) Rita was, therefore, a bit perplexed when one of the girls in her class, Linda, came up to have her work corrected and declared with unusual confidence that "the answer to where water comes from is *the ocean*." Rita indicated on the girl's paper that this answer was incorrect, but Linda was surprised by this judgment and insisted that she was right.

Rita was hesitant to contradict Linda because the girl was so confident about her answer. Although Rita disagreed with her, she sensed a conflict brewing and wanted to avoid it. So she tried to understand more about what Linda was thinking. "I said to her: 'Well, I don't understand. Explain it to me.' I was fumbling around and I was trying to figure out what she meant. It finally turned out that she knew, but she couldn't verbalize it for quite a while. After asking her questions and having her look at the workbook page, [Linda] said, 'The clouds pick the water up. I don't know how, but it puts the water from the ocean back in the clouds.'" Rita decided in this exchange that Linda "knew" what she was supposed to learn from the lesson even though her answer did not match the answer in the teacher's guide.

The potential conflict between perspectives on what it means to "know" something was momentarily resolved when Rita agreed with Linda that her answer was indeed correct. The equilibrium between Linda's understanding and the textbook's standards of knowledge was short-lived, however, when the other students in the class took an interest in Rita's judgment. As Rita recalled, "Linda went running back to the rest of the group and told them she wasn't wrong. The other kids started arguing with Linda because they saw it the way I saw it *and* the way the answer book saw it. But Linda could prove she was right." Rita had exacerbated an underlying contradiction in her classroom when she told Linda that her answer was correct. The conflict came to the surface because Linda was a member of a group of students studying the same material. Moreover, they had all been using the teacher's guide as the standard by which to judge the correctness of their answers. Their complaint was that Rita had applied a familiar standard to judging their answers but had used another standard to evaluate Linda's. Unless Rita did something to manage this conflict, it threatened to become a more difficult classroom problem.

One student, Kevin, confident that *his* answer was right because it matched the answer in the teacher's guide and because Rita had told him it was right, led the class in an argument with Linda and, by implication, with their teacher. In Rita's words: "One of the kids, Kevin, said Linda was really dumb because the ocean was where the water started out, and it ended up in clouds just before it rained. It wasn't that he didn't get her explanation, but he just dismissed it because I had told him earlier that his answer was right and he also knew that was the answer the book wanted. That's why she came up to me in the first place: to get confirmation that she was right because Kevin had said she was wrong." Like Rita, Kevin "got" Linda's explanation. Yet her individual understanding of the matter was not his concern. He "dismissed" Linda's explanation (as Rita herself had done at first) because it did not match what the book and his teacher said was "right," and he began an argument in order to settle the matter. If the teacher and the textbook were to be taken seriously, he argued, Linda could not also be right.

Rita's job here, as in my situation, might be viewed as requiring a choice between dichotomous alternatives. If she were to practice "child-centered" teaching, she would favor defending Linda's way of thinking while rejecting the textbook's authority. If she were to practice "curriculum-centered" teaching, she would judge Linda's knowledge using the written curriculum in the teacher's guide as the standard. Those students whose answers agreed with the book's answer were pushing her toward the latter, while Linda was pushing her toward the former.

Rita's Argument with Herself

Rita did not represent her work in this situation as making such a forced choice, however. Instead, she reviewed a series of complicated arguments she had with herself on the issues involved. She contended on the one hand that the question in the workbook was not very clear; its ambiguity made her less inclined to trust the answers in the teacher's guide. In addition, by reflecting on her conversation with Linda, she recognized that the girl really understood the "cycle of water," whereas those students who put down "clouds" might only have looked at the illustration in the book. Rita articulated this skepticism about impersonal measures of students' knowledge in a conversation she had with some other teachers about the incident: "I think too often kids get marked wrong for things that really aren't wrong. I mean, if you corrected Linda's paper and she wasn't around to explain her answer, she would never have had the chance to defend herself or say that this is the way I think. I mean, that's what happens on those Stanford Achievement Tests. They're not given any room for individuality of thought." Rita accepted Linda's answer as a valid representation of the girl's understanding. Yet, she also thought that both she and Linda should concur with the answer in the book. Rita related her thinking about this incident to her first year of teaching; she had read the teacher's guides very carefully that year and "tried to stay one step ahead of the kids" because she was trying to teach material she had not learned before. Even later, she relied heavily on the teacher's guide; she typically referred students directly to the "answer book" to check their own work so that she could spend time on helping others who were slower to finish their assignments. Rita argued that if she let Linda "get away with" her nonstandard interpretation of the question in the science book, she might be undermining her students' trust in these books as well as her own ability to guide her students' learning. For this teacher and her students, textbooks carry a great store of meaning about the nature of what is to be learned. So Rita was torn: she could produce good reasons for accepting Linda's answer as correct and she could also produce good reasons for marking it wrong.

Rita could not win this argument with herself about how to evaluate Linda's answer; like me, she was her own antagonist. Whether she announced to the class that Linda was right and thus implied that what the book said did not matter, or that Linda was wrong because she had interpreted the "cycle of water" in her own way, the consequences would be more overt conflict. While some might see such additional conflict as educationally productive, Rita, in her circumstances, clearly did not.

Rita's Inner Tensions as a Tool of Her Trade

Rita drew on her own conflicted concerns to arrive at her decision about what to do in this situation. Her conviction that she should not choose between Linda and the textbook was based on her personal capacity to value different, potentially contradictory kinds of knowledge. This was part of the "person she wanted to be." She had begun teaching and had been reasonably successful at it without much understanding of science. She had also grown up believing that the people who write books are smarter than she is — even smarter than her teachers. The public knowledge she learned in school from books had allowed her to achieve the position of teacher. So she had reason to trust the "rightness" of the knowledge represented by the standard curriculum. At the same time, however, she believed that much of what she knew could not be contained in books or measured by tests. She knew that she understood things she had figured out for herself, and sometimes she saw these ideas more clearly than those she had read in books. Rita was, therefore, concerned about the limitations of standard measures of knowledge, but her concern was not unconflicted.

Several months later Rita expressed the same ambivalent view of knowledge that formed the basis of her deliberations in this case in a conversation about the way a standardized test had been used to assess her own knowledge. She thought the test was not a very good tool for measuring what would make her a successful learner, but she also recognized that the test had some meaning to people who did not know her. She believed it would be "unfair" to deprive students of the instruction they might need to do well on such tests, even while she argued that the tests do not necessarily measure one's capacity for understanding. "If they don't have a serious attitude about tests," she said, "they're never going to make it in college. They have to have some respect for this information because it's controlling where they are going to go in life. I realize that society is not going to change before they get out of my classroom, and I don't want to put my burdens on the kids. You have to respect these tests, as I do, because I had to take them too. It's a ticket for the next place you want to go." Because Rita had not resolved her own feelings about the value of the sort of knowledge represented by scores on standardized tests, she had been in an effective position to use herself to mediate the conflict between conventional knowledge and individual understanding in the situation with Kevin and Linda. Her personal conflict about the value of standardized knowledge was a resource she drew upon in order to do her work in this classroom situation.

As the person responsible for settling disputes among her students about who is right, Rita represented the possibility of bringing these potentially contradictory ways of knowing together in the public arena of the classroom. Rather than siding with Kevin or Linda, she told them they were both right. She improvised. "I finally said to Kevin and Linda that they were both right. And I left it at that, and I let them handle it from there. (But I was kind of listening to what they would do.) Linda understood exactly what she was trying to get across. Kevin understood it also. But they understood on two different planes. I understood on a third one. I don't think there was any need for clarification, but there was a need for them to know they were both right."

Rita made no stark choices. She did not throw out the textbook and tell Kevin and Linda it didn't matter, nor did she tell Linda that she was wrong because she did not conform to the book's expectation. She accepted both of their answers on "two different planes" while putting herself on a "third plane," where she could value both Kevin's standards and Linda's divergence from them.

Coping Rather Than Solving

Rita constructed a way to manage the tension between individual understanding and public knowledge without resolving it. Since she had some authority as the teacher in this situation, Kevin and Linda took her judgment seriously, even though it was ambiguous. Both of them came out with a different, more complex view of knowledge. Kevin was told that the answer in the teacher's guide is not the only right answer in the public setting of the classroom, while Linda was told that the textbook answer has validity even though she sees things differently. Rita managed to deflect the vehement competition between these two students by issuing a more complex set of rules for judging one another's answers.

In my math class, I made it more difficult to draw the line between teaching that favored girls and teaching that favored boys. By muddying the waters with small-group instruction, I pushed the social conflicts that this dichotomy suggested further into the background. Rita did a similar thing in the area of instruction when she said Kevin and Linda were both right. She confused their ability to judge one another's knowledge and thereby mediated the conflict between them. As in my situation, she did not eliminate the original conflict; rather, she avoided it so as to avoid additional conflicts. This way of submerging the conflict below an improvised, workable, but superficial resolution is, of course, quite different from what many cognitive psychologists or curriculum experts would advocate.

Images of Teachers' Work and Their Implications for Improving It

These two stories portray the teacher as an active negotiator, a broker of sorts, balancing a variety of interests that need to be satisfied in classrooms. The teacher in each story initiates actions as solutions to particular environmental problems and defines herself as the locus of various alternative perspectives on those actions. Conflicts among these perspectives arise in the teacher, both presently within the classroom and in the way she interprets her own past experience. In order to do her job, the dilemma-managing teacher calls upon this conflicted "self" as a tool of her trade, building a working identity that is constructively ambiguous. While she works at solving society's problems and scholars' problems, she also works at coping with her own internal conflicts. She debates with herself about what to do, and instead of screening out responsibilities that contradict one another, she acknowledges them, embraces the conflict, and finds a way to manage.

What does this image of the teacher as a dilemma manager suggest about the nature of teachers' work and how to improve it? Images of teaching frame our construction of the tasks teachers perform; our sense of the work involved in successfully accomplishing these tasks forms the basis for designing improvements. Whether the actions of the two teachers I have described here should be thought of as typical strategies or be promoted as expedient practices will remain open to question. These stories are intended only to illustrate an image of teachers' work that can help us think about the nature of classroom practice. In order to learn something from the image about how to improve practice, it is necessary to compare it with other images of teachers in the literature and to examine the influence these images have had on the kind of help we give teachers when they face classroom problems.

Most commonly, *teachers are assumed to make choices among dichotomous alternatives*; to promote equality *or* excellence; to build curriculum around children's interests *or* around subject matter; to foster independence and creativity *or* maintain standards and expect everyone to meet them.[17] These choices are thought to enable teachers to avoid dilemmas in their everyday practice. An example of this perspective can be found in the way Mary Haywood Metz analyzed the manner in which a group of teachers responded to the work tensions produced by the desegregation of their schools.[18] Metz defined keeping classroom order and promoting student learning as "contradictory imperatives" for teachers and concluded that those she observed could not both maintain standards of behavior in the classroom and nurture students' commitment to learning; instead, they divided themselves into opposing camps. Part of the work of these teachers, in this view, was to figure out whether classroom order or students' commitment was more important to their success as teachers, and then to choose between them. Thus it would seem appropriate that help from outsiders appear in the form of arguments to teachers about why they should pay more attention either to classroom order or to student commitment. Much pre-service and in-service teacher education today takes this form. Professors and staff developers use evidence from research, rationales drawn from educational philosophy, or personal charisma to convince teachers that one approach is better than its opposite.

Another view of pedagogical work is illustrated by Gertrude McPherson's picture of the "small town" teacher.[19] She describes teachers' conflicts entirely in terms of contradictory external pressures. In this image, *the teacher is a person besieged by other people's expectations*. She cannot teach because of the need to defend herself against the inconsistencies in what students, administrators, colleagues, parents, and public officials expect her to do. Managing conflict is part of the teacher's job in this view, but it is seen as a source of "unhappiness and frustration" rather than as a means by which the teacher defines herself. McPherson's view carries with it a sense of what must be done to improve teaching practice: there is very little worthwhile work that can be accomplished by the teacher "as long as the goals of our educational system are unclearly defined. . . . internally inconsistent, [and] inconsistent with dominant and often themselves inconsistent values in our larger society."[20] More current literature on teacher stress takes a similar view: unless the goals of the teacher's job are redefined, the only positive steps a practitioner can take to reduce the harmful effects of the tension produced by conflicting expectations are engaging in regular physical exercise and maintaining a healthy diet.[21] These attitudes toward teaching regard the contradictions in teaching as problems to be solved by altering the way education is organized and conceptualized by society. In this view, society needs to become more consistent about its own goals and what it expects of teachers, thus eliminating conflict .

Yet another way of portraying teaching, one which that be thought of as a response to this abstract hope for unified goals, arises out of the work of social science researchers and government policymakers. These problem solvers have teamed up to find ways to help teachers increase student achievement. They turn away from conflicts that might arise in the classroom and assume that *the teacher is a technical-production manager* who has the responsibility for monitoring the efficiency with which learning is being accomplished. In this view, teaching can be improved if practitioners use researchers' knowledge to solve classroom problems.[22] The teacher's work is to find out what researchers and policymakers say should be done with or to students and then to do it. How much time should be spent on direct instruction versus seatwork? How many new words should be in stories children are required to read? If the teacher does what she is told, students will learn. Taking this perspective suggests that practical conflicts can be avoided if researchers' solutions are correctly implemented by teachers.

Some educational scholars reject this image of the teacher as a "black box" through which researchers' knowledge passes into the classroom.[23] In their view, *the teacher has an active role in deciding how to teach*; she makes decisions by putting research findings together with the information available in the classroom environment to make choices about what process will produce the desired objectives. Because cognitive information processing has been used as the model in these studies of teacher decision making, however, a "decision" is seen only as a process of mathematically ordering one's choices on the basis of unequally weighted alternatives.[24] At each point in the thinking process, the decider is assumed to see clearly which of two alternative routes is preferred to reach a given goal.[25] Therefore, improving teaching involves simplifying alternatives by screening out contradictory concerns so that any reasonable person would make the same correct choice using the same information. The process is mechanical, not personal; it is the sort of thinking one can imagine would be done better by unbiased machines than by people.[26] This theory, therefore, cannot help teachers to figure out what to do about the sort of unsolvable conflicts in their work that I have described.[27]

These images of teachers — as cognitive information processors, as implementers of researchers' knowledge about how to produce learning, as stressed and neurotically defensive, and as members of opposing camps — portray the conflicts in teaching as resolvable in one way or another. In contrast, the image of the teacher as dilemma manager accepts conflict as a continuing condition with which persons can learn to cope. This latter view does not replace the idea that the teacher plays conflicting roles in society, or the idea that it is useful to note patterns in the relationship between behaviors and their outcomes in order to make productive decisions; but it puts the teacher in a different problem-solving relationship to the social conflicts and behavioral patterns in her work. It suggests that, in addition to defending against and choosing among conflicting expectations, she might also welcome their power to influence her working identity. The major difference, then, between the image of the teacher as dilemma manager and the other images I have described is that the dilemma manager accepts conflict as endemic and even useful to her work rather than seeing it as a burden that needs to be eliminated.

There are, of course, many incentives for teachers and scholars to want to eliminate conflict and to think of classroom problems as solvable. If pedagogical problems could be separated one from another rather than entangled in a web of contradictory goals, then they could be solved in some sort of linear progression — shot down like ducks coming up in a row at a penny arcade. Thinking of one's job as figuring out how to live with a web of related problems that cannot be solved seems like an admission of weakness. Sorting out problems and finding solutions that will make them go away is certainly a more highly valued endeavor in our society. Strategies that merely enable us to "cope" or "manage" go against our deep-seated hopes for making progress by gaining control over our interactions with one another. Many people — including teachers — believe that if only scholarship in psychology and the social sciences could come up to the levels achieved by the natural sciences, and if only, with the help of technology, individuals could achieve the ideal of control over the environment represented in such scholarship, then everyone could live happily ever after. The work of managing dilemmas, in contrast, requires admitting some essential limitations on our control over human problems. It suggests that some conflicts cannot be resolved and that the challenge is to find ways to keep them from erupting into more disruptive confrontations.

This connection of limitation with dilemma management needs to be clarified, because we have come to identify classroom management with the teacher's ability to control students' behavior and direct them in learning tasks. This common usage most closely parallels the nonschool definition of a manager as a person who controls or directs the affairs of others. Such control is certainly an essential part of the teacher's job. I use the term "manage" in a different sense, however. To manage to do something can also mean to contrive to do it, implying that the capacity for invention or improvisation is a necessary part of the manager's repertoire. This usage suggests that a manager is one who is able to find a way to do something and that action and invention are fused together in the management process. We might also think of people as managing when they are able to continue to act or even to thrive in adverse circumstances. The teacher's work involves just this sort of invention and action in situations where potential adversity makes solving some kinds of problems inadvisable.

In order to do the work of teaching, as I have portrayed it, one needs to have the resources to cope with equally weighted alternatives when it is not appropriate to express a preference between them. One needs to be able to take advice from researchers but also to know what to do when that advice is contradictory, or when it contradicts knowledge that can only be gained in a particular context. One needs to hold at bay the conflicting expectations of those who have the power to determine whether one can succeed as a teacher or not and at the same time use those expectations as references in self-definition. One can be committed to a particular ideology or its opposite while recognizing the limitations of taking any single-minded view of such complicated processes as teaching and learning in schools. One needs to be comfortable with a self that is complicated and sometimes inconsistent.

Perhaps it is our society's belief in the existence of a solution for every problem that has kept any significant discussion of the teacher's unsolvable problems out of both scholarly and professional conversations about the work of teaching. But there may be other explanations as well. It may be that many teachers are able to carry on with their work as if there were no conflicts in what they are expected to do, or that there are in fact no conflicts in the way they define their jobs. It also may be the case that the sorts of people who become teachers and stay in teaching do not have the intellectual capacity to recognize the complications in the work that I have described.[28] These possibilities certainly deserve our attention.

But if dilemma managing is a significant part of the work of teaching, there are several questions that deserve further examination. First, there are questions about *frequency*. I have argued only that it is possible for teachers to work in ways that suggest that some classroom problems are better managed than solved. How much of a role does this sort of work play in what teachers do? How often do dilemmas of the sort I have described arise in classrooms? How often are they "managed" rather than "resolved"? What are the characteristics of teachers who do more dilemma managing than others? What are the characteristics of classrooms in which dilemma management is common?

A second category of questions can be grouped around understanding and evaluating what teachers actually do when they manage dilemmas. My emphasis in this essay has not been on the particular strategies used by the teachers but on the more general elements of the work involved. What different kinds of *strategies* are used in classrooms to cope with unsolvable problems? How could they usefully be grouped? Are there better and worse ways of keeping classroom conflict under the surface? How do the strategies teachers use compare with those used by other professionals who face dilemmas?

We also need to know more about what kind of *resources* teachers have available to cope with contradictions within themselves and in their work. How do they learn to cope, or learn that it is an appropriate thing to do? What characteristics of their working environment make dilemma managing more or less possible? How can teachers who have trouble coping with conflict get better at it? What role do supervisors, formal course work, other life experiences, and colleagues play in the development of the teacher's capacity for actively tolerating ambiguity? How are the personal resources required to manage pedagogical dilemmas related to the skills that researchers and policymakers use to address educational problems or the knowledge that scholars use to analyze the tensions in the work of teaching? What resources besides skill and knowledge might teachers bring to this aspect of their work?

Our understanding of the work of teaching might be enhanced if we explored what teachers do when they choose to endure and make use of conflict. Such understanding will be difficult to acquire if we approach all of the problems in teaching as if they are solvable, and if we assume that what is needed to solve them is knowledge that can be produced outside the classroom. In order to pursue the questions I have listed here, we shall need to adopt an image of teaching that takes account of the possibility that the teacher herself is a resource in managing the problems of educational practice.

Notes

1. My distinction between theory and practice here follows that developed by Joseph Schwab in his studies of curriculum development. Schwab has observed that the particulars of time, place, person, and circumstance that surround questions of what and how to teach are incongruent with the order, system, economy, and generality required to build a good theory; see Schwab, "The Practical: Arts of Eclectic," in *Science, Curriculum, and Liberal Education: Selected Essays*, ed. Ian Westbury and Neil J. Wilkof (Chicago: University of Chicago Press, 1978), p. 322.

2. See, for example, Susan Florio and Martha Walsh, "The Teacher as a Colleague in Classroom Research," in *Culture and the Bilingual Classroom*, ed. Henry T. Trueba, Grace P. Guthrie, and Kathryn H. Au (Rowley, MA: Newbury House, 1981), 87–101; Eliot Eisner, "Can Educational Research Inform Educational Practice?" *Phi Delta Kappan, 65* (March 1984), 447–452; and Leslie L. Huling, Myron Trang, and Linda Cornell, "Interactive Research and Development: A Promising Strategy for Teacher Educators," *Journal of Teacher Education, 32* (1981), 13–14.

   Christopher Clark and Penelope L. Peterson have recently emphasized that descriptive research on how teachers make interactive decisions in the classroom should be done as a basis for further theory building about teacher thinking; see their "Teacher's Thought Processes." Occasional Paper No. 73, Institute for Research on Teaching (East Lansing, MI: Michigan State University, 1984), p. 76.

3. Schwab describes the value of such "deliberation" as a method for studying the teaching process in "The Practical 4: Something for Curriculum Professors to Do," *Curriculum Inquiry, 13* (1983) 239–265. His notions are expanded, particularly with relation to deliberative exchanges among differing aspects of one's self, by Lee Shulman in "The Practical and the Eclectic: A Deliberation on Teaching and Educational Research," *Curriculum Inquiry, 14* (1984), 183–200.

4. The "particularistic" nature of the teacher's perspective has been described by Arthur S. Bolster, "Toward a More Effective Model of Research on Teaching," *Harvard Educational Review, 53* (1983), 294–308. The context-specific character of work in classrooms as it ap-

pears to practitioners has been examined by Walter Doyle in "Learning the Classroom Environment: An Ecological Analysis," *Journal of Teacher Education, 28* (1977), 51–55, and "Paradigms for Research on Teacher Effectiveness," *Review of Research in Education,* vol. 5, ed. Lee Shulman (Itasca, IL: Peacock, 1977), pp. 163–198. Philip Jackson compared teachers' propensity for "anecdotal" descriptions of their work with the more abstract quality of academic writing about teaching. See Jackson, "The Way Teachers Think," in *Psychology and Educational Practice,* ed. Gerald S. Lesser (Glenview, IL: Scott, Foresman, 1971), pp. 10–34.

5. The personal quality of teachers' knowledge is emphasized by Sharon Feiman and Robert Floden. See their "Cultures of Teaching" in *Handbook of Research on Teaching,* 3rd ed., ed. Merlin C. Wittrock, 1986. Gary Fenstermacher argues for considering the effect of the teacher's own concerns and personal history on the decisions she makes in the classroom in "A Philosophical Consideration of Recent Research on Teacher Effectiveness," in *Review of Research in Education,* vol. 6, ed. Lee Shulman (Itasca, IL: Peacock, 1979), pp. 186–215.

6. I have chosen the feminine gender for pronouns that apply to teachers throughout this manuscript because the majority of teachers are women.

7. Schwab, "The Practical: A Language for Curriculum," in Westbury and Wilkof, p. 289.

8. See, for example, Bryan Wilson, "The Teacher's Role: A Sociological Analysis," *British Journal of Sociology, 13* (1962), 15–32; Charles Bidwell, "The School as a Formal Organization," in *Handbook of Organizations,* ed. James G. March (Chicago: Rand McNally, 1965), pp. 972–1022; and Ann Lieberman and Lynn Miller, "The Social Realities of Teaching," *Teachers College Record, 80* (1978), 54–68.

9. The language of "dilemmas" to describe classroom problems has also been used by Ann Berlak and Harold Berlak in *The Dilemmas of Schooling: Teaching and Social Change* (London: Methuen, 1981). However, their analysis focuses on cultural contradictions and opportunities for social change as they are manifest in teachers' dilemmas and gives less attention to the practical work involved in managing dilemmas in the classroom.

10. See Schwab, "The Practical: Arts of Eclectic," p. 318; for a comparison between the knowledge produced by social science research and the knowledge practitioners use in their work, see Charles E. Lindholm and David K. Cohen, *Usable Knowledge: Social Science and Social Problem Solving* (New Haven, CT: Yale University Press, 1979); and also David K. Cohen, "Commitment and Uncertainty," Harvard University, unpublished manuscript, 1981.

11. Descriptions of teacher thinking have emphasized the choice between alternative courses of action as the outcome of teacher decisionmaking, based on models of cognitive information processing. See, for example, Richard J. Shavelson, "Teachers' Decision Making," in *The Psychology of Teaching Methods: The 75th Yearbook of the National Society for the Study of Education,* Part I, ed. Nathaniel L. Gage (Chicago: University of Chicago Press, 1976), pp. 143–165; John Eggleston, ed., *Teacher Decision Making in the Classroom* (London: Routledge & Kegan Paul, 1979); and Christopher Clark and Robert Yinger, "Research on Teacher Thinking," *Curriculum Inquiry* (1977), 279–304.

12. *Funk and Wagnalls' Standard College Dictionary* (New York: Harcourt Brace and World, 1963), p. 372. For a psychological description of the contradictory imperatives that can arise within the person of the teacher, see Angelika C. Wagner, "Conflicts in Consciousness: Imperative Cognitions Can Lead to Knots in Thinking," Paper presented at the First Symposium of the International Study Association on Teacher Thinking, Tilburg University, The Netherlands, October 1983.

13. For example, such dichotomous categories are used to examine teachers' work in Harry L. Gracey, *Curriculum or Craftsmanship: Elementary School Teachers in a Bureaucratic Setting* (Chicago: University of Chicago Press, 1972); George Spindler, "Education in a Transforming American Culture," *Harvard Educational Review,* 25(1955), 145–156; and Mary Haywood Metz, *Classrooms and Corridors: The Crisis of Authority in Desegregated Secondary Schools* (Berkeley: University of California Press, 1978). In contrast, views of the teacher derived from the social psychology of George Herbert Mead and others in "the Chicago School" present a more complex picture: for example, Willard Waller in *The Sociology of Teaching* (New York: Wiley, 1932); and Philip Jackson in *Life in Classrooms* (New York: Holt, Rinehart and Winston, 1968). The Berlaks, in *The Dilemmas of Schooling,* p. 133, de-

scribe the teacher's job in the face of contradictions as "transformation," by which they mean the invention of a pedagogical process that joins opposing poles of a cultural contradiction; in their view, the teacher has the capacity to be a vehicle whereby "the contending presses of the culture at least for the moment are synthesized and thus overcome."

14. See Carl Bereiter, "Schools Without Education," *Harvard Educational Review,* 42 (1972), 390–414; see also John D. McNeil, "A Scientific Approach to Supervision," in *Supervision of Teaching,* ed. Thomas J. Sergiovanni (Alexandria, VA: Association for Supervision and Curriculum Development, 1982), pp. 18–34.

15. This position is characteristic of those educational reformers whose philosophy of learning is built on theories of individual cognitive development.

16. I had the oppportunity to observe and work with Rita Cerone over three years as part of the Teacher Development Project in the Division for Study and Research in Education, Massachusetts Institute of Technology. This project is described in my "Teaching about Thinking and Thinking about Teaching," *Journal of Curriculum Studies,* 16, (1984), 1–18. Quotes of Rita's remarks are taken from transcripts of meetings of the teacher participants in that project and transcripts of my individual interviews with Rita, which occurred over a three-year period. The name "Rita Cerone" is a pseudonym, as are all student names used in this manuscript.

17. See, for example, Gracey, *Curriculum or Craftsmanship;* Jackson, "The Way Teachers Think"; Bidwell, "The School as a Formal Organization"; and Spindler, "Education in a Transforming American Culture."

18. Metz, *Classrooms and Corridors.*

19. McPherson, *Small Town Teacher* (Cambridge, MA: Harvard University Press, 1972).

20. McPherson, *Small Town Teacher,* p. 215.

21. Kathleen V. Hoover-Dempsey and Earline D. Kendell, "Stress and Coping in Teaching: An Integrative Review of the Literature," Paper presented at the annual meeting of the American Educational Research Association, New Orleans, April 1984.

22. See, for example, Nathaniel L. Gage, "An Analytic Approach to Research on Instructional Methods," in *The Social Psychology of Teaching,* ed. Arnold Morrison and Donald McIntyre (Harmondsworth, Eng.: Penguin Books, 1972); Robert E. Slavin, "Component Building: A Strategy for Research-Based Instructional Improvement," *Elementary School Journal,* 84 (1984), 255–269; John D. McNeil, "A Scientific Approach to Supervision"; and Jere Brophy and Thomas Good, *Teacher-Student Relationships: Causes and Consequences* (New York: Holt, Rinehart, and Winston, 1974).

23. Hilda Borko, Richard Cone, Nancy Russo, and Richard J. Shavelson, "Teachers' Decision Making," in *Research on Teaching: Concepts, Findings and Implications,* ed. Penelope L. Peterson and Herbert T. Walberg (Berkeley, CA: McCutcheon, 1979).

24. See Shavelson, "Teachers' Decision Making" in Gage, *Psychology of Teaching Methods;* Eggleston, *Teacher Decision Making in the Classroom;* and Clark and Yinger, "Research on Teaching Thinking."

25. This model is outlined in Clark and Peterson, "Teacher's Thought Processes," pp. 63–69.

26. The problems with mechanical information processing as the ideal model for describing human decision making in situations fraught with conflict have been cogently outlined in David Braybrooke and Charles Lindblom, *A Strategy of Decision: Policy Evaluation as a Social Process* (New York: Free Press, 1963), pp. 246–247. More recently, Joseph Weizenbaum has argued against assuming that human judgment is comparable to even the most sophisticated computers, in *Computer Power and Human Reason: From Judgment to Calculation* (San Francisco: Freeman, 1976).

27. Richard Shavelson and Paula Stern, "Research on Teachers' Pedagogical Thoughts, Judgments, Decisions, and Behavior," *Review of Educational Research,* 51 (1981), 471.

28. Jackson proposes this possibility in *Life in Classrooms,* pp. 144–148.

The author would like to acknowledge the helpful comments of Gemmette Reid, Marvin Lazerson, and David K. Cohen on earlier drafts of this paper.

"You Can't Just Say That the Only Ones Who Can Speak Are Those Who Agree with Your Position": Political Discourse in the Classroom

MELINDA FINE

How do teachers engage students in meaningful discussions on contemporary is-sues about which the teachers themselves often have strong opinions while simulta-neously creating an open atmosphere in the classroom in which students can ex-press and discuss a wide range of ideologies? What do teachers do when students express beliefs that oppose their own? What role should teachers play in creating an atmosphere in which students can take on social, political, and moral issues, think critically with each other about these issues, and learn in the process? In this chapter, Melinda Fine investigates these questions in a middle school classroom, examining the dynamics playing out in the discussion of controversial issues sur-rounding a curriculum on the Holocaust. Fine asserts that students are most cer-tainly able to handle discomfort, disagreement, and heated discussion in the learning process, and are more resilient than most adults believe. She concludes that educa-tion in a democracy demands that teachers and students engage highly charged and conflictual issues in the classroom that are still unresolved in the wider society, and that teachers and students must work to deal constructively and openly with the wide range of political and social ideologies that they bring into the classroom.

Cambridge, Massachusetts, lies just across the Charles River from Boston. Known best for its stately, well-kept colonial homes and the ivy-clad brick buildings of Harvard University, this 350-year-old city is generally per-ceived as a White, middle-class, intellectual enclave. While this perception is at least partially true, this densely packed city of almost 100,000 is in fact far more heterogeneous than its popular image suggests. One-fifth of all Cambridge resi-dents are foreign-born, and one-half of these arrived during the past decade. A ma-jority of the city's African Americans, as well as immigrants from Cape Verde, Brazil, Southeast Asia, Central America, and Haiti, tend to reside in neighbor-hoods that look quite different from the tree-lined streets and white-trimmed man-sions surrounding Harvard University.

Harvard Educational Review Vol. 63 No. 4 Winter 1993, 412–433

The Medgar Evers School is located in one of the poorer neighborhoods of Cambridge.[1] Here, mostly Black, Latino, Haitian, and Asian families live in multifamily homes that are usually close together and often in need of paint or new siding. Many of Medgar Evers' students come from the large housing project just across the street; 44 percent of the student population qualifies for free or reduced-price lunches. Because of the city's desegregation program, however, the school's roughly six hundred K–8 students are more racially balanced than the neighborhood in which the school is located: in 1992–1993, the school was 43 percent White, 34 percent African American, 16 percent Asian, and 7 percent Latino.

Medgar Evers is a long, three-story, beige concrete building of irregular geometric design. Surrounded by few trees, the school appears cold and austere when viewed from the street. Once inside, however, one gets an entirely different impression. Classrooms, offices, the school library, and the auditorium spin off from an airy central space that is open from the third floor to the basement. Sunlight streams in through skylights on the school's slanted roof, infusing all three floors of the building with light. Terracotta-tiled floors, clean hallways, notices for bake sales and other school events, as well as abundant displays of student artwork make the school feel cheery and welcoming. An enormous map of the world hangs on a wall across from the school's central office. This map is covered with push pins, each connected to a string that leads to a flag representing the country pinpointed. "We have children and families in our school representing *at least* sixty-four countries of the world," a card next to the map states. "We want to encourage children to become familiar with the world map, to identify all of the countries of origin, and to help celebrate our diversity!"

I have visited a classroom in this school nearly every day for the past four months, acting as a participant/observer while carrying out research for my doctoral dissertation in education. I have come to study how the teacher and students in one classroom grapple with an interdisciplinary social studies unit called "Facing History and Ourselves."[2]

This program seeks to provide a model for teaching history in a way that helps students reflect critically upon a variety of contemporary social, moral, and political issues. It focuses on a specific historical period — the Nazi rise to power and the Holocaust — and guides students back and forth between an in-depth historical case study and reflection on the causes and consequences of present-day prejudice, intolerance, violence, and racism.[3]

Facing History's decision to use the Holocaust as a case study and a springboard for exploring contemporary issues is complex and merits some discussion. When middle school teachers in Brookline, Massachusetts, created Facing History and Ourselves in 1976, relatively few Holocaust curricula existed. Perceiving the Holocaust to be a watershed event of the twentieth century, these teachers felt that their students should, indeed, learn about such a critical historical moment. At the same time, however, they felt that the Holocaust's "meaning" to students must lie not only in understanding its unique historical dimensions, but also in grappling with its more generalizable lessons about human behavior. Historically examining the escalation of steps through which individuals living under Nazi rule were made to follow Hitler — from the use of propaganda to influence one's thinking, to the threats against economic and personal security, to the use of terror to compel obedience — course designers sought to help students identify how opportunities for resistance were gradually eroded with the demise of German democracy and the rise of a totalitarian state. Using historical understanding as a catalyst for more personal, critical reflection, they intended to foster students' awareness of the social conditions that can undermine democracy and to promote their sense of moral and political responsibility as future citizens.

It might well be asked whether these goals could not also be achieved by undertaking a different, perhaps more relevant case study — of the Middle Passage (the transatlantic slave trade), for example, or the genocide of Native Americans. No doubt they could be. Program designers, teachers, and promoters do not argue that the Holocaust is the only genocide — or even the most important genocide — to teach about. In fact, Facing History has developed other curricular materials that deal more directly with these "closer-to-home" events, and the Facing History Resource Text includes a chapter on the Armenian Genocide.[4]

Program advocates do contend, however, that discussions about contemporary racism and violence may in fact be facilitated by focusing on a period of history more tangential to the cultural backgrounds of the course's ethnically diverse students. As Larry Myatt, a longtime teacher of the course and the director of an inner-city high school in Boston, says, Facing History offers "a way to talk about these issues in a *removed* way so that we don't hit people over the head with a two-by-four and say 'racism!' 'scapegoating!' "[5]

In keeping with the program's educational priorities, the semester-long curriculum is structured to move back and forth between a focus on "history" and a focus on "ourselves." Initial chapters of the program's resource book encourage thinking about universal questions of individual identity and social behavior. From here the course moves on to its more specific case study of prejudice and discrimination: an examination of the history of anti-Semitism, beginning as far back as ancient Rome. Students undertake a rigorous, multifaceted study of German history from 1914 to 1945, examining, for example, the impact of Nazi racial policies in education and the workplace, the nature of propaganda, and the various roles played by victims, victimizers, and bystanders during the Third Reich. These lessons provide critical historical content and serve as structured exercises for thinking about the choices that individuals, groups, and nations faced with regard to action and resistance. These exercises, in turn, prepare students for later discussions about how they themselves can assume responsibility for protecting civil liberties and becoming active citizens.[6]

Facing History's complex intellectual content is undergirded by a pedagogical imperative: to foster perspective-taking, critical thinking, and moral decision-making among students. It is specifically geared toward adolescents who are developmentally engaged in a fierce (and somewhat contradictory) struggle to become distinct individuals *and* to fit in with their peers. These students, curriculum developers argue, have the most to gain from a course that "raises the problem of differing perspectives, competing truths, the need to understand motives and to consider the intentions and abilities of themselves and others."[7] Rather than shying away from the conflicts that are inevitably generated when a diverse group of adolescents work to clarify their own beliefs and values, teachers encourage students to view complexity and conflict as potentially conducive to personal growth and social exchange.

I chose to observe the implementation of Facing History and Ourselves in the Medgar Evers school for specific reasons — reasons undoubtedly operative in my interpretation of the course and, consequently, important to acknowledge here.

First and foremost, I am a supporter of the program's goals. Educational efforts to foster moral and social responsibility are difficult undertakings, not only because of the conflictual nature of the material inevitably confronted by the students, but also because of the embattled position many such education programs — including Facing History — find themselves in today. I consider them socially necessary, nonetheless.

I also find compelling Facing History's claim that using historical subject matter somewhat tangential to the lives of racially diverse students may quite effectively reach and motivate students in multicultural urban settings. For this reason I have observed Facing History courses in several urban schools over the past few years, while completing my own doctoral work and serving as a research consultant to the Facing History organization.[8] My professional collaboration with Facing History has deepened my understanding of the program, but also demanded that I be vigilant in pushing myself to view its classroom practice in a critical light.

Consequently, while at the Medgar Evers school, I observed class daily for an eleven-week period. I hoped to learn how students and their teacher interpreted issues raised by the course, recognizing that their interpretations would no doubt shift during the semester and assuming, too, that they would at times produce conflict among classroom participants. I intended to describe how these conflicts were negotiated within the classroom.

To carry out my objectives, I felt that I needed to know as much as possible about the students, their teacher, and the school culture that surrounded the classroom study. I needed to have all classroom participants speak freely with me, and thus I needed to be known and trusted by them. These requirements dictated a qualitative, descriptive, phenomenological, and self-consciously personal approach to my subject, involving, among other things, participant/observation, in-class and post-class writing, lengthy individual interviews with students and their teacher, and ongoing review of students' written work.

My relations with the teacher and students were open and friendly. Over the course of the semester, I was invited to a bar mitzvah, sock hop, viola recital, and soccer match, and after the school year ended, I received a letter from one student asking me out to lunch. Since my intent was to get to know classroom participants and to let them get to know me, I never tried to hold myself aloof or maintain the stance of a completely distant, "objective" observer. Though I didn't, for the most part, participate actively in class discussion, I nonetheless tried to act in a style compatible with the school's "open" atmosphere. My constant, in-class writing was obvious to all present (in fact, students often teased me about how quickly I wrote), and I did comment on topics when asked by either the teacher or students. I also frequently asked, and was told, about students' basketball games, dances, baby-sitting, and dates. In turn, students asked and were told about me: that I was a teacher, an activist, and at that time a graduate student, and that I was writing a book about them.

I identify what I did and where I stand in relation to Facing History not to suggest that researcher "bias" qualifies the validity of my observations — as if some wholly neutral position were a preferable point of departure or even possible to attain. I believe all researchers stand in some relation to their subject; the reader simply deserves to know where I stand before watching these classroom events along with me.

* * *

It is an unseasonably hot day in May. The twenty-three students in Marysa Gonzalez's seventh/eighth-grade class sit fanning themselves with their spiral notebooks as late-morning sun pours into the classroom through a large, partially closed window on the far side of the room. Of the twelve girls and eleven boys in this room, six are African American, four are Asian, and thirteen are White, one of whom is a Latina. Nursing her latest sports injury, Jess limps to her seat clad in navy blue shorts and a University of Michigan tee-shirt. Abby sports a summer-bright turquoise shirt, matching socks, and white stretch pants. The top piece of her shoulder length, sandy-blond hair is pulled back in a clip, and her bangs remain loose and hanging. Sandra's clothing and hairstyle are almost identical. Alan and Josh each sport marginally punk hairdos. Alan wears an earring in his left ear. Chi-Ho's pressed, beige cotton shirt remains buttoned at both the neck and cuffs, and he removes his thick, black-rimmed glasses every now and then to wipe the sweat from his brow. Jamal and Amiri both wear oversized tee-shirts and baggy cotton pants.

The teacher, Marysa Gonzalez, searches intently through piles of paper on her desk. A handsome Latina in her late forties, her style is informal and unpretentious: she wears light khaki slacks, a loose-fitting red cotton shirt, and no makeup. Her long black hair, pulled back in a loose braid, is streaked with grey.

It is the eleventh and second-to-last week of the Facing History course. Using students' understanding of the Holocaust as a lens through which to approach more immediate concerns, Marysa focuses the remaining class discussions around contemporary political problems in order to highlight students' own social and political responsibilities. This way of bringing closure to the course is in keeping with the final chapter of the Facing History Resource Text:

> This curriculum must provide opportunities for students to explore the practical applications of freedom, which they have learned demand a constant struggle with difficult, controversial, and complex issues. . . . This history has taught that there is no one else to confront terrorism, ease the yoke and pain of racism, attack apathy, create and enforce just laws, and wage peace but *us*. . . . We believe that participating in decision-making about difficult and controversial issues gives practice in listening to different opinions, deciphering fact from opinion, confronting emotion and reason, negotiating, and problem-solving.[9]

Marysa circulates around the uncomfortably hot classroom handing out the syllabus for the week. Listing all reading and homework assignments for the next five days, the syllabus begins with a quote from radical community organizer Saul Alinsky, which is directly relevant to this week's discussion: "Change means movement, movement means friction, friction means heat, and heat means controversy. The only place where there is no friction is in outer space or a seminar on political action."

Intended as a comment upon political conflicts in the world at large, Alinsky's remark is equally telling about classroom dynamics. Over the next several days, students will view provocative documentary films about individuals and/or organizations holding controversial and differing political beliefs. These films (and related readings) are intended to impress upon students the importance of clarifying one's own political beliefs and raise complex questions about how a democratic and pluralistic society should best handle the conflicts generated by political diversity. In discussing these films, political differences within the classroom itself will be illuminated and debated, and dilemmas raised by the course's intellectual content will be mirrored in the lived curriculum of classroom dynamics.

From my perspective, these classroom dynamics reveal tensions about conflicting values and ideologies among teachers, students, and the Facing History curriculum itself, demonstrating the enormous complexity of the endeavor to catalyze critical, moral thinking among adolescent students. On the one hand, the Facing History program advocates bringing forth multiple points of view, developing students' understanding of multiple perspectives, and promoting tolerance among diverse peoples of often differing backgrounds. In the classes I have observed, teacher practice is to a considerable extent in keeping with these curricular values; teachers often actively engage with students of diverse political perspectives and encourage them to remain fair-minded and open to at least hearing alternative points of view. On the other hand, the program unequivocally rejects moral relativism, condemning social attitudes and beliefs that in any way repress or discriminate against individuals or social groups. Tensions inevitably arise when teachers and students differ in their feelings about which beliefs actually further or hinder these stated curricular objectives. Whose standards should determine what is morally "right" or "wrong"? Do these determinations align with an individual's own political beliefs? How should beliefs that some regard as "wrong" be handled in the classroom? What are the repercussions of silencing these viewpoints or, alternatively, allowing them to be voiced freely? As the recent controversy over New York City's "Children of the Rainbow" curriculum demonstrates, these questions are increasingly the subject of national educational debate.

Marysa and her students also clearly struggle with questions such as these. A close look at how they are dealt with here — within the safety of a trusted school community — may help to illuminate how they are negotiated within a broader social context. What follows, then, is a portrait of classroom life. It is intended not as an evaluative critique of the Facing History program's success or failure in meeting its stated goals, but rather as an analytic exploration of the dynamics encountered in attempting to do so. As a matter of both research inquiry and writing style, social science portraiture investigates, describes, and analyzes characters, settings, and events in context and in relation to one another, and is informed by an awareness of the researcher's own relationship with his or her subject.[10] Equally important, portraiture offers a style of writing designed to engage the reader in the particular experience described and, in so doing, give him or her a sense of a larger whole. I offer the following in the spirit of what the writer Eudora Welty has noted in another context: "One place comprehended can make us understand other places better."[11]

* * *

Friday, May 11

"Remember yesterday? What did we see?" Marysa asks about a film in which the subject of political difference is raised. Sandra answers, "A story about a man who taught his students that the Holocaust never happened, and that Jews wanted to rule the world." Abby adds, "He also said that all the banks and the finances were controlled by Jewish people." "Yeah," agrees Alan, "he thought there was an international Jewish conspiracy."[12]

Students take turns passionately describing "Lessons in Hate," an early 1980s documentary about Jim Keegstra, a popular and charismatic mayor and teacher in a small town in Alberta, Canada, who taught anti-Semitic beliefs to students for more than a decade. The film extensively documents Keegstra arguing that the Holocaust was a "hoax" that in no way singled out Jewish people. He also argues that the French revolution was a product of the "international Jewish conspiracy"; that John Wilkes Booth, the man who shot Abraham Lincoln, was a Jew; and that Jews caused the American Civil War. Young, vulnerable, and with little access to alternative beliefs or perspectives, Keegstra's students uncritically absorbed his teachings, or, in a few cases, adopted them ambivalently in order to receive a passing grade. More problematic still, Keegstra's statements were tacitly accepted by the school's principal and faculty and by most of the town's council and citizens. When the mother of one student finally challenged Keegstra's teachings, she was vehemently opposed by members of her community. The school board eventually fired Keegstra, but not until after a long and difficult battle had been waged that painfully divided members of the small town.[13]

The Keegstra film raises questions about how a community can tolerate conflictual beliefs among its members while still maintaining cohesion. Showcasing the struggles experienced by both Keegstra and those who oppose him, it demonstrates how difficult it can be to stand up for one's beliefs, regardless of their content. After what they have read, seen, and been taught throughout the semester, Marysa's students are outraged that anyone could minimize the horror of the Holocaust, much less deny its very existence. Distancing themselves from their Canadian peers, some make disparaging remarks about Keegstra's seemingly docile and gullible students:

Abby: It seems like these people just *feed* on people who are torn apart. They just suck them up by providing them with an excuse to hate! They probably want to find a way to place the blame on someone else just to explain their own situation.

Marysa: Exactly! What's the vocabulary word which describes that? (Several students shout out, "scapegoating!") Well, what can you do to help people when they're in this condition? What can you do to turn their beliefs around?

Josh: Kill them!

Marysa: What?! Kill them?!

Josh: Yes. If they say those things, and if they start a war or something, you have to fight back.

Alan: But if you go out and fight these people, and you kill six hundred or seven hundred of them, it won't stop *anything*! More will just come and fight back!

Marysa: What I'm *really* trying to push is that this is not just a problem that happened in history, a long time ago — the Dark Ages, when I was born. These issues are *here*, in the present. And you're a part of it. You have to be aware of it so *you* are not brainwashed or indoctrinated in the future.

For the next several minutes, students discuss the apparent differences between their own multicultural community and Keegstra's ethnically homogeneous school and town. Marysa asks students to identify similarities between Nazi doctrine and what Keegstra taught, and Abby brings up the international Jewish conspiracy theme. Drawing this argument closer to home, Marysa suggests parallels between the historical claim that Jews have controlled the financial industry and the present-day fear that Japanese increasingly dominate the U.S. economy. Chi-Ho raises his hand and quietly drops a bombshell: "I think that a Jewish international conspiracy *does* exist, but not quite as much as they say. So many people are talking about it, it must be some way true." "What?!" several students exclaim at once. Josh stares in disbelief at the boy who sits next to him, suddenly a stranger. Susie and Jess yell out in disbelief. Marysa responds in a strained but consciously even-tempered voice, "Chi-Ho, why do you think this?" Chi-Ho answers in a somewhat muffled voice, "I don't know, but I do." Marysa continues, "Don't you think that if there was a conspiracy it could have stopped the Holocaust?" "No, I don't," Chi-Ho replies, "because it's more recent. It's developed since the fifties only, I think." Marysa responds emphatically, "Chi-Ho, we need to talk!"

Animated one-on-one conversations spring up between students who sit next to each other in all corners of the room; the whole class seems to be buzzing. Abby raises her hand and (deliberately or not) turns up the heat several notches. She says, "I'm against what some people are doing with Israel, with the way it was established and with killing the Palestinians and everything. But that's different from an international Jewish conspiracy." "*What* are you talking about?" Josh exclaims furiously. "We weren't even talking about that!" Sandra adds critically, "What are you against now, Abby?" Abby answers, "I'm against the way the country was set up." Marysa asks incredulously and slightly sarcastically, "The UN vote?" Abby replies, "Not that, but what happened to the Palestinian people *through* that. Elie Wiesel and people like that were involved, and millions of Palestinian people were massacred and forced to leave their homes, just like in the Holocaust."

All hell breaks loose. It seems like everyone begins yelling at Abby, and Chi-Ho's earlier remark is left by the wayside. Abby steadfastly holds her ground. Though her words remain strong and her claims unqualified, she slumps further and further into her seat with each new attack by her classmates. She strikes me as being both scared and defiant. Confused about historical facts, Josh defends the state of Israel.

Josh: They were *attacked* in an eight-day war!

Abby: Well, it's still not right to be killing people to set up a country!

Josh: That's exactly what *we* did to set up *our* country!

Abby: So? I'm against *that*, too! I don't believe in that either!

Sandra (becoming increasingly exasperated): Well, what *are* you for? What *do* you believe in?

(Alison and Susie nod emphatically in agreement.)

Abby (matter-of-factly): I believe in control by the people.

Marysa: But how do you determine which people should have control, Abby? In the film we saw, the Canadian teacher thinks he should have control, 'cause he thinks he's right. How are you going to decide who gets to speak and who doesn't?

Students debate the conundrum of free speech for the remaining few minutes of class. Though Marysa has (perhaps self-consciously) shifted discussion away from a contentious and personalized debate, the classroom atmosphere remains charged.

I am scheduled to interview Abby later on this same day. As students get ready for lunch, I watch Abby self-consciously gather her books, seeming proud yet uncomfortable about being isolated. Calling out to her, I suggest that we can discuss the points she has raised during our interview, if she is interested; she smiles appreciatively.

Sandra, Alison, and Angela note my overture and come up to speak with me on their way out of the room. "Look, I don't know much about the Jewish religion, or any religion, really," Sandra says, "but isn't it true that in the Bible it says that the land was originally Jewish land, and that's why they wanted it? Or, why didn't the Jewish people just go to a different country?"

I try to answer as best as I can, explaining that Jews, Christians, and Moslems have all lived on the land, and that all have laid claim to it at different periods of history. "But doesn't the Bible say that the Jews were there *first?*," Angela retorts, "and then the Moslems came when the Jews went to Egypt?" Trying to grant each group its legitimacy, I speak to the importance of finding contemporary political solutions to the problem. Seeing myself more as a participant/observer than an arbiter of divergent viewpoints, I refuse to choose sides despite the girls' best efforts to make me do so. The three girls head off for lunch less angry but still visibly confused.

Josh leaves class upset by the comments made by both Abby and Chi-Ho. He speaks to Marysa for almost an hour after class, refusing to sit next to Chi-Ho and demanding that his seat be changed. In keeping with the curriculum's intent to foster students' ability to listen to alternative perspectives, Marysa tells me later:

> I tried to explain to Josh that Chi-Ho was the same person Josh thought he was before he made that statement. I told him that the way to respond to problems is not to refuse to speak to someone, but to talk together to try to figure it out and to help people to change their beliefs.

But "talking together" is not always easy. True to Alinsky's comment, "frictions" caused by Abby and Chi-Ho seem to circulate around the class as a whole (several students shout at Abby and Chi-Ho); between students and their teacher (Marysa expresses unequivocal disapproval of both students' comments); and, perhaps most poignantly, within students' individual relationships (friendships between Josh and Chi-Ho as well as Abby and Sandra are strained).

Marysa leaves class as upset as many of her students and uncertain about how to proceed. In fact, her confusion seems to have been manifest in her classroom dealings. Confronted with views she finds repugnant and even dangerous, she does, nevertheless, encourage students to remain open-minded, independent in their thinking, and respectful of difference. She even engages Abby and Chi-Ho in a critical debate, urging them to clarify their thinking and to defend their controversial points of view. At the same time, however, Marysa implicitly undermines the views of both of these students. By publicly acknowledging her disagreement with Abby and Chi-Ho, she uses her implicit authority as the "teacher" (the one empowered to design seating plans, assign homework and grades, and so forth) to undermine, rather than muzzle, these students' perspectives. Given the power differential between teacher and student, the critical debate between them is unevenly weighted.

For example, Marysa challenges Chi-Ho's remarks before the full classroom community, but then seeks to remove them from the public arena. "Chi-Ho, we need to talk," she says after only a brief exchange, simultaneously displacing disagreement to the private realm and suggesting that, once there, she will set the record straight. Moments later Marysa chooses not to intervene when several students jump on Abby, and her own questions of Abby sound slightly facetious. Finally, she eventually steers discussion away from the Middle East and toward freedom of speech in the midst of an unresolved debate.

Admittedly uncomfortable with the arguments raised and feeling unequipped to handle them, Marysa avails herself of her proximity to the Facing History and Ourselves national office and calls in staff member Steve Cohen to address the controversial issues raised by Abby and Chi-Ho. While I believe Marysa is making good use of an available resource, I also wonder whether she is bringing Steve in to quell controversy and, in essence, to set the record straight. A balding, wiry man in chinos and tennis shoes, Steve visits class a few days later.

Monday, May 14

"Why did Hitler choose to focus on the Jews?" Steve asks to open this morning's complex agenda. Alan replies, "He said that they were in charge of the money." Jess adds, "He said they were the people who put Germany in the economic state they were in." "Well, why did people believe it?" Steve continues. Abby says, "It's like that quote, 'If you tell a lie big enough and long enough, people will start to believe it.'" Steve asks, "Do you think that's true, from your own experience?" "Well, I've always been someone who doesn't like to just go along with what other people are saying," Abby replies, "but *yeah*, if you hear something long enough, it affects you . . . you kind of forget what your own principles are."

Steve bounces around the room, weaving around students' desks and speaking quickly in an animated voice that is often squeaky with excitement. Focusing directly on each student with whom he speaks, and referring to each by name, he engages the class in a discussion about how basic emotions and stereotypes take over when you "forget your own principles" and are "no longer able to think." "I want you to think about how stereotypes and propaganda work," Steve explains, "because, as you know, Hitler didn't invent anything new. Before Hitler, there was plenty of hatred of Jews." He continues with the following example:

> In the 1890s, a book appeared, and it was called . . . *Protocols of the Elders of Zion*. (Steve writes the title of the book on the board, and students copy it into their journals.) It appeared in Russian in 1890. And it explained that there was an *international* group of Jews who used to get together and meet in a Jewish cemetery in Prague, at night, and they would plan *everything* that was going to happen in the world. (Josh taps Chi-Ho on the shoulder, as if to suggest that he should listen closely.) This book was republished in England in 1919. It was republished in the United States in the 1920s — in a newspaper owned by Henry Ford, one of the two or three most important men in the country! In England it was published in *the* most important newspaper — the *Times* of London. And the

most interesting thing about this book is — it's a fraud! It's complete nonsense! It's made up! (Josh again prods Chi-Ho and whispers something to him; Chi-Ho smiles awkwardly.)

How do you know it's a fraud? Well, in the 1890s, this book was written by members of the Russian police force. (Steve writes "1890 — Russian police force" hurriedly on the board.) And how do you know that? Well, because this book was actually *copied* (Steve's voice cracks in excitement) from a book that was written in 1864 in France that didn't blame *Jews*, but that said the ruler of France, Napoleon III, was trying to take over the world (he writes "Napoleon, 1864" on the board). And everywhere where Napoleon appears in *this* book (Steve points to the original text), the word *Jews* appears in this one (he points to the words "Elders of Zion"). Think about this for a second! A French book in 1864 was copied by the Russians in 1890. The British copied the Russians. And the Americans copied the British. And it's a complete fraud! It's hocus pocus! It's untrue! It's a *lie*. And millions and millions of people believed it. (Pause). How come?

Susie: Because nobody told them any differently.

Alan: Because they believed it was written by someone who knew!

Josh: A lot of people want to blame somebody else for all of their problems.

Chi-Ho: Because then you're not responsible for what happens to people.

"Exactly!" Steve exclaims. "There are a lot of things that happen that are really beyond our control. An idea like this says — even if it's someone you hate, *somebody* is in control. Somebody is in charge of what's going on. And even if things are *lousy*, it's nice to be able to say, it wouldn't be lousy if it weren't for these bums. Let me show you how this happened in real life! This should take about five hours, but I'll do it in three minutes. You ready?" Students nod that they are.

For the next several minutes, Steve gives a remarkably clear and concise account of the infamous turn-of-the-century case in which Alfred Dreyfus, one of the few Jewish officers in the French Army, was falsely accused of giving military secrets to the Germans, convicted in two trials, and sentenced to prison on Devil's Island. "Many people said, 'How could Dreyfus have done it alone?' And others said, 'Aha, he didn't! He was part of this!' " (Steve points again to "Elders of Zion" on the board).

Abby asks, "Is that thing called the international Jewish conspiracy?" Steve explains: "In France, they called it the 'Syndicat.' And they referred to it as the 'international Jewish conspiracy.' There's a tremendous *power* in this kind of idea. Why were people so willing to believe it of Jews? Would they have believed it if this was . . . about Catholics? Would that have been popular in Europe?" "No," answers Sandra, "there are a lot of Catholics, so it wouldn't be as easy as singling out one Jew." Abby interjects, "What things you believe in will also depend upon the family you grow up in." Steve agrees, and draws the thorny issue of an international Jewish conspiracy to a close by reinforcing the curriculum's valuation of critical thinking. He says, "One of the things you're going to have to decide is whether you're going to believe what people say, or whether you're going to try to figure it out on your own."

Chi-Ho has remained conspicuously silent throughout this entire discussion. Often quiet in class, his behavior today is not unusual. Today's lecture, however, is given in response to his earlier remark, and it would seem to call for his participation. While only Josh makes a point of publicly acknowledging the connection between the previous class and today's by tugging at Chi-Ho's shirt-sleeve and whispering to him repeatedly, other students shoot furtive glances in Chi-Ho's direction. Chi-Ho seems to studiously ignore all meaningful looks. Though he appears to be listening throughout class and assiduously copies Steve's blackboard notes into his journal, he does not acknowledge that today's lecture was, however subtly, directed at him.

This is by no means the case with Abby when the second item on today's agenda is discussed. Referring to a set of maps of the pre- and post-World War I period, Steve shows how the world has changed since the fall of the Ottoman Empire. He points to the Middle East region and says: "There are White people, Black people, and Brown people living here. It's a whole Rainbow Coalition! After World War I, one of the major questions was — should people like this be able to rule *themselves*? And the winners of the war — France, Britain, and the United States — say 'No!' They give them independence with training wheels, and the winners of the war are gonna be the training wheels! These people end up living in countries which are *invented* after World War I. It's all a product of politics! Well, what kinds of problems might the 'training wheels' encounter?"

"They had to make sure the new boundaries wouldn't get people mad because they don't want to start another war," Alan answers thoughtfully. Nora adds, "They needed to keep people together with their own people so they'll be content." Drawing his finger across a large section of the map, Steve describes how Transjordan was ruled by the victorious British until 1948. "And who lived here?" he asks simply, pointing to Palestine. "Palestinians," Abby replies. Steve continues, asking, "Who were they, and what was their religion?" "They were Arabs," Abby responds. "They were Moslems, Jews, and Christians," corrects Steve. "To be a 'Palestinian' meant literally to live in Palestine. And they all lived under British rule."

For the next several minutes, Steve helps the class review what happened to Jews in the years leading up to and immediately following World War II. Josh remembers that Jews tried to get out of Europe, but often had no place to go. Angela believes many headed for Palestine because they had "religious ties there." Nora comments that it was often impossible to return to their homes because "they were taken by people, like their neighbors." Zeke adds that their possessions were taken, too.

"Lots of Jews lived in detention camps for two or three years after the war," Steve explains. "The Jews in Palestine want the European Jews to come there, but the Arabs and Christians don't want them to. The British have control of Palestine and they don't know what to do with it. Since the British can't figure it out, they give the problem to the United Nations, which functions as an international government with representatives from different countries. This is the U.N.'s big moment! Well, in 1947 the U.N. votes to divide Palestine again, into a state for Jews and a state for non-Jews."

"Is this when the eight-day war took place?" Josh interjects, reviving his previous comment. "No," Steve answers, "that took place later." Nora comments, "The U.N. is made up of representatives from all different countries, right? So, what did the Palestinian representative do?" Supportive and genuinely impressed, Steve exclaims, "That's a great question! There wasn't one, since Palestine was under British rule." "Well," Nora continues, "did the majority of the non-Jews in Palestine agree with the decision?" Steve responds, "Absolutely not! The majority of people were not happy. So in 1948 a war occurs — it's a small war compared to World War I and World War II — and in that war, the *Jewish* side of Palestine manages to survive, but the *non-Jewish* region gets taken — not by Israel, but by 'Transjordan.' . . . The Jewish part becomes Israel, but the non-Jewish part becomes Jordan and Egypt."

Abby is getting frustrated with Steve's version of history. She breaks in in a loud and exasperated voice, "But there was lots of violence between the Jews and non-Jews! A lot of people were killed! People were kicked off their homes. It was just like in the Holocaust!" Steve acknowledges the complexity of the situation but is direct in his rebuttal. Calmly and with authority, he asserts, "That's not quite true; part of it's true, but it's *very* complex. There were broadcasts telling people to leave their land, and many people *wanted* to leave because they wanted to get away from the war. When the Israeli government came in, they didn't know what to do with the Arab land. The people that fled their homes *do* end up living in camps, but that was the choice of the Jordanians, not the Israelis."

Abby objects, saying, "But they shouldn't have had to leave in the first place!" "They *chose* to leave," Steve responds, "There's *no* question that this displaced people and that people lost their homes who didn't want to. But there's also *no* question that extermination was *not* the policy. . . . The other thing is that many Jews in these Arab countries also lost *their* homes. One of the things that happens in times of war is that international human rights are *completely* neglected. This should make us think very closely about the policies of international government — they're *not* extermination policies, but they're also not policies that make it very easy for people to live their lives in the way they would like to." Abby isn't satisfied. "But if the Palestinians hadn't been kicked off . . ." she begins. Steve breaks in, "Do you mean the Palestinian non-Jews?" Accommodating Steve's language, Abby continues, "OK, if the Palestinian non-Jews hadn't been kicked off, why should they be so angry about not having their land?" "Oh, well! They've spent the past forty years living in camps and wanting to be on their parents' land!" Steve responds.

Most students have remained silent yet attentive during this exchange. Sandra sits close by Abby and does not come to her aid, despite Abby's frequent, beseeching looks in her direction. Josh only half-hides a smirk, seemingly pleased that Steve is taking Abby on. He now contributes to the discussion, "But there was another war!" and Steve replies, "There have been *lots* of wars. The tension Abby speaks to developed more after the land was taken in 1967. Many people believe that land should be exchanged for peace. There's a large Peace Now movement in Israel today saying that those territories should be given back to the Palestinian Arabs."

"But they *won* the war!" Josh repeats emphatically. "I learned that in Temple!" Steve responds by briefly highlighting different points of view within contemporary Israeli (Jewish) society. He is careful to distinguish between current policies and those on which the state was founded. Though he admits the existence of conflicting perspectives within contemporary Israeli society, he leaves less room for alternative interpretation when it comes to the founding of the state ("The tension Abby speaks to developed more after the land was taken in 1967," he says, and he suggests that Palestinians were not "kicked off" their land but "*chose*" to leave it). Though Steve is by no means alone in articulating this perspective (and in distinguishing it from current Israeli policies), it nonetheless reflects only one particular viewpoint in a complex and contentious historical debate.[14]

Some of Steve's other interventions are also grounded in a particular political stance. While acknowledging that the founding of the State of Israel was accompanied by some human rights violations, he denies that those violations were systematic or a matter of official policy. Moments later, he "corrects" Abby's language by recommending that she refer to Arabs as "Palestinian non-Jews" — a categorization that is itself not politically neutral, and arguably comparable to referring to Blacks as non-Whites or women as non-men. Like Marysa in the earlier classroom incident, Steve acts in somewhat contradictory ways, eliciting students' diverse viewpoints on the one hand while undermining the legitimacy of those with which he disagrees on the other.

Class nearly over, students begin to close their notebooks and put them inside their desks. Marysa and Steve turn to each other and begin speaking privately in the front of the room; they express pleasure and relief at having gotten through a potentially difficult session without drawing too much fire.

That neither Steve nor Marysa entirely transcended their own political beliefs in interpreting and responding to political differences within the classroom is not surprising; I would argue that no one can do so. These beliefs are a part of our internal make-up, as operative within these teachers as they are within my own interpretations of their practice. I did not leave my own political beliefs at the door when I entered the classroom; they were within me as I observed each class. These perspectives no doubt influenced how I interpreted classroom tensions between eliciting and muting student voice. As a Jewish woman strongly committed to a peaceful resolution of the Israeli-Palestinian conflict, I felt strongly opposed to Chi-Ho's remarks and to Abby's more extreme comments, even though I disagreed with how the teachers at times responded to both of these students.

Interviews conducted individually with Chi-Ho, Abby, Josh, and Sandra shortly after these classes took place support my interpretation of these classroom events as political in nature.[15] By "political" I mean to suggest not only the content of the classroom debate (in which a diversity of political views were expressed), but also the process by which it was negotiated (whereby controversial voices were silenced by those with greater authority and power). In these instances, power was exercised between students and their teachers; between Marysa and Steve; and among the students themselves. So, too, the relations among these players were hierarchical: some were given (or assumed) more authority to speak than others. And, depending on one's point of view, opposing positions were granted legitimacy or invalidated. In the process, some students felt silenced and subordinated, while others felt empowered and privileged.

In the course of our interviews, Chi-Ho and Abby express discomfort at feeling "unheard" and "misunderstood" in class, while Sandra and Josh enjoy the fact that these students were silenced. Expressing frustration with being "misunderstood," Chi-Ho remarks, "[Josh] wouldn't listen! . . . [It felt] terrible . . . I was disappointed. I *really* think that Marysa didn't really listen to me very carefully, and, if she *did*, she would understand what I meant."

Abby's response to the classes under study is multifaceted. She initially admits to being confused by Steve's alternative reading of historical events and expresses concern for (what she imagines to be) *his* discomfort. Portraying *herself* as the agent of her silencing (rather than Steve), Abby notes:

I *really* was confused by what he said, because, from what *I* had read (because my parents have a lot of books about that), it *really* was the total *opposite* of what he was saying. And, I mean, I *didn't* want to make a scene, so I didn't really, you know, say as much as I could have? I *didn't* want to totally contradict him, 'cause it would have made him feel uncomfortable. So I just kind of left it.

Moments later, however, Abby suggests that this self-censorship was not entirely voluntary. Though she hesitantly adopts Steve's terminology, she nevertheless defends her own perspective and argues that he was unable to hear it:

I thought about it a lot *during* and *afterwards* and, I *really* think that his point of view was *really, really* closed-minded! I mean, he thought about what I had to say, but he basically said it was totally wrong! . . . I was *trying to tell him* that from what *I've learned*, the situation between (pause) Palestinian non-Jews and the *Jews* was *very* oppressive, and one-sided, and it was really an awful situation! And he kind of *glorified* it in a way, and made it sound like it wasn't as violent as it really was!

While Abby eventually admits to having modified some of her own thinking in response to Steve, she seems frustrated that he has not done the same:

I didn't really mean *millions* because there weren't that many Palestinian non-Jews in the country. . . . *He* was right, because I thought about it and it wasn't really *extermination*. But they *really* wanted them to move off that land! And it was *their* homeland in the first place! And I *meant* that by taking them out of their home, as the Nazis did with the Jews, they put them in something that was like a *camp* where they weren't allowed to have any *human* rights that most people take for granted. I agree with him that the methods weren't exactly extermination but I *don't* agree with him when he says it wasn't as bad as in the *first* steps [of the Holocaust].

In contrast, neither Josh nor Sandra expresses discomfort with classroom dynamics, but they instead express pleasure in Steve's having silenced those with whom they disagree. Sandra notes with satisfaction, "When Steve came in and told Abby, 'You're wrong!' well, it was kind of funny, because she got like, *really mad*." Josh similarly notes, "Steve, he's great! He came in and he said this is total nonsense." Whispering "Don't tell her, but Abby talks a lot!" Josh takes pleasure in describing a contentious class in which his own beliefs reflect majority opinion while Abby's are seen as marginal. "I like when people make sure people know what's going on," he says later of Steve's also having put Chi-Ho in his place.

These excerpts suggest a confluence between my interpretation of classroom dynamics and students' experience of the course. Though students differed among themselves in their feelings about classroom dynamics, they shared my belief that both Marysa and Steve conveyed their own sense of "right" and "wrong" to the class and made sure, as Josh says, that "people know what's going on."

Tuesday, May 15

The day after Steve Cohen's visit, students return to the issue of contemporary political conflicts as originally intended by the curricular text. Walking toward the back of the class with a videotape in hand, Marysa begins: "We've talked about the thirties and the forties, and we've seen a movie about something happening in Canada in the eighties. Now we're going to look at our own home, the U.S. This documentary film is about the Ku Klux Klan teaching kids *your* age.[16] Imagine if you grew up in a town, an all-Black town, say, and you *adored* your teacher, and he told you all about all the horrible things Whites did — many of which I think are true. Would it be easy to believe it?" "It would be real easy," Jamal answers without hesitation, " 'cause he'd be my role model." "That's why indoctrination is so scary," Marysa continues, "and so important to understand. If you hear something again and again from someone you believe in, and you don't hear anything else, even though it may be one person's perspective, you'll probably believe it. . . . So in a way the diversity around you here, and the strengths from the differences of opinion you hear, and the strengths of the educational system you're in, encourage you to question and to learn different points of view. Try to think about that while you're watching this." Marysa pops the video cassette into the VCR, Angela hits the lights, and students settle down to watch TV.

"Klan Youth Corps" is a 1982 film about how the Ku Klux Klan recruits and trains American youth. Filled with riveting footage of actual night-time cross-burning ceremonies and stirring appeals made by the Klan's Imperial Wizard, the film documents 10- to 17-year-olds receiving instruction in racist ideology. The Imperial Wizard implores, "We will kill. We will stand in the streets. We will do what we have to to stop the niggers and the communists, won't we?" A counselor warns preteens at a Klan Youth summer camp that "many of the things you read in school are not the truth — they're just lies." And row upon row of cleanly scrubbed White boys and girls stand at attention and recite the Klan Youth Corps pledge in unison: "I pledge to practice racial separation in all my social contacts and to keep my forced contacts with other races on a strictly business basis. I pledge to oppose the false teaching that all races are equal or the same. I pledge that I will immediately go to the aid of any White person being attacked physically or verbally by a person of another race. I pledge that I will fight for the complete separation of all races in America and I will recruit others to do the same." The film is as direct as it is unnerving.

Marysa stops the tape and hits "rewind," while Angela turns on the lights. "Why don't people arrest the KKK?" Alison immediately asks. "They're protected by the First Amendment," Marysa replies. "Also, in a small town like that, people aren't going to stand up to it 'cause they'll probably believe it!" comments Alan. "They can pass out literature and wear their robes," Marlene adds, "but until they kill someone, or get caught killing someone, you can't do anything." Nora comments, "I understand that they're protected by the First Amendment, but I also think that they might abuse it. You never know how far they'll go."

Acknowledging that there's a big controversy about this, Marysa mentions the case in which members of the American Nazi Party won the right to march in Skokie, Illinois, after having been defended by the ACLU on the grounds of freedom of speech. The proud son of a prominent civil liberties attorney, Josh corrects Marysa matter-of-factly: "Freedom to assemble." Marysa continues, putting forth the traditional civil liberties argument, "If you stop *them*, who decides the next group that cannot speak?" Abby and Marysa debate this point:

Abby: I think society should be able to decide who should not speak.

Marysa: But "society" can fluctuate from time to time, group to group.

Abby: But the majority of society is not in support of oppression.

Marysa: What about people under Hitler?

Abby: If Hitler hadn't had the right to free speech, people wouldn't have believed him!

Marysa: Where do you draw the line? How do you decide who can and who can't speak? The First Amendment protects *everybody's* rights.

Abby: But millions of people don't agree with them!

Marysa: Let's say we wouldn't let socialists or communists speak.

Abby: But they're not oppressing other people!

Marysa: Capitalists feel they are.

Abby (laughing): Well, they're *wrong*!

Marysa: Abby, there's a bit of tunnel vision here that we have to speak about. You can't just say that the only ones who can speak are those who agree with your position!

As in the case of the two earlier classes described, this resource film and the discussion that followed raise the dilemma of how a democratic community that values free speech, diversity, and the open exchange of ideas can fairly address unpopular, controversial, or "wrong" points of view. Should those who voice these views simply be silenced, as Abby believes with regard to the KKK and to others who hold "oppressive" beliefs? And as Marysa — the individual holding the most power within the class — rejoins, who should define what constitutes "oppression" and be empowered to enact this silencing? As we have seen, answers to these questions are no simpler to find in the microcosm of the classroom than they are in Skokie, Illinois. Students' experiences of how issues raised by the film are handled in the classroom are contradictory. On one hand, they talk about valuing open-mindedness, a plurality of opinions, and the importance of free expression; on the other, at times they seek closure to controversies and rest easier in being told which opinions are "right."

For example, Sandra pays Steve a high compliment consistent with her valuation of "keeping an open mind": "You know, Steve doesn't just read one book and say, 'Well, this one book is right,'" she tells me during our interview. "He's the kind of person who reads lots of things, in depth." She criticizes Abby, in contrast, for failing to do the same: "Abby, she's not having an open mind! She's just so set about what she wants to believe."

But while Sandra values open-mindedness in theory, she herself finds it difficult to sustain. Overwhelmed by the diversity of opinions offered on the Middle East, she asks me to provide closure to this contentious debate, saying, "There's that issue about how the people were moved out. And Abby says some of the same things that were used in the Holocaust were used *there*, like murdering people, and some women were raped. And, then Steve said that they were *asked* to leave, and they left voluntarily. So I don't know which to believe! Because Abby said she's read it in books, and that Steve just learned it in *conservative* books, and, see, I don't know! So who is more, who is *more right*?" Disquieted by my refusal to grant either position full legitimacy, she eventually consoles herself in the best pluralist tradition: "There could be Steve's point of view, and [Abby's] point of view, and then mix them together and there could be something that they could come to."

Josh's approach to the problem is negotiated differently. At first glance he seems desirous of silencing those with whom he disagrees. He argues for "killing" people who hold beliefs like those of Holocaust revisionist Jim Keegstra and he appears equally dismissive of Abby's point of view. A longtime friend of Chi-Ho's, however, he is torn between an impulse to shut his friend out altogether (as manifested in his desire to move his seat) and an impulse to engage him in struggle (as manifested in his ribbing of Chi-Ho in class). He ultimately supports the second position, though he clearly has difficulty doing so. Evoking the words of his much-revered father, Josh says, "I've been taught that you do not start violence with people, and that the only way to prove yourself as a great person is to talk to people, to make them see that what they're saying is *so wrong*. This is what me and my father used to disagree on, but I'm beginning to believe him."

Abby seems to embody most dramatically the tensions between valuing open-mindedness and taking a clear moral stance. Reflecting the political priorities of her parents, she argues passionately in favor of social change and sees eliciting different points of view as essential to achieving it, saying, "I *really* believe that there needs to be some change in the world today! And I think a *really* important part of *change* is understanding what someone else is *thinking*. . . . If you just *come* out *say* what you think, and give *no* regard to what the *other* person is thinking, then that will create anger. And *resentment*. And they won't really be open to change." Knowing that the points of view of her fellow classmates are important in this regard, Abby continues, "I'm usually one of the only ones who is really speaking up, and I *really* want to know what other people think about what I'm saying . . . so maybe I could either argue it out, and *really* try to tell them what my point of view was, or just hear what other people are thinking about. . . . Because if they don't *speak*, I'm totally, totally closed off from anything that they're thinking about."

But while Abby campaigns eloquently for lively debates in which multiple points of view are brought out into the open, she argues equally well against granting each view legitimacy. Far from falling into a relativist trap, she asserts, "I *do* believe that there is *always* a *right* thing! And a lot of people have the impression that it's just your *opinion*. And your point of view. And they don't really give a chance to have one be right. It's just always 'They should be able to say that because that's their *opinion*.' And I really, really *don't* agree with that!" Directly challenging the civil libertarian line promoted by Marysa in reference to the KKK, she charges, "I think that the *right* thing should always be promoted and the people who think *otherwise* should not be allowed to speak!"

* * *

Students' contradictory yearnings for both closure and openness may be irresolvably in tension. Teachers' efforts to foster tolerance for alternative perspectives may be similarly at odds with their efforts to promote moral thinking. The ambiguities, conflicts, and tensions that arose during these three classroom sessions demonstrate the enormous challenge of debating contemporary social and political issues in the classroom.

There are those who oppose interjecting contemporary issues into the classroom for precisely these reasons. Conservative activists like Phyllis Schlafly, for example, have in the past attacked the Facing History and Ourselves program precisely because it encourages adolescents to reflect critically on current social issues. Condemning the program in national public hearings in 1984, she charged that it (and other so-called "therapy education" initiatives) could "depress the child" by "forc[ing] [him] to confront adult problems which are too complex and unsuitable for his tender years."[17] By causing the child to be "emotionally and morally confused," they could, she felt, lead to the "high rates of teenage suicide, loneliness, premarital sex, and pregnancies" that plague contemporary society.[18]

The Department of Education's National Diffusion Network — an agency that reviews curricula and funds their dissemination — reflected Schlafly's concerns in 1986–1988 when it denied funds to the Facing History program. The Department's action sparked a congressional hearing and heated debate among public-policy makers, educators, and other concerned citizens.[19]

But one need not look as far back as the mid-eighties to find opposition to classroom discourse on contemporary social and political debates. Only recently, the New York City Board of Education ousted Chancellor Joseph A. Fernandez, largely because of his support for initiatives that included AIDS education, condom distribution, and a curriculum that advocated tolerance for diverse social groups, including homosexuals. According to Carol Ann Gresser, the New York School Board's newly elected chair, parents were upset by Fernandez's promotion of a "social agenda" in the schools. "You can't bring into the classroom issues that haven't even been decided by the society," she said.[20]

I would argue exactly the opposite: one cannot possibly avoid bringing into the classroom issues over which society is still divided because students themselves are well aware of these issues and hungry to discuss them with their peers. The liveliness of the classroom sessions presented here testify to students' investment in just such debates. While these students were at times discomforted by what transpired in class, they were also vitally invested, excited, and engaged in the struggle. Though Sandra begged for closure, she tolerated not getting it; though Josh demanded separation from Chi-Ho, he remained sitting next to his friend; though Marysa opposed Abby, she engaged with her in open debate; though Abby felt intimidated, she hung in and held her ground. In short, while tempers were high, feelings impassioned, and intellects fiercely engaged, the group never closed down or fell apart. Highly conscious of their differences and the fault lines that divide them on specific issues, the class remained a community throughout. Their ability to do so reflects the skill with which Marysa created an environment of relative trust and safety within the classroom, and Facing History's engendering of personal, critical reflection no doubt contributed to that effort. But the strengths and capacities that students bring with them into this or any other classroom — their hunger to sort out where they stand and their ripeness for engaging in just such debates — must also be taken into account.

Thus, though opponents may argue that the inevitable consequence of such classroom interactions is either political indoctrination or the promotion of moral relativism, I would contend that neither is a necessary outcome nor an accurate characterization. What does seem inevitable is ambiguity and conflict — on this point, at least, advocates and opponents both agree. But here, too, programs encouraging engagement with social, moral, and/or political issues may offer a possible passageway through trouble — not by denying conflict through positing an unproblematized, homogeneous ideal, but by helping students to take well-thought-out stands and to listen closely to each other. Hopefully, by doing so they will learn to tolerate more fully the conflicts they will inevitably encounter in the world beyond the classroom. At their best, what programs like Facing History and Ourselves may offer students is not a blueprint for creating a single ideal community but practice in making webs among multiple ones. And that is essential to education in a democracy.

Notes

1. At the request of school administrators, the names of the school and its students and teachers have been changed.
2. Information about this curriculum can be obtained from Facing History and Ourselves, 16 Hurd Road, Brookline, MA 02146 (617-232-1595). The organization develops and disseminates curricular materials and runs an extensive training program to prepare teachers to teach the curriculum.
3. Throughout this article, the term "Holocaust" is used to refer to the Nazi genocide of Jews.
4. See Alan Stoskopf and Margot Stern Strom, *Choosing to Participate: A Critical Examination of Citizenship in American History* (Brookline, MA: Facing History and Ourselves, 1990); Margot Strom and William Parsons, *Facing History and Ourselves: Holocaust and Human Behavior* (Watertown, MA: Intentional Educations, 1982).
5. See Melinda Fine, "Collaborative Innovations: Documentation of the Facing History and Ourselves Program at an Essential School," *Teachers College Record*, 94, No. 4 (1993), 776.
6. Strom and Parsons, *Facing History*.
7. Strom and Parsons, *Facing History*, p. 14.
8. See Melinda Fine, "Facing History and Ourselves: Portrait of a Classroom," Special Issue: "Whose Culture?" *Educational Leadership* (1991/1992), 44–49; Fine, "Collaborative Innovations," pp. 771–789; Melinda Fine, "The Politics and Practice of Moral Education: A Case Study of Facing History and Ourselves," Diss., Harvard Graduate School of Education, 1991; and Melinda Fine, *Habits of Mind: Struggling over Values in America's Classrooms* (San Francisco: Jossey-Bass, 1995).
9. Strom and Parsons, *Facing History*, pp. 383, 387.
10. See, for example, Sara Lawrence Lightfoot, *The Good High School: Portraits of Character and Culture* (New York: Basic Books, 1983). For an excellent discussion of the similarities and differences between portraiture and other forms of social science inquiry, see Marue Walizer, "Watch With Both Eyes: Narratives and Social Science: Sources of Insight into Teachers' Thinking," Diss., Harvard University Graduate School of Education, 1987, pp. 12–47, 101–129.
11. Eudora Welty, *The Eye of the Storm: Selected Essays and Reviews* (New York: Vintage Books, 1979), p. 129.
12. All quotations of in-class comments are from written notes taken while class was in session.
13. "Lessons in Hate," distributed by Intersection Associates, Cambridge, Massachusetts, and available through the Facing History and Ourselves Resource Library.
14. See, for example, Zachary Lockman, "Original Sin," in *Intifada: The Palestinian Uprising Against Israeli Occupation*, ed. Zachary Lockman and Joel Beinin (Boston: South End Press, 1989), pp. 185–204.
15. All interviews with students were tape-recorded. Students' verbal emphases are indicated in the text in italics.
16. "Klan Youth Corps," distributed by the Anti-Defamation League of B'nai B'rith, New York, New York, and available through the Facing History and Ourselves Resource Library in Brookline, Massachusetts.
17. Phyllis Schlafly, *Child Abuse in the Classroom* (Illinois: Pere Marquette Press, 1984), pp. 435–437.
18. Schlafly, *Child Abuse*, p. 12.
19. For a fuller discussion of this controversy, see Fine, *Dilemmas of Difference*.
20. "A Full-Time Volunteer," *New York Times*, May 13, 1993, p. B3.

Arts as Epistemology:
Enabling Children to Know
What They Know

KAREN GALLAS

In this chapter, Karen Gallas explores the learning processes of the students in her first-grade classroom to find out how students come to know what they know. In their unit on insects, focusing on the theme of life cycles, the students and teacher use the arts as their central learning methodology. Students both learn and express their understandings of the academic content through a variety of art mediums: drama, poetry, visual arts, movement, and music. "True knowing," according to Gallas, involves "transformation and change" rather than memorization and regurgitation. Gallas as teacher is able to provide the opportunity for her students — even those who may be labeled as having some kind of learning deficiency or who begin their education outside of the educational "mainstream" — to attain this kind of true knowing by encouraging their impulses and instincts for the artistic way of learning and expressing. Reflecting on her experiences in her own classroom and the implications for the larger educational community, Gallas concludes that "the arts offer opportunities for reflection upon the content and the process of learning, and they foster a deeper level of communication about what knowledge is and who is truly in control of the learning process."

One afternoon in early June, six children and I crowd around a butterfly box watching a painted lady chrysalis twitch and turn as the butterfly inside struggles to break free. Juan, who is seated on a chair next to the box, holds a clipboard on his lap and is carefully sketching the scene. This is his third sketch of the day chronicling the final stage in the life cycle of the butterfly. It will complete a collection he began in early May, when mealworms arrived in our first-grade classroom. As he draws, the children agonize over the butterfly's plight. They have been watching since early that morning, and they all wonder if the butterfly will ever get out. Sophia smiles to herself and then begins to hum a tune.

"I'll sing it out," she says.

"Yeah, let's sing it out!" agrees Matthew, and all of the children begin to improvise a song. Juan looks up, smiles, and continues to sketch.

Harvard Educational Review Vol. 61 No. 1 February 1991, 40–50

Events such as these have become almost commonplace in my classroom. Over the course of the school year, this class of children questioned, researched, wondered, and discussed their way through a wide variety of subject matter and concepts. What distinguished their learning process from that of many other children, however, was the presence of the arts as an integral part of their curriculum: as a methodology for acquiring knowledge, as subject matter, and as an array of expressive opportunities. Drawing and painting, music, movement, dramatic enactment, poetry, and storytelling: each domain, separately and together, became part of their total repertoire as learners.

By describing the development of a unit on insects, this article will show how the arts can play an essential role in forming and extending all aspects of a curriculum. The concept of life cycles, which informed our study throughout, was the focus of several months of work for my first-grade class. Eighteen children, from a range of socioeconomic, racial, and cultural backgrounds, and including four different language groups, participated in this study from late winter through the month of June. What happened in this class could happen in any class of children. Each group brings a wide range of life experience to school, and, though we are often initially separated by language, culture, and racial barriers, I have learned that the creative arts, rather than labeling our differences, enable us to celebrate them.

Juan arrived in September from Venezuela, speaking no English but filled with joy at being in school. As I struggled during our first few weeks together to find out what he could and could not do (and found out that, according to my teacher's agenda, he could not do many things), Juan very graciously attempted to help me understand what he could do. He would tolerate a few minutes of my informal assessment activities and then use his one word of English: "Paint?" he would suggest cheerfully, and by that time I would agree. "Paint," for Juan, meant drawing, painting, modeling, or constructing, and it was his passion. As the weeks passed, I continued to be amazed by his talent and frustrated by his inability to learn the alphabet and basic readiness skills. However, Juan's own nonchalance about the process of learning to read and write was somewhat contagious, and I began to see that his art was presenting both what he had already learned at home and in school and what he desired to learn. It soon became clear that our forays into the world of number and letter recognition would be fruitless without Juan's skill as an artist. His visual representations became a catalogue of science information and science questions, and that information began to provide material for his involvement in reading and writing — and learning a new language. As Juan drew, we built a reading and speaking vocabulary from his pictures, and that vocabulary, together with his interest in representing science, also became the subject matter of his writing.

Juan was teaching me once again a lesson that I seem to have to relearn each year: when given the opportunity, listen to the children. They will show you what they know and how they learn best, and often that way is not the teacher's way. Because I am a teacher, my unspoken agenda is shaped by academic expectations: I am supposed to present concepts and skills, and the children are supposed to "master" those skills and concepts. Unfortunately, the journey toward mastery of a subject is often inextricably tied to instruments of assessment, presentation, and communication that are designed by and for teachers. Tests, workbook pages, teacher-led discussions, textbooks, charts — each of these assumes a commonality of experience that the children in a classroom may not share. Each artificially separates

Illustration by Juan

the process of mastery from that of individual expression. Each of these excludes the full participation of some portion of the population I teach.

How do young children convey their understanding of the world around them? Before they begin school, and even in the primary grades, most children depend on play, movement, song, dramatic play, and artistic activity as their means of making sense of the world. That these pastimes gradually give way to predominantly "adult" styles of communication is more a tribute to the power of traditional schooling and parental pressure than a statement of the natural process of expressive maturation. What unfolds each year in a classroom that places the arts as a centerpiece of the curriculum is simply a continuation of the early preoccupations of childhood. Children, unlike most of their teachers and parents, are comfortable using virtually all of the expressive modalities. Because one does not need to teach the "how" of the artistic process to them, their ability to use the arts for their own educational process is expansive.

Developing a multi-arts curriculum allows me to follow the children's own expressive interests while also using the artistic process as an integral part of the identification and expansion of their knowledge in different areas. This method goes beyond the use of art as an enhancement or enrichment of an already established curriculum and makes the arts central to the completion of the curricular process. For both teacher and child, the arts offer an expanded notion of classroom discourse that is not solely grounded in linear, objective language and thinking, but rather recognizes the full range of human potential for expression and understanding.

From the first days of our study of the life cycle of insects, we used basic creative and critical thinking skills to identify our existing knowledge base. What did these children know about insects, and what did they want to know? As a group, we brainstormed, sharing our common knowledge, and in the process generated questions we wanted to answer. Later we drew a semantic map to extend and relate our ideas.

What We Know About Insects	*Questions About Insects*
Birds eat them.	Are caterpillars insects?
They have six legs.	How many legs do beetles have?
Some are furry or slimy.	Do all insects have legs?
Some help trees.	Do all insects fly?
Some fly.	How do fireflies light up?
Some eat fruit.	Why do fireflies light up?
Some people eat them.	How do insects grow?
They could destroy the earth.	How do insects swallow?
Some eat wood.	Do they have teeth?
Some live underground.	How old can an insect get?
Some are dangerous.	How do they smell?
Some insects eat other insects.	How many kinds are there?
Most have antennae.	Do insects have lips?
Some have wings and don't fly.	Do they all hop?
Some insects are poisonous.	Do they smell with antennae?
Some help plants.	
Some insects eat plants.	
Some insects have stingers.	

Our study then began in earnest with observations of mealworms. We observed, sketched, and took notes on their behavior. Juan discovered in our second day of sketching that one of his mealworms was in the process of shedding its skin. Thus began the first in his series of meticulous sketches, both from live animals and from nonfiction books about insects. As a class, we spent the afternoons in the first week sketching, studying books and photographs, discussing entomological drawings by different artists, and observing the mealworms and caterpillars. On Friday we showed some of the sketches, and talked about what we were learning. The children were very impressed by the work, and those who hadn't been sketching asked Juan how he got so good.

"I practice a lot," he said, and our discussion continued about why we were sketching.

David: I'd heard people talk about this thing. I think it was a praying mantis, but I didn't know what it was. So I looked at a book, and then I drew it, and then I knew what it was.

Juan: Or if you don't know what a wing is and how it's made you can draw it and then you know.

A few days later, Adam was seated by himself, trying to sketch a picture of a monarch butterfly from a book. Since September Adam had struggled with fine motor tasks, such as drawing, cutting, or construction, but he was so impressed with the

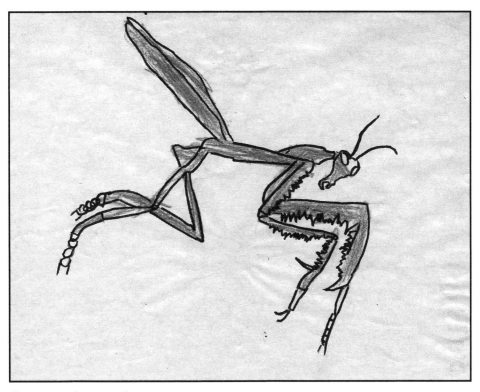

Illustration by David

work of other children that he had decided to try to do a sketch. As I watched, he was quite absorbed and had finished one wing, but the second wing was more difficult. He threw down his pencil, and I could see he was going to cry. "Don't stop, Adam," I said, and he nodded, wiped his eyes, and picked up the pencil.

Juan walked over to see what was wrong and offered a few suggestions. "You don't have to make it perfect today. Just draw it, then do more tomorrow." Adam went back to work. A few minutes later I saw him using the length of his forefinger to gauge how big the wingspread in the picture was. Juan came over to check, but said nothing. Adam continued until it was time to go home, and worked on the picture for another week until it was finished. He had done a beautiful, meticulous job, and he asked if I could make copies for the class to share.

It is intense artistic activity like this that begins in the early stages of learning and continues throughout a study that enables children to become immersed in a subject. The deep involvement in representing the form of an insect, whether it is one that has been observed or one only pictured in books, expands the child's basic knowledge of that organism and his or her ability to represent it both in thought and form. For Juan, visual representation is a natural process. It is his method for examining his world, as well as his means of externalizing what he is learning for others to share. For Adam, who excels in reading, writing, and abstract thought, but who often has a difficult time communicating and interacting with other children, the artistic process of drawing the monarch butterfly expands his own boundaries of symbolic representation and gives him a new way to reach out to other children. Adam often approached the learning process in a highly verbal and discursive manner, delighting in puns and playing on words or ideas in his speech and writing. These abstractions sometimes eluded his classmates, and thus the act of presenting himself in a visually compelling form became a new challenge for him as a learner.

One day early in our study, Carolyn made a special request. She had finished reading most of our nonfiction resource books, but she wanted to know if I had any poems about insects. I was sure I did, but I wondered why. She explained:

> A poem is a little short, and it tells you some things in a funny way. But a science book, it tells you things like on the news. . . . But in a poem, it's more . . . the poem teaches you, but not just with words.

Carolyn, whom I would often find throughout the year alone in the coat-cubbies writing poetry on scraps of paper, had reminded me that I had constructed my plans and gathered my resources too narrowly. Throughout the year as a class, we had used poetry as a way to gain more insight into whatever subject we were studying. Carolyn began to collect poems to read to the class about insects, and I reconsidered the place of poetry in this study. Her interest in metaphoric ways of knowing is not an isolated one. Poetry sometimes provides children with a window of insight that is broader than that offered in even the best nonfiction resources. Poetic form is often more suited to the thinking and writing of children than prose; it is spare, yet rich with sense impressions. It is a medium in which the images of wonder, curiosity, and analogic thinking, which so often characterize children's language, can flourish.

In the next week, our observations of insects continued outside, where each child found an insect habitat, observed the insect, sketched the habitat, and wrote field notes. Upon returning one afternoon, we shared our findings and began to discuss the relationships between our classroom study and our outdoor explorations. Soon after, we read *The Inch Boy* (Morimoto, 1986), a Japanese folk tale that describes the experiences of a character who never grows larger than an inch tall. The children were fascinated by the notion of living in the world as a tiny being. Adam wondered out loud what the world might be like for a tiny velvet spider mite: he had made the connection that I hoped would occur.

Jeffrey offered, "Well, what you might think is a hill would probably only be a pebble or a big piece of dirt."

"And," added Carolyn, "you might never see the blue sky, only just green and green and you'd think the top of the world was green." These ideas produced a lot of commotion, and before we left the meeting I asked the children to write a poem in the persona of an insect that they had observed. Sean chose the ant:

ANT

by Sean

I pretend I'm a ant
running and dodging birds.
Grass feels tickly under my feet.
Big trees shade me.

I climb a bush and I see buildings
houses and even other bugs too.
And then I see a watermelon seed
and I go off to carry it away with my friends.

After two weeks, the mealworms and caterpillars were pupating, and these observations, together with our classroom research and outdoor experiences, offered
an opportunity for us to compare the life cycles of several insects. Many children
had gained a great deal of new knowledge about different insects and their habits,
and their understanding had been shared in a variety of ways. I encouraged the
children to relate and expand their knowledge through movement and dramatiza-
tion. In small groups, they presented either the life cycle of an animal they had observed or one they had researched. Each group conferred, agreeing on an insect to
present, and then after some rehearsal mimed the stages of that insect's life cycle.
Sometimes each member of a small group enacted a different stage in that cycle,
while in other groups the members played out the transformation in unison. Brian
and Roberto lay on the floor, legs tucked against their sides, mirroring the slightly
visible legs on the mealworm pupa. I was surprised when they portrayed the transition from mealworm to pupa with such accuracy that even the timing of the twitch-
ing of the pupa was realistic.

For Brian, who might easily be labeled "attention deficit" because of his constant motion and distractibility, the action and focus of the movement experience
demonstrated how carefully he had observed and examined the mealworms, and it
also showed that Brian has the ability to translate his ideas into a kinetic modality
with great clarity. By offering him access to the arts of movement and enactment, I
have been able to see Brian's strengths: how carefully he observes and analyzes every detail of the world around him, and how creatively he solves challenging problems. Those strengths are often obscured by his behavioral problems, but when
Brian works through movement and drama, the behaviors that handicap him in
one situation become his gifts.

One of the more difficult tasks that I face as a teacher is moving children like
Brian beyond the level of acquiring new knowledge and ideas and asking them to
synthesize and apply their ideas to new and different contexts. It would be easy for
me to take a very basic approach to assessment and simply ask children to regurgi-
tate what they have learned, and we would have reached our goals: "Tell me the
facts of the life cycle of insects and label the stages on this diagram." Yet the act of
moving beyond simple knowledge acquisition toward true assimilation of learning
is the challenge for most children, and the process of assessing their learning in a
way that stimulates that growth is my challenge. True knowing means transformation and change, and it is that level of learning that I hope for but often find difficult to offer as a possibility to the children.

Fortunately, however, when given the opportunity, the children will provide me
with ideas to accomplish this goal. Sean, who is a talented artist, had become fascinated by the notion of relative size. He asked if he and Jeffrey could do a picture to
go with his poem. They spent a week working on a huge mural, drawing towering
blades of grass, large rocks, and giant sunflowers, then adding tiny insects trudging
up the huge plants. Sean's fascination, like Carolyn's, expanded my ideas of what
was possible, both for these children to grasp conceptually and for all of us to

achieve aesthetically. The union of critical and creative thinking that I had repeatedly observed taking place in the production of the mural, in Sophia's song about the struggle to complete a cycle, in Brian's translation of biological change into movement — this interaction that constantly occurs in the process of artistic activity is the key to an expansive curriculum.

Like the children, I must remain open to the potential of the arts to expand both my knowledge of the children I teach and my creative insight into the ongoing development of a curriculum. Many times I seem to miss opportunities to expand the children's experience because I am unable to see beyond the boundaries of my own goals for their learning. For example, Juan, our keen observer, in his careful scrutiny of all the pictures in our resource books, discovered a picture of a cocoon we had had in our room for several months but were unable to identify. The description in the book confirmed what we had observed in early May, when hundreds of tiny caterpillars came streaming out of the cocoon and then promptly took up residence in our garbage garden. There they crawled through the planters and wrapped themselves in pieces of leaves and potato skins. We were astonished and puzzled. The little caterpillars were, we read, called bagworms. Alison, who had brought us the cocoon in late winter, was terribly excited about the discovery. For several weeks we watched the survivors grow amidst the potato plants, which they preferred. They continued to cover themselves in leaves and debris.

At the same time, eight children, including Alison, had become involved in reading and sharing different "why" and "how" stories, such as *Why Mosquitoes Buzz in People's Ears* (Aardema, 1975) and selections from the *Just So Stories* (Kipling, 1902/1978), which explained occurrences in the natural world. For me, Juan's discovery of the bagworm and its habits, which struck us all as ludicrous but wonderful, and the children's interest in stories that offered humorous explanations of animal adaptation seemed to mesh with our class discussions of how animals and humans adapt to survive in their environments.

My realization that these events coalesced also addressed the challenge of developing an integrated arts curriculum that provides a range of arts experiences that will offer opportunities for *all* children to communicate their new knowledge and expanded understanding of the world. Every child is not a visual artist, like Juan or Sean, though some are; every child does not find expanded meaning through the poetic voice like Carolyn, though many do; and every child cannot represent an idea in movement or sound, like Brian and Roberto. The challenge, then, is to ensure that the range of experiences is broad enough to reveal each child's voice, and that those experiences spring from events that all of the children have shared in common.

Alison, whose shy demeanor and sparse language gives an impression of austere silence, is, in fact, a storyteller. Storytellers are often unknowingly discovered (and then eschewed by teachers) in the daily classroom event of sharing time. Their talents are rarely recognized in a classroom, because talk and telling is generally dominated by the teacher. Yet storytelling, as we know from studies of culture and folklore, is a way to pass on knowledge and information and is a dramatic event. Like drawing, music, and movement, it is also a preferred medium through which some children more adeptly clarify their relationship to the world and to their companions.

When I placed the challenge before the children of taking their new knowledge about insect life cycles and applying it to a different problem, Alison decided, with

Detail of illustration by Sean and Jeffrey

a few other children, that she wanted to make up a story to tell the class. Her story would explain how the bagworm came to carry the bag. At the same time, several other children decided to invent completely new insects based on their generalized knowledge of insects and draw or construct their imaginary habitats and life cycles. Alison proceeded to write a twelve-page story about the bagworm, which she edited and revised, realizing at one point that she had forgotten to explain allegorically that the female bagworm never comes out of the bag. When she finished, she told us a story in which the bagworm went from a tiny, unnoticed nuisance to a huge creature that ate everything in sight. In order to save themselves from the wrath of humans, the female worms decided to construct a bag to hide in, and they invited the males to join them. "But," said Alison in conclusion, "the males only stayed in the bags until they turned into moths, but the females were too scared to ever come all the way out, so they even laid their eggs inside of the bag, and then they died there." What Alison had described was the correct life cycle of those strange animals, but her vehicle for presenting it was entirely of her own invention.

The story enabled her to transform her observations and study of insects, and her involvement with a new literary genre, into a unique language event. In effect, Alison was creating her own folklore about a phenomenon she had observed in the world.

While Alison finished her project, other children created insects that were adapted to completely unique circumstances. I observed Ronit drawing a picture of her insect. She had labeled it with two parts: "head" and "body." I saw this and asked her to rethink what body parts an insect had. She looked at her drawing and back at me, then got up and went to fetch her science journal, opening it up to refer to a diagram we had used a few weeks earlier when we observed the mealworm beetles. On a new piece of paper, Ronit correctly redesigned her insect to include three body parts, colored it in with a bright yellow crayon, and began a third drawing of the insect in its habitat. As she drew, she told me it was going to live in the grass when it was an adult, and that it would get its food from buttercups.

"This is the actual size of my insect," she said as she drew a line which was about two inches long. Then she stopped, her eyes widened, and she gulped.

"Oops, that's way too big," and she grabbed the eraser once again. After drawing a line that was much smaller, she continued, "Aren't I smart? 'Cause I was thinking of him in the buttercups, so I had to make him smaller, or someone would come along and be terrified."

For Ronit, the art experience at this time became an opportunity to find out what she did or did not understand and to rethink her ideas in a new form. Watching her work on an artistic problem, I was able to see that Ronit had not understood some basic information, but I could also observe her quickly correcting herself and thinking through the problems that are inherent in this type of activity. An extremely creative child, Ronit's love of drawing, writing, and language shows great flexibility of thinking and sensitivity to imagery. The art experience in this instance stimulated her to clarify her basic information while also engaging her aesthetic viewpoint.

Late in June, as we approached the end of school, we talked about our studies of life cycles. I asked the children to brainstorm with me about what they thought of when they heard the word "metamorphosis." Here is what they said:

Metamorphosis

egg — mealworm — pupa — beetle
egg — tadpole — frog
egg — caterpillar — chrysalis — butterfly
egg — caterpillar — cocoon — moth
egg — larvae — mosquito
seed — plant — flower — fruit
water — rain — snow — ice
wind — tornado — cyclone — waterspout
egg — dinosaur — reptile — bird
egg — baby — grownup — death — dirt

We gathered for a movement and drama session after this, and I asked the children to describe, through movement, a metamorphosis that they had thought about or seen. Most of the children presented impressions of one of the ideas listed

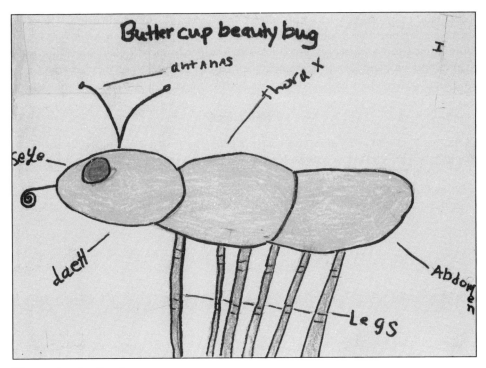

Illustration by Ronit

above. Finally, Brian, Jeffrey, and Lea, who had asked to go last, took their turn. They began with Brian enclosed between Lea's and Jeffrey's arms, as if in an embrace. Slowly, Lea and Jeffrey opened their arms and lifted Brian above them with his arms outstretched. He stood there as long as they could hold him and then the three toppled over together, flattened against the ground. Brian leapt up, took out an imaginary pencil, and began to write on Jeffrey's stomach. The other children, who had been mystified, jumped to their feet and shouted, "Tree! It's the life cycle of a tree!"

What we all understood by the end of this study was more than a collection of ideas about life cycles. What we understood from our experiences with the arts as subject matter and as inspiration was that knowing wasn't just telling something back as we had received it. Knowing meant transformation and change and a gradual awareness of what we had learned. For both children and teacher, the arts offer opportunities for reflection upon the content and the process of learning, and they foster a deeper level of communication about what knowledge is and who is truly in control of the learning process. As a pedagogical standard, the integration of the arts offers a rich resource for educators to infuse the learning experience at all levels with expansive and challenging perspectives.

The arts make it possible for all children, regardless of their differences, to participate fully in the process of education. They transcend the limitations placed on those children, like Juan and Brian, whose language, culture, or life experience is outside the mainstream of American schooling. They challenge children like Adam to expand their boundaries of personal expression and communication. They confirm the perspectives of children like Alison, Sean, and Carolyn, whose modes of communication and expression do not fit the predominant classroom discourse. They enable all children to recognize the breadth and depth of their learning.

References

Aardema, V. (1975). *Why mosquitoes buzz in people's ears.* New York: Dial Press.

Kipling, R. (1978). *Just so stories.* New York: Weathervane Books. (Original work published 1902)

Morimoto, J. (1986). *The inch boy.* New York: Puffin.

Tipping the Balance

JOSEPH CAMBONE

"Anne" is a teacher at a residential and day school for boys with severe emotional and behavioral challenges, an extremely complex learning environment that remains little known to the rest of society and the educational community at large. In this chapter, Joseph Cambone presents a portrait of Anne and her struggles to succeed and help her students learn. Anne works hard, thinks critically about her teaching, attempts to meet her students where they are, and holds a love for her students and her work that helps her maintain her focus on "strength and health, not pathology" in the teaching and learning process. Through Cambone's portrait, we bear witness to Anne's personal growth and professional development, her students' development as learners and members of a community, and the ways in which teaching and learning happens in this complex educational community.

Especially in times of darkness,
that is the time to love, that an act of love might
tip the balance.
— *Aeschylus*

Chaos

"I was some of the problem. My expectations were wrong." It is early October, a week after the lesson took place, and we are getting ready to watch it together on the videotape I have made. Anne sits with her Diet Coke, I with my pad and video paraphernalia. It is our first meeting, and I am struck (as I will be throughout our months of videotaping lessons and talking about them afterwards) by how honestly self-critical she is. "I remember thinking that I was glad we would see this on videotape," she says with a little laugh. She seems nervous, perhaps even embarrassed, about watching together what was clearly a difficult lesson. I had anticipated that. What I had not anticipated was her curiosity. More than anything, she is curious. She wants to see for herself where she made her errors, how she was part of the problem. For that opportunity, she is glad.

But I am puzzled: how could she have been the problem? I had obviously seen the lesson differently through the lens of the camera. These children are so difficult to manage, and the lesson seemed such a reasonable one to attempt! This group of

Harvard Educational Review Vol. 60 No. 2 May 1990, 217–236

five boys is the youngest in the long history of this residential treatment center. By all accounts, they are the most violent and disturbed for their age.*

Six-year-old Jeremy was born in a state institution and already has been in nearly ten foster homes. Small and thin, his dark hair is cut in a spiky brush-cut top that sets off his pale olive skin; he is cute, spunky, and talkative. Adults and children alike are drawn to him. But he is frequently confused and frustrated by almost all social situations and often becomes physically assaultive or sexually provocative.

Paul is seven. He and his family have been homeless until just recently, and there is evidence that he has been sexually abused in one of many shelters. The school is the first place that he has lived for any extended period of time. His round, deep-brown face is full of expression; his large almond-shaped eyes are always wide with what seems to be confusion and panic — and sometimes, thankfully, the glee of a little boy. He is known by almost all of the adults in the school by now, because his tantrums have been so exceedingly violent, frequent, and prolonged.

Six-year-old Steve had also been sexually abused before his adoption. Unlike the other boys, he is not a child who has tantrums often. Instead, he becomes oppositional, automatically shouting "NO!" at small requests or even when offered opportunities for fun. Often he sits, jaw set in his long, delicate face, brows furrowed, eyes squinting, whispering obscenities and taunts at the other boys. He is the only boy at grade level in his school work.

Samuel, eight years old, is a unique child, with average intelligence but pervasive neurological difficulties. In one-to-one situations, he is sweet and affectionate, never hesitating to hug adults or tell them how much he loves them. But he has spent very little time in classrooms or with groups of any kind. He is given to screaming episodes at the slightest provocation, leaving adults and students alike wondering at the cause.

Blond, blue-eyed, freckled Jamie is five years old, full of energy and continually on the move. He is unable to sit still for more than a few seconds at a time, always bumping into others, teasing and taunting them, poking his fingers at their sides. His activity level can escalate rapidly, easily disrupting the whole class; he is placed in "time-out" frequently. He is bright and verbal and quite engaging.

None of the boys has spent substantial time in school. Taken on their own, they are difficult to manage, demanding, and impulsive; put together, they interact explosively, provoking each other in a variety of ways — fighting, striking out at adults, throwing furniture and objects, and running away. Whenever I have seen the five together, chaos has not been far away. I thought the lesson went pretty well, considering the boys' behavior.

"Was this a bad lesson?" I betray my incredulity through my tone of voice. She laughs her laugh, intelligent and perceptive, always with the slight touch of apology, and answers, "Well, this was not as good a lesson as it could have been!" She explains:

> In terms of the process of a teacher . . . this has been a really hard group for me 'cause I've needed to change a lot of the things I'm doing. I'm constantly critiquing what I'm doing. And the group has been so out of control most of the

---

*I have changed the names of all adults and children to protect their confidentiality. However, to faithfully depict their experience, I have purposely retained their language.

time! On one level, I know that a lot of other people who have been here at the school even longer than I have said, "Oh my God! I can't believe that group!" And "I don't know how you deal with them every day." And "This is the most difficult group I've ever had in the art room!" And blah blah blah! So I know it's not me. But at the same time, I'm constantly knowing that I *do* need to change what I'm doing and that there are things that I can change to make it better. So I'm sort of constantly replaying that in my head.

Her eagerness to be self-critical seems layered, like so much of what she does; perhaps being self-critical helps fend off the impulse to blame the boys for their difficulties, as others sometimes do. Given their extremely troublesome behavior, it is easy to blame them. Perhaps, too, she is self-critical because she know that, in a way, she is in the spotlight; people are watching closely and with a certain amazement at how she'll handle the most difficult group they've seen in years.

Yet, the self-analysis goes much deeper, to what being a teacher means to her. Anne believes that being self-analytical is part of the "process of being a teacher." This process involves constantly re-evaluating assumptions about what works and what does not work in the classroom, not settling on one method; rather, developing a curriculum *in response to* the children. Anne believes that this year's plans cannot be based on last year's students.

So she is "glad" as we watch the tape of the lesson — glad for the opportunity to think over her assumptions, glad to think over her methods. And I am glad for the opportunity to watch her think as we begin to watch the videotape together.

Cathy's voice is getting tighter. It's the third week of school and already Anne has given this new teaching intern plenty of responsibility. The boys are getting restless, whispering, fidgeting on the L-shaped bench that wraps around the far left corner under the windows. There are usually five boys in the group, but Jeremy has already been removed from the room for trouble. Anne is setting up a new lesson and has not given them her full attention for just over a minute. The boys' energy is palpable, unfocused. She pulls the table out and puts the apples on it before them.

The PAUSE button gets pushed. "I wasn't well organized enough. I mean that is an immediate hindsight reaction . . . ." At first, I think she is referring to having the apples ready and the table in place. Butt she is referring to her disorganized mindset: she wasn't planning for the right children. "I've done this lesson at least twice before with other groups, and kids loved it. They were totally motivated to eat the apples . . . it was fun, a great lesson! . . . I sort of was stupid in saying ' . . . I can just do it off the top of my head!'" She watches the frozen action on the screen. ". . . I didn't really think enough about how different this group is from last year's — just how because it was successful last year . . . !"

She has focused on her interior organization for the lesson, while I have focused on how not being ready with materials causes tension to mount in the room. Ordinarily, a teacher can take at least sixty seconds or so of class time to arrange supplies for an activity, but not in this class — trouble begins brewing in those sixty seconds. Any time spent talking instead of doing something tempts fate; transitions between activities can be tortuous. I begin to understand her comments about organization. If she can move the boys smoothly from activity to activity, keeping them focused on objects by using their hands and eyes, she can divert their attention away from their own thoughts or each other. Nevertheless, it has to be the right activity. I push PLAY.

> *Samuel, strange and distant, starts making gulping noises, moving his head forward and back like a chicken when it walks. "Samuel, I can't put in a good sticker for you until you're not making noises. Samuel, look at me." Cathy is trying to regain his attention. He doesn't hear, lost in his own rhythm. Anne is moving quicker now but says nothing. Paul and Jamie are laughing together on the bench, mostly ignoring Cathy. James makes small kung-fu gestures. Paul laughs at the gestures Jamie uses and makes a few of his own. Jamie laughs and ups the ante; leaning back in his chair, he spreads his legs and pretends to play with his penis.*

Over the voices on the tape, Anne comments on Samuel. "It's very frustrating to figure out what to do with him! His biggest problem is being overstimulated, and he's in a group of extremely acting-out kids. The other kids are probably scary. . . ." She isn't sure he should remain in the class — maybe this school is the wrong place for him, maybe he needs something even more specialized. And Jamie is such a baby, not even six years old. He is so bright and eager, but overrun with impulses. She sees him play with his penis and wishes she could just let it pass by without comment. "It's something that [seems unimportant]. He plays with his penis on top of his pants . . . in some ways it is not atypical for a five-year-old. But with this group and knowing him. . . ." Cathy, who is less experienced, and less philosophical, seems frantic.

> *"Jamie, it looks to me that you need to go to time out." He leans toward her, purses his lips, sticks his tongue out a little, and makes a growling noise. Samuel mimics him, although he makes no sound. The defiance is contagious and Paul starts fidgeting wildly. Karen, the milieu therapist who is the third member of this team, takes Jamie by the hand and leads him out. Jamie hesitates and looks at Anne and says, "Ohhhh! What am I gonna do?" He seems befuddled. Was I doing something wrong, he seems to say; what did I do? "But when can I get my 'good' sticker?" he whines as he is withdrawn from the room. Anne turns to the remaining boys, face set in a serious look.*

When a child does something like what Jamie did, something that she thinks in itself is minor or manageable but could upset the others, she is distressed. "How much do you send one kid away from the group for something you think might upset the others in the group?" She returns to this question again and again, unable to answer it. The tension of this uncertainty about what approach to take marks the first weeks of school.

> *By now, Paul is in motion again, kneeling on his bench on all fours, swaying his buttocks back and forth. He is a ball of energy, but when he sees the adults' attention shift from Jamie back to him he jumps into a perfect sitting position.*
> *"Today we're going to talk about apples," she begins. She stands behind the table and puts out four different types of apples. The three boys give her rapt attention, as if they'd never seen an apple before. "Who can tell me something about these apples?" Hands shoot up in a great start to the lesson. Samuel says, "There's a red one, a green one, and [pointing to a golden delicious apple] a white one." "So they have different what . . .?" Samuel: "Colors." Anne: "Paul, what*

can you tell me about these apples?" He leaps off his bench and lurches toward the apples, leaning in as he goes. "No, stay in your seat, you'll get to touch them later." "But I have to show you!" He is pleading, he can't say it without touching. But she just continues speaking to the boys about the lesson. He inches backwards and sits down.

Fully animated, he points at one, learning forward, twisting in his seat, trying to find something important to say about the apple. His hand is outstretched, feeling the apple in the air as she calls on him again. "What can you tell me about these apples?" "They got skin on 'em? And stems?" Am I on the right track? He seems to ask as he works himself up to standing on one leg, knee still on the bench. His movement is getting larger; he can't sit still. "Good job, Paul." Now standing, he starts to sway, swinging his arms and hands up and down in the front of his body, then around to his back, then in front again. A little louder. "They have skin all around them." Anne acknowledges quickly, "Yes, they have skin all around them." Paul, voice filled with drama, "To make them warm!"

"What are you thinking?" I ask, hitting PAUSE. "Just how constantly in motion he is, that he has not been still once! . . . He's doing okay . . . although he is moving so fast . . . would it help him, would it be better or worse to make him stop and sit still?" She has him involved. His energy is ample but she is keeping it within boundaries. She makes a decision: "Right now, Paul moving his body around a lot is a minor problem compared to Paul being typically aggressive. It's sort of like saving my battles." She is constantly vigilant, watching them closely, collecting information, and sorting it on the fly.

She simply gestures to him to sit. Paul climbs back on the bench and kneels on it, facing away from the group, his head as a third point touching the bench. Samuel starts moving in his chicken motion, stops, starts again. Is he paying attention? "I like the red one and the dotted one," Steve says. Paul, up and moving again toward the apples asks, "You mean this one?" Anne loses none of her own momentum as she points and says, "Back on your seat, Paul." Once again he returns and lies across the bench.

The idea for the lesson is to use the senses to experience what is different and what is the same about apples. "We're going to see how they look, how the apples smell, how the apples feel, how the apples taste . . ., she says. Paul is on the move again. "Sit down," she says calmly and firmly without missing a beat. "This is a Macintosh. We're going to pass the apple around, and we're going to look with our eyes and say some words that tell what a Macintosh apple looks like."

Steve holds the apple and smiles. "It's cold!" he says. "There's a word for what it feels like. Remember that. But right now let's look at how it looks." She has a chart ready to write down words that tell how it looks, then feels, smells, and tastes. But it is too late, she has given them the apple to hold and the wheel's in motion. Paul takes the apple, gazing dreamily out the window as he rubs it between his hands, then smooths it against his face. "Now you guys are looking and feeling," Anne says aloud to herself. It's a statement of fact — things are already happening differently from what she planned. In truth, they are not "looking" at all, they are feeling. She planned a structured, sequential lesson on the five senses; they're interested only feeling.

She tries again to focus them, to redirect the lesson, to organize their learning. "I want boys to remember to look with their eyes. Now who can tell me a word about how this apple looks." Steve has caught on. He says, "It's red." Samuel Says, "It's juicy." But Anne is concentrating again on getting the squirming Paul back on track, "Paul, what's a word about how the apple looks?" *"It looks funny!" He is on his knees in front of her in a flash. "This could be a mouth and this could be a head." This time she lets him stay. After all, he has told her what it looks like. "Yes, but what color is it?" she asks. "It's red." Steve complains that he had already said that. No one hears him over Paul so he says, barely audible, his eyes slitted and angry, "It looks like a bum!" Paul has moved back to the bench and is walking on it like a crab with excitement. The tone in the room has changed but she isn't yet sure why. "I need everybody sitting quietly on the bench and eyes on me." There is a brief moment of stillness.*

When her simple request to sit quietly works, Anne decides not to make a big deal about everyone talking at once. She just stops and regroups. She wants to get on with the lesson and give each boy a chance to participate, but she needs a moment to get a handle on the tone of the room. She did not hear Steve's comment, and Samuel's was overshadowed by Paul's voice as well, but she picked up the change in tone, a shift away from exuberance and toward agitation. "Tone" is important to many of her decisions. It is an indication of the group's mood and level of tolerance. When she is made confident by the group's tone that they are doing well, she knows she can give an individual boy a little more latitude in his behavior, as she has with Paul. She draws on "knowledge of the individual kids and knowledge of the group dynamics. . . . If I feel like [a boy is] doing something that is going to set off the rest of the group, it's gotta stop right away. And if it looks like it's something that nobody else is paying attention to and the kid is still with what is going on, and it's going to cause a bigger problem to stop it than it is to let it keep going, then I might let it go." But in this case she misreads the tone, misunderstands why it has shifted, misses that the constant motion and commotion seem to be masking the boys' underlying confusion about what she wants. The tension is mounting among the children. They are offering ideas, talking about the apples. What does she want? They are mumbling what is important to them — "it's cold," "it's juicy" — but she is trying to focus them on seeing. Samuel is squirming and Steve has turned around in his seat, yawning, inattentive. She has lost them somehow.

After the lesson she realizes her error — the lesson was not suited for them. "We needed to cut out like twenty-five steps . . . . I've always taught the youngest kids who were emotionally disturbed and learning disabled and I felt like I had already pared everything down to the barest minimum. With this group, I need to go twenty steps below that." But in the moment, she wants to push them, "I'm used to pushing kids to that next level of thinking. . . . But the task I was asking them to do didn't make sense. I mean forget the difference between the eyes and the hands! Save the five senses for another lesson! That's a prerequisite skill they don't have yet." In this case, she has misjudged; has pushed too hard too soon, and the delicate balance of control was quickly lost.

"Paul, can you say what the apple looks like?" He jumps up and comes to her. She lets it go. He kneels. "There are little green spots and flat on the bottom. Flat here, flat here, and here it's busted." "Good job, Paul, now sit down." Paul, the showman, takes a bow before the group. Steve has been trying to speak again and gets pre-empted by Paul. Samuel giggles. Steve has been continually thwarted by

Paul's misbehavior and when Paul, perpetual motion on the bench, bounces around the bench toward Steve, Steve punches him in the side. Not hard, just enough. Paul hits him back. Anne is firm, calm, "Now Steve and Paul, each of you have three minutes to sit quietly and we're not going to go on until you're finished." The room bursts into pandemonium.

Anne's mind races to meet the crisis.

"It's moving so quickly and I don't feel I have time to think about what I'm saying. . . . "

Paul leaps up to run from the room but Cathy grabs him. Samuel starts rocking back and forth, head like a rag doll. Paul is yelling, "Fuck you, leave me alone, fuck you." "Paul, you have to the count of three to be back on your bench or you will leave the classroom. One, two . . ." Paul stops screaming and cursing, smiles at his classmates, cocky. Samuel gets quiet but then laughs and seems like a willing participant in the misbehavior. "Now the whole group is going to sit." When they hear this, the room bursts into chaos again. Paul grabs his crotch wildly and starts shouting suggestive words. Samuel laughs hysterically. Paul lifts his shirt and displays his stomach provocatively to Samuel, sing-songing, "BELLY-BUTTON!!" Anne takes his arm and begins to remove him.

"He's going to do something either dangerous or so outrageous that it is going to cause more of a problem."

Samuel starts to make noises. As Paul moves past the table with the apples on it, he picks one up and, still shouting sexual epithets for the boys, throws it at the wall. Anne takes both arms and walks him to time-out. Steve jumps from his chair and runs for the apple.

"This shouldn't be happening. I'm a bad teacher! If this is happening in my classroom, I should be able to have better control than this!!"

Samuel starts shrieking "FUCKER" over and over while he starts rocking. Finally, he jumps up and tries to run away.

"Can't we do anything to shut him up! He has good reason to be anxious . . . but we can't even be supportive!"

Cathy catches his arm, tries to hold Samuel and to get Steve back in his chair at the same time. Anne, at the other side of the room, has Paul pinned in a chair.

"An adult needs to put hands on him and physically stop him because otherwise he's going to run out of the classroom, knock something over, or do something potentially dangerous!"

He is kicking her and attempting to head-butt her, screaming.

"There's a part of me that is dealing with the physical reality — of not being able to physically put Paul down."

Karen returns Jamie to the room at just this moment.

" . . . this is a stupid time to bring Jamie into the room!"

Apparently, he has calmed down. Karen leaves Jamie in a chair on the far side of the room, takes Samuel from Cathy, and leaves the room with the shrieking Samuel. At the same time, Anne sees that Paul cannot remain and removes him from the room to the Crisis Center. Steve remains, looking innocent, on the bench.

"I can't remember whether Steve had been part of the initial problem or not. It all happened so quickly."

The class is over in ten minutes. It takes another thirty minutes to calm the children down and get on with the day. As we finish the tape, Anne is visibly frustrated, struggling to find what is going wrong, why she can't teach in the way she knows best and interact therapeutically with the boys as she has done in the past. "So much is happening at once . . . I need to be juggling so many things at once!" In the end, she circles back to where she began: "I was some of the problem. My expectations were wrong."

Insight

The huge old oak stands majestic in the center of the sprawling lawn, its last leaves driven away by the first rainy day of November. The manicured lawn, stretching gradually up the hill from the tree to the large, beige Victorian mansion, is dying green and sepia, and the last struggling marigolds are beginning to fade in the big barrel planters along the walks. Even in the rain, the campus is pretty. Sitting on a bluff over the river, the property was once a wealthy dairy farm. Now it is a school for emotionally disturbed boys, and the barn, with a copper weathervane atop its cupola, has been tastefully refitted for offices. The old carriage house matches the main house in style and color and is used as a crisis center. The very modern school building sits farther back on the prooperty, near the pasture that stretches up and out, rolling away toward the river; it is conservation land filled with birds. The mansion itself, called The House, is a residence for the boys, and although the inside is revamped for that purpose, the exterior retains its original grace. Canada geese fly overhead, leaving the river behind for the winter, and I breathe it all in as I amble up the walk, past Anne's classroom window, to my appointment with the principal to speak about Anne's work.

"FUCK YOU!"

Paul's voice pushes through the wall and crashes into the landscape. Samuel's piercing wail follows. Furniture is pushed over, and Paul's obscenities fuse with Samuel's sustained cries. I think about the video session Anne and I have planned for the afternoon, the conversation we will have, and the struggle she is involved in. I look one more time at the lovely campus and take another, deeper breath.

In the staff room at lunchtime, Anne is propped on the end of her seat, leaning toward her colleagues, talking rapidly, loudly, her food half eaten. Her usually pale face is drained further of color, tears fill her eyes. She is furious. Whatever I overheard an hour before led to something even more serious. I've never seen her angry — even when the children are outrageously provocative, she remains calm, her voice measured. I hesitate to ask what has happened and instead watch her two teacher colleagues listen carefully, offer words of encouragement, and validate her feelings of frustration and anger. They are good listeners, long practiced at "giving space," letting anger wind down before trespassing with their own thoughts and opinions. Yet it is clear that they are not listening out of obligation. They are sincere, they share her worry about the children, and they share many of her beliefs about teaching practice.

Almost in unison, all three look up at the clock. It is 11:55. By 11:56 they are gone. As always, they must be ready when the boys return from lunch, ready to maneuver them smoothly into the afternoon activity. Predictability, consistency, and challenge are words they use to explain their work, conditions they believe are requirements for these children. But making those beliefs manifest puts tremendous pressure on them; it requires them to wolf down meals, communicate economically, and quickly move on — even though they are personally upset. The heart of this school beats fast, pushes hard; it is difficult not to get caught up in the rapid-fire thinking, talk, and movement. Invariably, within twenty minutes of arriving, my pulse is racing, too.

At 3:00 that afternoon, Anne is still upset as she tells me the story. It began at "wake-up." The boys were resistant to getting out of bed and doing their morning routines. Breakfast was disagreeable, and by the time they reached the classroom, Anne, Cathy, and Karen had a difficult time settling the boys in. They had a full day ahead: reading, math, and writing, as usual. But a special event was planned for the morning. The "Animals as Intermediaries" folks were coming. These people are a group of naturists who come to the school with live, usually wild, but injured animals as part of a school-wide science program. Today they brought a field mouse and a dog. Anne had high hopes for this period. When they had come the week before, the activity was a great success. But today, Jeremy, in a rage because Steve got to hold the dog's leash and he did not, picked up a stapler and threw it at the dog, beginning a chain of problems that reverberated throughout the morning. Karen took Jeremy to the crisis center, where this behavior escalated, and before long Jamie was removed by Cathy for misbehavior as well.

Left alone with the three remaining boys, Anne continued with the planned curriculum and moved on into Big Books period. Big Books are just that: three feet tall, colorful, with large type. They are the basis for multiple language and reading activities. This is usually a successful time for all, but today the negative momentum of the morning pushed hard against the fun of Big Books. Steve ended up in time-out, Paul began running around the room, climbing on the window sill, and Samuel began to shriek, "because that's what he does whenever someone else is having trouble." Refusing to sit down when he was told to, Paul became physically abusive toward Anne, requiring her to hold him in a chair. When his behavior became even more assaultive, kicking and head-butting her, she attempted to put him in a full restraint, in which the child is maneuvered into a position where he cannot move his body, thus preventing harm to himself and others. He proved too wild and strong for her, and she was unable to control him. In the back of her mind, she knew the other two boys were watching closely to see if she could safely restrain Paul, and she knew she could not. She pulled back and let him run out of the room. The situation had shaken her and the other boys badly. "That was an upsetting scene because the other kids were watching me not be in control, physically in control of this situation. And then he [Paul] was running around campus being out of control."

To make matters worse, about five minutes after Paul was finally calmed down, his therapist insisted on having her regularly scheduled meeting with him, even though he had just assaulted a teacher and run around campus. Against Anne's strong objection, the therapist relieved Paul from his consequences and took him to get his lunch — in front of the boys who have just seen him assault their teacher. Anne was outraged. She tells me:

> . . . [he] sort of pranced into the lunchroom and got his lunch and all the other boys sort of looked at him and said "he just hit a teacher and ran around campus, what is he doing here?" And it was really very confusing. I was very angry because I didn't agree with that happening So that was sort of the straw that broke the camel's back . . . here was this child who had just done, in my mind, the two worst things he could have done! And there he was. And so I told his therapist to take him out of the lunchroom, that he couldn't be there, that he couldn't be near other boys and that I didn't want boys in my class to see him at all right now. And it was a little bit tense. . . .

She laughs a laugh that almost apologizes for her passion. But she is extremely serious: how can she be expected to make her classroom a safe place to learn if everyone doesn't give the children the same message about their behavior? These children can't differentiate the therapy session from the classroom; all adults are the same to them, and what the therapist sees as unconditional positive regard for Paul seems to seven-year-old Paul like getting off the hook. Anne's argument is quite persuasive; it has the force of belief, and her frustration is real.

Anne's frustrations are mounting. She is frustrated because it is already November and the chaos is continuing, frustrated that she can't deal with the children individually and therapeutically because so many things happen at once, frustrated that she cannot keep everyone safe, and particularly frustrated when she sees adults not working as a team. That, in fact, is the "straw that broke the camel's back."

Even though the feeling of chaos claims the balance of the day, there is a difference in the class. I had felt the difference earlier as I taped her lesson, felt that she might be making inroads into the chaos. Yet, it is evident as we begin to watch the tape together that she is not yet feeling any positive difference. The class still feels like bedlam to her. But it is clear to me that she is more confident about how to proceed. Closely watching her work with the children as she responds to whatever surprises they toss at her, I realize how intellectually agile she is. She enters a given period with a plan and a terminal goal, but her intellectual and emotional stance is open and ready: What will they do? What will they say? How will I respond so that I can keep them moving toward the goal and not lose them to answer or frustration? Each situation the boys present is a fresh problem to be solved in a series of steps toward a final goal. She draws on her earlier repertoire of activities, but she applies them in new ways, for different purposes.

Her work is not just responsive in the moment, though. Threaded through her talk about the class and evident in her actions with the boys are three principles that she has extracted from the chaos: these boys, individually, are clearly capable of higher intellectual and behavioral functioning; the problems they are presenting are group-management problems; the schedule of the day must be altered accordingly. By keeping these three ideas in mind, she limits the field of possible approaches: focus on their individual strengths, work to improve their interaction skills, and modify their environment to enhance their strengths and promote healthier interaction.

Three children and three adults sit huddled on the bench together, first an adult, then a child, then an adult, child, adult, child. Jeremy and Paul, she explains to Cathy and Karen, and for the ears of the three remaining boys, have been separated for the remainder of the day for their violent behavior.

I'm surprised. The remainder of the day? "[I am] trying to preserve the classroom space as a safe, calm space. Even if that means that four out of five need to leave it and then gradually come back one at a time. . . . But this . . . space needs to be preserved as a place where learning happens and where crazy behavior can't happen. . . ." I think back to her recurring dilemma: "How much do you send one kid away from the group for something you think might upset the others in the group?" She seems to have made a decision about how to proceed — make the classroom a place of learning and pull them back one at a time. This is a methodological decision that reflects Anne's adjustment to who these children are and the ways they think — they are young, inexperienced in school, and still unsure of what is required of them, and they are easily confused by what others say and do. She has decided to structure the environment in unambiguous, stark terms. The group-management problems can be resolved only if the children understand the environmental requirements: in this class, we learn; in this class, we do not act crazy. It is simply stated, over and over, in word and deed. It is for this reason that she is angry with Paul's therapist. By giving the message that consequences for violence could and will be suspended by one adult, but not another, the therapist undermines Anne's efforts.

Anne is finishing a read-aloud book. All five children seem mellow and affectionate. Jamie sees me and my video camera and comes up to look. Anne suggests that if the boys are interested and do a good job cleaning up and getting ready for the next period, I will demonstrate the camera. They hop to it, the transition goes smoothly, and one by one they sit on my lap and film their teachers and classmates. Then, just as easily, they hop back to their benches and begin writing class.

Anne shows them a large manila envelope, addressed and ready to go. It is a thank you letter to a museum they had toured the week before. "Remember yesterday we wrote a thank you letter to the Children's Discovery Museum. I got a big envelope. . . ." In it she put the oversized card that they had written as a group the day before. She tells them how she addressed the envelope and will send it. It is a brief lesson in letter writing. Quickly, she moves on and shows them the book they had made yesterday filled with the photos taken at the museum. On every page, a boy had pasted a photo of himself doing some fun thing at the museum. Under each photo he dictated a short sentence about what he did. "Here's Steve's picture. It says 'Steve liked the chain-reaction room!' and there's Samuel's picture, and it says, 'Samuel is jumping on the giant water bed!'" As she reads the captions under each picture, they give her all their attention, giggling with glee when their picture comes up.

"They said what to write and I *wrote* it, and they could *read* it," she says with excitement. "It was a record of their experiences: Jamie liked this, Paul liked this, Jeremy liked this. . . ." There is a remarkable difference in the presentation of this book from the presentation of lessons earlier in the year — the apples, for instance. Here, the short lesson is focused directly on the boys, what they thought, felt, saw, and did. The children laugh, ask questions, make comments. This way of doing things makes sense to them. They are in positive frames of mind. Characteristically, Anne decides to push them a little, to try something they don't like as much, and she pulls out the easel to begin a group lesson. She is always looking for an opportunity to push them harder, to acclimate them to school-like activities, to shift the balance in favor of academics.

> *"We'll keep this on the shelf in our room so that if you want to show anyone about our trip, you can." Anne sets up the easel as she speaks, "I thought that it is nice to have things to show about special things you've done. And this morning we did something special. Who can remember some of the things that we did this morning when the animals came to the class. . ."" At the slightest hint of a structured lesson, where questions will be asked and answers required, the boys' anxiety level goes up. Samuel starts rocking and making low noises; Jamie whines and sprawls on the bench. Cathy goes to Jamie, Anne to Samuel. Each talks quietly to the boys and they sit up. But Jamie is still fidgety. "I don't want to do this," he complains. Anne pushes ahead and asks Samuel what he liked about this morning. "I liked patting the dog." Anne writes the sentence on the easel. Not to be outdone, Jamie's hand shoots up. "I'm glad you've thought of something you liked, Jamie. What did you like?" His words spill from his mouth, he has so much he liked. "Wait, wait," says Anne with a smile, "let me get this all down!"*
>
> *They finish recording all the fun things they did. The lesson lasts less than three minutes. Anne gives them paper and markers and they draw pictures of what they remember, dictate sentences about the pictures to Anne, then copy what she has written under the pictures themselves.*

I run down with Anne what I've learned in the first moments of taping: the boys were able to look through my camera without incident, they have gone to a museum in another town on a field trip, and have engaged in a short lesson that, a month ago, would have led to a disruption. "How is it you were able to accomplish these things two days in a row?" First, she reminds me the period would never have been successful if all five children had been present. She would have had to do everything differently in that case. Then, as she speaks, she seems to be putting a name on what she has been doing, has been knowing, but did not yet put into words. "[I could do it] because there were these really salient things. We had gone on this trip and had this experience with the animals. They had been powerful or exciting or different experiences. It seemed like too good an opportunity to pass up! . . . I wanted to capitalize on these things and get them to do this . . . If they're gonna be able to do it [writing] at all, they'll be able to do it best when there's something they're really excited about." She has decided that, in part, managing the behavior of the group means getting them interested in what they are doing in class. The more they are interested, the more leverage she has to keep them out of trouble and in the group.

Using "salient" things make the difference. She has searched for and located what excites the boys in school, and has put more of the same in their way. Yet "salience" does not translate to doing whatever they want — an activity may be fun, but not salient. For Anne, salient activities are interesting to the boys *and* fulfill her academic or social goals for them as well. Her goals are clear. In the case of language arts, the older three boys (whom she considers first graders) will be writing stories on their own by June. The younger, kindergarten-aged boys will be dictating stories. From the beginning of September, "that's been the same goal. My feelings about how realistic it is go up and down a little bit." She laughs. Sometimes, it seems she laughs because her words sound absurd to her own ears, her beliefs and hopes incongruous in the current situation. Perhaps she should be happy with the small accomplishments and forget the terminal goals. "I'm too product-oriented!" she says, and laughs again.

Finding the salient content for her classes is important, but the day's organization is equally important to managing the group's behavior. Keeping them interested alone will not solve her problem of group management; when and how they do activities is just as important. Very early in the year, she decided that the afternoon schedule was too intense for these young children. With the slightly older children she had taught in the past, a half-hour each of language arts, science, and social studies activities made sense. For this year's youngsters, these artificial differentiations by content area didn't make sense. She believed the more important skills were learning to use language, to listen, to function as a group, and do group lessons, at least for now. Science, social studies, and writing became the materials she used, but what really mattered to Anne was ". . . balancing out each individual kid's academic, cognitive potential versus their behavioral, social needs . . . figuring out how to get them to do what they are capable of doing, [and] at the same time, keeping them in a group and having reasonable behavioral expectations for the group. . . ." She still had their academic goals in mind, but, "I needed to find a way to get all those experiences and all those goals done differently." And so she abandoned her formal writing period, as well as formal science and social studies, replacing them with a series of structured experiences in which the emphasis was less on content and more on group process. The activities she chose were still academic, but more spontaneous, more dependent on the prevailing moods of the class. The afternoon began to look more like pre-school or kindergarten and less like first or second grade.

The five boys loved being read to and would remain calm and attentive all through a picture book. So she read books about Pilgrims and Fizzwiggle the Cat. They enjoyed filmstrips, too, especially about insects or dinosaurs. They loved to draw. After each activity, the boys drew pictures and made things with their hands. All around the room hung drawings of Pilgrims and dinosaurs, insects and cats. Yet underneath each drawing or on a label beneath a string of clay beads were always words — a sentence about the art work. The early creations were labeled in an adult's neat hand; the later ones gradually gave way to the prehensile scrawl of kindergartners, silent testimony to the slow progression of the year, to "taking turns a little bit, not trying to accomplish all as quickly as I might have last year, by doing sometimes language art things, sometimes science things, sometimes social studies things. But the goals are still there. . . ."

Anne had set her goals for them long ago; it just has been unclear how to get to those goals. She is used to older children, and to setting goals for first and second graders. These children are kindergartners; the types of things she can teach, the ways she prefers to teach don't seem to work. Yet, she is making slow progress. She can keep three in the room at one time, sometimes without fights. Slowly, one by one, she will bring them back into the classroom. She can regroup them after a terrible morning and lead a productive afternoon. But the activity must be salient. She can cover some content with them. She just has to be flexible about when and how. She has to have the freedom to maneuver the schedule to match the mood.

Regression

"Yak! Yak! He's a Lego maniac!!
Yak! Yak! He's a Lego maniac!!
Yak! Yak! He's a Lego maniac!!"

Over and over, for nearly ten minutes, Jamie chants the phrase. He is flung across Anne's lap and she holds him tightly, a rag doll spent from anxiety, awaiting his state social worker's visit. The worker does not visit unless there is news, usually bad news: "We can't find your mommy." "We can't find your daddy." "We have a new foster home." "You'll be moving to a residential school." He doesn't know what Anne knows, that they have found his mommy and she has sent him some presents. She wants him back, is going to fight the state, which wants to put him up for adoption. This news will only overwhelm him more.

Anne is overwhelmed, too. As the weeks of struggle have turned into months, it is harder to hold on to the belief that she can make a difference, harder to resist being tipped into despair. And so she labors to balance herself between despair and belief. Now, she sits silently and Jamie chants his mantra in his futile battle to focus on one thing instead of the million thoughts and worries that are rushing at his mind. She is not unlike him. The desperate events of the past months rush at her and she does battle with them, she forces them into perspective by reminding herself why she does what she does. She is thinking, she tells me later, about nothing in particular and everything that has happened, numb and anguished at the same time.

> The past two weeks have been a complete regression back to less than zero. And until two days ago, pretty literally no teaching academics happened at all in the classroom. Two of the boys, Jeremy and Steve, we found out, have been involved in fairly extensive sexual activity on the weekends with one another. Both of them were pretty much basket cases for about two weeks and practically unable to be in class at all. [When they are in class] . . . the severity of [their] sexual and aggressive acting out [is so disruptive to others, that] Jamie has also, pretty much [been] unable to be in school. And with that much going on, Samuel, of course, spends a lot of time shrieking and has a lot of difficulty because things were pretty chaotic. So for almost two weeks, I did little else than restrain kids all day. And it was really miserable, and really awful.
>
> I finally felt that we were *getting* somewhere, like we were progressing toward some of the goals, that we were doing better as a group, and then everything fell apart, and it didn't make any sense, and I couldn't understand why. And then finding out why, having one of the boys disclose some of these things that were going on, on the one hand made it feel better because at least there was a reason for it! You know, it wasn't me, it wasn't the classroom, it wasn't just out of the blue!! But it also felt really bad. It was like we couldn't even keep these kids safe! That things were happening that are making their lives worse while they're in residential care! And that felt yukky — even though it wasn't my personal thing. It left me feeling very unhopeful about Jeremy's prognosis, very disheartened.
>
> In choosing to work with these kinds of kids, clearly I'm not just interested in academic teaching. I'm interested in social/emotional growth of kids. So I expect that some proportion of my time is gonna be spent dealing with social/emotional/ behavioral issues with kids and not just with teaching. But there is that part of it that feels like, "Well, for two weeks, all I did was restrain kids. I didn't have a classroom, I wasn't a teacher!" You know, I planned all this great curriculum that

I didn't get a chance to do. . . . The neat curriculum isn't as important to me as how the kids are doing altogether. It's frustrating to feel like you're working so hard to plan . . . here I am, I revamped all these things. I have all these new ideas and we're not even getting to try them because everyone is out of control all the time. And that feeling of, like I said in the beginning of the year, I said to my team who were new [this year], at Thanksgiving we're really going to see improvement. We didn't. That was wrong.

For pretty much two weeks, I've thought about the kids twenty-four hours a day. I've gone home and had dreams about them and felt very hopeless. It was a little bit better at the end of this week, 'cause better things started happening the past couple of days. At the same time that this is happening, I found out about a kid who graduated from here last year whose parents are about to terminate his adoption. And this was like a kid who wow! Here was one of our success stories! I had just told one of the parents of one of the kids in my class about this wonderful [story]: This boy came when he was seven-and-a-half, graduated when he was ten and went to public school, and he was doing so much better. Look how there is hope and success! And here his life is falling apart! And Jeremy is back to sucking the dicks of his friends when he is out of eyesight for ten seconds! And he is being really violent and really aggressive. And on one level, it made me feel really hopeless, and it's really shitty to feel hopeless about six-year-olds! And it's really hard to maintain the kind of energy that it takes to do this work when you're not feeling hopeful about it.

I guess I remind myself of the times when I feel hopeful, of the good things that can happen, and of my real belief that things will get better. I don't think I can fix them. I think I can help be part of making them healthier people. And if I didn't think that, I don't think I would do this kind of work. I think it's one of the reasons I like working with younger kids. . . . I wonder sometimes, especially with some of the more damaged kids, how much of that damage can be undone. The damage is there and it's always going to be there. But he's *six years old*! I'd like to think that all the time and effort and energy that's going into everything that I'm doing and that others are doing with him is going to mean that ten years from now he can lead some sort of productive, more normal life where he is not completely overrun by sexual and aggressive impulses 80 percent of the time! So I think . . . that [the] definition of success is different. . . . I've felt differently about it at different points in my professional growth. I feel differently about it for different kids. And it's really hard with such young kids to project what the ultimate hope might be for what they might be like.

I think [I have] high standards and push the kids and maybe cause more behavioral problems 'cause I'm pushing them to do things. It wouldn't be worth doing that if they were always going to be at a place like this for their whole lives. Like *who cares*, you know, how much socially appropriate behavior they learn, and if they learn how to read and do math and those kind of things! I think that there is always in the back of my head the thought and the hope that at some point down the road they're gonna go to some more normal setting. Whether they're gonna be adopted and stop living here or they go back to a public school at some point. Or that they stay at a place like this and are more successful there. You know or whatever. That there is a goal, that each one of these kids is capable of more higher functioning."

"Yak! Yak! he's a Lego maniac!!
Yak! Yak! He's a Lego maniac. . . ."

Progress

"Guess what? Our first book is about to be published!" She sits before the group, her voice full of excitement. Just one minute before, she had begun the transition from read-aloud time to writing. Everyone had enjoyed the book, had been huddled together on the bench, like puppies warming themselves against each other. Yet when Anne announced the transition, Paul threw himself back on the bench, spread his legs and started gesturing to his anus. Jeremy started yelling at him to stop. Jamie began yelling his request to get a book. Samuel started screaming. In a flash, without speaking, the three adults moved into action. Paul was removed to a chair on the other side of the room; Jeremy, refusing to move to time-out, needed to be quickly lifted off the bench and carried out. An adult sat next to Samuel and touched his arm and he quieted. As quickly as the disruption began, it was over. Paul was brought back to his seat — he had regained control quickly. Jeremy remained in the time-out chair but listened to what was going on. As if nothing has happened, Anne begins what will be a positive lesson.

"Guess what! Our first book is about to be published! Samuel decided that he was going to write about his dog and he wrote "Samuel and His Dog." Then he thought of a lot of different things all about his dog and he wrote them in his book. Samuel, can you come here and sit next to me while I show them your book? "My dog lived in the forest. My dog likes bones. . . . My dog's name is Sunshine!"

By early January, Anne had reinstituted a formal writing time at the boys' request. The first time one of the boys asked to write a book was during a free-choice period back in November (free choice comes at the end of every day; if they have done all their schoolwork, they can choose an activity of their own to do). Given their great love for read-aloud, it did not come as too big a surprise. Anne did not leap on the opportunity then; instead she "let this excitement keep on building on its own. A couple of months from now I will introduce it as a formal activity because they will be excited." She also waited because they still could not sit at a table together in November. They could listen to books, loved listening, in fact, but if they moved to work at tables, everything fell apart. She still needed to work on their ability to spend time together as a group.

The tone of the class seems very different. She finishes reading Samuel's book and begins to explain how boys can publish books they've written. She demonstrates how the books are constructed, with contact-paper-covered cardboard serving as a book jacket, shows how to glue the pages. She shows them the press-on letters they can use on the front for a title. Each page, she reminds them, must be illustrated as well. The explanation takes time and they sit paying attention. Occasionally, Paul bounces on his seat and Anne stops for a moment. "I'm going to wait until everyone pays attention." Paul immediately quiets down and gives his attention to the activity. "When each boy finishes his story, he can do this to his story to publish it." They like that idea a lot!!

Anne divides the group in two; Jamie and Jeremy go with Cathy, the others remain with her. This is a chronological division, the younger children will not be required to write. If they want to write, they can. What is important is for them to tell stories and have Cathy write them down. However, Anne believes that the other three boys need to begin to do their own writing and not just tell stories. She feels a pressure to get them to do first-grade work, but not at the expense of their learning to dislike writing. She worries about this being their first writing experience. She wants to guarantee that it is positive. Hence, they can write about whatever they choose and illustrate with the pictures they love to draw. Anne will then type their stories and ready them for "publication." Each finished story means the class has an "Author of the Day" who sits with the teacher in front of the group and has his story read. Only positive comments are allowed from the audience. Within a few weeks, fifteen or so books have been "published" and sit on the class bookshelf, to be taken out and read aloud, over and over again.

> *Paul dances to his chair at the table, swaying his buttocks back and forth. "Paul, go back to your bench. And when I see you sitting the right way, you can come up to the table." He sits for a brief moment while she settles Steve in. "OK, Paul, you can come over." He runs across the room and leaps on his chair. One leg goes up on the tabletop and he starts to climb. Anne calmly tells him to sit correctly and keeps reading from Steve's story of yesterday. "'Steve and Karen have a snowball fight.' That's good. Think about what you want to write today." Steve is not in a very good mood, it seems. When Anne turns to help Paul, Steve mumbles an obscenity toward Paul under his breath. Anne tells him to go back to his bench and to sit for a minute for speaking that way. As he leaves the table, he pretends to spit on Paul's work. Paul retaliates and pretends to spit on Steve's work. "Now, you have one minute on your bench as well." Paul erupts verbally, "He fuckin' spit on my fuckin' paper!" "Well," says Anne calmly, almost nonchalantly, "that doesn't mean you should do the same thing." "Loudmouth," says Steve toward Paul. I tense up and focus the camera closely on what will be a violent episode . . . nothing. They both sit back and wait quietly while Anne turns her attention to Samuel, who has ignored this whole altercation, busily readying the pieces of his publishable book.*

No screaming, no desks pushed over, no fists flying. Has she "fixed" them, I ask myself.

> *Steve moves his legs up underneath himself cross-legged. Paul does the same. Steve folds his hands, Paul does the same. One sticks out his tongue, the other sticks out his tongue. Anne and Samuel continue to talk about his story; they are laughing together and having fun, talking about the illustration that he needs to do. Miraculously, both Steve and Paul abandon their taunting and watch Anne. She finally brings Paul back to the table, opens his book with him and begins to read it. "What does this say?" she asks. He reads a page to her. "What will come next?" she asks. He falls to the work and starts writing his sentence. She has two of them working now. "Okay, Steve, now you can come to the table. What do you want to write about you and Karen today?"*

Earlier in the year, she had to send them out of the room for difficult behavior, get fun things happening in the room, then bring them back one at a time. Now, she can accomplish this same thing with them remaining in the room. " . . . It just took longer than I expected to get them acclimated into being in a classroom. I think in some ways, when I do look back on the year as a whole, I will say the first three months were spent getting the kids comfortable with the concept of being civilized in a classroom setting. It took that long to have them feel safe in a class and be able to contain themselves well enough to start doing anything else."

They do seem to feel safer, seem more confident in Anne, calmer in the environment. They seem to know what they are doing, the activities make sense. And it is clear that Anne feels good about them. Her frustration is not apparent, her body seems more relaxed, her voice almost gentle. Since safety and control no longer dominate the period, she can begin to push a little harder to get the boys to produce. For each boy, the issue to push on is different.

"Steve, what do you want to write?" "Me and Karen . . . uh . . ." He hands her a paper and demands she write down what he is saying. "You know what Steve, I don't have to write the word 'Karen,' you can copy it from right here." He flares up, "NO, you write Karen!!!" She ignores him, he is being obstinate, and she refuses to help. He takes it out on Paul. "Pussy!" he says at Paul, who just keeps working. Anne points to Steve's bench, and he goes there quietly. Samuel, in the meantime, is calling for her attention. He wants to show his drawing of his dog. It is just a bunch of legs in space. "Where is his body?" she asks. "I don't want to draw a body," Samuel replies. "Well, it's gonna be awfully hard for people to understand your picture, then." He draws another picture, but now only a body and no legs! "Now where are the legs?"

When she brings Steve back to the table, she still quietly insists that he copy words that he already knows or are written for him somewhere else in his story. As soon as he has trouble with a word that he doesn't yet know or hasn't written before, she is there to write it down. With Samuel, she continues to insist that he make a dog with legs, and the correct number of legs as well. The conversations overlap, the boys interrupt her, she deals with three questions at once. Instead of safety and control problems, these are new and welcome troubles, problems she is more accustomed to dealing with. Now that they are engaged in their work, they all want her attention simultaneously, they want their questions answered first, they cannot wait. This is, to her, "the classic writing time. Writing time in all of my classes felt that way, even with kids who can write and were further along. I know they are all working on their own thing and they all need my help all the time. They have no ability to understand you need to be helping other people as well. I pretend to be listening to all three of them constantly all of the time." She thinks about the problem that Steve is having today, his easy frustration and impatience with the task and with her. She wonders if it is because she is doing something wrong.

She lets Steve dictate a difficult sentence. "Anne . . . Anne . . . Anne," Samuel calls in his drooping whine. She responds, finally, when she has finished with Steve. But no sooner has she turned to Samuel than Steve is demanding from her that she spell the word 'to.' She moves back immediately and spells it. But he makes an error writing it, tries to erase, tears his page. "See! This fuckin' paper. . . ." She tries to help, suggests he tape the tear. "I hate you. . . . I'm going to stab you . . . no tape. . . . I want you to erase that damn letter!!!" Behind him, Samuel is droning over and over, "I'm on my last page, Anne . . . I'm on my last page, Anne . . . I'm on my last page, Anne." Paul asks for help. She speaks with Samuel, she answers Paul's question, she tapes Steve's page. . . .

The PAUSE button gets pushed on the video machine. "At this point, I was upset that Steve was getting as frustrated as he did, partly, I feel, with the way the writing program is set up, nobody should be getting frustrated. Partly, I was feeling that I was moving too fast with Steve in terms of what he was doing. But then I wasn't sure if his frustration was because I was moving too fast or if it was because he was having a cranky, needy day and even if it was not too hard for him, he would be feeling that way."

I smile to myself, and think back to September: "I was some of the problem. My expectations were wrong." I am amazed that she is being self-critical, now. Steve is being nasty even though she is being as helpful as seems possible. But it is a part of her personality, a drive within her, part of her "process of being a teacher." She believes these boys are capable, that learning for them should be fun, creative, exciting; it should focus on strength and health, not pathology. Teaching skills and competencies, she says, can be the most therapeutic thing of all. Yes, I think, for the teacher and the taught.

Belief

When I get out of my car on this April morning, about twenty boys are running up to class to begin their school day. Jostling, teasing, and generally doing what young boys do; they all race ahead of Samuel, who is struggling hard, and failing miserably, at doing what young boys generally do. His parents have tried to dress him "*a la mode*." He has new sneakers, a good windbreaker; he is holding a backpack along with the books that didn't fit in it, and straining to get his Walkman over his ears. All the while, he is trying to run and keep up with the others. But the Walkman slips off his head and falls to the ground. When he bends to reach for it, his books fall from his hand and the backpack follows. He flops on the sidewalk, not yet warmed after winter, and tries to reassemble his "look." His lack of coordination would be farcical if it were not so real.

In the front office, I pass young Jamie. He is angry as he walks with his therapist. "Where can I buy a gun?" he asks her. "I really need a gun!" His words smash against my ears like cymbals. My eyes meet his therapist's and she smiles wanly, takes him by the hand, and walks on.

I look at the children and I think about Anne and the work she does. How sustaining the power of belief must be for her! Although her resolve wavers, she believes in the children, in their ability to heal. She is convinced, truly, that she *must* make a difference. "I wonder sometimes, especially with some of the more damaged kids, how much of that damage can be undone. The damage is there and it's always going to be there. But he's *six years old*!" She possesses a kind of love for the children, some might say a foolish love, that keeps her pushing against the weight of their troubles, always trying to tip the balance in their favor.

I would like to acknowledge Dr. Sara Lawrence-Lightfoot, Donald Freeman, and Dr. Richard Small for their insightful critiques of earlier drafts of this portrait. Especially, I would like to thank "Anne" for generously fitting me into her already busy schedule, and for engaging in the reflective process with such vigor.

The Silenced Dialogue:
Power and Pedagogy in Educating
Other People's Children

LISA D. DELPIT

In this chapter, Lisa Delpit uses the debate over writing instruction to analyze the factors that underlie differing philosophies of teaching, particularly in relation to teaching students of color and poor students. Delpit identifies a "culture of power" at work in schools, revealing how the ways in which power is and is not used inside the classroom operate to either maintain the societal status quo or create change that can ultimately lead to achieving equity in educational experience for all students. Delpit concludes that teachers must teach all students the explicit and implicit rules of power, as well as the nature of the power relationships these rules create and represent, in order to begin the journey toward just and equitable educational opportunities for all children — other people's and our own.

A Black male graduate student who is also a special education teacher in a predominantly Black community is talking about his experiences in predominantly White university classes:

> There comes a moment in every class where we have to discuss "The Black Issue" and what's appropriate education for Black children. I tell you, I'm tired of arguing with those White people, because they won't listen. Well, I don't know if they really don't listen or if they just don't believe you. It seems like if you can't quote Vygotsky or something, then you don't have any validity to speak about your *own* kids. Anyway, I'm not bothering with it anymore, now I'm just in it for a grade.

A Black woman teacher in a multicultural urban elementary school is talking about her experiences in discussions with her predominantly White fellow teachers about how they should organize reading instructions to best serve students of color:

> When you're talking to White people they still want it to be their way. You can try to talk to them and give them examples, but they're so headstrong, they think they know what's best for *everybody*, for *everybody's* children. They won't listen, White folks are going to do what they want to do *anyway*.

Harvard Educational Review Vol. 58 No. 3 August 1988, 280–298

It's really hard. They just don't listen well. No, they listen, but they don't *hear* — you know how your mama used to say you listen to the radio, but you *hear* your mother? Well they don't *hear* me.

So I just try to shut them out so I can hold my temper. You can only beat your head against a brick wall for so long before you draw blood. If I try to stop arguing with them I can't help myself from getting angry. Then I end up walking around praying all day "Please Lord, remove the bile I feel for these people so I can sleep tonight." It's funny, but it can become a cancer, a sore.

So, I shut them out. I go back to my own little cubby, my classroom, and I try to teach the way I know will work, no matter what those folks say. And when I get Black kids, I just try to undo the damage they did.

I'm not going to let any man, woman, or child drive me crazy — White folks will try to do that to you if you let them. You just have to stop talking to them, that's what I do. I just keep smiling, but I won't talk to them.

A soft-spoken Native Alaskan woman in her forties is a student in the Education Department of the University of Alaska. One day she storms into a Black professor's office and very uncharacteristically slams the door. She plops down in a chair and, still fuming, says, "Please tell people, just don't help us anymore! I give up. I won't talk to them again!"

And finally, a Black woman principal who is also a doctoral student at a well-known university on the West Coast is talking about her university experiences, particularly about when a professor lectures on issues concerning educating Black children:

If you try to suggest that that's not quite the way it is, they get defensive, then you get defensive, then they'll start reciting research.

I try to give them my experiences, to explain. They just look and nod. The more I try to explain, they just look and nod, just keep looking and nodding. They don't really hear me.

Then, when it's time for class to be over, the professor tells me to come to his office to talk more. So I go. He asks for more examples of what I'm talking about, and he looks and nods while I give them. Then he says that that's just my experiences. It doesn't really apply to most Black people.

It becomes futile because they think they know everything about everybody. What you have to say about your life, your children, doesn't mean anything. They don't really want to hear what you have to say. They wear blinders and earplugs. They only want to go on research they've read that other White people have written.

It just doesn't make any sense to keep talking to them.

Thus was the first half of the title of this text born — "The Silenced Dialogue." One of the tragedies in the field of education is that scenarios such as these are enacted daily around the country. The saddest element is that the individuals that the Black and Native American educators speak of in these statements are seldom aware that the dialogue *has* been **silenced**.[a] Most likely the White educators believe

---

[a] **Silencing** is the suppressing of the ideas or views of others by a person or group of people in a setting where they have power granted to them by the group or society.

that their colleagues of color did, in the end, agree with their logic. After all, they stopped disagreeing, didn't they?

I have collected these statements since completing a recently published article (Delpit, 1986). In this somewhat autobiographical account, entitled "Skills and Other Dilemmas of a Progressive Black Educator," I discussed my perspective as a product of a skills-oriented approach to writing and as a teacher of process-oriented approaches. I described the estrangement that I and many teachers of color feel from the progressive movement when writing-process advocates dismiss us as too "skills oriented." I ended the article suggesting that it was incumbent upon writing-process advocates — or indeed, advocates of any progressive movement — to enter into dialogue with teachers of color, who may not share their enthusiasm about so-called new, liberal, or progressive ideas.

In response to this article, which presented no research data and did not even cite a reference, I received numerous calls and letters from teachers, professors, and even state school personnel from around the country, both Black and White. All of the White respondents, except one, have wished to talk more about the question of skills versus process approaches — to support or reject what they perceive to be my position. On the other hand, *all* of the non-White respondents have spoken passionately of being left out of the dialogue about how best to educate children of color.

How can such complete communication blocks exist when both parties truly believe they have the same aims? How can the bitterness and resentment expressed by the educators of color be drained so that the sores can heal? What can be done?

I believe the answer to these questions lies in ethnographic analysis: that is, in identifying and giving voice to alternative worldviews. Thus, I will attempt to address the concerns raised by White and Black respondents to my article "Skills and Other Dilemmas" (Delpit, 1986). My charge here is not to determine the best instructional methodology; I believe that the actual practice of good teachers of all colors typically incorporates a range of pedagogical orientations. Rather, I suggest that the differing perspectives on the debate over "skills" versus "process" approaches can lead to an understanding of the alienation and miscommunication, and thereby to an understanding of the "silenced dialogue."

In thinking through these issues, I have found what I believe to be a connecting and complex theme: what I have come to call "the culture of power." There are five aspects of power I would like to propose as given for this presentation:

1. Issues of power are enacted in classrooms.
2. There are codes or rules for participating in power; that is, there is a "culture of power."
3. The rules of the culture of power are a reflection of the rules of the culture of those who have power.
4. If you are not already a participant in the culture of power, being told explicitly the rules of that culture makes acquiring power easier.
5. Those with power are frequently least aware of — or least willing to acknowledge — its existence. Those with less power are often most aware of its existence.

The first three are by now basic tenets in the literature of the sociology of education, but the last two have seldom been addressed. The following discussion will explicate these aspects of power and their relevance to the schism between liberal educational movements and that of non-White, non-middle-class teachers and communities.[1]

1. Issues of power are enacted in classrooms.

These issues include: the power of the teacher over the students; the power of the publishers of textbooks and of the developers of the curriculum to determine the view of the world presented; the power of the state in enforcing compulsory schooling; and the power of an individual or group to determine another's intelligence or "normalcy." Finally, if schooling prepares people for jobs, and the kind of job a person has determines her or his economic status and, therefore, power, then schooling is intimately related to that power.

2. There are codes or rules for participating in power; that is, there is a "culture of power."

The codes or rules I'm speaking of relate to linguistic forms, communicative strategies, and presentation of self; that is, ways of talking, ways of writing, ways of dressing, and ways of interacting.

3. The rules of the culture of power are a reflection of the rules of the culture of those who have power.

This means that success in institutions — schools, workplaces, and so on — is predicated upon acquisition of the culture of those who are in power. Children from middle-class homes tend to do better in school than those from non-middle-class homes because the culture of the school is based on the culture of the upper and middle classes — of those in power. The upper and middle classes send their children to school with all the accoutrements of the culture of power; children from other kinds of families operate within perfectly wonderful and viable cultures but not cultures that carry the codes or rules of power.

4. If you are not already a participant in the culture of power, being told explicitly the rules of that culture makes acquiring power easier.

In my work within and between diverse cultures, I have come to conclude that members of any culture transmit information implicitly to co-members. However, when implicit codes are attempted across cultures, communication frequently breaks down. Each cultural group is left saying, "Why don't those people say what they mean?" as well as, "What's wrong with them, why don't they understand?"

Anyone who has had to enter new cultures, especially to accomplish a specific task, will know of what I speak. When I lived in several Papua New Guinea villages for extended periods to collect data, and when I go to Alaskan villages for work with Alaskan Native communities, I have found it unquestionably easier — psychologically and pragmatically — when some kind soul has directly informed me about such matters as appropriate dress, interactional styles, embedded meanings, and taboo words or actions. I contend that it is much the same for anyone seeking to learn the rules of the culture of power. Unless one has the leisure of a lifetime of "immersion" to learn them, explicit presentation makes learning immeasurably easier.

And now, to the fifth and last premise:

5. Those with power are frequently least aware of — or least willing to acknowledge — its existence. Those with less power are often most aware of its existence.

For many who consider themselves members of liberal or radical camps, acknowledging personal power and admitting participation in the culture of power is distinctly uncomfortable. On the other hand, those who are less powerful in any situation are most likely to recognize the power variable most acutely. My guess is that the White colleagues and instructors of those previously quoted did not perceive themselves to have power over the non-White speakers. However, either by virtue of their position, their numbers, or their access to that particular code of power of calling upon research to validate one's position, the White educators had the authority to establish what was to be considered "truth," regardless of the opinions of the people of color, and the latter were well aware of that fact.

A related phenomenon is that liberals (and here I am using the term "liberal" to refer to those whose beliefs include striving for a society based upon maximum individual freedom and autonomy) seem to act under the assumption that to make any rules or expectations explicit is to act against liberal principles, to limit the freedom and autonomy of those subjected to the explicitness.

I thank Fred Erickson for a comment that led me to look again at a tape by John Gumperz[2] on cultural dissonance in cross-cultural interactions. One of the episodes showed an East Indian interviewing for a job with an all-White committee. The interview was a complete failure, even though several of the interviewers appeared to really want to help the applicant. As the interview rolled steadily downhill, these "helpers" became more and more indirect in their questioning, which exacerbated the problems the applicant had in performing appropriately. Operating from a different cultural perspective, he got fewer and fewer clear clues as to what was expected of him, which ultimately resulted in his failure to secure the position.

I contend that as the applicant showed less and less aptitude for handling the interview, the power differential became ever more evident to the interviewers. The "helpful" interviewers, unwilling to acknowledge themselves as having power over the applicant, became more and more uncomfortable. Their indirectness was an attempt to lessen the power differential and their discomfort by lessening the power-revealing explicitness of their questions and comments.

When acknowledging and expressing power, one tends toward explicitness (as in yelling to your ten-year-old, "Turn that radio down!"). When de-emphasizing power, there is a move toward indirect communication. Therefore, in the interview setting, those who sought to help, to express their egalitarianism with the East Indian applicant, became more and more indirect — and less and less helpful — in their questions and comments.

In literacy instruction, explicitness might be equated with direct instruction. Perhaps the ultimate expression of explicitness and direct instruction in the primary classroom is Distar. This reading program is based on a behaviorist model in which reading is taught through the direct instruction of phonics generalizations and blending. The teacher's role is to maintain the full attention of the group by continuous questioning, eye contact, finger snaps, hand claps, and other gestures, and by eliciting choral responses and initiating some sort of award system.

When the program was introduced, it arrived with a flurry of research data that "proved" that all children — even those who were "culturally deprived" — could learn to read using this method. Soon there was a strong response, first from academics and later from many classroom teachers, stating that the program was terrible. What I find particularly interesting, however, is that the primary issue of the conflict over Distar has not been over its instructional efficacy — usually the students did learn to read — but the expression of explicit power in the classroom. The liberal educators opposed the methods — the direct instruction, the explicit control exhibited by the teacher. As a matter of fact, it was not unusual (even now) to hear of the program spoken of as "fascist."

I am not an advocate of Distar, but I will return to some of the issues that the program — and direct instruction in general — raises in understanding the differences between progressive White educators and educators of color.

To explore those differences, I would like to present several statements typical of those made with the best of intentions by middle-class liberal educators. To the surprise of the speakers, it is not unusual for such content to be met by vocal opposition or stony silence from people of color. My attempt here is to examine the underlying assumptions of both camps.

"I want the same thing for everyone else's children as I want for mine."

To provide schooling for everyone's children that reflects liberal, middle-class values and aspirations is to ensure the maintenance of the status quo, to ensure that power, the culture of power, remains in the hands of those who already have it. Some children come to school with more accoutrements of the culture of power already in place — "**cultural capital**,"[b] as some critical theorists refer to it (for example, Apple, 1979) — some with less. Many liberal educators hold that the primary goal for education is for children to become autonomous, to develop fully who they are in the classroom setting without having arbitrary, outside standards forced upon them. This is a very reasonable goal for people whose children are already participants in the culture of power and who have already internalized its codes.

But parents who don't function within that culture often want something else. It's not that they disagree with the former aim, it's just that they want something more. They want to ensure that the school provides their children with discourse patterns, interactional styles, and spoken and written language codes that will allow them success in the larger society.

It was the lack of attention to this concern that created such a negative outcry in the Black community when well-intentioned White liberal educators introduced "dialect readers." These were seen as a plot to prevent the schools from teaching the linguistic aspects of the culture of power, thus dooming Black children to a permanent outsider caste. As one parent demanded, "My kids know how to be Black — you all teach them how to be successful in the White man's world."

Several Black teachers have said to me recently that as much as they'd like to believe otherwise, they cannot help but conclude that many of the "progressive" educational strategies imposed by liberals upon Black and poor children could only be based on a desire to ensure that the liberals' children get sole access to the dwindling pool of American jobs. Some have added that the liberal educators believe themselves to be operating with good intentions, but that these good intentions are only conscious delusions about their unconscious true motives. One of Black an-

---

[b] **Cultural capital** refers to some types of cultural understanding — such as language, modes of social interaction, knowledge about the functioning of a system — that are valued commodities in a particular society or structure and can be used by an individual for advancement.

thropologist John Gwaltney's (1980) informants reflects this perspective with her tongue-in-cheek observation that the biggest difference between Black folks and White folks is that Black folks *know* when they're lying!

Let me try to clarify how this might work in literacy instruction. A few years ago I worked on an analysis of two popular reading programs, Distar and a progressive program that focused on higher-level critical thinking skills. In one of the first lessons of the progressive program, the children are introduced to the names of the letter *m* and *e*. In the same lesson they are then taught the sound made by each of the letters, how to write each of the letters, and that when the two are blended together they produce the word *me*.

As an experienced first-grade teacher, I am convinced that a child needs to be familiar with a significant number of these concepts to be able to assimilate so much new knowledge in one sitting. By contrast, Distar presents the same information in about forty lessons.

I would not argue for the pace of the Distar lessons; such a slow pace would only bore most kids — but what happened in the other lesson is that it merely provided an opportunity for those who already knew the content to exhibit that they knew it, or at most perhaps to build one new concept onto what was already known. This meant that the child who did not come to school already primed with what was to be presented would be labeled as needing "remedial" instruction from day one; indeed, this determination would be made before he or she was ever taught. In fact, Distar was "successful" because it actually *taught* new information to children who had not already acquired it at home. Although the more progressive system was ideal for some children, for others it was a disaster.

I do not advocate a simplistic "basic skills" approach for children outside of the culture of power. It would be (and has been) tragic to operate as if these children were incapable of critical and higher-order thinking and reasoning. Rather, I suggest that schools must provide these children the content that other families from a different cultural orientation provide at home. This does not mean separating children according to family background, but instead ensuring that each classroom incorporates strategies appropriate for all the children in its confines.

And I do not advocate that it is the school's job to attempt to change the homes of poor and non-White children to match the homes of those in the culture of power. That may indeed be a form of cultural genocide. I have frequently heard schools call poor parents "uncaring" when parents respond to the school's urging, that they change their home life in order to facilitate their children's learning, by saying, "But that's the school's job." What the school personnel fail to understand is that if the parents were members of the culture of power and lived by its rules and codes, then they would transmit those codes to their children. In fact, they transmit another culture that children must learn at home in order to survive in their communities.

"Child-centered, whole language, and process approaches are needed in order to allow a democratic state of free, autonomous, empowered adults, and because research has shown that children learn best through these methods."

People of color are, in general, skeptical of research as a determiner of our fates. Academic research has, after all, found us genetically inferior, culturally deprived, and verbally deficient. But beyond that general caveat, and despite my or others' personal preferences, there is little research data supporting the major tenets of process approaches over other forms of literacy instruction, and virtually no evidence that such approaches are more efficacious for children of color (Siddle, 1986).

Although the problem is not necessarily inherent in the method, in some instances adherents of process approaches to writing create situations in which students ultimately find themselves held accountable for knowing a set of rules about which no one has ever directly informed them. Teachers do students no service to suggest, even implicitly, that "product" is not important. In this country, students will be judged on their product regardless of the process they utilized to achieve it. And that product, based as it is on the specific codes of a particular culture, is more readily produced when the directives of how to produce it are made explicit.

If such explicitness is not provided to students, what it feels like to people who are old enough to judge is that there are secrets being kept, that time is being wasted, that the teacher is abdicating his or her duty to teach. A doctoral student of my acquaintance was assigned to a writing class to hone his writing skills. The student was placed in the section led by a White professor who utilized a process approach, consisting primarily of having the students write essays and then assemble into groups to edit each others' papers. That procedure infuriated this particular student. He had many angry encounters with the teacher about what she was doing. In his words:

> I didn't feel she was teaching us anything. She wanted us to correct each others' papers and we were there to learn from her. She didn't teach anything, absolutely nothing.
>
> Maybe they're trying to learn what Black folks knew all the time. We understand how to improvise, how to express ourselves creatively. When I'm in a classroom, I'm not looking for that, I'm looking for structure, the more formal language.
>
> Now my buddy was in [a] Black teacher's class. And that lady was very good. She went through and explained and defined each part of the structure. This [White] teacher didn't get along with that Black teacher. She said that she didn't agree with her methods. But *I* don't think that White teacher *had* any methods.

When I told this gentleman that what the teacher was doing was called a process method of teaching writing, his response was, "Well, at least now I know that she *thought* she was doing *something*. I thought she was just a fool who couldn't teach and didn't want to try."

This sense of being cheated can be so strong that the student may be completely turned off to the educational system. Amanda Branscombe, an accomplished White teacher, recently wrote a letter discussing her work with working-class Black and White students at a community college in Alabama. She had given these students my "Skills and Other Dilemmas" article (Delpit, 1986) to read and discuss, and wrote that her students really understood and identified with what I was saying. To quote her letter:

> One young man said that he had dropped out of high school because he failed the exit exam. He noted that he had then passed the GED without a problem after three weeks of prep. He said that his high school English teacher claimed to use a process approach, but what she really did was hide behind fancy words to give herself permission to do nothing in the classroom.

The students I have spoken of seem to be saying that the teacher has denied them access to herself as the source of knowledge necessary to learn the forms they need to succeed. Again, I tentatively attribute the problem to teachers' resistance to exhibiting power in the classroom. Somehow, to exhibit one's personal power as expert source is viewed as disempowering one's students.

Two qualifiers are necessary, however. The teacher cannot be the only expert in the classroom. To deny students their own expert knowledge *is* to disempower them. Amanda Branscombe, when she was working with Black high school students classified as "slow learners," had the students analyze RAP songs to discover their underlying patterns. The students became the experts in explaining to the teacher the rules for creating a new RAP song. The teacher then used the patterns the students identified as a base to begin an explanation of the structure of grammar, and then of Shakespeare's plays. Both student and teacher are expert at what they know best.

The second qualifier is that merely adopting direct instruction is not the answer. Actual writing for real audiences and real purposes is a vital element in helping students to understand that they have an important voice in their own learning processes. Siddle (1988) examines the results of various kinds of interventions in a primarily process-oriented writing class for Black students. Based on readers' blind assessments, she found that the intervention that produced the most positive changes in the students' writing was a "mini-lesson" consisting of direct instruction about some standard writing convention. But what produced the *second* highest number of positive changes was a subsequent student-centered conference with the teacher. (Peer conferencing in this group of Black students who were not members of the culture of power produced the least number of changes in students' writing. However, the classroom teacher maintained — and I concur — that such activities are necessary to introduce the elements of "real audience" into the task, along with more teacher-directed strategies.)

"It's really a shame but she (that Black teacher upstairs) seems to be so authoritarian, so focused on skills and so teacher directed. Those poor kids never seem to be allowed to really express their creativity. (And she even yells at them.)"

This statement directly concerns the display of power and authority in the classroom. One way to understand the difference in perspective between Black teachers and their progressive colleagues on this issue is to explore culturally influenced oral interactions.

In *Ways With Words*, Shirley Brice Heath (1983) quotes the verbal directives given by the middle-class "townspeople" teachers (p. 280):

"Is this where the scissors belong?"

"You want to do your best work today."

By contrast, many Black teachers are more likely to say:

"Put those scissors on that shelf."

"Put your name on the papers and make sure to get the right answer for each question."

Is one oral style more authoritarian than another?

Other researchers have identified differences in middle-class and working-class speech to children. Snow et al. (1976), for example, report that working-class mothers use more directives to their children than do middle- and upper-class parents. Middle-class parents are likely to give the directive to a child to take his bath as, "Isn't it time for your bath?" Even though the utterance is couched as a question, both child and adult understand it as a directive. The child may respond with "Aw Mom, can't I wait until . . . ," but whether or not negotiation is attempted, both conversants understand the intent of the utterance.

By contrast, a Black mother, in whose house I was recently a guest, said to her eight-year-old son, "Boy, get your rusty behind in that bathtub." Now I happen to know that this woman loves her son as much as any mother, but she would never have posed the directive to her son to take a bath in the form of a question. Were she to ask, "Would you like to take your bath now?" she would not have been issuing a directive but offering a true alternative. Consequently, as Heath suggests, upon entering school the child from such a family may not understand the indirect statement of the teacher as a direct command. Both White and Black working-class children in the communities Heath studied "had difficulty interpreting these indirect requests for adherence to an unstated set of rules" (p. 280).

But those veiled commands are commands nonetheless, representing true power and with true consequences for disobedience. If veiled commands are ignored, the child will be labeled a behavior problem and possibly officially classified as behavior disordered. In other words, the attempt by the teacher to reduce an exhibition of power by expressing herself in indirect terms may remove the very explicitness that the child needs to understand the rules of the new classroom culture.

A Black elementary school principal in Fairbanks, Alaska, reported to me that she has a lot of difficulty with Black children who are placed in some White teachers' classrooms. The teachers often send the children to the office for disobeying teacher directives. Their parents are frequently called in for conferences. The parents' response to the teacher is usually the same: "They do what I say; if you just *tell* them what to do, they'll do it. I tell them at home that they have to listen to what you say." And so, does not the power still exist? Its veiled nature only makes it more difficult for some children to respond appropriately, but that in no way mitigates its existence.

I don't mean to imply, however, that the only time the Black child disobeys the teacher is when he or she misunderstands the request for certain behavior. There are other factors that may produce such behavior. Black children expect an authority figure to act with authority. When the teacher instead acts as a "chum," the message sent is that this adult has no authority, and the children react accordingly. One reason this is so is that Black people often view issues of power and authority differently than people from mainstream middle-class backgrounds.[3] Many people of color expect authority to be earned by personal efforts and exhibited by personal characteristics. In other words, "the authoritative person gets to be a teacher because she is authoritative." Some members of middle-class cultures, by contrast, expect one to achieve authority by the acquisition of an authoritative role. That is, "the teacher is the authority because she is the teacher."

In the first instance, because authority is earned, the teacher must consistently prove the characteristics that give her authority. These characteristics may vary across cultures, but in the Black community they tend to cluster around several abilities. The authoritative teacher can control the class through exhibition of personal power; establishes meaningful interpersonal relationships that garner student respect; exhibits a strong belief that all students can learn; establishes a standard of achievement and "pushes" the students to achieve that standard; and holds the attention of the students by incorporating interactional features of Black communicative style in his or her teaching.

By contrast, the teacher whose authority is vested in the role has many more options of behavior at her disposal. For instance, she does not need to express any sense of personal power because her authority does not come from anything she herself does or says. Hence, the power she actually holds may be veiled in such questions/commands as "Would you like to sit down now?" If the children in her class understand authority as she does, it is mutually agreed upon that they are to obey her no matter how indirect, soft-spoken, or unassuming she may be. Her indirectness and soft-spokenness may indeed be, as I suggested earlier, an attempt to reduce the implication of overt power in order to establish a more egalitarian and nonauthoritarian classroom atmosphere.

If the children operate under another notion of authority, however, then there is trouble. The Black child may perceive the middle-class teacher as weak, ineffectual, and incapable of taking on the role of being the teacher; therefore, there is no need to follow her directives. In her dissertation, Michelle Foster (1987) quotes one young Black man describing such a teacher:

> She is boring, bo::ing.* She could do something creative. Instead she just stands there. She can't control the class, doesn't know how to control the class. She asked me what she was doing wrong. I told her she just stands there like she's meditating. I told her she could be meditating for all I know. She says that we're supposed to know what to do. I told her I don't know nothin' unless she tells me. She just can't control the class. I hope we don't have her next semester. (pp. 67–68)

But of course the teacher may not view the problem as residing in herself but in the student, and the child may once again become the behavior-disordered Black boy in special education.

What characteristics do Black students attribute to the good teacher? Again, Foster's dissertation provides a quotation that supports my experience with Black students. A young Black man is discussing a former teacher with a group of friends:

> We had fu::an in her class, but she was mean. I can remember she used to say, "Tell me what's in the story, Wayne." She pushed, she used to get on me and push me to know. She made us learn. We had to get in the books. There was this tall guy and he tried to take her on, but she was in charge of that class and she didn't let anyone run her. I still have this book we used in her class. It's a bunch of stories in it. I just read one on Coca-Cola again the other day. (p. 68)

To clarify, this student was *proud* of the teacher's "meanness," an attribute he seemed to describe as the ability to run the class and pushing and expecting students to learn. Now, does the liberal perspective of the negatively authoritarian Black teacher really hold up? I suggest that although all "explicit" Black teachers are not also good teachers, there are different attitudes in different cultural groups

---

* *Editor's note:* The colons [::] refer to elongated vowels.

about which characteristics make for a good teacher. Thus, it is impossible to create a model for the good teacher without taking issues of culture and community context into account.

And now to the final comment I present for examination:

"Children have the right to their own language, their own culture. We must fight cultural hegemony and fight the system by insisting that children be allowed to express themselves in their own language style. It is not they, the children, who must change, but the schools. To push children to do anything else is repressive and reactionary."

A statement such as this originally inspired me to write the "Skills and Other Dilemmas" article. It was first written as a letter to a colleague in response to a situation that had developed in our department. I was teaching a senior-level teacher education course. Students were asked to prepare a written autobiographical document for the class that would also be shared with their placement school prior to their student teaching.

One student, a talented young Native American woman, submitted a paper in which the ideas were lost because of technical problems — from spelling to sentence structure to paragraph structure. Removing her name, I duplicated the paper for a discussion with some faculty members. I had hoped to initiate a discussion about what we could do to ensure that our students did not reach the senior level without getting assistance in technical writing skills when they needed them.

I was amazed at the response. Some faculty implied that the student should never have been allowed into the teacher education program. Others, some of the more progressive minded, suggested that I was attempting to function as gatekeeper by raising the issue and had internalized repressive and disempowering forces of the power elite to suggest that something was wrong with a Native American student just because she had another style of writing. With few exceptions, I found myself alone in arguing against both camps.

No, this student should not have been denied entry to the program. To deny her entry under the notion of upholding standards is to blame the victim for the crime. We cannot justifiably enlist exclusionary standards when the reason this student lacked the skills demanded was poor teaching at best and institutionalized racism at worst.

However, to bring this student into the program and pass her through without attending to obvious deficits in the codes needed for her to function effectively as a teacher is equally criminal — for though we may assuage our own consciences for not participating in victim blaming, she will surely be accused and convicted as soon as she leaves the university. As Native Alaskans were quick to tell me, and as I understood through my own experience in the Black community, not only would she not be hired as a teacher, but those who did not hire her would make the (false) assumption that the university was putting out only incompetent natives and that they should stop looking seriously at any Native applicants. A White applicant who exhibits problems is an individual with problems. A person of color who exhibits problems immediately becomes a representative of her cultural group.

No, either stance is criminal. The answer is to *accept* students but also to take responsibility to *teach* them. I decided to talk to the student and found out she had recognized that she needed some assistance in the technical aspects of writing soon after she entered the university as a freshman. She had gone to various members of the education faculty and received the same two kinds of responses I met with four years later: faculty members told her either that she should not even attempt to be a teacher, or that it didn't matter and that she shouldn't worry about such trivial issues. In her desperation, she had found a helpful professor in the English Department, but he left the university when she was in her sophomore year.

We sat down together, worked out a plan for attending to specific areas of writing competence, and set up regular meetings. I stressed to her the need to use her own learning process as insight into how best to teach her future students those "skills" that her own schooling had failed to teach her. I gave her some explicit rules to follow in some areas; for others, we devised various kinds of journals that, along with readings about the structure of the language, allowed her to find her own insights into how the language worked. All that happened two years ago, and the young woman is now successfully teaching. What the experience led me to understand is that pretending that gatekeeping points don't exist is to ensure that many students will not pass through them.

Now you may have inferred that I believe that because there is a culture of power, everyone should learn the codes to participate in it, and that is how the world should be. Actually, nothing could be further from the truth. I believe in a diversity of style, and I believe the world will be diminished if cultural diversity is ever obliterated. Further, I believe strongly, as do my liberal colleagues, that each cultural group should have the right to maintain its own language style. When I speak, therefore, of the culture of power, I don't speak of how I wish things to be but of how they are.

I further believe that to act as if power does not exist is to ensure that the power status quo remains the same. To imply to children or adults (but of course the adults won't believe you anyway) that it doesn't matter how you talk or how you write is to ensure their ultimate failure. I prefer to be honest with my students. Tell them that their language and cultural style is unique and wonderful but that there is a political power game that is also being played, and if they want to be in on that game there are certain games that they too must play.

But don't think that I let the onus of change rest entirely with the students. I am also involved in political work both inside and outside of the educational system, and that political work demands that I place myself to influence as many gatekeeping points as possible. And it is there that I agitate for change — pushing gatekeepers to open their doors to a variety of styles and codes. What I'm saying, however, is that I do not believe that political change toward diversity can be effected from the bottom up, as do some of my colleagues. They seem to believe that if we accept and encourage diversity within classrooms of children, then diversity will automatically be accepted at gatekeeping points.

I believe that will never happen. What will happen is that the students who reach the gatekeeping points — like Amanda Branscombe's student who dropped out of high school because he failed his exit exam — will understand that they have been lied to and will react accordingly. No, I am certain that if we are truly to effect societal change, we cannot do so from the bottom up, but we must push and agitate from the top down. And in the meantime, we must take the responsibility to *teach,* to provide for students who do not already possess them, the additional codes of power.[4]

But I also do not believe that we should teach students to passively adopt an alternate code. They must be encouraged to understand the value of the code they already possess as well as to understand the power realities in this country. Otherwise they will be unable to work to change these realities. And how does one do that?

Martha Demientieff, a masterly Native Alaskan teacher of Athabaskan Indian students, tells me that her students, who live in a small, isolated, rural village of less than two hundred people, are not aware that there are different codes of English. She takes their writing and analyzes it for features of what has been referred to by Alaskan linguists as "Village English," and then covers half a bulletin board with words or phrases from the students' writing, which she labels "Our Heritage Language." On the other half of the bulletin board she puts the equivalent statements in "standard English," which she labels "Formal English."

She and the students spend a long time on the "Heritage English" section, savoring the words, discussing the nuances. She tells the students, "That's the way we say things. Doesn't it feel good? Isn't it the absolute best way of getting that idea across?" Then she turns to the other side of the board. She tells the students that there are people, not like those in their village, who judge others by the way they talk or write.

> We listen to the way people talk, not to judge them, but to tell what part of the river they come from. These other people are not like that. They think everybody needs to talk like them. Unlike us, they have a hard time hearing what people say if they don't talk exactly like them. Their way of talking and writing is called "Formal English."
>
> We have to feel a little sorry for them because they have only one way to talk. We're going to learn two ways to say things. Isn't that better? One way will be our Heritage way. The other will be Formal English. Then, when we go to get jobs, we'll be able to talk like those people who only know and can only really listen to one way. Maybe after we get the jobs we can help them to learn how it feels to have another language, like ours, that feels so good. We'll talk like them when we have to, but we'll always know our way is best.

Martha then does all sorts of activities with the notions of Formal and Heritage or informal English. She tells the students,

> In the village, everyone speaks informally most of the time unless there's a potlatch or something. You don't think about it, you don't worry about following any rules — it's sort of like how you eat food at a picnic — nobody pays attention to whether you use your fingers or a fork, and it feels *so* good. Now, Formal English is more like a formal dinner. There are rules to follow about where the knife and fork belong, about where people sit, about how you eat. That can be really nice, too, because it's nice to dress up sometimes.

The students then prepare a formal dinner in the class, for which they dress up and set a big table with fancy tablecloths, china, and silverware. They speak only Formal English at this meal. Then they prepare a picnic where only informal English is allowed.

She also contrasts the "wordy" academic way of saying things with the metaphoric style of Athabaskan. The students discuss how book language always uses more words, but in Heritage language, the shorter way of saying something is always better. Students then write papers in the academic way, discussing with Martha and with each other whether they believe they've said enough to sound like a book. Next, they take those papers and try to reduce the meaning to a few sentences. Finally, students further reduce the message to a "saying" brief enough to go on the front of a T-shirt, and the sayings are put on little paper T-shirts that the students cut out and hang throughout the room. Sometimes the students reduce other authors' wordy texts to their essential meanings as well.

The following transcript provides another example. It is from a conversation between a Black teacher and a Southern Black high school student named Joey, who is a speaker of Black English. The teacher believes it very important to discuss openly and honestly the issues of language diversity and power. She has begun the discussion by giving the student a children's book written in Black English to read.

Teacher: What do you think about that book?

Joey: I think it's nice.

Teacher: Why?

Joey: I don't know. It just told about a Black family, that's all.

Teacher: Was it difficult to read?

Joey: No.

Teacher: Was the text different from what you have seen in other books?

Joey: Yeah. The writing was.

Teacher: How?

Joey: It use more of a southern-like accent in this book.

Teacher: Uhm-hmm. Do you think that's good or bad?

Joey: Well, uh, I don't think it's good for people down this a way, cause that's the way they grow up talking anyway. They ought to get the right way to talk.

Teacher: Oh. So you think it's wrong to talk like that?

Joey: Well . . . [*Laughs.*]

Teacher: Hard question, huh?

Joey: Uhm-hmm, that's a hard question. But I think they shouldn't make books like that.

Teacher: Why?

Joey: Because they not using the right way to talk and in school they take off for that and li'l chirren grow up talking like that and reading like that so they might think that's right and all the time they getting bad grades in school, talking like that and writing like that.

Teacher: Do you think they should be getting bad grades for talking like that?

Joey: [*Pauses, answers very slowly.*] No . . . No.

Teacher: So you don't think that it matters whether you talk one way or another?

Joey: No, not long as you understood.

Teacher: Uhm-hmm. Well, that's a hard question for me to answer, too. It's ah, that's a question that's come up in a lot of schools now as to whether they should correct children who speak the way we speak all the time. Cause when we're talking to each other we talk like that even though we might not talk like that when we get into other situations, and who's to say whether it's —

Joey: [*Interrupting.*] Right or wrong.

Teacher: Yeah.

Joey: Maybe they ought to come up with another kind of . . . maybe Black English or something. A course in Black English. Maybe Black folks would be good in that cause people talk, I mean Black people talk like that, so . . . but I guess there's a right way and wrong way to talk, you know, not regarding what race. I don't know.

Teacher: But who decided what's right or wrong?

Joey: Well that's true . . . I guess White people did.

[*Laughter. End of tape.*]

Notice how throughout the conversation Joey's consciousness has been raised by thinking about codes of language. This teacher further advocates having students interview various personnel officers in actual workplaces about their attitudes toward divergent styles in oral and written language. Students begin to understand how arbitrary language standards are, but also how politically charged they are. They compare various pieces written in different styles, discuss the impact of different styles on the message by making translations and back translations across styles, and discuss the history, apparent purpose, and contextual appropriateness of each of the technical writing rules presented by their teacher. *And* they practice writing different forms to different audiences based on rules appropriate for each audience. Such a program not only "teaches" standard linguistic forms, but also explores aspects of power as exhibited through linguistic forms.

Tony Burgess, in a study of secondary writing in England by Britton, Burgess, Martin, McLeod, and Rosen (1975/1977), suggests that we should not teach "iron conventions . . . imposed without rationale or grounding in communicative intent, . . . [but] critical and ultimately cultural awareness" (p. 54). Courtney Cazden (1987) calls for a two-pronged approach:

1. Continuous opportunities for writers to participate in some authentic bit of the unending conversation . . . thereby becoming part of a vital community of talkers and writers in a particular domain, and
2. Periodic, temporary focus on conventions of form, taught as cultural conventions expected in a particular community. (p. 20)

Just so that there is no confusion about what Cazden means by a focus on conventions of form, or about what I mean by "skills," let me stress that neither of us is speaking of page after page of "skill sheets" creating compound words or identifying nouns and adverbs, but rather about helping students gain a useful knowledge of the conventions of print while engaging in real and useful communicative activities. Kay Rowe Grubis, a junior high school teacher in a multicultural school, makes lists of certain technical rules for her eighth graders' review and then gives them papers from a third grade to "correct." The students not only have to correct other students' work, but also tell them why they have changed or questioned aspects of the writing.

A village teacher, Howard Cloud, teaches his high school students the conventions of formal letter writing and the formulation of careful questions in the context of issues surrounding the amendment of the Alaska Land Claims Settlement Act. Native Alaskan leaders hold differing views on this issue, which is critical to the future of local sovereignty and land rights. The students compose letters to leaders who reside in different areas of the state seeking their perspectives, set up audioconference calls for interview/debate sessions, and, finally, develop a videotape to present the differing views.

To summarize, I suggest that students must be *taught* the codes needed to participate fully in the mainstream of American life, not by being forced to attend to hollow, inane, decontextualized subskills, but rather within the context of meaningful communicative endeavors; that they must be allowed the resource of the teacher's expert knowledge while being helped to acknowledge their own "expertness" as well; and that even while students are assisted in learning the culture of power, they must also be helped to learn about the arbitrariness of those codes and about the power relationships they represent.

I am also suggesting that appropriate education for poor children and children of color can only be devised in consultation with adults who share their culture. Black parents, teachers of color, and members of poor communities must be allowed to participate fully in the discussion of what kind of instruction is in their children's best interest. Good liberal intentions are not enough. In an insightful study entitled "Racism without Racists: Institutional Racism in Urban Schools," Massey, Scott, and Dornbusch (1975) found that under the pressures of teaching, and with all intentions of "being nice," teachers had essentially stopped attempting to teach Black children. In their words: "We have shown that oppression can arise out of warmth, friendliness, and concern. Paternalism and a lack of challenging standards are creating a distorted system of evaluation in the schools" (p. 10). Educators must open themselves to, and allow themselves to be affected by, these alternative voices.

In conclusion, I am proposing a resolution for the skills/process debate. In short, the debate is fallacious; the dichotomy is false. The issue is really an illusion created initially not by teachers but by academics whose worldview demands the creation of categorical divisions — not for the purpose of better teaching, but for the goal of easier analysis. As I have been reminded by many teachers since the publication of my article, those who are most skillful at educating Black and poor children do not allow themselves to be placed in "skills" or "process" boxes. They understand the need for both approaches, the need to help students to establish their own voices, but also to coach those voices to produce notes that will be heard clearly in the larger society.

The dilemma is not really in the debate over instructional methodology, but rather in communicating across cultures and in addressing the more fundamental issue of power, of whose voice gets to be heard in determining what is best for poor children and children of color. Will Black teachers and parents continue to be silenced by the very forces that claim to "give voice" to our children? Such an outcome would be tragic, for both groups truly have something to say to one another. As a result of careful listening to alternative points of view, I have myself come to a viable synthesis of perspectives. But both sides do need to be able to listen, and I contend that it is those with the most power, those in the majority, who must take the greater responsibility for initiating the process.

To do so takes a very special kind of listening, listening that requires not only open eyes and ears, but open hearts and minds. We do not really see through our eyes or hear through our ears, but through our beliefs. To put our beliefs on hold is to cease to exist as ourselves for a moment — and that is not easy. It is painful as well, because it means turning yourself inside out, giving up your own sense of who you are, and being willing to see yourself in the unflattering light of another's angry gaze. It is not easy, but it is the only way to learn what it might feel like to be someone else and the only way to start the dialogue.

There are several guidelines. We must keep the perspective that people are experts on their own lives. There are certainly aspects of the outside world of which they may not be aware, but they can be the only authentic chroniclers of their own experience. We must not be too quick to deny their interpretations, or accuse them of "false consciousness." We must believe that people are rational beings, and therefore always act rationally. We may not understand their rationales, but that in no way militates against the existence of these rationales or reduces our responsibility to attempt to apprehend them. And finally, we must learn to be vulnerable enough to allow our world to turn upside down in order to allow the realities of others to edge themselves into our consciousness. In other words, we must become ethnographers in the true sense.

Teachers are in an ideal position to play this role, to attempt to get all of the issues on the table in order to initiate true dialogue. This can only be done, however, by seeking out those whose perspectives may differ most, by learning to give their words complete attention, by understanding one's own power, even if that power stems merely from being in the majority, by being unafraid to raise questions about discrimination and voicelessness with people of color, and to listen, no, to *hear* what they say. I suggest that the results of such interactions may be the most powerful and empowering coalescence yet seen in the educational realm — for *all* teachers and for *all* the students they teach.

Notes

1. Such a discussion, limited as it is by space constraints, must treat the intersection of class and race somewhat simplistically. For the sake of clarity, however, let me define a few terms: "Black" is used herein to refer to those who share some or all aspects of "core black culture" (Gwaltney, 1980, p. xxiii), that is, the mainstream of Black America — neither those who have entered the ranks of the bourgeoisie nor those who are participants in the disenfranchised underworld. "Middle class" is used broadly to refer to the predominantly White American "mainstream." There are, of course, non-White people who also fit into this category; at issue is their cultural identification, not necessarily the color of their skin. (I must add that there are other non-White people, as well as poor White people, who have indicated to me that their perspectives are similar to those attributed herein to Black people.)

2. *Multicultural Britain: "Crosstalk,"* National Centre of Industrial Language Training, Commission for Racial Equality, London, England, John Twitchin, Producer.

3. I would like to thank Michelle Foster, who is presently planning a more in-depth treatment of the subject, for her astute clarification of this idea.

4. Bernstein (1975) makes a similar point when he proposes that different educational frames cannot be successfully institutionalized in the lower levels of education until there are fundamental changes at the post-secondary levels.

References

Apple, M. W. (1979). *Ideology and curriculum.* Boston: Routledge & Kegan Paul.

Bernstein, B. (1975). Class and pedagogies: Visible and invisible. In B. Bernstein, *Class, codes, and control* (vol. 3). Boston: Routledge & Kegan Paul.

Britton, J., Burgess, T., Martin, N., McLeod, A., & Rosen, H. (1975/1977). *The development of writing abilities.* London: Macmillan Education for the Schools Council, and Urbana, IL: National Council of Teachers of English.

Cazden, C. (1987, January). *The myth of autonomous text.* Paper presented at the Third International Conference on Thinking, Hawaii.

Delpit, L. D. (1986). Skills and other dilemmas of a progressive Black educator. *Harvard Educational Review, 56,* 379–385.

Foster, M. (1987). *It's cookin' now: An ethnographic study of the teaching style of a successful Black teacher in an urban community college.* Unpublished doctoral dissertation, Harvard University.

Gwaltney, J. (1980). *Drylongso.* New York: Vintage Books.

Heath, S. B. (1983). *Ways with words.* Cambridge, Eng.: Cambridge University Press.

Massey, G. C., Scott, M. V., & Dornbusch, S. M. (1975). Racism without racists: Institutional racism in urban schools. *Black Scholar, 7*(3), 2–11.

Siddle, E. V. (1986). *A critical assessment of the natural process approach to teaching writing.* Unpublished qualifying paper, Harvard University.

Siddle, E. V. (1988). *The effect of intervention strategies on the revisions ninth graders make in a narrative essay.* Unpublished doctoral dissertation, Harvard University.

Snow, C. E., Arlman-Rup, A., Hassing, Y., Josbe, J., Joosten, J., & Vorster, J. (1976). Mother's speech in three social classes. *Journal of Psycholinguistic Research, 5,* 1–20.

I take full responsibility for all that appears herein; however, aside from those mentioned by name in this text, I would like to thank all of the educators and students around the country who have been so willing to contribute their perspectives to the formulation of these ideas, especially Susan Jones, Catherine Blunt, Dee Stickman, Sandra Gamble, Willard Taylor, Mickey Monteiro, Denise Burden, Evelyn Higbee, Joseph Delpit Jr., Valerie Montoya, Richard Cohen, and Mary Denise Thompson.

This chapter is an edited version of a speech presented at the Ninth Annual Ethnography in Education Research Forum, University of Pennsylvania, February 5-6, 1988.

"How Come There Are
No Brothers on That List?"
Hearing the Hard Questions
All Children Ask

KATHE JERVIS

In this chapter, Kathe Jervis explores how children's experiences of race often go unnoticed or ignored by teachers, and how their questions about race go unaddressed. In her study of the initial year of a public middle school in New York City, Jervis found — in retrospect, through an examination of and reflection on her field notes — that students continually asked questions about race, culture, and ethnicity, particularly "Who am I in this school community?" and that teachers continually missed or ignored these opportunities for teaching and learning around these crucial issues in the educational lives of children. Jervis observes that even in a school that seeks to create a diverse and integrated school community, in which teachers assert a commitment to equity and openness around these complex issues, the silence about race is deafening. She argues that unless educators actively, constantly, and honestly explore the implications of race, culture, and ethnicity with each other and with their students, discussions that might be opened by children's questions will never happen. Jervis concludes that, although discussions about race are difficult, educators — especially White educators — need to focus attention on race and racism if children's questions about discrimination are ever to be a part of school discourse and if equity is truly going to be an attainable educational goal.

Bias, both conscious and unconscious, reflecting traditional and unexamined habits of thought, keeps up barriers that must come down if equal opportunity and nondiscrimination are ever genuinely to become this country's law and practice.
— *Supreme Court Justice Ruth Bader Ginsburg in* Pena v. Aderand,
a 1995 dissenting opinion on Affirmative Action

Teachers are in an ideal position . . . to attempt to get all of the issues on the table in order to initiate true dialogue. This can only be done, however, by seeking out those whose perspectives may differ most, by learning to give their words complete attention, by understanding one's own power, even if that power stems merely from being in the majority, by being unafraid to raise questions about discrimination and voicelessness with people of color, and to listen, no, to hear what they say.

— Lisa Delpit, *"The Silenced Dialogue: Power and Pedagogy in Educating Other People's Children"*

People who have no choice but to live their life in their black skins know racism when they see it. Racism is never subtle to the victim. Only White people say race doesn't matter.

— *Carrie Morris, Pathways School Faculty Member*

When I was hired to document the first year of a New York City public middle school, my job was to provide feedback and raise questions that would encourage more reflective practice, and then to write about the dilemmas facing this new school.[1] As I began this documentation at Pathways, as I am calling the school, I joined a faculty with whom I shared common values and a high degree of trust.[2] What I was to focus on was not set in stone; however, when I went over my notes at the end of the first year, the themes of race and ethnicity stood out prominently. Almost every incident that caught my eye seemed tinged by issues of equity, differences, and how children are known as part of their own cultures. Equally striking was the fact that, despite the faculty's expressed commitment to structures that supported equity and respected differences, my notes suggested that children's daily experience of race went undiscussed among the adults. I kept returning to how this school, which sought, according to its founding vision, "to enroll students with a diverse racial, economic, ethnic, and ability mix," in fact managed to avoid talking about race, even when events seemed to demand it.[3] I was further struck by how I, as a White staff member, had registered events without seeing them and had failed to understand earlier the meaning of what I had recorded.

Neither an evaluator nor a neutral observer, I was a documenter who was also fully engaged in working for the success of the school, and my role included staff responsibilities.[4] I had an advisory group that allowed me access to issues I might never have thought to raise were I not meeting with parents, reading student journals, and otherwise participating in the daily life of the school.[5] In addition to what I learned from my advisory, my data came from direct observations, interviews, casual conversations, faculty meeting notes, and school documents. I started with observations of children and actual events rather than the literature or theory.

My interpretation of selected school events begins in September 1990 and continues through June 1991. Though I have consciously tried to incorporate other faculty perspectives, this is my story, or at least one that I have shaped. Not everyone on the staff saw events the way I did. When a teacher asked me why I focused this article on race rather than on the development of curriculum at Pathways, I knew that what framed my question was not the burning issue for all faculty. I was in uncharted territory; race had not been a salient category in planning for the documentation. Racial boundaries provoke the deepest questions of personal identity and social structure, as well as the deepest silences, and an exploration of race is not what I or anyone else initially expected from this documentation. Only later, as

I created written pictures of daily school life, did I notice how children's questions about race and ethnicity dropped from the faculty's collective memory as soon as the moment of questioning came to an end, and how everyone on the staff, including me, missed what children seemed to be asking: "Who am I in this school community?"

This blindness to racial issues in schools has complex causes and deep roots. This blindness caused Pathways faculty to overlook, deny, or ignore issues of power embedded in race. We did not question who talked honestly, or who listened to whom, nor did individuals look critically at why some children became more central to the school's agenda than others. Faculty of color often vented their concerns outside of formal meetings. In the meetings, according to my notes, the majority White faculty did not appear to question their own perspectives, or ask whether there was a need to see kids more clearly in terms of their race and culture or to consider alternative interpretations of behavior.

Personal silence about race is common, and institutions like Pathways are shaped as much by what does not happen as by what does. Pathways' handpicked faculty had plunged into the hard work of founding a new school without anticipating the need for any overt discussion of race, and ingrained dominant societal norms prevailed by default.

All schools take refuge in silence about race to some degree, and many educators are novices at constructing multicultural, integrated school settings (Grant & Secada, 1990). What my documentation revealed is that racial issues were often invisible to the majority White faculty, or thought not to be about race. But like ultraviolet sun rays, damage from unexplored racial attitudes often appears long after the actual exposure. Building a successful integrated school means paying attention to people of color and attending to White racial attitudes before emergencies require it.

That society's problems play out in schools means that schools also offer an opportunity to open a dialogue about race and equality, yet this dialogue is never easy. At the heart of the story I am telling here is the striking ambiguity inherent in the individual incidents; people at Pathways disagreed about whether, and in what ways, events were racial. I have attempted to present enough details so readers can draw their own conclusions about what may be racial, adolescent, gender, happenstance, denial, or a mix of other factors that influence what happens in schools (McCarthy, 1993).

A lot occurred at Pathways that first year. Bringing into being an educational vision for sixth and seventh graders required instilling an ethos, setting standards, and establishing moral authority while simultaneously facing bureaucratic constraints, learning how to run a fire drill, and mollifying anxious parents. For this article, I set aside these monumental tasks and ignored many unique events that interacted with race. While readers may conclude from the incidents I have chosen to describe that Pathways faculty frequently got caught up in racial crises, that would be inaccurate and misleading.

Documenting Rarely Heard Stories

A colleague, Brenda Engel, influenced my approach to the work at Pathways. She makes a distinction between "documentation," which is a nonjudgmental and neutral selection of systematically collected documents reflecting a "complicated, many-faceted sequence of events that has occurred over a period of time so that it may be examined at leisure," and a "documented account," in which the documents are used to support a thesis (Engel, 1975, p. 3). This article is an example of the latter; I have chosen particular incidents, teased out from a complex whole, to address what I feel goes on everywhere, even in the "best schools," as adults and children try to untangle the larger societal issues that play themselves out in schools.

One purpose of a documenter is to function as a mirror, helping to make practitioners aware of their own practice. In my experience, once all the particulars of any incident are written down — what exactly was said or done — it becomes harder for faculty to stay with comfortable, unreflective thinking. The racial dynamics at Pathways likely mirror what happens in many schools facing similar challenges. In this article, I explore these dynamics and call attention to the deep levels of awareness necessary to change previously unexamined behavior.

This article evolved as I circulated drafts to all the staff, taking their comments into account with each revision. Though faculty talk about race was rare at the time of the incidents recorded here, I have included many of their responses to what I wrote. That the faculty engaged with me in this documentation effort is a tribute to their honesty, good faith, and their willingness to learn from the work.

During the rewrites, colleagues, friends, and family also added information, took issue with my viewpoints, and challenged me to clarify meaning, teaching me all along. For me, this is one way of socially constructing knowledge. Writing this piece has been a struggle to transform a still incomplete learning experience into more solid personal understanding.

What follows are glimpses of daily life at Pathways that invite educators to think about how we can begin and sustain the hard conversations about race that will allow us to hear — really hear — our own, as well as our children's, questions.

Creating a New School

Located on the edge of Harlem in a nineteenth-century elementary school building that just happened to have a vacant top floor, Pathways opened with its facility in a state of terrible disrepair. "As I was walking up the steps for the first time, I felt like I had spiders crawling around in my stomach. How come the school is so dreadfully damaged with cracks? What have I gotten myself into?" seventh grader Hector Zelaya wrote on the first day. To reach Pathways, Hector and his peers had to traverse the barren playground with its netless basketball hoops, climb up the long flights of stairs, the last of which smelled of wet plaster, and skirt the large buckets positioned to catch the water that dripped through the roof whenever it rained. Even the district office liaison called the setting "a hostile environment." Yet the staff was thrilled. Unlike the anonymous, bureaucratic junior highs with escalating dropout rates and demoralized faculties so often depicted in the press, Pathways was founded by teachers excited about exercising their own autonomy in a small, personal community.[6] Hector, one of many children who responded to the faculty's excitement, ended his essay saying, "When I got to class I felt at home and my worries were over. Now I know it's not just the outside; it's the inside and the people. I'm growing to like it on the first day and later on I'll love it (maybe)."

To build something where nothing existed before captured the founding director's imagination. Jan Palmer had not worked full time since before her oldest child was born. Her biological White and adopted Black children were now grown, and she was ready for the grueling hours that directing a school required. She was not even deterred by her temporary per diem status, which meant that her job showed up on the computer as a vacancy open to any high-seniority teacher.

Unlike their peers in a hiring system in which teachers are assigned to a school by a central office, alternative school directors have the luxury of hiring staff from among those applicants who wish to join their faculty. To select committed teachers who shared the values she considered crucial to founding a new school, Jan interviewed candidates, visited them on site, and invited them to observe her own classroom. She assessed their energy level, their willingness to work hard, and looked for evidence that children were at the center of their focus; too many worksheets, too much dependence on canned curriculum, or too much ego were grounds for rejection. As it turned out, none of the people she hired had weekend or after-school jobs, all were married, and all but the youngest had children. On the surface, we seemed more alike than different.

Nevertheless, we were a diverse staff. Don Jackson had previously taught for twenty years in "regular" junior highs, where he was often a minority White teacher. Carrie Morris, a seasoned African American teacher and former staff developer, was a twenty-year-plus veteran of the New York City Public Schools with more varied experience teaching children of all races than the rest of us. Bilingual, bicultural Lucy Lopez-Garcia, a Puerto Rican, moved comfortably within both Anglo and Latino cultures. A nursery school teacher only a few credits shy of a teaching credential, Lucy was delighted to work officially as an aide, but to function as a faculty member who was centrally important to colleagues, children, and parents in her role as an advisor and teacher of art. For Jim Serota, a White Ivy League graduate who had worked in an inner-city after-school program for two years, this was his first teaching job. Marilyn Ross, another young, White, first-year teacher, joined the staff part time in October. For several years, Jan and I been colleagues at a small, integrated middle school. When she decided to start a new school, I saw it as an opportunity to capture the experience in writing, and we conceived this documentation project, which built on my previous descriptions of classrooms and my twenty years of teaching.

The staff agreed with the vision statement that "a good school for preadolescents maintains a diverse community to educate children for life in a democratic society," but no one thought that implementing this vision was going to be easy. As Carrie told the deputy superintendent, "You have to engineer life in a diverse group to make it work. You can't leave it — any of it — to chance." This integrated faculty actively sought out White students to create a diverse student body and, at the same time, took care to keep those students from dominating academically. Although the staff did not spend planning time explicitly talking about race, they did engineer a four-pronged effort designed to achieve a fair and equitable school. First, the school recruited a cohort of academically proficient Black and Latino students, whose presence as role models confounded the stereotype of integrated schools in which Whites remain at the top of the academic hierarchy. Referred by an organization that prepared students of color for independent schools, these high-powered entrants became academic stars. Second, faculty planned heterogeneous classes, which prevented labeling children by their academic proficiency or lack of it. Third, teachers created openings for all kinds of talents to surface. They carefully mixed race, age, and abilities of students in subject matter classes, advisories, and special projects that required various skills. Fourth, they modeled respectful appreciation of differences through a year-long social studies curriculum, "Coming to America," which attempted to honor contributions from a variety of cultures.

The school enrolled sixty-three students. Although children do not actually come in standard demographic slots, convention requires labeling their heritages. We categorized slightly more than one-third of the student body as Latino, slightly over one-third as African American, slightly less than one-third as White, and two students as Asian. All students spoke English; many were bilingual in English and Spanish. Forty-three children applied for either free lunch (if their family of four had an annual income of less than $16,500) or for reduced-fee lunch (family income of less than $23,000). Reading and math scores ranged from the eighth to the ninety-ninth-plus percentile. When school began, no faculty member had taught children so diverse along so many dimensions, nor had their students been in such mixed classrooms before.

Few mortals succeed in meeting their highest goals, including the founders of schools in the first year. The stories I tell about race may suggest that this new middle school didn't come close to providing a good place for children, which would not be true. That Pathways students loved to come to school is amply documented in the essays I asked them to write in October, February, and June. Sixth grader Marie Diaz's June list distills the satisfaction that many students expressed in their essays:

Some things that I like about Pathways are:
1. On trips teachers aren't always watching what you do.
2. There's a lot of gossip going on.
3. The teachers are very, very friendly.
4. If you have a problem they will talk to you about it.
5. Teachers trust us.
6. I like science because we get to experiment with things, not just read a science book and then write a paragraph about what you read.
7. They take us to a lot of trips.

Further evidence that Pathways children enjoyed school comes from the official records: On the same day that Marie wrote her essay, a board of education attendance auditor tallied the books and concluded that Pathways had one of the highest teacher and student attendance rates of any school in New York City.

The small size, the strong advisory system, the care with which the faculty observed children, and the trust the school inspired meant that students exposed their feelings and that faculty took note of them. Yet despite conscientious attention to equitable structures and the teachers' concerted efforts to know children well, students' talk about race often caught faculty off guard. When race surfaced at unplanned moments, children's questions went unaddressed.

"He's Not One of Us, Is He?": A Child's Fleeting Question

It is easy to see race as an issue in a school where, day after day, the students in the top tracks are White and the students in remedial classes are primarily children of color. It is harder to make meaning from conversational snatches that easily get lost in the sweep of school life. The following 30-second incident has buried in it a child's real question. From my notes the first week of school:

> It is the first afternoon together in the park and the first full day of school. Don, a teacher (White) organizes a football game. Duke, a sixth grader (White), literally mows down Sam (White) on the other team, violating the agreed upon rules. Several kids (African American) complain. Duke calls them "Schmucks," and angrily retreats, muttering under his breath about how he knows the rules because he has played football all his life. Another teacher (White) encourages them to "forget it" and get on with the game, but several kids (all races) from both teams go immediately to Carrie (African American). They are baffled by Duke's behavior, by his insistence that he was playing correctly, by his belief that he had the right to knock Sam down, and his verbal epithet, which these kids took to be a racial slur. Arnold (African American) puts his arm next to Carrie's, and says seriously, "He isn't one of us, is he?"
>
> "What do you mean?" Carrie says. Arnold replies, "You know, his skin isn't dark. He called us 'Smokes'." (Field notes, September 13)

"He isn't one of us, is he?" is a basic human way to categorize the world. The disintegration of this football game exemplifies the subtle ways race seeps into children's consciousness. Arnold, as he compared his arm to Carrie's, thought that he heard his classmate say "smokes," referring to his skin color. Arnold's question and its accompanying gesture have become, for me, emblematic of the complicated, ambiguous nature of race and racism.[7]

Arnold did not hear "schmucks," the Yiddish word of derision in general use, which I heard clearly, and it may not have been a familiar word to him. So while Duke's insult was not a "racist" slur, this exchange illustrates the way Arnold made sense of his newly integrated world. This incident confirmed for me that when adults and children do not know each other and understand even less about each other's cultural backgrounds, race easily becomes the most salient personal attribute. Ambiguous remarks fall into the most obvious category, which is skin color, especially when students see color in discriminatory terms.

Nothing is inherently odd about noticing race and skin color, but in this society they are fraught with hidden meanings. Misinformation and lack of knowledge about race can be a minefield when no acceptable forum exists to raise questions. Although Arnold had never been in the same classroom with Whites before, and Duke had never been a racial minority at school, we never thought to create such a forum at Pathways. As a staff we were unprepared for students' barely articulated questions about this new racial mix. Whether due to conscious avoidance or unconscious denial, or a mix of both, I never talked to either child about what happened, nor did Carrie and I discuss it with each other or think to bring it to a faculty meeting. Arnold's question remained unexplored and Duke's behavior went unexamined. Pathways' curriculum, which was explicitly meant to be "gender fair and multicultural," openly addressed the question, "Who am I and how did my ancestors come to America?" yet it did not provide a place for Arnold to consider the implications of what he really wanted to know: "He isn't one of us, is he?"

The faculty listened to students and encouraged them to articulate their feelings, which paid off in personal relationships and mutual trust, but what was left unsaid or ignored about racial and cultural identity left children with a powerfully negative message. "People identify others by their skin color before their cultural identity," Carrie said after she read a draft of this article, and lamented that "little is embedded in any school's curriculum that really speaks to these issues."

Servant or Slave?

Before the staff was even in place, Pathways received a grant to hire a "playwright in residence" to teach all students "writers' workshop" twice weekly for six weeks. Jan hired Martin Cane, who came in mid-September to share his ideas with the faculty:

> Martin Cane, a young [White] playwright, arrived to meet the faculty. During the staff meeting, he explained how he is going to work: "First there will be a staged reading by professional actors of my own play. Putting on my play first means that I put myself on the line before I ask kids to do it. It is also a chance to have a common experience. Then kids will write scenes, from 2-10 pages and I will pick eight of them. The criteria for selection could be diversity of topic, how hard a kid worked, how passionate she is, how much of a breakthrough it is, or how much possibility it opens up for kids. After the scenes have been selected, professional actors will spend the day rehearsing plays with the student writers, and then there will be an all school event for families that night." (Field notes, September 12)

Faculty were impressed with Martin's values and program plans. In early October, he started teaching three sections of writers' workshop. His facility with language, his ability to provide students with instant phrases that got them unstuck, his energy and good actor's voice, and his swift pacing entranced me. After the first day, a sixth grader said about this master of language so skilled in releasing kids' imaginations, "That man sees things the rest of us don't see."

Martin's three back-to-back classes drained even his prodigious energy. Although the school tried to rearrange the schedule, Martin's own work prevented any shift. The emotions unleashed in his classes spilled out in unpredictable ways, especially when his energy ebbed. During the second week of Martin's program, he asked students to write about a scary emotion, and Bart, a White child, recalled an experience from several years earlier that still evoked his strong response. When Bart lived in South Africa, he found a poisonous snake in his garden, and he and a servant killed it. On hearing Bart read this story aloud, Sal, a Latino child, leapt up out of his chair and said, "You had slaves!" It was an accusation, not a question. Martin reddened, and said, "Servant is the word," and moved right on; this exchange took under thirty seconds.

Sal could not calm down, and after class he bullied Bart until a teacher intervened. Sal would not budge from his opinion that having a servant in South Africa meant that Bart's family was rich and owned slaves, both reasons to be hostile toward Bart. From that point on, this physically powerful child hectored the meeker Bart on many occasions.

Although this brief exchange between Sal and Bart appeared in my notes, and others witnessed it, we missed its racially loaded implications. We were inattentive to Sal and Bart when they most needed adult support to work through their strong feelings and to see the world through each others' eyes.

As a part-time, short-term artist-in-residence, Martin may have been the catalyst for this situation, but the regular faculty held the responsibility for helping children interpret it. If individual teachers are to see that children achieve a deeper understanding of class differences and racial issues, they need to generate opportunities for the whole faculty to discuss these topics among themselves. Had the school done so in this case, we might have seen that Sal needed a place to make his deep concerns about slavery explicit so that other students could recognize his perspective about the Black struggle in South Africa and come to understand what set him off. Faculty missed the chance to create such a forum. Instead, the only visible aftermath of this brief incident was Sal's continual picking on Bart, which then became an issue not of race, but of disciplining Sal for his "hot temper." It seems to me that adults' urge to curb unwanted behavior often shifts their focus from children to discipline, especially when rules can be invoked to cover situations, such as discussions of race, that make them uncomfortable.

"How Come There Are No Brothers on That List?"

Once the students had completed their play scenes, Martin chose eight of them to be staged by professional actors. He carefully described his process of selection:

> I made choices by first reading all the plays without regard for racial diversity or kids who needed support. I put scenes in three piles — strong, maybes, and rejects. Those in the third pile either were unfinished, had no investment, were unclear, or had no conflict — a central aim of my teaching. Then I reread them to see if I made any mistakes, but didn't move any into the "strong" pile. Then I shaped the performance evening, looking for humor, strong emotion, and a variety of subjects. All three classes had to be represented. Only after I met those criteria did I look at individuals for racial and gender balance. I chose one child who had come far and this would make a big difference to his growth. I couldn't help it that 6 out of the 8 selected plays were by girls. (Field notes, December 3)

On a Monday morning, two weeks after he had last taught, Martin returned to the first-period writing class, now overseen by regular Pathways faculty, and gave a moving introduction before announcing his final selections. He said with feeling, "My plays don't always get produced, and I have to accept that. It is part of being a playwright. I want you to know that when I tell you all of the plays were good, I really mean it. If I didn't believe the plays were good, I wouldn't say so." He named four children whose scenes were chosen and took them immediately to work with the professional actors. Other students quietly continued reading and writing.

Martin gave the same introduction to the second class, and took two children out. Only one boy, Derek, objected loudly, "My play was so fresh. It's not fair." Third period was different. This noisy class, for which Martin had the least energy, still did good work. Martin gave a short, less heartfelt version of what he had said to the other classes. Without talking about himself or the quality of the plays, he said wearily that "choosing play scenes was hard," and named two authors, who left with him to rehearse. Both of these winners were White, although those chosen from the other classes were children of color. After Martin's departure, Marilyn, a White faculty member newly hired to teach the writers' workshop, introduced an assignment, but the kids were not with her. Amid some commotion in the back of the room, Jerome, an African American, said rather tentatively, but in a voice loud enough to make everyone listen, "It's not my question, but someone wants to know, 'How come there are no brothers on that list?'"

Above the noisy responses — everyone wanted an answer — Jan took over. In the room to help with the play-scene logistics, she moved to the front of the class and began, "That is not true. The list is balanced." Pulling a list from her pocket, she read it aloud, naming an Asian and a Hispanic; when she got to Bianca, whose surname is Hispanic, she looked up and said, "Bianca is Hispanic." The class exploded. Everyone had something to say at the same time, and the voices got even louder before the crescendo peaked. Forgetting the original question of why no Black boys were chosen from this class, kids shrieked: "Bianca told me she was Black!" "How could anyone who talks like that be Hispanic?" "She has a Black attitude." The kids were astonished that anyone thought Bianca was Hispanic. Bianca's heritage is extremely complex; she is the biological child of a Latino father and a White mother, and the foster child of African American parents. Her peers saw her as Black. They totally overlooked the fact that if she were Black, then the list included at least one Black person. Bianca was not in this section of writers' workshop, so she could not answer questions about her background. For the adults in the room, all we thought we knew about supporting children's need for self-identification went down the drain, and the issue raised by Jerome — "How come there are no brothers on that list?" — went with it.

Voices were getting still louder when Lisa, an African American, changed the subject, which generated even more heat. "Why did I do this play anyway if it wasn't chosen?" she protested. "I spent half a week thinking of a topic and the other half writing seven pages. A waste. A pure waste." She was raging. Her anger at not being chosen despite her hard work sent hot sparks into the room. Serena, a Latina, answered her articulately and passionately: "Not everyone can be chosen. You still learn from writing." Energy whirled around the room and kids weren't in any state to listen. The period ended, mercifully for us, with a *deus ex machina* when two unplanned visitors arrived, almost as if in answer to our prayer for a diversion. Amid much chaos, the visitors offered us good wishes for our new school, and the class left for lunch. Jerome's question remained unanswered.

Although a child's whispered remark about the race of the winning playwrights should have alerted us to the conversation students were eager to have, we were more inclined to bury this uncomfortable 45-minute period in oblivion. Neither Jan, Marilyn, nor I brought it up informally or at any faculty meeting. The issues of children's racial and ethnic identity could have provided fertile ground for weeks of curriculum, but the pace of the day crowded out time for a topic that was hard for faculty to discuss and for which no particular space had been created within the school structure. Instead, we were embarrassed by a classroom eruption that took us beyond our own comfort level. To us, this noisy digression merely interfered with our pedagogical intentions, and we missed the opportunity for inquiry it might have provided. The issue of race as a factor in the selection process had disappeared from any formal discussion among children or faculty. The incident, however, did not end there.

The Pathways faculty worked hard to support children who struggled to find their own voices and act on their views. Lisa, still harboring strong feelings about why she wasn't selected, appropriately took this issue to her advisory, which wrote Martin the following letter:

12/3/90

To Mr. Martin Cane

In our Advisory we all discussed about how you chose the scenes for the plays.

1. I think we all understand that only a certain amount of people would be chosen. We all wish that we would be recognized for our work.
2. Before the plays were chosen you gave some people the idea that their plays were going to be chosen by giving them the idea that their work was Excellent.
3. What was the reason those people got chosen over the rest of us?

Lisa's initial outrage about how hard she worked on her play cut to the heart of the school's double message: We are inclusive until we decide to be exclusive. Lisa's concerns in class, mingled with the talk about race that charged the atmosphere, grew out of her sense of powerlessness when confronted with the subjectivity of the play-scene selections. She regained some control by going to her advisory. The advisory's letter, a mature, logical response devoid of the intense feelings she expressed in class, lacked explicit mention of race, perhaps because word had spread that Martin's list was, in fact, racially balanced. On it were a Black boy, a Black girl, two Latinas, a White boy, a White girl, an Asian girl, and Bianca with her complex background. Since evidence disproved the contention that there were no brothers on the list, the original question slipped back underground.

Had we adults who witnessed these complicated feelings listened more carefully and been more attuned to the crucial importance of students' questions about race, we might have discussed the explosive class at the next faculty meeting. Then all of us, including Lisa's advisor, who had not known about what happened, would have been better prepared to open conversations with children about racial exclusion and identity. Just because there was one brother on the list didn't mean the discussion should have ended.

Conversation about children's racial identity — so obviously ripe for exploration — never reappeared, at least not in any form that caught my attention. Only in hindsight did I see the possibilities for supporting children's understanding of their own heritages (Cohen, 1993). As for other fallout, a district colleague, one of our visitors who arrived in the midst of this classroom chaos, bruited it around that he was surprised discipline was so lax at Pathways. Such criticism was frequently leveled by adults in the school community when kids expressed volatile feelings about race, as in the struggle between Sal and Bart.

This incident might have been lost, except that I took notes. After I circulated a description of this episode to the staff as part of my first draft of this article, the faculty wondered what initially prompted LaTasha, an African American student, to question the composition of the play-scene list, and what caused Jerome to repeat her question. Why didn't LaTasha ask her own question? Was hers a casual query, which then sparked Jerome's urgent need to know? Why had the issue of race not come up during class sooner? Gender issues had been debated heatedly in other classes since the beginning of the year, yet talk about race had been essentially absent. Lucy speculated that perhaps Pathways' emphasis on belonging to a new school community, conveyed in the much-repeated phrase "we are all pioneers together," may have felt to the children like a "melting pot" philosophy that discouraged rather than invited discussions of differences. Did kids not feel safe enough to ask hard personal questions until now? And, even more disturbing, how much energy did kids of color spend wondering what was safe to say in a White teacher's class (Delpit, 1990)?

Equally significant was the issue of selectivity. No one absorbed what Martin had said in September: "The hardest task is to provide an inclusive experience and then be exclusive about it." Although children and teachers knew only eight plays would be selected, the reality hadn't sunk in. The children felt misled and took the route available through race to express their discomfort with a White male who closed the gate on their aspirations to be selected. A more established school might — just might — have thought more about the consequences of competitiveness interjected by an outsider.

These three vignettes caught faculty off balance. The following two incidents, involving Duke, who "mowed down" Sam in a football game the first day of school, and Derek, who also singled himself out on the first day, are weightier, with more apparent long-term consequences for these students and the school. While the stories differ, both boys shared a deep uncertainty about their place in school, and neither ever became fully part of the Pathways community.

Whites as a Minority

Changing demographics have produced a relatively new phenomenon in public education: White students as a racial minority in urban schools. Pathways staff believes that integration is worth preserving, but even if it were not — as many families of color are beginning to say — public schools are open to every child and all children deserve to be part of the school community. Only in retrospect were faculty able to raise the question, How do we serve all children together in the same educational institution?

That first year, faculty assumed that enough White children at Pathways were comfortable, so little attention was paid to the issue of "minority" White children. Faculty were disinclined to talk about children whose White skin already gave them a privileged position in society. Jan said later that the particular White children who were struggling were "finding out that in this school they are not the aristocracy." Carrie added, "It's good for their souls," but she also pointed out that "White kids are paying the price of a discriminatory society, as are Black and Latino kids."

My notes about Duke's experience as a White student at Pathways highlight one example of what teachers face if they want to integrate all children in a school community. White children do experience fewer problems in society; "Duke will always be able to get a taxi in the middle of the night," Carrie reminded me. Nevertheless, Duke needed to find a place at school. These excerpts from my advisory notes early in the year show my own inadequate and tentative responses as I threw myself into unfamiliar territory:

> One of the Black kids brought his sketch pad from home full of magic marker cartoons, and explained that he does them by eye, not by tracing. Everyone admired the drawings. When he came to a black-faced Mickey Mouse, Duke said, "Hey Mickey Mouse isn't Black." Kids said emphatically, "Why not?" and Duke backed off.
>
> Then, Bianca read her book report on *The Miss USA Pageant*. In the course of it, she was asked: "How did you know how old the new Miss USA was?" She answered, "I bin knowing it." Duke snapped, "You can't say that. It's not right." I said, "It may not be standard English, but it is absolutely correct in Bianca's home language. It means she has known it for a long time." (Field notes, September 18)

Though Duke's two contributions to this advisory session were sharply rebuffed, I never thought to explain to him why his peers and I objected. My notes from that day include another incident:

> The next thing I knew Jose was yelling, "Fight in the gym." When I arrived in the gym, Michael (African American) — and Duke were indeed fighting. Michael, feeling the sting of Duke's behavior over the last few days, said to me, "I don't like the way he has an attitude with teachers." I took Duke — the more upset — into the office; teary-eyed and angry, he said, "I'm one of the few White boys here. I grew up in an upper class White community and I'm not taking anything from anybody." I was surprised to hear a child use the term "upper class" and ignored it, but I wondered if he assumed that he would be treated differently from others. I quoted Jan's line reminding him America is changing and he will be better prepared to be a leader if he learns how to get on in a diverse group. I reiterated emphatically that this has to be a safe place for everybody — no fights, no snap judgments about the way others speak or draw. He agreed and pulled himself together while I went off to explain to Michael that fights are not allowed, and that while we have to teach Duke a few things, it isn't his responsibility to change Duke's attitude by himself. Relieved that I did not call his mother, he said, "Thank you for this talk." (Field notes, September 18)

At the time, I wondered about Duke's sense of entitlement — what I knew about his neighborhood or his family background gave me no clue to how he understood his self-proclaimed socioeconomic status. To my knowledge, he was a regular middle-class kid. Yet I never addressed his feelings of superiority, nor did I recognize that uncertainty and fear about this new school might be the real issue for him. Instead, I pointed out that White children do face fewer problems in society and told Duke he would be better prepared for today's society if he learned to lead by experiencing life as a racial minority. My reaction reflects an unexamined assumption about White privilege, and is one reason why people of color oppose integration that historically focuses on benefits for White children (Foster, 1993; Ladson-Billings, 1994). While I impressed upon the boys our desire to make the Pathways community safe for everyone, and I thought I made sense talking to Michael about Duke's prejudices, it never occurred to me to sit them down to talk with each other.

On October ninth, Duke apparently told a Latino fifth grader from the elementary school downstairs to "bug off" (at least that is what he said in his sanitized version). He admitted the child's only provocation was to be in the way. The offended child had threatened to bring an older brother and his friends to the playground "for protection," and Pathways students standing nearby (all Black, except for one White friend of Duke's) had refused to get involved. Understandably sensing danger, they had gone immediately to the Pathways office to report what had happened. The dangerous feeling lingered for a few days and to straighten things out with the elementary school, the building principal met with this fifth grader and the Pathways students who had witnessed the challenge. From my notes:

> The principal lectured the Pathways' kids on how they were outsiders in the neighborhood and tried to get them to see how the elementary kids felt with new non-neighborhood kids on the playground. At first it seemed like her lecture only exacerbated the middle school kids' feelings of nervousness and Duke's feelings of being in the minority. In talking it over in our own staff meeting we concluded her message about outsiders is so basic to the neighborhood ethic that we have to take it seriously. It was decided that rather than have the building principal and Jan supervise the playground for the next two weeks ("Two ladies for protection — no way," the men on the faculty said), kids would just be sent home immediately after school. Don pointed out what everybody needed to remember: "Duke doesn't understand that talk connects up with action much more quickly in this neighborhood. Duke has a lot to learn." (Field notes, October 15)

Faculty continued to watch Duke. By the time of his self-evaluation, we saw some small progress. This mid-semester exercise asked students, "What are the most important things you have learned?" On his first draft, Duke answered "math facts." The next day, on his final draft, he wrote instead, "I learned a lot about other kids." By Thanksgiving he had stopped reacting negatively to differences — at least out loud. He still had few friends and hung out only with White males, even when their most obvious commonality was being White. At the parent conference following this self-evaluation, his father agreed with us about Duke's social growth: "Yeah, things are better. He doesn't come home with stories anymore about how he's the only one who knows anything and everyone else is dumb."

Duke and Carrie had a good relationship, though she had no compunction about describing him, out of his hearing, as a racist. She often said, "after all, he is a kid." At Carrie's insistence, he stopped telling her offensive off-color jokes and apologized when she pointed out his arrogant behavior. He declared science with Carrie "my best subject." If given a choice in class with whom to work, he never chose a child of color. He did not socialize after school or join the basketball team, though he did play pickup games at lunch with racially mixed teams. He even played on the girls' kickball team when "they needed a good kicker." He knew a lot about baseball — statistics, history, strategy — but in the classroom Duke shared reluctantly, and others listened equally reluctantly. He affected the student body very little, except that kids were aware of his racial attitudes, as shown in my notes from the spring:

> The kids are watching a slide show in preparation for the three day camping trip. The quality of attention borders on the disrespectful. Many in the audience have never been to camp — or even away from home overnight, and nervous tension is high. The slides, shown by the camp director, picture much younger children —

all White. The (Black) boys on the back bench were loud and disruptive. One of them said derisively: "Look at all those Dukes up there." I was not meant to hear their remark and they didn't know that I did. When I reported this remark to the faculty, frankly thinking the kids had observed Duke well, Marilyn (White) rightly reminded me that, "If they had been White boys talking about a Black child, you wouldn't have hesitated for a minute to stop them." True. It never occurred to me to intervene. (It was easier for me to label Duke "racist" than initiate a hard conversation about "all those Dukes" with the boys on the back bench.) (Field notes, May 1)

Late in the spring, Duke began to talk about leaving Pathways. At first he said, "This school doesn't have enough extracurricular activities (though he never stayed for what they had), or that the "work isn't hard enough" (though I believed he didn't push himself to excel); finally, after some urging to be honest, he said it wasn't the school he didn't like, but he wanted to be where his friends were. In advisory, he did what was expected, joined games, and spoke when called on, but he was never central to the group. On a final assignment to write what was important about Pathways, he said:

> It's a small school. The teachers can get to know you better. They have time to work with you. In fact I think they get a little too personal. Like telling you to interact with people you don't really like instead of being with your friends. They worry too much about racism. They worry too much about your personal life instead of your academic life. I met a lot of nice people in my one year, but I really don't feel right here.

This essay matched what other children often noticed about Pathways' size and personal atmosphere. It also called attention to Duke's feelings of being separate and disconnected from the group. Late in the year, I tried to open a discussion with him about what I perceived as his narrowness in his choice of friends, and he didn't like it. Perhaps I didn't know how to talk about race effectively and had not created enough openings during the year for him to say what was on his mind.

Whether Duke is biased because of family or societal attitudes or is merely unhappy with his minority status is not really the issue. If integrated schools are going to succeed, it is imperative to find a way to include "all those Dukes" in the community. Duke never became an accepting or acceptable member of Pathways. Jan willingly admitted that "White children who come from the power structure with more experience and opportunities didn't get enough attention from us," while Carrie pointed out that "all children suffer from racism." The issues around White children may not be the most essential — children of color definitely pay a higher price for society's biases — but if public schools are to be successfully integrated, faculties will have to think harder about Whites as minorities, just as schools are now thinking harder about supporting children of color in predominantly White institutions.

For many White families, sending their children to schools where students are predominantly children of color requires giving up a privileged status gained by virtue of their White skin (McIntosh, 1988). Basic to the problem is this statement overheard at the district office: "If the mix is one-third Black, one-third Hispanic, and one-third White, White parents see the school as two-thirds non-White." Pathways is deliberately trying to achieve that one-third, one-third, one-third ratio in order to maintain an integrated setting. As part of managing that ratio, faculty must do more to insure that White parents are willing partners.

From the viewpoint of justly allocating school resources of faculty time and attention, that expenditure does not seem fair. To call for a big investment of faculty energy might create the impression of giving more of a scarce school resource to the dominant group. Children of color need an equal share of teachers' energy. Even in a school that is respectful of difference, it takes time-consuming, committed, moral leadership to build a school community based on the agreement that we are all citizens in this society together. Certainly, integration must be built on something other than a White, middle-class model for the benefit of Whites, as many Black families are now charging (Ladson-Billings, 1994). Yet, if White children are to learn to be comfortable when they number only a handful in a large group, they and their families will need this leadership. Such moral guidance to do what is right, rather than what is politically expedient for those in power, is not so easily given. My experience at Pathways and other schools suggests that many school communities are not yet prepared for what that leadership might entail.

Veteran White teachers may have thought about educating the increasing numbers of children of color, albeit often in terms of assimilating them into White middle-class norms. Many White teachers — who have rarely been a numerical minority themselves — have little empathy or knowledge about what would make the transition smoother for children who come from a predominantly White setting to a predominantly Black and Latino setting. I have already noted that the faculty made assumptions about White children's comfort levels. Indeed, it was easier for me to ignore Duke's lack of ease because he was White. In comparison with White faculty, Carrie's own racial experiences gave her more insight into Duke's minority status. Yet it was an unfair burden on Carrie to expect her to educate the faculty about race. White faculty already ask too much of faculty of color in interpreting students' behavior; this is work Whites must learn to do.

Do I Have a Place in This School?

The story of Derek's expulsion centers around the daunting challenge of educating other people's children as we would our own (Delpit, 1988). The "we" here refers to any of us who teach children across racial, ethnic, or class boundaries, which includes most teachers in today's urban settings. The background of this story is governance: Who sets the boundaries? Who is "the boss" of the school? What happens when standards of behavior are ignored or defied? In the foreground is Derek, who did not connect with enough Pathways adults to learn as we would like our own children to learn. The vision that every individual was valued faded when faculty seriously disagreed over Derek. Whether the staff used every means at their disposal to help him, and how they interpreted their responsibility or lack of it for Derek's predicament, is one of the story's unresolved and guilt-provoking themes. This story also calls attention to what happens when adults reach an impasse with a child who does not meet their standards of behavior.

Since Pathways faculty ostensibly shared the same values, governance by consensus worked fine when no one had passionate feelings and the issues were not loaded. Congenial meetings, good parties, and genuine friendships cemented faculty bonds. But in a crisis — and no one knew what form it would take until it happened — the method of consensus failed. We had no practice with confrontation, no precedent for resolving heated arguments, and no way to talk at meetings about differing perceptions of each others' actions. As a result, consensus collapsed in a crisis around Derek. No one heard his unarticulated question: "Where is my place in this school?"

From the staff viewpoint, Derek was trouble. Even on the first day of school, when kids were on their best behavior, Derek stood out. In my journal notes of the first all-school meeting, I speculated: "Derek didn't wait to sit on the rug when everyone else did, nor did he want to line up by height for Don's game. Was his reluctance related to his being one of the shortest boys in the school?" From that first day, this twelve-year-old African American boy could disrupt class merely by walking across the room on his way to the bathroom. He might provocatively pull his sweats up and down, or whack a child as he passed, which may have been an affectionate gesture but was disruptive nonetheless. He frequently refused to engage in anything even vaguely academic; thus he never became competent enough at school work to demonstrate that he was making progress.

Over the year, Derek's disrespect for adults — at least the White adults — escalated. Or, perhaps the White adults disrespected Derek by interpreting his behavior though narrow lenses, causing events to escalate.[8] Something about Derek locked faculty into battle with him. Derek was not a "middle-class" kid.[9] He may not have been well understood by White faculty, who focused on his "attitude" and failed to see how he was setting himself up for school failure right before their eyes. We need to understand more about children like Derek who often push adults beyond their own limits, but we also need to recognize how those limits relate to culture, class, and race.

With no one looking carefully at anything about this child except his transgressions, Derek became increasingly lost to view. School structures and faculty support that might have helped him find his way were absent. Yet Pathways faculty did have structures for paying attention to individual children. Each month, we scheduled a Descriptive Review, an activity designed to build a community based on shared knowledge about children, which entailed an in-depth look at one particular child. For each Descriptive Review, the faculty chose children who caused them to "tear their hair out" or who raised particular linguistic or pedagogical issues.[10] Based on those criteria Derek qualified, but each month we chose children who appealed to us more than Derek.

Of all the faculty, only Carrie got on well with Derek. Her ability to hear the hard-to-ignore children who were often disliked by others served him well. When she asked in a strong throaty tone, "Darling, what are you doing?" Derek frequently stopped his misbehavior and apologized in his own distinctive deep voice. Though I did not teach him, I saw how Derek's behavior aggravated those who were not as clearly connected to him as Carrie was. In the minor contretemps that teachers deal with daily, Derek managed to resist adult eye contact ("Please look at me when I am talking"), continue the offending infraction ("I asked you once to stop drumming on the table!"), and draw his friends into his court of appeal ("I wasn't talking, was I?"). Not everyone was as able to set clear boundaries for him as Carrie was. Perhaps Carrie's more ready acceptance of children like Derek who tested adult authority prevented her from calling sooner than others might have for drastic measures. And maybe she absorbed and took care of so much of his particular misbehavior that the rest of the faculty didn't need to signal for help. In any case, until Derek got into hopeless confrontations with the rest of the faculty, attention to other children took precedence over his annoying behavior and undone homework.

Derek's first real blow-up with an adult came in January. Everyone acknowledged that Derek was the star player on the basketball team, though something of a "hot dogger." When a referee called a foul on him during a regular intramural game, Derek lost his temper and kicked over a trash can. Carrie calmed him down and the school imposed no sanctions. In retrospect, some faculty considered this tolerance of Derek's unsportsmanlike behavior an egregious error. Later Don said, "We should have suspended him right then."

Even though Don was particularly vexed by Derek's behavior with other faculty members, he and Derek had no particular tension in their relationship. Don's math classes were popular, well organized and executed, with high standards for all children's achievement, and Derek behaved in them. In October, Derek wrote a description of his new teachers, including Don: "My math teacher plays too much, but I like him. When he gets to business he's strict." Don pointed out, "He may not have always done his homework, but he never gave me trouble in math class."

But skirmishes with Derek did take place elsewhere, especially outside the school walls. Field trips became increasingly hard for him when he refused to obey adults other than Carrie, even for seemingly simple instructions like, "The museum guard said to put your lunch away." As the year progressed, Derek began to cause so much trouble that Jan started a written record on him, which included such phrases as, "resisted authority . . . shouted out . . . refused to follow directions."

No one challenged Don in formal meetings when he reminded us of Derek's charismatic influence over other children. A teacher with over twenty years' experience, Don had a district-wide reputation for excellence. Former students remembered his teaching. Don quickly saw through logistical dilemmas, and staff accepted his authoritative solutions. As the ranking White male on this newly constituted faculty, his strong deep voice carried weight. The director listened. When Don repeatedly said that "Derek didn't care about us or the school," no one disagreed, nor did they counter his assertion that "Derek had too much power." Later in the year, everyone agreed with his conclusion that "Derek was unpredictable and all of us were thrown off balance."

Yet in retrospect, we saw that Derek never got into fights with other kids, came to school on time, was a star in basketball, had a good relationship with his advisor, and had lots of friends. Both girls and boys jockeyed to be part of his group at lunch. His inability or unwillingness to do academic work should have singled him out early for special attention, but it didn't. Students with more visible needs climbed to the top of the agenda, and as the year proceeded, Derek's name never came up at a staff meeting in answer to the regular question: "Who are you worried about?" By early spring, his inappropriate behavior with adults obscured any attempt to figure out how to support his academic learning.

By mid-April, Derek's behavior had become intolerable. When teachers tried to reason with him, distract him, or isolate him, he resisted by turning away, cursing, shouting, and kicking. Jan was usually unperturbable, able to tolerate children's idiosyncrasies and even their occasional misbehavior. But Derek's particular intransigence, his refusal to listen to adults, and the way he challenged them by resisting their requests broke down Jan's usually calm exterior. She could no longer see the twelve-year-old boy in front of her.

A crisis began to build on April 18th. From the school's "incident record":

> During gym, with no apparent provocation . . . Derek got angry. Carrie put her arm around him and started to talk to him, but he pulled away from her and hit a student who just happened to be behind him. Later in the office he threw his bookbag on the floor toward Jan, used the phone without permission, and was rude when told to hang up. (School records, April 18)

The crisis erupted on April 19th. Derek outraged the adults, first when he violated a serious school rule by returning twenty minutes late from lunch, and then when he interrupted an all-school meeting. At this meeting, planned by Carrie and the Student Advisory Council, students told their own stories of discrimination. From my notes:

> When Leonora tells a story, Derek yells, "No wonder they kicked you out of Woolworth's, you've got a dirty looking face." Sonia tells a story about how she, Erin, and Josie were on the subway in the Bronx and a policemen tore up Josie's Brooklyn bus pass. Derek shouts out, "What did you do?" Josie responds with where she was walking and Derek interrupts impatiently: "No, what did *you* do to make him tear up your bus pass?" He is agitated and can't be calmed down. Several stories later, Pam tells about gender bias she felt on the all school basketball team and Derek yells out that he doesn't think boys should have girls on this team. (Field notes, April 19)

Derek behaved as an audience of one, asking his own questions and injecting his opinions at will. The faculty cut him no slack. Carrie moved him off the floor and onto a chair immediately and, as she monitored the group, other adults took turns sitting next to him. At the time no one suggested that talk of discrimination against young Black males might have contributed to his agitated behavior. As someone who often stood out in a group, Derek may have easily identified with Leonora's panic and anger at being singled out. Derek's question, "What did you do?" was apt, but it went unheard as other than an unacknowledged interruption.

Right after the meeting, Jan asked Derek and several other boys to stay after school to account for their lateness. From her written description:

> Derek began to sing rather than listen. I asked him to leave the room and wait in the hall. He went instead to the gym and began to play basketball. When Don sent him back to the hall, he came into the classroom without permission, banged his bookbag on a desk, sat down and began to talk to his detained friends. He cursed at me and then at Don and threatened us physically. We told him to wait in the hall and we consulted with Carrie. We all agreed he should be suspended. I asked Carrie to tell him. (School records, April 19)

As his advisor, Carrie was Derek's official advocate and the liaison between home and school. As Carrie and Jan stood together to decide Derek's fate, Carrie was visibly exasperated. She was tired enough of Derek's behavior not to argue his case. She agreed to the suspension and sat him down directly to tell him. From my notes:

> About 3:00 Carrie and Derek sit down very close together on the stacked blue mats in the office. Derek is crying. As they lean their backs against the wall with their bodies almost touching, it seems a very personal contact. About 3:20, they

stand up and Carrie says "Goodbye, you have to go home right now."

Carrie then said to me that she told him she was going to call his mother, but not that he was suspended. She was moved by the talk with him. "I just can't suspend him until I talk to his mother." But rather than leaving, Derek went into the gym and began to play basketball. When Jan walked though the gym, she told him that since he was suspended, he should leave. Hearing that he was suspended, he lost control. He had a two-year-old tantrum with a twelve-year-old's vocabulary. He finally left, upset, but he left. (Field notes, April 19)

That was a public account. In my private journal I described Don's response to Derek's tantrum. I saw Derek as genuinely out of control, hence my comparison to a two-year-old. Derek's obscenities were hard to hear, but even harder for me to hear was Don's powerful White male voice saying to this distressed twelve-year-old: "Call the police. I'm going to call the police. . . . He is damaged goods." I had no idea what Derek absorbed in the midst of his own tantrum, but other teachers heard it. I was enraged, as were others, but no one, including me, took a public stand. Later, in the women's bathroom, several of us agreed that White males get away with a lot, but no one ever said anything directly to Don.

After Derek finally left that Friday afternoon, the faculty was worn down. His lateness from lunch, his resistance to the consequences, his worse than usual behavior in the meeting, and this last vivid outburst had taken their toll. Don and Jan decided to expel him rather than suspend him. Carrie did not argue for keeping him. She said with deep weariness, "Derek tries my soul," and wondered whether anything could be done to change his behavior.

On Saturday, Jan phoned each faculty member. Individual phone calls prevented faculty from hearing each other's deliberations, so it was harder to share their thinking, but it was the usual way faculty communicated on weekends and evenings. Don never wavered: "Derek is taking over this school and we can't have that." Faculty argued variously that you can't escalate a suspension to an expulsion over a weekend when the student was not at school; that it was morally wrong to accept Derek in the school community and then expel him without trying every option; that without due process or knowledge of the public school legal issues, expulsion was inadvisable; that expelling a child without warning is threatening to other children. Everyone did agree that Derek was a pain to have around. His mother was available only sporadically and his father even more rarely. If we could have magically pushed a button to send him to a better school where he got along with adults more easily, we would gladly have done it. Faculty agonized over where Derek could go, but Derek's options were limited, and even after the weekend, many of us felt Pathways was the best place for him to finish his sixth-grade year.

On Sunday night, the calls resulted in a plan created by Jan and Carrie for a Monday morning meeting with Derek and his parents. No expulsion, they agreed. But at the meeting, when Derek seemed to Jan to be unrepentant and lacking an understanding of his suspension, she decided on the spot to expel him. All the weekend talk about community, trust, and even the legal issues fell by the wayside in the face of Jan's reluctance to have Derek return to school. Afterwards, Jan said the school's inability to cope with Derek determined her decision, despite her Sunday-night intentions. Whatever caused Jan to lose faith in this child's possibilities, or the possibilities of Pathways, was in full gear at that meeting.

The school day proceeded as usual, but after school, the news of Derek's expulsion spread and feelings ran high. Faculty accepted the decision as a done deal, despite their discomfort with it. Carrie had vehemently opposed the expulsion in conversations with Jan, and admitted privately that she was startled and angry during the Monday morning meeting when Jan ignored their plans. She felt "Derek was contrite and near tears," but, she conceded, she would never, never contradict a director, especially in front of parents. Some faculty felt Jan heard only Don's view that expelling Derek was the right decision.

At the weekly staff meeting the next day, we mechanically dispensed with the regular agenda in thirty minutes in order to develop a written policy on suspension and expulsion that would prevent future lack of clarity. Given the uncertainties of a new institution, it was not surprising that faculty were so willing to set school-wide policy to cover discipline. Jan began by saying evenly and without affect:

> We need a policy for kids who are giving us trouble. I realize that somewhere last week I gave up on Derek. Something happened that made me not listen and I didn't realize it. There are things we didn't do. We didn't suggest counseling, we didn't suspend him, and we put up with things from him that we don't accept from others. (Field notes, April 23)

Jim wondered whether we should reconsider our decision to expel Derek or just move on. "I am still working on my feelings," he admitted, speaking for himself, but implicitly for the whole group. Don repeated his consistent position that whatever happened wouldn't have occurred if we only had had better rules, clearer discipline, and sharper boundaries for kids to know "what's what."

Jan and Don were still convinced expulsion was the correct decision. If a faculty could be characterized as depressed, this faculty was. The adults' anger and sadness mixed with Derek's classmates' surprise and confusion weakened everyone. Used to operating consensually, we had no experience openly disagreeing with Jan or with each other. Ousting Derek from the community made everyone feel badly, yet life with him had been undeniably hard. This decision brought to the surface differences in faculty values and assumptions about children, about schools, and about each other. The limits of the school's ability to support a difficult child were suddenly on view for everyone to see.

As usual, Don posed the question that framed the discussion: "What are the conditions for membership in this school community?" Marilyn, a first-year teacher, responded immediately, "You can think of communities that never expel members and ones that excommunicate. What kind of a community do we want to be?" The power of her question got lost as the talk returned to Derek. Carrie felt that Derek was more contrite at Monday's meeting than Jan's description portrayed. Considering the passionate feelings I heard her express in the halls, Carrie's tone at the staff meeting was moderate. She said evenly:

> I would rather err on the side of the child. The reason I didn't want to suspend Derek was because he'd be on the street all day or in the arcades. But after we accept kids, we have to include them and get them connected. We didn't act sooner because we had to get to other problems sooner. Derek's healthy. He defends himself. He's not resigned. That's a strength. In reality, it is easier not to have him, but are we being fair? (Field notes, April 23)

As much as Jan sympathized with the attempt to be fair, she wanted Derek gone — for reasons I believe even she did not understand at the time. Jan again reiterated that there had been no progress in Derek's understanding of his egregious behavior: "Derek couldn't retell what he did. It was not like he just left out chunks of the story, he didn't understand."

Don repeated what he had often said: "Derek is an incredibly powerful person. We cannot do anything for him. He is more powerful than we are." At 6 feet, 5 inches, Don's sheer physical presence is a factor in any meeting, and his forceful voice leaves nothing tentative about his contributions, whether he means them to be dogmatic or not. Softening his stance, Don added, "I feel a sense of failure, of course, but he did not respect us or care." No one presented any evidence to counter Don's statement. Not I or anyone else argued Derek's case. There was dead silence. Something intransigent in Don and Jan's position made it seem just as hard for me to get through to them as it was to discipline Derek on a field trip.

Jan then spoke in support of Don's opinion: "Kids have to be willing to listen, willing to change. There has to be a parent or an adult to work with." To which Carrie responded, without missing a beat, "But some kids don't have a parent and you have to work with that kid anyway."

The discussion returned to the need for a policy. Don pointed out, "The problem is not making a policy or writing it down, but in implementing it consistently. Discipline has to be consistent or it is nothing." At 5:05, Don stood up to signal that for him, the meeting was over.

After Don left, Carrie turned to me and said passionately what she did not say in the meeting: "Don's position disturbs me. You can't decide on boundaries and then expect kids to arrange themselves to fit. You can't have static boundaries when you work with children. Especially kids like Derek. I am still upset. You don't cut off a kid's finger when he touches the hot pie."

Talk about Derek went underground. The next day, when rehashing the staff meeting, Carrie observed, "We talked, but we didn't engage." Her perception matched mine. We agreed that the previous day's meeting was intense and fast paced and that faculty had differing perspectives; there was a little snapping, but no raised voices, no questioning, and no arguing. This unfinished incident left everyone tired and irritable. Underlying the tension was our inability to find a solution for Derek that worked for him and for us. The focus on a general policy kept the faculty distanced from Derek and obscured any recognition of his needs. Disagreement over the treatment of Derek prevented faculty from hearing this strong-voiced adolescent or each other. We retreated from the conflict.

It is easy to invoke society's hierarchies here: the unspoken constraints that kept a Black teacher from countering a White director or women from challenging male authority (Delpit, 1988; Fine, 1991). The small size of the faculty makes generalizing much like walking into quicksand, yet it is possible to see stereotyped power relations at work. In this case, Don, anticipating that his voice would be heard, repeatedly articulated his opinion and kept focused on translating it into action. Others did not challenge him, and those power relations became entangled with the issue of who speaks for an advisee. Carrie privately expressed feeling that Derek's fate was predetermined and that "I would be wasting my breath," which prevented her from advocating more strongly for his retention, even though she was his advisor. Her reluctance to speak on his behalf made it less likely that others would argue for him when she did not. Other teachers did not contradict Don when he described Derek's power to disrupt the school. Jan supported Don, since she felt the health of the school would suffer if Derek stayed. Don told me that because I did not teach Derek I could not know what other faculty faced, and his pointed logic reinforced whatever powerlessness I already felt. I and others remained mute. This interactive dynamic — Don and Jan expecting to have their opinions valued, and Carrie and I convinced that we would be dismissed — confirmed the conventional power relations between men and women, Blacks and Whites, directors and teachers.[11]

As Maxine Greene (1993) reminds us, "There are ways of speaking and telling that construct silences, create 'others,' invent gradations of social difference necessary for the identification of norms" (p. 216). Until we find another way, until power to speak is equalized and reciprocal so that *all* faculty can expect to be heard, children like Derek will not be well served.

School officials who set and legitimate boundaries have tremendous power over children's lives, and the interplay between institutional norms and individual adults' attitudes complicates what happens to students like Derek who do not meet standard expectations.[12] How to serve the Dereks of this world is not only an educational question, but also a political question that links power, discipline, and race. None of this speculation, all done in retrospect, could have helped us with Derek. Events occurred too quickly.

The following afternoon, the district office guidance counselor phoned Jan to summon her to a meeting with Derek's parents. Jan took the call in the school office as Don and I sat nearby. From my notes:

> Jan was calm and not at all defensive. She apologized for her first year naivete, gave details of Derek's behavior, told how hard it was to reach his parents, and listened. She could have been ordering supplies for all the emotion in her voice. It soon became clear that expelling a child is not an option. Jan was asked to appear in the Central Office with an incident report to meet with Derek's family. On the phone she was gracious and accepting. Off the phone she was upset. Don said ominously, "Can you imagine what he'll be like if he knows we have no recourse to expulsion? He'll be uncontainable." (Field notes, April 24)

After the meeting with Derek's parents, Jan reported that Derek would be back. Expulsion was legally indefensible because Derek never had the two non-contiguous five-day suspensions, which the district requires.

Jan modeled decorum for the staff and kids. Derek came back without a fuss, and with an agreement *not* to go on any school field trips without his mother or father. His parents never participated, and since trips were a central part of the curriculum, Derek was often absent. His return was also predicated on foregoing the three-day overnight camping trip, leaving him out of the pre-trip excitement. His presence reminded everyone of the expulsion controversy, which undoubtedly affected his treatment by adults and children. Carrie took responsibility for his last two months. This excerpt from my notes shows Derek's better and worse days:

> Derek came back and was better. He still had to be spoken to at the City Fair [not technically a trip but a district-sponsored requirement]. Carrie had to speak to him four times and called his father immediately. She said she could not take him

to the Central Park Challenge unless his father came. He said he would. On the day of the Challenge his father didn't show up and Derek was devastated. Carrie agreed to take him on the grounds that kids have to be in groups to learn how to behave. He was fine. When she talked to the mother about his father's not showing up, the mother said, "That's the story of Derek's life. He never shows up." (Field notes, May 15)

The decision to expel Derek was Jan's most naive decision of the year and, as she agrees, her biggest mistake. That she accepted Derek's return so readily and with such good grace helped rectify it, but Derek's place in the school community was already compromised and this experience took its toll on everyone. The next year, Derek's parents put him in Catholic school.

This child, who was caught in family and social circumstances beyond his control, called Pathways's basic values into question and brought faculty differences into focus. The last week in April I recorded in my journal that "I didn't take notes because it was too painful for everybody to see me carrying a notebook." In a number of small but perceptible ways that were tied to particular events surrounding Derek, our collegial bonds loosened. Don felt that Jan could have stopped Derek's misbehavior had she been a more powerful director. Carrie said that she couldn't stand Don talking negatively about children, as he sometimes did. Separated by these differences and by declining trust, faculty could no longer tap each other's knowledge or work out the human tangles.

Overall, the faculty poured astounding energy into educating children of all colors, and most children were treated as well as any parent would want. Black children are numerous enough at Pathways that it is hard to say that Derek's Blackness made it difficult for him to be treated respectfully by White faculty. But since Derek *is* Black, that fact cannot be divorced from his interactions with faculty. Some faculty thought Derek one of the most "difficult" students. In retrospect, it may have been easier — at least consciously — for White faculty to focus on his "attitude" rather than his race.

It is also hard to say whether Derek's Blackness affected Carrie's ability to connect with him. I cannot know whether her more solid relationship with Derek had anything to do with their shared race. She understood his strengths and his precarious stance in the world as a Black boy. Carrie included Derek in the school community and she didn't flinch at his misbehavior. But Derek needed more than what this one African American teacher could provide. Had Carrie felt less constrained by the dynamics described earlier, she might have convinced others that Derek was being shortchanged at school.

Dismissing Derek and other similar "problems" as too troubled for schools to educate is often easier than dealing with their difficulties, and many educators practice this kind of triage. Small schools should be particularly able to reach students like Derek, but these students must be known in all their complexity, not just as a thorn in the side of adults who have no investment in their lives. For such a promise of personalized schools to be fulfilled, faculties have to adopt Carrie's attitude about children. She often says, "When I am in a quandary about how to handle a child, I think 'What would I do if that child were my child?' and 'How would I want that child handled were my son or daughter in that situation?'" Parents have an urgency about their own children. We all need to feel the same urgency when we teach other people's children (Delpit, 1988).

Faculty Leadership: "Does Woolworth's Discriminate?"

In the spring, a spontaneous discussion on bias grew into a project involving every student at Pathways. The project originated in Advisory Council, Pathways's fledgling student government, and resulted in an all-school meeting on discrimination (the one where Derek so outraged the adults). Jan recounted how this topic arose in the first Advisory Council meeting:[13]

> After spring vacation, Carrie and I were all sitting around in a circle with about 12 kids, two from each advisory, and I asked, "What issues should we address here?"
>
> "Bias" Sudi answered. "People ask me to speak Chinese, even though I am Japanese. Or ask me about Korean green grocers as if I knew everything."
>
> Then older boys of color began to tell stories of how they were being treated in stores. "Racism," kids said. Carrie built on their responses by talking about the civil rights movement, fact finding, protests and sit ins. She said to me later, "These kids don't know history. They don't know how to protest. We have to do something." (Field notes, April 7)

While faculty managed to avoid talking about race by advocating more explicit rules and discipline policies, the students, under Carrie's leadership, confronted racial discrimination directly. After hearing kids' stories about police officers, store clerks, and the random person on the subway who said to Jessica's racially mixed group, "Whites shouldn't be with Black people," faculty readily agreed that teaching children to confront discrimination as they traveled around the city was essential to their well-being. Discussing circumstances facing children outside of school was clearly easier than discussing how race plays out in school with one another.

Every Thursday, during class time, and occasionally over pizza brought in for lunch, the Advisory Council met in Carrie's science classroom. The Council included three Whites, one Asian, four Hispanics, and four Blacks. Once the students decided to plan and practice for the all-school meeting on discrimination, Carrie proceeded. She had a clear goal, moved the discussion along at a pace that she dictated, elicited discussion from her questions, monitored the side conversations, noticed behavior beyond the norms, acted on some of it, and drew out the kids in order to help them understand what she wanted to teach:

1. A racist experience is anything that happens to you because of your race.
2. You can protect yourself against bias and not be diminished by it.
3. You can feel like a whole person after something unpleasant has happened to you.
4. Be careful what you call racist — not every discriminatory incident is racist. It might be against children, women, teenagers with loud voices, or teenagers in groups. Still people often discriminate against young boys of color who get stereotyped and judged by the color of their skin.

Carrie's entry into this teaching was through kids' shared stories. After hearing each story, she asked "How did you feel?" and "What recourse do you have?" By the second and third meeting, kids asked these questions themselves. At the end of every meeting, Carrie reminded kids of their belly button. "What is something that no one can take away from you? Your belly button is what holds you together. So when someone judges you unfairly, remember your belly button. No one can take that away from you. When you are angry have one thing that you can say that will pull you back together."

On April nineteenth, the Advisory Council sat on chairs in a circle surrounded by fifty children on the floor listening to their stories. The tone of this "fishbowl" was calm — except, as already described, for Derek. The largest boys struggled to keep their legs in a confined space, and this sensitive topic produced some nervous fidgeting, but students were interested in their classmates' dramatic, sometimes painful, stories:

> Lisa began: When Stella, Sudi and I were in Woolworth's looking around, a sales-lady stopped us and asked, "Who's here with you?" When we told her we weren't here with any adults, she said, "Sit in a corner and write a list of what you want and then come back."

> Juan told a variation: I was with some friends standing in line at the Woolworth's cash register getting ready to pay for a notebook and some White guys were ahead of us. They paid, but when it was our turn, the man at the door came over and asked us to empty our pockets.

> Bianca followed: When Jessica, Ramona and I were in Woolworth's and Ramona was buying a water gun, Jerome, Arnold, and their friends wanted to come in with us. The guard let us in, but not the boys. (Field notes, April 19)

The take-home lesson from these stories was that it matters how children present themselves in public. Students noticed that their adolescent voices can be as threatening as their skin color. The biggest boys of color had the biggest problems. In addition to bringing patterns to the surface, this public forum allowed children to testify to their pain and hear the community respond sympathetically to their stories of hurtful devaluation and exclusion.

When the meeting broke up and students moved to their homerooms, the subsequent smaller group discussions about discrimination were both intimate and orderly. Serious talk flowed easily without any of the out-of-control rage that occurred in December during the (admittedly more immediate) discussion of "How come there are no brothers on that list?" The formal process of the large meeting showed respect for everyone's perspective. Faculty agreed with the aims of the meeting: to give children a chance to tell their stories and learn some strategies to confront discrimination. However, and this is still the heart of the matter, Carrie made this meeting happen.

All children at Pathways benefitted from Carrie's charismatic personality, her commitment to academic achievement, her willingness to give freely of her time to kids (she preferred to have lunch with children rather than with adults), her consistency (if she said during class "see me later," she never forgot), her clear expectations (she insisted on complete sentences when children responded), and her scaffolding of what children needed to do as students (she practiced having them come into the room "like you have a purpose and something to do"). Yet it was Carrie's personal knowledge, her own experience with what children of color face, and her parenting of her own Black children that made it possible for her to run this assembly. Had she not been at Pathways, the assembly might never have happened.

Based on the Advisory Council assembly, Carrie developed an all-school project entitled "Does Woolworth's Discriminate?" Students conducted a controlled study of who was allowed to go into Woolworth's at lunchtime. They designed the study, sent groups with different racial makeups into Woolworth's at different times to test Woolworth's "admission policy," analyzed the data, and extrapolated the findings beyond their original sample. Advisory Council members modeled role-playing in each Advisory so that children would learn a technique to help them understand different perspectives. Then all the children role-played how to approach and respond to various acts of discrimination. Carrie received a grant to help other teachers construct similar curricula. "Does Woolworth's Discriminate?" was a model for honest talk with kids. Based on issues they care about, this project recognized that students felt secure in their own school community, encouraged them to raise questions about their problematic status in the outside world, and gave them the means to seek answers and develop actions to gain personal control.

As successful as this program was, programs do not eradicate racism; rather, beliefs and attitudes lead people to make changes. Individual transformation comes through reflecting on values that underlie programs and actions. At Pathways, more fundamental change came from thinking together about Derek and Duke than from any of the programs, curriculum, or initial structures that the school set in place.

Conclusion

One lesson that could be taken from this selective account is that even in the "best" schools, where faculty try hard to pay attention to individuals, Whites' blindness to race clouds their ability to notice what children are really saying about themselves and their identities. Safe spaces rarely exist in schools for adults or children to explore race, especially when Whites — who tend not to think of race all that often — determine the agendas, and teachers from other backgrounds become used to the absence of talk about race, or are convinced they will not be heard.

At Pathways, as in many schools, faculty members' personal backgrounds and assumptions about race, ethnicity, and class were little known to each other and not much explored. When school life went smoothly, our habits continued without examination. When conflicts arose, we had no way to untangle the knots. Faculty members need to be open with each other in order to have honest discussions. Such openness may not be possible in a new school, where the pace is like the title of John Adam's musical composition, *A Short Ride in a Fast Machine*. The first year at Pathways was exhilarating, but each day passed much too quickly to begin to have the extended discussions necessary to develop openness and honesty. Yet in my experience, even in an established school where a slower pace might allow for more conversational possibilities, race is often not well understood or thought to be a topic for discussion.

Talking honestly about racism may be the hardest thing faculties do in schools. Racial issues in America are complex, full of strong feelings and equally strong denials; anyone who has sat around a table with adults who feel awkward and tentative about having these conversations knows this is so. The initial task for educators may be to figure out how to make these conversations commonplace. How to do this within the already overloaded school day is not easy. Without a commitment from every person to participate and trust that others will listen and change, the effort is futile.

Teachers at Pathways and elsewhere are often good at observing who is stuck in math, whose writing needs help, who needs more skill in reading comprehension. Good teaching entails such observations. But until teachers, especially White teachers, get in the habit of looking more closely at the nuances of race and seeing patterns, building up evidence to anchor their impressions, sharing their conclusions with one another, and examining their own racial attitudes, they will not learn enough to provide for all children.

Only as I wrote up these glimpses of school life did I begin to hear, really hear, Carrie say, "People who have no choice but to live their lives in their Black skins know racism when they see it. Racism is never subtle to the victim. Only White people say race doesn't matter." Certainly, in our society, Whites in power are more interested in downplaying race, and it is Whites who decide what is and what is not racist (Sleeter, 1993; Tatum, 1992). What I learned from Carrie prompted me to write this article.

Complicating the dialogue about race is the ambiguity inherent in racial issues. However, the point is not to get the right labels — often no clear answer exists as to what is a racial incident, or whether an event involves bias, and if it does, whether it is conscious or unconscious. The very fact that it is difficult to say what is and is not a racial issue both makes it easier to avoid a discussion of race and gives an added edge to any exchange. Participants disagree not only about the substance of an issue, but also about what they are talking about. This makes conversation even harder, and it takes a committed faculty to keep talking (Burbules & Rice, 1991; Henze, Lucas, & Scott, 1993; Murphy & Ucelli, 1989; Olson, 1991).

The incidents related here focus on what faculty didn't hear, didn't understand, or didn't choose to pursue. This account does not relate the many times faculty stuck with kids to work through differences or put energy into including children in the community. Just as Marie Diaz's essay stands for many kids' responses to school, let sixth grader Serena Martinez's interview with me at the end of the year speak for faculty effort and children's learning:

> Serena [on handling racial conflict]: Each teacher helps you a lot because if there is a little problem they make it a BIG DEAL and that helps. Even though at the beginning you think, "Oh, this is boring; I don't want to do this because it's not going to change anything." Then you talk and you see the other side of the person and then you understand and then you know how they feel. It's nice when you talk it out. . . . At other schools after you have a fight with somebody, you don't resolve anything so there is still something in there and you still want to fight. Here you discuss the problems and you get to hear other people's sides. And you understand. (Taped interview, May 30)

This eloquent statement by a child confirms that not all opportunities to confront racial problems were missed. Carrie agreed: "When things arose, most individual racial incidents were handled well enough, quite well in fact. By that I mean kids understood their own responsibility and how it affected the outcome."

The staff learned from Derek's exile and Duke's withdrawal. Five years later, Pathways has become a stronger school for having lived through those serious missteps. In order to learn, faculties not only have to make mistakes, they also have to recognize them as mistakes. This documentation made what happened visible and discussable, and the following year the entire faculty began to talk about race more publicly. After the addition of more Latino and African American faculty, several outside researchers, and longer meetings with more overt conflict, this reflective faculty began to unlock the silences. Out of these experiences, several staff members have produced their own articles. More importantly, faculty now do better with the successors to Derek and Duke.

Attempts to educate *all* children in today's climate are fraught with pedagogical and social uncertainties that defy a single response. Many possible entry points exist, but developing structures for faculty members to reflect on their experiences and share their own perspectives is essential. Faculties need protected time during the day to talk, a willingness to question previously entrenched assumptions, and encouragement to be honest in collegial forums rather than in the hallways. As Lisa Delpit (1988) says, teachers need to be "unafraid to raise questions about discrimination and voicelessness with people of color, and listen, no, to *hear*, what they say" (p. 297). Connecting with each other and seeing the implications for educating children requires an alertness to what happens inside schools and out, a consciousness about how others see the world, a willingness to talk honestly, and a commitment to change the power relationships in the world.

When Whites in power don't hear the boiling lava that lies below the surface, they perpetuate silences about race. Then they are surprised when racial feelings erupt, although it is they who have paid no attention to the volcano.[14]

Notes

1. This work was funded by the Aaron Diamond Foundation, which is not responsible for the thinking expressed here.
2. Despite their permission to use real names, I have changed both the name of the school and the names of the teachers to preserve their privacy. I have also changed the names and details of children and their parents.
3. Initially drafted by the founding director and polished by me, this vision statement explicitly committed the school to an integrated, untracked student body. Faculty agreed to it in principle when they came to work at the school.
4. Although my position as a part-time documenter allowed me time and distance to reflect on my work as a member of the staff at Pathways, mine was not the outside perspective of an academic researcher (a tradition in which I have not been trained). Throughout my teaching career and involvement in teacher-research communities, one of my purposes in writing about classrooms has been to make practice explicit for a larger audience. Ultimately, what I write also contributes to improving my own practice as well. For further discussion of my work, see Jervis, Carr, Lockhart, and Rogers (1996).
5. At Pathways, every adult had an advisory of nine or ten students. Advisories met four days a week for an hour to discuss school and nonschool topics, read novels, celebrate birthdays, and sort out school experiences together. Advisors acted as liaisons with parents, advocated for advisees with other faculty, and talked individually to students about their progress and problems.
6. In New York City's thirty-two decentralized elementary and middle school/junior high districts, Mary Ann Raywid's (1990) definition of alternative schools applies: "Alternative schools are likely to be small; independently launched from program to program; separately operated without a great deal of external oversight or district-level coordination; internally less differentiated than other schools as to status and role; and quite variable from one program to another" (p. 96). New York's alternative schools draw from the whole city, but they generally strive for mixed abilities and diversity. It is important to note that Pathways' au-

tonomy is linked to its small size as well as to its status as an alternative school. A small faculty can more easily make up their own schedules, report cards, or curricula, and also decide to change them if they do not work well.

7. On the day of this incident in 1990, I recorded Arnold's words and gestures in my notebook. That night I typed up the incident, threw away my handwritten version, and forgot about it. Then in the fall of 1994, while sorting my files after yet another revision, I found one page of the original handwritten notes. On that page, but not in my typed notes, I had recorded that "a [White] teacher encouraged kids to 'forget it', when Arnold objected to Duke's behavior." In 1990, I had apparently "registered" that something, perhaps racial, went on between Arnold and Duke, but did not "see" that a White colleague urged kids to ignore it. Though somehow I knew to save that handwritten page, it took me years to understand, and then express, how White resistance to seeing, exemplified in my own actions as well as my colleague's advice to Arnold and Duke, is an enormously complicated aspect of racism.

8. See the chapter "African American Schoolchild in a Strange Land" in Janice Hale (1994) for a discussion of this interpretation.

9. See Knapp and Woolverton (1995) for a review of these issues.

10. Descriptive Review, developed by Patricia Carini and her colleagues in North Bennington, Vermont (Prospect Archive, 1986), is one method Pathways faculty used to help them understand children. In this process, a teacher collects, for presentation to other teachers, observations of one student's behaviors organized around a focusing question intended to illuminate some puzzling aspect of the child's school life. The presenting teacher describes the child fully, rendering physical gestures, temperament, relationships, interests, and approaches to formal academics in as detailed a way as possible. Other teachers ask questions to clarify the description. Then the group makes recommendations for practice. The underlying goal of a Descriptive Review is to describe a child as carefully as possible, to avoid evaluative judgments, and to develop strategies that build on the child's strengths.

11. Don's strongest reaction to my interpretation of this data was how he had not heard Carrie. "Was it really so hard for me to listen?" he asked. I noticed that the following year, when I attended several faculty meetings, he listened more carefully, and Carrie's voice became stronger. This may be a good example of documentation stimulating change.

12. For a discussion of standards, see Jervis and McDonald (1996).

13. Two representatives from each advisory were appointed by advisors or elected by advisories. That students came to the Council by different selection processes did not seem to be an issue, since they all felt it was an honor to serve. Carrie volunteered to oversee this Advisory Council. Jan, as director, worked with her, and I participated in the weekly meetings.

14. I would like to acknowledge Michelle Fine for suggesting this metaphor when she commented on a draft of this article.

15. As is standard feminist practice, I have included first and last names of authors.

References[15]

Burbules, Nicholas, & Rice, Suzanne. (1991). Dialogue across differences: Continuing the conversation.*Harvard Educational Review, 61,* 393–416.

Cohen, Jody. (1993). Constructing race at an urban high school: In their minds, their mouths, their hearts. In Lois Weis & Michelle Fine (Eds.), *Beyond silenced voices: Class, race and gender in United States schools* (pp. 289–308). Albany: State University of New York Press.

Delpit, Lisa. (1988). The silenced dialogue: Power and pedagogy in educating other people's children. *Harvard Educational Review, 58,* 280–298.

Delpit, Lisa. (1990). Seeing color: Review of *White Teacher. Hungry Mind Review, 15,* 4–5.

Engel, Brenda. (1975). *A handbook of documentation.* Grand Forks: University of North Dakota, North Dakota Study Group on Evaluation.

Fine, Michelle. (1991). *Framing dropouts: Notes on the politics of an urban public high school.* Albany: State University of New York Press.

Foster, Michele. (1993). Resisting racism: Personal testimonies of African-American teachers. In Lois Weis & Michelle Fine (Eds.), *Beyond silenced voices: Class, race, and gender in United States schools* (pp. 273–288). Albany: State University of New York Press.

Grant, Carl, & Secada, Walter. (1990). Preparing teachers for diversity. In W. R. Houston (Ed.), *Handbook of research on teacher education* (pp. 403–422). New York: Macmillan.

Greene, Maxine. (1993). Diversity and inclusion: Towards a curriculum for human beings. *Teachers College Record, 95,* 213–221.

Hale, Janice E. (1994). *Unbank the fire: Visions for the education of African American children.* Baltimore: Johns Hopkins University Press.

Henze, Rosemary, Lucas, Tamara, & Scott, Beverly. (1993, April). *Dancing with the monster: Teachers attempt to discuss power, racism, and privilege in education.* Paper presented at the annual meeting of the American Educational Research Association, New Orleans.

Jervis, Kathe, Carr, Emily, Lockhart, Patsy, & Rogers, Jane. (1996). Multiple entries to teacher inquiry: Dissolving the boundaries between research and teaching. In Linda Baker, Peter Afflerbach, & David Reinking (Eds.), *Developing engaged readers in school and home communities* (pp. 247–268). Mahwah, NJ: Lawrence Erlbaum.

Jervis, Kathe, & McDonald, Joseph. (1996). Standards: The philosophical monster in the classroom. *Phi Delta Kappan, 77,* 563–569.

Knapp, Michael S., & Woolverton, Sara. (1995). Social class and schooling. In James A. Banks & Cherry A. McGee Banks (Eds.), *Handbook of research on multicultural education* (pp. 548–569). New York: Macmillan.

Ladson-Billings, Gloria. (1994). *The dreamkeepers: Successful teachers of African American children.* San Francisco: Jossey-Bass.

McCarthy, Cameron. (1993). Beyond the poverty of theory in race relations: Nonsynchrony and social difference in education. In Lois Weis & Michelle Fine (Eds.), *Beyond silenced voices: Class, race, and gender in United States schools* (pp. 325–346). Albany: State University of New York Press.

McIntosh, Peggy. (1988). *White privilege and male privilege: A personal account of coming to see correspondences through work in women's studies* (Working Paper No. 189). Wellesley, MA: Wellesley College Center for Research on Women.

Murphy, Donald, & Ucelli, Juliet. (1989). Race, knowledge, and pedagogy: A Black-White teacher dialogue. *Holistic Education Review, 2*(4), 48–50.

Olson, Ruth Anne. (1991). *Language and race: Barriers to communicating a vision* (Reflective Paper No. 1). St. Paul, MN: Supporting Diversity in Schools.

Prospect Archive and Center for Education and Research. (1986). *The Prospect Center documentary processes.* North Bennington, VT: Author.

Raywid, Mary Ann. (1990). Successful schools of choice: Cottage industry benefits in large systems. *Educational Policy, 4*(2), 93–108.

Sleeter, Christine. (1993). White teachers construct race. In Cameron McCarthy & Warren Crichlow (Eds.), *Race, identity, and representation in education* (pp. 157–171). London: Routledge.

Tatum, Beverly Daniel. (1992). Talking about race, learning about racism: Application of racial identity development theory in the classroom. *Harvard Educational Review, 62,* 1–24.

This work unfolded over several years, and often I cannot untangle what I learned from whom. I am most indebted to my Pathways colleagues who met me for coffee, talked on the phone, and worked with me at home on Sunday afternoons. The file of their responses is thick and rich.

The Documentation Study Group responded to early drafts and kept me focused on the importance of the topic: David Bensman, Janet Carter, Priscilla Ellington, Heather Lewis, Sondra Perl, Jon Snyder, and Nancy Wilson. Others shaped my thinking by generously responding to drafts; their ideas are by now deeply embedded in the way the article evolved: Nancy Cardwell, Patricia Carini, Virginia Christensen, Beverly Falk, Michelle Fine, JoEllen Fisherkeller, Norman Fruchter, Maxine Greene, Herman Jervis, Steven Jervis, Elaine Joseph, Ann Lieberman, Maritza Macdonald, Hasna Muhammad (who heroically read three drafts), Peggy McIntosh, Diane Mullins, and Donald Murphy.

From 1991 through 1993 I participated in the Urban Sites Writing Network, a national teacher research group that deliberately invited equal membership of people of color and Whites. The result was a diverse network of National Writing Project teachers talking across cultural boundaries as we grappled with the complexities of urban classrooms in formal discussions and informal talk. It is here that I learned the importance of having the hard conversations.

I especially thank my husband, Robert Jervis, who encouraged me throughout. He pushed me to refine my thinking, and then patiently reread each new revision.

376

Lessons from Students on
Creating a Chance to Dream

SONIA NIETO

Where are the voices and ideas of students in efforts to improve schools and teach-
ing practices? This is the question that Sonia Nieto asks in this final chapter. She
talks to young people — junior and senior high school students — from a wide va-
riety of ethnic, racial, linguistic, and social-class backgrounds, and listens to what
they have to say about their schooling experiences. Then, using the power of the
students' own words and her understanding of what they are telling her, Nieto
communicates their messages to us. Nieto concludes that in order to achieve edu-
cational equity and high-quality educational experiences for all, students' critical
reflections and constructive ideas must be made key parts of the process of work-
ing toward those goals. Nieto's chapter ends this book with the message that stu-
dents are integral parts of the complex world of teaching, as both learners and
teachers, and their ideas and voices must be respected and valued by the educa-
tional community.

> How does it come about that the one institution that is said to be the gateway to
> opportunity, the school, is the very one that is most effective in perpetuating an
> oppressed and impoverished status in society? (Stein, 1971, p. 178)

The poignant question above was posed in this very journal almost a quarter
of a century ago by Annie Stein, a consistent critic of the schools and a re-
lentless advocate for social justice. This question shall serve as the central
motif of this article because, in many ways, it remains to be answered and continues to be a fundamental dilemma standing in the way of our society's stated ideals
of equity and equal educational opportunity. Annie Stein's observations about the
New York City public schools ring true today in too many school systems throughout the country and can be used to examine some of the same policies and practices
she decried in her 1971 article.

It is my purpose in this article to suggest that successfully educating all students
in U.S. schools must begin by challenging school policies and practices that place
roadblocks in the way of academic achievement for too many young people. Educating students today is, of course, a far different and more complex proposition
than it has been in the past. Young people face innumerable personal, social, and

Harvard Educational Review Vol. 64 No. 4 Winter 1994, 392–426

political challenges, not to mention massive economic structural changes not even dreamed about by other generations of youth in the twentieth century. In spite of the tensions that such challenges may pose, U.S. society has nevertheless histori- cally had a social contract to educate *all* youngsters, not simply those who happen to be European American, English speaking, economically privileged, and, in the current educational reform jargon, "ready to learn."[1] Yet, our schools have tradi- tionally failed some youngsters, especially those from racially and culturally domi- nated and economically oppressed backgrounds. Research over the past half cen- tury has documented a disheartening legacy of failure for many students of all backgrounds, but especially children of Latino, African American, and Native American families, as well as poor European American families and, more recently, Asian and Pacific American immigrant students. Responding to the wholesale fail- ure of so many youngsters within our public schools, educational theorists, sociol- ogists, and psychologists devised elaborate theories of genetic inferiority, cultural deprivation, and the limits of "throwing money" at educational problems. Such theories held sway in particular during the 1960s and 1970s, but their influence is still apparent in educational policies and practices today.[2]

The fact that many youngsters live in difficult, sometimes oppressive conditions is not at issue here. Some may live in ruthless poverty and face the challenges of di- lapidated housing, inadequate health care, and even abuse and neglect. They and their families may be subject to racism and other oppressive institutional barriers. They may have difficult personal, psychological, medical, or other kinds of prob- lems. These are real concerns that should not be discounted. But, despite what may seem to be insurmountable obstacles to learning and teaching, some schools are nevertheless successful with young people who live in these situations. In addition, many children who live in otherwise onerous situations also have loving families willing to sacrifice what it takes to give their children the chance they never had during their own childhoods. Thus, poverty, single-parent households, and even homelessness, while they may be tremendous hardships, do not in and of them- selves doom children to academic failure (see, among others, Clark, 1983; Lucas, Henze, & Donato, 1990; Mehan & Villanueva, 1993; Moll, 1992; Taylor & Dorsey-Gaines, 1988). These and similar studies point out that schools that have made up their minds that their students deserve the chance to learn do find the ways to educate them successfully in spite of what may seem to be overwhelming odds.

Educators may consider students difficult to teach simply because they come from families that do not fit neatly into what has been defined as "the main- stream." Some of them speak no English; many come from cultures that seem to be at odds with the dominant culture of U.S. society that is inevitably reflected in the school; others begin their schooling without the benefit of early experiences that could help prepare them for the cognitive demands they will face. Assumptions are often made about how such situations may negatively affect student achievement and, as a consequence, some children are condemned to failure before they begin. In a study by Nitza Hidalgo, a teacher's description of the students at an urban high school speaks to this condemnation: "Students are generally poor, uneducated and come from broken families who do not value school. Those conditions that produce achievers are somewhere else, not here. We get street people" (Hidalgo, 1991, p. 58). When such viewpoints guide teachers' and schools' behaviors and ex- pectations, little progress can be expected in student achievement.

On the other hand, a growing number of studies suggest that teachers and schools need to build on rather than tear down what students bring to school. That is, they need to understand and incorporate cultural, linguistic, and experiential differences, as well as differences in social class, into the learning process (Abi-Nader, 1993; Hollins, King, & Hayman, 1994; Lucas et al., 1990; Moll & Díaz, 1993). The results of such efforts often provide inspiring examples of success, because they begin with a belief that all students deserve a chance to learn. In this article, I will highlight these efforts by exploring the stories of some academically successful young people in order to suggest how the policies and practices of schools can be transformed to create environments in which all children are capable of learning.

It is too convenient to fall back on deficit theories and continue the practice of blaming students, their families, and their communities for educational failure. Instead, schools need to focus on where they *can* make a difference, namely, their own instructional policies and practices. A number of recent studies, for example, have concluded that a combination of factors, including characteristics of schools as opposed to only student background and actions, can explain differences between high- and low-achieving students. School characteristics that have been found to make a positive difference in these studies include an enriched and more demanding curriculum, respect for students' languages and cultures, high expectations for all students, and encouragement for parental involvement in their children's education (Lee, Winfield, & Wilson, 1991; Lucas et al., 1990; Moll, 1992). This would suggest that we need to shift from a single-minded focus on low- or high-achieving students to the conditions that create low- or high-achieving schools. If we understand school policies and practices as being enmeshed in societal values, we can better understand the manifestations of these values in schools as well. Thus, for example, "tracked" schools, rather than reflecting a school practice that exists in isolation from society, reflect a society that is itself tracked along racial, gender, and social-class lines. In the same way, "teacher expectations" do not come from thin air, but reflect and support expectations of students that are deeply ingrained in societal and ideological values.

Reforming school structures alone will not lead to substantive differences in student achievement, however, if such changes are not also accompanied by profound changes in how we as educators think about our students; that is, in what we believe they deserve and are capable of achieving. Put another way, changing policies and practices is a necessary but insufficient condition for total school transformation. For example, in a study of six high schools in which Latino students have been successful, Tamara Lucas, Rosemary Henze, and Rubén Donato (1990) found that the most crucial element is a shared belief among teachers, counselors, and administrators that all students are capable of learning. This means that concomitant changes are needed in policies and practices *and* in our individual and collective will to educate all students. Fred Newmann (1993), in an important analysis of educational restructuring, underlines this point by emphasizing that reform efforts will fail unless they are accompanied by a set of particular commitments and competencies to guide them, including a commitment to the success of all students, the creation of new roles for teachers, and the development of schools as caring communities.

Another crucial consideration in undertaking educational change is a focus on what Jim Cummins (1994) has called the "relations of power" in schools. In proposing a shift from coercive to collaborative relations of power, Cummins argues that traditional teacher-centered transmission models can limit the potential for critical thinking on the part of both teachers and students, but especially for students from dominated communities whose cultures and languages have been devalued by the dominant canon.[3] By encouraging collaborative relations of power, schools and teachers can begin to recognize other sources of legitimate knowledge that have been overlooked, negated, or minimized because they are not part of the dominant discourse in schools.

Focusing on concerns such as the limits of school reform without concomitant changes in educators' attitudes toward students and their families, and the crucial role of power relationships in schools may help rescue current reform efforts from simplistic technical responses to what are essentially moral and political dilemmas. That is, such technical changes as tinkering with the length of the school day, substituting one textbook for another, or adding curricular requirements may do little to change student outcomes unless these changes are part and parcel of a more comprehensive conceptualization of school reform. When such issues are considered fundamental to the changes that must be made in schools, we might more precisely speak about *transformation* rather than simply about reform. But educational transformation cannot take place without the inclusion of the voices of students, among others, in the dialogue.

Why Listen to Students?

One way to begin the process of changing school policies and practices is to listen to students' views about them; however, research that focuses on student voices is relatively recent and scarce. For example, student perspectives are for the most part missing in discussions concerning strategies for confronting educational problems. In addition, the voices of students are rarely heard in the debates about school failure and success, and the perspectives of students from disempowered and dominated communities are even more invisible. In this article, I will draw primarily on the words of students interviewed for a previous research study (Nieto, 1992). I used the interviews to develop case studies of young people from a wide variety of ethnic, racial, linguistic, and social-class backgrounds who were at the time students in junior or senior high school. These ten young people lived in communities as diverse as large urban areas and small rural hamlets and belonged to families ranging from single-parent households to large, extended families. The one common element in all of their experiences turned out to be something we as researchers had neither planned nor expected: they were all successful students.[4]

The students were selected in a number of ways, but primarily through community contacts. Most were interviewed at home or in another setting of their choice outside of school. The only requirement that my colleagues and I determined for selecting students was that they reflect a variety of ethnic and racial backgrounds, in order to give us the diversity for which we were looking. The students selected self-identified as Black, African American, Mexican, Native American, Black and White American (biracial), Vietnamese, Jewish, Lebanese, Puerto Rican, and Cape Verdean. The one European American was the only student who had a hard time defining herself, other than as "American" (for a further analysis of this issue, see Nieto, 1992). That these particular students were academically successful was quite serendipitous. We defined them as such for the following reasons: they were all either still in school or just graduating; they all planned to complete at least high school, and most hoped to go to college; they had good grades, although they were not all at the top of their class; they had thought about their future and had made some plans for it; they generally enjoyed school and felt engaged in it (but they were also critical of their own school experiences and that of their peers, as we shall see); and most described themselves as successful. Although it had not been our initial intention to focus exclusively on academically successful students, on closer reflection it seemed logical that such students would be more likely to want to talk about their experiences than those who were not successful. It was at that point that I decided to explore what it was about these students' specific experiences that helped them succeed in school.

Therefore, the fact that these students saw themselves as successful helped further define the study, whose original purpose was to determine the benefits of multicultural education for students of diverse backgrounds. I was particularly interested in developing a way of looking at multicultural education that went beyond the typical "Holidays and Heroes" approach, which is too superficial to have any lasting impact in schools (Banks, 1991; Sleeter, 1991).[5] By exploring such issues as racism and low expectations of student achievement, as well as school policies and practices such as curriculum, pedagogy, testing, and tracking, I set about developing an understanding of multicultural education as anti-racist, comprehensive, pervasive, and rooted in social justice. Students were interviewed to find out what it meant to be from a particular background, how this influenced their school experience, and what about that experience they would change if they could. Although they were not asked specifically about the policies and practices in their schools, they nevertheless reflected on them in their answers to questions ranging from identifying their favorite subjects to describing the importance of getting an education. In this article, I will revisit the interviews to focus on students' thoughts about a number of school policies and practices and on the effects of racism and other forms of discrimination on their education.

The insights provided by the students were far richer than we had first thought. Although we expected numerous criticisms of schools and some concrete suggestions, we were surprised at the depth of awareness and analysis the students shared with us. They had a lot to say about the teachers they liked, as well as those they disliked, and they were able to explain the differences between them; they talked about grades and how these had become overly important in determining curriculum and pedagogy; they discussed their parents' lack of involvement, in most cases, in traditional school activities such as P.T.O. membership and bake sales, but their otherwise passionate support for their children's academic success; they mused about what schools could do to encourage more students to learn; they spoke with feeling about their cultures, languages, and communities, and what schools could do to capitalize on these factors; and they gave us concrete suggestions for improving schools for young people of all backgrounds. This experience confirmed my belief that educators can benefit from hearing students' critical perspectives, which might cause them to modify how they approach curriculum, pedagogy, and other school practices. Since doing this research, I have come across other studies that also focus on young people's perspectives and provide additional powerful examples of the lessons we can learn from them. This article thus begins with "lessons from students," an approach that takes the perspective proposed by Paulo Freire, that teachers need to become students just as students need to become teachers in order for education to become reciprocal and empowering for both (Freire, 1970).

This focus on students is not meant to suggest that their ideas should be the final and conclusive word in how schools need to change. Nobody has all the answers, and suggesting that students' views should be adopted wholesale is to accept a romantic view of students that is just as partial and condescending as excluding them completely from the discussion. I am instead suggesting that if we believe schools must provide an equal and quality education for all, students need to be included in the dialogue, and that their views, just as those of others, should be problematized and used to reflect critically on school reform.

Selected Policies and Practices and Students' Views about Them

School policies and practices need to be understood within the sociopolitical context of our society in general, rather than simply within individual schools' or teachers' attitudes and practices. This is important to remember for a number of reasons. First, although "teacher bashing" provides an easy target for complex problems, it fails to take into account the fact that teachers function within particular societal and institutional structures. In addition, it results in placing an inordinate amount of blame on some of those who care most deeply about students and who struggle every day to help them learn. That some teachers are racist, classist, and mean-spirited and that others have lost all creativity and caring is not in question here, and I begin with the assumption that the majority of teachers are not consciously so. I do suggest, however, that although many teachers are hardworking, supportive of their students, and talented educators, many of these same teachers are also burned out, frustrated, and negatively influenced by societal views about the students they teach. Teachers could benefit from knowing more about their students' families and experiences, as well as about students' views on school and how it could be improved.

How do students feel about the curriculum they must learn? What do they think about the pedagogical strategies their teachers use? Is student involvement a meaningful issue for them? Are their own identities important considerations in how they view school? What about tracking and testing and disciplinary policies? These are crucial questions to consider when reflecting on what teachers and schools can learn from students, but we know very little about students' responses. When asked, students seem surprised and excited about being included in the conversation, and what they have to say is often compelling and eloquent. In fact, Patricia Phelan, Ann Locke Davidson, and Hanh Thanh Cao (1992), in a two-year research project designed to identify students' thoughts about school, discovered that students' views on teaching and learning were remarkably consistent with those of current theorists concerned with learning theory, cognitive science, and the sociology of work. This should come as no surprise when we consider that students spend more time in schools than anybody else except teachers (who are also omitted in most discussions of school reform, but that is a topic for another article). In the following sections, I will focus on students' perceptions concerning the curriculum, pedagogy, tracking, and grades in their schools. I will also discuss their attitudes about racism and other biases, how these are manifested in their schools and classrooms, and what effect they may have on students' learning and participation in school.

Curriculum

The curriculum in schools is at odds with the experiences, backgrounds, hopes, and wishes of many students. This is true of both the tangible curriculum as expressed through books, other materials, and the actual written curriculum guides, as well as in the less tangible and "hidden" curriculum as seen in the bulletin boards, extracurricular activities, and messages given to students about their abilities and talents. For instance, Christine Sleeter and Carl Grant (1991) found that a third of the students in a desegregated junior high school they studied said that *none* of the class content related to their lives outside class. Those who indicated some relevancy cited only current events, oral history, money and banking, and multicultural content (because it dealt with prejudice) as being relevant. The same was true in a study by Mary Poplin and Joseph Weeres (1992), who found that students frequently reported being bored in school and seeing little relevance in what was taught for their lives or their futures. The authors concluded that students became more disengaged as the curriculum, texts, and assignments became more standardized. Thus, in contrast to Ira Shor's (1992) suggestion that "What students bring to class is where learning begins. It starts there and goes places" (p. 44), there is often a tremendous mismatch between students' cultures and the culture of the school. In many schools, learning starts not with what students bring to class, but with what is considered high-status knowledge; that is, the "canon," with its overemphasis on European and European American history, arts, and values. This seldom includes the backgrounds, experiences, and talents of the majority of students in U.S. schools. Rather than "going elsewhere," their learning therefore often goes nowhere.

That students' backgrounds and experiences are missing in many schools is particularly evident where the native language of most of the students is not English. In such settings, it is not unusual to see little or no representation of those students' language in the curriculum. In fact, there is often an insistence that students "speak only English" in these schools, which sends a powerful message to young people struggling to maintain an identity in the face of overpowering messages that they must assimilate. This was certainly the case for Marisol, a Puerto Rican girl of sixteen participating in my research, who said:

> I used to have a lot of problems with one of my teachers 'cause she didn't want us to talk Spanish in class, and I thought that was like an insult to us, you know? Just telling us not to talk Spanish, 'cause they were Puerto Ricans and, you know, we're free to talk whatever we want, . . . I could never stay quiet and talk only English, 'cause sometimes . . . words slip in Spanish. You know, I think they should understand that.

Practices such as not allowing students to speak their native tongue are certain to influence negatively students' identities and their views of what constitutes important knowledge. For example, when asked if she would be interested in taking a course on Puerto Rican history, Marisol was quick to answer: "I don't think [it's] important. . . . I'm proud of myself and my culture, but I think I know what I should know about the culture already, so I wouldn't take the course." Ironically, it was evident to me after speaking with her on several occasions that Marisol knew virtually nothing about Puerto Rican history. However, she had already learned another lesson well: given what she said about the courses she needed to take, she made it clear that "important" history is U.S. history, which rarely includes anything about Puerto Rico.

Messages about culture and language and how they are valued or devalued in society are communicated not only or even primarily by schools, but by the media and community as a whole. The sociopolitical context of the particular city where Marisol lived, and of its school system, is important to understand: there had been an attempt to pass an ordinance restricting the number of Puerto Ricans coming into town based on the argument that they placed an undue burden on the welfare rolls and other social services. In addition, the "English Only" debate had become an issue when the mayor had ordered all municipal workers to speak only English on the job. Furthermore, although the school system had a student body that was 65 percent Puerto Rican, there was only a one-semester course on Puerto Rican history that had just recently been approved for the bilingual program. In contrast, there were two courses, which although rarely taught were on the books, that focused on apartheid and the Holocaust, despite the fact that both the African American and Jewish communities in the town were quite small. That such courses should be part of a comprehensive multicultural program is not being questioned; however, it is ironic that the largest population in the school was ignored in the general curriculum.

In a similar vein, Nancy Commins's (1989) research with four first-generation Mexican American fifth-grade students focused on how these students made decisions about their education, both consciously and unconsciously, based on their determination of what counted as important knowledge. Her research suggests that the classroom setting and curriculum can support or hinder students' perceptions of themselves as learners based on the languages they speak and their cultural backgrounds. She found that although the homes of these four students provided rich environments for a variety of language uses and literacy, the school did little to capitalize on these strengths. In their classroom, for instance, these children rarely used Spanish, commenting that it was the language of the "dumb kids." As a result, Commins states: "Their reluctance to use Spanish in an academic context also limited their opportunities to practice talking about abstract ideas and to use higher level cognitive skills in Spanish" (p. 35). She also found that the content of the curriculum was almost completely divorced from the experiences of these youngsters, since the problems of poverty, racism, and discrimination, which were prominent in their lives, were not addressed in the curriculum.

In spite of teachers' reluctance to address such concerns, they are often compelling to students, particularly those who are otherwise invisible in the curriculum. Vinh, an 18-year-old Vietnamese student attending a high school in a culturally heterogeneous town, lived with his uncle and younger brothers and sisters. Although grateful for the education he was receiving, Vinh expressed concern about what he saw as insensitivity on the part of some of his teachers to the difficulties of adjusting to a new culture and learning English:

> [Teachers] have to know about our culture. . . . From the second language, it is very difficult for me and for other people.

Vinh's concern was echoed by Manuel, a nineteen-year-old Cape Verdean senior who, at the time of the interviews, was just getting ready to graduate, the first in his family of eleven children to do so:

I was kind of afraid of school, you know, 'cause it's different when you're learning the language. . . . It's kind of scary at first, especially if you don't know the language and like if you don't have friends here.

In Manuel's case, the Cape Verdean Crioulo bilingual program served as a linguistic and cultural mediator, negotiating difficult experiences that he faced in school so that, by the time he reached high school, he had learned enough English to "speak up." Another positive curricular experience was the theater workshop he took as a sophomore. There, students created and acted in skits focusing on their lived experiences. He recalled with great enthusiasm, for example, a monologue he did about a student going to a new school, because it was based on his personal experience.

Sometimes a school's curriculum is unconsciously disrespectful of students' cultures and experiences. James, a student who proudly identified himself as Lebanese American, found that he was invisible in the curriculum, even in supposedly multicultural curricular and extracurricular activities. He mentioned a language fair, a multicultural festival, and a school cookbook, all of which omitted references to the Arabic language and to Lebanese people. About the cookbook, he said:

They made this cookbook of all these different recipes from all over the world. And I would've brought in some Lebanese recipes if somebody'd let me know. And I didn't hear about it until the week before they started selling them. . . . I asked one of the teachers to look at it and there was nothing Lebanese in there.

James made an effort to dismiss this oversight, and although he said that it didn't matter, he seemed to be struggling with the growing realization that it mattered very much indeed:

I don't know, I guess there's not that many Lebanese people in . . . I don't know; you don't hear really that much . . . Well, you hear it in the news a lot, but I mean, I don't know, there's not a lot of Lebanese kids in our school. . . . I don't mind, 'cause I mean, I don't know, just I don't mind it. . . . It's not really important. It *is* important for me. It would be important for me to see a Lebanese flag.

Lebanese people were mentioned in the media, although usually in negative ways, and these were the only images of James's ethnic group that made their way into the school. He spoke, for example, about how the Lebanese were characterized by his peers:

Some people call me, you know, 'cause I'm Lebanese, so people say, "Look out for the terrorist! Don't mess with him or he'll blow up your house!" or some stuff like that. . . . But they're just joking around, though. . . . I don't think anybody's serious 'cause I wouldn't blow up anybody's house — and they know that. . . . I don't care. It doesn't matter what people say. . . . I just want everybody to know that, you know, it's not true.

Cultural ambivalence, both pride and shame, were evident in the responses of many of the students. Although almost all of them were quite clear that their culture was important to them, they were also confronted with debilitating messages about it from society in general. How to make sense of these contradictions was a dilemma for many of these young people.

Fern, who identified herself as Native American, was, at thirteen, one of the youngest students interviewed. She reflected on the constant challenges she faced in the history curriculum in her junior high school. Her father was active in their school and community and he gave her a great deal of support for defending her position, but she was the only Native American student in her entire school in this mid-size city in Iowa. She said:

> If there's something in the history book that's wrong, my dad always taught me that if it's wrong, I should tell them that it is wrong. And the only time I ever do is if I know it's *exactly* wrong. Like we were reading about Native Americans and scalping. Well, the French are really the ones that made them do it so they could get money. And my teacher would not believe me. I finally just shut up because he just would not believe me.

Fern also mentioned that her sister had come home angry one day because somebody in school had said "Geronimo was a stupid chief riding that stupid horse." The connection between an unresponsive curriculum and dropping out of school was not lost on Fern, and she talked about this incident as she wondered aloud why other Native Americans had dropped out of the town's schools. Similar sentiments were reported by students in Virginia Vogel Zanger's (1994) study of twenty Latinos from a Boston high school who took part in a panel discussion in which they reflected on their experiences in school. Some of the students who decided to stay in school claimed that dropping out among their peers was a direct consequence of the school's attempts to "monoculture" them.

Fern was self-confident and strong in expressing her views, despite her young age. Yet she too was silenced by the way the curriculum was presented in class. This is because schools often avoid bringing up difficult, contentious, or conflicting issues in the curriculum, especially when these contradict the sanctioned views of the standard curriculum, resulting in what Michelle Fine has called "silencing." According to Fine, "Silencing is about who can speak, what can and cannot be spoken, and whose discourse must be controlled" (1991, p. 33). Two topics in particular that appear to have great saliency for many students, regardless of their backgrounds, are bias and discrimination, yet these are among the issues most avoided in classrooms. Perhaps this is because the majority of teachers are European Americans who are unaccustomed, afraid, or uncomfortable in discussing these issues (Sleeter, 1994); perhaps it is due to the pressure teachers feel to "cover the material"; maybe it has to do with the tradition of presenting information in schools as if it were free of conflict and controversy (Kohl, 1993); or, most likely, it is a combination of all these things. In any event, both students and teachers soon pick up the message that racism, discrimination, and other dangerous topics are not supposed to be discussed in school. We also need to keep in mind that these issues have disparate meanings for people of different backgrounds and are often perceived as particularly threatening to those from dominant cultural and racial groups. Deidre, one of the young African American women in Fine's 1991 study of an urban high school, explained it this way: "White people might feel like everything's over and OK, but we remember" (p. 33).

Another reason that teachers may avoid bringing up potentially contentious issues in the curriculum is their feeling that doing so may create or exacerbate animosity and hostility among students. They may even believe, as did the reading teacher in Jonathan Kozol's 1967 classic book on the Boston Public Schools, *Death at an Early Age*, that discussing slavery in the context of U.S. history was just too complicated for children to understand, not to mention uncomfortable for teachers to explain. Kozol writes of the reading teacher:

> She said, with the very opposite of malice but only with an expression of the most intense and honest affection for the children in the class: "I don't want these children to have to think back on this year later on and to have to remember that we were the ones who told them they were Negro." (p. 68)

More than a quarter of a century later, the same kinds of disclaimers are being made for the failure to include in the curriculum the very issues that would engage students in learning. Fine (1991) found that although over half of the students in the urban high school she interviewed described experiences with racism, teachers were reluctant to discuss it in class, explaining, in the words of one teacher, "It would demoralize the students, they need to feel positive and optimistic — like they have a chance. Racism is just an excuse they use to not try harder" (p. 37). Some of these concerns may be sincere expressions of protectiveness toward students, but others are merely self-serving and manifest teachers' discomfort with discussing racism.

The few relevant studies I have found concerning the inclusion of issues of racism and discrimination in the curriculum suggest that discussions about these topics can be immensely constructive if they are approached with sensitivity and understanding. This was the case in Melinda Fine's description of the "Facing History and Ourselves" (FHAO) curriculum, a project that started in the Brookline (Massachusetts) Public Schools almost two decades ago (Fine, 1993). FHAO provides a model for teaching history that encourages students to reflect critically on a variety of contemporary social, moral, and political issues. Using the Holocaust as a case study, students learn to think critically about such issues as scapegoating, racism, and personal and collective responsibility. Fine suggests that moral dilemmas do not disappear simply because teachers refuse to bring them into the schools. On the contrary, when these realities are separated from the curriculum, young people learn that school knowledge is unrelated to their lives, and once again, they are poorly prepared to face the challenges that society has in store for them.

A good case in point is Vanessa, a young European American woman in my study who was intrigued by "difference" yet was uncomfortable and reluctant to discuss it. Although she was active in a peer-education group that focused on such concerns as peer pressure, discrimination, and exclusion, these were rarely discussed in the formal curriculum. Vanessa, therefore, had no language with which to talk about these issues. In thinking about U.S. history, she mused about some of the contradictions that were rarely addressed in school:

> It seems weird . . . because people came from Europe and they wanted to get away from all the stuff that was over there. And then they came here and set up all the stuff like slavery, and I don't know, it seems the opposite of what they would have done.

The curriculum, then, can act to either enable or handicap students in their learning. Given the kind of curriculum that draws on their experiences and energizes them because it focuses precisely on those things that are most important in their lives, students can either soar or sink in our schools. Curriculum can provide what María Torres-Guzmán (1992) refers to as "cognitive empowerment," encouraging students to become confident, active critical thinkers who learn that their background experiences are important tools for further learning. The connection of the curriculum to real life and their future was mentioned by several of the students interviewed in my study. Avi, a Jewish boy of sixteen who often felt a schism between his school and home lives, for instance, spoke about the importance of school: "If you don't go to school, then you can't learn about life, or you can't learn about things that you need to progress [in] your life." And Vanessa, who seemed to yearn for a more socially conscious curriculum in her school, summed up why education was important to her: "A good education is like when you personally learn something . . . like growing, expanding your mind and your views."

Pedagogy

If curriculum is primarily the *what* of education, then pedagogy concerns the *why* and *how*. No matter how interesting and relevant the curriculum may be, the way in which it is presented is what will make it engaging or dull to students. Students' views echo those of educational researchers who have found that teaching methods in most classrooms, and particularly those in secondary schools, vary little from traditional "chalk and talk" methods; that textbooks are the dominant teaching materials used; that routine and rote learning are generally favored over creativity and critical thinking; and that teacher-centered transmission models prevail (Cummins, 1994; Goodlad, 1984; McNeil, 1986). Martin Haberman is especially critical of what he calls "the pedagogy of poverty," that is, a basic urban pedagogy used with children who live in poverty and which consists primarily of giving instructions, asking questions, giving directions, making assignments, and monitoring seat work. Such pedagogy is based on the assumption that before students can be engaged in creative or critical work, they must first master "the basics." Nevertheless, Haberman asserts that this pedagogy does not work and, furthermore, that it actually gets in the way of real teaching and learning. He suggests instead that we look at exemplary pedagogy in urban schools that actively involves students in real-life situations, which allows them to reflect on their own lives. He finds that good teaching is taking place when teachers welcome difficult issues and events and use human difference as the basis for the curriculum; design collaborative activities for heterogeneous groups; and help students apply ideals of fairness, equity, and justice to their world (Haberman, 1991).

Students in my study had more to say about pedagogy than about anything else, and they were especially critical of the lack of imagination that led to boring classes. Linda, who was just graduating as the valedictorian of her class in an urban high school, is a case in point. Her academic experiences had not always been smooth sailing. For example, she had failed both seventh and eighth grade twice, for a combination of reasons, including academic and medical problems. Consequently, she had had both exhilarating and devastating educational experiences. Linda had this to say about pedagogy:

> I think you have to be creative to be a teacher; you have to make it interesting. You can't just go in and say, "Yeah, I'm going to teach the kids just that; I'm

gonna teach them right out of the book and that's the way it is, and don't ask questions." Because I know there were plenty of classes where I lost complete interest. But those were all because the teachers just, "Open the books to this page." They never made up problems out of their head. Everything came out of the book. You didn't ask questions. If you asked them questions, then the answer was "in the book." And if you asked the question and the answer *wasn't* in the book, then you shouldn't have asked that question!

Rich, a young Black man, planned to attend pharmacy school after graduation, primarily because of the interest he had developed in chemistry. He too talked about the importance of making classes "interesting":

> I believe a teacher, by the way he introduces different things to you, can make a class interesting. Not like a normal teacher that gets up, gives you a lecture, or there's teachers that just pass out the work, you do the work, pass it in, get a grade, good-bye!

Students were especially critical of teachers' reliance on textbooks and blackboards, a sad indictment of much of the teaching that encourages student passivity. Avi, for instance, felt that some teachers get along better when they teach from the point of view of the students: "They don't just come out and say, 'All right, do this, blah, blah, blah.' . . . They're not so *one-tone voice*." Yolanda said that her English teacher didn't get along with the students. In her words, "She just does the things and sits down." James mentioned that some teachers just don't seem to care: "They just teach the stuff. 'Here,' write a couple of things on the board, 'see, that's how you do it. Go ahead, page 25.' " And Vinh added his voice to those of the students who clearly saw the connection between pedagogy and caring: "Some teachers, they just go inside and go to the blackboard. . . . They don't care."

Students did more than criticize teachers' pedagogy, however; they also praised teachers who were interesting, creative, and caring. Linda, in a particularly moving testimony to her first-grade teacher, whom she called her mentor, mentioned that she would be "following in her footsteps" and studying elementary education. She added:

> She's always been there for me. After the first or second grade, if I had a problem, I could always go back to her. Through the whole rest of my life, I've been able to go back and talk to her. . . . She's a Golden Apple Award winner, which is a very high award for elementary school teachers. . . . She keeps me on my toes. . . . When I start getting down . . . she peps me back up and I get on my feet.

Vinh talked with feeling about teachers who allowed him to speak Vietnamese with other students in class. Vinh loved working in groups. He particularly remembered a teacher who always asked students to discuss important issues, rather than focusing only on learning what he called "the word's meaning" by writing and memorizing lists of words. The important issues concerned U.S. history, the students' histories and cultures, and other engaging topics that were central to their lives. Students' preference for group work has been mentioned by other educators as well. Phelan et al. (1992), in their research on students' perspectives concerning school, found that both high- and low-achieving students of all backgrounds expressed a strong preference for working in groups, because it helped them generate ideas and participate actively in class.

James also appreciated teachers who explained things and let everybody ask questions because, as he said, "There could be someone sitting in the back of the class that has the same question you have. Might as well bring it out." Fern contrasted classes where she felt like falling asleep because they're just "blah," to chorus, where the teacher used a "rap song" to teach history and involve all the students. And Avi, who liked most of his teachers, singled out a particular math teacher he had had in ninth grade for praise:

'Cause I never really did good in math until I had him. And he showed me that it wasn't so bad, and after that I've been doing pretty good in math and I enjoy it.

Yolanda had been particularly fortunate to have many teachers she felt understood and supported her, whether they commented on her bilingual ability, or referred to her membership in a folkloric Mexican dance group, or simply talked with her and the other students about their lives. She added:

I really got along with the teachers a lot. . . . Actually, 'cause I had some teachers, and they were always calling my mom, like I did a great job. Or they would start talking to me, or they kinda like pulled me up some grades, or moved me to other classes, or took me somewhere. And they were always congratulating me.

Such support, however, rarely represented only individual effort on the part of some teachers, but rather was often manifested by the school as a whole; that is, it was integral to the school's practices and policies. For instance, Yolanda had recently been selected "Student of the Month," and her picture had been prominently displayed in her school's main hall. In addition, she received a certificate and was taken out to dinner by the principal. Although Linda's first-grade teacher was her special favorite, she had others who also created an educational context in which all students felt welcomed and connected. The entire Tremont Elementary School had been special for Linda, and thus the context of the school, including its leadership and commitment, were the major ingredients that made it successful:

All of my teachers were wonderful. I don't think there's a teacher at the whole Tremont School that I didn't like. . . . It's just a feeling you have. You know that they really care for you. You just know it; you can tell. Teachers who don't have you in any of their classes or haven't ever had you, they still know who you are. . . . The Tremont School in itself is a community. . . . I love that school! I want to teach there.

Vanessa talked about how teachers used their students' lives and experiences in their teaching. For her, this made them especially good teachers:

[Most teachers] are really caring and supportive and are willing to share their lives and are willing to listen to mine. They don't just want to talk about what they're teaching you; they also want to know you.

Aside from criticism and praise, students in this study also offered their teachers many thoughtful suggestions for making their classrooms more engaging places. Rich, for instance, said that he would "put more activities into the day that can make it interesting." Fern recommended that teachers involve students more actively in learning: "More like making the whole class be involved, not making only the two smartest people up here do the whole work for the whole class." Vanessa added, "You could have games that could teach anything that they're trying to teach through notes or lectures." She suggested that in learning Spanish, for instance, students could act out the words, making them easier to remember. She also thought that other books should be required "just to show some points of view," a response no doubt to the bland quality of so many of the textbooks and other teaching materials available in schools. Avi thought that teachers who make themselves available to students ("You know, I'm here after school. Come and get help.") were most helpful.

Vinh was very specific in his suggestions, and he touched on important cultural issues. Because he came from Vietnam when he was fifteen, learning English was a difficult challenge for Vinh, and he tended to be very hard on himself, saying such things as "I'm not really good, but I'm trying" when asked to describe himself as a student. Although he had considered himself smart in Vietnam, he felt that because his English was not perfect, he wasn't smart anymore. His teachers often showered him with praise for his efforts, but Vinh criticized this approach:

> Sometimes, the English teachers, they don't understand about us. Because something we not do good, like my English is not good. And she say, "Oh, your English is great!" But that's the way the American culture is. But my culture is not like that. . . . If my English is not good, she has to say, "Your English is not good. So you have to go home and study." And she tell me what to study and how to study and get better. But some Americans, you know, they don't understand about myself. So they just say, "Oh! You're doing a good job! You're doing great! Everything is great!" Teachers talk like that, but my culture is different. . . . They say, "You have to do better."

This is an important lesson, not only because it challenges the overuse of praise, a practice among those that María de la Luz Reyes (1992) has called "venerable assumptions," but also because it cautions teachers to take into account both cultural and individual differences. In this case, the practice of praising was perceived by Vinh as hollow, and therefore insincere. Linda referred to the lesson she learned when she failed seventh and eighth grade and "blew two years":

> I learned a lot from it. As a matter of fact, one of my college essays was on the fact that from that experience, I learned that I don't need to hear other people's praise to get by. . . . All I need to know is in here [pointing to her heart] whether I tried or not.

Students have important messages for teachers about what works and what doesn't. It is important, however, not to fall back on what Lilia Bartolomé (1994) has aptly termed the "methods fetish," that is, a simplistic belief that particular methods will automatically resolve complex problems of underachievement. According to Bartolomé, such a myopic approach results in teachers avoiding the central issue of why some students succeed and others fail in school and how political inequality is at the heart of this dilemma. Rather than using this or that method, Bartolomé suggests that teachers develop what she calls a "humanizing pedagogy" in which students' languages and cultures are central. There is also the problem that Reyes (1992) has called a "one-size-fits all" approach, where students' cultural and other differences may be denied, even if teachers' methods are based on well-meaning and progressive pedagogy. The point here is that no method can become a sacred cow uncritically accepted and used simply because it is the latest fad.

It is probably fair to say that teachers who use more traditional methods but care about their students and believe they deserve the chance to dream may have more of a positive effect than those who know the latest methods but do not share these beliefs. Students need more than such innovations as heterogeneous grouping, peer tutoring, or cooperative groups. Although these may in fact be excellent and effective teaching methods, they will do little by themselves unless accompanied by changes in teachers' attitudes and behaviors.

The students quoted above are not looking for one magic solution or method. In fact, they have many, sometimes contradictory, suggestions to make about pedagogy. While rarely speaking with one voice, they nevertheless have similar overriding concerns: too many classrooms are boring, alienating, and disempowering. There is a complex interplay of policies, practices, and attitudes that cause such pedagogy to continue. Tracking and testing are two powerful forces implicated in this interplay.

Tracking/Ability Grouping/Grades and Expectations of Student Achievement

> It is not low income that matters but low status. And status is always created and imposed by the ones on top. (Stein, 1971, p. 158)

In her 1971 article, Annie Stein cited a New York City study in which kindergarten teachers were asked to list in order of importance the things a child should learn in order to prepare for first grade. Their responses were coded according to whether they were primarily socialization or educational goals. In the schools with large Puerto Rican and African American student populations, the socialization goals were always predominant; in the mixed schools, the educational goals were first. Concluded Stein, "In fact, in a list of six or seven goals, several teachers in the minority-group kindergartens forgot to mention any educational goals at all" (p. 167). A kind of tracking, in which students' educational goals were being sacrificed for social aims, was taking place in these schools, and its effects were already evident in kindergarten.

Most recent research on tracking has found it to be problematic, especially among middle- and low-achieving students, and suggestions for detracking schools have gained growing support (Oakes, 1992; Wheelock, 1992). Nevertheless, although many tracking decisions are made on the most tenuous grounds, they are supported by ideological norms in our society about the nature of intelligence and the distribution of ability. The long-term effects of ability grouping can be devastating for the life chances of young people. John Goodlad (1984) found that first- or second-grade children tracked by teachers' judgments of their reading and math ability or by testing are likely to remain in their assigned track *for the rest of their schooling*. In addition, he found that poor children and children of color are more likely to face the negative effects of tracking than are other youngsters. For example, a recent research project by Hugh Mehan and Irene Villanueva (1993) found that when low-achieving high school students are detracked, they tend to benefit academically. The study focused on low-achieving students in the San Diego City Schools. When these students, mostly Latinos and African Americans, were removed from a low track and placed in college-bound courses with high-achieving students, they benefitted in a number of ways, including significantly higher college enrollment. The researchers concluded that a rigorous academic program serves the educational and social interests of such students more effectively than remedial and compensatory programs.

Most of the young people in my study did not mention tracking or ability grouping by name, but almost all referred to it circuitously, and usually in negative ways. Although by and large academically successful themselves, they were quick to point out that teachers' expectations often doomed their peers to failure. Yolanda, for instance, when asked what suggestions she would give teachers, said, "I'd say to teachers, 'Get along more with the kids that are not really into themselves. . . . Have more communication with them.' " When asked what she would like teachers to know about other Mexican American students, she quickly said, "They try real hard, that's one thing I know." She also criticized teachers for having low expectations of students, claiming that materials used in the classes were "too low." She added, "We are supposed to be doing higher things. And like they take us too slow, see, step by step. And that's why everybody takes it as a joke." Fern, although she enjoyed being at the "top of my class," did not like to be treated differently. She spoke about a school she attended previously where "you were all the same and you all got pushed the same and you were all helped the same. And one thing I've noticed in Springdale is they kind of teach 25 percent, and they kinda leave 75 percent out." She added that, if students were receiving bad grades, teachers did not help them as much: "In Springdale, I've noticed if you're getting D's and F's, they don't look up to you; they look down. And you're always the last on the list for special activities, you know?"

These young people also referred to expectations teachers had of students based on cultural or class differences. Vanessa said that some teachers based their expectations of students on bad reputations, and she found least helpful those teachers who "kind of just move really fast, just trying to get across to you what they're trying to teach you. Not willing to slow down because they need to get in what they want to get in." Rich, who attended a predominantly Black school, felt that some teachers there did not expect as much as they should from the Black students: "Many of the White teachers there don't push. . . . Their expectations don't seem to be as high as they should be. . . . I know that some Black teachers, their expectations are higher than White teachers. . . . They just do it, because they know how it was for them. . . . Actually, I'd say, you have to be in Black shoes to know how it is." Little did Rich know that he was reaching the same conclusion as a major research study on fostering high achievement for African American students. In this study, Janine Bempechat determined that "across all schools, it seems that achievement is fostered by high expectations and standards" (Bempechat, 1992, p. 43).

Virginia Vogel Zanger's research with Latino and Latina students in a Boston high school focused on what can be called "social tracking." Although the students she interviewed were high-achieving and tracked in a college-bound course, they too felt the sting of alienation. In a linguistic analysis of their comments, she found that students conveyed a strong sense of marginalization, using terms such as "left out," "below," "under," and "not joined in" to reflect their feelings about school (Zanger, 1994). Although these were clearly academically successful students, they perceived tracking in the subordinate status they were assigned based on their cultural backgrounds and on the racist climate established in the school. Similarly, in a study on dropping out among Puerto Rican students, my colleague Manuel Frau-Ramos and I found some of the same kind of language. José, who had dropped out in eleventh grade, explained, "I was alone. . . . I was an outsider" (Frau-Ramos &

Nieto, 1993, p. 156). Pedro, a young man who had actually graduated, neverthe-less felt the same kind of alienation. When asked what the school could do to help Puerto Ricans stay in school, he said, *"Hacer algo para que los boricuas no se sientan aparte"* (Do something so that the Puerto Ricans wouldn't feel so separate) (p. 157).

Grading policies have also been mentioned in relation to tracking and expecta-tions of achievement. One study, for example, found that when teachers de-emphasized grades and standardized testing, the status of their African American and White students became more equal, and White students made more cross-race friendship choices (Hallinan & Teixeira, 1987). In my own research, I found a somewhat surprising revelation: although the students were achieving successfully in school, most did not feel that grades were very helpful. Of course, for the most part they enjoyed receiving good grades, but it was not always for the expected rea-son. Fern, for instance, wanted good grades because they were one guarantee that teachers would pay attention to her. Marisol talked about the "nice report cards" that she and her siblings in this family of eight children received, and said, "and, usually, we do this for my mother. We like to see her the way she wants to be, you know, to see her happy."

But they were also quick to downplay the importance of grades. Linda, for in-stance, gave as an example her computer teacher, who she felt had been the least helpful in her high school:

> I have no idea about computer literacy. I got A's in that course. Just because he saw that I had A's, and that my name was all around the school for all the "won-derful things" I do, he just automatically assumed. He didn't really pay attention to who I was. The grade I think I deserved in that class was at least a C, but I got A just because everybody else gave me A's. . . . He didn't help me at all because he didn't challenge me.

She added,

> To me, they're just something on a piece of paper. . . . [My parents] feel just about the same way. If they ask me, "Honestly, did you try your best?" and I tell them yes, then they'll look at the grades and say okay.

Rich stated that, although grades were important to his mother, "I'm comfortable setting my own standards." James said, without arrogance, that he was "probably the smartest kid in my class." Learning was important to him and, unlike other stu-dents who also did the assignments, he liked to "really get into the work and stuff." He added,

> If you don't get involved with it, even if you do get, if you get perfect scores and stuff . . . it's not like really gonna sink in. . . . You can memorize the words, you know, on a test . . . but you know, if you memorize them, it's not going to do you any good. You have to *learn* them, you know?

Most of the students made similar comments, and their perceptions challenge schools to think more deeply about the real meaning of education. Linda was not alone when she said that the reason for going to school was to "make yourself a better person." She loved learning and commented that "I just want to keep con-tinuously learning, because when you stop learning, then you start dying."

Yolanda used the metaphor of nutrition to talk about learning: "[Education] is good for you. . . . It's like when you eat. It's like if you don't eat in a whole day, you feel weird. That's the same thing for me." Vanessa, also an enthusiastic student, spoke pensively about success and happiness: "I'm happy. Success is being happy to me; it's not like having a job that gives you a zillion dollars. It's just having self-happiness."

Finally, Vinh spoke extensively about the meaning of education, contrasting the difference between what he felt it meant in the United States and what it meant in his home culture:

> In Vietnam, we go to school because we want to become educated people. But in the United States, most people, they say, "Oh, we go to school because we want to get a good job." But my idea, I don't think so. I say, if we go to school, we want a good job *also*, but we want to become a good person.
>
> [Grades] are not important to me. Important to me is education. . . . I not so concerned about [test scores] very much. . . . I just know I do my exam very good. But I don't need to know I got A or B. I have to learn more and more.
>
> Some people, they got a good education. They go to school, they got master's, they got doctorate, but they're just helping *themselves*. So that's not good. I don't care much about money. So, I just want to have a normal job that I can take care of myself and my family. So that's enough. I don't want to climb up compared to other people.

Racism and Discrimination

> The facts are clear to behold, but the BIG LIE of racism blinds all but its victims.
> (Stein, 1971, p. 179)

An increasing number of formal research studies, as well as informal accounts and anecdotes, attest to the lasting legacy of various forms of institutional discrimination in the schools based on race, ethnicity, religion, gender, social class, language, and sexual orientation. Yet, as Annie Stein wrote in 1971, these are rarely addressed directly. The major reason for this may be that institutional discrimination flies in the face of our stated ideals of justice and fair play and of the philosophy that individual hard work is the road to success. Beverly Daniel Tatum, in discussing the myth of meritocracy, explains why racism is so often denied, downplayed, or dismissed: "An understanding of racism as a system of advantage presents a serious challenge to the notion of the United States as a just society where rewards are based solely on one's merits" (Tatum, 1992, p. 6).

Recent studies point out numerous ways in which racism and other forms of discrimination affect students and their learning. For instance, Angela Taylor found that, to the extent that teachers harbor negative racial stereotypes, the African American child's race *alone* is probably sufficient to place him or her at risk for negative school outcomes (Taylor, 1991). Many teachers, of course, see it differently, preferring to think instead that students' lack of academic achievement is due solely to conditions inside their homes or communities. But the occurrence of discriminatory actions in schools, both by other students and by teachers and other staff, has been widely documented. A 1990 study of Boston high school students found that while 57 percent had witnessed a racial attack and 47 percent would either join in or feel that the group being attacked deserved it, only a quarter of those interviewed said they would report a racial incident to school officials (Ribadeneira, 1990). It should not be surprising, then, that in a report about immigrant students in California, most believed that Americans felt negatively and unwelcoming toward them. In fact, almost every immigrant student interviewed reported that they had at one time or another been spat upon, and tricked, teased, and laughed at because of their race, accent, or the way they dressed. More than half also indicated that they had been the victims of teachers' prejudice, citing instances where they were punished, publicly embarrassed, or made fun of because of improper use of English. They also reported that teachers had made derogatory comments about immigrant groups in front of the class, or had avoided particular students because of the language difficulty (Olsen, 1988). Most of the middle and high school students interviewed by Mary Poplin and Joseph Weeres (1992) had also witnessed incidents of racism in school. In Karen Donaldson's study in an urban high school where students used the racism they experienced as the content of a peer-education program, over 80 percent of students surveyed said that they had perceived racism to exist in school (Donaldson, 1994).

Marietta Saravia-Shore and Herminio Martínez found similar results in their ethnographic study of Puerto Rican young people who had dropped out of school and were currently participating in an alternative high school program. These adolescents felt that their former teachers were, in their words, "against Puerto Ricans and Blacks" and had openly discriminated against them. One reported that a teacher had said, "Do you want to be like the other Puerto Rican women who never got an education? Do you want to be like the rest of your family and never go to school?" (Saravia-Shore & Martínez, 1992, p. 242). In Virginia Vogel Zanger's study of high-achieving Latino and Latina Boston high school students, one young man described his shock when his teacher called him "spic" right in class; although the teacher was later suspended, this incident had left its mark on him (Zanger, 1994). Unfortunately, incidents such as these are more frequent than schools care to admit or acknowledge. Students, however, seem eager to address these issues, but are rarely given a forum in which such discussions can take place.

How do students feel about the racism and other aspects of discrimination that they see around them and experience? What effect does it have on them? In interviews with students, Karen Donaldson found three major ways in which they said they were affected: White students experienced guilt and embarrassment when they became aware of the racism to which their peers were subjected; students of color sometimes felt they needed to overcompensate and overachieve to prove they were equal to their White classmates; and students of color also mentioned that discrimination had a negative impact on their self-esteem (Donaldson, 1994). The issue of self-esteem is a complicated one and may include many variables. Children's self-esteem does not come fully formed out of the blue, but is *created* within particular contexts and responds to conditions that vary from situation to situation, and teachers' and schools' complicity in creating negative self-esteem certainly cannot be discounted. This was understood by Lillian, one of the young women in Nitza Hidalgo's study of an urban high school, who commented, "That's another problem I have, teachers, they are always talking about how we have no type of self-esteem or anything like that. . . . But they're the people that's putting us down. That's why our self-esteem is so low" (Hidalgo, 1991, p. 95).

The students in my research also mentioned examples of discrimination based on their race, ethnicity, culture, religion, and language. Some, like Manuel, felt it from fellow students. As an immigrant from Cape Verde who came to the United States at the age of eleven, he found the adjustment difficult:

> When American students see you, it's kinda hard [to] get along with them when you have a different culture, a different way of dressing and stuff like that. So kids really look at you and laugh, you know, at the beginning.

Avi spoke of anti-Semitism in his school. The majority of residents in his town were European American and Christian. The Jewish community had dwindled significantly over the years, and there were now very few Jewish students in his school. On one occasion, a student had walked by him saying, "Are you ready for the second Holocaust?" He described another incident in some detail:

> I was in a woods class, and there was another boy in there, my age, and he was in my grade. He's also Jewish, and he used to come to the temple sometimes and went to Hebrew school. But then, of course, he started hanging around with the wrong people and some of these people were in my class, and I guess they were . . . . making fun of him. And a few of them starting making swastikas out of wood. . . . . So I saw one and I said to some kid, "What are you doing?" and the kid said to me, "Don't worry. It's not for you, it's for him." And I said to him, "What?!"

Other students talked about discrimination on the part of teachers. Both Marisol and Vinh specifically mentioned language discrimination as a problem. For Marisol, it had happened when a particular teacher did not allow Spanish to be spoken in her room. For Vinh, it concerned teachers' attitudes about his language: "Some teachers don't understand about the language. So sometimes, my language, they say it sounds funny." Rich spoke of the differences between the expectations of White and Black teachers, and concluded that all teachers should teach the curriculum *as if they were in an all-White school,* meaning that then expectations would be high for everybody. Other students were the object of teasing, but some, including James, even welcomed it, perhaps because it at least made his culture visible. He spoke of Mr. Miller, an elementary teacher he had been particularly fond of, who had called him "Gonzo" because he had a big nose and "Klinger" after the *M.A.S.H.* character who was Lebanese. James said, "And then everybody called me Klinger from then on. . . . I liked it, kind of . . . everybody laughing at me."

It was Linda who had the most to say about racism. As a young woman who identified herself as mixed because her mother was White and her father Black, Linda had faced discrimination or confusion on the part of both students and teachers. For example, she resented the fact that when teachers had to indicate her race, they came to their own conclusions without bothering to ask her. She explained what it was like:

> [Teachers should not] try to make us one or the other. And God forbid you should make us something we're totally not. . . . Don't write down that I'm Hispanic when I'm not. Some people actually think I'm Chinese when I smile. . . . Find out. Don't just make your judgments. . . . If you're filling out someone's report card and you need to know, then ask.

She went on to say:

I've had people tell me, "Well, you're Black." I'm not Black; I'm Black and White. I'm Black and White American. "Well, you're Black!" No, I'm not! I'm both. . . . I mean, I'm not ashamed of being Black, but I'm not ashamed of being White either, and if I'm both, I want to be part of both. And I think teachers need to be sensitive to that.

Linda did not restrict her criticisms to White teachers, but also spoke of a Black teacher in her high school. Besides Mr. Benson, her favorite teacher of all, there was another Black teacher in the school:

The other Black teacher, he was a racist, and I didn't like him. I belonged to the Black Students Association, and he was the advisor. And he just made it so obvious: he was all for Black supremacy. . . . A lot of times, whether they deserved it or not, his Black students passed, and his White students, if they deserved an A, they got a B. . . . He was insistent that only Hispanics and Blacks be allowed in the club. He had a very hard time letting me in because I'm not all Black. . . . I just really wasn't that welcome there. . . . He never found out what I was about. He just made his judgments from afar.

It was clear that racism was a particularly compelling issue for Linda, and she thought and talked about it a great deal. The weight of racism on her mind was evident when she said, "It's hard. I look at history and I feel really bad for what some of my ancestors did to some of my other ancestors. Unless you're mixed, you don't know what it's like to be mixed." She even wrote a poem about it, which ended like this:

But all that I wonder is who ever gave
them the right to tell me
What I can and can't do
Who I can and can't be
God made each one of us
Just like the other
the only difference is,
I'm darker in color.

Implications of Students' Views for Transformation of Schools

Numerous lessons are contained within the narratives above. But what are the implications of these lessons for the school's curriculum, pedagogy, and tracking? How can we use what students have taught us about racism and discrimination? How can schools' policies and practices be informed through dialogue with students about what works and doesn't work? Although the students in my study never mentioned multicultural education by name, they were deeply concerned with whether and in what ways they and their families and communities were respected and represented in their schools. Two implications that are inherently multicultural come to mind, and I would suggest that both can have a major impact on school policies and practices. It is important that I first make explicit my own view of multicultural education: It is my understanding that multicultural education should be *basic for all students, pervasive in the curriculum and pedagogy, grounded in social justice, and based on critical pedagogy* (Nieto, 1992). Given this interpretation of multicultural education, we can see that it goes beyond the "tolerance" called for in numerous proclamations about diversity. It is also a far cry from the "cultural sensitivity" that is the focus of many professional development workshops (Nieto, 1994). In fact, "cultural sensitivity" can become little more than a condescending "bandaid" response to diversity, because it often does little to solve deep-seated problems of inequity. Thus, a focus on cultural sensitivity in and of itself can be superficial if it fails to take into account the structural and institutional barriers that reflect and reproduce power differentials in society. Rather than promoting cultural sensitivity, I would suggest that multicultural education needs to be understood as "arrogance reduction"; that is, as encompassing *both* individual *and* structural changes that squarely confront the individual biases, attitudes, and behaviors of educators, as well as the policies and practices in schools that emanate from them.

Affirming Students' Languages, Cultures, and Experiences

Over twenty years ago, Annie Stein reported asking a kindergarten teacher to explain why she had ranked four of her students at the bottom of her list, noting that they were "mute." " 'Yes,' she said, 'they have not said one word for six months and they don't appear to hear anything I say.' 'Do they ever talk to the other children?' we asked. 'Sure,' was her reply. 'They cackle to each other in Spanish all day' " (Stein, 1971, p. 161). These young children, although quite vocal in their own language, were not heard by their teacher because the language they spoke was bereft of all significance in the school. The children were not, however, blank slates; on the contrary, they came to school with a language, culture, and experiences that could have been important in their learning. Thus, we need to look not only at the individual weaknesses or strengths of particular students, but also at the way in which schools assign status to entire groups of students based on the sociopolitical and linguistic context in which they live. Jim Cummins addressed this concern in relation to the kinds of superficial antidotes frequently proposed to solve the problem of functional illiteracy among students from culturally and economically dominated groups: "A remedial focus only on technical aspects of functional illiteracy is inadequate because the causes of educational underachievement and 'illiteracy' among subordinated groups are rooted in the systematic devaluation of culture and denial of access to power and resources by the dominant group" (1994, pp. 307–308). As we have seen in many of the examples cited throughout this article, when culture and language are acknowledged by the school, students are able to reclaim the voice they need to continue their education successfully.

Nevertheless, the situation is complicated by the competing messages that students pick up from their schools and society at large. The research that I have reviewed makes it clear that, although students' cultures are important to them personally and in their families, they are also problematic because they are rarely valued or acknowledged by schools. The decisions young people make about their identities are frequently contradictory and mired in the tensions and struggles concerning diversity that are reflected in our society. Schools are not immune to such debates. There are numerous ways in which students' languages and cultures are excluded in schools: they are invisible, as with James, denigrated, as in Marisol's case, or simply not known, as happened with Vinh. It is no wonder then that these young people had conflicted feelings about their backgrounds. In spite of this, all of them spoke about the strength they derived from family and culture, and the steps they took to maintain it. James and Marisol mentioned that they continued to speak their native languages at home; Fern discussed her father's many efforts to maintain their Native American heritage; Manuel made it clear that he would always consider himself first and foremost Cape Verdean. Vinh spoke movingly about what his culture meant to him, and said that only Vietnamese was allowed in the home and that his sisters and brothers wrote to their parents in Vietnamese weekly. Most of these young people also maintained solid ties with their religion and places of worship as an important link to their heritage.

Much of the recent literature on educating culturally diverse students is helping to provide a radically different paradigm that contests the equation *education = assimilation* (Trueba, 1989). This research challenges the old assumptions about the role of the school as primarily an assimilationist agent, and provides a foundation for policy recommendations that focus on using students' cultural background values to promote academic achievement. In the case of Asian Pacific American youth, Peter Kiang and Vivian Wai-Fun Lee state the following:

> It is ironic that strengths and cultural values of family support which are so often praised as explanations for the academic achievement of Asian Pacific American students are severely undercut by the lack of programmatic and policy support for broad-based bilingual instruction and native language development, particularly in early childhood education. (Kiang & Lee, 1993, p. 39)

A study by Jeannette Abi-Nader of a program for Hispanic youth provides an example of how this can work. In the large urban high school she studied, students' cultural values, especially those concerned with *familia,* were the basis of everyday classroom interactions. Unlike the dismal dropout statistics prevalent in so many other Hispanic communities, up to 65 percent of the high school graduates in this program went on to college. Furthermore, the youth attributed their academic success to the program and made enthusiastic statements about it, including this one written on a survey: "The best thing I like about this class is that we all work together and we all participate and try to help each other. We're family!" (Abi-Nader, 1993, p. 213).

The students in my research also provided impassioned examples of the effect that affirming their languages and cultures had on them and, conversely, on how negating their languages and cultures negated a part of them as well. The attitudes and behaviors of the teachers in Yolanda's school, for example, were reflected in policies that seemed to be based on an appreciation for student diversity. Given the support of her teachers and their affirmation of her language and her culture, Yolanda concluded, "Actually, it's fun around here if you really get into learning. . . . I like learning. I like really getting my mind working." Manuel also commented on how crucial it was for teachers to become aware of students' cultural values and backgrounds. This was especially important for Manuel, since his parents were immigrants unfamiliar with U.S. schools and society, and although they gave him important moral support, they could do little to help him in school. He said of his teachers:

If you don't know a student there's no way to influence him. If you don't know his background, there's no way you are going to get in touch with him. There's no way you're going to influence him if you don't know where he's been.

Fern, on the other hand, as the only Native American student in her school, spoke about how difficult it was to discuss values that were different from those of the majority. She specifically mentioned a discussion about abortion in which she was trying to express that for Native Americans, the fetus is alive: "And, so, when I try to tell them, they just, 'Oh, well, we're out of time.' They cut me off, and we've still got half an hour!" And Avi, although he felt that teachers tried to be understanding of his religion, also longed for more cultural affirmation. He would have welcomed, for example, the support of the one Jewish teacher at school who Avi felt was trying to hide his Jewishness.

On the contrary, in Linda's case, Mr. Benson, her English teacher, who was also her favorite teacher, provided just that kind of affirmation. Because he was racially mixed like Linda, she felt that he could relate to the kinds of problems she confronted. He became, in the words of Esteban Díaz and his colleagues, a "sociocultural mediator" for Linda by assigning her identity, language, and culture important roles in the learning environment (Díaz, Flores, Cousin, & Soo Hoo, 1992). Although Linda spoke English as her native language, she gave a wonderful example of how Mr. Benson encouraged her to be "bilingual," using what she referred to as her "street talk." Below is her description of Mr. Benson and the role he played in her education:

> I've enjoyed all my English teachers at Jefferson. But Mr. Benson, my English Honors teacher, he just threw me for a whirl! I wasn't going to college until I met this man. . . . He was one of the few teachers I could talk to . . . 'cause Mr. Benson, he says, I can go into Harvard and converse with those people, and I can go out in the street and "rap with y'all." It's that type of thing. I love it. I try and be like that myself. I have my street talk. I get out in the street and I say "ain't" this and "ain't" that and "your momma" or "wha's up?" But I get somewhere where I know the people aren't familiar with that language or aren't accepting that language, and I will talk properly. . . . I walk into a place and I listen to how people are talking and it just automatically comes to me.

Providing time in the curriculum for students and teachers to engage in discussions about how the language use of students from dominated groups is discriminated against would go a long way in affirming the legitimacy of the discourse of *all* students (Delpit, 1992). According to Margaret Gibson (1991), much recent research has confirmed that schooling may unintentionally contribute to the educational problems of students from culturally dominated groups by pressuring them to assimilate against their wishes. The conventional wisdom that assimilation is the answer to academic underachievement is thus severely challenged. One intriguing implication is that the more students are involved in resisting assimilation while maintaining their culture and language, the more successful they will be in school. That is, maintaining culture and language, although a conflicted decision, seems to have a positive impact on academic success. In any case, it seems to be a far healthier response than adopting an oppositional identity that effectively limits the possibility of academic success (Fordham & Ogbu, 1986; Skutnabb-Kangas, 1988). Although it is important not to overstate this conclusion, it is indeed a real possibility, one that tests the "melting pot" ideology that continues to dominate U.S. schools and society.

We know, of course, that cultural maintenance is not true in all cases of academic success, and everybody can come up with examples of students who felt they needed to assimilate to be successful in school. But the question remains whether this kind of assimilation is healthy or necessary. For instance, in one large-scale study, immigrant students clearly expressed a strong desire to maintain their native languages and cultures and to pass them on to their children (Olsen, 1988). Other research has found that bilingual students specifically appreciate hearing their native language in school, and want the opportunity to learn in that language (Poplin & Weeres, 1992). In addition, an intriguing study of Cambodian refugee children by the Metropolitan Indochinese Children and Adolescent Service found that the more successful they became at modeling their behavior to be like U.S. children, the more their emotional adjustment worsened (National Coalition, 1988). Furthermore, a study of Southeast Asian students found a significant connection between grades and culture: in this research, higher grade point averages correlated with the *maintenance* of traditional values, ethnic pride, and close social and cultural ties with members of the same ethnic group (Rumbaut & Ima, 1987).

All of the above suggests that it is time to look critically at policies and practices that encourage students to leave their cultures and languages at the schoolhouse door. It also suggests that schools and teachers need to affirm, maintain, and value the differences that students bring to school as a foundation for their learning. It is still too common to hear teachers urging parents to "speak only English," as my parents were encouraged to do with my sister and me (luckily, our parents never paid attention). The ample literature cited throughout this article concerning diverse student populations is calling such practices into question. What we are learning is that teachers instead need to encourage parents to speak their *native* language, not English, at home with their children. We are also learning that they should emphasize the importance of family values, not in the rigid and limiting way that this term has been used in the past to create a sense of superiority for those who are culturally dominant, but rather by accepting the strong ethical values that all cultural groups and all kinds of families cherish. As an initial step, however, teachers and schools must first learn more about their students. Vinh expressed powerfully what he wanted teachers to know about him by reflecting on how superficial their knowledge was:

> They understand something, just not all Vietnamese culture. Like they just understand something *outside*. . . . But they cannot understand something inside our hearts.

Listen to Students

Although school is a place where a lot of talk goes on, it is not often student talk. Student voices sometimes reveal the great challenges and even the deep pain young people feel when schools are unresponsive, cold places. One of the students participating in a project focusing on those "inside the school," namely students, teachers, staff, and parents, said, "This place hurts my spirit" (Poplin & Weeres, 1992, p. 11). Ironically, those who spend the most time in schools and classrooms are often given the least opportunity to talk. Yet, as we saw in the many examples above, students have important lessons to teach educators, and we need to begin to listen to them more carefully. Suzanne Soo Hoo captured the fact that educators are losing a compelling opportunity to learn from students while working on a project where students became coresearchers and worked on the question, "What are the obstacles to learning?" a question that, according to Soo Hoo, "electrified the group" (1993, p. 386). Including students in addressing such important issues places the focus where it rightfully belongs, said Soo Hoo: "Somehow educators have forgotten the important connection between teachers and students. We listen to outside experts to inform us, and consequently, we overlook the treasure in our very own backyards: our students" (p. 390). As Mike, one of the coresearchers in her project, stated, "They think just because we're kids, we don't know anything" (p. 391).

When they are treated as if they do know something, students can become energized and motivated. For the ten young people in my study, the very act of speaking about their schooling experiences seemed to act as a catalyst for more critical thinking about them. For example, I was surprised when I met Marisol's mother and she told me that Marisol had done nothing but speak about our interviews. Most of the students in the study felt this enthusiasm, and these feelings are typical of other young people in similar studies. As Laurie Olsen (1988) concluded in an extensive research project in California in which hundreds of immigrant students were interviewed, most of the students were gratified simply to have the opportunity to speak about their experiences. These findings have several implications for practice, including using oral histories, peer interviews, interactive journals, and other such strategies. Simply providing students with time to talk with one another, including group work, seems particularly helpful.

The feeling that adults do not listen to them has been echoed by many young people over the years. But listening alone is not sufficient if it is not accompanied by profound changes in what we expect our students to accomplish in school. Even more important than simply *listening* is *assisting* students to become agents of their own learning and to use what they learn in productive and critical ways. This is where social action comes in, and there have been a number of eloquent accounts of critical pedagogy in action (Peterson, 1991; Torres-Guzmán, 1992). I will quote at length from two such examples that provide inspiring stories of how listening to students can help us move beyond the written curriculum.

Iris Santos Rivera wrote a moving account of how a Freirian "problem-posing" approach was used with K-6 Chicano students in a summer educational program of the San Diego Public Schools in 1975 (Santos Rivera, 1983–1984). The program started by having the students play what she called the "Complain, Moan, and Groan Game." Using this exercise, in which students dialogued about and identified problems in the school and community, the young people were asked to identify problems to study. One group selected the school lunch program. This did not seem like a "real" problem to the teacher, who tried to steer the children toward another problem. Santos Rivera writes: "The teacher found it hard to believe in the problem's validity as an issue, as the basis for an action project, or as an integrating theme for education" (p. 5). She let the children talk about it for awhile, convinced that they would come to realize that this was not a serious issue. However, when she returned, they said to her, "Who is responsible for the lunches we get?" (p. 6). Thus began a summer-long odyssey in which the students wrote letters, made phone calls, traced their lunches from the catering truck through the school contracts office, figured out taxpayers' cost per lunch, made records of actual services received from the subcontractors, counted sandwiches and tested milk temperatures, and, finally, compared their findings with contract specifications, and found that there was a significant discrepancy. "We want to bring in the media," they told the teacher (p. 6). Both the local television station and the major networks responded to the press releases sent out by the students, who held a press conference to present the facts and answer reporters' questions. When a reporter asked who had told them all this, one nine-year old girl answered, "We found this stuff out. Nobody had to tell us anything. You know, you adults give yourselves too much credit" (p. 7). The postscript to this story is that state and federal laws had to be amended to change the kinds of lunches that students in California are served, and tapes from the students in this program were used in the state and federal hearings.

In a more recent example, Mary Ginley, a student in the doctoral program at the School of Education at the University of Massachusetts and a gifted teacher in the Longmeadow (Massachusetts) Public Schools, tries to help her second-graders develop critical skills by posing questions to them daily. Their responses are later discussed during class meeting time. Some of these questions are fairly straightforward ("Did you have a good weekend?"), while others encourage deeper thinking. The question posed on Columbus Day, "Was Columbus a hero?" was the culmination of much reading and dialogue that had previously taken place. Another activity she did with her students this year was to keep a daily record of sunrise and sunset. The students discovered to their surprise that December 21 was *not* the shortest day of the year. Using the daily almanac in the local newspaper, the students verified their finding and wrote letters to the editor. One, signed by Kaolin, read (spelling in original):

Dear Editor,

Acorting to our chart December 21 was not the shotest day of the year. But acorting to your paper it is. Are teacher says it happens evry year! What's going on?

As a result of this letter, the newspaper called in experts from the National Weather Service and a local planetarium. One of them said, "It's a fascinating question that [the pupils] have posed. . . . It's frustrating we don't have an adequate answer."(Kelly, 1994, p. 12). Katie, one of the students in Mary's class, compared her classmates to Galileo, who shook the scientific community by saying that the earth revolved around the sun rather than the other way around. Another, Ben, said, "You shouldn't always believe what you hear," and Lucy asserted, "Even if you're a grown-up, you can still learn from a second-grader!"

In the first part of this article, I posed the question, "Why listen to students?" I have attempted to answer this question using numerous comments that perceptive young people, both those from my study and others, have made concerning their education. In the final analysis, the question itself suggests that it is only by first listening *to* students that we will be able to learn to talk *with* them. If we believe that an important basis of education is dialogue and reflection about experience, then this is clearly the first step. Yolanda probably said it best when she commented, "'Cause you learn a lot from the students. That's what a lot of teachers tell me. They learn more from their students than from where they go study."

Conclusion

I have often been struck by how little young people believe they deserve, especially those who do not come from economically privileged backgrounds. Although they may work hard at learning, they somehow believe that they do not deserve a chance to dream. This article is based on the notion that all of our students deserve to dream and that teachers and schools are in the best position for "creating a chance" to do so, as referred to in the title. This means developing conditions in schools that let students know that they have a right to envision other possibilities beyond those imposed by traditional barriers of race, gender, or social class. It means, even more importantly, that those traditional barriers can no longer be viewed as impediments to learning.

The students in my study also showed how crucial extracurricular activities were in providing needed outlets for their energy and for teaching them important leadership skills. For some, it was their place of worship (this was especially true for Avi, Manuel, and Rich); for others, it was hobbies (Linda loved to sing); and for others, sports were a primary support (Fern mentioned how she confronted new problems by comparing them to the sports in which she excelled: "I compare it to stuff, like, when I can't get science, or like in sewing, I'll look at that machine and I'll say, 'This is a basketball; I can overcome it' "). The schools' responsibility to provide some of these activities becomes paramount for students such as Marisol, whose involvement in the Teen Clinic acted almost like a buffer against negative peer pressure.

These students can all be characterized by an indomitable resilience and a steely determination to succeed. However, expecting all students, particularly those from subordinated communities, to be resilient in this way is an unfair burden, because privileged students do not need this quality, as the schools generally reflect their backgrounds, experiences, language, and culture. Privileged students learn that they are the "norm," and although they may believe this is inherently unfair (as is the case with Vanessa), they still benefit from it.

Nevertheless, the students in this research provide another important lesson about the strength of human nature in the face of adversity. Although they represented all kinds of families and economic and social situations, the students were almost uniformly upbeat about their future and their lives, sometimes in spite of what might seem overwhelming odds. The positive features that have contributed to their academic success, namely, caring teachers, affirming school climates, and loving families, have helped them face such odds. "I don't think there's anything stopping me," said Marisol, whose large family lived on public assistance because both parents were disabled. She added, "If I know I can do it, I should just keep on trying." The determination to keep trying was evident also in Fern, whose two teenage sisters were undergoing treatment for alcohol and drug abuse, but who nevertheless asserted, "I succeed in everything I do. If I don't get it right the first time, I always go back and try to do it again," adding, "I've always wanted to be president of the United States!" And it was evident as well in the case of Manuel, whose father cleaned downtown offices in Boston while his mother raised the remaining children at home, and who was the first of the eleven children to graduate from high school: "I can do whatever I want to do in life. Whatever I want to do, I know I could make it. I believe that strongly." And, finally, it was also clear in the case of Rich, whose mother, a single parent, was putting all three of her children through college at the same time. Rich had clearly learned a valuable lesson about self-reliance from her, as we can see in this striking image: "But let's not look at life as a piece of cake, because eventually it'll dry up, it'll deteriorate, it'll fall, it'll crumble, or somebody will come gnawing at it." Later he added, "As they say, self-respect is one gift that you give yourself."

Our students have a lot to teach us about how pedagogy, curriculum, ability grouping, and expectations of ability need to change so that greater numbers of young people can be reached. In 1971, Annie Stein expressed the wishes and hopes of students she talked with, and they differ little from those we have heard through the voices of students today: "The demands of high school youth are painfully reasonable. They want a better education, a more 'relevant' curriculum, some voice in the subject matter to be taught and in the running of the school, and some respect for their constitutional and human rights" (1971, p. 177). Although the stories and voices I have used in this article are primarily those of individual students, they can help us to imagine what it might take to transform entire schools. The responsibility to do so cannot be placed only on the shoulders of individual teachers who, in spite of the profound impact they can have on the lives of particular students, are part of a system that continues to be unresponsive to too many young people. In the final analysis, students are asking us to look critically not only at structural conditions, but also at individual attitudes and behaviors. This implies that we need to undertake a total transformation not only of our schools, but also of our hearts and minds.

Notes

1. I recognize that overarching terms, such as "European American," "African American," "Latino," etc., are problematic. Nevertheless, "European American" is more explicit than "White" with regard to culture and ethnicity, and thus challenges Whites also to think of themselves in ethnic terms, something they usually reserve for those from more clearly identifiable groups (generally, people of color). I have a more in-depth discussion of this issue in chapter two of my book, *Affirming Diversity* (1992).
2. The early arguments for cultural deprivation are well expressed by Carl Bereiter and Siegfried Englemann (1966) and by Frank Reissman (1962). A thorough review of a range of deficit theories can be found in Herbert Ginsburg (1986).
3. "Critical thinking," as used here, is not meant in the sense that it has come to be used conventionally to imply, for example, higher order thinking skills in math and science as disconnected from a political awareness. Rather, it means developing, in the Freirian (1970) sense, a consciousness of oneself as a critical agent in learning and transforming one's reality.
4. I was assisted in doing the interviews by a wonderful group of colleagues, most of whom contacted the students, interviewed them, and gave me much of the background information that helped me craft the case studies. I am grateful for the insights and help the following colleagues provided: Carlie Collins Tartakov, Paula Elliott, Haydée Font, Maya Gillingham, Mac Lee Morante, Diane Sweet, and Carol Shea.
5. "Holidays and Heroes" refers to an approach in which multicultural education is understood as consisting primarily of ethnic celebrations and the acknowledgment of "great men" in the history of particular cultures. Deeper structures of cultures, including values and lifestyle differences, and an explicit emphasis on power differentials as they affect particular cultural groups, are not addressed in this approach. Thus, this approach is correctly perceived as one that tends to romanticize culture and treat it in an artificial way. In contrast, multicultural education as empowering and liberating pedagogy confronts such structural issues and power differentials quite directly.

References

Abi-Nader, J. (1993). Meeting the needs of multicultural classrooms: Family values and the motivation of minority students. In M. J. O'Hair & S. Odell (Eds), *Diversity and teaching: Teacher education yearbook 1* (pp. 212–236). Fort Worth, TX: Harcourt Brace Jovanovich.

Banks, J. A. (1991). *Teaching strategies for ethnic studies* (6th ed.). Boston: Allyn & Bacon.

Bartolomé, L. (1994). Beyond the methods fetish: Toward a humanizing pedagogy. *Harvard Educational Review, 64*, 173–194.

Bempechat, J. (1992). *Fostering high achievement in African American children: Home, school, and public policy influences.* New York: ERIC Clearinghouse on Urban Education, Teachers College, Columbia University.

Bereiter, C., & Englemann, S. (1966). *Teaching disadvantaged children in the preschool.* Englewood Cliffs, NJ: Prentice Hall.

Clark, R. M. (1983). *Family life and school achievement: Why poor Black children succeed or fail.* Chicago: University of Chicago Press.

Commins, N. L. (1989). Language and affect: Bilingual students at home and at school. *Language Arts, 66*, 29–43.

Cummins, J. (1994). From coercive to collaborative relations of power in the teaching of literacy. In B. M. Ferdman, R-M. Weber, & A. G. Ramírez (Eds.), *Literacy across languages and cultures* (pp. 295–331). Albany: State University of New York Press.

Delpit, L. (1992). The politics of teaching literate discourse. *Theory into Practice, 31*, 285–295.

Díaz, E., Flores, B., Cousin, P. T., & Soo Hoo, S. (1992, April). *Teacher as sociocultural mediator.* Paper presented at the Annual Meeting of the AERA, San Francisco.

Donaldson, K. (1994). Through students' eyes. *Multicultural Education, 2*(2), 26–28.

Fine, M. (1991). *Framing dropouts: Notes on the politics of an urban public high school.* Albany: State University of New York Press.

Fine, M. (1993). "You can't just say that the only ones who can speak are those who agree with your position": Political discourse in the classroom. *Harvard Educational Review, 63*, 412–433.

Fordham, S., & Ogbu, J. (1986) Black students' school success: Coping with the "burden of acting White." *Urban Review, 18*, 176–206.

Frau-Ramos, M., & Nieto, S. (1993). "I was an outsider": Dropping out among Puerto Rican youths in Holyoke, Massachusetts. In R. Rivera & S. Nieto (Eds.), *The education of Latino students in Massachusetts: Research and policy considerations* (pp. 143–166). Boston: Gastón Institute.

Freire, P. (1970). *Pedagogy of the oppressed.* New York: Seabury Press.

Gibson, M. (1991). Minorities and schooling: Some implications. In M. A. Gibson & J. U. Ogbu (Eds.), *Minority status and schooling: A comparative study of immigrant and involuntary minorities* (pp. 357–381). New York: Garland.

Ginsburg, H. (1986). The myth of the deprived child: New thoughts on poor children. In U. Neisser (Ed.), *The school achievement of minority children: New perspectives.* Hillsdale, NJ: Lawrence Erlbaum.

Goodlad, J. I. (1984). *A place called school.* New York: McGraw-Hill.

Haberman, M. (1991). The pedagogy of poverty versus good teaching. *Phi Delta Kappan, 73*, 290–294.

Hallinan, M., & Teixeira, R. (1987). Opportunities and constraints: Black-White differences in the formation of interracial friendships. *Child Development, 58*, 1358–1371.

Hidalgo, N. M. (1991). *"Free time, school is like a free time": Social relations in City High School classes.* Unpublished doctoral dissertation, Harvard University.

Hollins, E. R., King, J. E., & Hayman, W. C. (Eds.). (1994). *Teaching diverse populations: Formulating a knowledge base.* Albany: State University of New York Press.

Kelly, R. (1994, January 11). Class searches for solstice. *Union News*, p. 12.

Kiang, P. N., & Lee, V. W-F. (1993). Exclusion or contribution? Education K–12 policy. In *The State of Asian Pacific America: Policy Issues to the Year 2020* (pp. 25–48). Los Angeles: LEAP Asian Pacific American Public Policy Institute and UCLA Asian American Studies Center.

Kohl, H. (1993). The myth of "Rosa Parks, the tired." *Multicultural Education, 1*(2), 6–10.

Kozol, J. (1967). *Death at an early age: The destruction of the hearts and minds of Negro children in the Boston Public Schools*. New York: Houghton Mifflin.

Lee, V. E., Winfield, L. F., & Wilson, T. C. (1991). Academic behaviors among high-achieving African-American students. *Education and Urban Society, 24*(1), 65–86.

Lucas, T., Henze, R., & Donato, R. (1990). Promoting the success of Latino language-minority students: An exploratory study of six high schools. *Harvard Educational Review, 60*, 315–340.

McNeil, L. M. (1986). *Contradictions of control: School structure and school knowledge*. New York: Routledge & Kegan Paul.

Mehan, H., & Villanueva, I. (1993). Untracking low achieving students: Academic and social consequences. In *Focus on Diversity* (Newsletter available from the National Center for Research on Cultural Diversity and Second Language Learning, 399 Kerr Hall, University of California, Santa Cruz, CA 95064).

Moll, L. (1992). Bilingual classroom studies and community analysis: Some recent trends. *Educational Researcher, 21*(2), 20–24.

Moll, L., & Díaz, S. (1993). Change as the goal of educational research. In E. Jacob & C. Jordan (Eds.), *Minority education: Anthropological perspectives* (pp. 67–79). Norwood, NJ: Ablex.

National Coalition of Advocates for Students. (1988). *New voices: Immigrant students in U.S. public schools*. Boston: Author.

Newmann, F. M. (1993). Beyond common sense in educational restructuring: The issues of content and linkage. *Educational Researcher, 22*(2), 4–13, 22.

Nieto, S. (1992). *Affirming diversity: The sociopolitical context of multicultural education*. White Plains, NY: Longman.

Nieto, S. (1994). Affirmation, solidarity, and critique: Moving beyond tolerance in multicultural education. *Multicultural Education, 1*(4), 9–12, 35–38.

Oakes, J. (1992). Can tracking research inform practice? *Educational Researcher, 21*(4), 12–21.

Olsen, L. (1988). *Crossing the schoolhouse border: Immigrant students and the California public schools*. San Francisco: California Tomorrow.

Peterson, R. E. (1991). Teaching how to read the world and change it: Critical pedagogy in the intermediate grades. In C. E. Walsh (Ed.), *Literacy as praxis: Culture, language, and pedagogy* (pp. 156–182). Norwood, NJ: Ablex.

Phelan, P., Davidson, A. L., & Cao, H. T. (1992). Speaking up: Students' perspectives on school. *Phi Delta Kappan, 73*, 695–704.

Poplin, M., & Weeres, J. (1992). *Voices from the inside: A report on schooling from inside the classroom*. Claremont, CA: Claremont Graduate School, Institute for Education in Transformation.

Reissman, F. (1962). *The culturally deprived child*. New York: Harper & Row.

Reyes, M. de la Luz (1992). Challenging venerable assumptions: Literacy instruction for linguistically different students. *Harvard Educational Review, 62*, 427–446.

Ribadeneira, D. (1990, October 18). Study says teen-agers' racism rampant. *Boston Globe*, p. 31.

Rumbaut, R. G., & Ima, K. (1987). *The adaptation of Southeast Asian refugee youth: A comparative study*. San Diego: Office of Refugee Resettlement.

Santos Rivera, I. (1983–1984, October-January). Liberating education for little children. In *Alternativas* (Freirian newsletter from Río Piedras, Puerto Rico, no longer published).

Saravia-Shore, M., & Martínez, H. (1992). An ethnographic study of home/school role conflicts of second generation Puerto Rican adolescents. In M. Saravia-Shore & S. F. Arvizu (Eds.), *Cross-cultural literacy: Ethnographies of communication in multiethnic classrooms* (pp. 227–251). New York: Garland.

Shor, I. (1992). *Empowering education: Critical teaching for social change.* Chicago: University of Chicago Press.

Skutnabb-Kangas, T. (1988). Resource power and autonomy through discourse in conflict: A Finnish migrant school strike in Sweden. In T. Skutnabb-Kangas & J. Cummins (Eds.), *Minority education: From shame to struggle* (pp. 251–277). Clevedon, Eng.: Multilingual Matters.

Sleeter, C. E. (1991). *Empowerment through multicultural education.* Albany: State University of New York Press.

Sleeter, C. E. (1994). White racism. *Multicultural Education, 1*(4), 5–8, 39.

Sleeter, C. E., & Grant, C. A. (1991). Mapping terrains of power: Student cultural knowledge vs. classroom knowledge. In C. E. Sleeter (Ed.), *Empowerment through multicultural education* (pp. 49–67). Albany: State University of New York Press.

Soo Hoo, S. (1993). Students as partners in research and restructuring schools. *Educational Forum, 57,* 386–393.

Stein, A. (1971). Strategies for failure. *Harvard Educational Review, 41,* 133–179.

Tatum, B. D. (1992). Talking about race, learning about racism: The application of racial identity development theory in the classroom. *Harvard Educational Review, 62,* 1–24.

Taylor, A. R. (1991). Social competence and the early school transition: Risk and protective factors for African-American children. *Education and Urban Society, 24*(1), 15–26.

Taylor, D., & Dorsey-Gaines, C. (1988). *Growing up literate: Learning from inner-city families.* Portsmouth, NH: Heinemann.

Torres-Guzmán, M. (1992). Stories of hope in the midst of despair: Culturally responsive education for Latino students in an alternative high school in New York City. In M. Saravia-Shore & S. F. Arvizu (Eds.), *Cross-cultural literacy: Ethnographies of communication in multiethnic classrooms* (pp. 477–490). New York: Garland.

Trueba, H. T. (1989). *Raising silent voices: Educating the linguistic minorities for the twenty-first century.* Cambridge, MA: Newbury House.

Wheelock, A. (1992). *Crossing the tracks: How "untracking" can save America's schools.* New York: New Press.

Zanger, V. V. (1994). Academic costs of social marginalization: An analysis of Latino students' perceptions at a Boston high school. In R. Rivera & S. Nieto (Eds.), *The education of Latino students in Massachusetts: Research and policy considerations* (pp. 167–187). Boston: Gastón Institute.

About the Contributors

Adrienne Alton-Lee is Director of the Understanding Learning and Teaching Institute in Wellington, New Zealand. Her current work involves the development of collaborative research teaching case studies in the ERUDITE Programme (Educational Research Underpinning Development in Teacher Education). She is coauthor of "Towards a Gender-Inclusive School Curriculum: Changing Educational Practice" in *Women and Education in Aotearoa, Vol. 2*, edited by S. Middleton and A. Jones (with P. A. Densem, 1992), and "Research on Teaching and Learning: Thirty Years of Change" in *Elementary School Journal* (with G. A. Nuthall, 1990).

Lilia I. Bartolomé, Associate Professor of Education at the University of Massachusetts, Boston, is interested in the sociocultural and ideological dimensions of linguistic-minority education. Her recent publications include *The Misteaching of Academic Discourse: The Politics of Language in the Classroom* (1998) and "Dancing with Bigotry: The Poisoning of Racial and Ethnic Identities" in *Harvard Educational Review* (with D. Macedo, 1997).

Deborah P. Britzman is Associate Professor on the Faculty of Education at York University in Toronto. She is interested in psychoanalysis and education, and in the study of difficult knowledge in learning and teaching. Her publications include *Lost Subjects, Contested Objects: Toward a Psychoanalytic Inquiry of Learning* (1998) and *Practice Makes Practice: A Critical Study of Learning to Teach* (1991).

Joy MarieLouise Caires is currently completing a double major in English and Religion, with a focus in Biblical Studies, at Smith College, Northampton, Massachusetts.

Joseph Cambone, Director of the Walker-Wheelock Institute for Equity in Schools in Boston, is interested in the change process in schools, in particular the effects of change on teacher cognition and practice. His publications include "Time for Teachers in School Restructuring" in *Teachers College Record* (1995), and "Braided Curriculum in the Inclusive Classroom" in *Journal of Emotional and Behavioral Problems* (1994).

Liveda C. Clements is a Cash Control Specialist at Mellon Trust in Medford, Massachusetts. She is a 1998 graduate of Boston University, where she had a major in political science and a minor in economics. She is interested in creative writing.

R. W. Connell, Professor of Education at the University of Sydney, Australia, is concerned with social justice and educational change. His research includes work on gender, class inequality, globalization, and intellectuals. He is author of *Masculinities* (1995) and *Schools and Social Justice* (1993).

Brent Davis is Assistant Professor on the Faculty of Education, York University, North York, Ontario. His primary research interests include mathematics education, cognitive studies, teacher education, and curriculum theory. His recent publications include "Basic Irony: Troubling Foundations of School Mathematics" in *Journal of Mathematics Teacher Education* (in press), and *Teaching Mathematics: Toward a Sound Alternative* (1996).

Lisa D. Delpit, Benjamin E. Mays Professor of Urban Educational Leadership at Georgia State University in Atlanta, is interested in urban education. Her recent publications include *The Real Ebonics Debate* (coedited with T. Perry, 1998) and *Other People's Children: Cultural Conflict in the Classroom* (1995). She was awarded a MacArthur Fellowship in 1990.

Melinda Fine is an independent consultant and a Visiting Scholar at New York University's Institute for Education and Social Policy. Her research interests center around creating educational programs to foster social responsibility and moral development, educational equity for girls, and civic conscience. She is author of *Habits of Mind: Struggling Over Values in America's Classrooms* (1995) and "Facing History and Ourselves: Portraits of a Classroom" in *Educational Leadership* (1992).

Karen Gallas is Principal of Bellevue Santa Fe Charter School in San Luis Obispo, California, where she also teaches kindergarten. Her professional interests focus on language and literacy, multi-arts integration in elementary curriculum, and the acquisition of discourse. She is author of *Sometimes I Can Be Anything: Power, Gender, and Identity in a Primary Classroom* (1998) and *Talking Their Way into Science: Hearing Children's Questions and Theories, Responding with Curricula* (1995).

Karen Hale Hankins is a first-grade teacher at Whit Davis Elementary School in Athens, Georgia. Her professional interests center around narrative as theory, data, and method, as well as issues of social justice in the classroom. She is author of "Silencing the Lambs" in *Class Action: Teaching Social Justice in Elementary and Middle Schools* (edited by J. Allen, in press), and "One Moment in Two Times" in *Teacher Research* (1996).

Simon Hole teaches fourth-graders at Narragansett Elementary School in Narragansett, Rhode Island. His current interests include the use of narrative inquiry as a research methodology and a pedagogical strategy. His published works include "Working Together, Learning Together: Collegiality in the Classroom" in *Teaching and Change* (1997), and "Room for All" in *Writing within School Reform* (edited by G. McEntee, 1996).

Jeff Howard, President of The Efficacy Institute in Lexington, Massachusetts, is interested in driving greater student achievement through mobilization of effort. He is author of "You Can't Get There from Here: The Need for a New Logic in Education Reform" in *Daedalus* (1995), and "The Third Movement: Developing Black Children for the 21st Century" in *The State of Black America* (1993).

Kathe Jervis is a Senior Research Associate at the National Center for Restructuring Education, Schools, and Teaching at Columbia University's Teachers College in New York City. Her professional interests center around daily classroom life, teacher reflections and research, and children's thinking. She is author of *Conducting a School Quality Review in a Crosscultural Setting* (1998) and *Eyes on the Child: Three Portfolio Stories* (1996).

J. Alleyne Johnson (Jennifer E. Obidah) is Assistant Professor in Emory University's Division of Education Studies, located in Atlanta. Her professional interests center around the social and cultural context of urban schooling, including issues of violence and multicultural education. She is author of "Listen to the Children" in *Schools, Violence and Society* (edited by S. Spiner, in press), and "Born to Roll: Graduate School from the Margins" in *Multicultural Research: A Reflective Engagement* (edited by C. Grant, in press).

Mieko Kamii is Associate Professor of Psychology and Education at Wheelock College in Boston, as well as Director of the Center on College, School, and Community Partnerships. Her research interests include children's cognitive development and learning, and teachers' professional development and learning. She is author of "Standards and Assessment: What We've Learned Thus Far" in *The Web* (1996), and "Cultural Divide" in *Fieldwork: An Expeditionary Learning Outward Bound Reader* (edited by A. Mednick and E. Cousins, 1996).

Magdalene Lampert is Professor of Education at the University of Michigan, Ann Arbor, where she directs the Teacher Development through Video project. She is interested in the study of teaching in the context of practice. Her recent published works include *Teaching, Multimedia and Mathematics: Investigation of Real Practice* (1998) and *Talking Mathematics: Studies of Teaching and Learning in School* (1998).

Kari Larsen, a sophomore at the Pilot School in Rindge and Latin High School in Cambridge, Massachusetts, was born in Qui Nhon, Vietnam. She is a member of a lively family that includes her adoptive parents and five brothers and sisters who represent many different nationalities and cultures. (*Editors' note:* This information is from 1988, when we originally published her work. No more recent information is available.)

Robert Parris Moses is President of the Algebra Project, which he founded. A mathematics educator, curriculum developer, and teacher trainer, his goal with the Project is to establish a pedagogy of mathematics that expects and encourages every student to succeed at algebra in middle school, and supports their efforts to do so. He is currently teaching at the Lanier High School in Jackson, Mississippi.

Christian Neira is a Corporate and Litigation Associate at the law firm of Paul, Weiss, Rifkind, Wharton & Garrison in New York City, where he is a member of the Latin America practice group. He is active in Prep for Prep, an organization that recruits and trains minority students and supports their educational success in secondary school and at the college level.

Sonia Nieto is Professor of Language, Literacy, and Culture at the School of Education, University of Massachusetts, Amherst. Her research interests include multicultural education, Puerto Rican children's literature, and the education of Puerto Ricans in the United States. She is author of *The Light in Their Eyes: Creating Multicultural Learning Communities* (in press) and *Affirming Diversity: The Sociopolitical Context of Multicultural Education* (1992).

Graham Nuthall is Professor of Education at the University of Canterbury, Christchurch, New Zealand. His current research interests center around learning and teaching in classrooms from both a cognitive and a sociocultural perspective. He is author of "Learning How to Learn: The Evolution of Students' Minds through the Social Processes and Culture of the Classroom" in *International Journal of Educational Research* (in press), and "The Way Students Learn: Acquiring Knowledge from an Integrated Science and Social Studies Unit" in *Elementary School Journal* (in press).

John Patrick, prior to his retirement, was a Senior Lecturer at the Christchurch College of Education, Christchurch, Aotearoa New Zealand, where his research focus was teaching skills and the influence of learners' self-concepts on learning. He is coauthor of "Take Your Brown Hand Off My Book: Racism in the Classroom" in *SET: Research Information for Teachers* (with A. Alton-Lee and G. Nuthall, 1987).

Nan Stein is a Senior Researcher at the Wellesley College Center for Research on Women, located in Wellesley, Massachusetts. Her research interests center around gender violence in schools, including bullying, sexual harassment, dating violence, and hazing. Her most recent publications on this topic include *Between the Lines: Sexual Harassment in K-12 Schools* (1998), and "Slippery Justice" in *Educational Leadership* (1996).

Carol Stumbo is Director of the Region 8 Service Center of the Kentucky Department of Education, located in Prestonburg. Her major research interests center around the professional development of teachers. She is author of "Changing a State" in *The Nearness of You* (edited by C. Edgar and S. N. Wood, 1996), and "Giving Their Words Back to Them" in *Students Teaching, Teachers Learning* (edited by A. Branscome, D. Goswami, and J. Schwartz, 1992).

Dennis J. Sumara is a Professor on the Faculty of Education of York University, North York, Ontario. His professional interests center around teacher education, curriculum studies, and English language-arts education. He is coeditor of *Action Research as a Living Practice* (with T. Carson, 1997), and author of *Private Reading in Public: Schooling the Literary Imagination* (1996).

Susan McAllister Swap (deceased) was Chair of the Department of Professional Studies and Professor of Education and Psychology at Wheelock College in Boston. Her published works include *Enhancing Parent Involvement in Schools* (1987), *Managing an Effective Staff Development Program* (1987), and *Building Home-School Partnerships with America's Changing Families* (with L. Braun, 1987).

Robert Tremmel is an Assistant Professor and Coordinator of English Education at Iowa State University, Ames. His major professional interest is English education. His most recent publications are *Zen and the Practice of Teaching English* (in press) and *Crossing Crocker Township* (in press). His articles have appeared in *Journal of Teaching Writing, Freshman English News, English Education,* and *Journal of Aesthetic Education.*

Kathryn Zamora-Benson is a student at Boston University.

About the Editors

Ethan Mintz, a doctoral candidate in Administration, Planning, and Social Policy at the Harvard Graduate School of Education, was cochair of the Editorial Board of the *Harvard Educational Review* in 1997–1998. Prior to coming to Harvard, he was an actor in New York and used drama in his work as a teacher in the New York City public schools. His current research focuses on how students and teachers create knowledge in the classroom through drama and explores the impact of drama on student learning, teaching methods, and classroom culture.

John T. Yun is a doctoral candidate in Administration, Planning, and Social Policy at the Harvard Graduate School of Education. His research interests include issues of equity ranging from desegregation and school choice to school funding and the economic returns to education. He is also a former high school science teacher.